Exam 70-219

MCSE

Windows® 2000
Directory Services
Design

TRAINING GUIDE

New
Riders

Scott E. Archer

MCSE TRAINING GUIDE: DESIGNING A WINDOWS© 2000 DIRECTORY SERVICES INFRASTRUCTURE

International Standard Book Number: 0-7357-0983-1

Library of Congress Catalog Card Number: 00-100507

Printed in the United States of America

First Printing: September, 2000

04 03 02 01 00   7 6 5 4 3 2 1

Interpretation of the printing code: The rightmost double-digit number is the year of the book's printing; the rightmost single-digit number is the number of the book's printing. For example, the printing code 00-1 shows that the first printing of the book occurred in 2000.

Trademarks

Warning and Disclaimer

Use of the Microsoft Approved Study Guide logo on this product signifies that it has been independently reviewed and approved in complying with the following standards:

- ◆ Acceptable coverage of all content related to Microsoft exam number 70-219, titled Designing a Windows© 2000 Directory Services Infrastructure

- ◆ Sufficient performance-based exercises that relate closely to all required content

- ◆ Technically accurate content, based on sampling of text

PUBLISHER
David Dwyer

EXECUTIVE EDITOR
Al Valvano

ACQUISITIONS EDITOR
Stacey Beheler

MANAGING EDITOR
Gina Brown

PRODUCT MARKETING MANAGER
Stephanie Layton

MANAGER OF PUBLICITY
Susan Petro

DEVELOPMENT EDITOR
Chris Haidri

PROJECT EDITOR
Linda Seifert

COPY EDITOR
Daryl Kessler

TECHNICAL REVIEWERS
John Alumbaugh
Emmett Dulaney
John Griffin
Dennis Sauer

SOFTWARE DEVELOPMENT SPECIALIST
Michael Hunter

INDEXER
Christine Karpeles

PROOFREADER
Debbie Williams

COMPOSITOR
Marcia Deboy

MANUFACTURING COORDINATOR
Chris Moos

Warning and Disclaimer

This book is designed to provide information about Windows 2000 Directory Services Design. Every effort has been made to make this book as complete and as accurate as possible, but no warranty or fitness is implied.

The information is provided on an as-is basis. The authors and New Riders Publishing/MTP shall have neither liability nor responsibility to any person or entity with respect to any loss or damages arising from the information contained in this book or from the use of the discs or programs that may accompany it.

Use of the Microsoft Approved Study Guide Logo on this product signifies that it has been independently reviewed and approved in complying with the following standards:

- Acceptable coverage of all content related to Microsoft exam number 70-219, entitled Designing a Microsoft Windows 2000 Directory Services Infrastructure.

- Sufficient performance-based exercises that relate closely to all required content.

- Technically accurate content, based on sampling of text.

CONTENTS AT A GLANCE

PART VI   Final Review

PART VII   Appendices

Table of Contents

PART II: Analyzing Business Requirements

PART III: Analyzing Technical Requirements

8 Impact of Active Directory   337

PART IV: Designing a Directory Service Architecture

PART V: Preparing For Implementation

15 Designing an AD Implementation Plan   773

PART VI: Final Review

About the Author

Scott E. Archer lives in Indianapolis, IN with his wife Tiffany, daughter Kira (4), and son Ethan (2). He graduated from Purdue University in 1996 with a BS in Computer and Information Science and has been in the computer business for nine years. He is currently a Senior Consultant for FrontWAY, a national network and eBusiness consulting company where he's been working zombified recently because some book has been consuming his sleep time! Windows 2000 has been installed on his laptop since Beta 1, and has been his core focus since that time. Scott holds MCSE+Internet, MCT, and CCNA certifications and plans to continue on both Microsoft and Cisco tracks.

When he is not in front of a computer, he enjoys watching and playing basketball, doing home improvement projects, trying to figure out noncomputer related hobbies, and playing with the kids.

If you have any noncomputer related hobby ideas, please send them to `sarcher@frontway.com`. You can send questions or comments about the book there too!

Emmett Dulaney, MCSE, MCP+I, i-Net+, A+, Network+, CNA is the author of over a dozen books on certification. The former Certification Corner columnist for *Windows NT Systems Magazine*, he is the cofounder of D S Technical Solutions and an instructor for Indiana University/Purdue University of Fort Wayne, Indiana.

About the Technical Reviewers

John Griffin

John Griffin wrote his first FORTRAN IV program in 1969. Since then he has worked in a variety of consulting, networking and development positions. He has been a guest speaker at HP World and many technology expos throughout his career. His two passions in life (besides his wife) are woodworking and raising Australian Shepard puppies. Currently, John is the lead eCommerce developer for Iomega Corp. in Roy, Utah.

John Alumbaugh

John Alumbaugh, MCSE, CNE, MCT, A+,Network +, is the Principle Consultant for the Operating Systems and Collaborative Solutions team for FrontWAY Indianapolis, a Network and eBusiness consulting company. John has 13 years experience in the IT industry and is responsible for Windows 2000 Readiness at FrontWAY Indianapolis.

Dennis Sauer

Dennis Sauer, CNE, CNA, MCSE, MCNE, MCNI, is a former high school foreign language teacher that got interested in computers in 1990. He has worked in technical support and systems administration and more recently in consulting. He is currently an IT Field Consultant at Roche Diagnostics Corporation in Indianapolis and is responsible for supporting Roche's external customers.

Dedication

Scott E. Archer

This book is dedicated to my family:

Tiffany: You have no idea how thankful I am to have you as my wife. You have grown to understand me better than I think I understand myself. Thank you for allowing me to be me, to pursue my dreams, and for backing me every step of the way.

Kira and Ethan: There is nothing more special than the way you make me feel when I get my hugs and kisses. You are my inspiration.

Mom & Dad: Whether you believe it or not, all that hard work you put into me paid off. Thanks for not giving up on me. I think I finally get it!

Acknowledgments

I have a lot of people to thank for this opportunity:

Mary Foote and Dustin Sullivan: I know you're not there anymore, but I owe my sincere gratitude to both of you for opening that door just enough so I could push my way through it. I wish both of you the very best.

John Alumbaugh: This never would have happened if it weren't for you. Thanks so much for your guidance, suggestions, and encouragement.

Chris Haidri, Stacey Beheler, Linda Seifert, and Chris Zahn: Thanks for keeping on me in such a way I didn't feel pressured. Thanks also for your feedback, direction, and the overall way you handled this project. I feel it went smoothly because of your direction.

To all NRP employees and contractors behind the scenes doing the "dirty work": WOW! You have a huge job and do it so well. My sincere gratitude goes out to you.

Chris, Lea, Sean, John, Mike, Dennis: You all have and continue to encourage me to be the best I can be. Please continue being one step ahead of me so I continue to have something to strive for!

To anyone else who cheered me on during the long hours and late nights of writing—thank you.

Tell Us What You Think

As the reader of this book, you are the most important critic and commentator. We value your opinion and want to know what we're doing right, what we could do better, what areas you'd like to see us publish in, and any other words of wisdom you're willing to pass our way.

As the Executive Editor for the Networking team at New Riders Publishing/MTP, I welcome your comments. You can fax, email, or write me directly to let me know what you did or didn't like about this book—as well as what we can do to make our books stronger.

Please note that I cannot help you with technical problems related to the topic of this book, and that due to the high volume of mail I receive, I might not be able to reply to every message.

When you write, please be sure to include this book's title and author as well as your name and phone or fax number. I will carefully review your comments and share them with the author and editors who worked on the book.

Fax: 317-581-4663

Email: **nrfeedback@newriders.com**

Mail: Al Valvano
         Executive Editor
         New Riders Publishing
         201 West 103rd Street
         Indianapolis, IN 46290 USA

How to Use This Book

New Riders Publishing has made an effort in its *Training Guide* series to make the information as accessible as possible for the purposes of learning the certification material. Here, you have an opportunity to view the many instructional features that have been incorporated into the books to achieve that goal.

CHAPTER OPENER

Each chapter begins with a set of features designed to allow you to maximize study time for that material.

List of Objectives: Each chapter begins with a list of the objectives as stated by Microsoft.

Objective Explanations: Immediately following each objective is an explanation of it, providing context that defines it more meaningfully in relation to the exam. Because Microsoft can sometimes be vague in its objectives list, the objective explanations are designed to clarify any vagueness by relying on the authors' test-taking experience.

OBJECTIVES

This chapter completes the coverage (which was partially completed in Chapters 5 and 6) of the following Microsoft-specified objective for the Designing a Microsoft Windows 2000 Directory Services Infrastructure exam:

Evaluate the company's existing and planned technical environment.

- **Analyze security considerations.**

▶ The purpose of this objective is to get you familiar with the new Windows 2000 security features. There's a vast number of new and different security mechanisms in Windows 2000. It is essential that you know and understand these features as you plan and design a Windows 2000 directory services integration.

CHAPTER 7

Analyzing Security Requirements

Chapter Outline: Learning always gets a boost when you can see both the forest and the trees. To give you a visual image of how the topics in a chapter fit together, you will find a chapter outline at the beginning of each chapter. You will also be able to use this for easy reference when looking for a particular topic.

STUDY STRATEGIES

▶ Understand the core underlying functions of Active Directory, such as Lightweight Directory Access Protocol (LDAP) and Domain Name System (DNS). Being able to break down Active Directory down into manageable and comprehensible sections will make it easier to design.

▶ Be able to identify Windows NT 3.5x and 4.0 domain models and how to map those to Windows 2000 and Active Directory.

▶ Do not focus solely on the technical aspects of Windows 2000. It is a business system as much as it is an operating system, and you need to understand how to effectively model the operating system according to business objectives.

▶ Read up on DNS because it is core to Active Directory. If you feel you don't have a good understanding of it, you may want to read part of Chapter 10, "DNS and Active Directory," now.

Study Strategies: Each topic presents its own learning challenge. To support you through this, New Riders has included strategies for how to best approach studying in order to retain the material in the chapter, particularly as it is addressed on the exam.

INSTRUCTIONAL FEATURES WITHIN THE CHAPTER

These books include a large amount and different kinds of information. The many different elements are designed to help you identify information by its purpose and importance to the exam and also to provide you with varied ways to learn the material. You will be able to determine how much attention to devote to certain elements, depending on what your goals are. By becoming familiar with the different presentations of information, you will know what information will be important to you as a test-taker and which information will be important to you as a practitioner.

EXAM TIP

Granular Security Administration
Unlike Windows NT 4.0, Windows 2000 offers granular security administration through the Delegation of Authority Wizard. Administration of specific OUs can be delegated to members of those OUs. This flexible new method of sharing administrative control is likely to appear in exam scenarios.

Exam Tip: Exam Tips appear in the margins to provide specific exam-related advice. Such tips may address what material is covered (or not covered) on the exam, how it is covered, mnemonic devices, or particular quirks of that exam.

Note: Notes appear in the margins and contain various kinds of useful information, such as tips on the technology or administrative practices, historical background on terms and technologies, or side commentary on industry issues.

---

728   Part IV   DESIGNING A DIRECTORY SERVICE ARCHITECTURE

INTRODUCTION

Unless your Windows 2000 install is confined to a single office and a small group of users, it will likely be requested to integrate with an existing directory service. As pointed out frequently in this book, directory services are not new. Novell's NDS, for example, has been around for several years already and is a tried and true directory service. Consequently, you will rarely find an organization looking (at least initially) for a pure Active Directory environment.

Microsoft's interoperability strategy is based on a four-layer framework that covers the integration of the following:

◆ Network

◆ Data

◆ Applications

◆ Management

NOTE

Integration of ... This chapter does not cover the integration of operating systems at all these levels. If you want to read additional material, refer to the *Interoperability Capabilities* guide posted on TechNet.

Their philosophy is simple: By supporting key standards, Windows 2000 can interoperate with virtually any other standards-based operating platform.

The migration of Windows NT to Windows 2000 may involve the integration and coexistence of Active Directory with Windows NT. This chapter opens with a short discussion of that, and then moves into the non-Microsoft platform integration and coexistence. After that, the discussion turns to Active Directory and Exchange 5.5/2000 coexistence, as your Exchange customers are bound to be interested in integrating the Exchange Directory and Active Directory. The chapter wraps up with a discussion of the Services for UNIX interoperability features.

EXAM TIP

Coverage of Coexistence Although there is an incredible amount of detail in real-world coexistence scenarios, it's important to keep in mind that when taking a Microsoft exam, the answer will most likely include a Microsoft-based solution. Also, because of the granularity of this topic, coexistence scenarios will probably remain very high-level ones.

COEXISTENCE WITH WINDOWS NT

Plan for the coexistence of Active Directory and other directory services.

As you migrate from Windows NT to Active Directory, you might need to coexist for an extended period of time (depending on domain structure). Because of this, and because Microsoft wrote

Objective Coverage Text: In the text before an exam objective is specifically addressed, you will notice the objective is listed to help call your attention to that particular material.

FIGURE 9.8
Your Windows Installer package must reside on a network share accessible to users.

STEP BY STEP

9.1 Creating a New Package for Distribution

1. Create a test OU and a test user within that OU. Nothing special needs to be done as far as configuration.

2. Create a new GPO for that OU, and open the GPO to edit.

3. Expand Software Settings under User Configuration and right-click Software Installation.

4. Select New, Package.

5. In the Open dialog box, type the Universal Naming Convention (UNC) pathname (even though it may be local) to the MSI file for the Windows 2000 admin tools. This should be comparable to Figure 9.8.

6. Click Open. The MSI file is added to the list of software packages assigned to users of that OU (see Figure 9.9).

Step by Step: Step by Steps are hands-on tutorial instructions that walk you through a particular task or function relevant to the exam objectives.

Figure: To improve readability, the figures have been placed in the margins wherever possible so they do not interrupt the main flow of text.

---

296   Part III   ANALYZING TECHNICAL REQUIREMENTS

> **WARNING**
>
> **Authorization Data** Keep in mind that authorization data is application service specific and does not support user authorization in heterogeneous environments.

Kerberos v5 contains an encrypted field for applications to use for authorization data in the session ticket. Windows 2000 uses the authorization data to carry SIDs for user and group membership. The server-side Kerberos security provider uses this authorization data to build security access tokens, which represent the user on the system. It can then use this data to impersonate the client before attempting to access local resources protected by ACLs.

Two additional fields, implemented as Boolean flags, are used in the delegation of authentication features supported by Kerberos. The *proxy* and *forwarding* fields in session tickets can be set to allow servers to obtain session tickets for other servers on behalf of the client.

IN THE FIELD

IT'S ALL IN THE NAME OF SECURITY

One very good example of where you would benefit from the delegation of authentication (forwarding) feature of Microsoft's implementation of Kerberos is with a two-tier, Web-enabled email access package.

Consider the scenario in which back-end mail servers for an organization are inside the firewall and front-end Web-based email access servers (such as Outlook Web access) are on a secure DMZ. A client may securely log on to Active Directory using the X.509 certificate PKI extensions of Kerberos by connecting to the front-end Web servers. These servers then may forward the user's request to log on to a domain controller. Once authenticated, the user would then be able to access email.

Exactly how this process works is covered in the Kerberos reference material at the end of this chapter, but you can see easily that a main benefit is that the front-end server can be configured to perform delegated tasks for only specific clients—a very powerful security implementation.

Warning: In using sophisticated information technology, there is always potential for mistakes or even catastrophes that can occur through improper application of the technology. Warnings appear in the margins to alert you to such potential problems.

In the Field Sidebar: These more extensive discussions cover material that perhaps is not as directly relevant to the exam, but which is useful as reference material or in everyday practice. In the Field may also provide useful background or contextual information necessary for understanding the larger topic under consideration.

CASE STUDIES

Case Studies are presented throughout the book to provide you with another, more conceptual opportunity to apply the knowledge you are developing. They also reflect the "real-world" experiences of the authors in ways that prepare you not only for the exam but for actual network administration as well. In each Case Study, you will find similar elements: a Background of the case, a Problem Statement, and an Analysis.

CASE STUDY: ONLINE LICENSE COMPANY (OLC)

BACKGROUND

OLC is a company created by the Indiana Bureau of Motor Vehicles to provide a new service to licensed drivers. This new service provides drivers the opportunity to renew licenses and license plates over the Internet. OLC is an extension of the Indiana Bureau of Motor Vehicles and therefore shares the bureau's records database.

PROBLEM STATEMENT

The pressure from a newly elected "high-tech" governor to provide these services caused the OLC development team to rush delivery of the system. In doing so, it did not implement adequate security and has recommended to OLC that the bureau implement new security features.

Lead Developer
"There is no certificate-based security on this Web site. All traffic goes through port 80 and is unencrypted. This is true for all personal information, license numbers, credit card info—

CURRENT SYSTEM

The system was developed using Active Server Pages (ASP) and Dynamic HTML (DHTML), which work together to provide user interface functionality, and an ODBC connection to the state's UNIX-based Informix database. The entire Web system runs on a Windows NT 4.0 platform and uses a TCP/IP connection (via ODBC) to the database.

OLC Data Analyst
"My responsibility is to pull data from the Informix database and process it. I use an IP connection to the UNIX side and have to log on to both the UNIX OS and the Informix database. Seems a little *too* secure to me!"

A Licensed Driver
"*Wow!* I registered both cars in a matter of 10 minutes. That sure beats sitting in the BMV office for three hours. I don't know why anyone would ever use the offices anymore—I really don't. This system is awesome. One thing that

---

Background: The Background lists of the key problems or issues that need to be addressed in the Case Study.

Problem Statement: A few paragraphs describing a situation that professional practitioners in the field might face. A Problem Statement will deal with an issue relating to the objectives covered in the chapter, and it includes the kinds of details that make a difference.

Electrico employs about 5,000 people and is operationally managed from Indianapolis with divisions in El Paso (Manufacturing), Seattle (Product Development), Los Angeles (Sales), Buffalo (Shipping), and Chicago (Receiving). Electrico has been trailing its competition in terms of revenue for the past two years despite a steady increase in sales. Consequently, its executives have been studying its two main competitors and have made two distinct findings:

- Both of its main competitors utilize the Internet to sell product and supply their distribution channels with product.

- Both competitors include representatives from their corresponding IT organizations on every key strategic decision they make.

Immediately following these findings, Electrico called an executive meeting in which the following decisions were made:

- For the company to remain competitive, it must start putting an emphasis on technology.

- All IT projects should be outsourced from this point forward so the company can concentrate on its core competency.

a few 486 and low-end Pentium computers on the desktop running Windows 95 and a terminal emulation package to access the mainframe. IT has been reluctant to "fix" anything that was not "broken" and consequently has fallen behind the competition. Electrico executives have focused more on the bottom line in the past two years than on the business and now realize how the lack of focus on technology has jeopardized the company. They immediately got the appropriate funding to begin the project. Their goal is to change the way they do business.

BUSINESS ANALYSIS

Electrico has hired WayFront, Inc., a national consulting firm specializing in network and eBusiness solutions, to help take its business to the next level. WayFront understands technology, and more importantly, how to align business with technology to build a symmetric and high-tech business model. WayFront, after only a few days of high-level nontechnical discussions with Electrico, is ready to begin a series of discussions that will enable it to design a business solution to Electrico's problems. The following sections discuss WayFront's approach in detail.

Analysis: This is a lengthy description of the best way to handle the problems listed in the Case Study. In this section, you might find a table summarizing the solutions, a worded example, or both.

CHAPTER SUMMARY

KEY TERMS

- Kerberos
- NTLM
- SSL/TLS
- Public Key Infrastructure (PKI)
- Session ticket
- Ticket-granting ticket (TGT)
- Long-term key
- IPsec

The Internet is driving the need for increased security in all aspects of the computer network. Smarter software and people in the business means there are smarter hackers on the Internet.

Windows 2000 consists of three types of identity authentication: NTLM, Kerberos, and SSL/TLS. It wants to use Kerberos by default, but can only do so in a pure Windows 2000 environment. NTLM is still around for backward compatibility. Finally, SSL/TLS and X.509 certificates are available for certificate-based authentication.

Windows 2000 contains native support for public key infrastructure (PKI). The following make up the Windows 2000 PKI:

Key Terms: A list of key terms appears at the end of each chapter. These are terms that you should be sure you know and are comfortable defining and understanding when you go in to take the exam.

Chapter Summary: Before the Apply Your Knowledge section, you will find a chapter summary that wraps up the chapter and reviews what you should have learned.

EXTENSIVE REVIEW AND SELF-TEST OPTIONS

At the end of each chapter, along with some summary elements, you will find a section called "Apply Your Knowledge" that gives you several different methods with which to test your understanding of the material and review what you have learned.

Chapter 7   ANALYZING SECURITY REQUIREMENTS   **327**

APPLY YOUR KNOWLEDGE

Exercises

7.1   Creating a Group Policy Object

This exercise walks you through creating a GPO to specify security settings that will override the domain password security policy for a given OU.

Estimated Time: 10 Minutes

1. Open the Active Directory Users and Computers utility on your domain controller.

2. Create a new user in the default Users container. Name this user **Exercise71** and make sure you give it the same logon name. You will use this user throughout these exercises. *Do not assign this user a password and do not make any changes to the password configuration window.*

3. Create an OU by right-clicking the icon for your domain, then selecting New and Organizational Unit.

4. In the Name box (see Figure 7.10), type **Exercise71** and click OK.

FIGURE 7.10
Create your OU with the name Exercise71.

5. Right-click the Exercise71 OU and select Properties. Click on the Group Policy tab (see Figure 7.11) and click the New button. Name your new GPO **Exercise71GPO**.

FIGURE 7.11
The Group Policy tab on the Exercise71 OU, where you're creating a new GPO.

6. Click the Edit button to open the Group Policy Editor. Under Computer Settings, expand the Windows Settings folder, then expand Security Settings.

7. Expand Account Policy to reveal the Password and Account Lockout policies.

8. Click on the Password Policy (the password policy choices are shown in Figure 7.12) and change the Minimum Password Length to 7 characters.

Exercises: These activities provide an opportunity for you to master specific hands-on tasks. Our goal is to increase your proficiency with the product or technology. You must be able to conduct these tasks in order to pass the exam. When applicable, you can find solutions to Exercises in the "Answers to Exercises section."

Review Questions: These open-ended, short-answer questions allow you to quickly assess your comprehension of what you just read in the chapter. Instead of asking you to choose from a list of options, these questions require you to state the correct answers in your own words. Although you will not experience these kinds of questions on the exam, these questions will indeed test your level of comprehension of key concepts.

Exam Questions: These questions reflect the kinds of multiple-choice questions that appear on the Microsoft exams. Use them to become familiar with the exam question formats and to help you determine what you know and what you need to review or study more.

---

274   Part III   ANALYZING TECHNICAL REQUIREMENTS

APPLY YOUR KNOWLEDGE

Review Questions

1. What are the four major performance areas that should be represented in all baseline performance analyses?

2. What is the most efficient RAID configuration for a file server? Why is it not recommended?

3. What is the default configuration for the Windows 2000 server service?

4. What action must you perform before you can monitor the E: drive partition on your local computer?

5. What must you verify about the company and its users before you begin sampling data for a baseline?

6. What utility should you use to determine if Microsoft Exchange RPC data is saturating a WAN link?

7. Why would you consider using a utility, such as Microsoft Access, to view performance information?

Exam Questions

1. You wish to optimize the performance of the page file on a Windows 2000 server. What hard disk configuration would be the optimal storage medium for the page file?

   A. RAID 0

   B. RAID 1

   C. RAID 2

   D. RAID 5

2. You suspect your company's Sales and Marketing Ethernet segment is saturated. You wanted to use the System Monitor to quickly determine the utilization on that segment; however, the Network Segment object is not available. What is most likely the cause of this problem?

   A. SNMP is not installed on the computer being used for the analysis.

   B. Network Monitor Agents are not installed on the computer being used for the analysis.

D. Fine-tune the server service by selecting the Maximize Throughput for Network Applications setting.

8. Jim has just been hired at MLM Corp. as the LAN/WAN Manager, and his first task is to optimize the network. He uses a sniffer to determine what type of network traffic is in use. He determines that nearly half of the network's 80% usage is due to TCP/IP broadcast traffic from the 480 users. What should Jim do to relieve the network from excessive broadcast traffic?

   A. Install a packet optimizer.

Answers to Review Questions

1. Memory, processor, disk subsystem, and network subsystem. All four of these areas include objects that monitor the critical areas of any given server in any given role. See "What Data Should I Capture?"

2. RAID 0 (striping) is the most efficient RAID configuration across the board because of its incredibly fast read from and write to capability. RAID 0, however, has a serious drawback. It provides no fault tolerance, so if you lose a disk

---

Answers and Explanations: For some of the exercises, each of the Review and Exam questions, you will find thorough explanations located at the end of the section.

Suggested Readings and Resources

1. Microsoft TechNet Articles:

   • Configuring Enterprise Security Policies. Available on September 1999 and later TechNet CDs.

   • *Windows 2000 Reviewers Guide—Section 3:* Addressing Customer Challenges and Requirements. Available on July 1999 and later TechNet CDs.

   • MS Security Configuration Toolset. Available on January 2000 and later TechNet CDs.

   • Configuring Enterprise Security Policies. Available on September 1999 and later TechNet CDs.

   • Windows 2000 Security—Default Access Control Settings. Available on July 1999 and later TechNet CDs.

   • Windows 2000 Certificate Services. Available on July 1999 and later TechNet CDs.

2. Microsoft White Papers:

   • Secure Networking Using Windows 2000 Distributed Security Services

   • Introduction to the Windows 2000 Public Key Infrastructure

   • Introduction to Microsoft Windows 2000 Security Services

   • Single Sign On in Windows 2000 Networks

   • Encrypting File System

   • IP Security (IPsec) for Windows 2000

   • Security Configuration Tool Set

   • Windows 2000 Kerberos Authentication

   • Windows 2000 Kerberos Interoperability

Suggested Readings and Resources: The very last element in every chapter is a list of additional resources you can use if you want to go above and beyond certification-level material or if you need to spend more time on a particular subject that you are having trouble understanding.

Introduction

MCSE Training Guide: Windows 2000 Directory Services Design is designed for advanced users, technicians, or system administrators with the goal of certification as a Microsoft Certified Systems Engineer (MCSE). It covers the Designing a Microsoft Windows 2000 Directory Services Infrastructure exam (70-219). This exam measures your ability to analyze business requirements and design a directory service architecture. In addition, the test measures the skills required to analyze the business requirements for desktop management and design a solution for desktop management that meets business requirements.

This book is your one-stop shop. Everything you need to know to pass the exam is in here, and Microsoft has approved it as study material. You do not have to take a class in addition to buying this book to pass the exam. However, depending on your personal study habits or learning style, you may benefit from buying this book *and* taking a class.

Microsoft assumes that the typical candidate for this exam will have a minimum of one year's experience implementing and administering network operating systems in medium to very large network environments.

How This Book Helps You

This book takes you on a self-guided tour of all the areas covered by the Designing a Microsoft Windows 2000 Directory Services Infrastructure exam and teaches you the specific skills you'll need in order to achieve your MCSE certification. You'll also find helpful hints, tips, real-world examples, and exercises, as well as references to additional study materials. Specifically, this book is set up to help you in the following ways:

◆ **Organization.** The book is organized by individual exam objectives. Every objective you need to know for the Designing a Microsoft Windows 2000 Directory Services Infrastructure exam is covered in this book. We have attempted to present the objectives in an order that is as close as possible to that listed by Microsoft. However, we have not hesitated to reorganize them where needed to make the material as easy as possible for you to learn. We have also attempted to make the information accessible in the following ways:

- The full list of exam topics and objectives is included in this introduction.

- Each chapter begins with a list of the objectives to be covered.

- Each chapter also presents an outline that provides you with an overview of the material and the page numbers where particular topics can be found.

- The objectives are repeated where the material most directly relevant to it is covered (unless the whole chapter addresses a single objective).

- The CD-ROM included with this book contains, in PDF format, a complete listing of the test objectives and where they are covered within the book.

◆ **Instructional features.** This book has been designed to provide you with multiple ways to learn and reinforce the exam material. Following are some of the helpful methods:

- *Case studies.* Given the case study basis of the exam, we designed this *Training Guide* around them. Case studies appear in many chapters and also serve as the basis for exam questions.

- *Objective explanations.* As mentioned previously, each chapter begins with a list of the objectives covered in the chapter. In addition, immediately following each objective is an explanation in a context that defines it more meaningfully.

- *Study strategies.* The beginning of the chapter also includes strategies for approaching the study and retention of the material in the chapter, particularly as it is addressed on the exam.

- *Exam tips.* Exam tips appear in the margins to provide specific exam-related advice. Such tips may address what material is covered (or not covered) on the exam, how it is covered, mnemonic devices, or particular quirks of that exam.

- *Review breaks and summaries.* Crucial information is summarized at various points in the book in lists or tables. Each chapter ends with a summary as well.

- *Key terms.* A list of key terms appears at the end of each chapter.

- *Notes.* These appear in the margins and contain various kinds of useful information such as tips on technology or administrative

practices, historical background on terms and technologies, or side commentary on industry issues.

- *Warnings.* When using sophisticated information technology, there is always the potential for mistakes or even catastrophes that occur because of improper application of the technology. Warnings appear in the margins to alert you to such potential problems.

- *In the Fields.* These more extensive discussions cover material that may not be directly relevant to the exam but which is useful as reference material or in everyday practice. In the Fields may also provide useful background or contextual information necessary for understanding the larger topic under consideration.

- *Exercises.* Found at the ends of the chapters in the "Apply Your Knowledge" sections, exercises are performance-based opportunities for you to learn and assess your knowledge.

◆ **Extensive practice test options.** The book provides numerous opportunities for you to assess your knowledge and practice for the exam. The practice options include the following:

- *Review questions.* These open-ended questions appear in the "Apply Your Knowledge" sections at the end of each chapter. They allow you to quickly assess your comprehension of what you just read in the chapter. Answers to the questions are provided later in a separate section titled "Answers to Review Questions."

- *Exam questions.* These questions also appear in the "Apply Your Knowledge" section. Use them to help you determine what you know and what you need to review or study further.

Answers and explanations for them are provided in a separate section titled "Answers to Exam Questions."

- *Practice exam.* A practice exam is included in the "Final Review" section. The "Final Review" section and the practice exam are discussed later in this list.

- *ExamGear.* The special *Training Guide* version of the *ExamGear* software included on the CD-ROM provides further opportunities for you to assess how well you understood the material in this book.

> **NOTE** For a description of the New Riders *ExamGear, Training Guide* software, please see Appendix D, "Using *ExamGear, Training Guide Version.*"

◆ **Final Review.** This part of the book provides you with three valuable tools for preparing for the exam.

- *Fast facts.* This condensed version of the information contained in the book will prove extremely useful for last-minute review.

- *Study and exam tips.* Read this section early on to help you develop study strategies. It also provides you with valuable exam-day tips and information on exam/question formats such as adaptive tests and case study-based questions.

- *Practice exam.* An practice exam is included. Questions are written in styles similar to those used on the actual exam. Use it to assess your understanding of the material in the book.

The book includes several other features, such as the section titled "Suggested Readings and Resources" at the end of each chapter that directs you toward further information that could aid you in your exam preparation or your actual work. There are valuable appendices as well, including a glossary (Appendix A), an overview of the Microsoft certification program (Appendix B), and a description of what is on the CD-ROM (Appendix C).

For more information about the exam or the certification process, contact Microsoft:

Microsoft Education: 800-636-7544

Internet: `ftp://ftp.microsoft.com/Services/MSEdCert`

World Wide Web: `http://www.microsoft.com/train_cert`

CompuServe Forum: GO MSEDCERT

WHAT THE DESIGNING A MICROSOFT WINDOWS 2000 DIRECTORY SERVICES INFRASTRUCTURE EXAM (70-219) COVERS

The Designing a Microsoft Windows 2000 Directory Services Infrastructure Exam (70-219) covers the Windows 2000 networking topics represented by the conceptual groupings or units of the test objectives. The objectives reflect job skills in the following areas:

◆ Analyzing Business Requirements

◆ Analyzing Technical Requirements

◆ Designing a Directory Service Architecture

◆ Designing Service Locations

Before taking the exam, you should be proficient in the job skills represented by the following units, objectives, and subobjectives:

Analyzing Business Requirements

Analyze the existing and planned business models.

- Analyze the company model and the geographical scope. Models include regional, national, international, subsidiary, and branch offices.

- Analyze company processes. Processes include information flow, communication flow, service and product life cycles, and decision-making.

Analyze the existing and planned organizational structures. Considerations include management model; company organization; vendor, partner, and customer relationships; and acquisition plans.

Analyze factors that influence company strategies.

- Identify company priorities.

- Identify the projected growth and growth strategy.

- Identify relevant laws and regulations.

- Identify the company's tolerance for risk.

- Identify the total cost of operations.

Analyze the structure of IT management. Considerations include type of administration, such as centralized or decentralized; funding model; outsourcing; decision-making process; and change-management process.

Analyzing Technical Requirements

Evaluate the company's existing and planned technical environment.

- Analyze company size and user and resource distribution.

- Assess the available connectivity between the geographic location of worksites and remote sites.

- Assess the net available bandwidth.

- Analyze performance requirements.

- Analyze data and system access patterns.

- Analyze network roles and responsibilities.

- Analyze security considerations.

Analyze the impact of Active Directory on the existing and planned technical environment.

- Assess existing systems and applications.

- Identify existing and planned upgrades and rollouts.

- Analyze technical support structure.

- Analyze existing and planned network and systems management.

Analyze the business requirements for client computer desktop management.

- Analyze end-user work needs.

- Identify technical support needs for end-users.

- Establish the required client computer environment.

Designing a Directory Service Architecture

Design an Active Directory forest and domain structure.

- Design a forest and schema structure.
- Design a domain structure.
- Analyze and optimize trust relationships.

Design an Active Directory naming strategy.

- Establish the scope of the Active Directory.
- Design the namespace.
- Plan DNS strategy.

Design and plan the structure of organizational units (OU). Considerations include administration control, existing resource domains, administrative policy, and geographic and company structure.

- Develop an OU delegation plan.
- Plan Group Policy object management.
- Plan policy management for client computers.

Plan for the coexistence of Active Directory and other directory services.

Design an Active Directory site topology.

- Design a replication strategy.
- Define site boundaries.

Design a schema modification policy.

Design an Active Directory implementation plan.

Designing Service Locations

Design the placement of operations masters.

- Considerations include performance, fault tolerance, functionality, and manageability.

Design the placement of global catalog servers.

- Considerations include performance, fault tolerance, functionality, and manageability.

Design the placement of domain controllers.

- Considerations include performance, fault tolerance, functionality, and manageability.

Design the placement of DNS servers.

- Considerations include performance, fault tolerance, functionality, and manageability.
- Plan for interoperability with the existing DNS.

HARDWARE AND SOFTWARE YOU'LL NEED

As a self-paced study guide, *MCSE Training Guide: Windows 2000 Directory Services Design* is meant to help you understand concepts that must be refined through hands-on experience. To make the most of your studying, you need to have as much background on and experience with Windows 2000 Server as possible. The best way to do this is to combine study with work on Windows 2000 Server. This section gives you a description of the minimum computer requirements you need to enjoy a solid practice environment.

- Windows 2000 Server and Professional

- A server and a workstation computer on the Microsoft Hardware Compatibility List

- Pentium 166Mhz (or better) processor

- 1GB (or larger) hard disk

- VGA (or Super VGA) video adapter and monitor

- Mouse or equivalent pointing device

- CD-ROM drive

- Network Interface Card (NIC) or modem connection to Internet

- Presence on an existing network, or use of a two-port (or more) miniport hub to create a test network

- 32MB of RAM (64MB recommended)

It is easier to obtain access to the necessary computer hardware and software in a corporate business environment. It can be difficult, however, to allocate enough time within the busy workday to complete a self-study program. Most of your study time should occur after normal working hours, away from the everyday interruptions and pressures of your regular job.

ADVICE ON TAKING THE EXAM

More extensive tips are found in the "Final Review" section's "Study and Exam Prep Tips," but keep this advice in mind as you study:

- **Read all the material.** Microsoft has been known to include material not expressly specified in the objectives. This book has included additional information not reflected in the objectives in an effort to give you the best possible preparation for the examination— and for the real-world experiences to come.

- **Do the Step by Steps and complete the exercises in each chapter.** They will help you gain experience using the specified methodology or approach. All Microsoft exams are task- and experienced-based and require you to have experience actually performing the tasks upon which you will be tested.

- **Use the questions to assess your knowledge.** Don't just read the chapter content; use the questions to find out what you know and what you don't. You also need the experience of analyzing case studies. If you are struggling at all, study some more, review, then assess your knowledge again.

- **Review the exam objectives.** Develop your own questions and examples for each topic listed. If you can develop and answer several questions for each topic, you should not find it difficult to pass the exam.

Remember: The primary object is not to pass the exam—it is to understand the material. After you understand the material, passing the exam should be simple. Knowledge is a pyramid; to build upward, you need a solid foundation. This book and the Microsoft Certified Professional programs are designed to ensure that you have that solid foundation.

Good luck!

NOTE

Exam-taking advice   Although this book is designed to prepare you to take and pass the Designing a Microsoft Windows 2000 Directory Services Infrastructure certification exam, there are no guarantees. Read this book, work through the questions and exercises, and when you feel confident, take the practice exam and additional exams using the *ExamGear, Training Guide Edition* test software. This should tell you whether you are ready for the real thing.

When taking the actual certification exam, make sure you answer all the questions before your time limit expires. Do not spend too much time on any one question. If you are unsure about a question, answer it as best as you can; then mark it for review when you have finished the rest of the questions. Note, however, that this advice will not apply if you are taking an adaptive exam. In that case, take your time on each question. There is no opportunity to go back to a question.

NEW RIDERS PUBLISHING

The staff of New Riders Publishing is committed to bringing you the very best in computer reference material. Each New Riders book is the result of months of work by authors and staff who research and refine the information contained within its covers.

As part of this commitment to you, the NRP reader, New Riders invites your input. Please let us know if you enjoy this book, if you have trouble with the information or examples presented, or if you have a suggestion for the next edition.

Please note, however, that New Riders staff cannot serve as a technical resource during your preparation for the Microsoft certification exams or for questions about software- or hardware-related problems. Please refer instead to the documentation that accompanies the Microsoft products or to the applications' Help systems.

If you have a question or comment about any New Riders book, there are several ways to contact New Riders Publishing. We will respond to as many readers as we can. Your name, address, or phone number will never become part of a mailing list or be used for any purpose other than to help us continue to bring you the best books possible. You can write to us at the following address:

New Riders Publishing
Attn: Executive Editor
201 W. 103rd Street
Indianapolis, IN 46290

If you prefer, you can fax New Riders Publishing at 317-817-7448.

You also can send email to New Riders at the following Internet address:

`nrfeedback@newriders.com`

NRP is an imprint of Pearson Education. To obtain a catalog or information, contact us at `nrmedia@newriders.com`. To purchase a New Riders book, call 800-428-5331.

Thank you for selecting *MCSE Training Guide: Windows 2000 Directory Services Design.*

ACTIVE DIRECTORY BASICS

1 **Understanding Active Directory**

This chapter provides a brief introduction to Active Directory and its design-related characteristics. In doing so, it provides important background information regarding the unification of directory services. No formal exam objectives are covered, but you will be better prepared to approach the exam objectives after reading this chapter.

This key feature of Windows has been in the works for some time. A unified directory service is just what you may already expect, a single directory providing various services to multiple directory service-enabled applications that may request them. Active Directory as a unified directory, as well as additional Active Directory facts, are presented in this chapter.

CHAPTER 1

Understanding Active Directory

OUTLINE

- ▶ Understand the core underlying functions of Active Directory, such as Lightweight Directory Access Protocol (LDAP) and Domain Name System (DNS). Being able to break down Active Directory down into manageable and comprehensible sections will make it easier to design.

- ▶ Be able to identify Windows NT 3.5x and 4.0 domain models and how to map those to Windows 2000 and Active Directory.

- ▶ Do not focus solely on the technical aspects of Windows 2000. It is a business system as much as it is an operating system, and you need to understand how to effectively model the operating system according to business objectives.

- ▶ Read up on DNS because it is core to Active Directory. If you feel you don't have a good understanding of it, you may want to read part of Chapter 10, "DNS and Active Directory," now.

INTRODUCTION

Microsoft's Active Directory is a directory service completely integrated with the Windows 2000 line of server and workstation products. It provides an extensible, flexible, and powerful set of features, tools, and utilities designed to scale from the smallest of home businesses to the largest worldwide corporate enterprises. Network administrators, management, developers, and users utilize Active Directory to gain access to resources.

This chapter focuses on the Windows 2000 architecture as it relates to Active Directory and on specific design related components of Active Directory itself. It confirms the fact that with the introduction of a new operating system (OS), a wide array of upgrade and migration scenarios are bound to appear. Design considerations for upgrading each of the four Windows NT domain models are discussed briefly and we also make a brief stop on Novell Street.

Finally, various development interfaces are introduced at a high level along with some of the new design-focused Windows 2000 features. Because this chapter addresses general concepts rather than specific objectives, a case study is not presented.

"DIRECTORY" DEFINED

If you are reading this book, you most likely already know what a directory is. You could call the yellow pages a directory, or a physician list, or an online search tool such as Yahoo! or AltaVista, or...you get the point! Directories of some fashion are all around us; heck, these days even when we flip channels on cable television we are presented with a channel guide—another directory.

Windows 2000 Active Directory directory services is essentially two parts:

◆ **Directory.** A directory is a physical storage container that contains anywhere from a few up to millions of various types of objects. The most popular directory is a phone book, which contains names, phone numbers, and addresses—types of objects.

◆ **Services.** The primary function of a service with regard to a directory is to make the information in the directory useful. The Web interfaces of popular search engines Yahoo.com, AltaVista.com, and Lycos.com are all examples of services that provide you easy access to the information in the directory—the Internet.

Now you have the "textbook" definitions of a directory and a directory service. Next let's take a look at Active *Directory* as a provider of *services*. Figure 1.1 illustrates this concept.

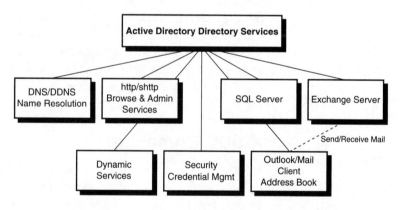

FIGURE 1.1
Active Directory as a service provider.

ACTIVE DIRECTORY IS A UNIFIED DIRECTORY

The notion of a single logon for access to all available network resources is not new; in fact, it can be argued that at one time a few years ago, it actually existed. Remember the mainframe and dumb terminal days? Okay, not the best reference, but it gets the point across. With the ever more complicated world of directory services and productivity standards and heterogeneous systems with a need to talk to one another, the need for a standards-based directory service is more apparent than ever.

Microsoft's Active Directory incorporates the Internet concept of a *namespace* with the operating system's core directory services. This allows administrators to unify the multiple namespaces that exist across heterogeneous applications throughout the enterprise. It uses the Internet standard Lightweight Directory Access Protocol (LDAP, which you'll learn more about in the next section) as its core protocol, which allows it to cross operating system boundaries and integrate multiple namespaces. It can manage other Network Operating System (NOS) directories and application-specific directories and helps reduce the administrative load required to maintain several dissimilar namespaces and their associated directory services.

X.500 Compliant

X.500 is the Open Systems Interconnect (OSI) directory standard. It defines a namespace, an information model, a functional model, and an authentication framework. Additionally, X.500 defines Directory Access Protocol (DAP), an OSI standard protocol for accessing an X.500 directory. DAP is extremely feature rich and carries a lot of overhead. Its clients rarely, if ever, use many of its features. Because DAP is so difficult to implement and requires so much raw power to run, an alternative protocol was created. This new protocol, LDAP, was created to leverage the relatively low overhead of the TCP/IP suite of protocols to access X.500 directories. Remember this: Active Directory is *not* an X.500 directory. It uses LDAP as the access protocol and supports the X.500 information model without having to host the entire X.500 overhead. X.500 directories accessed with LDAP remain intact and require no changes for LDAP to be successful.

LDAP Is Core

As previously stated, LDAP is the core protocol that enables Windows 2000 to leverage the benefits of X.500 style directories without the X.500 burden. LDAP defines the following components:

◆ **Data model**. Defines the syntax of data in the directory.

◆ **Organizational model**. Defines organization of data in the directory.

◆ **Security model**. Defines a manner in which data in the directory may be securely accessed.

◆ **Functional model**. Defines the operations used in querying and modifying data in the directory.

◆ **Topological model**. Defines how the directory service integrates with other directory services to form a global directory on the Internet.

One integral piece of Active Directory yet to be mentioned is another old Internet standard, Domain Name System (DNS). By utilizing DNS for name resolution within LDAP queries, Active Directory is able to support working with directory services running on non-Microsoft systems.

NOTE **DNS** Chapter 10, "DNS and Active Directory" is devoted to DNS and its integration with Active Directory.

Microsoft realizes that good applications need to support several industry standards, so it has built the following support into the native Active Directory implementation:

◆ Subsets of the 1993 Directory Access Protocol (DAP)

◆ 1993 Directory System Protocol (DSP)

◆ Directory Information Shadowing Protocol (DISP)

◆ Lightweight Directory Access Protocol (LDAP)

NOTE   **The LDAP Standard**   The LDAP (version 3) standard is defined by the IETF under RFC-1823. Active Directory supports both version 2 and version 3 of the LDAP implementation.

NOTE   **IETF RFCs**   Throughout this text, we will reference standards using IETF Request For Comments (RFC) numbers where appropriate. To access an RFC, connect to **http://www.ietf.org/rfc.html** and search for the appropriate RFC number.

Microsoft continues to work with standards organizations such as the Internet Engineering Task Force (IETF) to further refine standards with a goal that someday we'll be able to achieve seamless integration of standards-based directory services across the board.

ACTIVE DIRECTORY FEATURES AND BENEFITS

Active Directory features and benefits don't stop with X.500 and LDAP support. There are a considerable number of enhancements over the previous versions of Windows NT, which are highlighted in the following sections.

Support for Open Standards

Active Directory support for the DNS standard implementation is huge. It provides a common namespace between the Internet and your internal network. As discussed in the previous section, the support for LDAP and the X.500 functional model provides a common and intuitive query process for retrieving resources from the directory.

Active Directory uses RFC-822 standard naming formats, which are very similar to email addresses, as a "friendly" name. This friendly name can be used for email, printed on a business card, and logged on to the network.

Finally, LDAP URLs and X.500 names allow any client to access data from anywhere providing they work from an LDAP-enabled client and have security clearance. An LDAP URL is in this form:

```
LDAP://a_server.mycompany.com/CN=joesmith,OU=whitepapers,
OU=OpSys,OU=Windows2000,DC=Microsoft,DC=com
```

Most LDAP URLs are handled by the LDAP-enabled application program and remain unnoticed by users.

Rich Set of APIs

Without question, the biggest draw from the development community to Microsoft products is the rich set of Application Programming Interfaces (APIs). APIs provide a standard set of functions to which developers may write code. These functions allow access to Active Directory resources, thereby encouraging the development of application programs and tools that make use of the directory's services. The following sections describe the three major API sets.

ADSI

Active Directory Services Interface (ADSI) is a set of Component Object Model (COM) interfaces that give developers the ability to query and manipulate directory services without knowing specific information about how the directory services are implemented. ADSI is a part of the Open Directory Services Interface (ODSI), which is the Windows Open Systems Architecture (WOSA) standard for manipulating multiple directory services. ADSI objects are available to provide access to Windows 2000, Windows NT 4.0, NetWare 3.x through 5.x, and any other directory service that supports LDAP. It greatly simplifies the development of distributed applications as well as the administration of distributed systems because it abstracts the capabilities of directory services from different network providers and provides a single common set of APIs for managing distributed network resources. Figure 1.2 illustrates how clients and servers currently access directory services through proprietary API calls. Figure 1.3 introduces ADSI as a means of abstracting multiple directory services interfaces and representing them to the developer, administrator, or user in a standard set of COM objects.

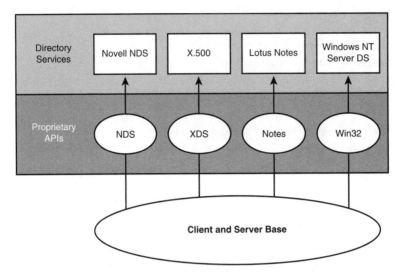

FIGURE 1.2

Heterogeneous directories and their corresponding proprietary API interfaces.

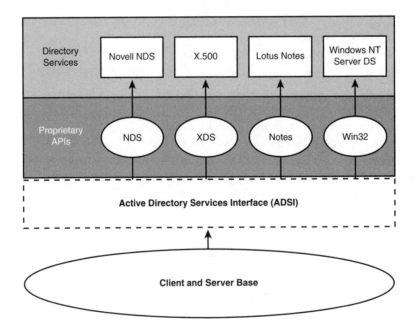

FIGURE 1.3

Heterogeneous directories abstracted by the ADSI and represented as a common set of objects.

The ADSI objects are designed to meet the needs of not only developers using traditional C and C++ but also the network administrator and the end-user. The following list highlights the intended usage of ADSI for the three groups.

◆ **Developers**. This area is what systems engineers and consultants would refer to as "hard core" developing. Developers use a compiled language such as C++ to write distributed applications to manage network resources, print queues, and more.

◆ **System Administrators**. This area of usage would include scripts written in an interpreted language, such as VBScript. System administrators would be able to develop small and minimally complicated script applets they could utilize over and over again. Common operations for this would be in the area of adding a large number of users to the directory and adding them to specific security groups.

◆ **Users**. Users would even have the ability to develop simple scripts that could query Active Directory with the help of a COM object. This query may yield such information as the number of print jobs in a queue for a specific group of users.

MAPI

The Messaging Application Programming Interface (MAPI), an "older" technology, is included in the Active Directory API set for backward compatibility with legacy MAPI-based applications. Microsoft encourages the use of ADSI to build new directory-enabled applications.

LDAP C API

The LDAP C API set is a solution for developers tasked with developing applications or toolsets that are required to work across many types of clients.

Drag and Drop Administration

Active Directory provides easy-to-use, yet powerful administration tools. These tools present objects in a hierarchical organization to the administrator, which gives him the ability to effectively model

Further Details on Pruning and Grafting   For more information on pruning and grafting, see the Microsoft Windows 2000 Distributed Systems Guide, which can be found on Microsoft TechNet, as well as at `http://www.microsoft.com/ windows2000`.

large organizations. The graphical user interface features a highly anticipated drag and drop control console tool. This tool is most useful in the restructuring of Active Directory domain objects using a process called pruning and grafting. To prune is to cut and to graft is to paste. If you, for example, create a large number of objects in the wrong place in the directory and need to move them to another area, you would utilize this process.

Extensible Schema

Sitting at the core of Active Directory is the schema. The schema defines *classes*, *attributes*, and *attribute syntax* (rules) for all Active Directory objects. When you right-click on an Active Directory object, such as the user object in Figure 1.4, you'll see several of the standard user object attributes, such as first name, last name, and so on.

Active Directory provides an installable interface to the schema through the Microsoft Management Console (MMC). From this interface (shown in Figure 1.5), on a domain controller specified as the Schema Master, an administrator may *extend* the schema to include additional objects and object attributes after modification of the schema has been enabled.

Suppose, for example, a company develops an application that utilizes an employee's Social Security number. The schema by default does not provide an attribute for the Social Security number, so the administrator would need to add it to and associate it with the user object class. We'll cover the schema and modification policies in more detail in Chapter 13, "Developing a Schema Modification Plan." For now, just understand that the schema may be extended to include custom attributes.

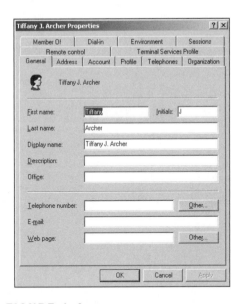

FIGURE 1.4

Tiffany J. Archer user object displaying the standard user object attributes.

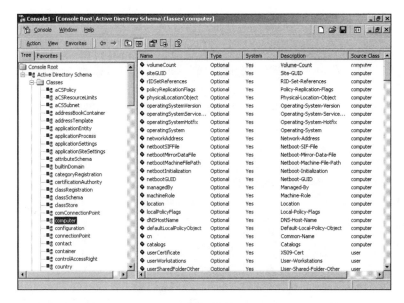

FIGURE 1.5
The Active Directory schema, displayed in the Microsoft Management
Console, may be extended to include additional classes and attributes.

Global Catalog Servers

To enable for all domains the ability to locate objects across an
entire Active Directory forest, special servers called *global catalog
servers* maintain partial directory information from all domains in
a forest. The global catalog servers provide users with quick returns
on Active Directory queries. Global catalog servers contain a replica
of all objects in each domain in the forest, but only a specific subset of each object's attributes. This "abbreviated catalog" is generated
through a special partial replication process. If a global catalog
server cannot satisfy a query within its partial replica, it forwards
the request to the source domain's full database replica for
fulfillment.

Multi-Master Replication Model

Active Directory is a true distributed database. Instead of having a single *primary* domain controller and several *backup* domain controllers, such as previous versions of Windows NT, Windows 2000 implements Active Directory domain controllers as equals.

It is estimated that 99 percent of the activity to which Active Directory must respond is query (read) activity. The remaining 1 percent is update (write) activity. This fact is highly responsible for the need to distribute databases. Creating multiple replicas of the directory and keeping them consistent significantly increases the number of queries that can be processed with little or no performance degradation. This disbursement and synchronization of Active Directory information is known as *multi-master replication.*

NOTE

Multi-Master Exceptions There are a few exceptions to the notion of "all domain controllers are created equal," so Microsoft created the operations masters, which will be discussed in detail in Chapter 12, "Designing an OU and Group Policy Management Structure."

Backward Compatibility

Microsoft generally does a pretty good job of providing a smooth transition from one platform to another, and that doesn't change with Windows 2000, although it does require quite a bit more planning! Active Directory operates in *mixed mode* by default. Mixed-mode (as opposed to native-mode) domains are domains in which Active Directory domain controllers may exist simultaneously with down-level Windows NT 3.51 and Windows NT 4.0 domain controllers. In this situation, Active Directory domain controllers work and act just like down-level domain controllers. We'll discuss upgrade design considerations in various chapters in Part IV, "Designing a Directory Service Architecture."

NOTE

Mixed and Native Modes Mixed-mode operation will be essential during the Windows 2000 migration process, but it is important to point out that is has several limitations. Once you complete a migration, you should set your sights on a native-mode implementation plan to leverage the full benefit of Windows 2000.

Name Resolution Services

One other area of interest in terms of backward compatibility is name resolution services. Mixed-mode domain controllers still understand NetBIOS. Native-mode domain controllers give you the option of eliminating NetBIOS name resolution in lieu of dedicated SMB ports. This provides for more efficient name resolution. Since several applications (including Microsoft BackOffice 4.5) still have NetBIOS roots, removal of NetBIOS is not likely to be an option for a while.

It is important to realize that native-mode Windows 2000 still understands NetBIOS. *You* control whether it continues to do so. Many people have the misconception that once you go to native mode, you lose NetBIOS—that is simply not true.

Interoperability

Interoperability is an extremely broad topic, especially when it is used in reference to Microsoft products. This section focuses on Active Directory interoperability with Novell NetWare and Microsoft Exchange, and then takes a look at future interoperability endeavors.

NetWare

At the time of this writing, Microsoft had released the second release candidate of the Microsoft Directory Synchronization Services (MSDSS) utility (packaged with Services for Netware 5.0). This utility provides one- or two-way synchronization between Active Directory and Novell Directory Services (NDS), and one-way synchronization between Active Directory and the Novell Bindery. This utility requires Novell's Windows 2000 client (4.7) on the server and cannot co-exist with other NetWare interoperability solutions, such as Gateway Services for NetWare.

Two-way synchronization gives the administrator the option to use the Active Directory Users and Computers user interface or the Novell NDS administration utilities to make changes to directory objects. One-way synchronization forces the administrator to make all directory changes in Active Directory.

Exchange

Windows 2000 introduces a plethora of new technologies for building solutions, among which are integration solutions for both Microsoft products and other third-party products through the use of ADSI. Microsoft Exchange 5.5 is the first Microsoft product to make use of ADSI (and other technologies such as Collaborative Data Objects) to provide collaboration and information sharing between Exchange 5.5 and Active Directory through the use of an Active Directory Connector (ADC). Administrators of Exchange can leverage the next-generation administration tools of Windows 2000 to manage down-level Exchange servers and synchronize the Exchange and Windows 2000 directories. This synchronization must be configured and is not without limits.

Exchange 2000—and, on a broader scale, the next generation of Microsoft BackOffice products—will be tightly integrated with Windows 2000 and Active Directory, and will take full advantage of the Windows 2000 security model, replication, authentication, and more.

Future Interoperability

Microsoft introduced the Joint Development Program (JDP) for select alliance partners to develop applications that (among other things) leverage Active Directory services. We can expect to see several applications spawn from this program throughout the life-cycle of Windows 2000. Additionally, it would be safe to assume that a very high percentage of the development community will be creating and upgrading applications to leverage the benefits of Active Directory.

The Windows 2000 API sets, specifically the ADSI and LDAP C APIs, provide the foundation for the development of Active Directory-aware applications, including interoperability packages.

Scalability

Remember Microsoft Exchange 4.0? Do you see any similarities between the Exchange directory and Active Directory? The Exchange 4.0 directory structure and its *extensible storage engine* (ESE) provide the foundation for Active Directory. The ESE provides the following two benefits that Microsoft was able to capitalize on in migrating it to a general-purpose directory service:

◆ **Multiple indexes.** The ESE provides multiple indexes for fast data retrieval.

◆ **Efficient storage for sparse objects.** Sparse objects are objects that support many different properties but do not always have values for all of them.

Active Directory supports multiple stores (the directory database) and each store is capable of reaching sizes up to 17TB, which is millions of objects per store.

Dynamic DNS

Domain Name System (DNS) is an Internet standard name resolution service that maps fully qualified domain names (FQDNs) to IP addresses. The Windows 2000 implementation of DNS includes some major enhancements over the traditional DNS, which enable it to become the core name resolution backbone on both sides of the corporate firewall. The following list outlines these major enhancements:

◆ **Service Resource Records (SRV RR).** SRV records (as these are commonly called) are used to specify the location of a server for a specific protocol, service, and domain. They are defined in RFC-2052.

◆ **Dynamic update protocol.** Dynamic update protocol provides a means of automatically updating primary DNS zone data. The dynamic update protocol is defined in RFC-2136. This is where the "dynamic" comes in with Dynamic DNS (DDNS).

◆ **Incremental zone transfer.** Incremental zone transfer allows for the partial transfer of a DNS zone file to its replication partners. This partial replication sends only modifications to the requesting server, and therefore drastically decreases the overhead involved in transferring an entire zone file. Incremental zone transfer is defined in RFC-1995.

◆ **Active Directory integrated zones.** If you opt to use the Microsoft implementation of DNS, you can store your zone files in Active Directory and take advantage of its replication topology. This option alleviates the hassle of maintaining flat text files for your DNS zones.

> **NOTE**
>
> **DNS or DDNS?**   DNS and DDNS both refer to Domain Name System. A DNS that supports dynamic update protocol may be referred to as DDNS or DNS. In this book, we will use both at times, but DNS in general.

Integration with TCP/IP Services

Windows Internet Name Service (WINS) and Dynamic Host Configuration Protocol (DHCP) have both been revised to provide support for dynamic DNS. We address DHCP and WINS integration with DNS in Chapter 10.

Non-Microsoft DNS Servers

If you choose to use a third-party DNS server for your Active Directory implementation, such as one you may have implemented already at a corporate level, it must support both the dynamic update protocol and SRV records. Specific BIND implementations of DNS will support both of these technologies.

Public/Private Key Infrastructure

Windows 2000 implements a distributed security model based on the MIT Kerberos v5 authentication protocol. Kerberos is used for distributed security within a tree, and incorporates the native Windows 2000 Access Control Lists (ACLs) for both public and private key security. Active Directory replaces the registry as the store for the security system and manages user accounts, domains, and group accounts as a trusted component within the Local Security Authority (LSA).

For objects that do not have Kerberos credentials, Active Directory supports the use of X.509 v3 public key certificates. In this scenario, an outsider such as a subcontractor would be granted secure access to specific internal information. The X.509 v3 specifications require certificates be issued by a trusted certificate authority, such as Verisign.

MIGRATION FROM PREVIOUS VERSIONS OF NT

The transition to Windows 2000 should be a methodically planned strategic process that takes into account not only the existing Windows NT infrastructure, but also strategic business initiatives,

company goals, administrative requirements, and company direction. Take your time in reading this next sentence, and make sure
you remember it as you read through this book: *The complexity of
migrating to Windows 2000 is not in the upgrade process itself, but in
the planning process where you determine the position of the company
now and the direction of the company in the 3–5-year future and
develop an upgrade strategy that meets the needs of every business objective.* Parts II and III of this book will be dedicated to helping you
prepare for these types of migrations.

The remainder of this section focuses on the four Windows NT
3.5x and 4.x domain models and describes the process by which
each model should be approached in terms of a Windows 2000
upgrade.

We will not cover the Windows 2000 and Active Directory installation processes in this book; however, you will see references to
pertinent resource materials throughout.

Table 1.1 lists the recommended in-place upgrade strategy for
Windows NT 3.5x and 4.x servers and domain controllers to
Windows 2000.

TABLE 1.1

LEGACY WINDOWS NT SERVER TO WINDOWS 2000 SERVER UPGRADE PATH

Legacy Version of Windows NT	*Upgrade to Windows 2000*
Windows NT 3.51 or 4.0 PDC	Domain Controller
Windows NT 3.51 or 4.0 BDC	Domain Controller or Member Server
Windows NT 3.51 or 4.0 Member Server	Member Server

IN THE FIELD

ISSUES WITH WINDOWS NT 3.51 AND WINDOWS 2000

There are two problems having to do with Windows NT 3.51 operating in Windows 2000 domains. They both have to do with users
and groups that belong to domains other than the logon domain.

continues

continued

The first problem involves applications running on a Windows NT 3.51 server in a resource domain. When a remote user attempts to access such an application, only the groups in the account domain of that user are used in constructing the security token. Groups from any resource domain are ignored. If the user is a member of a group in a resource domain, he may be denied access to the application.

The second problem involves System ID (SID) history for accounts that have been moved from one domain to another. Windows NT 3.51 cannot process SID history attributes from a domain other than the one from which the user is currently logging on. Therefore, the SID in the SID history file is not added to the user's token.

Microsoft's Recommended Migration Approach

Microsoft recommends that you do an incremental in-place upgrade. Through this process, you can slowly and methodically upgrade servers to Windows 2000, while maintaining all the functionality of your underlying Windows NT networks. This process is also transparent to client computers, which may continue logging on to the domain as they always have.

The following steps contain the generalized high-level, step-by-step processes recommended for the migration to Windows 2000. These steps are not detailed and should not be referenced during an actual migration. Derivations of each of these steps can be applied to all four migration processes. They are presented to give you exposure to the high level processes you can expect to perform during migration.

1. Analyze the business requirements. See Part II, "Analyzing Business Requirements."

2. Analyze the technical requirements. See Part III, "Analyzing Technical Requirements."

3. Develop a project plan and supporting documents. See Part V, "Preparing for Implementation."

4. Execute the project plan.

The following steps highlight the general steps you might take to migrate a single Windows NT domain to Windows 2000:

1. Verify that a full backup of the domain controllers (PDCs and BDCs) exists.

2. Remove a BDC from the network. By taking a BDC offline, you ensure that you have a current, untouched copy of your SAM database available in case of disaster.

3. Upgrade the PDC to your first Windows 2000 domain controller. This first domain controller will become your "root" server in the Windows 2000 domain.

4. Verify the functionality of the upgraded PDC. At this stage, clients may continue to log on as if the PDC were still a Windows NT 4.0 server.

5. Once you are satisfied, bring the offline BDC back online and upgrade it to Windows 2000 as an additional domain controller in the same domain. For multiple-domain models (single master, multi master, and complete trust), you'll need to repeat this process for each account database. Additionally, it is recommended for the multi master and complete trust models to create a "phantom" top-level domain and insert all account domains as children of this phantom domain. Chapters 10 and 11 provide more detailed description of domain namespace options, including the phantom domain.

6. Finally, upgrade all member servers and workstations at your leisure. Because they will not be Active Directory domain controllers, these servers and workstations may be upgraded before, during, or after the project.

7. After all computers are upgraded to Windows 2000 Server or Professional, you may opt to turn to native mode to receive the added functionality of nested groups, universal groups, and change and configuration management utilities.

NOTE

Antiques You probably have noticed that we've "ignored" Microsoft operating systems prior to Windows NT 3.5x. If you have Windows NT servers previous to version 3.5x, you should upgrade them to version 3.5x or 4.x before attempting a Windows 2000 upgrade.

Single Domain Model

The single domain model is by far the most simplistic domain model to migrate to Windows 2000. There are always options to split the single domain into multiple child domains of a single parent, but this is not recommended unless the business direction requires it. Be sure to develop and stick with a migration plan and an Active Directory design that best fits the needs of your company. In Figure 1.6, SingleDom, Inc., a company utilizing the single domain model, performs an upgrade to Windows 2000 and Active Directory. Notice the offline area. It is a key part of ensuring that you'll have the ability to recover from disaster during the upgrade process.

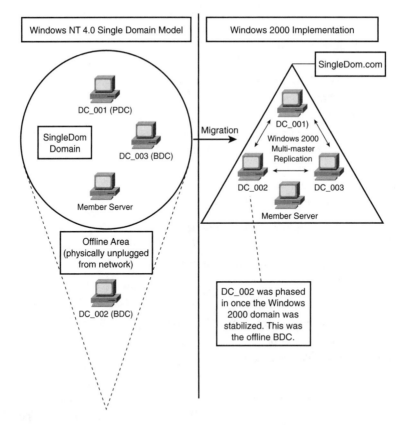

FIGURE 1.6

Migration of the Windows NT single domain model to Active Directory.

Single Master Domain Model

The single master domain model presents a few options for the migration process. Depending on the business model, administrative model, and infrastructure of the company, the migration team may decide to collapse resource domains and utilize a single Active Directory domain model. The removal of resource domains can greatly reduce administrative overhead and lead to a more manageable network. The most notable reason for implementing Windows NT single master domain models centers around the limitations of the SAM database size of 40MB. This reason is no longer valid in Windows 2000 and you should consider collapsing the resource domains into Windows 2000 organizational units (OUs). The same scenario applies if resource domains were created to delegate administrative control. On the other hand, if you find the creation of resource domains falls into one of the following categories, then you would want to keep them as child domains of your master domain.

◆ Support for decentralized administration

◆ Support for multiple domain policies

◆ Support for international differences

◆ Isolation of domain replication traffic

◆ Balancing of domain replication traffic

It is very important to identify the necessity of resource domains during the planning phase of your migration. You do not want to collapse a resource domain if the reason for its existence falls one of the categories within the preceding list. In Figure 1.7, MasterDom, Inc., a company utilizing a single master domain model with two resource domains, decided to collapse the resource domains into OUs of masterdom.com.

> **NOTE**
>
> **Organizational Units** OUs provide a means by which you can partition a domain into a hierarchical structure. They are used mainly for administrative purposes. Chapter 12 explains OUs in more detail.

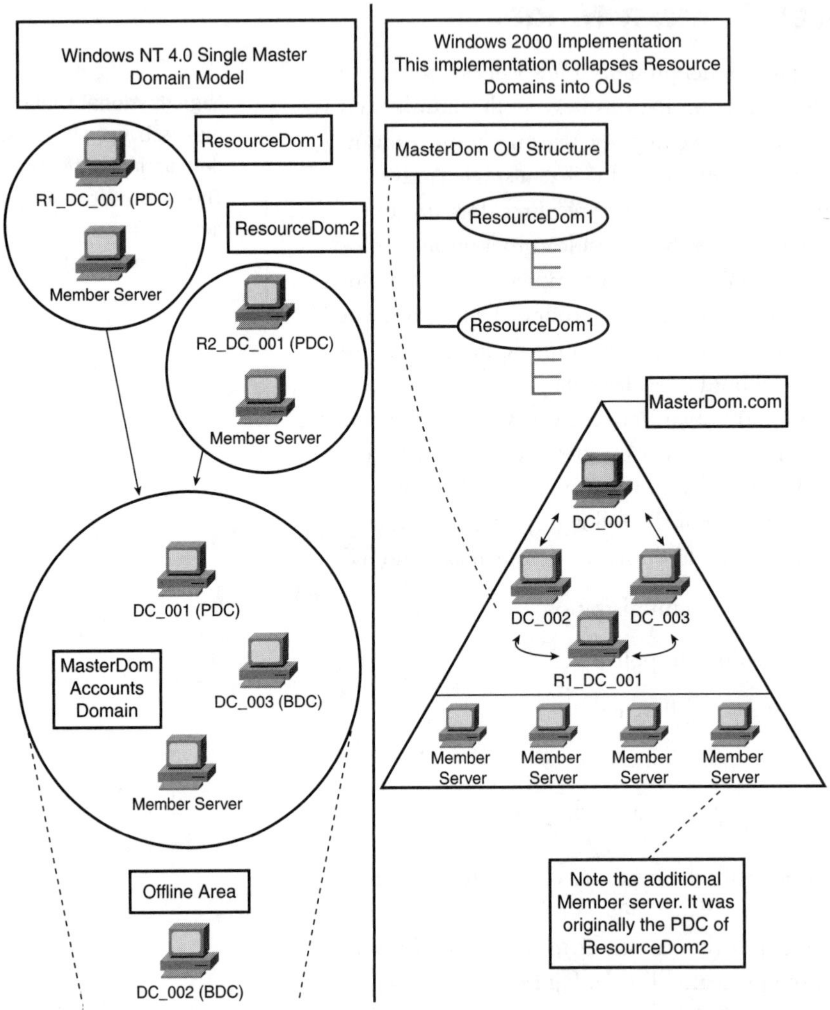

FIGURE 1.7
Migration of the Windows NT single master
domain model to Active Directory.

Multiple Master Domain Model

In a multiple master (multi-master) domain model, two or more master account databases exist on the network and provide the account base for one or more resource domains each. Each master domain trusts all other master domains, and each resource domain trusts all master domains. However, the master domains do not trust the resource domains. This scenario presents some additional challenges to the migration team. The best solution for migrating the multi-master model is to create a brand new phantom top-level root domain (company.com) and upgrade all master domain PDCs to child domains of the phantom root domain (master1.company. com) and (master2.company.com).

The resource domains should collapse to organizational units in the domain from which they were resources. Alternatively, one of the master domains could be selected to be the root of the Windows 2000 domain tree, and all other master domains could become child domains of it. This would probably create some tension between administrative teams in competing for that top-level domain spot since security can filter down from the top. Figure 1.8 depicts a company utilizing the multiple master domain model that chose to use a phantom top-level root domain in its migration.

NOTE

Why Phantom Domains? A phantom root-level domain may be utilized for numerous reasons. In this case, we chose to use one to keep both master domains operating at the same hierarchical level within the domain tree.

Complete Trust Domain Model

Anyone who's been in the Windows NT world for any length of time undoubtedly has heard other names for the complete trust model—names that cannot be mentioned in this book. Active Directory can ease the pain and suffering administrators often go through when they are responsible for a complete trust model. Migrating a complete trust model to Windows 2000 would enable a company to design a much more streamlined and manageable architecture.

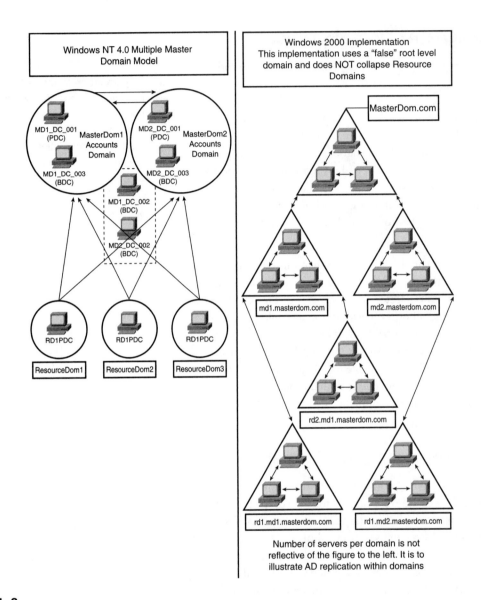

FIGURE 1.8
Migration of the Windows NT multiple master
domain model to Active Directory.

There are a few approaches to consider for this migration process, and the one you choose should match your business objectives and administrative structure. First, as with the multi-master model, consider creating a phantom top-level domain. This domain would do little more than provide the namespace for the rest of the directory. You could then migrate all domains to Windows 2000 as child domains of the phantom domain. This approach is the most attractive, again, because all account domains are treated as equals. This approach does not scale well, however, if administrative control needs to be centralized. The other approach is to structure the existing domains around your organizational and administrative hierarchy. For example, if in your complete trust model you have a specific domain for your corporate office, you may want to make that your top-level domain. All other domains would fall under it in a hierarchical tree. This would give the corporate office the opportunity to gain administrative control over all domains in the tree, but would also create opportunity for domain-level administration. This is referred to as a *hybrid* administration model. Figure 1.9 shows how a company using a complete trust model might implement Windows 2000 and Active Directory. In this figure, domain1 was the focal point of corporate control and so was used as the top-level Active Directory domain.

Novell NetWare

Microsoft includes an updated NetWare Migration Tool with Windows 2000. The Directory Service Migration Tool can be used to migrate NetWare 3.x, 4.x, and 5.x Bindery, and NDS based objects as well as volume data to Windows 2000. The tool is designed to work in a three-step process:

1. Create and model a view from NetWare.

2. Configure a view to Active Directory.

3. Migrate NetWare volumes to Windows 2000.

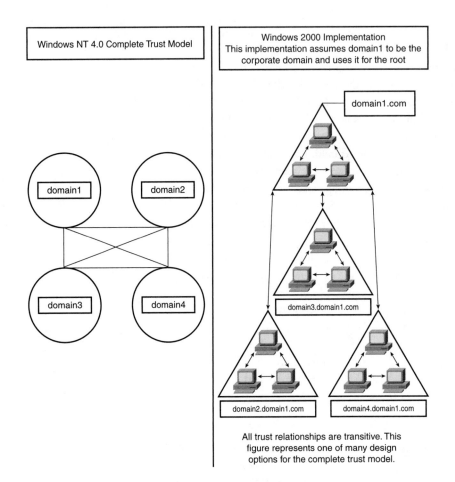

FIGURE 1.9
Migration of the Windows NT complete trust
domain model to Active Directory.

One of the problems with previous versions of the Netware Migration utility was that there wasn't much you could do with the NetWare structural information—that is, information from NDS or the Bindery basically came across as is, and then you had to go back and spend numerous hours reconfiguring it to fit your needs. The Directory Service Migration Tool introduces the concept of modeling directory data before you perform a migration. This powerful feature allows you to perform operations on data, such as modifying object data to fit your needs. For example, you can create, delete, and move objects, or add users to groups. You can also define options for setting passwords.

After you have modeled your data to fit your needs, you can perform an operation called *configuring a view to Active Directory*. This operation shows the source (NetWare) and destination (Active Directory) containers for your modeled objects. At this point you can commit your modeled data to Active Directory, which will create all the objects based on your view in Active Directory. Once this operation finishes, it is a good practice to use the Windows 2000 Directory Management Tools to verify successful directory migration.

Finally, you can migrate NetWare volumes to Windows 2000 using the Directory Service Migration Tool. You can migrate files, security attributes, and volume objects using a wizard-based utility.

PLANNING, PLANNING, PLANNING

As you've probably been able to guess, Windows 2000 deployment, and specifically Active Directory design, requires quite a bit of up-front planning and analysis. The entirety of Part II of this book is dedicated to business analysis, something we've rarely, if ever, seen in an *MCSE Training Guide* (or MCSE exam). As you read on, keep in mind that Microsoft developed Windows 2000 with the *business* needs of business in mind, not just the technology interests of the IT department. That alone plays a major role in way the material in this book is presented, as you are about to see. The goal of Windows 2000 is to change the way businesses operate by making them more efficient, scalable, and, of course, more cost efficient by reducing the total cost of ownership.

CHAPTER SUMMARY

KEY TERMS

- directory
- unified directory
- service
- resources
- Active Directory
- Application Programming Interface (API)
- namespace
- Lightweight Directory Access Protocol (LDAP)
- X.500
- Directory Access Protocol (DAP)
- Domain Name System (DNS)
- Dynamic DNS
- Internet Engineering Task Force (IETF)
- Active Directory Services Interface (ADSI)
- Messaging Application Programming Interface (MAPI)
- LDAP C API
- Component Object Model (COM)
- pruning and grafting
- schema
- global catalog
- mixed mode

Active Directory is a directory service completely integrated with Windows 2000. A *directory* is a collection of objects and services providing a method for making directory information accessible for users. Active Directory is a unified directory, which means that it provides the capability for other directories to integrate their services to form a single directory service.

Active Directory introduces the Internet concept of a namespace within the core Windows 2000 operating system. Active Directory (AD) is designed around and integrates tightly with the DNS namespace and uses LDAP as its core standard protocol. LDAP was derived from X.500 DAP standards as a means to "lighten" the load of a full X.500 implementation, which is extremely resource intensive.

AD incorporates a rich set of APIs, including the ADSI, MAPI, and LDAP C APIs. ADSI provides a set of COM objects that allow developers, and the occasional brave systems engineer, to write code to interface with Active Directory services. MAPI functionality is carried over from previous versions of Windows NT for backward compatibility reasons. Although many applications continue to use MAPI, it is expected that MAPI will be replaced by ADSI and other more robust APIs in the near future. Finally, the LDAP C API exists primarily for the C or C++ developer tasked with developing distributed applications.

Pruning and grafting, two relatively new terms in the Microsoft genre, are supported under the drag-and-drop administration functionality. To *prune* is to cut and to *graft* is to paste. These procedures can work together to move a large group of objects between domains or OUs.

The Active Directory schema—a database of objects, attributes, and attribute syntax—can be extended to support new objects and/or additional object attributes and attribute syntax.

Global catalog servers are servers earmarked to partake in a partial replication process with all domains in the forest. The result of this partial replication is a server with slices of all other domain directory databases. One advantage to having global catalog servers in an

CHAPTER SUMMARY

enterprise implementation of Windows 2000 is quicker and easier cross-domain lookups.

Active Directory can scale to support millions of objects, with an *estimated* hard database size limit of 17TB. It includes a new version of DNS—Dynamic DNS—in which resource records may be dynamically updated using the dynamic update protocol. It also supports incremental (partial) zone transfer.

Migrations from previous versions of Windows NT should be scrutinized extensively before execution. All four previous domain models have a boilerplate upgrade path. However, all cases are unique and it's always possible that an exception ends up being a showstopper.

Part II of this book is dedicated to the planning and analysis of the business model in preparation for Windows 2000 and Active Directory.

KEY TERMS
- native mode
- Novell Directory Services (NDS)
- service resource record (SRV)
- dynamic update protocol
- incremental zone transfer
- Active Directory integrated zone

> ## APPLY YOUR KNOWLEDGE

Exercise

1.1   Installing the Active Directory Schema Manager

This exercise demonstrates how to prepare for and install the Active Directory Schema manager. The schema manager is not installed by default, and there are a few requirements you need to meet before you can install the schema manager.

Estimated Time: 10 minutes

1. Log on to your Windows 2000 domain controller as the administrator.

2. Insert the Windows 2000 server CD and browse to the i386 (or alpha) directory.

3. Double-click the adminpak.msi file. Follow the directions on screen to install the Admin Tools.

4. Click Finish to complete the installation.

5. Click Start, then Run, and type `mmc /a`. This opens the Microsoft Management Console in Administrative mode.

6. Click the Console button, and click Add. Choose the Active Directory Schema snap-in and click Add and then close the Add Stand-Alone Snap-In window.

7. Click OK to close the Add/Remove Snap-In window. The Active Directory Schema snap-in should appear in the left MMC pane.

8. Expand the Schema snap-in to reveal object classes and attributes.

Review Questions

1. What is the core protocol of Active Directory and from where was it derived?

2. Around what namespace is Active Directory designed?

3. Name the three Active Directory API sets. Which one provides a COM interface to Active Directory?

4. The Active Directory schema consists of what three things?

5. What is the name given to the server that participates in partial directory replication with every domain in the forest?

6. Name four benefits of Microsoft's Dynamic DNS.

7. The Microsoft Windows 2000 Private Key Infrastructure is based on what authentication protocol?

8. True or false: When migrating a single domain model with three domain controllers to Windows 2000, you should always migrate a BDC first. Explain your answer.

9. If you choose to utilize a third-party DNS server for your production Windows 2000 network, what feature *must* it support?

10. Define a directory and a directory service.

APPLY YOUR KNOWLEDGE

Exam Questions

1. You have just installed the Active Directory Schema management tool and now have access to the Active Directory Schema MMC utility. You wish to create a new schema object for your Project Management team and add a few custom attributes to it. What two steps must you take before you can perform the desired operations?

   A. Stop the Active Directory directory service.

   B. Enable the schema operations master server for modification.

   C. Install the schema operations master server.

   D. Log on to the schema operations master server as a member of the Schema Admins group.

2. You are the administrator for a single master domain model network. You will be tasked with administering the network after Windows 2000 is implemented and you need to understand the multi-master replication model. Which three of the following statements are true in a multi-master replication model?

   A. All domain controllers have a read/write copy of the directory database for their domain.

   B. Once you go to Multi-Master mode, no down-level clients will be able to log on.

   C. There is no concept of a primary domain controller (PDC) with a Windows 2000 domain using the multi-master replication process.

   D. 99% of the activity to which the Active Directory directory service must respond is read activity; the other 1% is write activity.

   E. All domain controllers have a read/write copy of the directory database for each domain.

   F. Some operations do not work well in a multi-master environment and therefore Active Directory maintains special single master of operations servers.

3. You have just completed the population of the Sales OU, which included 500 users, 50 printers, and 15 security groups. Your manager pats you on the back and says, "Great job, but the objects were supposed to go in the Marketing OU!" What should you do?

   A. Use pruning and grafting to move the objects to the Marketing container.

   B. Use cut and paste to move the objects to the Marketing container.

   C. Use drag and drop to move the objects to the Marketing container.

   D. Use delete and redo to move the objects to the Marketing container.

4. You have just completed the implementation of Windows 2000 and Active Directory across your organization. The development staff is requesting a meeting with you to discuss leveraging the richly populated Active Directory database to further develop the company intranet. What technology should they use to access this directory information?

   A. LDAP C API

   B. MAPI

   C. ADSI

   D. ODBC

APPLY YOUR KNOWLEDGE

5. You are in the process of adding a new domain controller (W2KSRV002) to your existing Active Directory domain. You want to make sure you have DNS name resolution with this new server. What should you do to verify that you have DNS resolution?

   A. Ping another computer using its hardware MAC address.

   B. Ping another computer using its IP address.

   C. Map a drive to another server using the Net Use command.

   D. Ping another computer using its fully qualified domain name.

Answers to Review Questions

1. Lightweight Directory Access Protocol, or LDAP, is the core Active Directory protocol. Active Directory supports versions 2 and 3 of LDAP. LDAP was derived from the X.500 Directory Access Protocol (DAP) as an alternative to carrying the significant overhead that DAP requires. See "LDAP Is Core."

2. Active Directory is designed around the Domain Name System (DNS) namespace. Careful consideration should be given to naming Active Directory domains, so that they scale at the same rate as the DNS database does. See "Support for Open Standards" and "Dynamic DNS."

3. Active Directory provides three sets of feature-rich APIs: ADSI, MAPI, and LDAP C API. ADSI provides a set of COM objects to developers for access to the Active Directory database. See "Rich Set of APIs."

4. Objects, object attributes, and attribute syntax. Please see Exercise 1.1 for hands-on experience with the Active Directory schema. See "Extensible Schema."

5. The global catalog server participates in partial replication, a process by which all domains in a domain tree replicate a partially scaled-down model of their active directory database. The global catalog server is then used to provide cross-domain directory queries. See "Global Catalog Servers."

6. Microsoft Dynamic DNS provides the following four key benefits:

   • **SRV resource records.** Used to specify the location of a server for a specific protocol, service, and domain.

   • **Dynamic update protocol.** Provides a means of automatically updating the zone data on a zone's primary DNS server.

   • **Incremental zone transfer.** Allows for the partial transfer (modifications only) of a DNS zone file to its replication partners.

   • **Active Directory integrated zones.** Allows for the storage of DNS zones in Active Directory, which, in turn provides for replication of zone data.

   See "Dynamic DNS" for more details.

7. The Microsoft Windows 2000 Private Key infrastructure is based on the MIT Kerberos v5 authentication protocol. Kerberos is used for distributed security within a tree and incorporates the native Windows 2000 ACLs for both public and private key security. See "Public/Private Key Infrastructure."

8. False. You should take a fully synchronized BDC offline and upgrade the PDC first. This ensures that the current SAM database is updated first. Once you verify that all is well, you then upgrade all your BDCs and other computers. See "Microsoft's Recommended Migration Approach."

9. Non-Microsoft DNS servers must support, at the very minimum, SRV resource records. It may be impractical to implement a very large Windows 2000 network without support for dynamic update as well, because you would have to manually update SRV records. See "Non-Microsoft DNS Servers."

10. A directory is a physical storage container that contains from a few up to millions of various types of objects. A directory service provides a function that makes information in the active directory useful. See "'Directory' Defined."

Answers to Exam Questions

1. **B, D.** Before extending the schema, an administrator must be logged on to the domain as a member of the Schema Admins group. Additionally, the schema needs to be enabled for modification. This is performed on the Change Schema Master window presented by performing a right-click on the Active Directory Schema snap-in and selecting Operations Masters. See "Extensible Schema."

2. **A, D, F.** Each domain controller in Windows 2000 will contain its very own read/write copy of the Active Directory database for its domain only. This makes option A correct, but option E incorrect. There is no concept of a "multi-master

mode." Multi-master is a term used to describe Windows 2000 Active Directory replication. Down-level clients can still log on to the Windows 2000 domain as long as NetBIOS has not been removed. There is a concept of a PDC in Windows 2000. It is an Operations Master role called the PDC emulator. It mimics down-level PDCs so that down-level clients and servers can operate. 99% of the anticipated Active Directory activity will be read and the other 1% will be write. Finally, it is true that some operations, such as schema modifications and domain name generation, are not designed to operate in a multi-master world—so Active Directory maintains single master of operations roles, which are described in detail in Chapter 12. See "Multi-Master Replication Model."

3. **A.** Pruning and grafting is a process by which you may restructure certain aspects of Active Directory domains. Pruning and grafting is similar to the "cut and paste" technique available in many applications, but only in theory. If you answered drag and drop, give yourself half credit, because pruning and grafting are tools within the Drag and Drop administration initiative. Finally, delete and redo is always an option, but not nearly efficient enough to be considered a solution for this question. See "Drag and Drop Administration."

4. **C.** ADSI provides developers with a "portal" to Active Directory services and information. MAPI is used to interface with messaging applications, such as Microsoft Exchange. The LDAP C API could be used in this situation, but is not an efficient solution because it operates at a much lower level than ADSI. Open Database

APPLY YOUR KNOWLEDGE

Connectivity (ODBC) is used primarily for access to ODBC-compliant database applications, such as Microsoft SQL Server or Access. See "ADSI."

5. **D.** To be properly resolved by a DNS server, a computer must first be represented by a DNS server host record. Non-dynamic DNS servers must be updated with this information manually.

Microsoft Dynamic DNS servers have the capability of allowing dynamic updates from Windows 2000 clients and servers, and from DHCP and WINS servers who can act as a proxy to down-level clients. You can tell if a particular computer has DNS name resolution by pinging a FQDN, such as `server1.microsoft.com`. See "Dynamic DNS."

Suggested Readings and Resources

1. Windows 2000 (and Active Directory) white papers. `http://www.microsoft.com/windows2000`.

2. Cone, Boggs, and Perez. *Planning for Windows 2000*. New Riders, 1999.

3. Microsoft TechNet Articles.

   • "Active Directory Logical Structure."

• "Aligning Business and IT Goals."
• "Business Opportunities with Windows 2000."
• "Designing the Active Directory Structure."
• "Planning for Windows 2000 in the Enterprise."

Analyzing Business Requirements

This chapter creates a roadmap to prepare you for the business analysis process. Although it does not specifically cover any Microsoft exam objectives, it serves as an important step in setting the stage for the analysis and the objectives to come.

CHAPTER 2

Planning and Conducting Your Business Assessment

OUTLINE

▶ Be able to categorize the company relative to the industry in which it competes, as well as how it and its internal IT organization interoperate. Interoperability between business and IT is increasingly becoming a factor in today's business.

▶ Understand the difference between a strategy and a tactic. You will need to create a strategy and understand how to execute it during the business analysis.

▶ Know and understand the key Active Directory-related Windows 2000 feature sets. Understand not just what they are, but also how they can benefit the business.

▶ Know how to extract the right information at the right time. Understand that the way a company gathers, manages, and uses information could be the difference between success and failure.

▶ Stay on the business side of things during the business analysis. Don't talk technically; executives tune that out and you will have a very difficult time getting them back.

▶ Understand key areas of business to discuss during the business analysis. Remember that technical information is not what you need; you need to understand the business's vision, including its goals and business problem statements.

INTRODUCTION

Now that you've had exposure to the key technology benefits of Windows 2000 and Active Directory, you're ready to begin the business analysis process.

Like any process, the business analysis requires that you have a strategy. This chapter helps you define your deliverables, and from those deliverables, derive a strategy that will help you extract the information representative of those deliverables.

This chapter helps you categorize the company at a general level and with regard to its IT organization, and explains why that's important. It also presents a subset of the Windows 2000 feature set and explains the benefit of each feature as it pertains to the business.

Finally, you are presented with a list of key pieces of information you need to take from this analysis and a brief description of what to expect from each piece. This list represents the basis of the next chapter and the meat of the exam objectives in Part II, "Analyzing Business Requirements."

BUSINESS ANALYSIS PLANNING FRAMEWORK

If someone asked you to go down to Joe's desk and fix his network connection, chances are you'd go and fix it without a single thought about planning the fix. That's good. Something as simple as Joe's problem should be handled fairly easily by anyone reading this book. If someone asked you to go to BigCo International, a 5,000-person company, and implement a Windows 2000 solution, you'd probably not view it the same as Joe's situation. That's good, too! You've made the distinction between a purely *tactical* solution, and a solution that requires a *strategy*.

It's important to make the distinction between a tactical solution and a strategic solution. A *strategy*, as defined by dictionary.com, is an elaborate and systematic plan of action, and a *plan* is a scheme, program, or method worked out beforehand for the accomplishment of an objective. A *tactic* is an expedient for achieving a goal. So, a strategic solution can be understood as an elaborate and systematic scheme, program, or method worked out beforehand for the accomplishment of an objective, and a tactical solution is a goal-driven solution to a single problem.

With a complex solution like Active Directory design as your overall objective, the importance of a well-thought-out strategy should be apparent. A well-prepared strategy will utilize tactics as the techniques to carry out the strategy. In a meeting, strategy relates to your planned meeting agenda, and tactics refer to the techniques you use to conduct the meeting.

Create Your Strategy

Now that we've defined what a strategy is, how do we create one? If you've ever created a project implementation plan, you've created a strategy. Think of it as a roadmap to get from point A to point B taking into consideration obstacles along the way. In the case of the business analysis, our approach is going to be at a bit higher level. We want to create a strategy with the goal of extracting the information we need about the business, so we can design a solution to the problem.

Think of your strategy as a strategy to better understand your client's strategy for taking its business to the next level. The following list defines the areas of business from which you must extract information:

- ◆ Business vision

- ◆ Business goals and problems

- ◆ Organization of the company

- ◆ Geographical scope and company model

- ◆ Company processes

- ◆ Influences that affect company strategy

We explain each of these areas of business later in this chapter. To form your strategy, it is recommended that you create a checklist and add to it as you traverse this chapter. Leave a short amount of space at the top, and then start with a section labeled "Extract this information" and list the six preceding bulleted items. We drill down into them slightly more in this chapter and go in depth in the following chapter, so leave space between each bullet.

Before we cover those areas in more detail, you should jump over to the Windows 2000 Active Directory feature set and make sure you understand the pertinent Active Directory features and benefits. Having this knowledge before you begin the business analysis will help you begin to visualize solution scenarios. The following section provides you with this abbreviated feature set.

Windows 2000 Feature Set

To list the entire Windows 2000 feature set is out of the scope of this book, so we list the features that specifically pertain to Active Directory. Again, understanding the business benefits these features provide will help you provide your client with the best solution for his or her problem. This is the second step of your strategy. You may want to write on your checklist the task "Review Active Directory feature set." Table 2.1 lists the feature set.

> **NOTE**
>
> **Digital Nervous System** Don't confuse the acronym for Domain Name System (DNS) with the Digital Nervous System. The digital nervous system is more commonly referred to as *Digital DNA*.

TABLE 2.1

WINDOWS 2000 ACTIVE DIRECTORY FEATURE SET

Feature/Service	Description	Benefit(s)
Digital Nervous System (Digital DNA)	A system that represents a person digitally within an organization.	Highly structured information and communication flow, knowledge management, and business processes.
Built on DNS	DNS is the most widely used locator service in the world, used exclusively on the Internet. DNS maps a fully qualified domain name to an IP address.	Scalability. Windows 2000 Active Directory is designed around DNS, which scales from a single entry to supporting the entire Internet.

Feature/Service	Description	Benefit(s)
Active Directory Services Interface (ADSI)	ADSI abstracts the capabilities of several disparate directory services and unites them into a single set of directory service interfaces for easy management.	Greatly simplifies the development of directory-enabled applications. Greatly reduces the complexity of distributed systems management.
Global Catalog	Global catalog servers hold a partial replica of all domains in the tree and a subset of all object properties.	Performance. Allows users to quickly search for objects, wherever they are.
Extensible Schema	Ability to customize the "built-in" objects and attributes to fit the needs of your organization.	Important information, outside that of default Windows 2000 fields, can be published for users to access.
Multi-Master Replication	Changes can be made on any domain controller in the domain and be automatically replicated to other domain controllers.	Allows for extremely high availability of the directory for changes at any time. Scales to meet the needs of enterprise domains.
MIT v5 Kerberos Authentication	Replaces NTLM as the primary authentication protocol across all of Windows 2000.	Fast, single logon to Windows 2000 Server environments and to disparate systems that support v5 Kerberos.
Microsoft Management Console (MMC)	Common console for administrators to view network functions and perform management tasks.	Better organization for administrators and their toolsets. Lower cost of ownership for the desktop.

continues

TABLE 2.1	*continued*

WINDOWS 2000 ACTIVE DIRECTORY FEATURE SET

Feature/Service	*Description*	*Benefit(s)*
Group Policy	Application deployment, scripts, and policy options from an MMC snap-in.	Automate such tasks as application installation, user profiles, desktop system updates.
Remote Installation Services	A remote workstation can boot using PXE (pre-boot execution environment) and attach to a Windows 2000 server to install Windows 2000 Professional.	Remote OS installation services can be set to provide an array of host installation and configuration services.
IntelliMirror Technologies	Users can go to any PC on the corporate network and always have access to their files, applications, and settings. An administrator can assign, publish, or remove software to the directory to be picked up by specific users. Administrators may centrally administer desktop settings and have the ability to lock down computers.	Users' data is always available, and users' view of the network is always consistent. Administrators can deploy software without ever leaving their seats. Administrators can lock down computers and force users to store data on the server, minimizing the chances of data loss.
Distributed File System (DFS)	DFS implements a single name for disparate file system resources at a site.	Makes it easy for users to find and manage data on the network. To the users it looks as if they are storing data in one location, whereas behind the scenes, DFS may have it routed to several different areas.

Feature/Service	Description	Benefit(s)
Dynamic DNS (DDNS)	DDNS is a standard for dynamically updating records in the DNS database. DDNS integrates with Active Directory, or may use flat text files.	Reduces DNS administration costs by removing the need to statically add and replicate DNS zone data. Allows for the removal of NetBIOS in the future.
Connectors	Connectors, such as the Active Directory Connector, allow Active Directory to communicate with disparate directory services, such as Exchange, NDS, and Windows NT.	Fewer directories to manage. Simplified administration using new MMC tools.

These few features don't cover all the Active Directory features by a long shot, but you should be able to use the information in the Table 2.1 to your advantage when you are visualizing the solution set for a client. If you want a complete listing of the Windows 2000 feature sets, look up the article "Windows 2000 Server Feature Tables" in Microsoft TechNet.

COMPANY CATEGORIZATION

Another thing you'll want to consider doing as you develop your strategy is categorizing the company. By categorizing the company relative to the industry, as well as IT (we explain shortly), you can better understand the line of business the company is in. If, for instance, you are consulting for an automotive company, you don't want to go in and ask a question such as, "What kind of software do you write?" It just wouldn't make sense, and you'd end up losing credibility. The following two sections explain what we mean by categorizing the company. Update your checklist by adding this information in the space you left at the top.

Relative to the Industry

If you don't already know it from past experiences with the company, you should do a bit of research on the company. Specifically, you should know the market in which the company competes, such as automotive, consumer electronics, manufacturing, distribution, and so on. You should also ask for or locate a mission statement. Additionally, it would be beneficial to know who the company's competitors are and research them as well. The Internet is a superb resource for this kind of research. With an understanding of the company's market space, competition, and mission, you can tailor your strategy to align with its business.

Relative to IT

When you categorized the company relative to the industry, you probably didn't have much trouble figuring out which market segment they competed in and who their competition was. What about categorizing the company relative to IT?

Different companies treat IT in different ways. Some let business drive fundamental improvements in IT, others let new information technology drive business goals, and still others treat IT as if it were simply a cost center—another drain on company profits. It's important to get an overall picture of how the company as a whole and the IT organization as a whole work together (or don't) toward common goals. You may choose to use the terminology *IT-centric* or *business-centric* for those companies that, respectively, let IT drive the business or allow business decisions to force IT to take reactionary action.

IN THE FIELD

SOME REAL-WORLD FACTS ABOUT MANAGING IT

Microsoft and a major independent consulting firm conducted a study on a number of large companies that consistently do an excellent job of using IT to deliver substantial value to their organizations. The survey revealed that those companies' successes were based on managing IT functions *just like any other strategic business functions and processes.* So in that context, the IT organization within those large companies was neither a costly drain nor a fix for all problems.

WHAT TO GAIN FROM THE ANALYSIS

You now have a fundamental understanding of the key elements that make up the business analysis. Now let's take a look at the key areas from which you need to extract information in order to come up with a solution.

There are many avenues you can take to get this information, but it is recommended you plan a meeting or series of meetings. You will need representation in these meetings from key company executives that influence and/or decide the strategic direction of the company. You also will need representation from the IT organization, such as the CIO or Director of IT.

The six following sections describe how to extract the information. Chapter 3, "Analyzing the Results of the Business Assessment," will address how to take this information and perform an analysis on it.

Business Vision

A business vision is essential to the success of the company. Every company has a vision, whether stated or not—otherwise the company wouldn't exist. A vision states where the company will be X years down the road. Your job is to extract that vision from the powers that be. You should use an interview process, a strategic series of questions that gets the right information at the right time. Remember your categorization of the company? This is where the payoff is: in the formulation of your questions.

Here are some sample questions. Parentheses are used to denote the premise of the question. Your questions may be similar or totally different than these, depending on your situation.

◆ What is your business vision? (general, icebreaker)

◆ Where do you see your company in three, five, and 10 years? (general).

◆ Do you see your competition moving in the same direction? (competition-focused)

◆ Do you see your core business processes growing faster than, slower than, or side-by-side with technology? (question to help determine IT-centric versus business-centric)

◆ How does your organization plan to manage its intellectual data? (information management)

◆ Are you anticipating and preparing for networking capabilities that allow resources from around the world to collaborate in real time? (awareness of emerging technology)

◆ Are you prepared to transport voice, data, and streaming video over your WAN? (checking awareness of emerging technology)

As you ask these questions, refer to the initially stated vision and see what doesn't match up. These and similar questions will provide you with a clear picture of not only the company's vision, but how it plans to leverage new technology to realize its vision.

Business Goals and Problems

Although the company's vision is certainly important, you must remember that you are performing an analysis of the business in preparation for the Active Directory design process. The vision will give you a picture of the end of the tunnel. Defining the business goals will light the tunnel, and correctly addressing relative business problems in the organization will ensure that the light is not a train!

Business goals and problems can best be described as desired end results and areas the company has identified as needs for strategic or planned improvement, respectively. Microsoft's famed slogan "Where do you want to go today?" is a great way to kick off a meeting to define these goals and business problems because it asks a very simple, yet thought-provoking question: "In what direction do you want to take your company?" Your job in this phase is to help the company define its goals and objectives for doing this project, and analyze business problems the company is or has been facing. This is where you get the "why" of the project.

Again, the questions in the following list are not all-inclusive, but are a representative subset of the type of questions you'll want to ask in determining the goals and business problems. Remember, this interview will have an IT twist since you are now talking about the project.

◆ Can you list your goals and objectives relative to this project? (If they have them, use them!)

◆ Where is your business today with regard to directory services and IT in general?

◆ Where should your business be when the project is completed?

◆ What are some of the challenges you are facing now and how do you plan to alleviate them?

◆ What are your expectations of Windows 2000 and specifically Active Directory?

◆ Do you have immediate or future wishes to connect disparate directory services?

Make sure you take copious notes during this interview, as you should prepare a detailed "business goals and stated business problems deliverable" document so you and the company have agreement on these points. It's a good idea to have this document signed by both parties.

Organization of the Company

This section and the next section, "Geographical Scope of the Company," feed off one another in an iterative fashion. In the organizational analysis of the company, you need to discuss things like the company management model; the vendor, partner, and customer relationships; and merger and acquisition plans. The tie-in with the next section occurs really in the analysis of the management model because often you see the management hierarchy built around the geographic layout of the company.

The interview process for the organizational structure analysis should happen as explained in the following sections.

Management Model

◆ Describe your company management model. (You are looking for a structure of management that is in place at the company.)

◆ Describe your company management model three years into the future. What changes will have taken place?

Company Organization

◆ How is the overall organization of the company centered? Is the company organized around the geographical scope? Products? Departments? IT?

◆ What organizational changes do you anticipate within the next three years?

Vendor, Partner, and Customer Relationships

◆ What vendor programs are in place currently?

◆ Do you allow vendors to access your network? Do you access theirs? For what purposes?

◆ What are your future vendor relationship plans?

◆ Do you currently use—or have future plans to use—electronic commerce to do business with vendors?

◆ How many partner relationships do you currently maintain?

◆ Do you see the number of partner relationships growing in the future? How?

◆ Do you currently use—or have future plans to use—electronic commerce to do business with partners?

◆ Do you allow partner access to your network? Will you in the future?

◆ Do you have a customer service department? If so, how do they currently service customers?

◆ Do you plan to leverage new technology to improve your customers' service experience? If so, what technology will you use? When?

◆ How does your Web site currently fit into the vendor, partner, and customer relationships category? How will it in three years? Why?

Merger and Acquisition Plans

◆ Does your company have plans to acquire another company or companies in the next three to five years? How about merging with another company?

◆ Do you have a plan to blend a newly acquired company into your network? Is it a phased plan?

◆ Do you have a plan to allow for network-based communication to flow between your company and a company you've merged with?

Determining the amount of free access to your network you'll give to an outsider—such as a vendor or customer—has a significant impact on the design of Active Directory, especially in the design of the security model. The previous information will be used in several other areas of Active Directory design as well, which will be discussed in Chapter 3.

Geographical Scope of the Company

Determining the geographical scope of the company is not difficult. Determining how the company operates functionally within that scope is. You'll need to ask questions that extract information about both the current and future geographical positioning of the company and how it plans to operate within or between those bounds.

Functional company models relate to how they manage resources, distribute product, and so on, and have a direct influence on how they design their network infrastructure. Typical company models and generalized descriptions are as follows:

◆ **Regional.** Management of the company is divided into large multi-state sections, usually with multiple locations. One location is designated to be the regional headquarters. Company has national presence.

◆ **National.** Management of the company is centrally located at a corporate campus. Company has national presence.

◆ **International.** Management of the company is centrally located in each division. Divisions are typically per continent.

◆ **Subsidiary.** Company operates as several entities or business units, usually with different names, all reporting to a parent "umbrella company." Each entity has its own management hierarchy and all entities share a common board of directors.

◆ **Branch Office.** Company operates as a separately managed division at every branch location. Branch managers typically report to corporate executives at the central corporate office.

The preceding descriptions are not textbook by any means and should not be taken as such. They should give an accurate enough description of the differing company models as they relate to geographical scope for you to place the company you are working with. You should ask questions regarding the geographical scope and company model as follows:

◆ Categorize your company in terms of geographical scope. (You can list the previous company models to help elicit a response.)

◆ Discuss company operations relative to the previous answer. Ask questions such as the following: Are there separate business units within the company or at each location? Do you have different management methodologies in different offices? Are different networks in place at different locations or are you standardized?

◆ How do your different locations affect communication?

◆ Are time zones a problem when communicating? (For example, how do you handle communications between the U.S. and Singapore?)

◆ Do you have offices that speak different languages? How do you address that issue?

◆ How do your different locations affect the flow of information?

◆ What are the differences between your various international offices in terms of policies and procedures?

The preceding questions give you the information you need to determine how to structure the Active Directory domain and organizational unit structure. You will analyze this information in Chapter 3 and discuss the Active Directory design in Chapter 11, "Designing the Active Directory Structure."

Key Company Processes

Company processes define how the company operates internally as well as externally. They define how it gathers disparate data and turns it into useful information, manages that information, and communicates that information. Bill Gates says in his book *Business @ the Speed of Thought* that "how you gather, manage, and use information will determine whether you win or lose." He goes on to talk about the digital nervous system and how the concept of knowledge management is the key to the success of a company. We'll incorporate the digital nervous system into the analysis of key company processes in Chapter 3. We'll focus on the following four company process classes: information flow, communication flow, service and product life cycles, and decision-making.

Service and product life cycles refer to the preparation, deployment, maintenance, and removal of a product in a production environment. Figure 2.1 illustrates these four areas and associates activity with each.

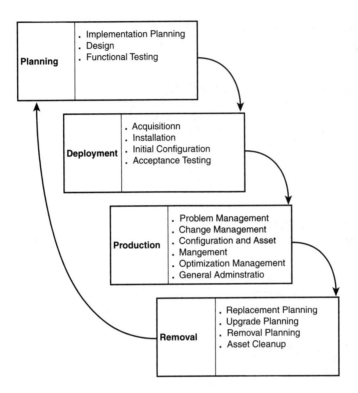

FIGURE 2.1
The service and product life cycle.

The service and product life cycle refers to the process of preparing, deploying, maintaining, and removing software and product from computing environments.

With emerging technologies and fierce competition in the industry, product life cycles are decreasing quickly, which is driving up service costs in the removal and re-deployment areas. Services define the tools users use to do their jobs. They can be anything from hardware and software to human resources and they sit at the core of the service and product life cycle. We'll ask the appropriate questions to try to extract the information we need to help reduce cost in these areas.

Decision-making is a broad topic, and we'll channel it to the context of process in this section. You'll see it reappear throughout the business and technical analyses in different contexts. For this section, we'll ask questions that pertain to identifying key decision-makers that influence the flow of information and communication within the organization.

Information and Communication Flow

◆ Do you have an information repository now? Do you have plans to implement one in the future?

◆ How do you communicate information across the company?

◆ Do you receive feedback on information? Do you do anything with that feedback? Why or why not?

◆ Can you put together virtual teams of people from different geographical locations? Can you give them a common virtual office?

◆ Do you utilize a company intranet?

◆ Do you utilize a workflow application to control the flow of information throughout the company?

Service and Product Life Cycle

◆ How do you determine when to replace an application or service?

◆ What is the cost associated with the replacement process?

◆ Do your help desk personnel typically have to go desk to desk to complete an installation of new software?

Decision-Making

◆ Who are the key decision-makers in the area of information and communications processes?

◆ Are there multiple levels of decision-making that need to occur in order to gain final approval?

◆ Is there typically a waiting period when a decision is pending? Is there a cost in lost productivity associated with the waiting time?

◆ What are the key influences that drive decisions? External influences? Competition?

As with other sections, these questions are not all-inclusive, but are designed to get the information you need for this assessment. The final section, "Company Strategy Influences," somewhat overlaps the earlier section "Key Company Processes," as you will see.

Company Strategy Influences

As alluded to in the previous section, there are several key influences that may affect the company's strategic direction. These influences can come from several places: the explosion of the Internet, competition, cost, and just about any other competitive business-related factor you can think of. In this section, we focus on the following key company influences: company priorities, projected growth and growth strategy, laws and regulations, tolerance for risk, and total cost of ownership.

We will remain consistent with the rest of the chapter by presenting sample questions in preparation for analyzing the results in the next chapter.

Company Priorities

- ◆ List the top five company priorities in order of precedence.

- ◆ What could influence the company to shift priority away from one or more of these five?

- ◆ Can you identify where a majority of factors originate that influence the strategic company direction to the point that you would consider shifting priorities?

Growth and Growth Strategy

- ◆ What role does internal growth play in strategy?

- ◆ What role does external (merger or acquisitions) growth plan in strategy?

- ◆ Do you have a plan in place to control growth?

Laws and Regulations

◆ List the laws and regulations that currently influence the company strategy.

◆ If a new law were passed that fundamentally shut down an area of your business, how would you cope?

◆ Are you ready to scale your network to compensate for laws and regulations?

Tolerance for Risk

◆ Do you have a risk management plan in place?

◆ What do you consider risk? How do you avoid it? How do you cope with it?

◆ How much risk will it take to influence the company strategy?

Total Cost of Ownership (TCO)

◆ Do you have a current TCO figure?

◆ Has this figure caused you to change your company strategy?

◆ Have you done a Return on Investment (ROI) study based on your TCO study and Windows 2000? Why or why not? Are the numbers substantial?

We'll get into TCO and ROI studies in the next few chapters. For now, it is important to associate them with risk and the potential to affect the strategic influence of the company.

BUSINESS ANALYSIS DELIVERABLES

The result of any assessment or analysis should be a deliverable or set of deliverables. This section discusses some common deliverable documents you'll find are needed at the close of the business analysis. Keep in mind that not all analyses will require all of these deliverable documents, and others may require additional special purpose deliverables.

It is also important to take a step back here to understand where you are in the Active Directory design process. You might be thinking you're ready to build a vision/scope document, or even begin work on the implementation plan. Not yet. At this point, you're not ready to build any formal documents. The deliverables described briefly in the following sections will help you get to that point, but they focus on communicating back to the customer how *you* understand their business to be. You will re-visit a number of these documents further on in the project process (and this book), and they will help form the basis of a vision/scope document and project implementation plan.

Business Goals and Problems Document

Whether you conduct interviews, hold facilitated open discussion meetings, or have individual one-on-one conversations to determine the business goals and define business problems, the end result should be re-statement of these goals and problems, as you understand them. This business goals and problems document is of utmost importance because you are going to tell the company how you interpreted this information. This should facilitate additional communication to fine-tune the business goals and further discuss current business problems.

Gap Analysis

The Gap Analysis facilitates the comparison of the existing business with where it envisions itself sometime in the future. It specifically looks at current state compared with future state on a single objective level and analyzes the gap in between. From this analysis, a determination of *how* to get there can be drawn.

There are two parts to the Gap Analysis: one that analyzes gaps in the current versus desired state of the business, and another that analyzes gaps in the current versus desired state of the technical environment.

Risk Assessment

Because projects rarely, if ever, are completed without some sort of problem or unexpected blip in the process, you must perform a risk assessment and present a risk management plan as a deliverable. The best solution to a potential risk is to have it identified before it happens, and have a plan in place to deal with it. This is called *mitigating* risk. You should have some data now on how the company views risk—specifically, what its tolerance of risk is.

CHAPTER SUMMARY

You need to spend a bit of time preparing a strategy for conducting your business analysis. A *strategy* is an elaborate and systematic scheme, program, or method worked out beforehand for the accomplishment of an objective. Your objective for conducting the business analysis is to extract the information you need to determine what the strategic direction of the business is in the following areas:

◆ Business vision

◆ Business goals and problems

◆ Organization of the company

◆ Geographical scope and company model

◆ Company processes

◆ Influences that affect company strategy

You must have good working knowledge of the Windows 2000 feature set relative to Active Directory before you conduct the analysis. This will allow you to begin visualizing potential solutions and will help drive communications.

You should categorize the company relative to the industry, such as automotive, manufacturing, distribution, and so on, and also relative to its IT organization. For example, if you categorize a company as a manufacturing company, you can formulate your questions relative to that industry. The way a business views its IT organization is

KEY TERMS

- strategic solution
- tactical solution
- vision
- objective
- geographical scope
- company model
- business model
- influence
- business-centric
- IT-centric
- Gap Analysis
- deliverable
- growth
- service and product life cycle
- laws and regulations
- risk

CHAPTER SUMMARY

becoming increasingly important. With the explosive use of the Internet as a business medium, the IT department is playing more of a strategic role in the business. Categorize the company as *IT-centric* if IT drives fundamental business changes, *business-centric* if business drives fundamental IT changes, or *hybrid* if the business views IT as a strategic business partner, like other departments. Understanding this during the analysis will allow you to recommend or suggest fundamental changes to the strategic direction of the company.

Potential deliverables of the business analysis include a goals and problems document, Gap Analysis, and risk management plan.

APPLY YOUR KNOWLEDGE

Exercise

2.1 Creating an Analysis Strategy

Exercise 2.1 gets you familiar with strategy. Its purpose is to step you through the process of creating a strategy to prepare for the business analysis.

You have been given the task of designing the Windows 2000 Active Directory for Migration Masters, Inc. This project is a major part of the overall Windows 2000 migration from NT 4.0. Your first goal is to prepare a strategy for extracting Migration Masters' business reasons for the migration. You should be able to gather all of the information with the exception of the internal IT relationship from outside the Migration Masters doors.

The following steps will prompt you with questions you should use in preparation for the business analysis process. It may help if you relate these questions to a company you are familiar with.

Estimated Time: 10 minutes

1. Who is Migration Masters?

2. In what industry does Migration Masters compete?

3. What product or service does Migration Masters offer its clients?

4. Who are Migration Masters's chief competitors and what do they do on the outside that's fundamentally different than Migration Masters?

5. Does Migration Masters have an internal IT staff?

6. How does Migration Masters view its internal IT staff? As a cost center? As a driver of change? As a strategic business unit?

7. What is Migration Masters's mission statement?

8. Where does Migration Masters operate geographically?

Review Questions

1. In which area of the service and product life cycle would you find change management taking place?

2. Before you begin your business analysis, it is essential to have what?

3. What technology has become a key driver for strategic business change?

4. How would you categorize a company that relies on its IT department to drive strategic business objectives?

5. How would you categorize a company that forces its IT department to react to changes in its business strategy?

6. What is a company process?

7. What is a business problem?

8. What should be the outcome of the business analysis?

Exam Questions

1. You are a consultant preparing to embark on a Windows 2000 planning project. You will be responsible for creating procedures to manage software throughout its lifecycle. What four phases of the service and product life cycle should you become familiar with?

APPLY YOUR KNOWLEDGE

A. Preparation, Planning, Deployment, Maintenance

B. Planning, Deployment, Maintenance, Removal

C. Planning, Coding, Shipment, Installation

D. Vision, Planning, Maintenance, Support

2. You are a business development manager for a consulting company. You have been asked to integrate with your client to help develop strategic technology solutions. You find that your client does not know the difference between a strategic solution and a tactical solution. How would you best describe the difference between the two?

A. Strategic solutions are solutions to the task-level areas of a tactical solution.

B. A strategic solution is an elaborate or systematic scheme, worked out beforehand for the accomplishment of an objective. A tactical solution is a goal-driven solution to a specific problem.

C. A strategic solution generally requires less planning than a tactical solution.

D. A tactical solution is an elaborate or systematic scheme, worked out beforehand for the accomplishment of an objective. A strategic solution is a goal-driven solution to a specific problem.

3. As the CIO of a company, you wish to describe information flow, communication flow, service and product life cycles, and decision-making. These are examples of which area of analysis?

A. Communications

B. Operational Structure

C. Goals and Problems

D. Key Company Processes

4. You are a consultant in charge of performing a business analysis for your client. You wish to extract specifics on how information flows within the organization. Which two of the following would be appropriate questions to ask your client?

A. Do you currently utilize a workflow application to control information according to formalized rules?

B. How do you manage the service and product life cycles within the organization?

C. Who are the key decision-makers within the company?

D. Do you utilize a corporate intranet?

5. You are the IT administrator for Xennox Corporation. Users in the organization want you to provide them a fast, single logon to Windows 2000. Which feature set of Windows 2000 would you turn to for this?

A. IntelliMirror

B. Group Policy

C. MIT v5 Kerberos Authentication

D. Dynamic DNS

6. You are a consultant working with the Application Development team leader for Xennox Corporation. He mentions to you that his

APPLY YOUR KNOWLEDGE

developers are having trouble keeping up with the API interfaces for all of the directories. Which feature set of Windows 2000 greatly simplifies the development of directory-enabled applications by abstracting the disparate directories of many platforms?

A. Active Directory Service Interface

B. Group Policy

C. IntelliMirror

D. Extensible Schema

7. You've just left a meeting in which the company's CIO mentioned that there is no hope of implementing any e-commerce solutions for at least two years. Which area of the business analysis can you turn to for more information about *why* that's the company's belief?

A. Operational Structure

B. Goals and Problems

C. Organizational Structure

D. Company Processes

Answers to Review Questions

1. Maintenance. Change management occurs during the production life of a product. Change must be anticipated and managed effectively in order to deliver a high quality service. See "Key Company Processes."

2. A strategy, which is a sophisticated plan. Getting prepared for a meeting is a form of a strategy. See "Business Analysis Planning Framework."

3. The Internet. The explosive growth of e-commerce is causing many companies to fundamentally change they way they conduct business. See "Company Categorization."

4. IT-centric. Companies that center around the IT organization are considered IT-centric. IT-centric companies base strategic business direction on only the IT organization. See "Relative to IT."

5. Business-centric. Business-centric companies typically do not include the IT organization in key business decisions; rather, they often treat IT as a liability. See "Relative to the Industry."

6. Defines how a company operates internally. Company processes at a high level define how companies operate internally. Some company processes include communication flow and information flow. See "Key Company Processes."

7. Business problems are areas the company has identified as needs for strategic or planned improvement. See "Business Goals and Problems."

8. A set of deliverables. A completed business analysis results potentially in several documents, called deliverables, that provide feedback, assessments, and other information relative to the analysis. See "Business Goals and Problems."

Answers to Exam Questions

1. **B.** Preparation, Deployment, Maintenance and Removal define the service and product life cycle. If you are going to be responsible for managing a software product or products throughout the life

APPLY YOUR KNOWLEDGE

cycle, you need to become familiar with what each phase of the service and product life cycle involves. See "Service and Product Life Cycle."

2. **B**. A strategic solution is an elaborate or systematic scheme, worked out beforehand for the accomplishment of an objective. A tactical solution is a goal driven solution to a specific problem. A strategy might be preparing the dialog of a presentation, and a tactic might be the technique you use to communicate that strategy during the presentation. See "Business Analysis and Planning Framework."

3. **D**. Information flow, communication flow, service and product life cycles, and decision-making are all examples of key company processes. Company processes relate to how a company operates internally and, in particular, how they manage intellectual capital, information. Communication is a part of information flow, the operational structure refers to the company model and geographical scope, and goals and problems represent why a company is seeking a solution to a problem. See "Key Company Processes."

4. **A, D**. There are many questions you might ask that arguably could pertain to information flow. Options A and D both discuss topics that directly relate to information and how it is managed or disseminated. Workflow applications typically integrate with intranets and messaging platforms to control the flow of information. Options B and C could pertain to information, but are targeted at a specific type of information, not how information flows. See "Information and Communication Flow."

5. **C**. MIT v5 Kerberos authentication protocol provides for a fast, single logon to the Windows 2000 server environment, as well as disparate systems that support Kerberos. Dynamic DNS refers to name resolution, Group Policy refers to administration and software installation, and IntelliMirror refers to desktop management. See "Windows 2000 Feature Set."

6. **A**. The Active Directory Services Interface (ADSI) greatly simplifies the development of directory-enabled applications by abstracting the interfaces of disparate directories and presenting them in uniform COM objects. This way, developers must know and understand one method of entry into the directory services, not one for each directory service. The schema refers to the Windows 2000 object and attribute type definition, Group Policy relates to administration and software distribution, and IntelliMirror relates to desktop management. See "Windows 2000 Feature Set."

7. **B**. When you perform the business analysis, a key to understanding why the company is considering or ruling out particular solutions is realizing its goals and problems. Additionally, the long-term strategic vision of the company will yield information about where it wants to be several years down the line. The Operational and Organizational structures refer to the management model and company model, and the Company Processes include items such as information and communication flow and decision-making, so only the Goals and Problems assessment might help you figure out the strategic impediments (real or imagined) that are envisioned down the road for the company. See "Business Goals and Problems."

APPLY YOUR KNOWLEDGE

Suggested Readings and Resources

1. Microsoft TechNet Articles.

   - "Aligning Business and IT Goals."
   - "Planning, Deploying, and Managing Highly Available Solutions."
   - "Creating the Windows 2000 Vision/Scope Document and Risk Management Plan."
   - "Identifying Windows 2000 Features That Meet Enterprise Goals."

2. Gates, William H. III. *Business @ The Speed of Thought.* Warner Books, 1999.

3. Heiman, Stephen E. and Sanchez, Diane. *The New Strategic Selling.* Warner Books, 1998.

This chapter steps you through the analysis of the business assessment outlined in Chapter 2, "Planning and Conducting Your Business Assessment." It is one of the key chapters addressing the Analyzing Business Requirements section of the Microsoft-supplied guidelines for the exam.

Analyze the existing and planned business models.

- Analyze the company model and the geographical scope. Models include regional, national, international, subsidiary, and branch offices.

- Analyze company processes. Processes include information flow, communication flow, service and product life cycles, and decision-making.

▶ When you are tasked with designing a strategic solution to a problem, you must understand a broad range of factors that influence that problem. Windows 2000 and Active Directory were designed to wrap around the business model and become a more strategic part of business than any other operating system ever has been. Therefore you must pay very close attention to the business itself. The geographical scope of the company will influence the way you design your Active Directory domains and organizational units, and will play a large role in how you use sites to manage replication traffic. Likewise, company processes define how the company operates in terms of information and communication. The way a company manages information and communication (knowledge) will influence almost all facets of Active Directory design.

Analyze the existing and planned organizational structures. Considerations include management model; company organization; vendor, partner, and customer relationships; and acquisition plans.

CHAPTER 3

Analyzing the Results of the Business Assessment

OBJECTIVES

▶ In much the same way as the geographical scope of a company influences the design of Active Directory, the organizational structure influences how you organize the objects within the directory to promote ease of administration and delegation of authority. The company's relationships with outside vendors, partners, and customers will determine how external access to the directory is managed, and more importantly, how security of those areas in the directory is implemented. Acquisition plans will roll into the aforementioned access and security areas, and will also present you with scalability scenarios to consider during your design phase.

Analyze factors that influence company strategies.

- Identify company priorities.
- Identify the projected growth and growth strategy.
- Identify relevant laws and regulations.
- Identify the company's tolerance for risk.
- Identify the total cost of operations.

▶ Whereas the previous objectives have direct influence on Active Directory design, this objective works at a higher level. It is important to identify factors that influence company strategies because the company's goals and objectives are based upon its strategies. The goals and objectives identify where a company wants to be in the future, which has a direct impact on key design scenarios for the directory. If strategy changes, that causes objectives to change, which filter down to your design plans. This is where a risk management plan becomes so important.

OUTLINE

STUDY STRATEGIES

- ▶ Take the necessary time to do Exercise 3.2, which has you view an online seminar focused upon knowledge management. This seminar will help you get a real-world understanding of decision-making drivers, information and communication flow, and other general business-related processes.

- ▶ Make sure you have a good general understanding of a digital nervous system. If the text in this chapter is insufficient for you, read the Enterprise Identity white paper mentioned in the additional resources list at the end of this chapter.

- ▶ Because the information in this chapter is abstract, it's important that you find something to relate it to. The Electrico case study is a great starting point, but if you're able to take it a step further and relate it to an actual company or client of yours, then you'll be in a better position to comprehend the information rather than just "reading" it.

- ▶ Pay attention to the sections on company strategy influences and again relate them to actual companies with which you do business. It's very important that you understand how things like mergers, law, regulations, and risk can affect a company's forward-looking strategy.

- ▶ Make sure you read the In the Field sidebars throughout this chapter. They help explain and support technology and processes beyond the scope of the chapter.

INTRODUCTION

Now that we've created the framework for conducting the business analysis, we'll apply it to a real-world situation. This chapter introduces Electrico Corporation, a consumer electronics organization that designs, produces, and distributes consumer electronics products around the world. You'll learn more about Electrico in the case study.

The entire focus of this chapter is dedicated to the framework for performing the business analysis set up in the previous chapter. Quite a bit of material will be derived from the case study. We'll go deeper here than in the previous chapter, and actually step through the analysis and draw some conclusions about the information extracted in the case study.

You may be wondering when we're going to start talking about Active Directory design and get away from this business analysis stuff. We are currently gathering the information we are going to use as input to the Active Directory design process. As stated previously, Windows 2000 and Active Directory are designed with an emphasis on the business. The material we cover in this part of the book will focus largely on *what* you need to understand about the business to effectively design Active Directory to meet both the business and technology needs of the company. The better you understand the areas of business outlined by this and future chapter objectives, the more successful you're apt to be when it comes time to crank out a design.

This chapter is one of the lengthiest chapters in the book, and covers quite a few test objectives. Once we get through this chapter, we'll get moving toward the technology side of the assessment, and then on to the design of Active Directory.

For now, though, let's take a look at the Electrico case study.

CASE STUDY: ELECTRICO CORPORATION

BACKGROUND

Electrico Corporation is an Indianapolis-based consumer electronics organization that designs, manufactures, and distributes consumer electronics products all over the world. Worldwide, Electrico employs about 5,000 people and is operationally managed from Indianapolis with divisions in El Paso (Manufacturing), Seattle (Product Development), Los Angeles (Sales), Buffalo (Shipping), and Chicago (Receiving). Electrico has been trailing its competition in terms of revenue for the past two years despite a steady increase in sales. Consequently, its executives have been studying its two main competitors and have made two distinct findings:

- Both of its main competitors utilize the Internet to sell product and supply their distribution channels with product.

- Both competitors include representatives from their corresponding IT organizations on every key strategic decision they make.

Immediately following these findings, Electrico called an executive meeting in which the following decisions were made:

- For the company to remain competitive, it must start putting an emphasis on technology.

- All IT projects should be outsourced from this point forward so the company can concentrate on its core competency.

- Electrico must rethink its business vision and analyze its business problems.

- Electrico should turn to Microsoft Windows 2000 to help strategically realign the company with IT.

PROBLEM STATEMENT

Electrico's current IT infrastructure consists of Novell NetWare 3.x and 4.x servers, all running in Bindery mode. Its line of business applications resides on an IBM mainframe. It still has quite a few 486 and low-end Pentium computers on the desktop running Windows 95 and a terminal emulation package to access the mainframe. IT has been reluctant to "fix" anything that was not "broken" and consequently has fallen behind the competition. Electrico executives have focused more on the bottom line in the past two years than on the business and now realize how the lack of focus on technology has jeopardized the company. They immediately got the appropriate funding to begin the project. Their goal is to change the way they do business.

BUSINESS ANALYSIS

Electrico has hired WayFront, Inc., a national consulting firm specializing in network and eBusiness solutions, to help take its business to the next level. WayFront understands technology, and more importantly, how to align business with technology to build a symmetric and high-tech business model. WayFront, after only a few days of high-level nontechnical discussions with Electrico, is ready to begin a series of discussions that will enable it to design a business solution to Electrico's problems. The following sections discuss WayFront's approach in detail.

Company Categorization

Before entering a meeting room, WayFront has properly categorized Electrico as a leader in the

continues

CASE STUDY: ELECTRICO CORPORATION

continued

consumer electronics market. Its strengths are its products and customer service, its weaknesses are a lack of direct sales and focus on IT, key benefits its competitors have over Electrico.

From the initial discussions it had with Electrico, WayFront was able to categorize Electrico as a *business-centric* company in terms of its relationship with IT.

No formal meetings between the two companies were needed for WayFront to make these determinations.

The following sections all occur in business meetings between Electrico executives, key line of business representatives, and WayFront consultants and business development managers. These sections are presented in question (WayFront) and answer (Electrico) format.

Business Vision
Purpose: To understand the vision of the company.

[Q]. What is your current business vision?

[A]. (Electrico CEO). It needs to change. It was focused on increasing product quality and utilizing new sales methodologies to increase revenue. After looking bottom line at our competition, we now recognize that we need to focus our attention on technology and how we use it to sell our product.

[Q]. Where do you see your company in 3–5 years?

[A]. (Electrico CEO). I see us struggling if we don't find a solution to our problem. I would like to see us as a company others model themselves after, a company with the right mix of business and IT that maintains product sales numbers double that of what we maintain now.

[Q]. What if your network could become a tool for increasing product quality and promoting new sales methodologies?

[A]. (Electrico CEO). That would be great in theory, but how do you make that happen? (Electrico CIO). Let's not worry about how, let's keep this conceptual. I think that is a great idea.

[Q]. What if you could use the Internet to sell your products all over the world?

[A]. (Electrico CEO). That would probably take care of our revenue problems, but it may create some others in logistics.

[Q]. Logistics are a valid and warranted concern. What if you could use that same technology to create a managed process that both benefits you logistically and does not burn bridges with your current distributors?

[A]. (Electrico CEO). That would be great!

[Q]. One final question. Do you see your competition moving in the same direction, that is, a technology-driven direction?

[A]. (Electrico CIO). I think they're already there with the technology on the front end, but I don't think they've wrapped their entire organization around the same logic.

CASE STUDY: ELECTRICO CORPORATION

Business Goals and Problems
Purpose: To develop a list of goals and business problems.

[Q]. Can you list your goal for this project?

[A]. (Electrico CEO). Our goal... We definitely need to start focusing on technology to help the business along. We can't compete without it. (Electrico CIO). I've seen several Windows 2000 seminars and am impressed with Microsoft's focus on the business in developing this operating system. That's the main reason we are interested in putting it to use.

[Q]. What are your problems in terms of how functional areas of your business operate or interoperate?

[A]. (Electrico CEO). We don't have a central repository to store information. We have information on several Novell servers, the IBM mainframe, in email folders, and on paper. It's too difficult to manage that way. Since the data is stored in so many places, all the different logins are an issue. (Electrico CIO). We don't have an effective communication process either. Several times we've had to scrap product designs because somebody did not communicate flaws efficiently. That's just one example. Our internal IT department is not a factor in our business processes; they react to business needs and are forced to come up with solutions that are not planned or tested. Sometimes they work, but more often than not, they don't, or don't get implemented in time to solve the problem. This is a big cost to our company. (Electrico CEO) And while we're on money, the cost of managing our network is outrageous. (LOB Rep) Our outside

sales people have a difficult time keeping up-to-date on marketing materials and other key pieces of information because they are never in the office. They can dial in, but that process is slow and tedious. The same goes for our vendor and partner base. They cannot currently access our system and need to.

[Q]. In a perfect world, describe how you'd like to see your key business processes, such as design of your product, the development of marketing materials for your product, or strategic IT interaction flow.

[A]. (Electrico CIO). In a perfect world we'd be able to share information between teams of developers, designers, and testers on the technical level, and between sales, marketing, and our external partners and vendors on a business level. Our internal processes, such as new employee integration would initiate processes to create network and email accounts, prepare a cubicle or office, and assign a phone extension. Other key processes would be streamlined as well.

[Q]. What if you could create a digital nervous system that not only allowed, but promoted, information gathering, storing, and sharing between any employee in the company?

[A]. (Electrico CIO). I believe you are referring to knowledge management, which is another key technology I've been studying for a while. If we could apply business rules to such a technology, I think we'd be on the right track. Right now, it's just too hard for our user base to locate resources on the network and make use of them.

continues

CASE STUDY: ELECTRICO CORPORATION

continued

Company Organization
Purpose: To discover how the company is managed, and how vendor, partner, and customer relationships are viewed. Also to discover information about mergers and acquisitions.

[Q]. You mentioned your vendors and partners earlier—how does Electrico manage vendor and partner relationships?

[A]. (Electrico CEO). Currently we have a portion of our outside sales organization dedicated to managing the relationship with our vendors. This team devotes 100 percent of its time to making sure our products end up in the distribution channel at the right time, in the right quantity, and so on. Our partnerships are a much smaller part of our business. We currently partner with only one other company. This company provides employees for our manufacturing plants in Mexico. Our corporate HR staff manages this partner relationship from here. There is not a lot of interaction between the two.

[Q]. Do you currently allow partners or vendors to access your network? How about future plans for this?

[A]. (Electrico CEO). No. We have a strict security policy in place that does not allow any external party to access the network. I don't think we'll change that in the future unless we can guarantee security, although we'd like to start using the Internet to do business with vendors and partners.

[Q]. How does your customer service department interact with your customers? Do you see that changing in 3–5 years?

[A]. (Electrico CEO). Customer Service currently uses direct mailings to our customer base to promote warranty registration. They also man an 800 number for customer issues and route calls to the appropriate places, such as product support, billing information, etc. In the future we'd like to expand our customer service center to provide a broad array of product-specific services that are currently handled by the product teams themselves. The problem for the customer service reps has been a lack of information pertaining to the product line.

[Q]. How do you utilize your Web site in the areas of vendor, partner, and customer relationships?

[A]. (Electrico CIO). We dropped budgeting for our Web site when we started having money issues. Consequently, we have nothing more than a static Web site that lists our product line. This site is rarely updated and is currently outdated by three months. We would like to enhance this site to fit the needs of our customers.

[Q]. Describe your high-level company management model.

[A]. (Electrico CEO). We run everything from here. We have an executive board of directors and executive directors for each of our product lines. We also have departmental directors that report directly to me. All of these positions are located here. On the middle tier, we have branch managers, resource managers, and product managers. These positions are spread out around our offices, distribution centers, and manufacturing facilities in the U.S., Canada, Mexico, and

CASE STUDY: ELECTRICO CORPORATION

Europe. Under these positions are "tier three" managers, who play more of a team leader role during projects.

[Q]. Do you see the management model changing in the next 3–5 years?

[A]. Yes. We've been discussing making a few changes, but have not implemented them. We are looking to distribute some managers when we go to a regional operation.

[Q]. Do you plan to grow your business within the next 3–5 years through mergers or acquisitions?

[A]. (Electrico CEO). Yes. We've discussed the possibility of purchasing an Asia-based company to grow our business in that market. A merger with the same company is a possibility if we cannot acquire them.

Geographical Scope and Company Model
Purpose: To find out where the company operations are located. To understand how the company operates within the geographical scope.

[Q]. You mentioned previously how the company was geographically dispersed. Can you elaborate on this?

[A]. (Electrico CEO). Sure. We are headquartered out of Indiana and have a small campus of three buildings there. We have regional operations in Buffalo, Chicago, Los Angeles, Seattle, and El Paso in the U.S., and London in Europe. Our Canadian operation in Vancouver serves as an extension of our Seattle operation, and our El Paso operation serves as a hub for our Mexico plants located in Juarez. We have several smaller operations that report either directly to corporate

in Indiana, or to one of the regional headquarters I just mentioned.

[Q]. So it sounds like your company model is best described as a mix between national and regional—is that accurate?

[A]. (Electrico CEO). Yes. (Electrico CIO). Well, from a reporting perspective he's right, but from an infrastructure perspective we operate more like a hub-and-spoke, because all WAN connections come here first. That was a result of explosive growth and poor planning.

[Q]. So it's safe to assume you'll be doing some infrastructure work in conjunction with this project?

[A]. (Both). Yes.

Company Processes
Purpose: To understand company processes as they relate to information and communication flow, as well as service and product life cycles and decision-making.

[Q]. Do your product teams change? If so, how do you manage those teams, communications, and information?

[A]. (Electrico CIO) Our product teams are usually permanent because our products don't change much from one revision to the next. We do, however, appoint short-term teams to conduct research and research analysis. Email is our principal means of communicating the needs of teams back and forth. It works but is inefficient when we need to give the teams access to

continues

CASE STUDY: ELECTRICO CORPORATION

continued

resources they need to do their jobs. We'd like to be able to automate the team creation process period. That would involve providing the team with disk space for collaboration, access to secure documents, access to printers, and additional software.

[Q]. What if you could create virtual teams, provide them with network space to collaborate, an interactive Web interface, and boundless integration (members can be from anywhere in the world)?

[A]. (Electrico CIO). That would fundamentally change the way we do business, which I think we can all agree is a good and needed thing. I'd be interested in seeing a solution concept in a test lab.

[Q]. How do you determine when to replace a certain product from your product line with a new version? How about a line of business applications?

[A]. (Electrico CIO). Good question. Internally, talking about applications replacement, we replace something when it stops working. That is literally how we've made decisions in the past. We recognize that needs to change fundamentally. We have a bit more structure when it comes to our product line. We use a standard product life cycle model to rev our products and have been pretty successful.

[Q]. Do you use any type of decision support system that provides you with the knowledge you need to make decisions? If not, where do you get the information you need to substantiate a decision?

[A]. (Electrico CIO). We do not have any decision support systems in place. It really depends on the type of decision we make as to what we base it from. We trust managers to make fair decisions for, say, vacation time, based on workload, available time the requesting employee has for vacation, the employee's performance—those things. Now if we're making a strategic decision, something that affects the direction of the company, those decisions are made after meetings where we discuss market research, performance (dollar wise), cost (if applicable)—things like that. Information that to us is not readily available, we have to go out and get it.

[Q]. How do you structure your decision-making process? I mean, are there various levels of decision-making before something is approved? Is there veto-ability? How much time does this process take?

[A]. (Electrico CEO) From a high level, we empower our management staff to make some decisions that do not require approval. For those decisions that require approval, we typically use cost to determine who has the final say. Some decisions can be overturned by executive directors or the board, but that rarely happens. Our process is pretty quick. Most decisions are approved within 48 hours, depending on what's being decided.

[Q]. Do you employ any sort of workflow application that applies your business rules and facilitates communication and tracks correspondence?

CASE STUDY: ELECTRICO CORPORATION

[A]. (Electrico CIO). No. We send a bunch of emails to people we know have the final say. In the future, we'd like to look at such a system.

**Influences That Affect Company Strategy
Purpose: To see what internal or external instigators will cause the company to change its strategy.**

[Q]. Can you list your top three company priorities in order of precedence?

[A]. (Electrico CEO). Our top priority is to increase sales volume and to remain competitive in our market. Second, implement the technology that allows us to do that. Third, educate our staff.

[Q]. What influences would make you change any of these priorities?

[A]. (Electrico CEO). Market conditions influence consumers. If market conditions are such that consumers quit buying our products for an extended period of time, it could cause us to refocus our strategy. Other influences are our competitors and how we match up with them in sales volume reports, technology, mergers and acquisitions, and the law.

[Q]. What are the relevant laws and regulations that influence your strategy?

[A]. (Electrico CEO). There are a plethora of regulations governing the transmission of digital signaling across the airways. There are too many to list, but they drive us nuts because they are constantly changing as new technologies emerge. There are really no laws; you see more laws in the service provider arena, say for a satellite system.

[Q]. Has Electrico ever performed a Total Cost of Operations assessment? If so, where are your problem areas?

[A]. (Electrico CIO). We've never performed a formal TCO assessment, but I can tell you that there is significant cost in the maintenance of the Novell Server network and the client base. We keep increasing our help desk staff to compensate for poor trouble ticket resolution time, but it doesn't seem to help much. We spend a lot of time trying to fix problems that shouldn't have happened in the first place.

[Q]. How much risk are you willing to take to realign your business with IT in mind?

[A]. (Electrico CEO). Obviously we don't want to do anything stupid, but at the same time we have an immediate need to get something in place. We'll sacrifice the money to replace instead of upgrade, we'll accept the risk associated with planning and design so we can do the job right.

[Q]. Where do you draw the line between acceptable risk and jeopardizing the well-being of the company?

[A]. (Electrico CEO). That's a very hard line to draw; I guess it depends on how we feel collectively about a certain risk. I'd like to have a risk management plan in place so we know what to do if we run into something.

NOTE

Tips for the Envisioning Session
One recommendation for the setting of this stage of the analysis is a conference room with a white board. A recommendation for the format is a facilitated discussion between the key design architects and business managers on the solution design team. Executive management should not attend this discussion.

ENVISIONING THE FUTURE

A clear and concise vision provides direction and inspiration for the entire company, if it is done right.

Envisioning the future is probably one of the more difficult things company executives do these days. There are so many things that can influence how people see the future. Remember Year 2000? The Internet? How many corporations anticipated they'd be selling product direct to anyone who wanted it around the world by 1998? How many companies back in the 1920s predicted the stock market would crash and the Great Depression would occur? The point we're trying to drive home is that a good vision is one that takes into consideration things that may influence the strategic direction of the company for years to come.

Electrico stated during the interview process that its vision needs to change. Does it? Your job during the interview process is to listen when appropriate, and ask the right questions when appropriate. You are trying to add value to the business by designing a technical solution that addresses their problems. To do that, you must thoroughly understand both where they are (current state) and where they want to go (vision).

Current State

Electrico stated the following vision during the meeting:

> *"It needs to change. It was focused on increasing product quality and utilizing new sales methodologies to increase revenue."*

Your task is to analyze this quote and the answers to your interview questions and draw some conclusions about the current vision of the company. You may decide you want to make some comments about the vision, but you should remember that some companies may not be open to suggestions about changing it.

In Electrico's case it's pretty easy, since the CEO already told us it needed to change. Our course of action then will be to analyze the answers to our questions from the meeting to determine where Electrico wants to position itself in its industry over the next 3–5 years.

It would be a good idea here to go ahead and break down the company's current vision statement. Even in Electrico's case, this will give us additional insight into the current state of the company. For example, in looking at Electrico's current vision, you can draw two conclusions:

◆ Electrico is a company dedicated to producing high-quality products.

◆ New sales methodologies have or will be introduced to the organization.

The second bullet in the preceding list is interesting. You have a vision statement that references *new* methodologies. If you run into something that doesn't quite sit right, like this, you should question the company. After further questioning, Electrico states that they constantly run their sales force through the Miller-Heiman Strategic Selling courses, which have been so effective, they've been added to the company vision.

Now you understand the current vision of the company. Where does it see itself in the next 3–5 years?

How Will the Company Change?

More important than the current state is how the company will change in the next 3–5 years. The vision statement identifies specific goals that are required for the continued growth of the company. In this section, you will analyze the information pertaining to the future positioning of the company and draw a conclusion based on that information.

Electrico is sure of one thing—it needs to focus on technology more than in the past if it is to continue to compete in the industry. WayFront, in its analysis, uses this statement as a starting point. During the interview, the Electrico CEO stated that they would struggle if they didn't find a solution to their problems. The

NOTE

When discussing network operating systems, the typical life cycle is between three and five years, so you'll see references throughout this chapter to the future as the next 3–5 years.

problems were identified as no e-commerce solution, and not enough involvement of IT in strategic business decisions. Already, WayFront can draw a conclusion: *Electrico must involve IT in strategic planning efforts.* Additionally, the Electrico CEO, in setting his sights high, stated he would like to see Electrico as a company others model themselves after with the right alignment of business and IT. A second conclusion can be drawn here: *Electrico wishes to design a world-class business infrastructure, one in which both business and IT collaborate to determine strategic business direction.* Finally, in the same statement, the Electrico CEO states that this alignment of IT and business would double the sales volume that it currently maintains. A final conclusion can be drawn from this statement: *Electrico must utilize the business and IT alignment to double its sales volume within five years.*

"What If?" Analysis

In the case study, WayFront used "What if?"-based questioning to determine the business needs of the organization. The "What if?" question is very effective in a high-level analysis because the sky really is the limit. For example, WayFront asked questions geared at sparking this interest of Electrico and getting them to think in a certain way about the way they do business. Questions such as *"What if your network could become a tool for increasing product quality and promoting new sales methodologies?"* demand a response that usually requires a bit of thinking. In this case, WayFront incorporated Electrico's existing vision into a "what if" question and gave it an IT twist. The response was positive but with a bit of apprehension.

Sometimes companies are reluctant to change anything—especially companies that have been around a while. WayFront was able to detect this apprehension, *"but it may create some problems with logistics"* and roll that consideration into the next question, *"What if you could use that same technology to create a managed process that both benefits you logistically and does not burn bridges with your current distributors?"* The result, something potentially show-stopping, was turned completely around into something positive.

Concluding the Business Vision Analysis

How you perform the analysis of the business vision, or any other section of the business analysis, is up to you. The goal is to take the information you were able to extract from the meeting, organize it, and make sense of it. In this case, we used a conference-room setting with a facilitated discussion format. We took our notes from the meeting, discussed them, and drew conclusions from them. The next step is to take the results of the analysis and put them into a useful format.

Figure 3.1 illustrates how you might organize your findings in the business vision analysis. In Electrico's case, you will present these findings to the executives and come up with a vision for the company moving forward. In all cases, you will take these findings and apply them in your design proposal.

Electrico Corporation. Business Vision Analysis Results

Current Vision Statement:	Focused on increasing product quality and utilizing new sales methodologies to increase revenue.
Conclusions Drawn From Analysis	1. Electrico must involve IT in its strategic planning efforts.
	2. Electrico wishes to design a world-class business infrastructure, in which both business and IT collaborate to determine strategic business direction.
	3. Electrico must utilize the business and IT alignment to double its sales volume within 5 years.
Future Vision (from analysis of data)	Increase product sales volume by developing and maintaining a world-class relationship between business and IT, and utilizing a top-notch network infrastructure to gather, organize, and manage knowledge.

FIGURE 3.1
Electrico Corporation. Results of business vision analysis.

ANALYZING BUSINESS PROBLEMS

The first step in planning workable solutions is to analyze the business problems and create project objectives. The most efficient way to organize the objectives definition is through the use of a table (see Table 3.1) that maps business problems to project objectives. We will pick up our discussion of the Electrico case study later in this section.

Business Goal

The business goal is usually associated with the overall goal for the project. In Electrico's case, the business goal can be stated as *"To start focusing on technology to help the business along."* It is important to clearly define this business goal, because the goal will serve as strategic direction for the project. The business goal is a statement, and the project objectives both support that statement and address one or more specific business problems.

Problem Analysis

> **NOTE**
>
> **Project Reference**   Just to clarify, we are treating the business analysis as a project that consists of one or more project team members. The client in this case is the business you're assessing, even if the project team is itself a part of that business.

Once you've defined the business goal, the next step is to analyze the business problems and come up with project objectives that address those problems. As an analyst, your goal in performing this analysis is multi-fold: First, you want to understand what your client's problems are. What are the business problems and how can we fix them? In general, what are the client's expectations for the project? Second, you want to begin to look at project scope. What is it going to take to make this project successful? What will the personnel requirements be? How long will the project take? Finally, you want to organize the problems and objectives into short- and long-term categories that address specific business concerns. Typically your longer-term category will consist of anything that addresses ROI or TCO.

The following sections outline the business problem analysis process.

Problem-Objective Table

The first step in performing the business problem analysis is to map the business problem to a project objective. A conference room discussion and a white board are a perfect setting for this activity.

To determine what the business problems are, review your notes from the meeting. On the white board, write down anything you and your project team consider a business problem. Once you have exhausted your notes, remove duplicate problems, condense similar problems into one, and verify with the company with which you're working that these problems are accurate.

The end result of this discussion should be a table such as Table 3.1. Table 3.1 acts as a precursor to the following sections by displaying the problem-objective relationships from the Electrico case study. Keep in mind that this is an Active Directory design book, so issues that do not pertain to that do not appear in this list.

> **NOTE**
>
> **Project Objectives** At this stage in the problem analysis, we have not yet discussed our project objectives. We have inserted them in Table 3.1 to make it complete, and will discuss how we came up with them in the following section.

> **NOTE**
>
> **Direct Problem-Objective Mapping** An effective way to address each business problem is to create an objective that addresses that problem. A one-to-one mapping between problems and objectives is recommended wherever possible.

TABLE 3.1

BUSINESS PROBLEM AND OBJECTIVE RELATIONSHIP—ELECTRICO

Business Problem	*Project Objective*
Too many logons are necessary to get to the information needed for a simple task.	Utilize Active Directory and directory connectors to provice a single logon.
Systems do not facilitate adequate communication among departments.	Design the Active Directory structure so that it provides the framework for collaboration and communication.
The cost of managing the network is too high.	Design Active Directory to facilitate simplified network management. Make the MMC a single source of administration.
External users, including Electrico employees, vendors, and partners, cannot get to the data they need in an adequate fashion from outside the company.	Develop a security policy that authenticates employees, vendors, and partners and allows specific access to the directory based on security credentials.
	Create a new remote access system utilizing Virtual Private Networking (VPN) technology.
Employees have a difficult time finding the resources they need from the network.	Use Active Directory to store information about all objects on the network.
There is no way for employees to manage intellectual material.	Prepare Active Directory to incorporate Microsoft Exchange Server 2000 WebStore and Workflow.

Objective Definition Stage

The next step in the business problem analysis is to prepare project objectives to address each problem. To do this, you'll treat each business problem individually, and create an objective to solve that problem. Your objectives will be an extremely high-level selection from your solution set, which in this case is Windows 2000, and more specifically, the Active Directory design subset of solutions. This is where your knowledge of Windows 2000 and Active Directory becomes key.

We'll start the objective definition with the list of problems from the white board. For each problem, we must identify a solution, an objective that addresses the problem. In the case of Electrico, we came up with six problems (refer to Table 3.1). Because Table 3.1 already lists the project objectives, we'll discuss how we came up with them.

Problem #1: Too many logons are necessary to get to the information needed for a simple task. Over the years, Electrico has added systems "just in time" to get the job done. Consequently it has ended up with quite a few systems that do not communicate with one another. A side effect of this situation is the number of times a user must authenticate to a different system to get the information he needs. At Electrico, it's possible that a user would need to log in to the Novell network, the IBM mainframe, and the email package just to find one piece of information. To alleviate this problem, it needs a unified directory with a single logon. No need to go any further. You have your objective. **Objective #1: Utilize Active Directory and directory connectors to provide a single logon.**

Problem #2: Systems do not facilitate adequate communication among departments. More often than not, you'll find that organizations do not communicate well. We'll all probably go to our graves trying to get to the root cause of that problem. What we can do is provide a more robust environment that promotes (and sometimes demands) good communication. There will always be that human factor around to ruin everything, but there is nothing we can do about that. We know from our meeting that Electrico in part blames its systems for inadequate communication. To *help* resolve Electrico's communication problems, we need to provide a platform that promotes collaboration, team communication, messaging, and conferencing, all of which cannot be provided by Active Directory in and of itself. This is an example of a case in which you'd want to promote the integration of additional technology that addresses this problem. Microsoft Exchange 2000 provides not only messaging and scheduling capabilities, but also a world-class knowledge-management platform, which just happens to address all of the above issues.

So, in summary, we draw our objective in the form of providing a platform that promotes collaboration and communication. **Objective #2: Design Active Directory structure so that it provides the framework for collaboration and communication.**

Problem #3: The cost of managing the network is too high. This is another area that hinders the efficiency of businesses. When you get right down to it, bottom-line costs drive how, and how well, businesses perform. A company without an IT focus, such as Electrico, tends to treat its IT department as a cost center, a necessary evil that just frankly costs the business too much money. Businesses are starting to come around now and realize the benefit of strategic IT involvement in the core business. This, among other things, changes the way they look at IT costs. Once they begin to reap the benefit of technology in the core business operation, the whole cost center thing seems to disappear. Another side of this is when the IT infrastructure is such that management becomes a costly operation. Such is the case with Electrico: It has too many systems to manage and hence has compensated by hiring additional staff. Its goal is to reduce this cost, yet better its internal system, a goal that proper implementation of Windows 2000 and Active Directory should resolve. **Objective #3: Design Active Directory to facilitate simplified network management. Make the MMC a single source of administration.**

Problem #4: External users, including Electrico employees, vendors, and partners, cannot get to the data they need in an adequate fashion from outside the company. This problem is complex. When you step back and look at why the problem exists, you'll see there are two problems: the company security policy and the remote access services. For that reason, this problem is addressed using two objectives: one that addresses security, and another that addresses remote access. In terms of security, Electrico's long-standing company security policy states that non-employees simply

> **NOTE**
>
> **Importance of Microsoft Exchange**
> Because Exchange is out of the scope of this book, we can't go any further into it, but do recommend you understand its capabilities, as they are a great complement to Windows 2000.

do not get access to the network—period. With the information age in full swing, Electrico needs to be persuaded a bit to revise their security policy to allow partners and vendors access to the information they need access to. With Windows 2000 Public Key Infrastructure (PKI), Kerberos Authentication, X.509 Certificates, IPsec, and other encryption protocols, it is possible to open only specific doors on the network for specific users, therefore keeping confidential company information protected. The remote access services in use by Electrico are old, slow, and antiquated. This inhibits the external sales employees from getting the information they need when they need it. So we must architect a new remote access system to alleviate this problem. **Objective #4: (Security) Develop a security policy that authenticates employees, vendors, and partners and allows specific access to the directory based on security credentials. (Remote Access) Create a new remote access system utilizing Virtual Private Networking (VPN) technology.**

Problem #5: Employees have a difficult time finding the information and resources they need from the network. This problem is a gruesome side effect of growth in several areas. As the company grew, additional systems were added to address growing business needs. Although on the surface these systems got the job done, underneath they began to create minor problems for the users. The users had to go to several locations to find the resources they were looking for. As the company grew, these problems became larger. Now the problems are so big, they're starting to reverse the benefit of the additional systems. You can address this problem by utilizing Active Directory as your resource repository—that is, publishing all network resources to a single searchable directory so users can easily find and use them. **Objective #5: Use Active Directory to store information about all objects on the network.**

Problem #6: There is no way for employees to manage intellectual material. This problem is another one of those problems that arises from rapid, uncontrolled growth. Smaller organizations have the ability to manage information well, because there are usually one or two people generating that information and they manage it themselves. When you get into larger organizations, this process becomes less manageable because you have several people and systems responsible for generating information, and those who use the information may have nothing to do with putting it together. Microsoft has invested in significant research into the development of knowledge and how to manage it. While Active Directory and Windows 2000 do not specifically perform functions that allow you to manage knowledge, Exchange 2000 does. This is yet another use for Exchange in the Electrico environment. The Windows 2000 Active Directory design for Electrico should consider the integration of Microsoft Exchange 2000's WebStore and workflow functionality.

The Active Directory design that will promote the incorporation of these technologies is the design itself—that is, highly structured domains and organizational units, and well-planned security groups. **Objective #6: Prepare Active Directory to incorporate Microsoft Exchange Server 2000 WebStore and Workflow.**

> **NOTE**
>
> **More About Exchange** You can read more about the Microsoft Exchange WebStore and Workflow functionality at `http://www.microsoft.com/exchange/prodinfo/2000/default.htm`.

IN THE FIELD

PROJECT SCOPE AND TEAMS

Once you've defined your project objectives, you should start to think about the scope of your project. For most large projects, you'll create more than one project team, and you should begin to define those teams as the project objectives and scope become clear. The scope of a project defines its boundaries (what will and will not be done). Windows 2000 scopes generally will be large, since many corporations will wrap infrastructure and hardware upgrades in with them. Moreover, it's not uncommon to build different project teams for DNS design, Active Directory design, security, training, rollout, and more. A word to the wise: Begin your team building and resource planning early in the process.

COMPANY ORGANIZATION

Analyze the existing and planned organizational structures. Considerations include management model; company organization; vendor, partner, and customer relationships; and acquisition plans.

The analysis of the company organizational structure is where things are going to start getting complicated and even a bit abstract. When discussing the organizational model relative to Active Directory, everything seems to tie in some way to everything else. A change in one area filters through dependent areas and, before you know it, you can have a mess on your hands. The goal here is to get the right information to do the design. This section uses parts of the Electrico case study to demonstrate a pseudo real-world look at company organization. Before we start, take a step back and think about what we really need to accomplish here in this section. Your goal in performing this analysis is to understand the management model; vendor, partner, and customer relationships, and merger and acquisition plans of the business so you can adequately design Active Directory to satisfy the current and future needs of each.

Existing and Planned Management Models

The existing and planned management models of the organization play a key role in the design of the Active Directory security groups, organizational units, sites, and potentially delegation of administrative control. Having a good understanding of the current and planned management models will allow you to design a solution that both satisfies the existing needs, and has the ability to scale up or down with company growth or cutbacks.

The first step in performing this analysis is to extract the key information about the management model from the meeting notes. The key statements about the company management model at Electrico are as follows:

◆ "We run everything from here." All key decisions are made from the corporate headquarters.

◆ "We have an executive board of directors…," "We also have departmental directors…," "On the middle tier… These positions are spread out…," "Under these positions are 'tier three' managers…"

◆ "We are looking to distribute some managers when we go to a regional operation."

These bullets give us a high-level view of the management model as it exists now, and what the future holds. In performing an analysis on this information, you want to ask yourself questions such as the following:

◆ Does the management model coincide with the geographical scope of the company? (Geographical scope will be discussed in the next section.)

◆ What roles do different levels of management perform and does this impact the design concept for Active Directory?

◆ What role does the management model play in Active Directory security policies? Will there be a need for delegated control to management?

◆ How will changing the management model impact the design of Active Directory?

◆ What special considerations must be given to the executive management and board of directors?

◆ How does the IT management model integrate with the rest of the company? What special considerations will IT management need?

You may need to set up additional meetings with the company to discuss the management model in more detail, specifically to see how it plans to incorporate its managers into the directory. You may find that IT management is the only division of the management model that needs to be considered; however, other companies will incorporate other areas of management—hence the complexity. In any case, the end result of this analysis should be a requirements specification for Active Directory design with the company management model in mind. Furthermore, your specification should include a section on how the management model is expected to change, and how those changes will impact the design. Enter change, risk, and problem management. If these areas are not something you've dealt with in the past, get to know and understand them now because they will be your saving graces throughout this process.

In examining Electrico's management model, we see a relatively complex, multi-tiered management model that is spread out across the geographical scope of the company, as illustrated in Figure 3.2. Keep in mind that, although complex, Electrico's model has been simplified quite a bit so we can effectively convey the materials in this section.

> **NOTE**
>
> **Change, Risk, and Problem Management** Detailing change, risk, and problem management is out of the scope of this book. These areas of project management will be referred to throughout this book. It is highly recommended that you understand these processes and where they fit into the design process. Check the "Suggested Readings and Resources" list at the end of this chapter for reading material on these subjects.

Different companies will incorporate different levels of management into Active Directory design. In most cases, including Electrico, IT management and administration (discussed in detail in Chapter 4, "Analyzing the IT Administration Model") will be the focal point for your design, and other areas of management will provide input for security policies, delegation of control, vendor and partner integration, and merger and acquisition planning. The remaining subsections in this section describe the analysis of these areas.

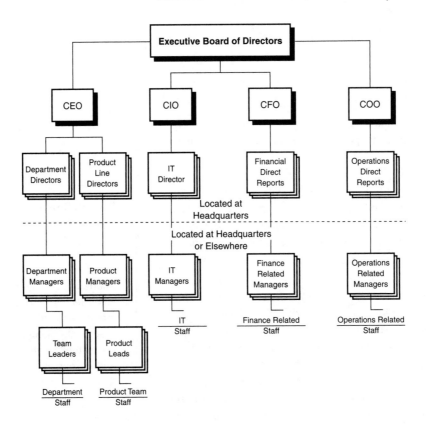

FIGURE 3.2
The Electrico management model.

Existing and Planned Vendor, Partner, and Customer Relationships

We're going to take a bit of a diversion in discussing this section. The digital nervous system, Microsoft's initiative to digitize the DNA of a company, presents us with an interesting view of vendor, partner, and customer relationships, as well as employee-to-employee relationships. The Community Management module of the digital nervous system discusses utilizing the Internet as a medium to facilitate these relationships. We'll discuss the Electrico vendor, partner, and customer relationships in the context of Community Management. You'll find later in the chapter that another digital nervous system module, Identity Administration, is used to discuss the key company processes within Electrico.

The explosion of the commercialized Internet has increased the need for efficient collaboration between a company and its key vendors, partners, and customers. The concept of a digital community promotes the use of the Internet to allow vendors, partners, customers, and even employees to quickly find and share the right information at the right time. More importantly, using the Internet to facilitate this collaboration means that it can be done from anywhere in the world, any time of the day. Of course, these relationships must be managed.

Digital community management manages relationships between internal and external identities. For example, an employee of Electrico may need to access a resource inside the company firewall from the outside. Because she is an employee, she is granted access through an authentication process to her resource, whereas a vendor, based on a PIN, may not even see the logon window to attempt to log on to an internal resource. This is an example of authentication, one of three components of community management: authentication, rendezvous, and authorization.

Authentication

Authentication, in general, is a verification process. Within Windows NT, it gives you access to network resources based on your user ID and password. Within the digital nervous system, it verifies your *identity*. Electrico has a strict policy against allowing vendors and partners access to their network because of security concerns.

N O T E

Extranets The process of extending an internal network to the Internet is called creating an extranet. *Extranets* are Web-accessible portions of a company's secure internal network. These portions do require authentication. Web access to a messaging server (Outlook Web Access to Exchange) is an example of an extranet.

Authentication securely identifies identities through the use of a username and password, or other set of security credentials.

Windows 2000 supports MIT v5 Kerberos authentication, X.509 certificate authentication, PKI (Public Key Infrastructure), and smart-card authentication mechanisms. This comprehensive set of digital authentication processes provides top-notch security to the internal network. Active Directory can use any of these authentication mechanisms to validate users and provide access to all valid resources within the company network (inside or outside the firewall).

With the explosion of eBusiness over the past few years, cases like Electrico's are becoming the minority. More companies are extending their internal networks to the Internet to allow vendors and partners to exchange information electronically.

IN THE FIELD

THE APPLICATION OF AN EXTRANET

There are a variety of uses for extranets. One of the more popular is that of Virtual Private Networks (VPNs), which are extensions of the corporate network that use a secure connection over the Internet to allow authenticated access for users with credentials. Many companies are replacing costly remote access services (RAS) with VPNs for a number of reasons. At the top of the list is cost. A company with a bank of 200 modems to support remote access can replace all 200 modems with a single (albeit fast) connection to the Internet and a VPN router or OS service. All that's then required for remote access through the VPN is access to the Internet and a VPN client. This solution proves to be much more cost effective over the long run than the traditional dial-in RAS connection. Vendors, partners, and customers can take advantage of extranets to gain limited access to the company information specific to their needs.

Rendezvous

More and more companies are setting up eCommerce storefronts on the Internet to sell their wares direct, and provide rich information to their customers. They are providing areas for customers to get information and support, send comments, or download updates

to products. Connecting vendors, partners, and customers to
these resources, or to each other, is called rendezvous, the second
component of community management.

Simply stated, *rendezvous* is the process of allowing people to
connect to resources and other people. Rendezvous can play an
important role in vendor, partner, and customer relationships
because it provides a simple method for them to locate the resources
they need to locate. You can think of rendezvous in the context of a
simple address book—a resource to which all users have access, and
which provides a method of connecting them to one another.

Active Directory provides the foundation for rendezvous in its
support for Internet standard protocols such as DNS and LDAP.
Through the use of these protocols, a company can populate and
expose specific attributes of its internal directory to the extranet for
use by validated vendors, partners, and customers.

Authorization

The final component of community management is authorization.
Authorization uses a person's identity and context (both discussed
later in this chapter) to grant access to resources. Do not confuse
this process with authentication. In the context of a digital nervous
system, *authentication* verifies your identity, and authorization uses
that identity information to grant access to resources. Authorization
is what ensures the security of the internal network and network
resources. Authorization works side by side with provisioning (also
discussed later in this chapter) to ensure that an authenticated user
has access not only to the tools to do her job (provisioning), but
also the access to resources (authorization) she needs to do her job.

Very important to the digital nervous system is a consistent security
model. Active Directory provides this model, mainly by its ability
to support a single logon and its ability to pass logon credentials to a
requesting application. For example, Ken logs on to Windows 2000
and Active Directory Kerberos authenticates him. When he needs
to access another system, perhaps an Active Directory aware database
system that requires authentication, Active Directory simply passes
Ken's logon credentials.

Electrico

With community management and the digital nervous system in mind, we'll now resume the analysis of Electrico's case study and see how a digital nervous system can be leveraged to better manage vendor, partner, and customer relationships.

The following bullets from the Electrico case study contribute to our analysis of its vendor, partner, and customer relationships:

◆ No partners or vendors are permitted to access Electrico's network because of a strict security policy. Plans to modify that policy hinge on how technology can ensure security. Electrico would like to begin using the Internet to do business with vendors and partners.

◆ Electrico uses an internal customer service department to provide phone-based service to its customers. It has plans to enhance this area of the company to provide additional services without requiring the aid of product teams.

◆ A portion of the outside sales organization currently manages the relationships with Electrico's vendors.

◆ Electrico's HR department manages the relationship with its only partner, which provides the company employees for its Mexico-based manufacturing facilities.

◆ Electrico currently has a static, out-of-date Web site that displays information about its products. They have dropped budgeting for the management of this site. They would like to pick back up with the site and tailor it to customer needs.

In Electrico's case, we need to examine a few different areas of Active Directory design. First is the customer service organizational unit. Currently the customer service department manually handles service calls covering a wide range of topics. It cannot provide detailed product support because of the lack of training and pertinent information about the products. Electrico has existing plans to expand the department, and provide it with the information needed to provide product support. This means that the department as a whole will need access to specific information across OU boundaries in Active Directory. Setting up Active Directory security groups and providing sufficient permissions to product information for those security groups will allow customer service access to that data. Additionally, if Electrico created an extranet and incorporated the aforementioned digital nervous system processes, it could allow breakthrough support via its extranet and allow the customer service representatives to collaborate with customers, vendors, and partners.

The second area is in the vendor and partner relationship realm. Electrico currently uses outside sales staff to manage its vendor relationships, so when creating the OU design in the directory, you must consider this additional duty. This additional duty requires the specified sales individuals to have access to the information they need to provide to vendors, so simple permissions will probably handle this requirement. As Electrico looks to the future, it would like to utilize the Internet as a means to manage vendor relationships and provide for electronic data interchange (EDI). Among other things, this creation of an extranet is going to require Active Directory integration, management, and most definitely a security policy, all of which define a digital nervous system. The most common way to incorporate an extranet with the LAN and the Intranet is to create a demilitarized zone (DMZ) and locate all extranet servers on the DMZ. Figure 3.3 illustrates a simple DMZ.

The final area of consideration is the company Web site enhancements to provide customers with a rich, interactive, and functional experience. The relationship between the Web site and Active Directory lies in the services Electrico chooses to provide its customers, as well as vendors, partners, and employees. Remember that community management and its core components—authentication, rendezvous, and authorization—extend Active Directory to the Internet and provide the same level of security as inside the firewall. Electrico's chief concern about a functional Web site with access to internal data was security. You need to pick up on that and identify Active Directory and accompanying services as solutions to this problem.

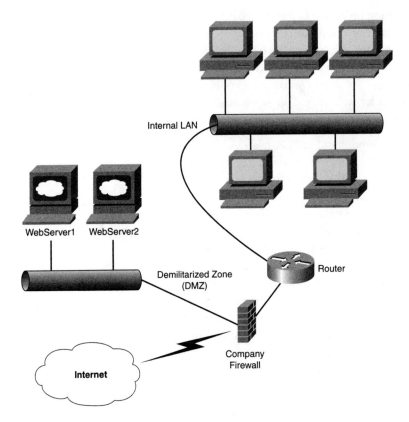

FIGURE 3.3
A simplified view of a Demilitarized Zone (DMZ).

Expected Areas of Growth

Growth within a company typically occurs in three areas: internal through new hires, mergers with other companies, and acquisitions of other companies. In a majority of cases, internal growth does not affect the design of directory services, as new employees usually hire into the functional business model. Consequently, the two major types of growth you need to be aware of in your design are mergers and acquisitions.

IN THE FIELD

GROWTH BEYOND THE BUSINESS MODEL

It is important that you not rule out internal growth from becoming a factor in Active Directory design. While it is true that most companies—especially well-established companies—do not grow rapidly enough internally to affect Active Directory design, there are cases in which this is not true. Consider the "dot com" industry. Many start-ups begin by offering a single service and then, if successful, grow rapidly to offer a much wider variety of services. Of course, one of the measurements of success is the company's ability to scale and do so rather quickly and easily. The methodically planned Active Directory structure will enable these organizations to grow vertically within the business model, as well as horizontally to extend the business model.

Mergers

It seems like every time you turn on the news, you're hearing about some multi-billion dollar *merger* between two gargantuan companies. Step back and think for a minute how big a job the IT organizations of those two companies have in front of them. Let's just say sleep deprivation comes to mind! In fact, if you've ever been a part of a large merger, you'll recall that the standardization of line of business systems, email, and even the network operating systems didn't happen overnight; in fact, it probably didn't happen for months or even years after the merger was final. The two companies probably went about business as usual for a while, just like nothing ever happened, and waited for the long, slow process of standardization to take place. How the two companies interoperate during this convergence time is what we're analyzing here.

Before Windows 2000, when two companies merged, how did they facilitate communication across the company? How did employees from one company access resources on the other company's network? How did they exchange email? What if one company was Windows NT and the other was NetWare? These are just some of the questions the IT organizations of each company had to answer. Microsoft recognized the stress IT organizations, and businesses in general, had to endure during a corporate merger. They designed Windows 2000 and Active Directory to simplify the interoperability and migration aspects that typically make up the IT end of a merger. As you plan the Active Directory design for a merger, keep the following in mind:

◆ **Domain and OU design.** Design the domain and OU structure such that additional domains and OUs may be added without affecting the "original" ones.

◆ **Synchronization and migration toolset.** Know your "merger" toolset with Windows 2000. These are your synchronization and migration tools. Windows 2000 provides four main interoperability tools:

- *NetWare integration and migration tools.* Windows 2000 includes tools to both integrate with, and migrate from NetWare. The integration tools provide for up to two-way synchronization of Active Directory and Novell's NDS. The migration tools provide a method to migrate NetWare users, groups, and volumes to Windows 2000.

- *Services for UNIX.* The goal of Services for UNIX (SFU) is to provide a comprehensive set of tools to help bridge the gap between UNIX and Windows for users and administrators.

- *Services for Macintosh.* Windows 2000 services for Macintosh provide Appleshare-compatible directory authentication and file and printer sharing capabilities using the Appletalk protocol.

- *Single sign-on for host systems.* Through the use of SNA server and Windows 2000, you can provide integration with host systems using the RACF and ACF-2 security protocols.

◆ **Third-party tools and utilities.** There are several companies offering synchronization and migration utilities for Windows 2000. Entevo, FastLane, and Mission Critical all offer migration utilities that facilitate a managed and phased migration process.

◆ **Meta directory solutions.** Meta directories will sit atop an organization's differing directories, such as the ERP directory, Active Directory, Novell NDS, and Exchange Directory, and provide a single point of administration to all directories. This ensures that all directories are "in synch" with one another. Microsoft acquired ZoomIT Corporation specifically to enhance its meta directory product Via.

◆ **Directory consolidation.** Consolidation is essentially moving the "identity" information from one directory to another and upgrading the applications to a version supported by the target directory (presumably Active Directory). Exchange 5.5 to 2000 is a good example of this.

◆ **Standards.** Always keep development of standards near the top of your list. This is a longer-term objective, but one that you'll need to begin addressing as soon as the two companies announce the merger.

> **NOTE**
>
> **Even More About Exchange**   There are several references in this book to Microsoft Exchange. One of many good resources for additional Exchange information is the official Exchange Web site at `http://www.microsoft.com/exchange`.

Acquisitions

Acquisitions activity refers to one company purchasing another. Typically the purchasing organization will integrate the other organization into its network. The bullets listed for mergers in the previous section also apply to acquisitions. Additionally, you should consider the following issues for acquisitions, which will be discussed at length in Chapters 10, 11, and 12:

◆ **Domain model integration.** Determine whether the acquired company will be integrated into the existing domain structure, or will become a new domain.

◆ **Active Directory sites.** Depending upon connectivity to the newly acquired company, you may need to consider controlled Active Directory replication through the use of sites. This of course comes after the domain model integration.

IN THE FIELD

PLAN FOR ORGANIZATIONAL CHANGE

One thing mergers and acquisitions are sure to bring about is change. Change is a nemesis to some and is welcomed by others. How companies cope with change—whether they proactively plan for it or just react to it—often determines success or failure. The following excerpt is from an excellent Microsoft TechNet article, "MS Solutions Framework: Managing Organizational Change."

continues

continued

"In other words, the organizations that succeed at change do so by considering the people who are affected by, will have to live with, and are often crucial to effecting the change in question. Even better, not only does managing the human aspects of an organizational change initiative help ensure the successful implementation and use of the technical solution, it sets the groundwork for implementing future solutions…"

You should read that entire article if you're planning M&A strategies, or if your organization is simply restructuring or facilitating some other form of change.

COMPANY OPERATING SCOPE

Analyze the existing and planned business models.

The operational scope of the company defines how it distributes and manages its resources. It plays a key role in both the physical and logical design characteristics of Active Directory, namely, in the design of sites and subnets, placement of operation masters, administration, and replication. In this section, we'll utilize our meeting notes with Electrico to determine how the company is geographically dispersed, and how the company operates relative to its geography.

There are two parts to the geographical scope of a company; where the offices are located, and how they are interconnected. The latter aspect will be discussed in more detail during the analysis of technical requirements in Part III, "Analyzing Technical Requirements." In this chapter, however, we are more concerned about discovering *how* the company operations are organized *within* the geographical scope. This *how* characteristic is called the company model, and is typically one of regional, national, international, subsidiary, or branch office. We'll first discuss the geographical scope of the company, then how the company operates within that scope.

> **NOTE**
>
> **A Handle on the Basics** This section assumes that you have a basic understanding of sites and subnets, and Active Directory replication. If you don't, the chapters in Part IV, "Designing a Directory Service Architecture," cover both topics at length.

Geographical Scope

Arguably the best way to visualize the geographical scope of an organization is to draw it on a piece of paper. Figure 3.4 shows a diagram drawn according to the Electrico geographical scope.

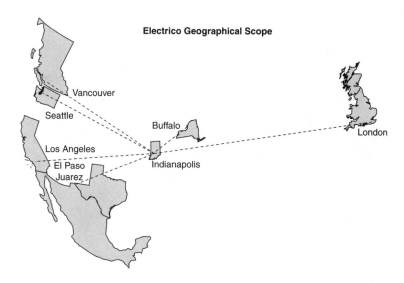

FIGURE 3.4
The geographical scope of Electrico.

You can immediately assert that Electrico *physically* is an international company, because it has operations outside the United States. The next step is to assign a number to each location on the diagram. This number should roughly correspond to the number of employees at each physical location. That number of employees has a direct impact on how you structure your Active Directory domains. For example, if Electrico had 50,000 employees at its Mexican manufacturing facility, 25,000 in El Paso, 30,000 in LA, and 40,000 in Seattle, and you wanted to use a regional domain structure, that would be 145,000 people in the single western region domain, which may work just fine, but imagine replicating that many objects across the WAN links! This example exaggerates a bit (by 140,000!) on the number of people Electrico employs, but gets the point across. Figure 3.5 shows the updated diagram.

One last thing you'll want to be aware of when you analyze the geographical scope is growth potential. Use dotted lines to indicate future expansion.

NOTE

Network Topology If you have a network topology diagram at this stage of the business assessment, use it to analyze the geographical scope of the company.

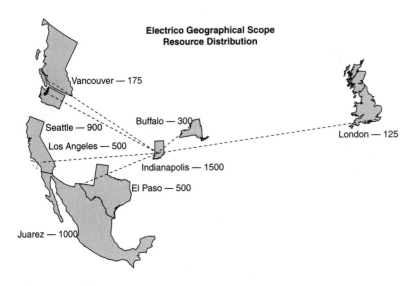

Electrico Geographical Scope Resource Distribution

Vancouver — 175

Buffalo — 300

London — 125

Seattle — 900

Los Angeles — 500

Indianapolis — 1500

El Paso — 500

Juarez — 1000

FIGURE 3.5
Electrico's distribution of resources.

Company Operational Model

Large international companies are more apt to run their businesses by geographical scope than a local company is. If you think about it, you wouldn't want to run an international company solely from the United States; there are just too many factors that affect how businesses operate overseas that differ from the U.S. Figure 3.6 shows the geographical scope of Electrico, along with its operational divisions. You can see that the operational divisions of Electrico are all located in the U.S., even though there are manufacturing and distribution facilities internationally. These international facilities are managed locally because of international differences, Foreign Trade Zone policies, and time differences, but report back to specific operational divisions in the US, so they really operate as pseudo-branch offices.

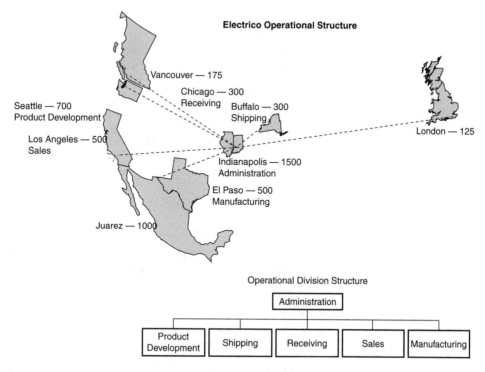

FIGURE 3.6
Electrico's operational environment.

There are many different ways a company can divide and manage its resources throughout its geographical scope. This simple, yet effective, method for mapping out both the physical locations and the operational divisions should work across the board with minor modifications. Additionally, you'll want to consider the connectivity between physical sites in terms of available bandwidth and performance requirements before you begin your design. These technical factors are discussed in detail in Part III of this book.

IN THE FIELD

THE APPLICATION OF GEOGRAPHICAL SCOPE

The geographical scope of operations determines the physical structure of Active Directory. As you will read in Part IV, Active Directory sites define the physical structure by acting as a replication boundary.

continues

continued

With Windows NT, administrators had two choices when faced with connecting two physically separate locations: Join the same domain across the WAN link, or create a new domain in the remote location. Windows 2000 provides a means to abstract the physical layer altogether in its implementation of sites. A site can contain multiple domains, or a domain can be part of multiple sites—in other words, sites are implemented independently from the logical structure of Active Directory. The two sites separated by a WAN link can be split into two separate sites and remain part of the same domain. Replication traffic can be scheduled for off-peak hours using site links.

The following sections describe the popular company operational models, which are typically based on geographical scope, bandwidth/connectivity, and how resources are managed. With each model, we'll decide what type of Active Directory design best fits the model.

National Model

The *national* model is best described as a hub-and-spoke model with no endpoints on the spokes. In other words, all administration and management of company resources is controlled centrally at the company hub, or headquarters. The Active Directory single domain model would fit well with this company because it would allow centralized administration of all aspects of the directory.

Subsidiary Model

Subsidiary companies are usually companies that a parent company creates. For example, suppose a large computer integration firm on the up-and-up decides it wants to focus its business practices in four areas. Consequently, it splits the company into four new companies, each with a specific focus on technology. This is relatively common in the computer industry. The new companies are likely wholly owned subsidiaries of the parent company. Typically, these companies operate under their own names and have their own management staff and executive directors. Usually, a board of directors sits atop all four companies, forming an "umbrella." In this case, there are a couple of options for Active Directory design. First, and probably the best, design for running separate (yet not separate) companies is a multiple tree forest design. This will allow for disjoint namespaces for each tree (company), but still allow for mediated cross-company communications and resource sharing. Alternatively, if the same namespace is desired, you could use a single tree with four second-level child domains. Figure 3.7 illustrates these two options.

Branch Office Model

The *branch office* operational model is very similar to the national model in that there is typically a hub-and-spoke model. With the branch office model, however, the spokes have endpoints, meaning that the branch offices stand on their own and are not completely run by the central hub. The recommended Active Directory configuration for the branch office operational structure is a single domain with organizational units for each branch office. This way an administrator could delegate administrative control to the branch level with relative simplicity.

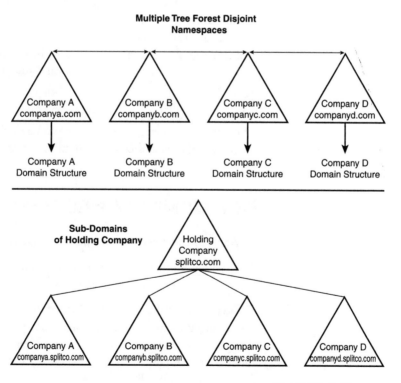

FIGURE 3.7
Two options for capturing your domain-sub-domain relationships.

Regional Model

If a company splits its operations out regionally, such as Electrico, a couple of options for the Active Directory design exist. First, a single domain could be used with organizational units making up the regions and "sub" organizational units within each region comprising the branch office locations. This configuration is recommended if the company wishes to centrally manage the directory. If decentralized or hybrid control is desired, then a multiple-branch tree, much the same as in the second part of Figure 3.7, could be used, with the regions being the second-level domains. Microsoft recommends that, for efficiency, the number of second-level domains does not exceed six.

International Model

If the company operates as a true international company, you should design Active Directory according not only to the operational and IT administration structure, but also with international differences in mind. To support international differences, Microsoft recommends that multiple domains be used. The second part of Figure 3.7 illustrates a domain model that would suit an international company.

When you reach the technical parts of this book, you will find information supporting the above recommendations. Chapters 10 and 11 specifically address the structuring of Active Directory.

KEY COMPANY PROCESSES

Analyze the existing and planned business models.

We're going to utilize the digital nervous system vision again, this time to discuss key company processes.

The explosion of the commercial use of the Internet *has* fundamentally changed the way businesses operate; it has fundamentally changed the way we communicate and exchange information. Think about it, five years ago when you went to purchase a used car, what did you do? If you're like most people, you picked up a copy of *Wheels and Deals* and made some phone calls. Now think about how you'd handle that same process today. Chances are you'd hop onto the Internet, search for used cars in your area, and get all the information about the car you need. You can even buy the car over the Internet and have it delivered to you if the information you've read is satisfactory to you. Needless to say, the Internet has become an extremely valuable tool.

When we talk about key company processes, we are talking about how a company communicates, how it manages and exchanges information, and how it makes key decisions. Microsoft has invested an extraordinary amount of money researching how businesses manage intellectual knowledge. That research resulted in the digital nervous system initiative. Microsoft's vision for a digital nervous system is that computerized processes will allow a company to perceive and react to its environment, sense competitive challenges, and organize timely responses. How well a company reacts to the changing business will be a direct reflection on the health of its internal digital processes. We'll address some key areas of the digital nervous system vision in the following sections.

Information and Communication Flow

Microsoft develops great software, but how it uses, manages, and distributes information is a fundamental key to its success. Information is not just white papers, TechNet articles, and slide decks; in fact it is much more than the tangible objects we typically associate it with. We'll focus on information and a company's digital nervous system as we discuss information and communication flow in business.

The core unit of a digital nervous system is a digital identity. A digital identity simply represents a person and his associated attributes. In today's enterprise business, a person's digital identity is represented separately in every directory in use by the organization. It's represented once with one set of attributes in the Windows NT SAM, once in the HR SAP module with another (different) set of attributes, once in Exchange with yet a different set of attributes, and again in any application that requires its own directory database. Furthermore, the attributes from each directory, such as last name and phone number, overlap. The pain is obvious. Every time something changes with that person's identity, all of these directories must be updated.

Enterprise Identity Management

The concept of Enterprise Identity Management represents a holistic approach to managing an organization's digital nervous system. It is a vision that represents the future of how a business processes knowledge, information and communication, and identity data within a unified directory system. It is a core function of a digital nervous system and is comprised of the following three modules:

- Identity Administration
- Community Management
- Identity Integration

We'll discuss only identity administration in this section. We discussed community management previously regarding managing vendor, partner, and customer relationships. We will not discuss identity integration in the context of this chapter; however, the concept of identity integration will arise in Chapter 14, "Planning for Coexistence," when we discuss Active Directory integration with disparate directory systems.

> **NOTE**
>
> **Enterprise Identity Management**
> If you want more information on Enterprise Identity Management, please see the Microsoft TechNet article "Enterprise Identity Management Solutions with Windows 2000 and the Active Directory."

> **NOTE**
>
> **Understanding What Comprises the Digital Nervous System**   A digital nervous system is not any one software, hardware, or process. It is a combination of people, processes, and technology that together form a unified structure for identity management within an organization.

Identity Administration

Identity administration represents the blending of businesses' relationships with their employees, technical infrastructure, and business processes. Its goal is to align identity management with business processes; so, for example, when an employee moves from one business unit to another within a company, her identity is simply moved within the company's digital nervous system, and she inherits all the necessary rights, permissions, software, and items like a cell phone, pager, new office extension, and more, automatically. Identity administration is composed of three major functions: existence, context, and provisioning. When the Electrico CIO stated that he'd like to automate the creation of short-term project teams, he was referring to a process that existence, context, and provisioning would manage well.

Existence

When a person is hired, a typical organization will immediately add that person to the HR module of its Enterprise Resource Planning (ERP) system. That user will report to his boss, get assigned to a cube or office, and usually wait for a phone extension, computer, cell phone, pager, network account, email account, and probably a slew of other accounts he will need to perform his job. He has to wait because organizations, unless extremely organized and communication happy, do not flush information about a new hire through the channels quickly or efficiently.

The existence function within the Identity Administration module of a digital nervous system refers to a single entry point to the digital nervous system. A typical company will utilize its HR system as the point of identity creation, although depending on the company's processes, it may use any number of other systems. Regardless of the starting point, the existence process is responsible for ensuring, for example, the new employee has everything he needs to do his job. It triggers account creation in the messaging system and NOS, in database packages, it sets rights, permissions, grants dialup access, and fires off requests for additional devices, such as a cell phone or Palm Pilot. All of this is automatic, transparent, and is triggered by simply creating a new account in the directory system specified as the entry point.

Through the combined use of Active Directory, ZoomIT technology, and business rules, you can create the existence process and make it totally transparent across the company.

In the case of existence, Active Directory provides the hierarchical structure, security, group policies and IntelliMirror technologies, and MMS provides business rules that sit atop Active Directory and define the flow of information throughout the enterprise. MMS also provides the meta-directory technology that allows Active Directory to integrate with various other directory systems.

There are two important items in the Electrico case study that apply to this section. We'll introduce them here and carry them throughout the rest of the discussion of identity administration. These items are outlined here:

NOTE **ZoomIT** Microsoft acquired ZoomIT Corporation and is coordinating quite a bit of its digital nervous system initiative around its capabilities as a meta directory. You can find several informative articles on what is now Microsoft MetaDirectory Services (MMS) by searching for MetaDirectory at Microsoft TechNet.

◆ Electrico uses short-term research and analysis teams when they prepare to revise a product from their product line. The creation of these teams is manual, as requests flow through email. A waiting period exists before the team is created, then disk space for collaboration, access to secure documents, access to printers, and additional software all must be manually configured for each member of the team.

◆ Electrico is interested in a workflow application to facilitate communications at several levels within the organization.

Before a short-term research team can become productive, an administrator must create shared disk space and apply security for each user in the group. He then must distribute software manually to every member of the group, and make sure each can connect to additional network resources.

By creating a digital nervous system for the organization, this process can be streamlined into only a couple of steps by changing the context of the existence of each user on the team, and allowing business rules to handle the rest.

Context

The second function of Identity Administration is context. *Context* refers to the management of a person's digital identity.

A person is constantly moving throughout the company, whether it's from one physical location to another, on and off project teams, or as a result of promotions or changes in job role. This movement represents a change in that person's context. The context function within the digital nervous system is based on these types of parameters, so when a person requires fundamental change, updating the context ensures the enterprise environment responds to those changes by providing the person whatever it is he or she needs. For example, if a person's job role changes and that person now needs access to additional software and a color printer, his or her context is updated to reflect that, and the digital nervous system is able to respond to those needs.

Active Directory provides the mechanism to build the framework of a digital nervous system. Using the hierarchical structure, security groups, and group policy, you can create the context for a user. MMS provides Active Directory with the ability to detect changes in identity information and react according to business rules. With these technologies in place, when a user, for example, moves into a new job in a different location, the administrator needs to simply move the user object in Active Directory to the new location, which changes the context of the user, which changes the user's identity, which triggers business rules, which applies the appropriate security and group policies to the user in his or her new location. Group policies deliver the software the user needs and he or she can immediately access the appropriate resources needed to do the new job.

You can see now how, in Electrico's case, changing the context of each team member's identity by, say, adding them to a new group called "Product X Research," triggers business rules that can provide the team members with access to shared disk space, network resources, and the other necessities they need to do their job. But *how* does it all work?

Provisioning

Provisioning is the process of dynamically providing users with the software, permissions, and other tools they need to do their job. It is based on a person's digital context.

The Active Directory design features that promote provisioning are, again, its hierarchical structuring, security policies, and group policy. Additionally, provisioning promotes the use of the IntelliMirror suite of technologies, as well as Quality of Service. MMS plays a critical role with its business rules, giving Active Directory the ability to detect certain changes and take action according to these business rules.

Workflow

We've discussed the need to automate the creation of research teams for Electrico, but have not addressed its needs for workflow, or have we? One would typically associate workflow applications with the intranet and messaging solutions. But if you look at a digital nervous system, it can be argued that, when you add MMS business rules to Active Directory, you have the foundation of a workflow process. In fact, Active Directory does provide the identities required for workflow, and a workflow designer being packaged with the Exchange 2000 messaging and collaboration platform provides the robust functionality to create workflow applications.

Decision-Making

A benefit of streamlined business processes—especially the management and dissemination of intellectual capital (information and knowledge) across the enterprise—is enhanced, well-informed decision-making. A digital nervous system provides a structured environment in which information and communication flow is enhanced numerous times over, and knowledge about people, places, and things (users, locations, and resources) is stored in one location. This enhanced management of knowledge has been proven in many case studies to not only enhance, but speed up the decision-making process.

The Electrico executives state the following about their decision-making processes:

◆ When questioned about how they make decisions to upgrade or replace software, Electrico says they replace it when it no longer works.

◆ Electrico does not use any decision support system. They trust managers to make fair HR-related decisions. They spend time in meetings, doing research, and collecting information to make strategic decisions.

◆ When determining who has final decision power, Electrico bases that determination on the amount of money a particular decision will cost the company.

When a company does not have the knowledge to make informed decisions, it typically makes bad ones. When you perform your business analysis, the key thing to understand about the company's decision-making is what information they base decisions upon. In Electrico's case, how they make decisions is heavily based on trust in some areas, and time-consuming research in others.

As stated earlier, knowledge management is the cornerstone to enhancing the decision-making process. The ability to get the right information in the right format in the right amount of time could have a large impact on the decision itself. Take for instance the stock market: Before computers, pagers, cell phones, and all the other devices from which we get up to the millisecond (a bit exaggerated) stock prices, all we had was the newspaper to rely on for stock information. Granted, back then stocks didn't fluctuate quite as much as they do now, but, if you looked in the Tuesday morning paper and saw that 3M was selling for $3.00 per share, by the time you called the broker and requested a purchase Tuesday afternoon, the price may have already gone up to $50.00 per share. Today, you have next-to-real-time updates and can make an enhanced decision to buy quickly. Information is in the right place at the right time.

Because decision-making sits atop knowledge, information, money, communication, and a slew of other influences, your goal in enhancing the decision-making process is to enhance some or all of its influential areas. We discussed knowledge management a bit and how Exchange 2000 provides an "engine" of sorts for efficient storage of knowledge, or intellectual capital. We discussed information and communication flow in the context of a digital nervous system. We are now going to discuss the influences that can lead a company to change its strategies (a decision). All of these areas directly affect how a company makes decisions.

Product and Service Life Cycles

How efficiently a company manages its core network products and services is playing more of a role than in years past. The product and service life cycles define an end-to-end view of services, rather than the traditional rotation of hardware and software. Business processes rely on the underlying infrastructure to provide services to enable a job to be done. These services consist of tools or products, such as a word processor or spreadsheet. If these tools are unavailable, essential jobs don't get done.

Consider the explosion of businesses relying solely on the Web for income. What happens if their Web servers go down? Remember eBay and that dark 24 hours they went through back in early June 1999? Their stock dropped 9% that day. Because eBay at that point was servicing about 600 million hits a month on their auction site, being down for one day cost them about 20 million hits, probably some very important customer loyalty, and who knows how much money.

Where does eBay's moment in the negative spotlight fit in with the product and service life cycle? Well, when its systems went down, the company was trying to launch a revamped version of its site because the life cycle of the original eBay had "expired."

Today, society exists in a just-in-time (JIT) world that changes very quickly. This world is made of people, processes, and technology, which all must coexist as one cohesive unit. People cannot function without process. Process cannot function without technology. Technology cannot function without people—well, theoretically at least! This blend of people, process, and technology is illustrated in Figure 3.8.

The service and product life cycle outlines how people, processes, and technology work together to provide end-to-end services for the organization. Figure 3.9 illustrates the service and product life cycle.

How a company managed its service and product life cycle before Windows 2000 is probably not how they handle it with Windows 2000 and Active Directory. Software installation and maintenance utilities, such as Group Policy and the IntelliMirror technologies, not only change the way software is installed; they also change the planning, deployment, production (management) and retirement of software. Electrico currently uses reactionary tactics to retire, plan, and deploy new applications and services throughout its enterprise. This methodology is rarely successful, and from a TCO standpoint, can be very costly in the area of help desk support.

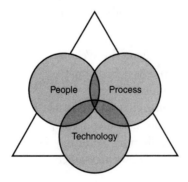

FIGURE 3.8
A cohesive unit can be formed by people, process, and technology.

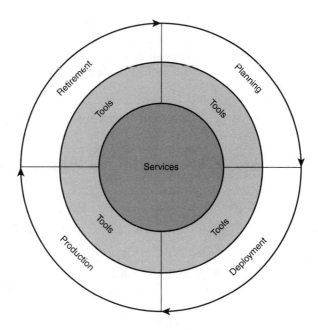

FIGURE 3.9
The service and product life cycle.

Two new features of Windows 2000—the Windows Installer, and Software Installation and Maintenance—are designed to help companies overcome challenges in deploying and managing software in the enterprise.

Windows Installer

The Windows Installer uses a new file format (.msi), which replaces the traditional setup.exe. MSI files deliver a higher level of sophistication to software and installation maintenance. The Windows Installer yields the following three advantages:

◆ **Custom installations**. The administrator may opt to leave items such as clip-art out of an installation package. The "clip-art" option will still be visible within the application, but will have to be automatically installed the first time a user selects it.

N O T E **More Windows Installer** There are also Windows Installer versions for Windows NT 4.0 and Windows 9x, but with those versions you do not have the added benefit of coupling with the Windows 2000 software installation and maintenance utilities.

N O T E **Requires Windows 2000 on Servers and Clients** Software installation and maintenance features are only available when both the server and client computers are running Windows 2000. This is because Windows 2000 uses group policy objects to function.

◆ **Resilient applications**. If a critical file is inadvertently (or maliciously) deleted, the application will automatically reinstall that file from the installation source without interrupting work.

◆ **Clean removal**. Applications are removed safely without damaging any other applications by removing shared files.

Software Installation and Maintenance Technology

Software installation and maintenance technology allows you to deploy and manage software centrally through the use of Group Policy, without ever having to visit the desktop.

Software installation and maintenance aligns very closely with the service and product life cycle, as detailed in Table 3.2.

IN THE FIELD

PLANNING GROUP POLICY

As you begin to structure your Active Directory domains and OUs, consider one key fact about group policy. Group policy objects can be created only at the site, domain, and OU levels within the directory. Designing an Active Directory that will support group policy objects is a crucial step in the design process. If you have, for example, an Active Directory structure that consists of a single site, a single domain, and no OUs, you will not easily be able to distribute custom software packages to specific groups of users. By creating an OU structure and strategically placing users within that structure, you have much more flexibility when assigning or publishing software through Group Policy.

TABLE 3.2

Software Installation and Maintenance in the Service and Product Life Cycle

Life Cycle Phase	Software Installation and Maintenance Function	Description
Planning	Package acquisition	You must have an .msi (package) file before you can deploy. Three options exist for package acquisition: • Obtain from vendor • Create your own (re-packaging) • Use a .zap file. ZAP files are loosely related to Windows .INI files and are used when .msi files are not available. ZAP files may only be used to *publish* applications, not *assign* them.
	Package modifications	Similar to installer (.msi) files, but with an .mst extension. A modified package file allows you to create custom installations of applications for specific usage scenarios.
Deployment	Application assignments	When administrators use Group Policy to assign applications, the applications appear (to the client) as if they were installed on the computer, but are not installed until the user attempts to open an associated file, or invokes the program through desktop or Start menu shortcuts.
	Application publishing	When administrators use Group Policy to publish applications, this is transparent to the user. Users can install the published application through add/remove programs (such apps show up as available software) or by document invocation.
Maintenance	Maintenance (general)	Applying upgrades and redeploying software is simplified greatly for published or assigned apps. Administrators can use the application assignments or publications to apply service pack upgrades, and so on.
Removal	Forced removal	Software is removed from a computer automatically. Forced removal is mandatory.
	Optional removal	Gives users the ability to uninstall an assigned or published application from their computers.

Company Strategy Influences

Analyze factors that influence company strategies.

Every company should be able to identify factors that cause its operations to change, shift focus, or otherwise influence its forward-looking strategy. Some companies are very good at dynamically shifting focus in strategic areas based on some market indicator.

Some companies have tunnel vision and don't pay close enough attention to the very influences that end up driving them into the ground.

This section discusses the analysis of factors that influence company strategies. We'll utilize Electrico once again to bring to light some real-world scenarios.

Conducting an Influence Interview

When you discuss factors that influence company strategies, you should use an open discussion session with as many stakeholders from the company as possible. This ensures that all major areas in which a company strategy may be influenced will be adequately represented. These five strategic areas of business will be the focus of the following sections:

◆ Company priorities

◆ Growth

◆ Tolerance for risk

◆ Laws and regulations

◆ Total Cost of Operations

You might be wondering how these areas pertain to Active Directory design. Remember that Active Directory was developed by Microsoft to wrap around the strategic business needs of the organization. Factors that influence strategic change within a company drive the need to strategically realign Active Directory with business. This will become more prevalent in the following sections.

Company Priorities

What are company priorities? In layman's terms, they are the most important "things" to a company. The identification of company priorities during your business analysis will help you determine the underlying network capabilities needed to support those priorities. It's just like anything else: You have to know what you're planning for before you can plan for it.

There are several ways to determine a company's priorities. You can simply ask what they are, conduct an interview, use a survey, take a vote—it's not too difficult. The difficulty will come in determining which takes precedence over the others. Depending upon the size of the audience, you'll come up with several *opinions* of company priorities, and you'll need to have company executives sort them out and *prioritize* them for you.

In our case study with Electrico, we asked for the top three priorities. Electrico responded with the following:

◆ Increase sales volume and remain competitive in our market.

◆ Implement the technology to do so (remain competitive).

◆ Train our staff.

Whether you'll be able to come up with a prioritized list like this is debatable. Some organizations will easily be able to list three or more priorities; others will need quite a bit of help.

Once you have the top priorities identified, you can begin the decomposition process and determine the best way to support each one. Electrico, for example, wishes to implement the technology that will support increased sales volume and allow them to continue to compete in their market place. We already know that in order to do that, they're going to have to take their business to the Web, because that is where their competition is having them for lunch. Where you would become so important to the success of Electrico is right in the middle of priorities number 1, 2, and 3. It is going to be *your* directory design that allows them to take their business to the Web and hence *your* design that allows them to increase sales volume and remain competitive in their market, and generally *your* design that aligns the business and its needs of the company. It's essential to make sure your Active Directory design properly aligns with company priorities.

IN THE FIELD

ACTIVE DIRECTORY DESIGN TO PROMOTE SALES

One option for Active Directory design to support increased sales volume comes directly from our discussion about a digital nervous system. Your design itself won't increase sales, but your design to support more informed decision-making, ease of administration,

continues

continued

and in general a more cohesive enterprise will allow the company's employees to focus on their jobs rather than on getting to the information they need, or fixing computer-related problems. Active Directory is there to provide services to the employees when those services are required. If the design falls short or does not provide these services at the right times and places, the company will be hard pressed to increase sales.

Issues Surrounding Growth

A company's growth through mergers and acquisitions or through new hires can cause it to drastically shift focus rather quickly. Knowing the growth potential of a company and, more importantly, the growth strategy of a company, will help you prepare an Active Directory design that scales with the business.

A growth *strategy* can be loosely defined as how a company plans to utilize its growth. For example, CompanyA and CompanyB compete head to head in the computer systems integration market. They both do hardware breakfix, desktop support, network design and integration, product sales, and education. CompanyA merges with a large Value Added Reseller (VAR), and CompanyB acquires a company specializing in security. After a year, CompanyA has dropped its services and education divisions, and has become integrated with the VAR. CompanyB is still going strong in its original areas, and has added a huge focus on security. This example illustrates how growth through mergers and acquisitions can totally change a company's strategies (the case with CompanyA), or shift or widen them (the case with CompanyB).

Your understanding of the future growth plans for the company plays a critical role in the design of Active Directory. Using the preceding example, if you knew at design time that CompanyA would merge with the VAR, you would have designed Active Directory according to merger plans with the VAR. You might have gone as far as to investigate the VAR's internal systems to determine how best to prepare CompanyA for the merger. For CompanyB, you might have incorporated business unit OUs into the design, so the security company's network could have been collapsed into a single OU within CompanyB.

Tolerance for Risk

Risk. How much of it is a company willing to take? Where does it come from? What are its consequences? These are just a few of the questions you will be faced with when you begin to talk about risk. We are not developing a risk management plan here; we are looking at risk as a factor that may influence company strategy.

Many areas, such as business operations, organization, and infrastructure, may influence a company's tolerance for risk. For example, during your business and IT analysis, you determine that SlowPipe, Inc. has an existing 56K WAN connection between Site1 and Site2. Site1 performs all management tasks for Site2, so therefore your Active Directory design calls for only one domain. Your plan to control replication traffic using Active Directory sites was shot down by SlowPipe management because it wants the local domain controller in Site2 to be constantly up to date for LDAP lookups. This situation (though a bit corny) presents an interesting situation. SlowPipe will not replace the 56K line, yet they expect to replicate uncompressed domain information across it while continuing to work efficiently from Site2. The risk they are not willing to take is the expenditure to update that line. Good faith from you in this case would be to document this situation and submit it to SlowPipe management as an issue that may reduce Site2 productivity once implemented. You could classify this case as a high tolerance for risk in terms of replication and latency for Site2, or low tolerance for risk in terms of the cost of replacing the WAN connection.

> **NOTE**
>
> **Risk Management Planning**
> Developing a risk management plan is a task that is typically subordinate to the project plan. We will not develop one here but want to point out its importance. You can read more about developing a risk management plan for Windows 2000 projects in the Microsoft TechNet article *"Creating the Windows 2000 Vision/Scope Document and Risk Management Plan."*

Laws and Regulations

Depending on the business, laws and regulations pertaining to business operations may come into play. Identifying these pertinent laws and regulations will help you determine how to implement certain features of your design.

An international company, for example, must contend with laws regulating strong encryption. It is illegal in some foreign countries to use 128-bit encryption in any application, including an operating system. This alone may influence your design in the area of group policy objects assigning or publishing strong encryption software, such as Internet Explorer.

It would be nice if all laws were as easy to identify as the strong encryption law. The fact is, they're not, especially for technologists and even business people not familiar with the company's line of work. Because of this, it is highly recommended that you extract this information from a company's lawyers. The lawyers should be able to come up with a list that is relevant to the company's business. From this list, you'll need to figure out how these laws might, or do, influence the company, and roll that into your design.

Total Cost of Operations

If you try hard, you can tie just about anything we've discussed in our business analysis back to money. That shouldn't be too big a surprise; its effective use is what makes a company thrive. A buzzword you've undoubtedly grown accustomed to is *TCO*. Total Cost of Operations (or Ownership) is a comprehensive model that helps managers understand the direct, budgeted costs and the indirect, unbudgeted costs associated with a particular asset throughout its life cycle.

> **NOTE**
>
> **TCO Assessment Is a Complex Topic**
> Assessing the TCO for an organization is an extremely time-consuming and detailed task. We will not perform a full TCO analysis in this book. If you would like to read some good information on TCO, see the Microsoft TechNet article *"The MS TCO Model: Applying the MS Solutions Framework to Reduce TCO."*

Microsoft and Interpose developed a three-pronged approach to TCO. It encompasses people, processes, and technology (sound familiar?). The goal is to balance and coordinate improvements between people, processes, and technology to help make businesses operate more cost effectively, while maintaining or increasing profitability.

Performing a TCO assessment may influence company strategies in many ways. It may uncover costs that can be immediately eliminated, allowing a shift in budgeting to other areas of the business. Conversely, it may uncover areas of the business that are grossly under budgeted, causing the company to take appropriate action.

Goals for a TCO Assessment

Some companies choose to invest very little money in underlying IT infrastructure, and receive very little value in return. Other companies invest gobs of money in IT, and the return on that investment makes every dime worth it. On the other hand, there are those companies that invest very little money in IT, but get an excellent return, and those who invest gobs and get nothing. Common to all businesses, strategic IT expenditures should accomplish at least one of the following goals:

◆ Increase the organization's profits by driving down costs.

◆ Maintain profits by protecting revenue or avoiding future costs.

You can examine these goals in terms of value creation. How does the business expect to gain capital on these expenditures? Table 3.3 describes four different types of value creation.

TABLE 3.3

VALUE CREATION 101

Value Creation	Description
Value restructuring	Value restructuring refers to using a technology solution to restructure the way a company does business, resulting in fundamental improvement.
Value acceleration	Value acceleration refers to using a technology to realize benefits now, rather than later.
Value linking	Value linking refers to the snowball effect the added benefits in technology in one area can have on another area.
Flexibility	Flexibility refers to planning and deploying technology that will support future growth.

Flexibility is a key type of value creation to take away from this section. Designing flexibility into Active Directory will help the company avoid future costs associated with growth or changed strategies. For example, if you had a small startup expected to grow rapidly over the next year through acquisitions, then you'd design the infrastructure for that company so it would support the added growth of not only people and traffic, but also the associated technology. The same design principles apply to Active Directory—design growth and scalability into Active Directory from the beginning, and you can avoid future and costly redesign effort.

CHAPTER SUMMARY

KEY TERMS

- envisioning
- current state
- Miller-Heiman
- "What if?" analysis
- business process
- business problem
- project objective
- Problem-Objective table
- community management
- authentication
- rendezvous
- authorization
- geographical scope
- operational model
- digital nervous system
- Enterprise Identity Management
- digital identity
- identity administration
- existence
- context
- provisioning
- Windows Installer technology
- Software Installation and Maintenance technology

Performing the analysis of the business requirements is a crucial step in determining the needs of business, and mapping those needs to your Active Directory design. There are several ways to conduct your business analysis, including roundtable discussions, surveys, "what if" scenarios, and meetings with key stakeholders. You should consider using a combination of these methods, and any others you see fit to extract and analyze the information below:

- ◆ Envisioning the future
- ◆ Business problems
- ◆ Company organization
- ◆ Company operating scope
- ◆ Key company processes
- ◆ Company strategy influences

The envisioning process is one of the more difficult tasks business executives face, not because it's inherently difficult, but because there are so many factors that influence direction. In your analysis of business vision, you must understand the current state of the company before you analyze the vision. You can't get to point B if you don't know where point A is.

Business problems are problems the company has now that they want to fix: problems that cost money, or problems with process, law, directory services, and information and communication flow. Once you understand a problem, you can create an objective to help the business overcome that problem. In your analysis of the business problems, make sure you define the business goals first, so you know where you are going. These goals should be in line with the vision. Then you address the current problems. The best way to get an overall understanding of the types of problems within a business is to talk to as many people as possible. Once the company is satisfied that all major problems are noted, you analyze them, taking into account what you know about the business, and create objectives for strategically solving those problems. This phase may run the length of the business analysis.

CHAPTER SUMMARY

Analyzing the organizational structure of the business may become a bit abstract relative to the Active Directory design. Relating the business management model to the design of Active Directory is a very difficult task, especially for large organizations spread across the world. To tackle this process, look at the geographical scope of the company and analyze how management works within that scope. Determine whether business management (that is, management outside of IT) even needs to be considered in the design of Active Directory. If so, determine the role management will play. Vendor, partner, and customer relationships also need to be considered for current and future integration with Active Directory. Consider using the Community Management module from the digital nervous system initiative to encourage organizations to standardize authentication, rendezvous, and authorization processes for internal employees as well as external partners, vendors, and customers. Finally, extract and analyze information pertaining to the expected growth of the company. Companies may grow in a number of ways, including internal hiring, mergers, acquisitions, and the formation of conglomerates, subsidiaries, and more. Having knowledge of an upcoming merger before you roll out Active Directory will not only give you the ability to plan that into your design, but will also save the companies involved thousands—even millions, in some cases—of dollars in re-engineering down the road.

The operating scope of a company defines how it distributes and manages its resources. There is the physical geographical scope of the company to consider, as well as the operational model the company uses within that scope. Understanding the geographical scope of the company will help you determine the domain structure and where your well-connected and not-so-well-connected sites are. The operational structure (such as national, regional, and branch office) within the geographical scope will help you understand how the company is managed, where resources are located, and so on. It will provide insight for the design of Active Directory, specifically in areas like domain design, international considerations, Active Directory sites, and more.

A company's key internal processes impact several areas of the Active Directory design. Consider using the Enterprise Identity

KEY TERMS

- Total Cost of Operations (Ownership)
- value creation
- value restructuring
- value acceleration
- value linking
- flexibility
- strategy influences

CHAPTER SUMMARY

Management module within the digital nervous system initiative to encourage the business to standardize and unify its directory services across the board. Processes like information and communication flow, service and product life cycles, and decision-making define how a business operates. Consider the implications of changing processes to align with Windows 2000 and Active Directory design initiatives. Also consider the implications of changing processes.

There are many factors that influence a company's strategic direction. Factors such as growth, money, laws and regulations, risk, and so on need to be addressed during the analysis. These items should be addressed relative to their ability to change the strategic positioning of the company. After these factors are identified, they should be communicated to all stakeholders and should be incorporated into the design planning process.

APPLY YOUR KNOWLEDGE

Exercises

3.1 Identify Business Analysis Components

In this exercise, you will examine several statements from a business analysis discussion and associate them with the appropriate phase or phases of the business analysis.

Estimated Time: 5 Minutes

1. Review the statements in Table 3.4. Associate each statement with a business analysis phase from the right column by connecting them with a line. Each statement will be associated with exactly one phase.

2. Compare your answers with the correct solution shown in Table 3.5.

TABLE 3.4

DATA FOR COMPLETING EXERCISE 3.1

Statement	Business Analysis Phase
"We'll need a solid method for authenticating and authorizing partners so we can properly distinguish them from customers."	Envisioning
"Our strategy may change if the merger happens."	Business problem analysis
"A single point of entry and management is optimal. That way, when someone moves to another department, or gets married for that matter, we have only one place to make changes."	Company organization
"We have offices in the U.S., Europe, Asia, and the South Pacific."	Company operating scope
"Right now, we can't communicate efficiently because of the number of systems that don't talk the same language."	Key company processes
"If the market continues to grow at this rate, we'll continue to grow the breadth of our business. Otherwise, we'll focus on our successes, and build them in depth."	Company strategy influences

APPLY YOUR KNOWLEDGE

TABLE 3.5

EXERCISE 3.1 SOLUTION

Statement	Answer	Business Analysis Phase
"We'd need a solid method for authenticating and authorizing partners so we can properly distinguish them from customers."	Company organization (vendor, partner, and customer relationships)	Envisioning
"Our strategy may change if the merger happens"	Company strategy influences (growth strategy—merger)	Business problem analysis
"A single point of entry and management is optimal. That way, when someone moves to another department, or gets married for that matter, we have one place to make changes."	Key company processes (information and communication flow)	Company organization
"We have offices in the U.S., Europe, Asia, and the South Pacific."	Company operating scope (geographical scope)	Company operating scope
"Right now, we can't communicate efficiently because of the number of systems that don't talk the same language"	Analyzing business problems	Key company processes
"If the market continues to grow at this rate, we'll continue to grow the breadth of our business. Otherwise, we'll focus on our successes, and build them in depth."	Envisioning	Company strategy influences

3.2   Understand Knowledge and Information Flow

In this exercise, you will visit the Microsoft seminar online Web site and watch a presentation on Knowledge Management. The purpose of this exercise is to support the sections on information and communication flow, decision-making, and company processes with application-level information. This is an optional exercise.

You must have Internet access to carry out this exercise. In addition, a sound card and speakers are needed to hear the audio portion of the online seminar.

Estimated Time: 45 Minutes

1. Open your Web browser (we recommend Internet Explorer) and navigate to:

```
http://www.microsoft.com/Seminar/1033/
20000224kmsolutionshh1/seminar.htm
```

2. Once the embedded Windows Media Player initializes, click the Play button.

3. Enjoy the presentation and think carefully about how the points raised during the seminar relate to topics covered in this chapter!

3.3   Analyze Customer Relationships

In this exercise, you will walk through a sample strategic business interview focused on extracting the organization's views on vendor, partner, and customer relationships. You should read through this exercise and record answers appropriate for your own business, to get a feel for the type of information that should be discussed during such an interview.

APPLY YOUR KNOWLEDGE

Estimated Time: 5 Minutes

1. On the average, would you say that the 80/20 rule applies to your external customer base? (80% of your business comes from 20% of your customers.)

   _____

   _____

   _____

2. What is your main form of communication with your customers?

   _____

   _____

   _____

3. Do you maintain communications with customers after a sale? If so, how? Do you have a lot of return buyers?

   _____

   _____

   _____

4. Do you have business partners? If so, how do you engage them?

   _____

   _____

   _____

5. Do you allow your business partners access to internal company knowledge? If so, how? Is this process secure?

   _____

   _____

   _____

6. Do you allow your customers access to internal company knowledge? If so, how? Is this process secure?

   _____

   _____

   _____

7. What is your vision for customer relationship management moving forward? How do Active Directory and the concept of a digital nervous system fit in with this vision, if at all?

   _____

   _____

   _____

8. How do you communicate with your product vendors? How does your future vision differ from the current process, if at all?

   _____

   _____

   _____

9. Do your employees take part in collaborative online discussions with vendors? With partners? With customers? With other employees?

   _____

   _____

   _____

APPLY YOUR KNOWLEDGE

10. Who are your main competitors and how do they manage vendor, partner, and customer relationships?

_____

_____

_____

Review Questions

1. In which phase of the business analysis should community management be discussed?

2. What is the role of a digital nervous system in an enterprise environment?

3. What has Electrico been forfeiting because of the lack of focus on aligning business and IT goals?

4. Which five areas of business should be your focus when you hold the discussion on the key company influences that affect strategy?

5. What are the two major types of growth you should focus on when performing the business analysis?

6. What should be the end result of every business problem identified in the business analysis?

7. If your company centralizes all of its business operations to a headquarters office, but has locations around the country, which operational model does your company have?

8. What are the four phases of the service and product life cycle?

9. In which phase of the business analysis will you analyze the information pertaining to the future positioning of the company?

10. Which area of company management will typically become the focal point for your Active Directory design in terms of management and administration?

Exam Questions

1. You are the CIO for a major communications firm. You wish to distribute your IT budget in the most effective way possible. Which of the following goals (at a minimum) should strategic IT expenditures accomplish?

   A. Increase the organization's profits by driving costs down.

   B. Maximize return on investment.

   C. Keep the company on the leading edge of technology.

   D. Incorporate the best hardware, software, and services into the organization.

2. You are a consultant contracted to assist in the strategic development of a company's digital nervous system. You wish to describe the vision of a digital nervous system in the context of service and product life cycles. Which three items should you refer to as one cohesive unit when explaining the service and product life cycle?

   A. Technology

   B. Finances

   C. Hardware

   D. Software

   E. People

   F. Processes

3. How would you describe the interview process in the Electrico case study in terms of how it was approached to extract information? (Choose two.)

   A. There was too much involvement from high-level executives and not enough representation from other functional areas within Electrico.

   B. Representation of Electrico personnel was adequate, but the question pool could have been larger and more detailed.

   C. Functional area (such as departmental and product) management should have been the only representation from Electrico for this meeting.

   D. Electrico attorneys should have been present at the interviews from the very beginning.

4. You are a project manager in charge of driving the upcoming Windows 2000 migration for your client. Because of project volume, you wish to begin assembling the appropriate project resources as soon as possible. At which point in the business analysis should you start to develop project teams according to scope?

   A. Before the business analysis starts.

   B. Immediately after you've concluded the business analysis.

   C. You should not consider project teams or scope until long after the business analysis.

   D. Immediately after you've defined your project objectives.

5. You are a consultant for Emmitt Corporation. The IT director is considering an upgrade to Windows 2000. Currently, his major challenge is managing software once it has been installed on user desktops. Which one of the following statements could you make about the advantages Microsoft Windows Installer technology could yield to address the IT director's challenge?

   A. MSI allows you to assign applications, publish applications, and manage applications.

   B. MSI provides for custom installations; self-healing, resilient applications; and clean and safe removal of software.

   C. MSI provides an opportunity for administrators to add custom graphics, subscribe to channels, and recompile the code.

   D. MSI allows you to provide support INI files for setup.exe, force the destination location for installs, and automatically complete the name and organization fields during setup.

6. You are a business and technology consultant for a large consulting firm. XYZ Corp. has engaged you to design Active Directory for its new Windows 2000 infrastructure. You have not worked with XYZ Corp. before. What should you do before you have your first face-to-face meeting with XYZ Corp.? (Choose three.)

   A. Determine XYZ Corp.'s competition.

   B. Categorize XYZ Corp. relative to its IT staff.

   C. Analyze the problems identified by XYZ Corp.

APPLY YOUR KNOWLEDGE

D. Categorize XYZ Corp. relative to its market.

E. Prepare your project teams for the initial meeting.

F. Analyze XYZ Corp.'s digital nervous system.

7. You have just completed the analysis of Speed-Search Corporation's network in preparation for a massive Windows 2000 upgrade. You recommend that they roll out Windows 2000 Professional on all workstations and Windows 2000 Server on all member servers so they can start to reap the benefits of some new features. What type of value creation have you just provided SpeedSearch?

A. Value linking

B. Value acceleration

C. Flexibility

D. Value restructuring

8. You are a consultant for a high-level network and eBusiness firm. The CEO for a century-old manufacturing company has approached you about a problem. The cost of managing his 19 different directory systems has begun to take its toll and he is worried that high-tech competitors will shut out his company unless it acts fast. The company already has Windows 2000 in place. What technology would you recommend the firm invest in to help alleviate the CEO's concerns?

A. It should invest in upgrading all directory services to versions that support Windows 2000 and Active Directory.

B. It should invest in developing a digital nervous system using Active Directory and

MMS (ZoomIT) technology to create digital identities with a single point of administration.

C. It should invest in development of a parallel system that would contain a purpose-built proprietary directory application for the entire company.

D. It should invest in Active Directory connectors to connect all 19 directories to Active Directory and use Active Directory as the single point of administration.

9. You are the design consultant for a manufacturing corporation. During your business analysis, you discover that the executive team does not allow financial reports to be published on the company intranet because they are concerned that individuals other than those intended might intercept the data. Consequently, the financial reports must be hand-delivered to each executive team member on a weekly basis. What is this behavior an example of?

A. The company's low tolerance for risk driving its internal processes.

B. The company's high tolerance for risk allowing internal processes to function smoothly.

C. The company keeping a close eye on cost.

D. The company following its own internal laws and regulations.

10. You are the Web administrator for your company. Your company wishes to provide secure access to a secure subset of information for its vendors, partners, and customers. The solution must be accessible from the Internet, must be encrypted,

and must integrate with the Active Directory security model. Choose the best possible implementation scenario for this task.

A. Create an intranet for the vendors, partners, and customers, and require that they authenticate to Active Directory before gaining access.

B. Create an extranet for the vendors, partners, and customers, and require that they authenticate to Active Directory before gaining access. Assign a certificate to the extranet and require 128-bit encryption.

C. Create an extranet for the vendors, partners, and customers, and require that they authenticate to Active Directory before gaining access.

D. Create an intranet for the vendors, partners, and customers, and require that they authenticate to Active Directory before gaining access. Assign a certificate to the intranet and require 128-bit encryption.

Answers to Review Questions

1. Organizational structure. Community management is an Enterprise Identity Management module within the digital nervous system. It focuses on providing a framework for implementing and managing the authentication, rendezvous, and authorization operations for outside resources, such as vendors, partners, customers, and other employees. See "Existing and Planned Vendor, Partner, and Customer Relationships."

2. A digital nervous system represents a leap toward digitizing company processes, such as information and communication flow; vendor, partner, and customer relationships; and more. See "Key Company Processes."

3. Money. The cost of maintaining internal systems, the help desk, and reactionary implementations of hardware and software is driving the TCO through the ceiling, and the ROI through the floor. See "Total Cost of Operations."

4. Company priorities, growth, tolerance for risk, laws and regulations, and TCO. These five areas cover a majority of factors that influence company strategies, although this may not be an exhaustive list. See "Company Strategy Influences."

5. Mergers and acquisitions. These two areas of growth are going to be the ones you need to watch out for. In mergers you'll typically combine the infrastructures of the two companies, and in acquisitions you may replace or combine the infrastructure of the acquired company with that of the acquiring company. See "Issues Surrounding Growth."

6. A project objective. Once you have good representation of the existing business problems, you and your project team prepare project objectives to address those problems. See "Analyzing Business Problems."

7. National operational model. More often than not, you can categorize a company's operational model as national if they use the hub and spoke configuration. Typically there will be a hub, or headquarters that manages everything, and

APPLY YOUR KNOWLEDGE

satellite offices around the country that report back to the headquarters. See "Company Operating Scope."

8. Preparation (Planning), Deployment, Production (Management), Removal (Retirement). Names in parentheses represent different terminology for the same phase. See "Product and Service Life Cycles."

9. Envisioning. Understanding a company's vision for the future is just one step in understanding the company and how you can help it prepare for the next 3–5 years, or longer. See "Envisioning the Future."

10. IT Management. Most companies don't include areas of management outside IT for directory administration. This does *not* mean you can ignore them in your design. Business processes such as information and communication flow include all management divisions and may affect the directory design. See "Existing and Planned Management Models."

Answers to Exam Questions

1. **A.** At a minimum, strategic IT expenditures must strive to increase revenue by driving down TCO. Maximizing ROI is an attainable by-product of this. C and D refer to tactical IT expenditures more than they do strategic expenditures, and are therefore not considered correct in the context of this question. See "Total Cost of Operations."

2. **A, E, F.** In today's just-in-time society, change occurs rapidly. For this reason, people, processes, and technology must work together to plan for

and cope with change. Finances by definition support people, processes, and technology. People, processes, and technology use hardware and software. See "Product and Service Life Cycles."

3. **A, B.** When we conducted the interview with the CEO, CIO, and LOB representatives, we thought we had an adequate representation of Electrico personnel. By the time we got into the analysis, we realized we needed to organize some more meetings to extract specific information. C is not correct because we do need executive representation. D is not correct because only a small portion of the interview required input from attorneys. See "Case Study: Electrico Corporation" and "Analyzing Business Problems."

4. **D.** You should start preparing your project teams and scope after you've defined the project objectives. This way, you have a general idea of the types of specialized talent (Exchange, Active Directory Design, SMS, Infrastructure) you need on your teams. If you attempt to define your teams before any analysis, you will end up changing them several times as you discover what it is you'll actually be focusing on. If you wait until after the entire business analysis, your project teams will have to re-discuss business requirements. See the In the Field sidebar named "Project Scope and Teams."

5. **B.** The Windows Installer technology provides the following three benefits:

   • **Custom installation.** Administrators may choose to leave optional components uninstalled until first use.

- **Resilient applications.** If an application is missing a file required to execute, such as a DLL, it will download it from the installation point in the background.

- **Clean and safe application removal.** Applications are removed without causing damage to other applications.

Option A describes a couple of group policy functions, which "enable" Windows Installer technology in the enterprise, but are not a benefit of it. Option C describes Internet Explorer customization using the IEAK, which is unrelated. Option D describes the automated setup of Windows 2000 Professional using the setup information manager, and is also unrelated. See "Windows Installer."

6. **A, B, D.** Before you set foot in the door at XYZ Corp., you need to do a bit of research on the company as a whole. Use the Internet or other tools to determine its line of business so you can categorize it relative to its market (manufacturing, distribution, electronics, or the like). You also, if possible, should make an initial assumption as to its relationship with IT, mainly determining whether it is business-centric, IT-centric, or hybrid. Finally, determine its chief competition. You cannot successfully analyze business problems (answer C) until you've discussed them with XYZ Corp. (while this can happen over the phone, it typically does not). Additionally, you cannot build project teams (answer E) until you have solidified project objectives and determined scope. The analysis of a digital nervous system (answer F) definitely requires your being on-site and heavily involved in company processes. See "Case Study: Electrico Corporation" and "Analyzing Business Problems."

7. **B.** Value acceleration, which occurs when you apply strategic technology to receive benefits now instead of later. Rolling out Windows 2000 on workstations and member servers will allow SpeedSearch to begin to use some of the new Windows 2000 features immediately. Value linking refers to the act of benefits spreading from one area to others. Flexibility refers to providing technology that will support future growth. Value restructuring refers to fundamental restructuring in the way a company operates. See "Total Cost of Operations" and Table 3.3, "Value Creation 101."

8. **B.** They should invest in Active Directory with MMS (ZoomIT) technology to create digital identities within the digital nervous system. Answer A is incorrect because it is improbable that all 19 directories in use would have upgraded versions that support Active Directory. Answer C is incorrect because the use of a proprietary directory application is a step in the opposite direction—Microsoft is very big on standards-based development. Answer D is incorrect because it is impossible to use Active Directory connectors to connect all other directories to Active Directory, because very few connectors actually exist. See "Information and Communication Flow."

9. **A.** Because the executive team is uncomfortable posting financial reports on the intranet, they have a low tolerance for risk in that area. This means that using the intranet to distribute the report—which is much easier and more cost effective than the current way—is a risk they're unwilling to take. Answer B is incorrect because it states the exact opposite—that the company has a high tolerance for risk and therefore would

APPLY YOUR KNOWLEDGE

not have a problem posting the report. Answer C refers to cost, and could be a factor in the decision to manually distribute the report, but since over the long run a manual distribution would cost more with postage, distributors, and time, this answer is not considered correct. Finally, internal laws and regulations (typically implemented policies and procedures) are typically a reflection of an organization's tolerance for risk. See "Tolerance for Risk."

10. **B.** The Web administrator must create an extranet, require authentication to Active

Directory, and to enable encryption, assign a certificate to the extranet. The Kerberos authentication protocol contains extensions for Public Key Infrastructure and can therefore authenticate Internet users via X.509 certificates to Active Directory. The definition of an extranet involves extending an intranet outside the firewall, and therefore answers A and D are incorrect. Answer C fails to include a certificate for encryption and therefore falls short of satisfying the requirements. See "Existing and Planned Vendor, Partner, and Customer Relationships."

Suggested Readings and Resources

1. Microsoft TechNet Articles.

    - MS Solutions Framework: Risk Management.

    - MS Solutions Framework: Managing Organizational Change.

    - Network Services Architecture Strategic Plan for XYZ Communications.

    - Planning for Windows 2000 in the Enterprise.

    - Identifying Windows 2000 Features that Meet Enterprise Goals.

    - Enterprise Identity Management Solutions with Windows 2000 and the Active Directory.

    - Creating the Windows 2000 Vision/Scope Document and Risk Management Plan.

    - Business Opportunities with Windows 2000

    - Planning, Deploying, and Managing Highly Available Systems.

    - Aligning Business with IT Goals.

2. Gates, William H. III. *Business @ the Speed of Light.* Warner Books, 1999.

3. Cone, Boggs, and Perez. *Planning for Windows 2000.* New Riders, 1999.

This chapter continues the analysis of business requirements by assessing the structure of IT management. We've separated this chapter from the rest of the business analysis because it deserves special attention. After all, it's the IT department! For uniformity, we'll continue our discussion of Electrico, but this time focus on IT.

Analyze the structure of IT management. Considerations include type of administration, such as centralized or decentralized; funding model; outsourcing; decision-making process; and change-management process.

▶ This objective views the structure of IT from a business perspective by analyzing the business operations within the IT department. How the group determines its funding model, how it utilizes outsourcing, and how it handles the decision-making process all describe the business side of the IT department. How IT manages the enterprise describes the type of administration.

CHAPTER 4

Analyzing the IT Administration Model

OUTLINE

▶ Focus on the differences between the three IT administration models. Make sure you read and understand the section that describes these models so you can appropriately identify them.

▶ Pay close attention to the differences between TCO and ROI.

▶ Apply the Microsoft Rapid Economic Justification framework and its five phases to a real environment. A Giga-validated REJ analysis is published at the following Internet address:

`http://www.microsoft.com/WINDOWS2000/guide/`
`server/profiles/csbn.asp`

Definitely read this if you have difficulty with the REJ portion of this chapter.

▶ Understand the cost-benefit equation, the 4×7 Benefit Matrix, and the business assessment roadmap to an extent that you know where and for what reason each can be used.

▶ If you have the opportunity, run through the information covered in this objective with your own company's IT management and administration staff.

▶ This chapter touches briefly on TCO and ROI assessments. If you want to gain a more complete understanding of these assessments, take some extra time and perform Exercise 4.3.

INTRODUCTION

Ahhh. It's nice to be back in the IT world, isn't it? After the lengthy Chapter 3, "Analyzing the Results of the Business Assessment," covered nothing technical, you'd think we'd start getting down and dirty with some technology in this chapter. Well, sorry. Before we can do that, we need to take a good look at the structure of IT management, from a business perspective.

This chapter focuses on the IT organization within a company and how it operates within the company model. We'll look first at the type of IT administration and how it is structured within the company and geographical scope. We'll focus on three administrative models: centralized, decentralized, and hybrid. Each of these models represents a slightly different way of managing a company's IT assets.

Second, we'll examine the IT funding model by examining how IT approaches funding projects. Funding is a broad topic and we'll touch on several economic areas that may influence the funding model, such as Total Cost of Ownership (TCO), Return on Investment (ROI), Total Economic Impact (TEI), cost/benefit analyses, and financial metrics.

Third, we'll discuss the approaches to outsourcing. We'll discuss the advantages and disadvantages to outsourcing, and analyze the company's views on outsourcing in the areas of risk, security, control, and more.

Fourth, we'll discuss the decision-making processes within the IT organization and how they affect IT as a whole.

Finally, we'll discuss the IT change-management processes in the area of administration and control. Change is inevitable in IT and it's important that an IT organization manage change well using a standardized process.

CASE STUDY: THE ELECTRICO IT ORGANIZATION

BACKGROUND

Electrico is a large consumer electronics organization based in Indianapolis, IN. Worldwide, Electrico employs about 5,000 people, 78 of whom are associated with its internal IT organization. The geographical scope of the company spans two continents, North America and Europe, and will potentially expand into Asia within the next two years.

PROBLEM STATEMENT

The IT organization has managed to keep Electrico's digital infrastructure operational and competitive for several years. Recently, however, Electrico has fallen behind the competition in terms of revenue. After some analysis, they have attributed it to a lack of focus on the IT intelligence of the company. Network operating systems have not been revved in six years, which has produced a deficiency in the technical abilities of much of its IT staff. Additionally, the distribution of IT resources across the company only loosely fits with the hybrid administration model. There are no standardized change-management processes in place, which over the years has caused numerous problems with Novell servers across the company.

CIO

"I take responsibility for not pushing technology integration within the business. I became consumed with helping create new selling initiatives and focused too much on the technology of our product. We on the board have done a complete 180 and are now poised to rebuild our technology group."

NetWare Administrator

"The only reason I've not left this company is because of the people and the relaxed environment. I've basically fallen two years behind in the NOS space because we've been stuck with NetWare 3.12. I've taken it upon myself to study both Novell NDS and Windows NT over the past few years and have recommended we do something numerous times, to no avail. Now Microsoft has released Windows 2000, I know nothing about it, and of course, we're moving to it. I'm worried about my job."

CURRENT IT MODEL

Figure 4.1 illustrates the distribution, type, and number of IT resources across the company. The accompanying organizational chart illustrates the reporting structure within the IT organization. The IT administration model is considered a hybrid model, with some services being managed centrally, but a majority being managed on a per-server basis due to differing needs and response time. Electrico currently does not outsource any of its operations, nor does it incorporate a standards model for administration. Funding is almost nonexistent within the department due to a lack of focus on IT value-added services. All decisions within the company can be vetoed by management or executives higher up the corporate ladder.

continues

CASE STUDY: THE ELECTRICO IT ORGANIZATION

continued

Network Manager

"Every person we have on staff outside the corporate campus here in Indy is a person we had to fight tooth and nail to get. The powers that be required that we keep costs (salaries) down to what you'd typically pay a help desk person. The talent we needed was on the server end in quite a few of our offices around the country. We got what we could for the money, and they've worked out okay, but the learning curve was huge for them and it's not fair."

Mainframe Ops Manager

"I've been at this company for 27 years. When I started, we didn't have much to manage—just this big box behind me, which, by the way, is original equipment. When we replaced dumb terminals with PCs, my group, which was the only group then, was suddenly tasked with supporting all these new computers. It took the CEO two years to approve another team of administrators. I can see the pain the network and support staff are going through now. I'm glad to see this new focus on IT, though."

ENVISIONED IT MODEL

With a complete rebuilding of the relationship between IT and business operations in the works, Electrico plans to completely restructure its IT organization. They would like to incorporate centralized administration utilizing a single Windows 2000 domain and Active Directory, with decentralized on-site help desk support at every location. The help desk will be delegated minimal administration authority, such as resetting passwords and creating/deleting user accounts. They will outsource high-end network and infrastructure services and re-assign existing employees who qualify for specific administration duties. All outsourced individuals will report up through the network manager. They would like to move toward a unified directory services architecture in which all directories within the organization may be managed via Active Directory or a meta-directory solution. Decision-making will become more dynamic by empowering employees at certain levels to make decisions with no approval required up to a certain financial metric. Finally, Electrico wishes to incorporate standards into the IT organization and a change-management process to control change.

CIO

"We see this opportunity to really create a top-notch IT organization. I think the challenge is going to be aligning the business and IT worlds parallel enough that they work together efficiently. I think there will be some bumps along the way, but in the end I think it'll work out."

CASE STUDY: THE ELECTRICO IT ORGANIZATION

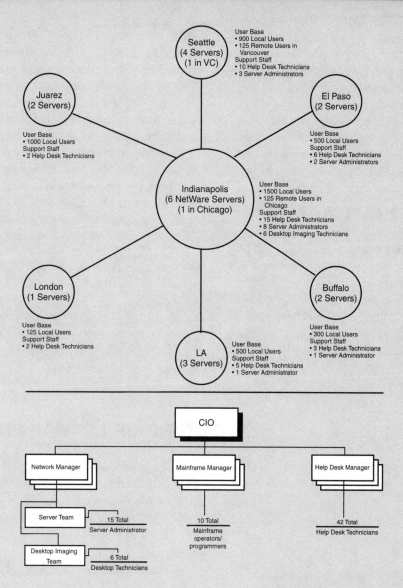

FIGURE 4.1

Distribution, type, and number of IT resources across the geographical scope of Electrico.

continues

CASE STUDY: THE ELECTRICO IT ORGANIZATION

continued

Help Desk Manager

"We are all excited, nervous, and a bit skeptical of the new focus on IT. We've all had a chance to examine the proposed IT model and feel that it's going to make our jobs extremely difficult because of the new technology. We don't want to see them outsource the help desk like they are doing with the server end, so we've all enrolled in Windows 2000 Professional training classes."

ECONOMIC METRICS

Parallel to the IT restructuring, Electrico will attempt to manage costs and develop funding metrics based on annual TCO studies and ROI analyses incorporated with every large project. IT management will provide the business executives (via the CIO) total economic impact (TEI) figures prior to receiving funding approval for projects whose cost is greater than a certain dollar amount.

CFO

"We now recognize the importance IT plays in the overall business. We also realize how costs can pile up if they are not managed closely. Our goal in managing the IT expenditures is to verify that these expenditures will yield a positive return before the life cycle of the proposed solution is over. For that, we need TCO and ROI. Using the results of the TCO and ROI studies, the total economic impact of the solution may be presented to the board. We (the board) consider the TEI of a major project considerably valuable because it does not just look at hard-dollar costs, it also looks at the economic benefits the solution will have over time for the organization."

STRUCTURE OF IT MANAGEMENT

The company's IT organization is going to provide the framework for the basic building blocks of Active Directory. From a management and administration perspective, the way the company plans to administer Active Directory will determine where you create domains, OUs, sites, and subnets. Additionally, the skillsets of IT resources will help determine how you implement group policy, security, remote access, and many other features of Windows 2000.

On the other end of the spectrum, the decision-making processes and funding affect Active Directory as well, albeit from a different level. Let's face it, without the funding, we couldn't do much of anything within IT. We're seeing more companies turn to strategic economic assessments to discover, analyze, and justify IT expenditures (decision-making). Total Cost of Ownership assessments, or some variation of them, are almost commonplace in the IT organization these days, and return on investment analyses are often a required supplement to TCO. Both TCO and ROI, as well as Total Economic Impact (TEI) and cost/benefit analyses will be covered later in this chapter.

TYPE OF ADMINISTRATION

Windows 2000 is a unique and powerful operating platform because of its ability to conform to the business model and type of IT administration in the organization. This flexibility presents a huge window of opportunity for organizations to realign their administrative staff with the needs of the business.

There are three types of IT administration present in business today: centralized, decentralized, and hybrid. The goal of this section is to discuss each type of administration in the context of the business model and, in particular, the operational structure of the company relative to the geographical scope. When you analyze an organization's administrative structure, you will want to look for these types of administration, how many administrative resources are required, and how the administrative processes may be streamlined or automated to become more efficient. You'll take this data, the operational and organizational structures of the business, and key company processes and combine them with the available IT resources and skillsets to determine how you should design Active Directory to support the organization moving forward.

| EXAM TIP | **Administration Versus Management** In Chapters 2 and 3, there were references to the network management and business management models. Remember that administration type is closely related to the network management model, as you may see either or both of these terms on the exam. |

Centralized Administration

Centralized administration refers to a dependency on an individual or team in a single location for administration of the network and network resources. Consider Electrico's corporate headquarters in Indianapolis—if you ignore the rest of the world, the three buildings that make up the Indianapolis headquarters are administered centrally by the corporate IT administration team. This can be loosely related to a "single point of administration."

Resource distribution is contained at a single site and the administration team at that site is responsible for administering the entire network. Companies tend to start out by centralizing administration because typically the number of required resources is less than that of other types of administration.

Your goal in performing the analysis of the structure of IT management is to determine whether the current structure is adequate considering the rest of the environment. In some cases you won't see a need to change it, and that's fine; just be aware of the other options, which may fit better with the business model and existing IT resources. Your analysis of the different IT administrative groups—such as the user account administrators, infrastructure administrators, and help desk—will help you determine whether the centralized type of administration is right for the company.

Decentralized Administration

You see decentralized administration models in medium- to large-sized enterprises where typically the geographic scope of the company plays a role in positioning administrative resources. Decentralized administration is used when IT administrative resources are spread throughout the organization and are responsible for managing a specific part or resource set (such as printers) of the organization's network.

You will occasionally find decentralized administration within a large organization with one physical site that has several business units or divisions. Sometimes, each business unit is responsible for a specific area of administration. These situations can be addressed using delegation of administrative control within Active Directory. We will discuss delegation of administration in Chapter 12, "Designing an OU and Group Policy Management Structure."

Hybrid

The hybrid type of administration is a combination of both centralized and decentralized administration. In large enterprises with vast resource and technology distribution, hybrid administration is most likely what you'll see. A good example of a hybrid approach is in the environment of a national systems integration company. The corporate headquarters typically manages all directory services centrally, but each branch manages resources—such as printer and file shares—locally.

Hybrid administration may be the most difficult to get your arms around in terms of an analysis, since resources and management are usually spread out.

Impact on Active Directory Design

When designing the Active Directory administrative structure, you'll concentrate on two basic building blocks: domains and OUs. We will discuss domains and OUs in detail in Part IV, "Designing a Directory Service Architecture."

A *domain* is both an administrative boundary and a security boundary. Administrative privileges do not extend past domain boundaries, and each domain has its own security policy that applies to all security accounts within the domain.

An *OU* is a container that organizes objects within a domain into logical subgroupings. These subgroupings define your administrative hierarchy. It is the OU design that is key to supporting the company's type of administration.

According to Microsoft, the best way to design the OU hierarchy is to mirror the way Active Directory will be administered. OUs should be used to replace Windows NT 4.0 resource domains, as well as in preparation for delegation of administrative control. As previously stated, we'll discuss OU design in great detail in Part IV of this book. For now, it's important you understand the relationship between the type of administration and the OU structure.

IT Administration at Electrico

We know from the Electrico case study that they currently utilize a hybrid type of IT administration. The mainframe computer is administrated centrally, and the Novell servers, at all levels, are administrated separately, by each of the designated offices in Figure 4.1. A few exceptions to this are Vancouver and Chicago, which are managed from Seattle and Indianapolis, respectively. We also know the structure of the IT department in terms of an organizational chart. Most IT resources are not located in Indianapolis, but still directly report to Indianapolis-based management.

The envisioned IT environment at Electrico changes dramatically. They will implement a single Windows 2000 domain, centrally control all administration, and delegate user password resets and account management to help desk personnel, which will be staffed at every location. Furthermore, Electrico will outsource high end networking services and keep a staff of server administrators in Indianapolis only. All other server administrators will be offered help desk team lead positions or transfers to Indianapolis, or will be let go.

To get from the present state to the envisioned state, Electrico will have to perform the following tasks (at a minimum):

◆ Reassign all server personnel not located in Indianapolis.

◆ Redesign its organizational chart and reporting structure.

◆ Train its IT staff on Windows 2000.

◆ Hire new help desk staff for Vancouver, Chicago, and all other satellite offices that require help desk support.

◆ Implement the new system.

The Active Directory structure for the new type of IT administration would resemble Figure 4.2.

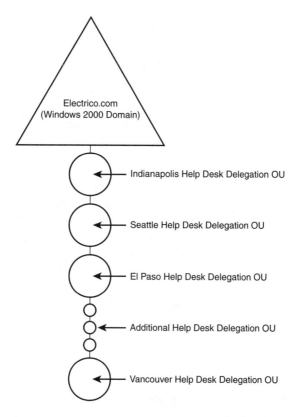

Electrico.com
(Windows 2000 Domain)

Indianapolis Help Desk Delegation OU

Seattle Help Desk Delegation OU

El Paso Help Desk Delegation OU

Additional Help Desk Delegation OU

Vancouver Help Desk Delegation OU

FIGURE 4.2
Electrico high-level domain and OU structure.

By choosing to go with a single-domain model, Electrico will implement a worldwide solution that shares a common directory, security policy, namespace, and type of administration. These cost-reducing decisions will benefit both the IT organization and the business as a whole because the company will be operating as a unified company, not several disparate companies as the previous network and type of administration may have dictated.

FUNDING MODEL

A funding model is a broad topic that covers a vast area of economics in the business. We will focus our discussion on the funding model from the structure of IT management perspective.

Historically, most IT organizations in businesses reported up through the CFO or the COO and were viewed as non-revenue generating cost centers. Nowadays, we are seeing a shift in the positioning of IT in the business. The IT organization is fast becoming a strategic part of business, and often no longer reports up through the CFO. Chief Information Officers (CIOs) are replacing CFOs as IT overseers and are focused on providing IT organizations with strategic technology-driven direction.

We mentioned that IT organizations do not typically generate revenue. From a budgeting perspective, then, how IT justifies its expenditures is extremely important. Up until a few years ago, IT was a cost to the business. Computers were great for the techno-folks, but a mountain to climb for most business people who had not been exposed to technology. To businesses, especially those that had operated for decades without computers or with dumb terminals and a mainframe, the move to a computer on every desktop was impractical, costly, and a waste of time. Today, however, things are different. The Internet is mainstream, technology as a whole is moving out of its infancy, and businesses are beginning to see value in aligning their strategic vision with technology.

One thing still remains and probably always will. Most IT organizations do not generate revenue. To get the budgeting dollars it needs, IT has to prove to the business that investing in technology will be a sound investment, and it must do this in a language business will understand—dollars. Businesses won't invest in technology without justification of some sort of positive return, just as you wouldn't invest money in the stock market without justifying that move by the potential for financial return on your investments.

This section will focus on providing economic justification for the incorporation of Windows 2000 and Active Directory. We'll discuss this economic justification in terms of a cost-benefit analysis, which incorporates TCO and is essentially an ROI deliverable, through the application of Microsoft's Rapid Economic Justification (REJ) framework.

IN THE FIELD

CONDUCTING A TOTAL COST OF OWNERSHIP (TCO) ASSESSMENT

We've mentioned TCO in every chapter so far and really have not given you a clear picture of what exactly it is. Microsoft's definition of TCO is a "comprehensive model designed to help enterprises understand the total cost of owning and using IT component assets over time." TCO is a planning tool, and is a much simpler concept than you might imagine. When implemented within a standard framework with validated industry-average data, TCO assessments can result in easier technology implementation and cost justification, reduced customer costs, and improved quantification of business value that can enhance the measurement of ROI.

TCO in its most basic form is based on the following principles:

- **Baseline metrics.** Enterprises should create a baseline TCO by first evaluating their own TCO and then comparing it to the TCOs of other companies in their industry.

- **Problem recognition.** TCO problems should be recognized and the impact of potential risks and planned solutions assessed.

- **Change validation.** After implementing changes, the TCO should be recalculated to verify that the change has had a positive impact.

A TCO will provide you with the information to make high-level IT policy decisions, as well as an understanding of all budgeted and unbudgeted costs. The Microsoft (and Interpose) TCO model uses seven categories to group budgeted costs:

- Hardware and software costs

- Management costs

- Development costs

- Support costs

- Communication costs

- End-user costs

- Downtime costs

continues

continued

There is much more information available about TCO on the Web, in Microsoft TechNet, and on the corner of every CIO's desk. This In the Field sidebar was derived from the Microsoft TechNet article "The MS TCO Model: Applying the MS Solutions Framework to Reduce TCO." You can find additional information by searching the Microsoft TechNet CD or **http://www.microsoft.com/technet** using the keyword "TCO."

Rapid Economic Justification Framework

The rapid economic justification framework provides IT professionals with an efficient method to analyze the economic performance of IT investments, plan for resources, and gain capital appropriation for IT projects—in other words, to perform an ROI assessment. The REJ framework is composed of five phases:

◆ Business assessment

◆ Solution

◆ Cost-benefit analysis

◆ Financial metrics

◆ Risk

These phases are illustrated in Figure 4.3.

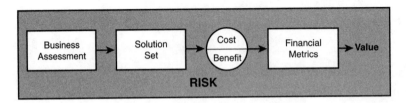

FIGURE 4.3
The Rapid Economic Justification framework.

Business Assessment

Having a clear understanding of the business drivers and key project stakeholders plays a crucial role in how you present your case on value. Different people and groups of people perceive value in different ways. Your goal in this phase is to determine who the key owners of business processes are through the use of critical success factors. A business assessment roadmap like the one in Table 4.1 provides you with a clear and consistent roadmap to extract that information.

Solution

Using the key business process stakeholders you defined in phase 1 (refer to Table 4.1), you will collaborate and determine how you can implement Windows 2000 Active Directory to better align the business with the critical success factors. A common approach here is the "what if…" method, which is designed to demonstrate the benefit of a solution. For example, "What if you could centrally administer all your remote locations?"

TABLE 4.1

BUSINESS ASSESSMENT ROADMAP

Stakeholders	Critical Success Factors	Strategy	Key Performance Indicators	Current	Desired	Process	Owners
CEO							
CIO							
CFO							
IT managers							
LOB managers							
Others							

IN THE FIELD

CONDUCTING A RETURN ON INVESTMENT (ROI) STUDY

Much like TCO, we've mentioned ROI in every other breath so far. So what exactly is ROI? Return on Investment is the analysis of the current or potential impact a new technology has on the business objectives and TCO. Simply stated, it pinpoints the benefits from the money spent to incorporate a new system, new technology, or even new process.

Arthur Andersen conducted a 100+ page study on Windows 2000 Professional and Server that detailed the ROI impact of migrating from Windows NT 4.0 Workstation or Server. This section contains excerpts from those studies, which may be found in Microsoft TechNet by searching on "ROI Impacts for Corporate Customers."

The Arthur Andersen study suggests the following four-step approach to analyzing ROI impacts:

1. **Identify relevant areas of the IT profile matrix.** The IT profile matrix defines the area of IT you are studying, and what drivers in that area you are studying. For example, you may be studying infrastructure in the areas of manageability, availability, and so on.

2. **Review ROI analysis.** In this area, the organization will review the ROI impact areas, such as manageability and availability, to determine which specific features of the technology being analyzed (Windows 2000) apply to its environment.

3. **Review business initiatives.** Outline business initiatives that pertain to the organization. Then analyze these initiatives to determine whether the technology impact helps these initiatives achieve the desired goal.

4. **Review detailed test results.** Used to further refine the findings in steps 1–3.

For more information on ROI, please see the aforementioned Arthur Andersen study in Microsoft TechNet.

Cost-Benefit Analysis

The cost-benefit analysis is the focus of the phased approach in the framework. This is the justifying aspect that will be incorporated with the financial metrics and risk and presented to the key stakeholders of the project. The REJ framework provides a method by which you cannot only generate a list of itemized benefits of the investment (part of TCO), but also provides a way to connect the benefits to the business needs. In essence, the cost-benefit analysis uses TCO as a tool. Table 4.2 illustrates the REJ framework cost-benefit analysis approach.

TABLE 4.2

THE COST-BENEFIT EQUATION

Step	Scope	Approach
Analysis	Well-known categories that provide credibility	TCO, value creation, and ROI processes
Profiling	All project-associated benefits	4×7 benefit matrix (see Table 4.3)
Quantification	Speaks in terms of dollars	Quantification tools such as Expected Monetary Value, Five Steps to Productivity, and so on.

> **NOTE**
>
> **4×7 Benefit Matrix**   You can read additional information about the 4×7 Benefit Matrix in the Arthur Andersen study "ROI Impacts for Corporate Customers," which is listed in the following two TechNet articles: "Microsoft Windows 2000 Professional: ROI Impacts for Corporate Customers," and "Microsoft Windows 2000 Server: ROI Impacts for Corporate Customers."

Benefits can be expressed in many different ways. When you perform your cost-benefit analysis, you must consider the importance of expressing the benefits of the project relative to the needs of business. Table 4.3 presents the aforementioned 4×7 benefit matrix, which is used to illustrate the impact the solution has on both the IT and business areas.

TABLE 4.3

4×7 BENEFIT MATRIX

	Systems Technology	Systems Management	Systems Development	Individual Tasks	Business Functions	Business Process	Value Chain	Total Revenue
Increase Revenue								
Reduce Costs								
Protect Revenue								
Avoid Costs								

WARNING

Technical Folks Beware   It is not expected that IT professionals be able to perform this phase on their own. Since the metrics need to be expressed in marginal earnings per share and economic value added (EPS & EVA, respectively), a financial analyst or line of business manager should provide assistance.

Financial Metrics

Key to the success of the REJ framework method for determining ROI is projecting the impact of the integration of Windows 2000 and Active Directory fiscally in the balance sheet. This phase is where you would compare cost-saving options such as outsourcing, contracting, and leasing.

Risk

As always, a risk assessment should be incorporated as a final step in this process. A side note here about risk: Risk assessments and the management of risk should be an ongoing processes throughout the life cycle of any project. You can read more about risk in references previously cited.

Outsourcing

Organizations are finding that, as business changes, they are unable to master every aspect of their own business, as they may have done in years past. They have turned to outsourcing the operations that are not part of the core business, but still must be there to make the business successful. Outsourced IT operations are one of the most—if not *the* most—common areas for outsourcing.

Outsourcing is becoming an extremely popular option within organizations, particularly in the area of help desk support. Typically what happens in organizations that outsource is they keep control of the operation, but transfer the responsibility for solution delivery to the third-party company. In many cases, you will be playing the role of that third party when you engage clients in your Active Directory design projects. Keep that in mind as you read through this section; it represents an interesting point of view. There are a number of pros and cons in the outsourcing area, so we'll try to focus on the impact of outsourced operation on the design of the Windows 2000 and Active Directory solution from the company outsourcing operations's point of view.

Why Do Companies Outsource Operations?

Companies outsource operations for a variety of reasons. From a financial point of view, companies don't have to concern themselves with paying salaries, benefits, or training costs. Additionally, they don't have to worry about office space, cell phones, laptops, and other devices. Finally, and probably most importantly, outsourcing non-focus areas of business allows the company to focus on its core business, and not on the technology to support that business.

From a scheduling and staffing perspective, companies are able to fluctuate the size of outsourced operations to scale with busy and slow times of the year. This fact alone significantly optimizes the cost of supporting the outsourced operations because companies only pay for services as they need them.

Finally, companies providing resources for outsourced operations typically focus on technology and are therefore experts in specified areas.

IN THE FIELD

THE OTHER SIDE OF GOOD...

As with just about anything else, there are some precautions companies that outsource operations—especially IT operations—need to take. For example, a company that outsources its server administration must guard against the hired help creating "back doors" for access to the network. Additionally, by giving a third party administrative access to the network, that third party may be able to gain access to confidential information.

Whatever the case, companies that outsource should not overlook the possibility of the third-party organization overstepping its bounds, stealing confidential information, or maliciously creating security holes on the network.

Management of Outsourced Operations

Your objective relative to outsourced operations is to identify which areas of the IT organization utilize third-party companies on a regular basis, and determine how this affects the design of Active Directory. You should approach this area using a four-step process as outlined here:

1. Identification

2. Control

3. Security

4. Management

Identification

The first logical step in analyzing outsourced operations is to identify which operations are outsourced. There is no rocket science involved here, just a conversation with appropriate IT management. The information you want to capture is the unit of IT that is outsourced (such as the help desk, server support, or design), the extent of the outsourcing (such as all, partial, or problem based), and the level of service provided by the outsourced operation (such as tactical problem-based support or strategic design).

Control

One of the risks a company must address when it chooses outsourcing as a means of staffing a part of its business is the level of control it will retain, and the level of control it will give to the outsourced company. You'll see varying levels of control; some companies retain a very tight grip on control and decision-making, while others rely on the outsourced company to participate in controlling that aspect of its business. Regardless, you need to understand who has control of the day-to-day operations. You can capture this information again by interviewing the internal management in charge of the relationship. Another aspect you need to assess here is the communication between the outsourced company and the internal management residing over that relationship. From this assessment, you should also be able to determine the reporting structure for the outsourced company.

Security

Whenever a third party gets involved in any area of IT, the internal security team should get involved and put together a security policy to govern that relationship. Your goal is to determine what level of access an outsourced company has to the enterprise network. A good starting place for this information is the security team if it exists. If not, interview both the outsourced person in charge, or the internal manager of that outsourced group. Obviously, a server administration group is going to have more security clearance requirements to the network than a help desk group. This must be considered and properly integrated into the Active Directory design.

Management

The company must manage all outsourced operations in order to remain in control of its business. We've made reference to the "manager of the outsourced relationship"; this person will play a key role in providing you with information about the relationship in the areas of identification, control, and security both currently and looking forward with the design of Active Directory.

Electrico's Plans for Outsourcing

As stated in the case study earlier in this chapter, Electrico plans to outsource its high-end network and infrastructure services. To perform these tasks, the outsourced company needs complete administrative authority over the entire network. The outsourced teams will report up through the Electrico network manager, who will both manage and control the relationship with the outsourced company. The outsourced company will be responsible for providing project-based end-to-end solutions for Electrico. They will be working side by side with Electrico server administration personnel.

Using the preceding requirements, we know that the outsourced company will be designing Active Directory, and therefore will need administrative access to the network. This is the sort of unique situation that most companies will monitor very closely. If Electrico had opted to outsource help desk operations instead, then one of the design objectives that would typically be inserted into the plan is delegation of administrative control for the help desk, so they could change passwords, but nothing else.

DECISION-MAKING PROCESS

We're going to pick up the discussion on decision-making from Chapter 3 and go one step further in our analysis of it for IT. You'll recall in Chapter 3 we discussed decision-making in terms of information and knowledge. To make key informed decisions, the decision-makers use information and knowledge, and they use it at the right time for a specific decision. That's where the phrase "information at the right place at the right time" comes from, and a digital nervous system plays a key role in enhancing the decision-making processes by delivering information at the right place and time.

From an IT perspective, we need to model the decision-making processes a bit, and categorize them into two buckets: static and dynamic. IT, more so than other areas of business, defines potentially a unique organizational structure. In some cases, we see a "traditional" static hierarchical organizational chart, in which decision-making flows from the top down. Conversely, the dynamics of the industry have found their way into the internal IT organization of some companies to form a more dynamic organizational chart. For example, many software development companies these days are moving away from the traditional 8–5 workday, and are instead
providing employees with the luxury of deciding for themselves when they want to work. These employees must meet certain metrics and of course, must produce quality products on time, just like anyone else. The interesting part of this model is the dynamic nature of the business relative to the organizational chart. These employees are empowered to make their own decisions (within reason, of course), and then typically gain approval from somewhere else, which may have a bit more power to make decisions until it in turn must filter up, and so on. The impact on the design of Active Directory exists in the areas of availability and the ability to scale with the dynamics of the organization.

CHANGE MANAGEMENT PROCESS

Dynamic organizations, new technology, process improvements, and a slew of other business drivers have all become realities in the marketplace today. A crucial and often dreaded effect of technology in this world is change. Change is one of the most overlooked and underappreciated, and least accepted issues that people, technical or not, must cope with in today's society. Let's face it: Nobody wants to change a good thing—there's an element of risk involved that leads to apprehension that a comfort level may be compromised.

A key area you need to understand about an organization as a whole is how its members cope with change. After all, you are getting ready to impose a quite drastic change on the way they work. When you engage with a customer to do a project, be sure to not only take a look at the change-management processes they have in place, but also try to determine how they deal with change. Some companies may not even have the ability to accept change in some specific areas of their business; for example, a company's old infrastructure may not be able to support flexible data access, increased load due to changing processes, or high encryption. You'll find change to be a very broad subject area, but if you concentrate on determining the change processes they have in place, how they cope with change, and your ability to detect the indications of change, then you'll have understood the foundation of change.

EXAM TIP

Understanding Change Management Will Serve You Well Change management refers in large part to project management, which is outlined in the Microsoft Solutions Framework (MSF). Understand the life cycle of MSF to be prepared for questions that present you with a project plan scenario or questions about "phases" of change management. More information on MSF can be obtained from `http://www. microsoft.com/MSF`.

Documented Change-Management Standards

On occasion, you'll find a company that has implemented a change-management standard. In this case, part of your analysis should be the consideration of entering the Windows 2000 and Active Directory implementation into the company's documented change control process. This will ensure uniformity throughout the organization and will allow the management of change internal to the company.

NOTE

Project Change Management This is not the same as your project scope change management process. This is the company's internal change management process. You will implement your own change management process to control change within the scope of your project.

Your Ability to Detect Potential Change

As you assess the current operating environment, your ability to detect potential changes or consequences of change within the organization makes you a valuable asset to the organization. We mentioned an ailing infrastructure earlier and the fact that it would probably fail the company at some point in the future. You need to also be aware of how upcoming change in any area of the organization may affect the existing systems in place. This change could be as small as a change in the way expense reports are to be turned in. Consider the company that uses a manual process for expense report validation. If the company wishes to implement an automated system with workflow processes for expense report validation, you should think about the infrastructure and its ability to support the additional traffic, the messaging system and its ability to support workflow processes, and the existing hardware and its ability to support the additional technology. There are many such changes that happen in business every day, and most of them are forgotten soon after because the existing systems and infrastructure accepted the change. Your job is to uncover the exception to this rule.

Considering Change in Active Directory Design

When you begin the design process for Active Directory, you'll want to consider change-management standards in place at the organization. Aside from having the ability to scale with changes to the structure of the company, Active Directory also needs to provide the framework for any automated change control processes the company has in place. Active Directory and Windows 2000 in general were designed from the ground up with a focus on providing the ability to change with the ever-changing business. Simply moving objects from one place to another can make most organizational changes extremely simple. For the more complicated changes organizations go through, several utilities, such as pruning and grafting, are available to assist in incorporating the change into the digital environment.

STANDARDS DOCUMENTATION

As with any assessment, any documentation you can create or pick up along the way is always beneficial. Always ask for documentation regarding the subject matter so you don't end up reinventing the wheel.

CHAPTER SUMMARY

There are three types of IT administration options within the IT organization:

◆ **Centralized.** All resources on the corporate network, both local and remote, are administrated from one central location.

◆ **Decentralized.** Resource administration is distributed throughout the company according to geographical scope, resource distribution, and other factors. There is no single point of administration.

◆ **Hybrid.** A combination of both centralized and decentralized administration. For example, the corporate office might control the corporate directory but leave local file and print share administration to each office.

The IT administrative model is important when it comes to the design of Active Directory. You will (in the context of the company) take the structure of IT management and use it to design your OU hierarchy. OUs provide a great deal of flexibility, including the delegation of control and the logical grouping of users and groups into specific hierarchies.

Most IT organizations do not generate revenue for the business and are therefore faced with scrutiny when spending any amount of money. It is extremely important for IT organizations to justify expenditures. The Microsoft Rapid Economic Justification (REJ) framework was developed to provide IT managers a quick method to justify cost. It does this by presenting a business with a cost-benefit analysis. Total Cost of Ownership (TCO), a huge buzzword in the IT world, is a great tool for providing dollars-and-cents positioning for an organization, but it fails to justify expenditures. Return on Investment (ROI), another buzzword, focuses on hard numbers and takes an extraordinarily long time to prepare. The REJ

KEY TERMS

- centralized administration
- decentralized administration
- hybrid administration
- Total Cost of Ownership (TCO)
- Return on Investment (ROI)
- resource distribution
- funding model
- cost-benefit analysis
- cost-benefit equation
- Rapid Economic Justification
- 4×7 benefit matrix
- outsourcing
- change management

CHAPTER SUMMARY

goes beyond the traditional itemized list of benefits for IT budget owners by providing analysis, profiling, and quantification of IT benefits to apply to business tasks, functions, and processes that can benefit from the technology.

Organizations are discovering that it is just plain financially smart to seek help from external organizations in the areas outside its core competencies. Outsourcing has become a way of life for organizations large and small. When you analyze the IT organization in preparation for the Active Directory planning process, you need to pay special attention to the outsourced operations. Some organizations use outsourced help desks, and may or may not give them any domain administration rights. When the company moves to Windows 2000, the company may decide to give the outsourced organization the delegated right to change passwords. It is this type of information you need to concentrate on. You can usually get this type of information from the managing party in charge of the outsourced relationship.

The attention you give to the decision-making processes within IT organizations is a bit different from that which you give to the rest of the business, mainly because IT controls the computing environment. You should understand the types of information and knowledge that key decision-makers use to make decisions, and try to create better access to this information with your Active Directory design. You should also categorize the IT organizational structure into one of two categories: static or dynamic. Static environments use the nice hierarchical structure of management, with decision-making flowing down. Dynamic organizations are more "free spirited" and empower their employees to make their own decisions (up to a specific point). The difference between these two categories may impact the way you design Active Directory.

Change management is a crucial part of the IT environment. Organizations rarely implement standard change management procedures and often feel the pain of not doing so. When you enter into an engagement for an organization, you should make every effort to get your project included in their change management process. Additionally, you should have your own change management processes in place for the project, and abide by them.

APPLY YOUR KNOWLEDGE

Exercises

4.1 Fill in a 4×7 Benefit Matrix

From the list below, populate the appropriate box within the 4×7 benefit matrix in Table 4.4. All entries in the list will be used at least once. You will find the solution in Table 4.5.

Estimated Time: 5 Minutes

- Microsoft Management Console (MMC)
- Improved information and communication flow
- Workflow processes
- Active Directory Services Interface (ADSI)
- Remote Installation Services (RIS)
- Disk quotas
- Group policy
- IntelliMirror
- Terminal Services for legacy PC integration
- Advanced searching capability
- Cost-benefit matrix
- Outsourcing
- Rapid Economic Justification (REJ)

TABLE 4.4

EXERCISE 4.1

	Systems Technology	Systems Management	Systems Development	Individual Tasks	Business Functions	Business Process
Increase Revenue						
Reduce Costs						
Protect Revenue						
Avoid Costs						

APPLY YOUR KNOWLEDGE

TABLE 4.5

EXERCISE 4.1 SOLUTION

	Systems Technology	*Systems Management*	*Systems Development*	*Individual Tasks*	*Business Functions*	*Business Process*
Increase Revenue	N/A	N/A	N/A		Improved information and communication flow	
Reduce Costs	Disk Quotas, RIS	MMC, Group Policy, IntelliMirror	ADSI, RIS	Advanced searching capability		Workflow processes
Protect Revenue	N/A	N/A	N/A		Cost/Benefit Matrix	REJ
Avoid Costs	Terminal services for legacy PC integration			RIS		Outsourcing

4.2 Determine the Type of IT Administration

In this exercise, you will identify the types of IT administration models described in the text blocks.

Estimated Time: 5 minutes

1. For each block of text, use the space provided to categorize the described type of IT administration as centralized, decentralized, or hybrid.

   NorthSide Company has one office in downtown Chicago. This is its only office, which employs 1,000. It is comprised of 10 business units, each with its own IT administrative requirements. Each business unit employs at least one IT professional who is responsible for day-to-day support for only that business unit. One of these business units is the IT department, which is responsible for its own administration, as well as administrating only directory services throughout the other business units.

   Answer _____

   SouthSide Company has 13 offices across the southern U.S. Each office is connected via WAN connection to the central corporate office. All servers, with the exception of a single local file and print server, are located at the corporate office. All IT resources are located at the corporate office as well. All IT operations are managed countrywide from the central office. IT administrators manage remote servers using a Terminal Services session.

   Answer _____

   EastSide Company has five offices throughout the Silicon Valley. This technology firm operates financially as a single entity, but operationally and administratively as separate companies. Each office has its own IT staff responsible for all facets of IT administration for that office only. The IT strategy board, which contains IT representation from all offices, meets monthly to discuss synergy and direction. At no time does any one office administrate—or influence the administration of—another office.

Answer _____

WestSide Corporation is considering purchasing the NorthSide, SouthSide, and EastSide

Companies. Assuming WestSide is a new corporation that does not wish to change the type of administration within the other companies, what will likely be the resulting type of administration once the purchases take place?

Answer _____

2. The answers to the above are contained in Table 4.6.

TABLE 4.6

EXERCISE 4.2 SOLUTION

Company	Type of Administration	Explanation
NorthSide Co.	Hybrid	You may be inclined to label this type of administration centralized because it is confined to a single building, but because each business unit has its own IT administration staff, certain areas of administration are decentralized. Because the IT department does manage the directory services for the entire organization, both centralized and decentralized administration exist here, and hence the type of administration is hybrid.
SouthSide Co.	Centralized	Although there are several physical locations, only a single IT administrative group exists at the corporate office. Because this group is responsible for all IT administration, the type of administration is centralized.
EastSide Co.	Decentralized	Because each office stands alone with its own IT administration, the type of administration is decentralized. Even though the IT administrative teams from each office strategize on a monthly basis, there is no overlap in administration.
WestSide Corp.	Hybrid	If you merge centralized, decentralized, and hybrid types of administration, the resulting type will definitely wind up being hybrid. Typically in these situations, the purchasing company will develop a new top-down administrative approach.

APPLY YOUR KNOWLEDGE

4.3   Calculating TCO and ROI Using the TCO and ROI Advisor

In this exercise, you will utilize the Microsoft TCO and ROI Advisor utility located both on the CD accompanying this book (*<drive>*:\tco_roi) and on the Web at `http://www.microsoft.com/TCO/offcal.asp`.

This exercise is *optional.* The TCO and ROI calculations are complex and undoubtedly new to most technologists. We highly recommend you walk through this utility carefully and read the incorporated help files.

> **NOTE** **Study the Process, Not the Particulars** The TCO and ROI Advisor was developed specifically for Microsoft Office 97 migrations and therefore will seem outdated. Keep in mind that it's not the exact focus and details of the utility itself that you should concern yourself with here—it is the process employed by the utility.

Estimated Time: 60 Minutes

1. You must have Microsoft Excel installed on your system for this exercise to work.

2. Execute the file desk_tco.exe from one of the two aforementioned locations. Follow the installation procedures to allow the utility to install.

3. Open the TCO and ROI Advisor utility from the TCO & ROI Tools Programs menu option.

4. Follow the nine-step wizard process to generate a TCO and ROI report. Use real or arbitrary data. Click the Help button at each step to learn more about the information on that step.

5. Analyze the resultant Excel Workbook report. Pay close attention to the first worksheet and utilize the mouseover tips for each column heading with a red arrow in the upper-right corner.

6. Navigate through the rest of the workbook worksheets.

Review Questions

1. If you manage your entire organization's IT environment from your corporate headquarters, what type of IT administration are you using?

2. Information in the right place at the right time enhances what key process?

3. What analysis should you perform to help justify the total economic value of a proposed technology?

4. You have just performed a TCO assessment for the organization you'll be designing Active Directory for. What step of the cost-benefit equation have you just completed?

5. What approach utilizes a combination of people, processes, and technology?

6. If the help desk staff at Electrico does not enroll in Windows 2000 professional classes, how might this affect the future of their jobs?

7. You have just proposed a new method of administrating the network at Electrico. To them, what have you really proposed?

8. What are the key influences on the decision-making process?

9. Your strategy for managing operations for a specific group within IT has shifted to managing day-to-day operations management only. What might you have done with this group?

Exam Questions

1. You are the project manager for a company to which Electrico outsources its server and networking components. During a meeting with the Electrico network manager, he explains to you that he feels apprehensive about the outsourcing situation. What might be the cause of this apprehension?

   A. The increased cost of outsourcing network and server IT components has caused him to feel apprehensive.

   B. The decreased cost of outsourcing network and server IT components has caused him to feel apprehensive.

   C. Because his direct reports no longer have control over day-to-day operations with the network and servers, he feels like he has lost control.

   D. Because he no longer owns the network and server operations responsibility, he may be apprehensive about the outsourced company managing the job correctly.

2. What process provides a framework for making high-level IT policy decisions, as well as an understanding of all budgeted and unbudgeted costs?

   A. The funding model

   B. Rapid economic justification

   C. Total Cost of Ownership

   D. Return on Investment

3. You are engaged by an organization to analyze the impact of investing in a certain technology. What might you do to perform this analysis?

   A. ROI assessment

   B. TCO assessment

   C. Rapid economic justification assessment

   D. 4×7 benefit matrix

4. You are analyzing the IT management structure and come across a portion of the organization that is outsourced. Who is the key individual that can provide you details on that outsourced relationship?

   A. Outsourced company manager

   B. Individual on outsourced team

   C. IT director

   D. Management of outsourced relationship

5. Suppose Electrico had decided to outsource its help desk operation instead of network and infrastructure. How would this change the security configuration within Active Directory?

   A. Would require granular delegated administration

   B. No change

   C. Would require X.509 certificate-based authentication

   D. Would require PKI authentication

6. You complete your analysis of the IT management structure for Electrico. As a deliverable,

APPLY YOUR KNOWLEDGE

you provide them with your recommendations to completely change the structure of IT management. What process should Electrico have in place that will help them cope with this action?

A. Rapid economic justification

B. Standards documentation

C. Change management

D. Decision-making process

7. Your conceptual OU design consists of OUs named *north_region, south_region, east_region,* and *west_region.* Each OU's Managed By field contains a security group that relates to groups of administrators in different locations. What does this design reflect about the type of administration?

A. The type of administration is centralized.

B. The type of administration is decentralized.

C. The type of administration is hybrid.

D. The type of administration is either hybrid or decentralized.

8. You have just completed a balance sheet that examines buying versus leasing and hiring versus outsourcing. Which phase of the Rapid Economic Justification framework should you perform next?

A. Risk assessment

B. Financial analysis

C. Cost-benefit analysis

D. Business assessment

9. You are the project manager for an integration firm assigned to drive a Windows 2000 assessment for your client. You conduct a meeting with the IT director, CIO, and other key players from the business and technology sides of your client's organization. You wish to collect critical success factors from the group. Which tool should you approach this task with?

A. 4×7 benefit matrix

B. Cost-benefit equation

C. Business assessment roadmap

D. TCO assessment

Answers to Review Questions

1. Centralized administration. An organization managing all resources from a single location is using centralized administration. See "Type of Administration."

2. Decision-making. Decisions are based on several factors, but two key factors influence all decisions. Information and knowledge play crucial roles in the decision-making process and are most effective when presented in the right place at the right time. See "Decision-Making Process."

3. Cost-benefit analysis. The cost-benefit analysis uses TCO and a host of other tools to provide economic justification for the incorporation of a particular technology or process. See "Cost-Benefit Analysis."

4. Analysis. The analysis step of the cost-benefit equation provides a toolset (including TCO) to

use to analyze the solution within the scope of the business. See "Rapid Economic Justification Framework."

5. TCO. Microsoft's TCO approach utilizes the combination of people, processes, and technology to achieve its goals. See "Total Cost of Ownership TCO Assessment."

6. They might be outsourced. Having the right skillset to support its user base is critical to a help desk staff. If Electrico's help desk staff did not get up to speed on Windows 2000 Professional, they could be replaced by a third-party company. See "Outsourcing."

7. Change. You propose change along with any proposal you present to a company. This is important to remember, because without question, someone resilient to change will complain. See "Change Management Process."

8. Information and knowledge. To make strategic business decisions, the decision-makers need to have knowledge and access to solid supporting information, among other things. See "Decision-Making Process."

9. Outsourced it. Typically when companies outsource a division of their business, they retain high-level management control over that area of business. See "Outsourcing."

Answers to Exam Questions

1. **C.** Companies often feel they are losing control when they outsource any operations. Typically, outsourcing an area of business results in a decreased cost, so A is not correct. Decreasing cost is usually not a cause of apprehension, so B

is not correct. D may be a correct answer in some cases, but organizations typically retain management over outsourced operations and therefore would not have to worry about them being properly managed. See "Outsourcing."

2. **C.** Total Cost of Ownership is a comprehensive model designed to help enterprises understand the total cost of owning and using IT component assets over time. It provides businesses with information that helps them make high-level IT policy decisions, as well as an understanding of all budgeted and unbudgeted costs. The funding model describes all economic facets within IT and is therefore too broad a topic to be correct. Rapid economic justification is a five-step framework that provides IT professionals with an efficient method to analyze the economic performance of IT investments and is therefore also too broad a topic to be correct. ROI describes return on IT investments and is used as input for TCO. See the In the Field sidebar "Conducting a Total Cost of Ownership (TCO) Assessment."

3. **A.** To analyze the impact of a certain technology on the organization, you should perform a Return on Investment assessment. ROI assessments pinpoint the benefits that money spent to incorporate a new technology has on business objectives and TCO. TCO assessments are aimed at providing information about the total costs of owning and using an IT asset over time. Rapid economic justification is a five-step framework geared toward providing information on the economic performance of IT expenditures. The 4×7 benefit matrix may be used as a vehicle to describe the type and area of a specific technology's benefits. See the In the Field sidebar "Conducting a Return on Investment (ROI) Study."

APPLY YOUR KNOWLEDGE

4. **D.** To get a detailed and current view of the out-sourced relationship, you need to speak with the company manager of the outsourced relationship. This person will most likely have access to all the pertinent information you would need. The IT directory may know of the relationship, but will not be involved (typically) in the details. The outsourced manager will be able to give you the perspective of the outsourced company, but not the company itself. Individual outsourced employees will not know the details on the rela-tionship and therefore will not be of assistance. See "Outsourcing."

5. **A.** To go from outsourcing network and infra-structure to outsourcing the help desk requires a new strategy on security. An outsourced network infrastructure requires that the outsourced com-pany have complete control over the network. Help desk operations require a very different approach. Windows 2000 allows you to delegate granular-level permissions to OUs and other users. This granularity is perfect for the out-sourced help desk because it allows administrators to grant the right to reset passwords to the help desk without giving it full administration rights. The two authentication mechanisms don't apply here, and because there is a change needed, choice B is incorrect. See "Outsourcing."

6. **C.** Because change is eminent in the IT industry, IT organizations should have a change manage-ment process in place. This process will help them cope with and react to change in an effi-cient and planned manner. Rapid economic justification refers to a five-step framework geared toward providing information on the economic performance of IT expenditures. Standards documentation should be part of a change management process—but is not meant to help companies cope with change. A fluent decision-making process will assist with coping, but will be a part of change management. See "Change Management Process."

7. **D.** The type of administration in this scenario could be anything but centralized. Because each OU is managed by a different group of adminis-trators in a different geographical location, that rules out centralized administration only. Because portions of the directory may or may not be administered from a central location (which would make it hybrid), you cannot say for sure that decentralized administration is used, and hence must acknowledge that both hybrid and decentralized are possibilities. See "Type of Administration."

8. **A.** The financial metrics ensure that the impact of the solution is being projected in the balance sheet and therefore describes the phase you just completed. The next logical phase is the risk assessment, which is an ongoing part of the REJ framework and should be an ongoing part of any project. The cost-benefit analysis and business assessment steps within REJ fall prior to the financial metrics step and are therefore incorrect. See "Rapid Economic Justification Framework."

9. **C.** You create a business assessment roadmap to organize key high-level project information, such as critical success factors and key performance indicators. Both the cost-benefit equation and the 4×7 matrix utilize information and build the solution from the business assessment roadmap. TCO refers to the cost of assets within the orga-nization. See "Business Assessment."

APPLY YOUR KNOWLEDGE

Suggested Readings and Resources

1. Microsoft TechNet Articles.
   - Economic Analysis of the Impact of IT
   - MS Windows 2000 Server: ROI Impacts for Corporate Customers
   - MS Windows 2000 Professional: ROI Impacts for Corporate Customers
   - MS Solutions Framework: Managing Organizational Change
   - The MS TCO Model: Applying the MS Solutions Framework to Reduce TCO

2. Microsoft White Papers. `http://www.microsoft.com/windows2000`. Utilize the search engine to search acronyms such as REJ, TCO, and ROI.

ANALYZING TECHNICAL REQUIREMENTS

This chapter begins the coverage of the following Microsoft-specified objective for the Designing a Microsoft Windows 2000 Directory Services Infrastructure exam:

Evaluate the company's existing and planned technical environment.

- **Analyze company size and user and resource distribution.**

- **Assess the available connectivity between the geographic location of work sites and remote sites.**

- **Assess the net available bandwidth.**

▶ When it comes to designing Active Directory, the size of the company makes a big difference. Additionally, the available bandwidth between a company's physical locations will govern the way you design the Active Directory physical structures, such as sites and subnets. It is very important that you estimate the impact the Active Directory traffic flow will have on the existing network, so you don't overload it.

CHAPTER 5

Analyzing the Physical Environment

STUDY STRATEGIES

▶ To get the most out of an infrastructure analysis, incorporate information such as number of users, WAN hardware, and WAN connection speeds with the network topology diagram. Having this information in one location will go a long way toward gaining an understanding of the network as a whole.

▶ Before you attempt to make any recommendations based on an analysis of the infrastructure, make sure you know and understand any Service Level Agreements (SLAs) pertaining to the availability of infrastructure-related services. These SLAs will definitely influence your view of the state of the infrastructure.

▶ Create tables to help you keep track of the physical infrastructure. You should use several small tables instead of one large table for readability's sake.

▶ Make sure you understand how to calculate net available bandwidth. Know how to analyze the network to accurately represent this number.

INTRODUCTION

Waahooo! Finally the technical stuff! We're going to take off here and really start to dig into the technology architecture of the organization. In this chapter and the four that follow, you'll perform a detailed physical IT assessment. The goal of this assessment is to provide up-to-date technical documentation of the current environment. Additionally, and simultaneously, you'll be documenting the planned changes to the technical environment according to the technology team or teams within the organization.

The physical assessment will be broken into several high-level areas, as illustrated by the following bulleted list:

◆ User and resource distribution

◆ Infrastructure assessment

◆ Network topology

◆ Name resolution services

◆ Hardware analysis

◆ Network management tools

Each of these areas carries a significant amount of importance relative to the design of the directory services infrastructure. The documentation you pull together during the physical assessment can be utilized in the project management process (along with the business data) to provide current state input for the Gap Analysis, which will tell you exactly where you are and where you want to be. All you'll have to do is figure out how to get there.

> NOTE
>
> **Recycling Y2K Assessments**
> Some organizations have performed a detailed physical network assessment during Year 2000 preparations. Keep this in mind because you may be able to use some or all of that information.

INTERVIEW THE INFORMATION TECHNOLOGY TEAM

Suppose you're a consultant. You walk into a new organization you've never worked with before, and you are tasked with documenting their entire networking infrastructure. You'd be pretty overwhelmed if you didn't have the support of the internal staff, right?

Even if you're employed by the company, you need to solicit the help of the technology team(s) in charge of the specific technologies (such as infrastructure or server support) you'll be assessing. If you were asked to teach a class, but had never taught before, chances are you'd find someone who had and pick their brain before you gave it a shot. This is really the same thing. The technology team lives with the specific product or technology day in and day out. That alone provides quite a bit of value to you during an assessment.

The important thing here is that you leverage the expertise of the people who manage the environment if they are willing and able to help. If not, dig in—you're going to have to go it alone.

How Many People and Where Are They?

One of the first things you need to find out about the company is the geographical distribution of its employees. We addressed this task in Chapter 3, "Analyzing the Results of the Business Assessment," so if you already have those numbers, verify their validity and use them— if not, get them in any way possible. You simply need to get the number of employees at each physical location. Make sure you obtain the expected growth percentage for the next 3 to 5 years and apply that to the current number of employees. These numbers are extremely important to have so you can set expected traffic volume expectations on the infrastructure and assist the company in making decisions about hardware or WAN link upgrades.

In addition to the number of users per location, you need to obtain the number of physical offices within each location. Understand that geographical locations alone will do you no good if each location contains multiple physical offices, so make sure you take that into consideration.

The format in Table 5.1, or something similar to it, should be used to keep track of the user distribution.

TABLE 5.1

SAMPLE CHART FOR EVALUATING CURRENT AND FUTURE GEOGRAPHICAL DISTRIBUTION OF USERS

Location Name	Type of Location	Number of Buildings	Expected 3–5 Year Growth (Buildings)	Number of Users	Expected 3–5 Year Growth (Users)
Chicago	Headquarters	3	3	1500	1750
New York	Regional office	1	2	500	650
Indianapolis	Satellite office	1	1	15	20
Orlando (Future)	Satellite office	1	1	0	45

You can expand this table as we move through the chapter by adding additional columns. Because all physical characteristics of the network will be associated with a location (and for cosmetic purposes within this book), we'll split the assessment into several tables. You can always refer to the location name when associating with other tables.

ENTERPRISE INFRASTRUCTURE ASSESSMENT

Evaluate the company's existing and planned technical environment.

After you've determined the geographical layout of the organization and planned growth, you're ready to move forward with an infrastructure assessment. During this infrastructure assessment, you'll probably uncover quite a bit more than you expected. It usually works out that way. Take this assessment seriously; you'll use it down the road in determining your directory services design specifications. The following subsections provide a roadmap for assessing the general environment.

> **NOTE**
>
> **Enterprise Computing Roadmap** Microsoft has developed a planning model called the Enterprise Computing Roadmap whose purpose is to assist IT managers in determining when and where new products fit within the enterprise. The model is vendor non-specific, so it can be used across the board. You can read more about it in the Microsoft TechNet article "Identifying Windows 2000 Features That Meet Enterprise Goals."

Network Topology

Site boundaries, site connections, message routing, directory replication, and system administration all depend on network topology. The key elements that affect a network topology are

◆ Network type

◆ Inter-network links

◆ Network size

◆ Bandwidth

◆ Traffic patterns

◆ Protocols

These elements are discussed in the following sections. The initial tangible you will want to come up with is a network diagram. If you've performed a business analysis according to Chapters 2 and 3, you already should have such a diagram. Make sure it displays a graphical representation of the network and details the type of WAN connections and speeds as well as physical locations. You should be able then to associate the number of users from the previous section to this diagram. Figure 5.1 illustrates a sample network topology diagram.

You'll notice the dotted-line area of the network topology diagram. This designates future growth plans. You will probably have to add this to your diagram, as most companies (unfortunately) won't have this done for you. Having both the current and future topology on the same diagram will provide you with the information you need to plan the future WAN scalability.

NOTE

Purpose of the Network Topology Diagram   The network topology diagram does not necessarily need to conform to the key elements list of parameters. The main purpose of this diagram is to illustrate the interconnected locations that form the network.

EXAM TIP

Knowledge of Networking Basics The Windows 2000 design exams assume a specific level of knowledge originally addressed by the Networking Essentials exam. It is a good idea to have taken the Network Essentials exam before attempting any design test.

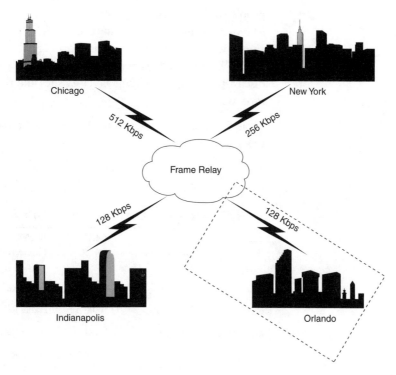

FIGURE 5.1
Sample network topology diagram.

Connection Types and Speed of Each

A more detailed network topology diagram may show the type of LAN as well as the WAN. Typical speeds for LANs are not less than 10MB and are always considered well-connected; conversely, typical WAN speeds may be considerably slower, ranging from 9.6K to more than 9GB. When determining the placement of Active Directory domain controllers within the enterprise, there are a few "loose" rules you should follow. We say loose here because different people could interpret areas of well-connected computers differently. Microsoft defines a "well-connected" (WAN) computer network as any network with the slowest connection greater than or equal to 512K. We'll take a look at these rules in Chapter 11 when we discuss the design of Active Directory sites and the replication processes.

Table 5.2 describes how you might want to represent the connection types and speeds:

TABLE 5.2

LAN/WAN CONNECTION TYPES AND SPEEDS

Location Name	LAN Connection Type	LAN Speed	WAN Connection Type	WAN Speed
Chicago	FastEthernet	100MB	Frame Relay	512K
New York	FastEthernet	100MB	Frame Relay	256K
Indianapolis	Ethernet	10MB	Frame Relay	128K
Orlando	FastEthernet	100MB	Frame Relay	128K

You'll want to make sure you include all network types for each location, both LAN and WAN, and even wireless and metropolitan area solutions. Additionally, if the corporation utilizes any type of SANs (Storage Area Networks), we highly suggest you record the topology for those as well.

Physical Network

Obtaining the network topology diagram and applying whatever modifications to it is a good start in determining what you are dealing with in terms of an enterprise network. Breaking out the jeans, T-shirt, and packet sniffer is even better. A key element in determining just what is going on in the enterprise is to identify all the hardware and software that makes it happen. We're not talking about ProLiant servers and Windows NT Oses; we're talking about the true infrastructure: the routers, switches, hubs, gateways, and other devices that spend their lives in the trenches, directing traffic and making sure one corner of the network can talk to all the others.

We'll begin our look with the core infrastructure devices and work our way through to the QoS (Quality of Service) initiatives and enabling software services. We'll introduce some tools that can significantly reduce the cost and time involved in gathering this information, and discuss how to leverage the native report and query capabilities of these tools to present your findings.

One thing we want to make clear right now. It is essential that you document any problems you uncover during this analysis. Any significant problems having to do with the infrastructure must be fixed prior to the implementation of Windows 2000 and Active Directory. If you begin implementation with anything but a stable networking backbone, you are setting yourself up for failure. In short, fix problems and stabilize the network before you move into the implementation phases.

Routers

The router is the heartbeat of the WAN. If the router goes, the WAN goes, just like that. For this reason you must pay particularly close attention to the router, its OS and firmware versions, protocols, services, interfaces, and traffic load. In this chapter, we'll concentrate on just a few of these parameters; we've dedicated a couple of future chapters to dig deeper into the performance, security, and access elements of the infrastructure.

For the router documentation, you can develop a huge table that lists everything this and the next few chapters will discuss, or you could break it down into something a bit more manageable, which is what we'll do in every part of this chapter, with the exception of Table 5.3. For each router in each location, collect the following information:

◆ Class, type, and model

◆ WAN, LAN, and specialty slots total

◆ WAN, LAN, and specialty slots used

◆ Speed of each interface

◆ Firmware version

NOTE **IPv6** With the explosion of the Internet and the need for a larger TCP/IP address space, you may be inclined to collect IPv6 support information for the IP-based infrastructure components. You can find out more information about IPv6 support in Windows 2000 at the following Internet address:

`http://msdn.microsoft.com/ downloads/sdks/platform/tpipv6. asp`

◆ OS version

◆ Protocols bound to each interface

◆ Complete IP address of each interface (IP, mask, gateway, name servers, and so on)

NOTE

Active Directory Sites   Generally speaking, Active Directory sites should be created for every segment of the business that is not connected by a well-connected WAN link. We'll hit sites and subnets along with the rest of the physical AD design later in the book.

You may be wondering what all this has to do with designing a directory services infrastructure. Remember that your solution needs to be efficient in order to be effective. The information you collect about the routers and other network devices allows you to size the network. This means you can determine when and where there may be potential problems with the efficiency of traffic flow before they exist and can design Active Directory accordingly.

Table 5.3 provides a sample router inventory sheet. This is pretty detailed. You may not need to get this detailed, depending on your environment and project scope.

Don't forget: The IP addressing information should be recorded per interface.

EXAM TIP

Sites Versus Domains Versus OUs   The distinctions involved in creating sites, OUs, and domains are tricky. To effectively challenge this exam, it is critical to know when to choose a site, an OU, or a domain. Always keep in mind that, when deciding about design considerations in the real world (bandwidth, management type, administration type, growth strategy, GPO placement, namespace, and so on), you *should not overlook* company politics. Fortunately most of the questions you'll see on the exam involve considerations that are more technical than political.

Although this information may be time consuming to get, it will save you valuable time in the future when you start planning and sizing your infrastructure. For example, you'll be able to refer to this chart when you plan your site and subnet design in the Active Directory, and will not need to revisit the router network. One other thing that will significantly enhance the visual representation of the network is to incorporate this data with your network topology diagram.

TABLE 5.3

ENTERPRISE ROUTER INVENTORY SHEET

		Router Brand, Type, and Model								
		Class Backbone	*Type Cisco*	*Model 7000*	*Class Access*	*Type Cisco*	*Model 2620*	*Class Access*	*Type Ascend*	*Model 5150*
Location *Role*		*Indianapolis* *Backbone node*			*Chicago* *VPN connection I*			*Indianapolis* *Internet access*		
Total Ports	WAN	0			2			1		
	LAN	16			1			1		
	Specialty	0			1			0		
Used Ports	WAN	16			2			1		
	LAN	2			1			1		
	Specialty	0			1			0		
Interface Speeds	WAN Int 1	N/A			T-1 (1.544MB)			128K ISDN		
	WAN Int n	N/A			T-1 (1.544MB)			N/A		
	LAN Int 1	1GB			100MB			10/100MB		
	LAN Int n	1GB			N/A			N/A		
	Special Int 1	N/A			Voiceover IP			N/A		
Firmware Version		1.00.234			1.00.233			1.00.455		
OS Version		12.0.5T			12.0.4T			4.33		
Protocol Bindings	WAN Int 1	N/A			TCP/IP			TCP/IP		
	WAN Int n	N/A			TCP/IP			N/A		
	LAN Int 1	TCP/IP, IPX/SPX			TCP/IP			TCP/IP, IPX/SPX		
	LAN Int n	TCP/IP, IPX/SPX			N/A			N/A		
	Special Int 1	N/A			TCP/IP			N/A		

continues

TABLE 5.3 | *continued*

ENTERPRISE ROUTER INVENTORY SHEET

		Router Brand, Type, and Model								
		Class *Backbone*	*Type* *Cisco*	*Model* *7000*	*Class* *Access*	*Type* *Cisco*	*Model* *2620*	*Class* *Access*	*Type* *Ascend*	*Model* *5150*
Location *Role*		*Indianapolis* *Backbone node*			*Chicago* *VPN connection I*			*Indianapolis* *Internet access*		
IP Addressing	IP Address	10.1.1.1			10.1.5.1			204.222.222.17		
Scheme (per interface)	Mask	255.255.255.0			255.255.255.0			255.255.255.240		
	Gateway	10.1.1.254			10.1.5.254			204.222.222.1		
	Hostname	Mybackbone			Myvpnaccess			Myisdnrouter		
	Name server	10.1.1.253			10.1.1.253			N/A		

After you have the router network documented, you need to consider the company's plans for growth or reorganization of the network. You can be of great value to the company in suggesting ways they can restructure their network to better fit their planned business and technology direction with this data. You need to understand the company's plans for growth so you can determine if any additional routing needs are required, and if so, document them with "dotted lines" and incorporate them into your plans.

IN THE FIELD

THE GROWING BUSINESS

With the explosion of the Internet and the services it provides, more and more companies are struggling to keep a competitive advantage in their market space. Companies need to strategically align technology with their business if they are to keep an edge over their competition. This technology alignment starts with a good, solid networking infrastructure, which makes it possible for a strategic and effective implementation of the NOS, which makes it possible for the effective use of information and communication throughout the company, which makes it possible for informed decision-making. This cycle all starts with routers, switches, and other internetworking equipment that will support the software that is fast becoming the lifeblood of an organization.

Switches

Another layer of the network infrastructure incorporates switches. You'll need to collect some data on the switches mainly for sizing and expected growth. The information you need to collect will be far less detailed than for the router, so you can relax a bit!

The switch is the core of the local network. It allows for directed packet forwarding between hosts, creating what's called a "virtual circuit." The main benefit of a switch over the previous generation hub is that a switch reduces the collision zone of packet data to almost nothing. When assessing the switches in the network, you should collect the following data:

◆ Manufacturer and model

◆ Number of ports

◆ Number of ports used

◆ Stackable (Y/N)

◆ Dedicated backplane for stacking (Y/N)

◆ Manageable (Y/N)

◆ Management address

Table 5.4 provides a sample switch assessment.

TABLE 5.4

SAMPLE SWITCH ASSESSMENT

Location	Manufacturer	Model	Number of Ports	Number of Ports Used	Stackable?	Independent Backplane for Stacking?	Manageable?	Management IP Address
New York	Cisco	3524	24	20	Yes	Yes	Yes	102.0.0.1
Indianapolis	Cisco	2924	24	18	Yes	No	Yes	102.0.0.2
Chicago	Cisco	3512	12	2	Yes	Yes	Yes	192.0.0.3

NOTE

More on Switching   If you are interested in reading more about switching technology, take a look at the Cisco Press excerpt at:

`http://www.cisco.com/cpress/cc/`
`td/cpress/ccie/ndcs798/nd2002.htm`

Although not exam-worthy, this information will give you deeper visibility into switching technology.

You'll find that this information, especially the information on the stackability of the switch, is crucial to have when determining the growth implications within the company. Some newer switches introduce a "backplane" to provide for fast and easy stacking of the switches without consuming any ports. This is definitely important in sizing the network for the future. Switches filled to capacity will need to be either replaced or stacked with additional switches if growth suggests it. In general, make sure you have enough scalability left in the existing switches before you embark on implementation.

Hubs

One suggestion here. Get rid of hubs and replace them with switches. Switches are much faster, more manageable, and absurdly more efficient. If you or the company you work for have not seen any reason to replace hubs with switches, you will after Windows 2000 is in place. This is not because Windows 2000 prefers switches over hubs—it doesn't care. The amount of traffic created by Windows 2000 on the network, however, will undoubtedly wreak havoc in the collision zone of a hub, which will bring the network to its knees, but this won't happen with a switch. Enough said.

Bridges and Other Devices

NOTE

Bandwidth Managers   Bandwidth managers utilize QoS-type technology to aggregate and prioritize network bandwidth by analyzing packets that pass through them. For example, mission-critical application data floating across the network may be given high priority, whereas streaming video may be given low priority. This increases the availability and performance of business mission-critical application data.

Any other devices that function on the LAN or WAN should be documented as well. Bridges in particular should be inventoried in much the same way the routers were, mainly because their function on the network is to provide a connection between two networks. Chances are if you have a bridge on the network, it's old and you have two different network topologies, such as Ethernet and Token Ring. If you run into this situation, check to see what the future plans are in terms of standardizing the network topology. If you can standardize on one topology, you can reduce cost and standardize products and peripherals that utilize the physical network. Otherwise, document each side of the bridge for project planning's sake. Other network devices, such as gateways, bandwidth managers, and so on, should be documented as well.

Name Resolution Services

WINS and DNS (and in some cases LMHOSTS and HOSTS files) make up the core IP name resolution services in a Windows NT environment. SAP and RIP broadcasts are abundant in a Novell environment. Your job is to determine not only when, where, and how these services are being utilized, but also to what extent they are being utilized. This is one area in which a packet sniffer may come in handy, and we'll discuss the use of a sniffer later in this chapter.

Because SAP and RIP are broadcast-based protocols, you'll first need to identify whether they are in use on the network, then determine whether they are needed moving forward. Both SAP and RIP packets have been known to saturate a network, and should be eliminated if the network does not use them. To determine the extent of their use, you'll need a network monitor or sniffer. Collect data for a day or two to get an accurate look, and make a decision as to whether it's a problem. We'll cover SAP and RIP, as well as various other protocols in the protocol analysis, later in this section.

Both DNS and WINS services reside on servers. Client computers use directed broadcasts to communicate with them, resulting in considerably less network utilization than a pure broadcast-based protocol. Use a table such as Table 5.5 to record information on WINS and DNS.

> **NOTE**
>
> **LMHOSTS and HOSTS Files**   Before WINS and DNS services were available, organizations made use of static text files to provide name resolution services for Windows. LMHOSTS is the text file version of WINS and provides NetBIOS name-to-IP address resolution. HOSTS is the text file version of DNS and provides FQDN-to-IP address name resolution. Both files may still be in use in some networks.

TABLE 5.5

SAMPLE **WINS** AND **DNS** INVENTORY INFORMATION

Server	*WINS*	*DNS*	*Subnet*
Server1	Yes	Yes	10.1.1.0
Server2	No	Yes	10.1.5.0
Server3	Yes	No	10.1.9.0

It's important to include the subnet the servers are on with this table so you have an idea of the WAN traffic that may be generated by these two services. Based on what you know about the networking infrastructure so far, you should be able to determine whether the current configuration will be sufficient for the next 3–5 years.

If not, you now have information to support your reason to move these services around (or, in the case of DDNS, eliminate WINS).

IP Addressing Schemes

DHCP is almost mainstream in corporations now because of its ability to remove the IP address management burden from the network manager.

When you look at the IP addressing schemes in an organization, you need to record the different methods they use to configure client IP addresses. The following three methods are mainstream:

◆ DHCP server

◆ QIP servers

◆ Manual IP configuration

DHCP Server

By far the most popular method is Dynamic Host Configuration Protocol (DHCP). If you find that a DHCP server is providing IP configuration for the corporation, your job is pretty simple. Record the server and scope configuration of the server running DHCP. The result of this analysis should resemble Table 5.6.

TABLE 5.6

SAMPLE DHCP SERVER CONFIGURATION DATA

Server Name	Location	Number of DHCP Controlled - Subnets (Scopes)	Global Options	Scope Options	IP Address Range	Exclusions	Lease Time
MrDHCP	Chicago	15	DNS Servers	Router	10.1.1.10 to 10.1.1.240	10.1.1.25 to 10.1.1.50	3d
			DNS Domain Name				
			WINS Servers				
			WINS Node Type				

The incorporation of DDNS as the core name resolution and service locator service within Windows 2000 presents a problem with legacy operating systems. The problem is simple: Legacy operating systems have no concept of DDNS, and therefore have no idea how to keep their resources' records up to date. In this case, DHCP acts as a proxy by managing the updates of the "A" (name-to-IP) and "PTR" (IP-to-name) records in DDNS. In a pure Windows 2000 environment (Windows 2000 on both client and server), the Windows 2000 Professional client manages the DDNS "A" record on its own. DHCP still manages the "PTR" record.

There is one other new feature with DHCP. In Windows 2000, the Active Directory must authorize all DHCP servers using a secure administrative account. This is in an attempt to protect against "rogue" DHCP servers (DHCP servers that are not supposed to be on the network). We'll cover more on this topic in Chapter 7, "Analyzing Security Requirements."

QIP Servers

QIP servers are hot. They provide robust IP management services for the enterprise. In terms of DHCP, QIP servers offer standards-based, many-to-one DHCP fail-over, IP address "check before assign" capabilities, the ability to assign IP addresses to older BOOTP clients, and the ability to update DDNS servers with client information. This is much like the DHCP we'll see in Windows 2000. If you find QIP servers on the network, you need to approach them in much the same way as you approach DHCP servers.

Manual IP Configuration

Manual TCP/IP configurations should be reserved for servers and infrastructure devices only. If a corporation still utilizes manual IP configurations on its client workstations, make it top priority to convert them to DHCP (or QIP) if at all possible.

Visiting every desktop to record the manual IP setting is not necessary during this assessment. Documenting all subnets within the organization is. You should record the IP subnets and the number of nodes per subnet at minimum, and also include plans for migrating to a centrally controlled IP management system.

This section brings up an interesting issue. Find out why the organization hasn't gone to a centrally controlled IP system, such as DHCP. It may be that its routers don't support the forwarding of DHCP data for some reason, and it hasn't upgraded yet. If you do run into such a case or one similar to it, you need to document it in the assessment and list it as a high priority item that needs to be addressed. As stated previously, the success of your Windows 2000 implementation is largely dependent upon the underlying infrastructure.

Protocol Analysis

Because Windows 2000 is built around Internet standards, it's fitting that we focus on TCP/IP in this book. We don't want to take (too much) away from the slick IPX/SPX protocol pioneered by Novell, but even they have acknowledged that TCP/IP is the now and the future by incorporating it into the core NetWare platform.

The protocol analysis, although cut-and-dried, can be time-consuming and extremely detailed. At its simplest level, a protocol analysis could be a listing of the protocols currently used on the network, such as TCP/IP and IPX/SPX. A detailed protocol analysis could get down to the TCP and UDP packet volume over time on a specific interface. How detailed you get depends on the scope of your project and what SLAs you need to uphold.

A general rule of thumb is to use as few protocols as possible throughout your network. Keep this in mind while performing the protocol analysis so you can identify unnecessary protocol overhead. This is another good fit for the sniffer because just looking at the servers will not give you the answer. Client computers determine the protocol used in a "discussion," and you aren't going to spend the time to hit 5,000 PCs to see what protocols they have bound. Regardless of the method you use to determine the protocols in use, the end result should be some sort of a list of protocols with a plan to get as close to a TCP/IP-only network as possible.

As you perform the protocol analysis, you are collecting statistics and looking for problem areas. We'll pick on IPX for an example. In fact, this example is probably the most influential reason IPX is not recommended in WAN-type environments. IPX uses SAP (Service Advertising Protocol) and RIP (Routing Information Protocol) to announce services and network routes on the network. Both protocols broadcast updates every 60 seconds. In a LAN situation, this typically is not a problem. In a WAN environment, however, where you have a lot of servers and small WAN links, SAP and RIP have the potential to saturate the network. It takes a relatively poor and unplanned network design for this to happen, but there are such networks out there.

Bandwidth

We've discussed the bandwidth in terms of capacity and connectivity, but have not gotten much deeper than that. This section takes a look at sizing up the available bandwidth and preparing for future initiatives that may demand more bandwidth, or require better and more efficient management of existing bandwidth.

Net Available Bandwidth and SLAs

Net available bandwidth is the total bandwidth minus the utilized portion of bandwidth. You can calculate this by establishing a baseline utilization and subtracting it from the size of the link. It is important that you know your net available bandwidth when preparing for future integration of bandwidth intensive operations such as voice and video. Furthermore, many IT organizations set performance-based Service Level Agreements (SLAs) based on the amount of available bandwidth. It is important that you uncover any such SLAs that may be affected by future integration of network services. IT management is a good place to start if you need to find documented SLAs.

Table 5.7 illustrates the calculation of average utilization on a T-1 line (1.544MB total throughput).

TABLE 5.7		

CALCULATING AVERAGE BANDWIDTH UTILIZATION OF T-1 LINE

Time	Percent Utilization	Running Utilization Average
8:00a.m .	40%	40%
10:00a.m.	53%	46.5%
12:00 Noon	42%	45%
2:00p.m.	65%	50%
4:00p.m.	61%	52.2%
6:00p.m.	20%	46.83%
8:00p.m.	2%	40.43%
10:00p.m.	80%	45.38%
12:00 Midnight	80%	49.22%
2:00a.m.	30%	47.3%
4:00a.m.	80%	50.27%
6:00a.m.	10%	46.91%

We can deduce from the table that the T-1 is 46.91% utilized on the average, with peak utilization of 80% overnight during scheduled backup and replication processes. To get the net available bandwidth from these numbers, we need to do some math. Remember, *available* bandwidth refers to the amount of bandwidth that is *not* in use.

Nonutilized network bandwidth = (100% − 46.91%) = 53.09%. 53.09% of total bandwidth is .5309 × 1.544 = .8197MB. This means that the net available bandwidth is .8197MB, or 819.7KB.

If your plans are not to remove any services, just add them, you have 819.7KB of available bandwidth to play with. If there are SLAs that directly relate to the amount of available bandwidth, those must be considered. For example, if a simple SLA states that bandwidth utilization must not rise above 90%, you know you've only got 10% to play with. This is a good place to recommend an upgrade, if necessary.

Quality of Service (QoS)

We've mentioned Quality of Service (QoS) a few times and haven't really addressed what it's all about. In short, QoS refers to bandwidth management. It's the technology that enables administrators to specify bandwidth for priority services, such as a mission-critical line of business application services.

It is important to point out that standard Ethernet does not support QoS. IEEE 802.1p (IP Precedence) and 802.1q (VLAN, or Virtual Local Area Network) standards must be implemented along with QoS-enabling protocols, such as RSVP (Resource Reservation Protocol) and RTP (Real-Time Protocol) to enable the benefits of QoS. For more information on IEEE 802.1q and 802.1p, refer to the Microsoft TechNet article "Description of 802.1p Signaling."

More often than not, you're going to find QoS initiatives on the future end of an analysis, not the current end. Chapter 6, "Analyzing Performance-Related Requirements," will discuss more on Windows 2000 QoS Services.

> **NOTE**
>
> **Quality of Service Standard** IETF RFC-2212 defines the QoS standard generally accepted by the IEEE. Also, if you are interested in reviewing the IEEE 802.1 standards specification, you can obtain more information by visiting **http://standards.ieee. org/catalog/IEEE802.1.html** (this information does cost, though).

Telecommuting

One final piece of the bandwidth puzzle has to do with remote access and telecommuting. The 1990s saw a great shift in telecommuting because of the highly available, inexpensive, and fast dial-up access to the Internet and the corporate office. As we head into the twenty-first century, industry experts expect the number of telecommuters to rise significantly.

New and emerging technologies that leverage the Internet as an extension of the office are becoming an increasingly important part of business. One such technology is the Virtual Private Network (VPN). VPNs allow organizations to utilize the Internet as a WAN connection, in many cases eliminating the need to install expensive Frame Relay or point-to-point connections. One thing you'll need to consider with VPNs, however, is the amount of hardware and bandwidth resources it will require.

> **EXAM TIP**
>
> **Working from Home** The onset of broadband access around the world has made telecommuting more feasible and prevalent than ever. Skill at designing remote access and Virtual Private Networks is now critical for Windows 2000 design success and may very well be an integral part of the exam.

TOOLS AND UTILITIES TO HELP WITH ANALYSIS

All the items we've discussed so far would take some time to complete in an enterprise setting. For this reason it is important to mention that in some circumstances it may be beneficial to use a network management or inventory utility to collect this data. There are some great utilities available for a price. If the organization currently uses a network management or inventory tool capable of collecting the data you need to collect, consider using it. If not, you have a decision to make. The general rule of thumb should be to use the tool if you can implement it network wide and collect your data quicker than you can do it manually. Some of the more popular tools capable of collecting some or all of the information needed in this chapter are listed in Table 5.8.

TABLE 5.8

NETWORK MANAGEMENT AND DIAGRAMMING SOLUTIONS

Application	Manufacturer	Description
NetworkIT Pro	Computer Associates (http://www.ca.com/solutions/enterprise/networks/)	"Best of Breed" application built on the UniCenter TNG framework that is ideal for enterprise network management.
NetView	Tivoli (http://www.tivoli.com/products/index/netview/)	End-to-end network manager. Offers dynamic updates of network devices, auto discovery, and so on.
DM/Suite	FastLane (http://www.fastlane.com/products/dmsuite)	Offers field-tested Directory Management applications, allowing enterprises to effectively plan, deploy, and manage Windows 2000. This is an end-to-end Windows 2000 migration suite of products.
Visio	Microsoft (http://www.microsoft.com/office/visio)	Popular diagramming tools with the capability to autogenerate diagrams of networks.

All the tools mentioned in Table 5.8 include native-query and report-generation features that can be a significant bonus to your analysis. For example, these tools may be able to provide any or all of the data we've discussed in this chapter with a simple click of a button. Make sure you leverage the benefits of these utilities if you choose to use them.

CASE STUDY: eFLY AIRLINES

eFly Through the Chapter   This case study is presented all in one location for easy reading, but you're well-advised to go back and make sure you notice the ways in which various topics presented throughout the chapter come to bear upon particular aspects of the situation faced by the company in this case study. Then, after you've thought about the current state of this company and the analysis of their physical environment that must be done to effectively plan for the most successful migration possible to Windows 2000 and Active Directory, keep the details of the case study in mind because you will be encountering them a few times during the upcoming Exam Questions section.

BACKGROUND

eFly Airlines is a new regional carrier for a large airline corporation. It operates in the midwestern United States and is headquartered in St. Louis, MO. eFly has airport hubs and small offices in Indianapolis, IN, Chicago, IL, Minneapolis, MN, and Memphis, TN. It books reservations only via the Web or its parent carrier. For Web-based reservations, it frequently offers discounted tickets.

eFly was formed by its parent corporation, which purchased three small regional carriers and combined them into this one company.

PROBLEM STATEMENT

CEO

"Our biggest problem now that we've leveled off is maintenance. We all got used to working 15-hour days to get this thing off the ground (no pun intended) and expected that to decrease once we reached a comfort level with our new airline routes and reservation system. We've done that and everyone except the IT guys are back to about eight-hour days. The IT guys are tasked with integrating our new systems with those of our parent carrier, a task that requires a lot of planning and dedication."

IT Director

"The IT staff here is responsible for the monitoring and optimization of our Web servers. Since these are mission-critical servers, they are watched very carefully. Additionally, we are responsible for the integration of our SQL 6.5 database with the UNIX reservation and ticketing systems. We've been fighting performance-related problems lately, and I'm pretty sure it has to do with our nonstandard infrastructure."

Web Developer

"We are really part of something good here at eFly, and that's why we stick around and do all this extra work. We need to continue to do so but focus a bit more on the network as a whole and how our regional offices communicate. I have this Web site under control now!"

continues

CASE STUDY: eFLY AIRLINES

continued

CURRENT SYSTEM

Ticket Buyer

"I like the services eFly has to offer. I get a little paranoid about entering my credit card information when using its online ticketing system because I don't see the little security icon on my Web browser."

Web Developer

"I had to turn Secure Sockets Layer off a couple of times because it was causing problems integrating with UNIX. I think I have that resolved now."

Infrastructure Specialist

"When I asked for an infrastructure diagram on my first day with the company, and they couldn't produce one, I knew I was in trouble. In the two weeks I've been with the company, I've come to realize there are absolutely no standards within this organization."

CURRENT ENVIRONMENT

IT Director

"Our reservations and ticketing systems run on an HP/UX system and are part of our parent company's systems. Our membership and tracking services run on a SQL 6.5 database and our Web servers run on Windows NT and IIS 4.0. Our internal systems run a mixture of Windows NT and Novell NetWare that's left over from the smaller companies that were combined to form eFly."

Infrastructure Specialist

"You can definitely tell this company was put together in a hurry. In St. Louis, where most of the systems exist, we have Windows NT. The HP/UX doesn't come into play internally. At our hubs, we have mostly airline maintenance activities and logbooks. Connectivity varies between these sites. To Indy and Memphis, we have 128K Frame Relay connections, to Minneapolis we have a 56K and to Chicago we have a 256K Frame Relay connection. We have both Cisco and Nortel (Bay) routers and switches throughout the company."

Help Desk Manager

"Our offices run Windows 95 and 98, and Windows NT Workstation 4.0. Protocols vary from IP only to IP and IPX. Some Windows NT workstations actually have DLC installed so they can print directly to a networked printer. The only standard applications are Microsoft Office 97, LogBooks, and our Web-based time system, TimeBill."

ENVISIONED SYSTEM

IT Director

"I'd like to see us standardize on a single operating platform that will enable Internet and UNIX integration, enhanced security and performance, lower TCO, and extreme simplification of administration. In short, I'd like to go to Windows 2000."

CASE STUDY: eFLY AIRLINES

Infrastructure Specialist

"While I like both Cisco and Bay, I'd like to implement standards across the board. That means replacing one with the other. My preference is Cisco because I've got seven years experience working with it and have relationships with Cisco people. Our Frame Relay network is not bad, but I'd like to see everything up to about 256K, especially if we're looking at Windows 2000."

Help Desk Manager

"We desperately need to standardize on a single desktop OS. Windows 2000 Professional should enhance the way our people work. It's also supposed to be more reliable, faster, and more robust than our current systems. Applications-wise, I don't know. I think our current systems are okay—they do what we need—but maybe we should look into some upgrades. I really like the Web-based technologies."

SECURITY

Outside Security Consultant

"eFly really doesn't have the right infrastructure in place to enable any sort of enhanced security. They need to standardize on something, and go with it. Then they can develop a security infrastructure. I'd recommend moving to Windows 2000 and utilizing Kerberos for authentication and security. They can leverage Kerberos not only internally, but also with the HP/UX system."

IT Director

"We are only beginning to understand how important security is to our organization. Having a Web-based front end to our mission-critical business application really puts us at risk for malicious attack. I think we need to focus our security attention first to IIS and then to the rest of the organization."

Web Developer

"I'd like to figure out why connectivity with the HP/UX is sometimes lost with SSL configured. I am hoping that a move to Windows 2000 and IIS 5.0 fixes this intermittent problem."

PERFORMANCE

Infrastructure Specialist

"I'd like to upgrade all the routers to RISC architecture. I'd like to remove all hubs and replace them with manageable switches. I'd like to upgrade our corporate headquarters backbone to fiber connectivity all the way to the servers."

Indianapolis Maintenance Crew

"When I enter logs, I'd like to not have to wait five minutes for the next screen to appear. I have jets to service; I can't be fooling around with these computers."

continues

CASE STUDY: eFLY AIRLINES

continued

IT Director

"I'd like to incorporate Network Load Balancing Services with the front-end Web servers. We expect to increase volume drastically over the next few years. We currently get about 50,000 hits per week on our Web servers and expect that to double in the next three years. We also need to take a proactive approach at managing our growth. I'd like to implement performance monitoring standards so we can keep an eye on the current real-time numbers and, more importantly, do some trend analysis and stop problems before they become major issues."

MAINTAINABILITY

IT Director

"The first thing we need to do is provide Windows 2000 training to all of our support staff. I am focused on understanding how it helps reduce TCO through simplified administration."

IT Administrator

"We need to design the new system around our geographical scope of operations and our business model. We plan to centralize administration here in St. Louis, so that means we'll need an effective and efficient way of replicating changes out to our hubs."

Infrastructure Specialist

"I am the infrastructure "team" right now. My goal is to have everything standardized so I can sit in my office and perform routing maintenance on all of the infrastructure devices. I also plan to run volume reports so we keep a good handle on our traffic and receive alerts when we need to make changes."

AVAILABILITY

IT Director

"Our Web-based systems need to be available 24×7×365—period, end of story. I think there are technologies out now that offer *five nines* (in other words, 99.999%) uptime. These servers are our business, so it is well worth the investment."

Customer Service Administrator

"My job depends on our SQL database being up and operational. I take about 50 calls per day and about two thirds of them require my accessing data. I work 8 to 5 daily, so during that time, it has to be up."

Infrastructure Specialist

"If I get approval for implementing what I want, we'll never have to worry about connectivity problems. I want to replace all infrastructure equipment with new, as well as provide redundant WAN connections."

CHAPTER SUMMARY

As you prepare to perform a physical analysis of the network, it is important that you talk to the IT teams that are responsible for these systems currently. You can find out some valuable information and potentially save quite a bit of time and money by asking a few simple questions.

The geographical distribution of the company resources directly affects the core of the Active Directory sites and subnets design, replication, management, and various other areas of Windows 2000. Construct a table that lists the geographic location, office name, number of users, and expected growth rates. This will give you something to refer to as you diagram the network. A network diagram is an enhancement to the visualization of the network. If you don't have one, create one or obtain one as early into the assessment as possible. Use dotted lines to draw in future growth, as it will allow you to see both today and into the future.

Document LAN and WAN speeds in and between all offices. Additionally, document the type of network, such as FastEthernet, ATM, Frame Relay, Fiber, and so on. Moreover, document the physical devices attached to these networks. Physical devices, such as routers, switches, and bridges, do not run Windows 2000, but they provide a platform for it to enable its services, which makes them every bit as important as the OS itself. You'll want to collect information on the manufacturer and model of the device, firmware, processor and memory (if applicable), protocols, protocol configuration, and more, and update a table with this information.

For Windows 2000 to function properly, you must incorporate name resolution services. To do this well, you must know what is in use on the network, and what the desired name resolution services are. DNS and WINS (and/or potentially LMHOSTS and HOSTS files) both provide name resolution for TCP/IP-based services. SAP and RIP are used by IPX to advertise services and routing information. Whatever the case, determine what is used currently, what is desired for the future, and how to get from now to then.

There are three popular ways to configure client TCP/IP addresses: DHCP, QIP, and manual configuration. Determine what is currently

KEY TERMS

- enterprise infrastructure assessment
- network topology
- bandwidth
- connection type
- LAN (local area network)
- WAN (wide area network)
- MAN (metropolitan area network)
- Ethernet
- FastEthernet
- Token Ring
- Frame Relay
- QoS (Quality of Service)
- router
- switch
- hub
- bridge
- WINS
- DNS
- Service Advertising Protocol (SAP)
- Routing Information Protocol (RIP)
- TCP/IP
- IPX/SPX
- collision zone
- DHCP server

CHAPTER SUMMARY

KEY TERMS

- QIP server
- SLA (Service Level Agreement)
- telecommuting

NOTE

Current Use of IP Services The current usage of TCP/IP services—such as DHCP, QIP, or manual—may end up being one or more of each. For example, consider the case in which a corporate office uses DHCP but can't figure out how to forward DHCP requests across a WAN link—so satellite offices use manual addressing. Be aware of such situations.

in use on the network and what is desired for future management. The push should be for Windows 2000-based DHCP since it incorporates features to allow for legacy operating systems to take part in DDNS. Moreover, this version of DHCP incorporates with Active Directory security to try to eliminate rogue DHCP servers.

Subtracting the utilized bandwidth from the total bandwidth derives net available bandwidth. Knowing the net available bandwidth in conjunction with any Service Level Agreement (SLA) allows you to accurately determine whether the additional traffic generated by Windows 2000 will suggest an upgrade. Pay special attention to telecommuting and remote access, because new and emerging technologies, such as VPN's, are demanding faster, more reliable access to the organization from the public Internet.

Finally, utilize Network Management tools and their native query and report generating processes to your advantage. They can significantly reduce the amount of time involved in performing the physical analysis. They can also enhance the presentation of data with charts, graphs, and so on.

APPLY YOUR KNOWLEDGE

Exercises

5.1 Determine Net Available Bandwidth

This exercise presents you with a table depicting network bandwidth utilization. You will be tasked with determining three different classifications of net available bandwidth: minimum, maximum, and average.

Estimated Time: 20 Minutes

TABLE 5.9

EXERCISE 5.1

Time	Utilization
12:00 Midnight	2%
2:00 a.m.	89%
4:00 a.m.	13%
6:00 a.m.	44%
8:00 a.m.	80%
10:00 a.m.	73%
12:00 Noon	50%
2:00 p.m.	67%
4:00 p.m.	68%
6:00 p.m.	31%
8:00 p.m.	12%
10:00 p.m.	1%

> **NOTE**
>
> **Bandwidth Utilization** It is important to understand that when assessing bandwidth utilization in the real world, you need to use a much smaller time increment to get an accurate reading. Your network sniffer should be able to take a reading once every five seconds or so.

1. Determine the minimum, maximum, and average net available bandwidth, using the data from Table 5.9. Calculate numbers based on the understanding that information was collected on a T-1.

2. This time assume the data collected came from an Ethernet (10MB) network, and perform the same calculations as in Step 1.

Table 5.10 illustrates one of many approaches to the problem set forth in Exercise 5.1.

APPLY YOUR KNOWLEDGE

TABLE 5.10

EXERCISE 5.1 SOLUTION

Time	Utilization	Running Average Utilizations
12:00 Midnight	2%	2%
2:00 a.m.	89%	45.5%
4:00 a.m.	13%	34.67%
6:00 a.m.	44%	37%
8:00 a.m.	80%	45.6%
10:00 a.m.	73%	60.2%
12:00 Noon	50%	58.5%
2:00 p.m.	67%	59.71%
4:00 p.m.	68%	60.75%
6:00 p.m.	31%	57.44%
8:00 p.m.	12%	52.9%
10:00 p.m.	1%	48.18%

The darker shaded area of Table 5.10 illustrates the maximum utilization. The lighter shaded area illustrates the minimum utilization.

The following list details the minimum, maximum, and average net available bandwidth, assuming the preceding data was collected on a T-1:

◆ **Maximum net available bandwidth.** Minimum utilization is 1% at 10 p.m. 1% of 1.544MB is .01544MB. 1.544 – .01544 is 1.52856MB, which is the maximum net available bandwidth.

◆ **Minimum net available bandwidth.** Maximum utilization is 89% at 2 a.m. during backup over WAN. 89% of 1.544 is 1.37416.

1.544 – 1.37416 is .16984MB (~173.9K), which is the minimum net available bandwidth.

◆ **Average net available bandwidth.** Average utilization is 48.18%. 48.18% of 1.544 is .7439. 1.544 – .7439 is .8001 (~819.3K), which is the average net available bandwidth.

The following list details the minimum, maximum, and average net available bandwidth, assuming the preceding data was collected on an Ethernet (10MB) network:

◆ **Maximum net available bandwidth.** Minimum utilization is 1% at 10 p.m. 1% of 10MB is .1MB. 10 – .1 is 9.9MB, which is the maximum net available bandwidth.

◆ **Minimum net available bandwidth.** Maximum utilization is 89% at 2 a.m. during backup over WAN. 89% of 10MB is 8.9MB. 10 – 8.9 is 1.1MB, which is the minimum net available bandwidth.

◆ **Average net available bandwidth.** Average utilization is 48.18%. 48.18% of 10MB is 4.818. 10 – 4.818 is 5.182MB, which is the average net available bandwidth.

5.2 Determine Appropriate Action

For each of the scenarios in the left column of Table 5.11, select the appropriate option in the right column that best addresses the action that would lead toward a solution for that scenario.

Estimated Time: 5 Minutes

APPLY YOUR KNOWLEDGE

TABLE 5.11

EXERCISE 5.2

Scenario	Solution
"We have offices in 17 different geographical locations and have a Frame Relay connection between this office and and each of the 16 others."	Perform a protocol analysis.
"We have only three small sites here in the main campus, but we didn't keep good records of the equipement we used to connect them."	Perform an automated (software-assisted) infrastructure hardware inventory.
"We have 188 locations throughout the U.S. We are uncertain whether each of the locations is connecting using the standard router package."	Perform a manual infrastructure hardware inventory.
"We currently use TCP/IP, IPX/SPX, NetBEUI, and DLC protocols on all of our Windows NT servers. NetWare was just removed from our network."	Prepare a network topology diagram.

TABLE 5.12

EXERCISE 5.2 SOLUTION

Scenario	Solution	Explanation
"We currently use TCP/IP, IPX/SPX, NetBEUI, and DLC protocols on all of our Windows NT servers. NetWare was just removed from our network."	Perform a protocol analysis.	Because the company still uses IPX/SPX on its servers, it would stand to reason that a protocol analysis is in order since NetWare servers have been removed. (IPX/SPX may not be required anymore.)
"We have 188 locations throughout the U.S. We are uncertain whether each of the locations is connecting using the standard router package."	Perform an automated (software-assisted) infrastructure hardware inventory.	If you are dealing with a large number of locations that are all connected, performing a manual infrastructure inventory can be overwhelming and quite time consuming. In this case, you'd want to use a utility that would help automate an infrastructure inventory.
"We have only three small sites here in the main campus, but we didn't keep good records of the equipment we used to connect them."	Perform a manual infrastructure hardware inventory.	In cases where you have a limited number of locations and a manageable amount of infrastructure equipment to assess, a manual collection would prove beneficial—unless you already have an automated utility in place.
"We have offices in 17 different geographical locations and have a Frame Relay connection between this office and each of the 16 others."	Prepare a network topology diagram	When looking at the geographical layout of an organization, you should automatically think of a network topology diagram to represent the network as a whole.

APPLY YOUR KNOWLEDGE

5.3 Analyze the Network Topology

In this exercise, you will test your ability to pick out key points about a network topology from a conversation.

Estimated Time: 15 Minutes

1. Read this excerpt carefully:

   "Now that our new design is complete, I want to recap the structure so that we are all on the same page. RIOcom now operates from a regional standpoint. Our new offices are in L.A., New York, Newark, Houston, and Denver—and we still obviously have our corporate headquarters here in Chicago. Since we've gone to the regional model, we no longer have the remote agencies to consider in our infrastructure; all those employees either work from home or were integrated into one of the regional offices. The ones who work from home use local ISPs to connect to the Internet and then VPN into here for corporate system access. Accounting folks: The new T-1 charge you'll see on the MCI bill is for this new VPN connection to the Internet. This is in addition to the T-1 point-to-points we have between here and New York, Denver, L.A., and Houston. We still have the 64K point-to-point between New York and Newark as well.

   Our company has grown quite a bit since last we met, so let me break it down for you. Daryl's group in L.A. is now 447 strong, Larry's group in Houston is up 200% to 500 strong, Monica in Denver has her hands full with 250 agents, and Jan in the New York area manages about 600 agents between New York and Newark, 25% of whom work from the Newark office. And here in Chicago we are up to a whopping 750 agents and still growing!"

2. On a sheet of paper, draw the network topology diagram for RIOcom. Be sure to include the following components:

   - Names of all physical locations
   - Number of employees working out of each location
   - Network bandwidth between each location
   - Any special network considerations

3. Check your drawing against the solution shown in Figure 5.2.

APPLY YOUR KNOWLEDGE

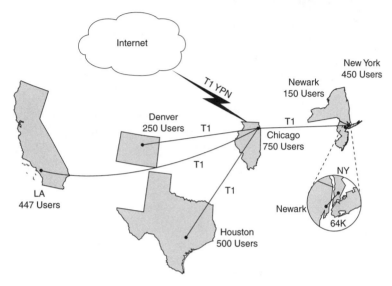

FIGURE 5.2
A sample RIOcom network topology diagram.

Review Questions

1. What is Microsoft's definition of a "well-connected" network?

2. What should you build or obtain to get a graphical representation of the network topology?

3. What device can be considered the heartbeat of a wide area network?

4. Which network device uses a "virtual circuit" to provide a dedicated path for communication between two computers?

5. When determining which switch to purchase, what should you look for in terms of scalability and efficient use of that switch?

6. Why are hubs not recommended anymore?

7. What are the two core name-resolution services in use today by Windows NT networks? What service will Windows 2000 allow an administrator to eliminate?

8. What feature of the Windows 2000 implementation of DHCP is directed at protecting the environment against rogue DHCP servers?

9. Which IEEE Ethernet standards provide a framework for implementing QoS?

10. List some benefits you gain from using network and/or asset management utilities to perform a physical IT assessment.

APPLY YOUR KNOWLEDGE

Exam Questions

1. It is end-of-year closing for ABC Corp. Sam, an IT administrator, just finished giving the accounting department users priority bandwidth for their mission-critical application. What technology is this an example of?

   A. QIP

   B. QoS

   C. VPN

   D. VLAN

2. You are a consultant working with the eFly infrastructure specialist. In preparing an Active Directory design, he explains that his goal is to isolate directory replication traffic local to each physical network segment. On which physical layer of Active Directory design should you recommend he focus his attention to accomplish his goal?

   A. Sites and subnets

   B. Users and groups

   C. Domains and trusts

   D. Security policies

3. A & T Corp. is a company that was formed as a result of A Co. and T Co. merging. Both companies are law firms and do an extensive amount of network-intensive work. Both companies run on NetWare. A 56K WAN line exists between the two offices and communication across that line has degraded quite a bit over the year they've been together. What may be causing the line to degrade?

   A. Backup operations

   B. LAN broadcasts

   C. SAP and RIP broadcasts

   D. Collisions

4. You are conducting an infrastructure workshop for an organization by using manual IP addressing. On which two IP-addressing services should you focus the workshop to explain the options for automatic IP address configuration?

   A. DHCP

   B. WINS

   C. QIP

   D. DNS

   E. SAP

5. You are an outside consultant contracted by eFly to help determine the best design for its internal infrastructure. Based on conversations with the eFly infrastructure specialist (as described in the case study), what should you recommend his first course of action be?

   A. Remove all infrastructure components and replace them with all new ones.

   B. Develop a network topology diagram.

   C. Determine all protocols in use on the network.

   D. Recommend an increase in bandwidth for all locations.

6. You are the IT director for your company and have been considering the removal of all NetWare 4.11 servers so you can have a pure Windows 2000 environment. What impacts will the removal of all NetWare servers have on your environment? (Choose two.)

   A. Decrease network utilization

   B. Increase network utilization

   C. Require the removal of IPX/SPX

   D. Allow for the removal of IPX/SPX

   E. Require the removal of TCP/IP

7. Suppose after performing a physical assessment for eFly, you find that all remote sites utilize hubs instead of switches. What can you say about the speed of local traffic at these sites?

   A. It is faster than in the corporate office.

   B. It is slower than in the corporate office.

   C. It is the same speed as in the corporate office.

   D. It uses virtual circuits.

8. Based on your understanding of the eFly network topology, how would you design the Windows 2000 site structure?

   A. Use a single site and let Windows 2000 handle the replication schedule.

   B. Use a site for Indy and Chicago, a site for Minneapolis, and a site for St. Louis and Memphis.

   C. Create a site for each physical location.

   D. You don't need to create any sites for eFly.

9. The infrastructure specialist for eFly Airlines wants to provide priority bandwidth to internal mission-critical applications. What device may he use to provide this functionality?

   A. Network Analyzer

   B. Bandwidth Manager

   C. Packet Sniffer

   D. Quality of Service

10. You are an infrastructure consultant for eFly Airlines. The infrastructure specialist has requested your services to assist in determining whether he needs to upgrade the WAN links between sites. At a minimum, what information should you collect before you can make any recommendations? Choose the best answer.

    A. You should collect information about each application in use on the network.

    B. You should collect information about the type of networking equipment on either side of the connection.

    C. You should collect information about the maximum, minimum, and average network utilization on each of the WAN connections.

    D. You should collect information about the protocols in use on each segment of the network.

APPLY YOUR KNOWLEDGE

Answers to Review Questions

1. Microsoft defines a well-connected network as any connected network whose slowest WAN connection is 512K or higher. See "Connection Types and Speeds of Each."

2. In order to visualize the entire topology of a network, it is highly recommended that you either build or obtain a network topology diagram. See "Network Topology."

3. The router can be considered the heartbeat of the WAN. If it goes down, unless there is a redundant link in place to take over, that connection is down. See "Routers."

4. A switch uses the concept of a virtual circuit to facilitate efficient communication between two computers. This virtual circuit is a dedicated collision zone, which significantly increases the efficiency of the communication. See "Switches."

5. As a general rule of thumb, you should make sure that any switch you purchase with the intent of adding to it contains a dedicated backplane for connecting multiple switches. This eliminates the utilization of Ethernet ports for this task and therefore provides for extended use. See "Switches."

6. Simply stated, a hub is one big collision zone, meaning all devices attaching to the hub "speak out loud" within the hub. This chatter increases collisions on contention-based networks and therefore reduces efficiency. See "Hubs."

7. Windows NT uses Windows Internet Name Service (WINS) for NetBIOS name resolution, and DNS for host name resolution. Windows 2000, with the incorporation of Dynamic DNS, gives the administrator an opportunity to remove NetBIOS, eliminating the need for WINS. See "Name Resolution Services."

8. Windows 2000 requires that Active Directory authorize all DHCP servers. This is meant to prevent nonproduction or malicious DHCP servers from providing client IP addresses. See "DHCP Server."

9. IEEE 802.1p (IP Precedence) and 802.1q (VLAN). 802.1p allows administrators to prioritize network traffic. 802.1q makes use of the never-implemented prioritization tag within VLANs. See "Quality of Service."

10. There are actually several benefits you gain from using network management utilities. Some are speed, reports and queries, charts, presentation of data, and accuracy. See "Tools and Utilities to Help with Analysis."

Answers to Exam Questions

1. **B.** Quality of Service enables network administrators to prioritize network bandwidth for specific applications and specific users. It requires IEEE Ethernet standards 802.1p and 802.1q with supporting protocols. See "Quality of Service."

2. **A.** Sites and subnets define the physical design of Active Directory. The purpose of a site is to form replication boundaries. This is usually done for segments of the company that are geographically separated by a not-well-connected WAN link. You can define well-connectivity based on your situation and the acceptable latency within the organization, or use the generally accepted and Microsoft-defined 512K minimum requirement. Subnets relate to IP segments and make up a site. See "Connection Types and Speeds of Each" in

APPLY YOUR KNOWLEDGE

this chapter, and in Chapter 11, "Designing the Active Directory Structure," see the section "Put Together a Site Plan."

3. **C**. SAP and RIP broadcasts can saturate a network if between them there are many NetWare servers on either side of a WAN connection. SAP and RIP broadcasts occur every minute. Every NetWare server addresses each SAP and RIP packet every time they are sent out. Options A and D do make a case for being correct, but in the context of the question, C is the only answer that works. See "Protocol Analysis."

4. **A, C**. DHCP and QIP are TCP/IP addressing services that allow servers to automatically assign IP addresses to requesting clients, eliminating the need to manually assign IP addresses to each client. DNS and WINS are both TCP/IP-related name-resolution services and cannot assign IP addresses. SAP is the Service Advertising Protocol used mainly by NetWare servers to advertise their services on the network. See "IP Addressing Schemes."

5. **B**. A network topology diagram is a very important element that allows the infrastructure team to visualize the network as a whole. The other three answers represent actions that may be taken in the future, after studying the networking environment. See "Network Topology."

6. **A, D**. The removal of NetWare from the network would reduce (even if just slightly) the overall utilization of the network by eliminating SAP and RIP packet broadcasts. It would also allow the administrator to remove IPX/SPX from all servers, therefore providing the opportunity for an all-IP network. See "Protocol Analysis."

7. **B**. Switches pass data much more quickly than hubs do, mainly because of the use of virtual circuits, which eliminate collision zones found in hubs. See "Switches" and "Hubs."

8. **C**. Because every WAN link is pretty slow (by today's standards) you should create a site for each location that fails the "well-connected" test. You must have at least one site in every Windows 2000 network. This site is created by default and is named default-first-site-link. See the "Active Directory Sites" Note in the "Routers" section.

9. **B**. Bandwidth managers, such as Packeteer PacketShaper (`http://www.packeteer.com/products/index.cfm`), provide bandwidth prioritization and allocation services. These services allow network administrators to increase the efficiency of applications by providing them the bandwidth necessary for optimum performance. Network managers are applications that are used to manage network services and do not provide bandwidth prioritization services. Packet sniffers are used to collect packet-level information, such as TCP and UDP data from the network. Quality of Service (QoS), the general name given to the services that bandwidth managers provide, is not a device and is not considered a correct answer here. See "Bridges and Other Devices."

10. **C**. To determine whether the WAN connections need to be upgraded, you should at the very least collect the maximum, minimum, and average network utilization on each connection. Answers A, B, and D all approach being correct in that the information they propose you collect is beneficial. However, to determine whether the WAN connections need to be upgraded, you must know the utilization of each. See "Bandwidth."

APPLY YOUR KNOWLEDGE

Suggested Readings and Resources

1. Microsoft TechNet Articles.

   • Chapter 7: Planning Your Windows 2000 Server Installation. Windows 2000 Corporate Preview Guide. Available on July 1999 and newer TechNet CDs.

   • Planning, Deploying, and Managing Highly Available Solutions. Available on June 1999 and newer TechNet CDs.

   • Planning Windows NT Server 4.0 Deployment with Windows 2000 in Mind. Available on January 1999 and newer TechNet CDs.

   • *Managing Infrastructure Deployment Projects.* Available on August 1999 and newer TechNet CDs.

2. Cone, Boggs, and Perez. *Planning for Windows 2000.* New Riders Publishing, 1999.

3. Nielsen, Morten Strunge. *Windows 2000 Server Architecture and Planning.* Coriolis, 1999.

This chapter continues the coverage of the following Microsoft-specified objective for the Designing a Microsoft Windows 2000 Directory Services Infrastructure exam:

Evaluate the company's existing and planned technical environment.

- **Analyze performance requirements.**

- **Analyze data and system access patterns.**

- **Analyze network roles and responsibilities.**

▶ Virtually everything you do to or with a computer affects its performance or the performance of a network to which it is attached. This fact drives the need to consider performance situations in the planning phases of a Windows 2000 implementation. Establishing a performance baseline with the current system is critical to determining where a company operates performance-wise today and what their comfort level is with that performance. The trending and analysis of this performance data will help you determine whether a server or other network device needs to be replaced, phased out, upgraded, or left alone.

To properly choose the trending and analysis data, you must understand what the system is used for, how many users attach and utilize the server, and what kind of data they access when doing so.

The role of the server and its network-related responsibilities also play a crucial role in both performance and server optimization.

CHAPTER 6

Analyzing Performance-Related Requirements

OUTLINE

STUDY STRATEGIES

▶ Get to know your performance analysis toolsets. Any time you need to analyze performance on a Windows 2000 system, you should automatically think "System Monitor."

▶ Take time to get familiar with the business for which performance analysis is necessary. To properly characterize performance data, you must understand how the business operates and what its growth potential is. Performance is a very broad topic, so to be successful at getting what you want out of an analysis, you must know what you are looking for.

▶ Spend a good amount of time "playing" with System Monitor before you take the exam so you understand how it works. Experiment with the System Monitor counters while testing various types of applications and loads to see how they affect the overall performance of the system.

INTRODUCTION

Performance impacts everything, and everything impacts performance. If you step back and think about it, this statement is not that far-fetched; in fact, it's pretty true! In this chapter, we'll utilize a six-step approach to explain how to accurately forecast performance requirements based on current trends and analyses. We'll also discuss several of the server roles within an organization and the performance-related metrics unique to each.

Trending and analysis are two things organizations just flat out don't do on a consistent basis. We'll explain how performing these two operations as well as characterizing the workload can have a positive impact on proactive management of the network and its resources. Additionally, we'll discuss implementing standard trending and analysis features that will help organizations remain on top of their networks.

Finally, we'll jump into Windows 2000 and discuss some of the server roles and responsibilities relative to performance. We'll also discuss at a high level some of the new Windows 2000 integrated technologies that impact performance on both the hardware and software levels.

This chapter carries on the eFly Airlines case study introduced in Chapter 5, "Analyzing the Physical Environment." You might want to review that case study before beginning this chapter.

WHAT IS A PERFORMANCE ANALYSIS?

A *performance analysis* is just that: an analysis of performance. You probably perform several performance analyses per day if you work around computers. "Why is this thing so slow?" To answer that question, you need to take into consideration several performance-related influences. For example, let's assume that "thing" is a standard desktop computer attached to the eFly network at one of the remote hubs. To Sam, the user, the PIII-500 computer with 128MB of RAM and a 10/100MB Ethernet NIC does absolutely no better pulling data from the membership database in St. Louis than did his old 486. Why? To answer this question you must understand what affects performance and how to detect performance bottlenecks. To Sam, the PIII-500 is junk because he can't get his data quick enough. To the infrastructure expert, the problem is simple to detect; there is a network bandwidth deficiency between the local site and the hub in St. Louis. This "bottleneck" slows all traffic between the remote hub and St. Louis to whatever its speed is.

SUCCESSFUL APPROACH TO PERFORMANCE MONITORING

The infrastructure expert didn't guess that bandwidth was the problem—he knew it, because he understood how to detect a bottleneck based on existing systems and applications.

Although this chapter won't make you an infrastructure expert, it will certainly shed light on what you need to do to successfully monitor both the network and servers. It will also help you understand how and why to optimize your servers. We'll utilize a six-step approach to ensure a successful analysis:

1. Determine a baseline.

2. Quantify measurement information.

3. Determine bottlenecks.

4. Determine feasible response time.

5. Project future needs.

6. Implement a performance analysis and trending standard.

By following these six steps, you will ensure that performance-related bottlenecks can be detected and reduced or eliminated. Additionally, with the integration of long-term trending and scheduled analysis and reporting, you'll be setting the framework for proactive capacity planning.

LEVERAGE THE KNOWLEDGE OF IT RESOURCES

Before we jump into these steps, it is important to consider the people that live the environment day to day before you begin collecting and analyzing data. IT administrators, help desk staff, infrastructure teams, and knowledge workers (users) will be able to provide valuable insight on the performance factors they deal with frequently. In some cases, you may be pleasantly surprised to find that some meaningful performance information is already available to you. Ask key members of the IT staff what kinds of performance-related problems they handle. If nothing else, it may give you a good heads-up regarding specific hardware or software to monitor.

DON'T FORGET THE INFRASTRUCTURE

When thinking performance, the underlying support infrastructure is often slighted in deference to the server network. You don't want to spend a considerable amount of time and resources analyzing the current server hardware and software only to find the performance problems are hung up in the routers and hubs.

Although we'll focus our attention on server hardware and Windows NT and Windows 2000 performance metrics, we'll point out when and where a specific performance problem points to the underlying support infrastructure. In fact, before you even look at the server hardware and operating systems, take time to inventory the supporting network infrastructure as you did in Chapter 5. Look for potential performance dampeners, such as the use of hubs instead of switches, or old and overworked routers.

STEP 1: DETERMINE A BASELINE

To have something against which to compare future performance data, you must establish a baseline of performance data. To explain this process, we will utilize the Windows 2000 System Monitor, which is the next generation of the NT Performance Monitor.

EXAM TIP

Utilize Baseline Information
Having a baseline available will help you read between the lines of a scenario and determine if the network is healthy or not. When planning a Windows 2000 site, bandwidth is the key determining factor for site placement. If, for example, there is enough available bandwidth but it is 80% utilized, you will have to address the utilization or modify your design plan.

NOTE

Accessing the System Monitor
The Windows 2000 System Monitor is accessed by selecting the Performance option in the Administrative Tools (see Figure 6.1).

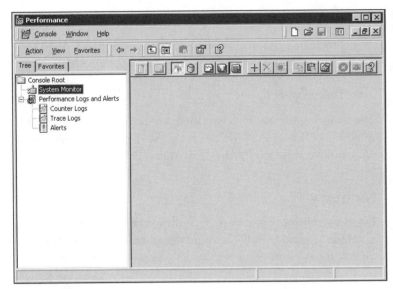

FIGURE 6.1

Windows 2000 System Monitor.

IN THE FIELD

PERFORMANCE MONITOR VERSUS SYSTEM MONITOR

Windows NT included a utility for analyzing performance called *Performance Monitor*. This utility, while adequate in its lifetime, was quite limited in what it could do. For example, when collecting performance data to a log file for future analysis, you were required to capture all counters for the selected object. Some objects contain 20 or more counters, so you can imagine the overhead this added to a server doing the logging. Additionally, analyzing the data was complex because you had to sift through all the different counters to come up with the data you needed. The Windows 2000 System Monitor fixes this problem by allowing counter-level logging, which pinpoints the data you want for a given situation, reduces the size of the log file, and reduces the complexity of the ensuing analysis.

What Data Should I Capture?

The System Monitor utility includes objects for capturing just about every performance-related attribute on a Windows NT or Windows 2000 server. Applications may also populate the System Monitor with objects specific to their usage. In this chapter, we'll focus on capturing data for the following system-critical performance objects:

> **NOTE**
>
> **Performance Objects** *Performance objects* refers to the actual objects, such as processor, memory, and so on, that the System Monitor application utilizes to capture performance-related data.

◆ Memory

◆ Processor

◆ Network subsystem

◆ Disk subsystem

The following sections highlight these key performance objects and what to look for on the physical system. We'll dig a bit deeper into each of these objects in "Step 3: Determine Bottlenecks."

Memory

Inadequate memory in a server will cause excessive paging and significantly reduced overall system performance. As a general rule of thumb, the more memory you can have in a system, the better—within reason.

Memory considerations should not stop at physical RAM. The page file, used for virtual memory in all versions of Windows, plays a crucial role in performance. In both Windows NT and Windows 2000, you can optimize memory performance by strategically locating the page file on nonsystem disks with low utilization (see Figure 6.2).

The memory object in System Monitor can be used to track a number of counters, such as Pages/Sec. Pages/Sec displays the number of requested pages that were not immediately available in RAM, that consequently had to be accessed from the hard disk page file. In Step 3, we'll discuss several additional memory object counters that can be used to detect memory bottlenecks.

Processor

Just about everything that happens on a computer involves the CPU. Even when a machine is sitting still with nobody logged onto it, the processor still needs to handle service interrupts and provide its services to any application or service that may need them. Different classes of processors (Alpha, Intel, Motorola, and so on) operate at different speeds and utilize different instruction sets to complete processing. Some are more efficient than others. Computers with more than one processor have the ability to split the load between them, therefore reducing the burden on each and increasing performance.

> **WARNING**
>
> **Too Much Memory?** Be careful to size your system with adequate memory and room to grow, but don't go out and blindly buy enough to fill a system to capacity. Consider the repercussions, such as a page file greater than 4GB for Windows 2000 Server.

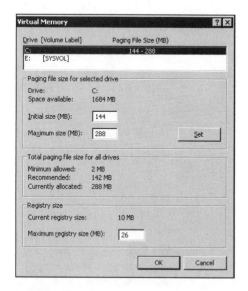

FIGURE 6.2
Windows 2000 virtual memory configuration.

The processor is used more on some systems than on others. For example, it is generally used more frequently on an application server than on a file and print server because of the increased number of services and drivers it must support.

The processor System Monitor object contains a slew of processor related counters. The ones we'll primarily focus on are %Processor Time, %Privileged Time, and %User Time. You'll learn more about each of these counters in Step 3.

Network Subsystem

As you can imagine, several factors might influence the overall performance of the network. Each of these factors must be individually analyzed to determine if its performance affects the overall performance of the network. Each can then be summarized to get an overall picture of network performance.

Table 6.1 describes each section of the network subsystem and some of the associated System Monitor objects used to monitor performance. The objects listed are not all-inclusive, but rather represent a majority of the common objects used to monitor network information.

You'll recall from Chapter 5 the physical inventory of networking hardware devices. This network subsystem analysis is just one area where that information will prove to be useful.

Disk Subsystem

In much the same way that the components of the network subsystem impact the overall performance of the network, the components of the disk subsystem influence the overall disk I/O performance. There are a number of components that make up the entire disk subsystem, and not unlike the network subsystem, a number of System Monitor objects must be analyzed both individually and together to get an accurate reading on disk performance.

Table 6.2 describes each section of the disk subsystem and some of the associated System Monitor objects.

> NOTE
>
> **Network Segment Object** The Network Segment object is only available after the installation of the network monitor agent. This object places the NIC in "promiscuous mode," which allows it to analyze all network traffic, not just traffic destined to it. Use this counter wisely, as it does increase the load on the server, which may skew data.

TABLE 6.1

NETWORK SUBSYSTEM AND ASSOCIATED SYSTEM MONITOR OBJECTS

Network Subsystem Component	Role	System Monitor Counters
Network Interface Cards	Provides throughput between the server resources and physical network	Server Network Interface
Number of Users	Network load factor	Server
Network Infrastructure Hardware	Routers, bridges, switches, hubs, and so on. Provide intelligent transport of data	Network Segment Network Interface
Network Protocols	Provides a common means of transporting data from computer to computer	TCP, UDP, IP, NBT, NetBEUI, NetBEUI Resource, Nwlink IPX, Nwlink SPX, Nwlink NetBIOS
Network Services	Serves a specific function on the network, such as name resolution	Network interface Network segment Objects specific to network services (such as WINS, DNS, DHCP, RAS)
Network Applications	Software that resides on the servers that provide services to clients and other servers	Application-specific objects
Directory Services	Provides network identity, security, authentication, and several other network services	Server

TABLE 6.2

DISK SUBSYSTEM AND ASSOCIATED SYSTEM MONITOR OBJECTS

Disk Subsystem Component	Role	System Monitor Counters
Controller(s)	Provides a means for reading and writing data to disk	Physical Disk
Caching	Improves disk performance by temporarily storing information on the controller	Physical Disk
RAID Controllers (hardware-based)	Provides options for significant improvement of disk I/O	Logical Disk Physical Disk
Type of Work	Based on applications, defines whether processes are disk bound (I/O intensive)	Logical Disk Physical Disk
Type of Drives	Describes disk access time, latency, and so on.	Physical Disk

System Monitor disk counters are not enabled by default. To enable them, you must make use of the `diskperf` command, which has a variety of options as described in Table 6.3.

TABLE 6.3

ENABLING AND DISABLING SYSTEM MONITOR DISK COUNTERS

Switch	Description
-y	Enables all disk counters at the next reboot
-yd	Enables only the physical disk counters at the next reboot
-yv	Enables only the logical disk or storage volume counters at the next reboot
-n	Disables all disk counters at the next reboot
-nd	Disables only the physical disk counters at the next reboot
-nv	Disables only the logical disk or storage volume counters at the next reboot
\\computername	Redirects the request to enable/disable disk counters on a remote computer

NOTE

Physical and Logical Disk Counters In case you need a refresher, *physical disk* counters measure the activity of a single physical hard drive, whereas *logical disk* counters measure activity on a partition or logical drive within a physical disk or set of disks.

Application Resources

In addition to the aforementioned "core" performance objects, it may be important to include some application-specific performance objects in your baseline. For example, if the company heavily uses Exchange throughout the enterprise (or in specific pockets), it would be quite beneficial to include counters from the Exchange performance object in the baseline. This object would record the Exchange-based activity (RPC calls, message volume, queue lengths, and so on) and can graphically present it in System Monitor.

Collecting Data for a Baseline

The process of collecting data for a baseline begins with choosing the correct data to capture. We described the four major components in this section for a reason; they should be collected under all circumstances. Additional data, such as WINS, DNS, and application-specific data like Exchange and SQL traffic, should be captured if it is in use on the particular network you are monitoring.

Data Gathering Timeline

After you've determined the objects and associated counters you are going to collect, you need to determine how often you want to log the data. It is recommended that your first set of data be captured at a maximum of every minute. This will yield a pretty large file, but will also give you an accurate representation of the counters. It is important to use a computer other than the one you are collecting data from to generate the logs, since the process of writing to the log file every minute might skew your results. Make sure this computer has adequate space to store the log files.

A good baseline can be completed in about three days of normal work activity. This brings up an important point; you want to make sure there is nothing "special" going on during your baseline. In other words, capture data while people are working normally.

Once you capture the three-day baseline, set up an automated logging process to capture data once every 5 or 10 minutes. This will provide you with ongoing data for trends and analysis work as you move forward with the performance analysis. Figure 6.3 illustrates where you make the changes to the logging interval.

System Monitor Logs

The System Monitor tool is capable of capturing data and exporting it to another application for analysis. Before you export it, however, you must somehow store the data as you are capturing it.

NOTE

The Use of Logs The System Monitor utility provides logging functionality so data may be captured over time and referenced at a later date for analysis.

NOTE

Log File Sizes Depending on what you log, the System Monitor log files when logging every 60 seconds can range anywhere from about 1MB to several hundred MB per 24-hour period.

NOTE

Performance Monitor Versus System Monitor Logs Performance Monitor logs in Windows NT 4.0 are only capable of capturing *all* counters within a specific object (such as memory). In Windows 2000's implementation of the System Monitor, you have the ability to select specific counters in the log view. This really cuts down on log file sizes and makes the data easier to manipulate.

The System Monitor logging option gives you the ability to capture data for long periods of time and store it in a format that can be easily opened in another application. One such format is a CSV (Comma Separated Value) file. CSVs may be imported into various data analysis tools, such as Microsoft Excel, SQL Server, Access, and many more. "Step Two: Quantify Measurement Information" discusses analysis of the log files further.

STEP 2: QUANTIFY MEASUREMENT INFORMATION

The second step is to quantify the performance information by creating a measurement database. In the first step, we discussed the objects and counters we needed to measure, and used the System Monitor utility to begin capturing data in a log file format. This short step discusses how to take that information from the performance log files and migrate it to an analysis tool.

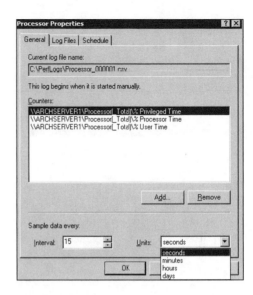

FIGURE 6.3
To change the logging interval, select the number of hours, minutes, or seconds on the general property page of your log settings.

Starting and Stopping the Logging Process

To capture the data for analysis, you must first define your log parameters, start the log, then stop the log and export the log file. Step by Step 6.1 describes the process of defining a log using the Windows 2000 System Monitor.

STEP BY STEP

6.1 Defining a Log in Windows 2000 System Monitor

1. Open System Monitor by clicking Start, Programs, Administrative Tools, Performance.

2. Expand Performance Logs and Alerts in the left Explorer window.

continues

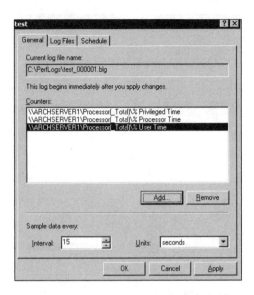

FIGURE 6.4
Completed System Monitor log configuration.

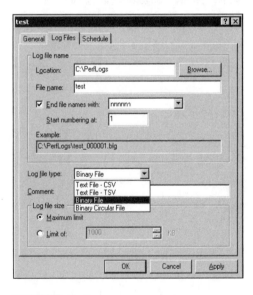

FIGURE 6.5
Log Files tab, which displays options for the log file.

continued

3. Click the Counter Logs option.

4. Right-click anywhere in the right pane and select New Log Settings.

5. Type any name for the log file and click OK.

6. Click the Add button to begin adding object counters to the log.

7. In the Add to Log dialog box, choose the server from which you want to log performance information.

8. Choose the objects and counters you wish to monitor and click Add. When finished, click Close. Your configuration should resemble that of Figure 6.4.

9. Click on the Log Files tab (see Figure 6.5).

10. In the Log File Type drop-down list, select Text File— CSV. This will allow you to export the logged data to a database for analysis. You may also change the filename and location for the log from this window.

11. Click the Schedule tab to customize the start and stop options. If you leave this alone, as soon as you save the log it starts to collect data.

12. Click OK to save and close the log. Keep in mind that it will start running unless you changed the schedule to manual or a later time. You can use the context menu on the log object you just created to start and stop it.

Preparing the Log File for Analysis

Once you have a log file ready for analysis, you must import it into an appropriate application. Any application that can read a CSV file should be able to open the log data.

STEP 3: DETERMINE BOTTLENECKS

The third step in the performance analysis is to determine where there are bottlenecks. Bottlenecks define a part or parts of a computer system as a whole that restrict the workflow and in general, cause a system to slow down. You'll use the performance data you captured in Step 2 to determine bottlenecks.

Workload Characterization

Finding a system bottleneck is not an exact science. You can't just look at the data and understand exactly where the bottlenecks exist. Because of this, you should use a workload characterization approach.

Workload characterization refers to the categorization of servers. For example, servers performing specific roles in the network environment have specific performance related expectations. The following sections discuss the popular server roles and where you should look for bottlenecks in each. In all cases, you should not ignore the four core performance objects introduced earlier in the section "What Data Should I Capture?"

File and Print Servers

The obvious use of a file and print server is to host file and printer shares that are accessed by users over the network. In some cases, these servers will also be used as installation points for applications. Because file and print servers host objects that require extensive disk access, disk I/O would be a good place to look for a bottleneck.

> **NOTE**
>
> **Analyzing Data Outside of System Monitor** Although you can use the System Monitor utility to analyze log file information, we recommend that you use an external utility so you can have more granular control over your data.

In short, make sure you analyze closely the performance counters captured for the physical and logical disk objects on file and print servers. One other area that influences the performance of file and print servers is the number of users accessing their resources at a given time. For these numbers, check the server sessions counter within the server object.

Application Servers

Application servers are unique in that their main purpose is to provide the server end of client/server software applications. Because they run one or more server-side applications, they require more RAM than file and print servers. For application servers, pay close attention to the memory and page file object counters. Additionally, because application servers require clients to connect over a network, you should investigate the server sessions counter within the server object, as well as the network related counters. You may also find high processor utilization on these servers and hence should keep an eye on the processor object counters.

Applications installed on application servers often populate the performance monitor object list with objects of their own. Make sure you utilize these objects and their associated counters to provide a picture of traffic patterns within the application.

Domain Controllers

The primary use of a domain controller is to validate logons. You should automatically investigate the logons/sec server object. In large enterprises where there are multiple domain controllers replicating account databases, network utilization will come into play, especially if replication occurs over a WAN link. Keep in mind that replication of the SAM account database originates from the PDC in a Windows NT 4.0 environment. In a Windows 2000 environment with multi-master replication, there is no PDC, and replication occurs in and between all replication partner domain controllers in the same domain, and between global catalog servers throughout the forest.

EXAM TIP

Application Server Performance Can Depend on Placement
Effective placement of application servers can improve performance. Plan to place each server in the location closest to its primary users. If users are across a WAN link, consider placing the server on the same side of the link as the users.

Memory Bottlenecks

Hands down, the most common type of bottleneck found in an NT server is a RAM (memory) bottleneck. To understand how to detect a memory bottleneck, we'll review quickly the memory model in Windows NT 4.0, which has not changed drastically in Windows 2000.

Paged and Non-Paged RAM

Memory, specifically RAM, is divided into two types: paged and non-paged. Paged RAM is virtual, which allows all applications to believe they have access to the entire installation of memory. Each application is given a bank of private memory addresses, which are mapped to physical memory. Non-paged RAM, on the other hand, must remain in main memory and cannot be read from or written to.

Virtual Memory

Virtual memory combines the RAM, disk, and file system cache to form a paging file that supplements the physical RAM. Data is stored on disk in a page file until needed and is then moved into physical memory. To make room for new data, existing data in main memory is then moved back to the page file.

IN THE FIELD

HARD PAGE FAULTS

One very clear indication of a memory bottleneck is the number of hard page faults over an extended period of time. Hard page faults occur when an application wants data from RAM and it's not there. Windows NT and 2000, to satisfy the request, must access the data from the much slower hard disks. Hard page faults in excess of more than 5 per second are a dead giveaway of a memory bottleneck.

Detecting Memory Bottlenecks

To determine whether RAM is experiencing a bottleneck, you should use the following memory object System Monitor counters:

◆ **Pages/Sec.** The number of requested pages that were not immediately available in physical RAM and, hence, had to be extracted from paged memory on disk.

◆ **Available Bytes.** The amount of available physical RAM. The number of available bytes will typically be low because the cache manager uses available memory for caching operations and returns it when needed.

◆ **Committed Bytes.** The amount of virtual memory that has either been committed to physical RAM or to the page file.

◆ **Pool Non-Paged Bytes.** The amount of RAM in the non-paged pool system memory area that is committed to operating system tasks.

Table 6.4 lists the above memory counters and describes thresholds you should look for.

TABLE 6.4

MEMORY OBJECT COUNTER VALUES THAT COULD INDICATE A MEMORY BOTTLENECK

Counter	Threshold	Potential Bottleneck Indicator
Pages/Sec	0–20	Consistently over 5
Available Bytes	Minimum of 4MB	Consistently under 4MB; this could indicate excessive paging
Committed Bytes	Less than physical RAM	Consistently larger than physical RAM
Pool Non-Paged Bytes	No increase; remain steady	Steadily increasing without ever decreasing; this could indicate a memory leak

---

Figure 6.6 illustrates how a System Monitor configuration may be used to find memory bottlenecks.

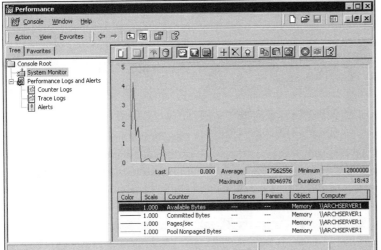

FIGURE 6.6
System Monitor configured for memory object counters.

Processor Bottlenecks

CPU-bound applications, excessive paging, and inadequacies in other areas of a computer, such as memory, can cause the CPU utilization to increase. CPU utilization from one server to the next may change drastically, even though the servers "seem" to be used by the same number of users. Application servers, for example, are particularly hard on the CPU because they are expected to do a lot of data processing. One thing you must take into consideration when analyzing processor utilization is the thought process behind the design of today's computers: An idle CPU is a wasted CPU. You can expect, therefore, that CPU utilization will rarely, if ever be 0 even if the server is "idle."

The following processor object System Monitor counters should be considered when trying to detect a processor bottleneck:

- ◆ **%Processor Time.** Amount of time the processor is busy.

- ◆ **%Privileged Time.** Amount of time a processor spends performing OS services.

- ◆ **%User Time.** Amount of time a processor spends performing user services.

Additionally, the following two system and server object System Monitor counters are important in determining processor congestion:

◆ **Processor Queue Length (system object).** The number of requests the processor has in its queue waiting to be executed.

◆ **Queue Length (server object).** The number of requests in the queue for the processor.

Table 6.5 describes what to look for in each of these processor-related counters. Figure 6.7 contains a graphical representation of the processor-related counters.

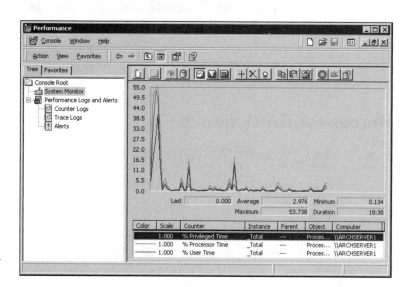

FIGURE 6.7

System Monitor configured to view processor-related counters.

TABLE 6.5

PROCESSOR-RELATED COUNTERS THAT CAN BE USED TO DETECT A PROCESSOR BOTTLENECK

Counter	Threshold	Potential Bottleneck Indicator
%Processor Time	Below 75%	Consistently over 75%
%Privileged Time	Below 75%	Consistently over 75%
%User Time	Below 75%	Consistently over 75%
System: Processor Queue Length	Less than 2	Consistently over 2
Server: Queue Length	Less than 2	Consistently over 2

If you detect a processor bottleneck, you have three options:

◆ Upgrade or replace the processor.

◆ Add an additional processor.

◆ Offload some of the CPU-intensive applications to a different server.

There is not a single recommended action for this scenario. You may even find that the reason a processor is overutilized is due to excessive paging due to lack of RAM. In this case, you could alleviate the problem by adding memory and possibly relocating the page file. This would primarily be a judgment call based on the current environment and planned technology implementations.

Network Bottlenecks

Pinpointing a network bottleneck is difficult. As we discussed earlier, there are several factors that may influence the overall performance of the network. To make things a bit easier, think of the network as two separate entities:

◆ Network infrastructure components, such as routers, switches, and hubs

◆ Server-based network elements, such as the NIC and protocol bindings

By delineating your network components this way, you can immediately split network bottleneck detection time in half with the correct data.

Network Infrastructure Components

In Chapter 5, we discussed the networking infrastructure components and some of the things to watch out for in terms of performance influences. We now are going to focus on how to determine if those components are in fact causing a bottleneck. This is one area where the Network Monitor utility will benefit you. This "sniffer" utility captures data packets as they travel across the network. Figure 6.8 illustrates the network monitor in action.

NOTE

"Native" Network Monitor The Network Monitor utility requires that Network Monitor Agents be installed from Windows NT/2000 Add/Remove Programs. Also, this "native" version is not as feature-rich as the version that ships with Microsoft Systems Management Server, which includes drivers for other operating systems (the native version includes drivers only for Windows 2000).

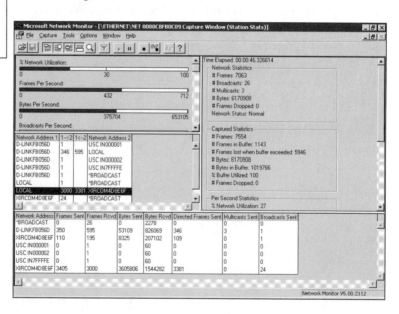

FIGURE 6.8

Network monitor in action on a network.

An analysis of the captured Network Monitor data should yield performance influences such as traffic patterns, protocols in use on the network, and source and destination addresses. You can deduce from this analysis where a particular problem may exist, trends in network utilization, and more. This information is best used as a supplement to the System Monitor data captured about the network segment.

Server-Based Network Elements

The server-based network elements consist of the NIC type and speed, number of users attaching, protocols, network services, applications, and directory services. A bottleneck can be located within any of these elements, or can be a result of a combination of two or more of them. This is where the complexity comes in. You must have some way to determine which networking element is the culprit. To do this, you must analyze all elements separately as well as together.

Network-Related System Monitor Counters

There are a number of network-related System Monitor objects, especially when each protocol stack is taken into account. You need to determine which objects to monitor given your environment. For example, if you are in a complete NetWare 3.x or 4.x environment, you would need to monitor IPX- and SPX-related information as well as SAP and RIP information.

The following list describes some of the network-related System Monitor counters. We stress *some* here; these do not comprise an exhaustive list of counters for the network segment:

◆ **Server: Bytes Total/Sec.** Describes the number of bytes the server has sent and received on the network. You can determine how busy the server is in terms of network I/O using this counter.

◆ **Server: Logons/Sec.** This counter is important to collect on domain controllers. It describes the number of local, over-the-network, and service account authentication attempts per second.

◆ **Server: Logons/Total.** This counter is important to collect on domain controllers. It describes the number of local, over-the-network, and service account authentications that have occurred since the performance data collection started.

◆ **Network Segment: %Network Utilization.** Use this counter in conjunction with the Network Monitor data. It describes the utilization of network bandwidth on the segment being monitored.

◆ **Network Interface: Bytes Sent/Sec.** Describes the number of bytes sent out to the network from a specific NIC.

◆ **Network Interface: Bytes Total/Sec.** Describes the number of bytes sent and received per second through a particular NIC.

Table 6.6 describes how these network-related System Monitor counters can be used to determine bottlenecks. Figure 6.9 illustrates what the System Monitor analysis for these counters looks like. Again, this is not all-inclusive, but does represent the most popular counters.

> **NOTE**
>
> **Adding Network Interface Counters**
> The network interface counters are added to a TCP/IP host only after the SNMP service is installed.

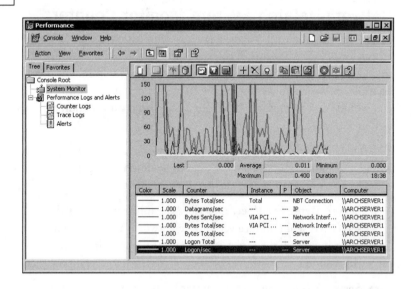

FIGURE 6.9
System Monitor representation of network-related counters.

TABLE 6.6

NETWORK-RELATED SYSTEM MONITOR COUNTERS

Counter	Threshold	Potential Bottleneck Indicator and Solution
Bytes Total/Sec (Server)	High, but not extreme	If number is extremely high and network utilization is low, consider adding a NIC and splitting the load between the two.
Logons/Sec (Server)	High, but not extreme	If number is extremely high and processor utilization is high, consider adding an additional domain controller.
Logons/Total (Server)	High, but not extreme	If number is more than 200, consider adding a domain controller.
%Network Utilization (Network Segment)	Up to 50% on switched networks; 30% otherwise	Analyze with Network Monitor, and trace and compare network traffic with utilization. Determine what network traffic can be reduced. May point to physical infrastructure.
Bytes Sent/Sec (Network Interface)	Dependent on NIC and protocols; should be a high number	If number is extremely high, consider adding a NIC or removing unnecessary protocols. Could be related to physical infrastructure as well. Analyze applications to determine traffic flow.
Bytes Total/Sec (Network Interface)	Dependent on NIC and protocols; should be a high number	If number is extremely high, consider adding a NIC or removing unnecessary protocols. Could be related to physical infrastructure as well. Analyze applications to determine traffic flow.

Protocols

You could have the most optimized network infrastructure possible and still have performance degradation due to the improper use of core networking protocols. A good rule of thumb is to utilize primary and secondary protocols. This provides a basic level of protocol fault tolerance. Which protocol is used in which role is up to the corporation, but we recommend in any environment that TCP/IP be the standard primary protocol. Our choice for the secondary protocol may come as a surprise if you expect NetBEUI to be recommended in this role; we instead recommend IPX/SPX (NWLink) because it is routable, whereas NetBEUI is not.

> **NOTE**
>
> **Protocol Binding Order** Pay close attention to the binding order of networking protocols, especially on client computers because it is the client that initiates the communications protocol with the server.

What we see in some corporations as we analyze the networking infrastructure is both inefficient and nonstandard protocol utilization. For example, one server might have TCP/IP and IPX/SPX (NWLink) installed, while others have TCP/IP and NetBEUI installed. In both cases, there is only one standard protocol. The other is "dead weight" and should be dropped if it doesn't serve a purpose.

With Windows 2000, it is not recommended that you standardize on TCP/IP—it is *required*. If there was ever any doubt which protocol should be first in the binding order, it has been cleared up with Windows 2000.

Name Resolution Services

A key element in any Microsoft network is name resolution services. WINS and DNS in particular have a bearing on the perceived performance of the overall network. In a Windows NT 4.0 network, WINS especially needs to be examined for optimal configuration. You may recall from configuring WINS through DHCP that you must specify a WINS/NBT Node Type before completing WINS configuration. Table 6.7 describes WINS/NBT node types and the name resolution processes for each:

TABLE 6.7

WINS/NBT NODE TYPES

Node Type	Name Resolution Process
0x1 = B-node (Microsoft modified B-node)	1. Check LMHOSTS cache. 2. Broadcast. 3. Check LMHOSTS file (Windows NT only).
0x2 = P-node	1. NetBIOS Name Server (WINS) only
0x4 = M-node	1. B-node 2. P-node
0x8 = H-node	1. Check whether name is local name. 2. Check cache of remote names (ARP). 3. WINS. 4. Broadcast. 5. LMHOSTS File (optional). 6. HOSTS File (optional). 7. DNS (optional).

The configuration of the NetBIOS over TCP/IP (NBT) node type is important to performance because its improper configuration may be generating unnecessary traffic in the form of broadcasts. The optimum configuration is H-node because it uses directed user datagram (UDP) packets to resolve names from a WINS server first, and only sends out broadcast packets if WINS is not available. Broadcasting does not cross networks, which means if B-node or M-node are being utilized, a significant amount of broadcast traffic is being produced that may or may not serve a purpose, depending on which network the recipient is on.

The point here is to take the time to identify how clients and servers are resolving NetBIOS names. We assume that WINS is in place in a Windows NT environment because of its ease of use and popularity. If broadcasts are being used over a name server, suggest changing it. Once the move to Windows 2000 is complete and DNS takes over the name resolution services, WINS and NetBIOS will eventually become a nonissue, but that time is still a while off in most cases.

NOTE

WINS/NBT Node Type To read more about WINS and the NetBIOS of TCP/IP name resolution processes, please see the TechNet article "NetBIOS over TCP/IP Name Resolution and WINS."

Addressing Network Subsystem Bottlenecks

If you determine that you do in fact have a network subsystem-related bottleneck, there are several viable options you have geared at helping you solve the problem. The following list highlights these options:

◆ **Add NIC(s) to the server.** By adding NICs, you have the ability to create a load balanced "team" of NICs. In this scenario, the network load could be evenly distributed between all NICs, thereby reducing the load on a single NIC.

◆ **Upgrade to a higher performance NIC.** If you have 10BT Ethernet card, upgrade to 100MB or 10/100MB or even FDDI if possible.

◆ **Upgrade the network infrastructure.** If the physical network is verifiably causing the problem, consider replacing hubs with switches; old routers with new; CAT III cable with CAT V, VI, or VII; and so on.

◆ **Add more servers and domain controllers.** If you find the performance problems are related to logon authentications, add a domain controller.

◆ **Segment the network.** Using TCP/IP subnetting, create several subnets with no more than 255 nodes permitted on each. This will reduce the broadcast zone by keeping broadcast traffic at home on the originating network.

Disk Bottlenecks

Performance problems related to the disk subsystem are a little easier to find than network-related problems. The disk subsystem consists of controllers, caching, type of work being performed, and the type of drives. You'll probably not be able to pinpoint a disk bottleneck without using the System Monitor counters because there is really no dead giveaway that points directly to the disk subsystem as the problem.

Use the following System Monitor disk object counters to detect a bottleneck:

◆ **%Disk Time.** Describes the total amount of time a disk is busy servicing read and write operations.

◆ **Disk Queue Length.** Describes the number of pending I/O requests for the disk.

◆ **Avg. Disk Bytes/Transfer.** Describes the average number of bytes transferred to or from the disk during read or write operations.

◆ **Disk Bytes/Sec.** Describes the rate at which bytes are transferred to or from the disk during read or write operations.

Table 6.8 lists these System Monitor counters and describes what we expect to see and what to look out for. Figure 6.10 illustrates the system performance monitor representation of disk subsystem counters.

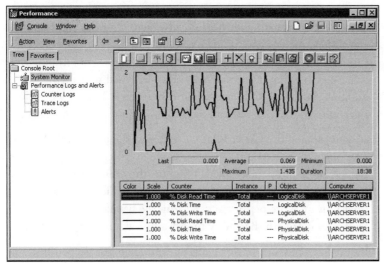

FIGURE 6.10
System Monitor representation of disk
subsystem-related counters.

TABLE 6.8

SYSTEM MONITOR DISK OBJECT COUNTERS

Counter	Threshold	Potential Bottleneck Indicator
%Disk Time	Keep under 50%	If disk utilization is consistently significantly over 50%, the disk is being punished.
Disk Queue Length	Keep under 2	If queue length is consistently over 2, it indicates disk congestion.
Avg. Disk Bytes/ Transfer	Higher the better	If number is steadily decreasing, it could indicate the impending failure of a hard disk, or could signify an increased requirement for data processing.
Disk Bytes/Sec	Higher the better	If number is steadily decreasing, it could indicate the impending failure of a hard disk, or could signify an increased requirement for data processing.

There are a number of actions you can take if you determine a bottleneck is occurring in the disk subsystem. You can add faster controllers, such as Fast SCSI-3, or on-board caching controllers if throughput is a problem. You can also offload users, applications, or other disk-busying influences to another less used server. Finally, examine the use of RAID arrays for disk storage. Table 6.9 describes the common RAID levels and rates them in terms of performance.

As you can see, the fastest RAID level across the board is RAID 0. The downfall of RAID 0—the reason we don't see it very much—is there is no fault tolerance. RAID 5 offers the most benefit because of its read performance. Most organizations are willing to take a (very small) hit on write performance to reap the benefits of RAID 5— fault tolerance with the ability to lose a disk without going down.

It's outside the scope of this book to drill down any deeper into RAID technologies, but if you're interested in more information, there is a great TechNet article called "Tuning Windows NT Server Disk Subsystems." We recommend that you read it if you are responsible for making servers fast!

TABLE 6.9

PERFORMANCE RATINGS FOR VARIOUS RAID LEVELS

RAID Level	*Random Read*	*Random Write*	*Sequential Read*	*Sequential Write*
0 (Stripe)	1	1	1	1
1 (Mirror)	2	2	3	2
5 (Stripe set with parity)	1	3	1	3

(1=Fastest, 2=Second Fastest, 3=Slowest)

Step 4: Determine Feasible Response Time

The need to determine how long a system *should* take to respond to a specific request is important. Often, users in the networking environment will complain of slow computers, saturated network, or something else related to the inefficiency of the network. Although they are sometimes right, they can be flat out wrong, too. You know that, your boss knows that, but how do you tell the user that? You can't just say "You're wrong" (wouldn't that be nice!). You have to show them that it's not just them.

Wouldn't it be nice if everyone could expect Server1 to respond to User1, User2, and User3 in exactly the same way in exactly the same amount of time? Yes it would—but we know that isn't possible all the time.

For this reason, you must take the information you collected in Steps 1–3 and use it to determine how a system should respond given its workload, hardware configuration, and role within the network. From this data, you can specify the limits of the system and communicate them. This will make everyone, especially management, aware of limits and will set performance-related expectations.

Step 5: Project Future Needs

Performing routine and accurate analysis on your performance data is a good practice to get into. With this data, you can determine trends and observe usage patterns that are not easily seen without performance data.

You will probably see more and more larger companies expecting significant performance gains when they move to Windows 2000. Although they may very well see those gains, Windows 2000 can only do so much. As you begin to project future needs, make sure you have an optimal configuration on which to base those needs; don't expect Windows 2000 to alleviate problems it has no control over, such as network infrastructure configuration or RAID array configuration.

To make a long story short, for you to accurately project the future needs of a company in terms of network infrastructure and servers, you have to keep a constant eye on performance indicators and trends. The next step discusses the implementation of such analysis and trending operations.

Step 6: Implement a Performance Analysis and Trending Standard

Establishing a performance-monitoring standard will help you proactively stay on top of performance-related issues. Additionally, it will help plan for resource and budgetary needs and can be used for preventative maintenance information.

Graphical Trend Reports

One way to present this information is in the form of standard trend reports that illustrate current usage patterns in comparison with historical usage patterns.

The chart in Figure 6.11 illustrates a typical trend report for the processor utilization on a server. In this report, you can see that from one reporting period to the next, the processor utilization increased significantly. IT managers can use this report to justify the purchase of an additional processor to proactively alleviate the potential processor bottleneck problem—before it happens. Now imagine the impact similar reports for memory, network, disk, and other metrics would have on an organization's ability to stop problems before they happen!

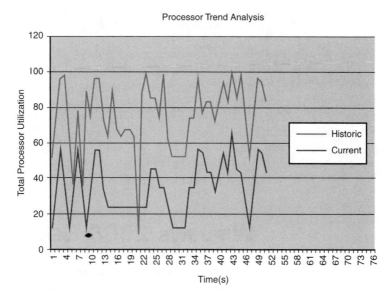

FIGURE 6.11
Processor performance trend report.

You can use the System Monitor to collect performance data for trend analysis. Be sure to set the file type to CSV if you plan to export it to Excel, Access, or other data analysis tools. Also, set the data sample interval significantly higher than the default. Collect data once an hour or so as a standard to keep the file sizes down.

Numerical Reports

Graphical reports are good for visualizing the data and for trend analysis. Numerical reports are important to show percentages; maximum, minimum, and average utilization; and other statistics not easily shown on a graph. While graphical trend reports sum up extended periods of time, such as a week, a month, or even a quarter on one page, numerical reports are best suited for daily analysis. Consider processor utilization: A numerical report would show maximum, minimum, and average utilization for a server's processor throughout the day. Figure 6.12 illustrates a simple report that could be automated without writing more than a few macros. It is simple, but effective.

Processor Utilization Report		
	Historical	*Current Week*
Average	34.35	74.88
Max	65	100
Min	12	8

FIGURE 6.12
Simple Excel-based utilization report for
current versus historical processor utilization.

WINDOWS 2000 SERVER ROLES

So where does all this performance analysis really impact Windows 2000 and directory services? Obviously, the four core performance areas have a great deal of impact with Windows 2000 and Active Directory, as well as any other OS on the market. We're now going to focus on the five major Windows 2000 server roles and rate the importance of each performance object to each role (see Table 6.10).

TABLE 6.10

PERFORMANCE OBJECT RATING WITHIN WINDOWS 2000 SERVER ROLES

Server Role	Processor	Memory	Network Subsystem	Disk Subsystem
Domain Controller	2	1	1	3
File/Print	3	2	2	1
Web Server	3	2	1	3
Database	1	2	2	1
Numerical Analysis	1	2	3	3

(1=Critical, 2=Important, 3=Unimportant)

Domain Controllers

In a Windows 2000 environment, domain controllers have several responsibilities, which include the following:

◆ Host Active Directory and related services.

◆ Authenticate clients and services.

◆ Host the Global Catalog.

◆ Provide Operations Masters services.

◆ Act as Kerberos Key Distribution servers.

◆ Provide WINS, DDNS, DHCP, DFS, and other services.

Basically, the network and memory are the crucial elements of domain controllers, although they can potentially perform quite a bit of processor-intensive work. The one thing that is not as important with Domain Controllers is the disk subsystem.

> **EXAM TIP**
>
> **Controller Roles and Placement are Critical** Being at ease with decisions about placement and the required number of operations master servers per segment/ domain/site is an absolute must for performing well on the exam.

File/Print Servers

A whole bunch of storage and quick access to and from it satisfies the critical needs of file and print servers. The CPU is not important in terms of processing power (although be careful not to under-power the server). You should pay close attention to the configuration of the disk subsystem. These servers should have large RAID 5 arrays for quick read capability and fault tolerance.

Web Servers

The Web and FTP servers really should have a single purpose for being on the network: validating and responding to user requests for Web pages. In some cases, Web servers process pages prior to transmission (such as is the case with Active Server Pages). In these cases, the CPU becomes more important. In all Web server cases, however, the optimization of the network subsystem is critical.

Database Servers

You could argue that all four components should be equally important in database servers. If you think about it, a fair number of "back office" applications can be considered database applications. Exchange Server is a good example. We've labeled mass storage as the key critical component of database servers, simply because they require massive amounts of storage. Optimization of the disk subsystem will have the most bearing on performance of these servers, although CPU, memory, and the network subsystem all vie closely for second.

Numerical Analysis Servers

Systems that are responsible for performing intense graphics operations, statistical analysis, or other CPU-intensive operations must obviously have the processing power to do so. In most cases, multiple CPUs are recommended for these systems along with a gob of memory for caching.

Server Service

One thing common to all NT servers but not mentioned yet is the configurable server service. The purpose of the server service is to establish sessions with remote stations and receive server message block (SMB) request messages from those stations. Its configuration (see Step by Step 6.2) affects the overall performance of the server by adjusting the amount of RAM on other system resources available for it to use. See Figure 6.13 for server service configuration options.

STEP BY STEP

6.2 Opening Server Service Configuration

1. If you are running Windows 2000, right-click the My Network Places icon and select Properties.

If you are running Windows NT, right-click the Network Neighborhood icon and select Properties.

---

2. If you are running Windows 2000, right-click the icon for your local area connection and select Properties.

If you are running Windows NT, click on Server Service.

3. If you are running Windows 2000, double-click File and Printer Sharing for Microsoft Networks.

If you are running Windows NT, click Properties.

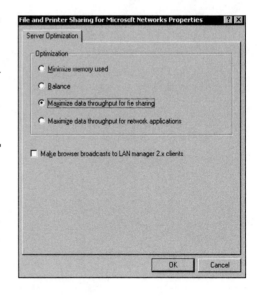

FIGURE 6.13
Server service configuration dialog box.

By default the server service in Windows NT is configured to maximize throughput for file sharing. This is unchanged in Windows 2000. Table 6.11 explains each of the server service optimization settings and when you should use each.

TABLE 6.11

WINDOWS NT/2000 SERVER SERVICE CONFIGURATION OPTIONS

Server Service Setting	Description	Use
Minimize Memory Used	Meant to accommodate up to 10 simultaneous users	Very small environments with fewer than 10 users
Balance	Meant to accommodate up to 64 simultaneous users	Small organizations where there exists a single server
Maximize Throughput for File Sharing	File cache access has priority over user application access; optimized for 64 or more connections	File server
Maximize Throughput for Network Applications	User application access has priority over file cache access; optimized for 64 or more connections	Application servers

Be sure you have a good understanding of the server role before making any changes to the server service. This change will require a reboot on both Windows NT and Windows 2000 servers.

NOTE

Client/Server Memory Management Tuning the server service to Maximize Throughput for Network Applications is only a valuable change for client/server applications that do not manage their own memory. SQL server, for example, manages its own memory, so a change to the server service would not make a difference in terms of SQL's performance.

Windows 2000 Features That Enhance Performance

In this final section, we'll highlight some of the new features in Windows 2000 that take performance to the next level. This is meant to be an introduction to these features and not a hardcore drilldown. The goal is for you to keep these in mind as performance-related objectives come up.

Symmetric Multi-Processing (SMP) Support

Windows NT supported multiple processors in a single server, but not nearly to the extreme that Windows 2000 does. Windows 2000 Server supports up to four processors in a single server; Advanced Server handles up to eight processors; and DataCenter Server can scale up to 32 processors in a single server.

Because of this scalability, the implementation of the SMP code has been enhanced to achieve better linearity of scaling on high-performance servers. The performance enhancements will be noticeable on higher-end systems—specifically, on eight-way or higher systems. This means Windows 2000 Advanced Server and Windows 2000 DataCenter Server will reap the SMP enhancement benefits the most.

CPU, Memory, and I/O Tuning

There have been a slew of enhancements to the areas of CPU, memory, and I/O tuning. Most of these enhancements are very low level and are not relevant even in this chapter. The ones that should interest you after reading this chapter are additional non-paged and paged pool memory that prevents fragmentation, and an increased file system cache size (from 512MB to 960MB) that reduces contention for system resources during context switching.

Enterprise Memory Architecture

Enterprise Memory Architecture (EMA) allows Windows 2000 Advanced and DataCenter Servers to take advantage of larger than 4GB physical memories. This allows applications that are EMA aware to take advantage of this additional physical memory by caching data, resulting in higher performance. SQL Server 7.0 Enterprise is EMA aware.

I_2O

Intelligent I/O (I_2O) is a new industry initiative that promotes the interoperability, performance, and ease of use of I/O subsystems. I_2O provides the following significant benefits:

◆ Offloads certain I/O operations, resulting in better CPU performance

◆ Facilitates adaptation of such technologies as RAID and Fiber Channel

◆ Provides the ability to write standardized device drivers that are OS-independent

◆ Offers the flexibility to change transports

Scatter/Gather I/O

Scatter/gather support enables increased I/O throughput for application data that is stored in noncontiguous memory. The key benefit to performance is that application programs will not have to work with an intermediate buffer that gets the data all as one chunk.

Kerberos Authentication Protocol

The default Windows 2000 authentication protocol is Kerberos version 5, although NTLM is still supported and utilized for down-level client authentication. The key performance benefit of Kerberos is the notion of ticket-based authentication. After the first time a client requests a resource on the network—perhaps a file share—a domain controller is out of the picture. The client can use the key and his ticket to authenticate to that resource until the ticket expires. This is unlike NTLM authentication, where every time a client wanted access to a network resource, it had to ask a domain controller and wait for permission.

Windows Load Balancing Services

Windows load balancing services (WLBS) allow you to put up to 32 servers in a "cluster" and balance the load of incoming TCP/IP traffic between them. Each server keeps itself updated by broadcasting its status every second. Overall network performance is enhanced by splitting the load between the WLBS servers. Although round-robin DNS is the most popular method to split the load between the load balanced servers, WLBS clusters actually direct new requests to the least utilized server in the cluster, resulting in a true optimization of server services.

CHAPTER SUMMARY

KEY TERMS
- baseline
- bottleneck
- Network Monitor
- Performance Monitor
- System Monitor
- System Monitor object
- System Monitor object counters
- SNMP (Simple Network Management Protocol)
- network segment
- workload characterization
- protocol binding

Analyzing performance requirements is more than just hooking up the System Monitor utility and collecting data. It's about understanding the business and how it uses technology. The technology needs to operate efficiently so the business does not suffer. Technology in this sense is really everything that makes up a network, with an emphasis on the core network backbone and servers. Infrastructure components, such as routers, play just as much a role in network utilization as the servers themselves.

We recommend you use a couple of tools to analyze the network. The first, the Windows 2000 System Monitor, is focused at monitoring hundreds of counters on a given server. The second, Network Monitor, will "sniff" the line and capture every piece of data traveling across it. You can use this data to see if there is any traffic on the wire that doesn't need to be there, and make plans to eliminate it.

As you monitor the performance of servers, you should always monitor at least the default counters for the following four object areas, no matter what type of server:

CHAPTER SUMMARY

◆ Processor

◆ Memory

◆ Disk subsystem

◆ Network subsystem

The following list describes a six-step approach to analyzing performance and system and data access patterns on the network:

1. **Determine a Baseline.** Use the System Monitor and Network Monitor utilities to gather baseline information that you can use in comparisons later in the process.

2. **Quantify Measurement Information.** Take the information you gathered in Step 1 and export it to a measurement tool, such as an Excel spreadsheet or Access database. Perform statistical analysis on it and generate graphical reports.

3. **Determine Bottlenecks.** Use the analysis from Step 2 to determine where bottlenecks exist. Take steps to alleviate these bottlenecks.

4. **Determine Feasible Response Time.** Based on your analysis of the current environment, determine what would be reasonable response times for specific applications, such as Exchange servers and Line of Business (LOB) applications. Set the proper performance-related expectations with management and end users and back up those expectations with real data.

5. **Project Future Needs.** Determine what the future performance-related needs of the company are going to be. These needs could be driven by several factors, such as growth plans or software application upgrades.

6. **Implement a Performance Analysis and Trending Standard.** Implement an on-going performance analysis process. Log files can be generated and then automatically ported to a database, which can in turn produce trend reports. This step allows the company to stay a couple of steps ahead by giving it the ability to anticipate where there may be a problem with performance bottlenecks. They can then proactively take measures to alleviate such a problem before it becomes a real issue.

KEY TERMS

• RAID

• SMP (Symmetric Multi-Processing)

• I_2O (Intelligent Input/Output)

• EMA (Enterprise Memory Architecture)

• Kerberos

• scatter/gather I/O

• Windows load balancing services

CHAPTER SUMMARY

Understanding the server roles and responsibilities within a network is important to the tuning and optimization of those servers. By rating the importance of the four major performance-related resources within these servers, you can create a focus on the trending and analysis reports. For instance, you could tailor reports for file and print servers that display up-to-the-minute information on disk read and write performance, as well as used and free space. Because you know that disk space is the most important for file and print servers, you can set up System Monitor to send you an alert if a certain threshold is passed.

Windows 2000 includes a plethora of performance-related enhancements, such as Kerberos v5 authentication, I_2O, scatter/gather I/O, EMA, and many more. You should conceptually have an understanding of what each of these enhancements means and where it is of value.

APPLY YOUR KNOWLEDGE

Exercises

6.1   Create a System Monitor Log

This exercise demonstrates how to create a Windows 2000 System Monitor log. You will generate logged data here to use later in analyses in Exercises 6.2 and 6.3.

Estimated Time: 15 Minutes

1. Open the Windows 2000 System Monitor by clicking Start, Programs, Administrative Tools, Performance.

2. Expand Performance Logs and Alerts and right-click Counter Logs.

3. From the context menu, select New Log Settings. Name this log PerfAnalysis.

4. Click Add to add objects and counters to PerfAnalysis.

5. On the Select Counters window (see Figure 6.14), click Use Local Computer Counters if you wish to monitor your own computer, or Select Counters from Computer if you wish to monitor a computer other than the one you are sitting at.

6. Select Processor from the Performance Object drop-down list. Select the Select Counters from List radio button and then choose the %Processor Time counter.

7. Select the Select Instances from List radio button and then _Total.

8. Click Add to add the processor counter.

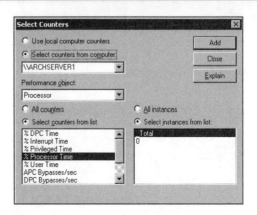

FIGURE 6.14
The Select Counters window.

9. Use the same process to add the following objects, counters, and instances:

   • Memory object, Pages/Sec counter

   • LogicalDisk object, %Disk Time, _Total

   • Server, Bytes Total/Sec

   • Network Interface, Bytes Total/Sec, *<the NIC on the computer you're monitoring>*

NOTE

Logical Disk Counters   Don't forget to turn on the disk counters by typing `diskperf -y`. Also, in order to see the Network Interface counters, you must have the SNMP service installed.

---

10. Once you've added all counters, click Close.

APPLY YOUR KNOWLEDGE

11. On the PerfAnalysis window, adjust the data sampling time down to every 5 seconds. Your PerfAnalysis log settings should resemble those in Figure 6.15.

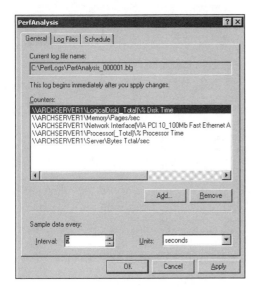

FIGURE 6.15
PerfAnalysis log settings after adding all counters.

12. Click the Log Files tab.

13. Change the Log File Type to Text File—CSV. This will sample the data and save it in a comma-separated file. This will be important for Exercise 6.3.

> **N O T E** **Log File Location**   While you're on the Log Files tab, make a note of the log file location. You'll need it in each of the next two exercises.

14. Click the Schedule tab. Change the At time in Start Log to about 5 minutes from now. Under Stop Log, click After and change the setting to 10 minutes. This will set PerfAnalysis to begin logging performance data 5 minutes from now and run a duration of 10 minutes. Click OK. PerfAnalysis should appear in the list of counter logs with a red icon.

> **N O T E** **Performance Data**   If you are running on a home network or in a test lab or other environment where there isn't much activity on the server you are monitoring, you should try to generate some traffic during the time the performance data is being logged.

6.2   Use the System Monitor to View Logged Data

This exercise demonstrates how you can utilize the System Monitor to analyze logged data.

Estimated Time: 5 Minutes

1. From the System Monitor main application window, click System Monitor in the left explorer window.

2. To change the focus of the System Monitor from real time to a log file, click the View Log File Data button.

APPLY YOUR KNOWLEDGE

3. In the Select Log File window, navigate to your log file. It should be named perfanalysis_000001.csv. Select it and click Open.

4. The System Monitor is now set to utilize the historical log file as its data. Click the + icon to add counters from your logged data.

5. Click the arrow to pull down the Performance Object list. Notice the only available counters are those you chose to record in the PerfAnalysis log.

6. Add all counters from all objects. Click Close when done. You should see the chart of your logged data, similar to that of Figure 6.16.

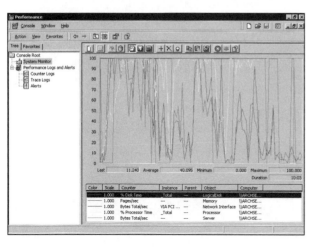

FIGURE 6.16
PerfAnalysis Chart view.

7. You can also view your PerfAnalysis data as a report by clicking the third button to the right of the View Log File Data button.

6.3 Utilize Microsoft Excel to Chart Performance Data

This exercise demonstrates the process by which you can analyze the PerfAnalysis data in an external analysis tool, such as Microsoft Excel.

Estimated Time: 10 Minutes

1. Launch Microsoft Excel. The version shouldn't matter, although this exercise is written to Excel 2000.

2. Open the PerfAnalysis log file. You'll need to adjust the column widths so you can see the data more easily.

3. Highlight columns B through F. You can ignore column A, which indicates the time the data sample was recorded.

4. Select Insert, Chart to start the Chart Wizard.

5. Choose Line from the Chart Type list. Choose the top-left line chart on the right side (see Figure 6.17).

APPLY YOUR KNOWLEDGE

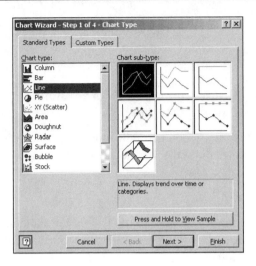

FIGURE 6.17
The Microsoft Excel Chart Wizard provides a slew of options for configuring a chart.

> NOTE
>
> **Excel Data Analysis**   Microsoft Excel is a robust data analysis tool and hence is full of options. We will follow a general charting path in this exercise, but keep in mind that you can do much more than just chart all data.

6. Click Next. You do not have to change anything here, but if you want to clean up the legend, click the Series button.

7. Click Next. You can give the chart a name and provide labels for your X axis (time) and Y axis (value) if you like.

8. Click Next. Save the chart as a new sheet. This will separate the chart and the data, but will make it much easier to read.

9. Click Finish. The chart appears and should somewhat resemble the System Monitor Chart view. Figure 6.18 shows a chart with data labels.

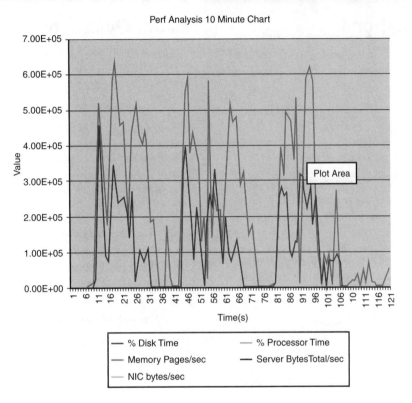

FIGURE 6.18
The final PerfAnalysis Excel chart with axis labels, legend updates, and a title.

APPLY YOUR KNOWLEDGE

Review Questions

1. What are the four major performance areas that should be represented in all baseline performance analyses?

2. What is the most efficient RAID configuration for a file server? Why is it not recommended?

3. What is the default configuration for the Windows 2000 server service?

4. What action must you perform before you can monitor the E: drive partition on your local computer?

5. What must you verify about the company and its users before you begin sampling data for a baseline?

6. What utility should you use to determine if Microsoft Exchange RPC data is saturating a WAN link?

7. Why would you consider using a utility, such as Microsoft Access, to view performance information?

8. I am a server. I don't care too much about the CPU or memory, but I really like disk space and network throughput. What type of server am I?

9. What are the two types of RAM and what is the main difference between them?

10. How would you determine whether there are SAP packets active on the network?

Exam Questions

1. You wish to optimize the performance of the page file on a Windows 2000 server. What hard disk configuration would be the optimal storage medium for the page file?

   A. RAID 0

   B. RAID 1

   C. RAID 2

   D. RAID 5

2. You suspect your company's Sales and Marketing Ethernet segment is saturated. You wanted to use the System Monitor to quickly determine the utilization on that segment; however, the Network Segment object is not available. What is most likely the cause of this problem?

   A. SNMP is not installed on the computer being used for the analysis.

   B. Network Monitor Agents are not installed on the computer being used for the analysis.

   C. You are not logged on with the appropriate rights to view the Network Segment object.

   D. You must first run the `diskperf -y` command and then reboot before you can see the Network Segment object.

3. The eFly IT director asks you to determine why the LogBooks application is running slowly from remote sites. You suspect a performance bottleneck. Which of the following answers represents the order in which you should attempt to find it?

APPLY YOUR KNOWLEDGE

A. (1) Check the speed of the WAN connection. (2) Check the physical networking devices from client to server. (3) Use System Monitor to determine segment utilization. (4) Use Network Monitor to trace LogBooks packets.

B. (1) Check the physical networking devices from client to server. (2) Use System Monitor to determine segment utilization. (3) Use Network Monitor to trace LogBooks packets. (4) Check the speed of the WAN connection.

C. (1) Use System Monitor to determine segment utilization. (2) Use Network Monitor to trace LogBooks packets. (3) Check the physical networking devices from client to server. (4) Check the speed of the WAN connection.

D. (1) Check the physical networking devices from client to server. (2) Use Network Monitor to trace LogBooks packets. (3) Check the speed of the WAN connection. (4) Use System Monitor to determine segment utilization.

4. You've been monitoring eFly's main Web server over the past two weeks. During that time, you've noticed a steady increase in the number of hits this server is getting from the Internet. If this trend keeps up, what should eFly do to spread the number of hits between multiple servers and thereby reduce the load?

A. Increase RAM and add a second processor.

B. Add a new server and incorporate an active/passive cluster.

C. Incorporate round-robin DNS to satisfy external requests to the Web server.

D. Add one or more additional Web servers and incorporate Windows load balancing services.

5. Suppose eFly purchases the next version of LogBooks, which does away with the client front-end and uses a Web browser instead. Given what you know about the current infrastructure at eFly, how would you determine if this configuration yields any performance advantage for a remote site?

A. Install the new version of LogBooks on a computer identical to the one the old version is on in the remote site. Use a benchmarking package to test the performance of each.

B. Upgrade to the new version of LogBooks and use a sniffer to monitor the usage of the WAN link. Compare this number to a historical sniffer baseline.

C. Create a performance baseline using the System Monitor before you upgrade to the new version. Complete the upgrade, then create another performance baseline and compare it with the original.

D. Install the new version of LogBooks. Utilize the Network Monitor to analyze the traffic flow of each package.

6. Amid all the confusion and chaos that parallels an aggressively growing company, eFly realizes that it doesn't have any graphical email capabilities. They plan to immediately replace the HP/UX text-based mailing system with a new dual-processor, 1GB of RAM server running NT 4.0 and Exchange Server 5.5. What performance bottleneck will Exchange Server produce if it is located only in St. Louis and all the other hubs have to connect remotely? Assume Outlook 2000 is the client of choice.

APPLY YOUR KNOWLEDGE

A. The NIC in the client will become a bottleneck.

B. The WAN connection between the sites will become a bottleneck.

C. The memory (RAM) in the Exchange server will become a bottleneck.

D. The disk subsystem in the Exchange server will become a bottleneck.

7. You've been monitoring the processor utilization on an application server over a period of two weeks. During that time you've seen a steady increase in total processor utilization. During the latest reporting period, it was steadily operating at 80%. Which of the following things might you suggest the company do to reduce processor utilization on this server?

A. Add an additional network interface card.

B. Add more memory (RAM).

C. Rebuild the disk subsystem so that only RAID 5 arrays are utilized.

D. Fine-tune the server service by selecting the Maximize Throughput for Network Applications setting.

8. Jim has just been hired at MLM Corp. as the LAN/WAN Manager, and his first task is to optimize the network. He uses a sniffer to determine what type of network traffic is in use. He determines that nearly half of the network's 80% usage is due to TCP/IP broadcast traffic from the 480 users. What should Jim do to relieve the network from excessive broadcast traffic?

A. Install a packet optimizer.

B. Switch to the IPX/SPX protocol.

C. Segment the network into two or more IP subnets.

D. Replace the network hubs with switches.

9. Support for what new feature allows Windows 2000 device drivers to operate for the same hardware under different operating systems?

A. Enhanced Memory Architecture (EMA)

B. Scatter/gather I/O

C. Intelligent I/O (I$_2$O)

D. Symmetric Multi-Processing (SMP)

10. Which of the following WINS/NBT node types will achieve optimum performance in a fully routed WAN environment?

A. B-Node

B. P-Node

C. M-Node

D. H-Node

Answers to Review Questions

1. Memory, processor, disk subsystem, and network subsystem. All four of these areas include objects that monitor the critical areas of any given server in any given role. See "What Data Should I Capture?"

2. RAID 0 (striping) is the most efficient RAID configuration across the board because of its incredibly fast read from and write to capability. RAID 0, however, has a serious drawback. It provides no fault tolerance, so if you lose a disk

you lose data. RAID 5 (stripe set with parity) is the most typical RAID configuration for file servers. It provides extremely fast reads, but is considerably slower to write to. Most organizations take the performance hit so they can protect data. See "Disk Bottlenecks."

3. Maximize Throughput for File Sharing. In this configuration, file cache access has priority over user application access and is optimized for 64 or more connections. This setting is recommended for file servers. See "Server Service."

4. You must turn the disk counters on by executing the diskperf -y command. If E: is a physical drive, you can execute diskperf -yd, and if E: is a logical partition, you can execute diskperf -yv. One of these commands must be executed before you can sample data from disks or disk partitions. If your counters return 0 all the time, you haven't run the diskperf utility. This is unchanged from Windows NT. See "Disk Subsystem," especially Table 6.3.

5. You must verify that nothing "special" is going on within the company that may cause the data you sample to become skewed. You want to have a "normal" workday with the company. Some infrastructure teams go as far as to not mention they will be capturing data on a specific day. See "Data Gathering Timeline."

6. Use the Network Monitor, which by default will capture all protocol types it knows about (including RPC) that are in use on the network segment. See "Network Infrastructure Components."

7. Database or data analysis utilities, such as Microsoft Access or Excel, allow you to perform robust manipulation on the data. In the case of historical performance data, these utilities provide robust analysis mechanisms that allow you to manipulate performance data in many different, useful ways. See "Step 6: Implement a Performance Analysis and Trending Standard."

8. A true file server wants gobs of disk space on a fast and reliable disk subsystem. It also wants a fast and reliable network connection. CPU and memory are important, as they are in any system. They are not as important as network and disk in this case. See "File/Print Servers."

9. Memory, specifically RAM, is divided into two types: paged and non-paged. Paged RAM is virtual, which allows all applications to believe they have access to the entire installation of memory. Each application is given a bank of private memory addresses, which are mapped to physical memory. Non-paged RAM, on the other hand, must remain in main memory and cannot be read from or written to. See "Paged and Non-Paged RAM."

10. Utilize Network Monitor to capture data on the network segment. Analyze the capture and search for SAP packet data. See "Network-Related System Monitor Counters."

APPLY YOUR KNOWLEDGE

Answers to Exam Questions

1. **A.** For optimal page file performance, RAID 0 (Disk striping) is the best choice. It ranks number one in both read and write performance. Raid 1 (Mirroring) is built for redundancy and suffers a bit in performance, there is no RAID 2, and RAID 5 (Stripe set with parity), is built for redundancy and availability and therefore is not the most optimal configuration for speed. For more information, see Table 6.9.

2. **B.** You must install the Network Monitor Agents for the Network Segment System Monitor object to become available. Installing SNMP enables the Network Interface System Monitor object. Anybody who can log on to a Windows NT or Windows 2000 computer can monitor performance. The diskperf -y command enables the System Monitor disk counters. See "Step 1: Determine a Baseline."

3. **A.** Check the speed of the WAN connection first. It is easy and takes no time at all. Next, check the physical networking devices from client to server; this should include any physical hardware between the client and server. Third, use System Monitor to determine the utilization on the network segment. Finally, use Network Monitor to trace LogBooks packets. Since this task is more time-consuming than any of the others, you should only do it when you have to. See "Step 3: Determine Bottlenecks."

4. **D.** Windows load balancing services allows you to cluster up to 32 servers and share a single virtual IP address between them. Adding RAM and processors may boost performance, but will not help distribute the load. Incorporating an active/passive cluster provides for availability, not load balancing. Round-robin DNS will evenly distribute load across all servers in a cluster; however, answer C refers to only a single server. See "Windows Load Balancing Services."

5. **C.** The best way to determine the impact on performance of a new version of software is to know precisely what the performance numbers were to start with, or in other words, create a baseline. Once you have a baseline, install the new software and let it stabilize. Create a new baseline using the same performance metrics as your original. Compare the two. The gap between the numbers should indicate a positive or negative performance difference. For more information, review the six-step process for forecasting performance requirements based on current trends and analyses, introduced in "Successful Approach to Performance Monitoring."

6. **B.** Because Exchange is going to be installed at the hub of the organization, remote sites must utilize remote procedure calls (RPCs) over the WAN. RPCs can carry quite a bit of overhead and can saturate a small WAN link. The client NIC most likely will not become a bottleneck. The RAM and disk subsystem in the server may present issues, but likely not before the smaller WAN links do. See "Step Three: Determine Bottlenecks."

7. **B.** There are several opportunities for decreasing this server's processor utilization, but of the available answers, only adding more RAM could decrease its utilization. Inadequate RAM can cause excessive paging, a processor-intensive operation that increases a processor's utilization. Adding a second NIC (answer A) might increase network throughput capacity, but would not affect processor utilization. Rebuilding the disk subsystem (answer C) might have a small effect on processor performance, but not to the extent that it would significantly decrease its utilization. The server service, regardless of tuning, requires the same amount of processor involvement, and therefore the particular setting in answer D would not decrease its utilization. See "Processor Bottlenecks."

8. **C.** To reduce broadcast traffic, you need to either get rid of applications that produce it, or work to isolate it. Because you can't get rid of it, you must isolate it. The net effect of isolating broadcast traffic is it reduces the number of nodes that receive broadcasts (remember that each node on a segment must process broadcast packets). Creating TCP/IP subnets is the best way to isolate this traffic. Utilizing a packet optimizer does not help isolate broadcast packets. Changing to the IPX/SPX protocol won't help since it is natively a broadcast-based protocol. Network hubs and switches have nothing to do with broadcast packets. See "Addressing Network Subsystem Bottlenecks."

9. **C.** I_2O provides a means by which device drivers can be written in a standard format that is supported across OS platforms. Scatter/gather support enables increased I/O throughput for application data that is stored in noncontiguous memory. Enhanced memory architecture is an architecture that allows applications to make use of larger than 4GB physical memories. Symmetric multiprocessing refers to support for more than one processor in the same computer. See "Windows 2000 Features That Benefit Performance."

10. **D.** The hybrid node type (H-node) configuration for NetBIOS name resolution is optimal for fully routed TCP/IP networks. Because it first attempts to directly contact a name server (WINS, for example), it can alleviate many broadcast messages that increase network utilization. H-node does support broadcast as a means of finding resources, but only resorts to that method after exhausting all others. The other node types—B-, P-, and M-nodes—all broadcast for services before using a name server. See "Name Resolution Services," particularly Table 6.7.

Suggested Readings and Resources

1. Microsoft Technet Articles.

   - Sheesley, John. "Understanding Memory Usage in Windows 2000." TechRepublic.com. Available on September 1999 and newer TechNet CDs.

   - "Performance Analysis and Optimization of MS Windows NT Server Part 1." Available on August 1997 and newer TechNet CDs.

   - "Performance Analysis and Optimization of MS Windows NT Server Part 2." Available on August 1997 and newer TechNet CDs.

   - "Planning, Deploying, and Managing Highly Available Solutions." Available on June 1999 and newer TechNet CDs.

   - Aubley, Curt. "Tuning Windows NT Server Disk Subsystems." *Windows NT Magazine*. Available on October 1999 and newer TechNet CDs.

   - "Domain Sizing and Capacity Planning for Windows NT Server 4.0." Available on September 1999 and newer TechNet CDs.

   - "Capacity Planning for Your Windows NT Server Network." Available on September 1997 and newer TechNet CDs.

This chapter completes the coverage (which was partially completed in Chapters 5 and 6) of the following Microsoft-specified objective for the Designing a Microsoft Windows 2000 Directory Services Infrastructure exam:

Evaluate the company's existing and planned technical environment.

- **Analyze security considerations.**

▶ The purpose of this objective is to get you familiar with the new Windows 2000 security features. There's a vast number of new and different security mechanisms in Windows 2000. It is essential that you know and understand these features as you plan and design a Windows 2000 directory services integration.

CHAPTER 7

Analyzing Security Requirements

▶ Read as much as possible about Kerberos. This chapter contains a bit more than an overview, but to really get a good handle on this complex authentication protocol, you should read the outside resource material suggested at the end of this chapter.

▶ Read as much as possible about PKI. Again, this chapter gives you some level of detail, but

you will serve yourself well to read the suggested material at the end of this chapter for a more in-depth understanding.

▶ Make sure that you do Exercise 7.2 to get an idea of how to install Certificate Services. We recommend you even take that exercise further and set up a standalone root CA and a subordinate CA.

INTRODUCTION

Security in an organization is essential for protecting the organization's data and other intelligence that may be in demand external to the organization. There has also been recent need to further secure areas of the internal network from current or past employees. All it takes is one disgruntled employee to reveal a secret to a competitor.

To create an effective security plan, you must consider every aspect of security. We'll emphasize securing Active Directory since directory services is the focus of this book. We'll open this chapter with some insight as to why security is so important, and how the Internet has exposed some companies' assets to the world without them even knowing it.

Determining what an organization has implemented in terms of security can be a daunting task. For this reason, it is important to solicit the help of the internal team (if it exists) responsible for securing the network.

We'll focus on Windows 2000 and its top-notch security infrastructure and when appropriate discuss how some implementations of NT security map up to Windows 2000. We'll discuss security in the areas of authentication, Active Directory, data transmissions, and the Internet.

We'll close with a section on configuring security in the enterprise using the built-in Windows 2000 security toolset and Group Policy Objects.

CASE STUDY: ONLINE LICENSE COMPANY (OLC)

BACKGROUND

OLC is a company created by the Indiana Bureau of Motor Vehicles to provide a new service to licensed drivers. This new service provides drivers the opportunity to renew licenses and license plates over the Internet. OLC is an extension of the Indiana Bureau of Motor Vehicles and therefore shares the bureau's records database.

PROBLEM STATEMENT

The pressure from a newly elected "high-tech" governor to provide these services caused the OLC development team to rush delivery of the system. In doing so, it did not implement adequate security and has recommended to OLC that the bureau implement new security features.

Lead Developer

"There is no certificate-based security on this Web site. All traffic goes through port 80 and is unencrypted. This is true for all personal information, license numbers, credit card info—everything."

OLC Director

"When you have the government pressuring you to get something done, well, you get it done. This new "high-tech" guy in charge now unfortunately knows just enough about technology to be dangerous. If he'd give us the initiatives and let us manage the development the right way, we'd make him look a lot better."

CURRENT SYSTEM

The system was developed using Active Server Pages (ASP) and Dynamic HTML (DHTML), which work together to provide user interface functionality, and an ODBC connection to the state's UNIX-based Informix database. The entire Web system runs on a Windows NT 4.0 platform and uses a TCP/IP connection (via ODBC) to the database.

OLC Data Analyst

"My responsibility is to pull data from the Informix database and process it. I use an IP connection to the UNIX side and have to log on to both the UNIX OS and the Informix database. Seems a little *too* secure to me!"

A Licensed Driver

"*Wow!* I registered both cars in a matter of 10 minutes. That sure beats sitting in the BMV office for three hours. I don't know why anyone would ever use the offices anymore—I really don't. This system is awesome. One thing that concerns me is I didn't see that little padlock icon I see on other sites where I use my credit card. I sure hope nobody stole my credit card number while I was doing this bit of business with the state government."

ENVISIONED SYSTEM

OLC would like to move the Windows NT 4.0 platform to Windows 2000 to take advantage of several security enhancements. Because internal OLC employees need to connect to the Informix

continues

CASE STUDY: ONLINE LICENSE COMPANY (OLC)

continued

database to query for new records, they must log on to the UNIX environment with different user-names and passwords. OLC would like to provide single sign-on services to its employees.

OLC IT Director

"We've been patiently waiting for Microsoft to release Windows 2000. Looks like the time is finally here. We are going to take advantage of the early adopters program and implement Windows 2000 throughout our organization."

Indiana BMV Director

"We're allowing OLC to do just about anything they want. I am really happy with my counterpart over there and truly believe he will do the best thing. Because we see the way people get their renewals and registrations changing to a computer-based operation, we've reallocated 50% of our funds to OLC."

SECURITY

Although measures were taken to make the code in the system secure, none were taken to secure the Web site or any data transmissions. OLC would like to provide authentic and secure connections for licensed drivers as they utilize the online services. Additionally, data connections and transmissions within the OLC offices must be secured at all times to prevent any possibility of eavesdropping.

OLC IT Director

"I want to make sure that even if someone did penetrate our internal network, he couldn't deci-pher what was traveling across the wire. To do that, we plan to require secured connections between all computers. For our external visi-tors—the drivers of Indiana—we want to make sure that everything they transmit is guarded."

BMV UNIX Administrator

"I am prepared to work with OLC employees to do whatever is necessary for them to do their jobs. I'd even like to help make it easy for them!"

PERFORMANCE

Performance is not too much of a concern in the OLC environment. New state-of-the-art servers and networking backbone are in place and working at optimal efficiency.

OLC IT Director

"Our unsecured site is fast now. We expect to take a slight performance hit with the implemen-tation of security structures, but the performance improvements to IIS 5.0 and Windows 2000 should even that out."

MAINTAINABILITY

Since a team of developers wrote all code inter-nally, OLC can easily maintain the system itself. All code must be checked in and out using Visual Source Safe, and standard code maintenance procedures are in place."

CASE STUDY: ONLINE LICENSE COMPANY (OLC)

BMV UNIX Administrator

"I am working on cross-training the OLC Administration team on the UNIX toolset for the administration and maintenance of the UNIX environment. I am scheduled to assist in the implementation of Windows 2000 and in doing so should be cross-trained on the Windows 2000 security toolsets."

OLC Development Manager

My team is working diligently on prepping the site for Windows 2000 security integration. We have a signed certificate from VeriSign and need to plan the rest of our security infrastructure."

THE NEED FOR SECURITY

Encryption systems, firewalls, and other security-related devices are extremely important in defining infrastructure security, but the most critical component is the server operating system. There are several variables, such as cost, maintainability, and impact on the business environment that must be weighed as corporations implement security plans across the network.

The Internet

The Internet is driving organizations to open up and interact with vendors, partners, and customers using new and often unproven technologies. To remain competitive, corporations quite often end up trading a well-thought-out security plan for just simply getting a server on the Internet to do eCommerce, a risk that could end up costing quite a bit more than the amount of profit the Internet can generate.

> **EXAM TIP**
>
> **eCommerce Is a Red Flag** When you see the word "eCommerce" in a question, be prepared to investigate certificate services and Public Key Infrastructure, which are core to the security architecture of an eCommerce site.

This drastic change in business is what causes some to expose too much of the wrong information to the wrong people. To implement a solid security plan, a security implementer must always be of the mindset that a hacker is out there, looming, waiting to break in and steal vital confidential documents. Companies such as OLC that are under pressure to deliver that new product or service swiftly often underestimate the value of security.

Disgruntled Employees

Disgruntled employees are dangerous. They know the environment and the people within it, and could cause harm without the proper precautions in place. Take, for example, the case of Iva Bincanned, a network administrator who has been with a company for a number of years. She developed relationships with other employees and was generally liked among her peers. When she was given a pink slip due to downsizing, she became very angry and wanted revenge. Because she was an administrator, it was easy for her to create a backdoor account she could use to access the network. When the other network administrators deleted her account, they did not delete her backdoor account. Iva dialed up the night she was let go, logged right onto the system, and proceeded to delete everything she had access to. She had given that account domain admin permissions.

Cases similar to Iva's happen every day. That's why security is so critical. Could this have been prevented? Probably.

KEEP AN OPEN MIND ON SECURITY

As you can well imagine, how an organization chooses to secure its intelligence from potential threats is a big deal. Too often, organizations take security too lightly—often with an "it won't happen to us" attitude. Those that do spend time focusing on security often do well at securing from external threats, only to get burned by someone inside the organization's firewall.

Security is not only a very broad topic, but also is an element that can differ significantly from place to place. State and federal government agencies and some of their contractors, for example, must consider the potential for espionage and/or political terrorism because of the types of activities these organizations perform. Companies on the cutting edge of technology typically don't deal with terrorism, but do have to concern themselves with leakage of confidential information about products, culture, corporate strategy, or other areas of the business.

Whatever the organization, there is always a lowest common security denominator, which is what we focus on in this chapter. You must make sure that in any real-world situation, you're taking into account the fullest set of needs of the particular organization with which you're working.

WINDOWS 2000 AUTHENTICATION

Security begins with the authentication process. Within Windows 2000, the authentication process starts with interactive logon. Interactive logon is the process of identifying a security principal (a user) against a domain or local machine account. Windows 2000 handles the security principal's security credentials transparently after a single successful logon. The transparent process is referred to as *network authentication*, a process by which Windows 2000 confirms security principals' identities with network resources.

> **NOTE**
>
> **Security Principal** Microsoft uses the term *security principal* to describe any entity that can initiate action. So, human users are considered security principals, and so are computers and services.

Windows 2000 authentication supports three core protocols: NT LAN Manager (NTLM), Kerberos, and Secure Sockets Layer/Transport Layer Security (SSL/TLS).

NTLM

The NTLM authentication protocol exists in Windows 2000 for the primary purpose of authentication with previous versions of Windows. NTLM is the core authentication protocol for Windows NT 3.5x and 4.0. You should determine whether you're going to carry on with support for NTLM, because you do have the opportunity to remove it from a Windows 2000 environment. When deciding whether to keep NTLM around, use Table 7.1 as a roadmap.

TABLE 7.1

CONSIDERATIONS FOR REMOVING NTLM

Environment	*Action*
The current network still has Windows NT and/or Windows 95/98 computers on it.	NTLM is required to continue supporting previous versions of Windows.
UNIX clients, not configured for the Kerberos protocol, use the existing Windows NT or Windows 2000 servers.	If UNIX computers are configured to use SMB (server message block), you must continue to support NTLM. If UNIX computers are configured to use TCP/IP standard applications like FTP and Telnet, NTLM can be eliminated.
Several UNIX clients are configured to use Kerberos. All of them use SMB to connect to Windows NT or 2000 servers.	You can eliminate NTLM if you configure the UNIX servers to authenticate to Windows 2000 using Kerberos.
Current Windows NT/2000 clients connect to a UNIX server using SMB.	If you continue to use SMB, you must continue to support NTLM. You can replace SMB with the network file system (NFS), which will free you to remove NTLM support.

Figure 7.1 graphically represents the NTLM authentication process.

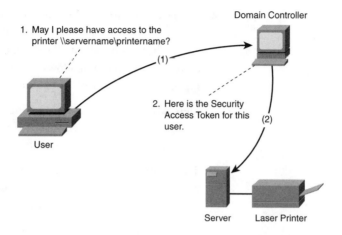

1. May I please have access to the printer \\servername\printername?

(1)

Domain Controller

2. Here is the Security Access Token for this user. (2)

User

Server   Laser Printer

FIGURE 7.1
The NTLM authentication process is based on security access tokens granted by the domain controller each time access to a resource is needed.

Kerberos

Kerberos is the default Windows 2000 authentication protocol. An entire book could be written about it. This section, as long as it may be, is really just a detailed overview of the protocol's implementation. We'll cover features of Kerberos throughout this chapter and, by its end, you should have a good understanding at where it fits within the security and authentication architecture of Windows 2000, as well as how it provides authentication services outside Windows 2000.

MIT Kerberos version 5 replaces NTLM as the default authentication protocol for Windows 2000. Kerberos is an industry-standard protocol that is supported by a wide variety of platforms. The Kerberos protocol defines the interactions between clients and its authentication service, the Key Distribution Center (KDC). The KDC uses Active Directory as its accounts database. The benefits of using Kerberos are as follows:

NOTE

Kerberos Authentication in Windows 2000 The Kerberos implementation in Windows 2000 conforms to Internet RFC-1510.

◆ **Faster session establishment.** An application server does not need to connect to a domain controller to validate credentials and authenticate a client. This enhances the scalability of application servers and allows them to concentrate on providing application services, not authenticating users.

◆ **Delegation of authentication.** This is the ability for one back-end server to impersonate a client and make connections with other back-end servers on behalf of that client.

◆ **Transitivity.** Users can authenticate anywhere in a domain tree because of the distributed nature of Kerberos and its KDCs. The KDCs in each domain trust tickets issued by other KDCs in the tree.

The name Kerberos comes from the Greek mythological figure "Cerberos," a fierce, three-headed dog that guarded the gates of the underworld. The three heads of Cerberos map to the three pieces of Kerberos: client, server, and trusted intermediary (the KDC).

Kerberos Background

Kerberos is a shared secret authentication protocol. This means that if only two people know a secret, then either person can verify the identity of the other by confirming that the other person knows the secret. For example, suppose Lea wants to send Rex a message, and Rex wants to make sure that message is from Lea before he acts on it. They decide to use a password to solve this issue. If Lea can somehow let Rex know she knows the password without flat-out telling him, the process is easy. The problem is that this can't be done securely. The logical way is to send the password bundled with the message, but then anybody sniffing the wire can intercept it. She could encrypt it, but would have to send the decryption key for Rex to unlock it, which would defeat the purpose.

Kerberos secret key cryptography solves this issue. Rather than sharing a password, communicating clients share a cryptographic key that only the two of them know. They use the knowledge of this key as verification of one another's identity. The only question remaining is how do Lea and Rex agree on a secret key? The answer is a trusted intermediary known as the Key Distribution Center.

> **EXAM TIP**
>
> **UNIX Interoperability and Single Sign On**   In exam scenarios, the involvement of Single Sign On (SSO) is a clue that Kerberos and UNIX authentication should be explored as a possible solution.

Key Distribution Center

The Key Distribution Center (KDC) is a service that runs on a secure server. In Windows 2000, the KDC runs on every domain controller. It manages a database of all security principals within its *realm*—the Kerberos equivalent of a Windows 2000 domain. Along with other information about security principals, the KDC stores a cryptographic key known only by the security principal and the KDC. This *long-term key* is used in exchanges between the security principal and the KDC. It is typically derived via a one-way hashing function based on the users password. This long-term key is returned by the KDC to the requesting client in the form of a ticket-granting ticket.

> **NOTE**
>
> **Hashing** All implementations of Kerberos v5 must support the DES-CBC-MD5 hashing algorithm, although other hashing algorithms are permissible.

Ticket-Granting Tickets

A *ticket-granting ticket* (TGT) is a special type of session ticket used for access to the KDC's services. This TGT contains an encrypted copy of the user's long-term session key that is derived at logon time by the KDC and is sent to the client's cache during the logon process. This TGT may be used to authenticate quickly with the KDC should a client need to replace an expired session ticket, or request a new one. The TGT saves time and resources by forcing the KDC to do a database lookup of the username and return its long-term session key only once, at logon time.

When a client (Lea) wishes to talk to a server (Rex), the request (TGT) is sent to the KDC. The KDC distributes a short-term session key to the client. Lea and Rex will use this session key for their conversation.

Session Tickets

The data structure used to return the session key to the client is called a session ticket. The *session ticket* is comprised of the client's copy of the session key encrypted with the secret key that the KDC shares with the client. The server's copy of the session key is embedded, along with information about the client, in the session ticket. The entire session ticket is then encrypted with the key that the KDC shares with the server. This session ticket is then cached on the client workstation and may be used to directly authenticate with the server until it expires.

> **NOTE**
>
> **Authenticator** In protocols that use secret key encryption, a client wanting to gain access to a server or service must present information in the form of an authenticator encrypted in the secret key. This authenticator must be unique and different every time the protocol is executed. Time can be considered a good authenticator.

To continue the example, when Lea wants to talk to Rex now, she sends a request to the trusted authority, the KDC, which returns her a session ticket. Upon receipt, Lea extracts her copy of the session key and stores it in volatile cache (when Lea goes to sleep, she forgets everything!). To talk to Rex, she sends him the session ticket (which is still encrypted with the server's secret key), and an authenticator, which is encrypted with the session key. The ticket and authenticator together become Lea's qualifying credentials in talking to Rex.

When Rex receives a request to talk from someone claiming to be Lea, he decrypts the session ticket using his secret key. Once decrypted, he extracts the session key and uses it to decrypt Lea's authenticator. Rex will know that the request to talk came from who the sender is claiming to be if he is able to decrypt everything successfully. If so, he and Lea establish a connection and begin their conversation. Figure 7.2 describes this entire process.

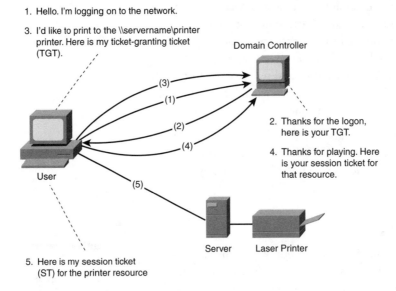

1. Hello. I'm logging on to the network.

3. I'd like to print to the \\servername\printer printer. Here is my ticket-granting ticket (TGT).

Domain Controller

(3)
(1)
(2)
(4)

2. Thanks for the logon, here is your TGT.

4. Thanks for playing. Here is your session ticket for that resource.

User

(5)

Server   Laser Printer

5. Here is my session ticket (ST) for the printer resource

FIGURE 7.2
The initial Kerberos authentication process.

The beauty of using session tickets is that the server has absolutely no responsibility in terms of remembering session tickets. It is totally on the client to retain the session ticket in its cache until the ticket expires. Another benefit is that session tickets are reusable, so every subsequent time a user needs to communicate with a server, it can use the cached copy of the session ticket for that server, as shown in Figure 7.3.

Kerberos Integration

Kerberos is fully integrated with the Windows 2000 security architecture for authentication and access control. WinLogon, the initial Windows domain logon service, uses the Kerberos security provider to obtain an initial Kerberos ticket. Other services, such as the redirector, use the Windows 2000 Security Support Provider Interface (SSPI) when they need to connect to the Kerberos security provider.

NOTE

SSPI The Security Support Provider Interface defines Windows security APIs for network authentication.

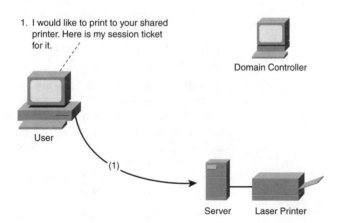

1. I would like to print to your shared printer. Here is my session ticket for it.

Domain Controller

User

(1)

Server   Laser Printer

FIGURE 7.3
Once a session ticket has been issued, subsequent connections to the server only require the client to present its session ticket for that server.

Kerberos v5 contains an encrypted field for applications to use for authorization data in the session ticket. Windows 2000 uses the authorization data to carry SIDs for user and group membership. The server-side Kerberos security provider uses this authorization data to build security access tokens, which represent the user on the system. It can then use this data to impersonate the client before attempting to access local resources protected by ACLs.

Two additional fields, implemented as Boolean flags, are used in the delegation of authentication features supported by Kerberos. The *proxy* and *forwarding* fields in session tickets can be set to allow servers to obtain session tickets for other servers on behalf of the client.

IN THE FIELD

IT'S ALL IN THE NAME OF SECURITY

One very good example of where you would benefit from the delegation of authentication (forwarding) feature of Microsoft's implementation of Kerberos is with a two-tier, Web-enabled email access package.

Consider the scenario in which back-end mail servers for an organization are inside the firewall and front-end Web-based email access servers (such as Outlook Web access) are on a secure DMZ. A client may securely log on to Active Directory using the X.509 certificate PKI extensions of Kerberos by connecting to the front-end Web servers. These servers then may forward the user's request to log on to a domain controller. Once authenticated, the user would then be able to access email.

Exactly how this process works is covered in the Kerberos reference material at the end of this chapter, but you can see easily that a main benefit is that the front-end server can be configured to perform delegated tasks for only specific clients—a very powerful security implementation.

Kerberos Interoperability

Kerberos v5 is implemented for a variety of operating platforms and can be used to provide a single point of authentication in a heterogeneous and distributed environment. This interoperability is based on the following characteristics:

◆ Identification of users through a common authentication protocol by principal name.

◆ Ability to define trust relationships between Kerberos realms (equal to Windows 2000 domains) and to generate ticket referral requests between realms.

◆ RFC-1510 compliant implementations.

◆ Support for Kerberos version 5 security token formats for exchanges and context establishment as defined by the IETF. (See RFC-1964 for more information.)

It is possible for Windows 2000 clients to authenticate to non-Windows 2000 Kerberos KDCs and vice versa. Clients that obtain initial Kerberos TGTs from a KDC in a non-Windows 2000 domain (realm) use the Kerberos referral process to request a session ticket from a Windows 2000 KDC. This referral ticket is created by inter-realm trust relationships. This process occurs when the Kerberos security provider on a Windows 2000 KDC attempts to find authorization data to generate a token. This data is likely not available when security principals authenticate to non-Windows 2000 Kerberos realms.

In our OLC case study, when internal Windows 2000 users need to access the Informix database on the UNIX platform, the Windows 2000 KDC will recognize that resource exists on the UNIX side and will refer client requests to a UNIX realm KDC via a trust relationship. The UNIX KDC then will generate session tickets for the Informix database.

Extensions for Public Key Authentication

Windows 2000 implements extensions to the Kerberos protocol to provide for public key authentication. The public key authentication allows clients to request an initial TGT using a private key. To answer this request, the KDC uses a public key obtained from an X.509 certificate stored with the user object in Active Directory.

These user certificates should be issued from a trusted Certificate Authority (CA), such as VeriSign's Digital IDs or Microsoft Certificate Server. After the initial private key authentication succeeds, standard Kerberos protocols for obtaining session tickets are used to connect the client to network services. This enhancement allows for interactive logon using smart cards. It is based on a draft specification submitted to the IETF working group for review. It is the objective of Microsoft, as well as several other third parties interested in public key technology, that the draft specification be amended to the industry-standard Kerberos specification.

Single Sign-On with Kerberos

A huge benefit to having an industry standard protocol as the core for authentication and security is the ability to step outside the Windows 2000 platform by creating trust relationships with other platforms. Operating platforms that support the MIT Kerberos v5 protocol are illustrated in Figure 7.4.

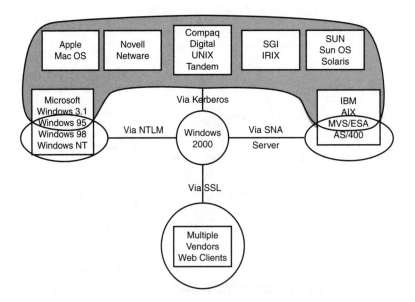

FIGURE 7.4

Microsoft's vision of providing SSO with other platforms.

Establishing the cross-platform trust with Kerberos is relatively easy, provided all the pieces are in place on both sides. The administrator creates a trust relationship between the Windows 2000 KDC and the other platform's KDC, which are in different realms. The Kerberos tickets are provided via cross-realm referrals. The Windows 2000 administrator simply sets up user accounts with rights and permissions for the incoming users to use, and that's it.

One downfall to SSO with Kerberos in a heterogeneous environment is the management of the connection. Some of the things that are managed in the background under Windows 2000 need to be manually handled in this environment. For example, when a trust is established in a heterogeneous environment, the administrator must manually synchronize keys between Active Directory and the other platform's KDC. Additionally, the administrator loses the single set of administration tools and a single repository for SSO information.

SSL/TLS

The final core authentication protocol is Secure Sockets Layer/ Transport Layer Security (SSL/TLS). Windows 2000 uses SSL/TLS and X.509 certificates to provide mutual authentication, message integrity, and confidentiality. The Windows 2000 implementation of SSL/TLS supports logon through the use of smart cards, and is used to protect connections on unsecured networks.

Authentication of External Users

Support for public key certificate-based authentication allows client applications to connect to secure Windows 2000 services as a proxy for users that don't have a domain account. A single Windows 2000 account can be used to provide secure access to one or many external users.

This means businesses can easily and securely share information with certain individuals from other organizations. You may recall our section on vendor, partner, and customer relationships in Chapter 3, "Analyzing the Results of the Business Assessment." This authentication protocol is what takes advantage of the single digital identity (domain account) associated with a customer, partner, or vendor. By authenticating users external to the company in essentially the same way that internal employees are authenticated—that is, against Active Directory—administrators have a single point of administration.

PUBLIC KEY INFRASTRUCTURE (PKI)

We've already broached the topic, so we'll segue into Public Key Infrastructure. PKI is a capability, not a "thing." It's important that we clear up that common misconception from the get-go.

The purpose of PKI is to make it easy for businesses to use public key cryptography. Get into the mindset of thinking PKI as soon as you hear eCommerce, intranet, Internet, extranet, collaboration, or any other potentially Web-enabled service.

Public Key Cryptography

Public key cryptography refers to the use of two keys: a public key designed to be shared, and a private key, which must be guarded. These keys complement each other, meaning that if you encrypt something with your public key, it can only be decrypted with the corresponding private key. This works both ways. Either way, the goal of public key cryptography—the ability to obscure data in such a way that it can only be interpreted by the intended party—is achieved.

Another component of PKI includes digital signing. This task is a way to prove the origin of a piece of data. This does not provide privacy of data.

Public key cryptography provides three core capabilities that are important to businesses. These three capabilities are highlighted using some potential business cases in Table 7.2.

TABLE 7.2

CAPABILITIES AND BUSINESS USE OF PUBLIC KEY CRYPTOGRAPHY

Capability	Business Use
Privacy	Encrypting email sent across the Internet to prevent eavesdroppers from reading contents
	Encrypting network traffic, such as Web site traffic entering a secure area when entering credit card information
	Encrypting video conference sessions established through NetMeeting
Authentication	Verifying a visitor to an intranet site so that user can access information secured from other users
	Proving to customers that they are at your Web site and not a Web site impersonating yours
	Providing critical data to customers in a way that assures them it is legitimate
Non-repudiation	Creating a solid and tamper-proof database of a customer's purchase history on an eCommerce site
	Signing electronic contracts that are legally binding

> **NOTE**
>
> **Non-Repudiation** Achieving non-repudiation means having the capability to prove beyond dispute that someone took a particular action.

Digital Certificates

Public keys are packaged as digital certificates, which contain a public key and a set of attributes, such as the keyholder's name. These attributes are relative to the keyholder and define the key-holder's identity, what he's allowed to do, and where the certificate is valid. This binding is appropriate because the certificate is digitally signed by the issuing CA to validate its authenticity.

A good analogy when discussing certificates is a standard credit card. Your Visa card contains a unique key in the form of the credit card number. It contains attributes, such as your name and the card's expiration date, and maybe even your picture. A trusted authority issues it, and its authenticity is sealed in the magnetized strip

Intermediate and Subordinate CAs
The structure of the Certificate Authority hierarchy goes from Root to Intermediate to Entity. Microsoft uses the term "subordinate" to describe any CA server that is not at the root level (hence, all Intermediate and Entity CAs). In the general hierarchy, Entity CAs are *subordinates* of Intermediate CAs, which are *subordinates* of Root CAs.

(assuming it cannot be tampered with). Anyone who trusts the issuing bank will allow you to use the card. Of course, how companies determine whether to accept or reject your credit card is where this analogy needs a bit of help.

Certificate authorities are a hierarchical grouping of public key certificate servers that are responsible for signing digital certificates they issue. This hierarchy can go as deep as needed, although there always will be a finite top level, known as the *root*. Figure 7.5 presents a certificate authority hierarchy.

The important thing about certificate authorities is that each certificate issued by a CA must be digitally signed and certified by the next higher level of CA. So (referring Figure 7.5) if you had a certificate issued by an entity certificate authority, it would have to be signed by the intermediate certificate authority, which would have to be signed by the root CA.

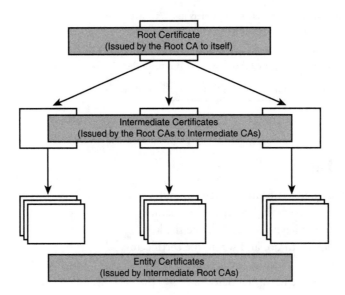

FIGURE 7.5
The certificate authority hierarchy may go as many levels deep as needed, but will always have a single root.

Windows 2000 provides two types of CAs: Enterprise and Standalone, which are discussed in the following sections.

Enterprise Root CA

An Enterprise CA is used at the root of a corporate CA hierarchy. It is typically installed if you will be issuing certificates to users or computers inside an organization that is part of a Windows 2000 domain, and hence require that all requesting users have an appropriate Active Directory-based identity. The requirements for an Enterprise CA are as follows:

◆ Active Directory, because Enterprise CAs use Active Directory to store certificates

◆ Windows 2000 DNS, which is required by Active Directory

◆ Administrative privileges on DNS, Active Directory, and CA servers

Typically, Enterprise CAs are configured to issue certificates only to subordinate Enterprise CAs.

Subordinate Enterprise CA

A subordinate Enterprise CA issues certificates to users and computers within an organization. It is not the most trusted CA because it is subordinate to another CA. All subordinate Enterprise CAs within a CA hierarchy are derived from a single Enterprise root CA. subordinate Enterprise CAs require the following:

◆ A parent CA, which could be an external commercial CA or an Enterprise root CA

◆ Windows 2000 DNS

◆ Active Directory

◆ Administrative privileges on DNS, Active Directory, and CA servers

Standalone Root CA

If you wish to deliver certificates only external to the corporation's directory, you will install a Standalone root CA. These Standalone CAs do not require requesting parties to have Active Directory-based accounts, and in fact will not issue certificates for logon to the directory. Standalone CAs are most commonly used to issue certificates to visitors to a Web site to provide a certain level of authenticity. OLC in the case study, for example, most likely would create a Standalone CA.

The only requirement for a Standalone CA is administrative privileges to the local computer.

Subordinate Standalone CA

As with Subordinate Enterprise CAs, it is a good security measure to create Subordinate Standalone CAs to issue certificates. A Subordinate Standalone CA issues certificates to entities outside a corporation, and requires the following:

◆ An association with a CA that will process its certificate requests; this most likely will be an external commercial CA (such as VeriSign), but also may be a Standalone CA or an Enterprise CA

◆ Administrative privileges on the local server

You can mix and match various levels of Enterprise and Standalone CAs in your organization. You can even have multiple hierarchies—meaning multiple root CAs. Additionally, you can factor in external commercial CAs, such as VeriSign or Thawte.

PKI Components

There are five components that make up a complete PKI. These five components are responsible for creating, validating, transporting, and using the digital certificates that PKI depends on. These components are as follows:

◆ **Certificate Authorities (CAs).** There are two additional responsibilities a CA has beyond what we've just discussed. The first is the decision as to what attributes it will include in a certificate and what mechanism it will use to verify those attributes before issuing the certificate. Second, the CA is responsible for issuing Certificate Revocation Lists (CRLs). If an owner's private key has been compromised or the holder is no longer associated with the issuer, the CA adds it to the CRL and publishes it so clients can check it. Once published, every authorization must first check this list before approval.

◆ **Certificate Publication Points (CPPs).** CPPs make certificates and CRLs publicly available inside or outside the organization. Publishers can use any kind of directory service, including X.500, LDAP, etc. to accomplish this task. They also can publish and distribute them on smart cards, CDs, Web pages, and so on. The industry standard is clearly LDAP.

◆ **Key and Certificate Management Tools.** When were certificates issued? Who holds them? Are there any old certificates? These are all questions organizations need to address with PKI. There is a management tool in Windows 2000 that allows you to manage certificates, CRLs, and more. It's called the MMC, and you hear plenty about it elsewhere in this book.

◆ **Public Key-Enabled Applications.** A well-written PKI-enabled application will make use of public key cryptography without the user ever knowing it. A key to the successful implementation of a PKI is in the applications that use it. Microsoft Outlook, IIS, IE, and Money are just a few of the applications that are "PKI-ready" out of the box.

◆ **Hardware Support.** PKI hardware is *optional*. The booming market demand for PKI has driven hardware manufacturers to develop cryptographic hardware, including smart cards, PC cards, and PCI cards that offer cryptographic accelerated processing. Keep your eye on this area of PKI; you'll probably be seeing smart cards in the mainstream within a few years, as well as biometric devices, such as retinal scanners and fingerprint readers.

IN THE FIELD

WHAT ABOUT THE DISK SPACE?

There are a few factors concerning hard disk capacity you must consider when you install Certificate Services as part of your PKI. The first thing you must consider is how many certificates will be issued by the CA. Project how many certificates will be issued for the life of the CA. A CA that issues a large number of certificates or that has a longer lifetime will require a larger certificate database.

continues

continued

The second factor is the size of each certificate. The certificate database includes all information in the certificates, including the public keys. Certificates that have larger public keys and that contain additional special information will consume more disk space per certificate issued.

Large certificate databases may grow to several hundred megabytes or even over a gigabyte. The best way to predict the growth rate for the size of a certificate database is in a lab using test certificates and watching the size of the database grow.

One additional factor you must include in your test lab is the Certificate Revocation List. Because these lists must be searched each time a certificate is requested, you should create multiple small CRLs. This will ensure that you don't degrade performance.

The Windows 2000 implementation of PKI builds on Microsoft's already robust PKI components. The foundation is built on interoperability, security, flexibility, and ease of use. The primary components of the Windows PKI are as follows:

◆ **Certificate Services.** Certificate Services are implemented as a core OS component. The service allows businesses to act as their own CA and issue and manage their own digital certificates.

◆ **Active Directory Directory Service.** Active Directory not only provides a central repository for network resources, but also is a PKI publication point.

◆ **PKI-Enabled Applications.** Internet Explorer, Microsoft Money, IIS, Outlook, and Outlook Express are all natively PKI enabled. A slew of third-party applications use the Windows 2000 PKI and are also PKI-enabled.

◆ **Exchange Key Management Service.** This is a component of the Exchange BackOffice application that allows for the retrieval and archiving of keys used to encrypt mail messages.

PKI Standards in Windows 2000

Standards bodies, such as the World Wide Web Consortium (W3C), the Internet Engineering Task Force (IETF), and the International Telecommunication Union (ITU) have been working hard with vested interest in promoting the interoperability between multi-vendor implementations of PKI. Microsoft has worked, and continues to work, alongside these impartial bodies to ensure the correct and fully interoperable implementation of the Windows PKI.

Table 7.3 lists the standards, definitions, and justification supported by the Windows 2000 implementation of PKI.

TABLE 7.3

Windows 2000 Support for PKI Standards

PKI Standard	Definition	Justification
X.509 Version 3	Defines content and format for digital certificates	Standard is needed for the exchange of certificates between vendors
CRL Version 2	Defines content and format for digital Certificate Revocation Lists	Standard is needed for the exchange of certificate revocation information between vendors
PKCS Family	Defines behavior and format for the exchange and delivery of public keys	Provides the ability for different vendors to request and move certificates using a standardized process
PKIX	Defines behavior and format for the exchange and delivery of public keys	Emerging PKI standard positioned to replace the PKCS standard
SSL Version 3	Defines encryption for Web sessions	Most widely implemented security protocol on the Internet; downfall—it is subject to export controls
SGC	Defines security similar to SSL without export complications	Allows 128-bit security and, in certain cases, is fully exportable
IPsec	Defines IP packet encryption for network sessions	Offers transparent and automatic encryption of network transmissions
PKINIT	Defines standard for using public keys for authenticating to networks that use Kerberos	Allows Kerberos to use digital certificates on smart cards as security credentials for authentication
PC/SC	Defines a standard for the integration of smart cards and computers	Open standard to which many smart card vendors' specifications adhere

Open Industry Security Standards

The Windows 2000 implementation of PKI inherits the security features built into Windows 2000. This is made possible because the major PKI components are part of the core OS. Because they rely on widely available, open Internet standards, PKI components reap the benefit of years of experience and maturity. Computer security and cryptography experts, who took significant input from computer, banking, financial, legal, and government experts, developed the security standards listed in Table 7.3. The end result is a rock-solid security infrastructure that meets the demands of real-world needs. Microsoft has been very careful to use mature security and encryption algorithms that have stood the test of time and prolonged public use. Table 7.4 lists Windows 2000's support for cryptographic algorithms.

TABLE 7.4

WINDOWS 2000-SUPPORTED CRYPTOGRAPHIC ALGORITHMS

Algorithm	Type
RSA	Public key encryption
DSS	Public key encryption
MD4	Hashing algorithm
MD5	Hashing algorithm
SHA-1	Hashing algorithm
RC2	Secret-key encryption
RC4	Secret-key encryption

Open Security Architecture

Because Windows 2000 offers an open security architecture, it integrates well with third-party PKIs. It is important to remember, however, that because of its integration with the OS, the Windows 2000 PKI provides the best, most seamless integration with Active Directory, native security protocols, and other security services.

MANAGING AND SUPPORTING INTER-BUSINESS RELATIONSHIPS WITH WINDOWS 2000 SECURITY

Many organizations today are opening up their networks to allow partners, vendors, suppliers, and customers secure access to specific areas. A majority of these corporations typically create a user account for the business partner or client to authenticate to. Because of the seamless integration with Active Directory, Windows 2000 security allows for simplified administration of these accounts. For example, XYZ Corp. could create a single user account for each external type of user, such as a partner, vendor, supplier, and customer. Using Active Directory organizational units, XYZ Corp. could easily delegate administrative authority to a user or group of users responsible for maintaining those relationships.

For assured security, companies like XYZ Corp. are implementing Virtual Private Networks between themselves and business partners in order to encrypt network traffic over the public network. These solutions are very popular because of the high value and low cost of implementing them.

ACTIVE DIRECTORY AND SECURITY

A fundamental relationship exists between Active Directory and the Windows 2000 security subsystem. Active Directory stores domain security policy information, such as domain-wide password restrictions and system access privileges, both of which have a direct impact on the use of the system. Windows 2000 implements object-based security, in which every object in the directory contains a security descriptor that defines access permissions that are required to read or write the object properties.

The security model provides a uniform and consistent implementation of access control to all domain resources, such as files, users, and printers, based on group membership. Furthermore, because of the tight integration between Active Directory and the security subsystem, the Windows 2000 OS is able to trust the security-related information stored with objects in the directory.

This relationship with security and Active Directory is achieved *only* by complete integration of Active Directory with the Windows 2000 OS.

Trust Relationships

Because Windows 2000 supports the creation of automatic two-way transitive Kerberos trusts between a child domain and its parent domain within a domain tree, the security and management tasks are greatly reduced in this area. With Windows NT 4.0, administrators not only had to manually create the trust and secure it with a password, but also had to manage two distinctly different SAM databases full of user credentials and, in most cases, had to synchronize user accounts and passwords with both domains. With Kerberos authentication under Windows 2000, a user can authenticate across domain boundaries to anywhere within the domain tree or forest without administrative intervention and, most importantly, without needing an account setup on the other domain.

Active Directory does support the creation of one-way manual "explicit" trust relationships. These types of trusts are still required for interoperability with down-level Windows NT domains and with other operating platforms. An explicit trust is required in our case study to integrate the UNIX and Windows 2000 operating systems. Figure 7.6 illustrates Windows 2000 trust relationships.

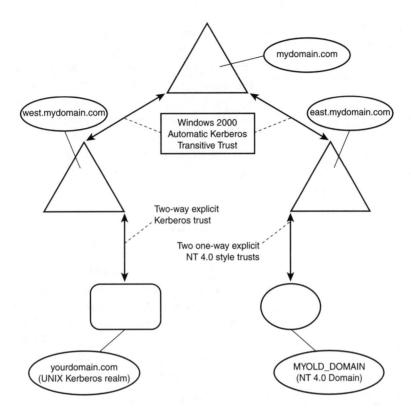

FIGURE 7.6
Windows trust relationships now can take two forms—automatic Kerberos trusts or one-way, manual, Windows NT-style trusts. In addition, the existence of UNIX may require an explicit two-way Kerberos trust.

Delegation of Administration

A highly touted new feature of Windows 2000 and Active Directory is the ability to delegate administrative authority. This process allows administrators to deputize special users or other administrators with granular and specific administrative duties. Granting the technology contact from a business unit the ability to reset passwords for a subset of users in that business unit would be a good example of delegated administration. This person would have no additional administrative powers—just the ability to reset passwords for a specific set of users. Imagine what you could do with this! In Windows NT, the only way to delegate any administrative authority was to give the person or persons requesting authority too much by sticking them in the Domain Admins group (or other built-in group), or to flat-out create another trusted domain. Windows 2000 has fixed that problem and then some by incorporating the Delegation of Administrative Control Wizard. We'll discuss delegation in much more detail in Chapter 12, "Designing an OU and Group Policy Management Structure."

Granularity

How many times have you as an administrator needed to allow a contractor the right to temporarily create user accounts, or perform some other administrative function, in your Windows NT domain? If you've ever been in that situation, you realized one of Windows NT's downfalls: no granular control. In the case of creating user accounts, it was literally an all-or-nothing Domain Admin role. Not a good position to be in when that contractor you trusted with the Domain Admin permission burns you by doing something stupid!

Windows 2000 incorporates an incredibly fine-grained access rights model. This model allows administrators to grant or deny access rights on the ACL of an object at the following levels:

◆ To the object as a whole, which includes all properties of the object

◆ To a grouping of properties, defined by property sets within the object. (Property sets are defined on the property set attribute of a property in the schema.)

◆ To an individual property of the object

By default, when an object is created in Active Directory, the creator of the object is granted uniform read/write access to all properties of the object.

Container objects also provide granular access with respect to who has permission to create child objects. For example, you can define who in the organization can create child objects, such as other containers or user and printer objects. This is a fabulous method of keeping Active Directory clean, because you can allow delegates to create only what they need.

Inheritance

Inheritance of access rights defines how access control defined at higher-level "parent" containers of the directory flows down to "child" containers and then to "leaf" objects. Generally speaking, there are two models for implementing inheritance: dynamic and static.

Dynamic Inheritance

Dynamic inheritance uses an algorithm to define the implicit and explicit permissions on an object. The *explicit* permissions are those assigned directly to that object. The *implicit* permissions are defined to parent containers of the object and are applied to it through inheritance. This greatly simplifies administration by allowing an administrator to effectively change the access permissions on thousands or millions of objects by simply changing them on the parent container of the objects. The drawback to this method is that each and every time a client requests read/write access to an object, Active Directory must dynamically calculate permissions on that object. In a large hierarchical OU structure, this process could slightly degrade performance.

Static Inheritance

Windows 2000 implements a static form of inheritance and refers to it as *Create Time inheritance*. This form of inheritance allows you to define the access control information that flows down to child objects of a container. When an object is initially created, Windows 2000 merges the default access rights with the rights that are inherited from the parent container. New access rights applied to parent-level containers may or may not be inherited by the object, depending on the options set within the object.

We'll discuss more about how this all works in Chapter 12.

Some Recommendations for Securing Active Directory

Because you have such a high degree of flexibility in securing Active Directory, you should take great care in designing a security standard.

As with Windows NT, you should always assign permissions to groups rather than users. The administration of user-level permission assignments, especially in a large corporate environment with several administrators, is cumbersome and simply not a good practice.

In addition to using groups to assign permissions, you should also set a standard for where you assign them. For example, don't make it a practice to assign permissions at the property level. As with user-level permissions, property-level permission assignments can make for an extremely difficult environment to keep a good handle on. You should consider assigning inheritable permissions at the domain level to enforce global security standards, and at the OU level to enforce decentralized security needs. Of course, where you choose to standardize your inheritable permissions will reign heavily on your administrative needs.

Be careful with the *Deny* permission. It works the same way the *No Access* permission works in the NTFS file system. A viable use of this permission is to deny a user in a group access to a particular object without removing the user from a group.

Keep a close eye on the users in the organization who have Domain Admin or Enterprise Admin permissions. Only a select group of individuals should have this type of access. Periodically, do a permissions audit to uncover any forgotten permissions assignments.

As with any NOS, change the Domain Admins group members' passwords frequently, and make them difficult to crack.

SECURING DATA TRANSMISSIONS

Your security policy should extend to the data transmissions flowing across the LAN and WAN. In Windows 2000, you can encrypt standard data transmissions using IPsec. IPsec is made up of the following four components:

◆ Encryption and encapsulation

◆ Authentication and anti-replay

◆ Key management and digital certificates

◆ Support for unique digital certificates

Windows 2000 Predefined IPsec Policies

IPsec stores its policy information in Active Directory. An IPsec policy consists of rules, filters, and negotiation policies that are retrieved from Active Directory when a system starts. IPsec is disabled by default, so to begin using it, you'll either have to create your own policy or choose from one of the three predefined policies:

◆ **Client (Respond Only).** This is used for computers that should not secure communications normally. For example, intranet clients may not require IPsec, unless it is requested by another computer. Implementing this policy on a computer enables it to respond appropriately to requests for secure communications via its default response rule, which tells it to negotiate with computers requesting IPsec. Only the requested protocol and port traffic for the communication is secured.

◆ **Server (Request Security).** This policy is used for computers that should normally secure communications, for example, servers that transmit sensitive financial data. If a computer employing this policy accepts unsecured data, it always requests IPsec in subsequent communications from the original sender. If the other computer is not IPsec-enabled, communications will continue unsecured.

◆ **Secure Server (Require Security).** This policy is used for computers that always require secure communications—for example, servers that transmit highly sensitive data such as top-secret classified government data. Computers employing this policy will reject incoming unsecured communications requests, and outgoing data is always secured. No unsecured communication is allowed by this policy.

All of the predefined policies are designed for computers that are members of a secure Windows 2000 domain. They may be assigned as is without further action, modified, or used as a template for defining custom IPsec policies.

EXAM TIP

IPsec Interoperability Computers utilizing IPsec can still communicate with computers that do not utilize IPsec, but the benefit of the extra security is lost.

IPsec for OLC

In our case study, OLC requires secure data transmissions internally. They have the option of using the predefined *Secure Server* IPsec policy, or customizing their own. Whatever they choose, they must require encryption on all data transmissions.

Predefined Rules and Filter Actions

Similar to the predefined policies, the default response rule for an IPsec policy is provided without need for modification. It may be activated without further action or customized to fit specific needs. It is automatically added to each new IPsec policy you create, but not automatically activated. The purpose of the default rule is to prepare any computers that do not require security to respond appropriately when another computer requests secure communications.

Similar to the predefined rules, predefined filter actions are provided for activation without any need of modification. Like the policies and rules, the filters can be modified to fit specific needs, or used as a template to create additional customized filter actions.

SECURITY IN THE ENTERPRISE

NOTE **Group Policy** Administrators use Group Policy to specify options for managed desktop configurations, software deployment or publication, and more for both computers and users. The security settings extension in Group Policy that we'll focus on here applies to computers only, with the one exception being public-key policies, which may be assigned to a user.

You should now have a fairly good understanding of the security technology associated with the Windows 2000 Active Directory. Now how do we use and enforce this security throughout the enterprise? The answer lies in the integration of the security configuration toolset with the group policy infrastructure. Group Policy (which will be discussed in more detail in Chapter 12) allows you to establish security policies within *Group Policy Objects (GPOs)*, which may be assigned at the site, domain, or OU levels in Active Directory. That said, the integration of the security configuration toolset with GPOs allows you to propagate centrally managed security policies out to all Windows 2000 computers at a site, domain, or OU level.

As you've probably figured out by now, pretty much everything is policy-based in Windows 2000. If you skipped learning Windows NT policies because you didn't use them, you're somewhat at a disadvantage, but not totally. The differences between Windows NT policies and Windows 2000 group policy are pretty big in terms of configuration and ease of use, and therefore can be picked up pretty easily.

Security Policy

Security policy defines a security configuration file that is stored as part of a Group Policy Object. You create these files using the Security Configuration Toolset. You can configure several types of security configuration files using the security configuration editor:

◆ **Account policies.** Account policies define the policies that affect user accounts. You can configure password, account lockout, and Kerberos policies here. Since workstations and member servers contain local accounts databases, password and account lockout policies can be configured locally as well as domain-wide. Kerberos policies do not apply to local accounts databases. In all cases, domain policies override local account policies.

◆ **Local policies.** Can configure local audit policy, user rights, and various configurable security options on a Windows 2000 system.

◆ **Event log.** The event log allows you to configure size, access, and retention parameters for application, system, and security logs.

◆ **Restricted groups.** You can apply policy to groups that are security sensitive, such as the Administrators group.

◆ **System services.** You can now apply security policies to individual system services and grant access to specific users to start, stop, or pause the service (refer to Figure 7.4).

◆ **Registry.** You can configure registry key level policies to provide granular control to each key.

◆ **File system.** You can configure access permissions for file system objects.

◆ **Public key policies.** Can configure encrypted data recovery agents for the Encrypting File System (EFS) domain-wide root and trusted certificate authorities.

◆ **IPsec policies.** Can configure the IPsec policies for computers within a given scope.

These policies can work together to form policies with a large and generalized scope, such as a domain-wide policy, or they can be saved as security configuration files with a specific purpose, such as defining a different minimum password length for a subset of users. These security files may then be attached to OUs as Group Policy Objects.

Precedence

There are three places—local machine, domain, and OU—where policies can be applied, which means they must carry some sort of priority ranking when being applied since a computer may exist in a domain under an OU. The order of precedence for applying security policy is as follows:

1. Local policy

2. Domain policy

3. OU policy

Local policy, which is defined on the computer itself, carries the least precedence. The domain policy sits in the middle, and the OU policy carries the most weight. The domain policy is applied to all computers in a given domain and then any specific OU policies are applied for computers that exist in OUs with defined policies. The net effect of all this is if there are conflicting policies, the domain policy overrides the local machine policy, and the OU policy overrides the domain policy. Figure 7.7 shows a GPO being created for an OU.

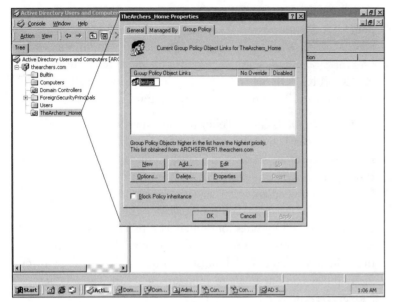

FIGURE 7.7
Group Policy Object being created for an Organizational Unit.

It is important to note here that unlike previous versions of Windows NT, Windows 2000 domain policy actually filters down to the workstation level. For example, in Windows NT 4.0 when you had a domain policy that forced the domain password to 15 characters, it was applied only to domain controllers (primary and backup). In Windows 2000, the same domain-wide password policy also applies to your workstations and member servers local accounts database.

> **EXAM TIP**
>
> **Placement of GPOs** Another critical skill to have mastered when approaching this test is the placement of Group Policy Objects. Pay particular attention to the material in this section.

Group Policy Versus System Policy

It is no secret that Windows NT system policies were cumbersome to create, implement, and manage. Microsoft has done a superb job in re-engineering policies and integrating them with the core OS in Windows 2000. Do not let the name "Group Policy" fool you. These policies really have nothing to do with groups, other than when you implement them, you typically "group" similar computers or users together in an OU and apply a Group Policy Object to it.

> **NOTE**
>
> **Registry Mode** System policy in Registry mode could be run under Windows NT to directly update a computer's registry; however, this was dangerous, and meant that administrators had to use two different modes to complete an update to a policy if they wanted to apply it immediately.

One of the key fundamental differences between NT system policies and Windows 2000 Group Policy is in the way they are applied. With Windows NT System Policies, an administrator uses the System Policy Editor in policy file mode to create an NTCONFIG.POL file and must save it the \\SERVERPDC\ netlogon share. The policy is not applied until the user logs on.

In Windows 2000, Group Policy has one mode that is somewhat of a cross between Policy File mode and Registry mode. Modifications made to a GPO are saved immediately to that GPO, but the change is not immediately implemented on the target machines. Instead, GPOs are refreshed automatically at given intervals during a process called *policy propagation*. Policy propagation is triggered by the target computer every 5 minutes for domain controllers, and every 60–90 minutes for member servers and workstations. The net benefit of this is in administration. Administrators have only one place to configure policy and one mode to configure policy in. The rest "just happens."

Domain Security Policy

During the initial configuration of Active Directory, the domain security GPO is created and attached to the domain object. The domain security policy is just that: a policy that is applied by default to all computers within a domain. The domain security file describes the following three security policy group settings:

◆ Password policy

◆ Account Lockout policy

◆ Kerberos policy

Step by Step 7.1 will assist you in opening the default domain security policy. You must be logged onto your Windows 2000 domain as an administrator for this to work.

STEP BY STEP

7.1 Opening the Default Domain Policy

1. Click Start, Programs, Administrative Tools, Active Directory Users and Computers.

2. Right-click your domain name in the left console pane and select Properties.

3. Select the Group Policy tab. The default domain policy appears as a Group Policy Object.

4. Highlight default domain policy and click the Edit button.

5. Under Computer Configuration, expand Windows Settings and then Security Settings.

6. The default domain policy security settings appear.

Expand the Account Policy item and then click on one of the three settings to view the default domain security configuration. Figure 7.8 illustrates the domain security policy.

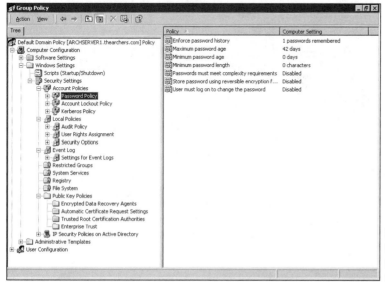

FIGURE 7.8

Windows 2000 domain security policy window containing the domain password policy configuration settings.

Domain Controller Security Policy

By default, all Active Directory domain controllers are added to the Domain Controllers OU. The domain controller security policy defines the security policy common to all domain controllers in that OU. The default domain controllers security policy is created when the first Active Directory domain controller joins the network. It can be opened in much the same way the default domain GPO can, the only difference being that instead of selecting properties from the domain object, you select properties from the domain controllers OU. Refer to Step by Step 7.1 and make the aforementioned replacement to view the default domain controller GPO.

The most significant settings made in the default domain controller GPO are the user rights assignments. User rights were moved out of the User Manager for Domains (in Windows NT 4.0) and into policy-based administration (in Windows 2000). Audit policy and security options policy are also defined in the default domain controllers GPO. This policy is applied with higher precedence than the default domain policy. Figure 7.9 shows the domain controller security policy settings.

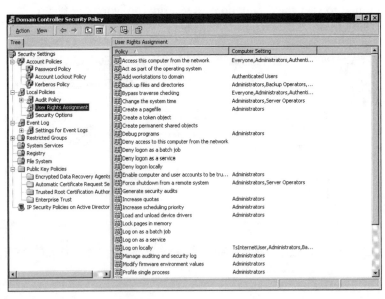

FIGURE 7.9

Windows 2000 domain controller security policy illustrating the default domain controller user rights settings.

A Word About Account Policies

The account policies security area is unique in terms of how it takes place on computers in the domain. All domain controllers receive their account policies from GPOs configured at the domain node, no matter where the domain controllers computer object lies in Active Directory. This is to ensure consistency across the domain for all domain accounts.

As far as workstations and member servers in the domain go, they follow the normal GPO hierarchy with account policy. Remember that Windows 2000 propagates the account policy down to the workstation level, so even the (Windows 2000 Professional) workstations local accounts database adheres to the domain policy.

> **NOTE**
>
> **Local Accounts Policy** It is possible to override the default domain policy on a workstation or member server. To do this, you add a workstation or member server's object to a new OU and apply a GPO to that OU with specific changes to the accounts policy. Because OU GPOs are last to be processed, their settings end up being applied even when previous GPOs contain conflicting settings.

PERSPECTIVE ON THE EXAM OBJECTIVE

Security is such a wide and deep topic that in order to get a good grasp on it, you need to put it in the right context. Our exam objective states that we need to *analyze (existing and planned) security considerations*. The content of this chapter has really focused on the major Windows 2000 security features centered around Active Directory because the focus of the exam is on designing a directory services infrastructure. You could argue that a directory services infrastructure really covers a lot more than Active Directory, so it would be in your best interest to read some of the reference material listed at the end of this chapter.

Security Policies

Some questions you may end up seeing on the exam are questions relating to defining a security policy. Security policies must address the following:

◆ Physical and location security

◆ Creating a security policy document

◆ Reacting to security exposure

A security policy includes guidelines and standards whose purpose is to eliminate security breaches that can lead to certain kinds of attacks and threats. Our case study in this chapter is a good example of a company in need of a security policy. OLC provides a great service, but without the proper security in place, the company could be heading for disaster. One thing is for certain; it is extremely difficult to cover all bases of security and implement a completely secure system without trading off some sort of functionality. For this reason, most companies, when forming a security policy, define what security means to them. This could be totally different from what it means to the next company. A security policy will address the following types of questions:

◆ What is acceptable network conduct and what is not?

◆ Who has access to what and why?

◆ Who is responsible for maintaining security policies?

◆ What data needs to be protected and from whom?

◆ How will security incidents be responded to?

◆ Will we have a password change and history policy?

◆ Who will be allowed access to the data center?

Of course, this is not an exhaustive list, but should get you thinking along the right lines.

CHAPTER SUMMARY

KEY TERMS

- Kerberos
- NTLM
- SSL/TLS
- Public Key Infrastructure (PKI)
- session ticket
- ticket-granting ticket (TGT)
- long-term key
- IPsec
- session key
- domain security policy
- domain controller security policy
- OU security policy
- authenticator
- Delegation of Administrative Control Wizard
- inheritance
- dynamic inheritance
- static inheritance
- encryption/decryption
- cryptography
- Group Policy
- Group Policy Object (GPO)
- Digital certificate
- Certificate Authority (CA)
- digital signature
- security principal
- Key Distribution Center (KDC)

The Internet is driving the need for increased security in all aspects of the computer network. Smarter software and people in the business means there are smarter hackers on the Internet.

Windows 2000 consists of three types of identity authentication: NTLM, Kerberos, and SSL/TLS. It wants to use Kerberos by default, but can only do so in a pure Windows 2000 environment. NTLM is still around for backward compatibility. Finally, SSL/TLS and X.509 certificates are available for certificate-based authentication.

Windows 2000 contains native support for public key infrastructure (PKI). The following make up the Windows 2000 PKI:

- ◆ Certificate Services
- ◆ Active Directory Directory Services
- ◆ PKI-enabled applications
- ◆ Exchange Key Management Services

Windows 2000 also includes native IPsec capabilities and has three built-in IPsec security policies that are integrated with the Group Policy.

The default domain and default domain controller security policies can be located by right-clicking the domain name and domain controller OU, respectively, within the Active Directory Users and Computers add-in.

CHAPTER SUMMARY

The default domain policy contains settings for account security, such as Kerberos, account lockout policy, and password policy, which are implemented already by default for every computer in the domain. Likewise, the default domain controller security policy contains settings for the local policies on all domain controllers. Local policies define audit policy, user rights assignment, and security options.

Read the related reference material that has been mentioned; it's especially important for this chapter because the topic is so broad. Also, be thinking about how you're going to move your existing environment to Windows 2000 in terms of security. As always, having something real-world to which you can relate the chapter content will provide you great benefit.

KEY TERMS
- realm
- hashing
- SSPI
- authorization data
- proxy and forwarding
- ticket referral
- X.509 certificate
- single sign on
- Certificate publication points
- Certificate Revocation List (CRL)
- Client (Respond Only)
- Server (Request Security)
- Secure Server (Require Security)
- policy propagation

APPLY YOUR KNOWLEDGE	

Exercises

7.1   Creating a Group Policy Object

This exercise walks you through creating a GPO to specify security settings that will override the domain password security policy for a given OU.

Estimated Time: 10 Minutes

1. Open the Active Directory Users and Computers utility on your domain controller.

2. Create a new user in the default Users container. Name this user **Exercise71** and make sure you give it the same logon name. You will use this user throughout these exercises. *Do not assign this user a password and do not make any changes to the password configuration window.*

3. Create an OU by right-clicking the icon for your domain, then selecting New and Organizational Unit.

4. In the Name box (see Figure 7.10), type **Exercise71** and click OK.

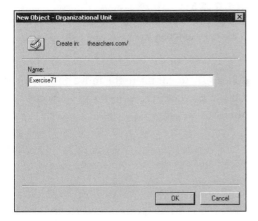

FIGURE 7.10
Create your OU with the name Exercise71.

5. Right-click the Exercise71 OU and select Properties. Click on the Group Policy tab (see Figure 7.11) and click the New button. Name your new GPO **Exercise71GPO**.

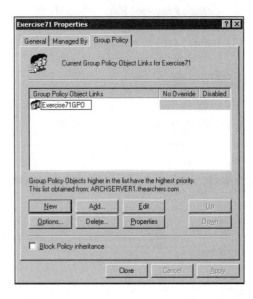

FIGURE 7.11
The Group Policy tab on the Exercise71 OU, where you're creating a new GPO.

6. Click the Edit button to open the Group Policy Editor. Under Computer Settings, expand the Windows Settings folder, then expand Security Settings.

7. Expand Account Policy to reveal the Password and Account Lockout policies.

8. Click on the Password Policy (the password policy choices are shown in Figure 7.12) and change the Minimum Password Length to 7 characters.

APPLY YOUR KNOWLEDGE

9. Change the Passwords Must Meet Complexity Requirements option to Enabled.

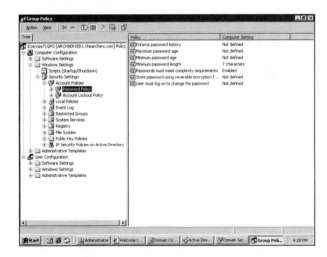

FIGURE 7.12
It's easy to make adjustments to the password policy in the Group Policy Editor.

10. Close the Group Policy configuration window. Close the Exercise71 OU properties window.

11. Click on the Users container to display your new user.

12. Right-click the Exercise71 user and select Move from the context menu. Choose the Exercise71 OU as the destination, as in Figure 7.13.

FIGURE 7.13
You can move the user to any of the selected containers. For this exercise, choose the Exercise71 OU.

13. Click OK to complete the move and then click on the Exercise71 OU to verify your user is there.

APPLY YOUR KNOWLEDGE

> **NOTE**
>
> **Log on Locally**   If you only have one computer and are using it as both the AD server and a "workstation," you'll first need to add the Exercise71 user to the Log on Locally right. You can do this by right-clicking the Domain Controllers OU, selecting Properties, selecting the Group Policy tab, editing the default domain controllers OU, and navigating to the User Rights Assignment local policy.

14. To see the results of your changes, log on to the Windows 2000 domain as Exercise71. Press Ctrl+Alt+Del and click the Change Password option. Attempt to change your password to something fewer than 7 characters. You should not be allowed. If you are, you may have to wait a bit for the policy settings to take place. Move on to Exercise 7.2 and check back later.

7.2   Setting Up a Certificate Authority

This exercise walks you through the process of setting up a certificate authority for your organization. You must be logged on to a domain controller with administrative privileges and have Internet access for this exercise to work properly.

Estimated Time: 30 Minutes

1. In the Control Panel Add/Remove programs utility, add Certificate Services from the Add/Remove Windows Components area.

2. Click Next. Accept the warning about not being able to rename the computer or join/remove it to/from a domain.

3. In the Certification Authority Type window (see Figure 7.14), select Enterprise Root CA. Click Next.

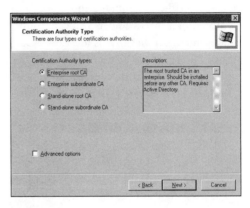

FIGURE 7.14
The Certification Authority Type window allows you to select from the four available types of CAs.

4. On the CA Identifying Information window, fill in information similar to that in Figure 7.15. The CA name is important because it will identify the CA in Active Directory. Click Next when you're done with this window.

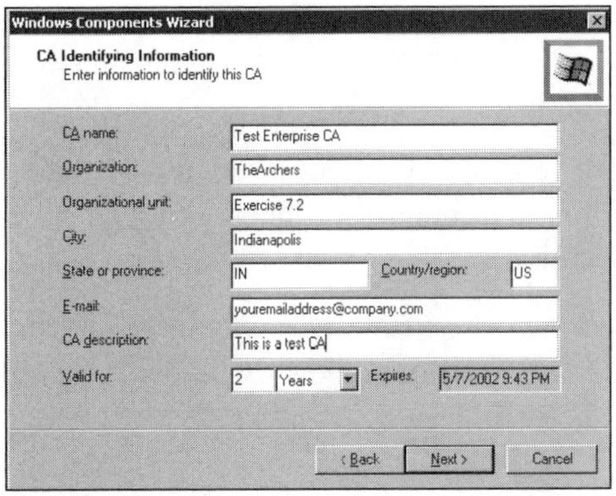

FIGURE 7.15
You must tell Active Directory some information about the new CA.

APPLY YOUR KNOWLEDGE

5. On the Data Storage Location window (see Figure 7.16), note the locations of the certificate database and log files. Then click the check box to allow certificate configuration information to be stored in a shared folder. You can point the management utilities to this location should Active Directory not be available. Click Next when finished. (At this point you may need your Windows 2000 Server CD).

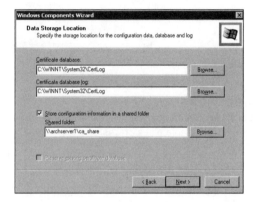

FIGURE 7.16
You can allow for certificate administration via a sharepoint in the event your Active Directory is unavailable.

6. Once the components are configured, click Finish.

7. To verify that Certificate Services is running, drop to a command window and type **net start**. Scroll up to find Certificate Services in the list.

8. To view the certificate configuration, open the Certificate Authority MMC under Administrative Tools (see Figure 7.17).

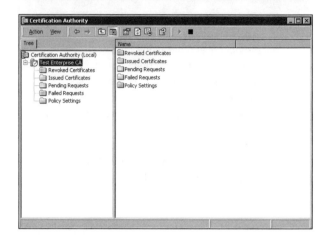

FIGURE 7.17
Use the Certificate Authority MMC to view and manage certificates.

> **NOTE**
> **Installing a Certificate** To install a certificate, you must create a custom MMC and add the Certificates snap-in. Once you do this, you can utilize that utility to request certificates from your Enterprise root CA, and the Certificate Authority utility to view and manage them.

Review Questions

1. What is the authentication process that involves the use of session tickets?

2. A trusted intermediary in Kerberos authentication is known as what?

3. What is the name of the Kerberos ticket that returns the client's long-term session key?

APPLY YOUR KNOWLEDGE

4. By assigning permissions to a group of objects instead of an object itself, you are making use of what?

5. Where does IPsec store its policy information?

6. What type of inheritance in Windows 2000 is referred to as *Create Time inheritance*?

7. Name the Windows 2000 security policies and the order in which they are applied.

8. Name two interoperability situations that require manual trusts to be created.

9. The process by which a KDC in a UNIX realm redirects a client request for a Windows 2000 resource to the Windows 2000 KDC is known as what?

10. What are the three authentication mechanisms available within Windows 2000?

Exam Questions

1. You are the administrator for a financial institution. The VPs need to exchange documents securely at all times. What predefined IPsec security policy should you implement on the VPs' computers?

   A. Client (Respond Only)

   B. Secure Server (Require Security)

   C. Server (Request Security)

   D. X.509 Certificates

2. You wish to change the `msft.nwtraders.com` domain logon password policy to allow 60 days between required changes. Where would you change this policy?

   A. The registry on a domain controller

   B. The default domain security policy

   C. The default domain controller security policy

   D. User Manager for Domains

3. A user calls the help desk to complain that his Windows 2000 Professional workstation keeps losing its password policy settings. Why would this be happening?

   A. There is a virus on the workstation.

   B. The user's registry is set to read-only.

   C. The domain policy is overriding his settings.

   D. The user is not saving his password policy settings.

4. Suppose the online services provided by OLC began to generate enough transactions that the company brought on temporary employees to help process the transactions. You wish to audit directory services access for these individuals only. How should you configure the security policy?

   A. Create an OU for the temporary users and create and assign a GPO with the appropriate settings to this OU only.

   B. Turn on directory service access auditing for the domain security policy.

   C. Turn on directory service access auditing for the domain controller security policy.

   D. Create a GPO with the appropriate setting and assign this GPO to each user object.

5. Randy is the administrator for a large manufacturing company with an outsourced help desk.

How can Randy allow the help desk manager the ability to reset passwords and create and delete user accounts for the help desk personnel only?

A. Create a new OU and make the help desk manager the owner of that OU. Move all help desk personnel into that OU.

B. Make the help desk a Domain Admin by adding her to the Domain Admins group.

C. Delegate administrative authority of the help desk manager user object. Assign the reset passwords and create and manage user accounts to that user object.

D. Delegate the administrative control of the HelpDesk OU by assigning the help desk manager the ability to reset passwords and create and manage user accounts.

6. Suppose you were a security consultant brought on by OLC to help define a security policy for their company. Which of the following best describes the areas in which you should you concentrate your efforts?

A. Creating a security policy document, positioning the firewall, reacting to security exposure

B. Reacting to security exposure, creating a security policy document, physical and location security

C. Physical and location security, reacting to security exposure, administrative personnel

D. Administrative personnel, reacting to security exposure, positioning the firewall

7. You are the security consultant for an organization. You wish to describe the Kerberos authentication process to this organization's technology team. Which of the following best describes the Kerberos authentication process?

A. The Kerberos authentication protocol is a service that runs on a secure server and manages a database of all security principals within its realm.

B. The core Kerberos authentication protocol uses X.509 certificates to provide mutual authentication, message integrity, and confidentiality.

C. Kerberos is an SMB-based authentication protocol that can be used to authenticate all previous versions of Windows clients.

D. Kerberos is a shared secret key authentication mechanism. If two computers wish to communicate, they can do so if and only if each computer can secretly and securely confirm the identity of the other.

8. What technology would you implement to assure OLC customers that they are at a secure and authentic site, not a site trying to impersonate the OLC site?

A. Kerberos Authentication

B. Public Key Cryptography

C. IP Security

D. NTLM

APPLY YOUR KNOWLEDGE

9. You are designing a security plan for a company whose network consists of 50 Windows 9x clients and 100 Windows 2000 Professional clients. The company is planning a move to Windows 2000 and Active Directory and is planning to use Group Policy Objects to control security settings throughout the company. What would you suggest the company do as it upgrades to Active Directory and implements the security policy?

   A. Upgrade the Windows 9x workstations to Windows NT Workstation.

   B. Nothing; everything will work with the security policy as is.

   C. Upgrade the 50 Windows 9x clients to Windows 2000 Professional.

   D. Add the Active Directory upgrade to the Windows 9x computers.

10. Joseph is employed as a financial analyst by OLC. His hobby, however, is computer networking. One day Joseph attaches a network monitoring device to the OLC network to intercept some passwords. Assuming that OLC has implemented its security plan, what type of data will Joseph likely see?

   A. Any non-TCP/IP related data, such as IPX/SPX frames or data from protocols other than TCP/IP

   B. Plain-text passwords only

   C. All TCP/IP related information that is not encrypted as well as all data from other protocols

   D. Data returned by name resolution servers, such as WINS and DNS

Answers to Review Questions

1. Kerberos is the default authentication and security protocol in Windows 2000. In short, the process involves the use of session tickets that employ shared secret keys between client and server. See "Kerberos."

2. The trusted intermediary in the Kerberos authentication process is known as the key distribution center (KDC). The KDC is responsible for issuing session tickets to client computers requesting network resources. See "Key Distribution Center."

3. The long-term session key is created at logon time via a one-way hash of the user's password. It is returned from the KDC to the client's cache in a ticket-granting ticket. The TGT is passed back to the KDC for subsequent requests to network resources. See "Key Distribution Center."

4. Windows 2000 employs object attribute inheritance, which allows administrators to assign permissions to parent objects, and have child objects inherit permissions from their parent. See "Inheritance."

5. IPsec stores its policy information in Active Directory. This provides for a single storage location for all security-related information and provides for seamless integration of IP security. See "Windows 2000 Predefined IPsec Policies."

6. Static inheritance is referred to as Create Time inheritance. At the time of an object's creation, Windows 2000 merges default security information with the settings of the parent object. After that, the object may or may not inherit its parent's security information. See "Static Inheritance."

7. Local security policy, domain policy, OU policy. These are the three default security policies and the order in which they are applied. Hence, the OU policy will override any of the previous two. See "Security Policies."

8. Manual trusts must be created to interoperate with down-level Windows NT domains as well as with heterogeneous systems, such as UNIX and IRIS. See "Trust Relationships."

9. A *referral process* occurs in situations where a request is processed by a KDC in one realm (or domain) for a resource in another realm (or domain). The referral process is simply the re-direction of the request to another KDC. See "Kerberos Interoperability."

10. Windows 2000 supports NTLM, Kerberos, and SSL/TLS authentication. Kerberos is the default and is used whenever possible. NTLM exists for backward compatibility with down-level clients or servers, and SSL/TLS provides secure authentication with X.509 certificates. See "Windows 2000 Authentication."

Answers to Exam Questions

1. **C.** You should configure the VPs' computers for the Server (Request Security) option. The Client (Respond Only) option should be configured for clients that need to respond appropriately for secure connections. The Secure Server (Require Security) option should be used only if all data transmissions on the network need to be secure. X.509 certificates are issued by Certificate Authorities and are used for secure Internet authentication. See "IPsec for OLC."

2. **B.** The default domain security policy is created when the first domain controller is added to a domain. It defines account policies in the areas of passwords, account lockout, and Kerberos. The default domain controller security policy defines policy only for domain controllers, and does not define password policy. The registry on domain controllers holds password policy, but is overridden by domain policy. The User Manager for Domains is where password policy was changed in Windows NT. See "Security Policy."

3. **C.** In Windows 2000, the domain-wide security policy extends to member servers and workstations that are members of the domain. The user may coincidentally have a virus but that's not the technical answer we're looking for! There is no explicit "save" operation when changing policy. See "Security Policy."

4. **A.** To make changes to any security policy, you should create and assign a GPO to an OU. Since the OU policy is the last to be applied, it will override any other security policy, including the domain-wide security policy. Domain controller security policy does control the audit policy on all domain controllers, but would set it for all objects, not just a subset of users. You should never assign GPOs to a user object—and you won't because you can't! See "Security Policy."

5. **D.** To assign a non-administrator temporary permission to perform a specific task, use the Delegation of Administrative Control Wizard. For proper implementation, assign the OU containing the objects you want affected a GPO enabling the help desk manager the granular permission needed to perform individual tasks. See "Active Directory and Security."

APPLY YOUR KNOWLEDGE

6. **B.** A security policy includes guidelines and standards whose purpose is to eliminate security breaches that can lead to certain kinds of attacks and threats. Because of the scope of security, you need to be sure you cover all bases, including physical and location security, creating a security policy document, and how the company should react to security. Options A, C, and D provided viable answers to the question, but focused too much on task-level security measures. See "Security Policies."

7. **D.** Kerberos is a shared secret key authentication protocol that makes use of a trusted intermediary (the KDC) to generate keys that can be used for secret exchanges between two computers. This secret key provides the ability for each computer to secretly and securely confirm the identity of the other. Answer A describes the Kerberos Key Distribution Center, which is only a part of the core authentication protocol. Answer B describes SSL/TLS authentication using X.509 certificates. The core Kerberos protocol as implemented in RFC-1510 does not support X.509 certificate-based authentication; however, the Microsoft extensions to the protocol do. Answer C describes NTLM authentication, which is the Microsoft proprietary predecessor to Kerberos. See "Kerberos."

8. **B.** A core business value to using public key cryptography is authentication. Proving to customers that they are at your Web site and not a Web site impersonating yours means customers

are satisfied and more at ease with your services. Both Kerberos and NTLM provide authentication services, and IPsec provides for security in data transmissions. See "Public Key Cryptography."

9. **C.** To control security settings throughout the company, all client computers must be capable of "being controlled." Windows 9x clients are not considered to be secure clients and should be upgraded to Windows 2000 Professional, an OS much more suited to businesses and one that can definitely partake in security plans. Adding the Active Directory patch to the 9x clients would allow them to search Active Directory, but would not do anything to secure them. An upgrade to Windows NT Workstation would provide added security, but would not allow for a centrally controlled security policy to be applied. See "Group Policy Versus System Policy" and "Security Policies."

10. **A.** Joseph will be able to see any non-TCP/IP data that is on the network segment he is monitoring. Because OLC's plans were to require IPsec for all internal communications, Joseph will see only encrypted garbage for IP data. Data returned by name resolution servers will be encrypted as well because it is IP data. Because OLC had planned to use the Kerberos authentication protocol, passwords will be encrypted as well. This information is covered throughout this chapter and its case study.

Suggested Readings and Resources

1. Microsoft TechNet Articles:

   - Configuring Enterprise Security Policies. Available on September 1999 and later TechNet CDs.

   - *Windows 2000 Reviewers Guide—Section 3:* Addressing Customer Challenges and Requirements. Available on July 1999 and later TechNet CDs.

   - MS Security Configuration Toolset. Available on January 2000 and later TechNet CDs.

   - Configuring Enterprise Security Policies. Available on September 1999 and later TechNet CDs.

   - Windows 2000 Security—Default Access Control Settings. Available on July 1999 and later TechNet CDs.

   - Windows 2000 Certificate Services. Available on July 1999 and later TechNet CDs.

2. Microsoft White Papers:

   - Secure Networking Using Windows 2000 Distributed Security Services

   - Introduction to the Windows 2000 Public Key Infrastructure

   - Introduction to Microsoft Windows 2000 Security Services

   - Single Sign On in Windows 2000 Networks

   - Encrypting File System

   - IP Security (IPsec) for Windows 2000

   - Security Configuration Tool Set

   - Windows 2000 Kerberos Authentication

   - Windows 2000 Kerberos Interoperability

This chapter covers the following Microsoft-specified objective and its four subobjectives for the Designing a Microsoft Windows 2000 Directory Services Infrastructure exam:

Analyze the impact of Active Directory on the existing and planned technical environment.

- **Assess existing systems and applications.**

- **Identify existing and planned upgrades and rollouts.**

▶ One of the early planning stages for Active Directory design should be to determine the compatibility of the existing systems and applications. Additionally, take into consideration the existing and planned systems upgrades and/or rollouts, as you may well be able to integrate some or all upgrade plans with Active Directory.

Analyze technical support structure.

▶ Drastic changes may be in store for an environment with the integration of Active Directory. The purpose of this subobjective is to discover and document the required technical support structure both pre- and post-Active Directory. The difference between the requirements is where the required changes to technical support will lie.

Analyze existing and planned network and systems management.

▶ Network and systems management utilities are the heart and soul of some corporations. The purpose of this objective is to analyze any such utility and its use within the network to uncover potential problems that could arise once Active Directory is introduced to the environment.

C H A P T E R 8

Impact of Active Directory

OUTLINE

STUDY STRATEGIES

▶ Familiarize yourself with the various systems management, asset management, and inventory collection utilities mentioned throughout this chapter. Knowing a bit about their purposes will help you understand where and how they should be used.

▶ Work on understanding exactly why removing NetBIOS is important. Also utilize the NBTSTAT utility with various switches to get a good grasp on the data and information it returns. It would also help to read about it in TechNet or even the Windows 2000 Server Help.

▶ Make sure you thoroughly understand the structure of IT management and in general the technical support structure as described in Chapter 4, "Analyzing the IT Administration Model." This will help you determine how the structure of the IT organization needs to change once Windows 2000 and Active Directory are in place.

▶ Read the white paper on Windows 2000 Management Services listed in the suggested readings at the end of this chapter to get a more thorough understanding of the initiative.

INTRODUCTION

The applications a company uses are critical to its survival. This chapter is dedicated to assessing the existing (pre-Windows 2000) applications and making a determination as to whether they will survive as is in an Active Directory-centric environment. It is important to consider not only the impact Active Directory will have on these applications, but also the impact Windows 2000 in general will have on these applications, so we'll address both as we describe existing systems and applications throughout this chapter.

We'll cover four objectives that may impact, or be impacted by, Active Directory. The assessment of existing systems and applications is only the first area. We'll also look at a few critical areas that tie in with the applications a company uses. One of these areas is its technical support structure. Practically every company has a technical support structure—it doesn't matter whether there's a formal help desk or application support structure, as long as there are people tasked with taking care of problems that occur with the network or with specific tasks or applications.

We'll also discuss plans for upgrades and rollouts. We'll discuss this objective in terms of standards and whether a company would be better off waiting to roll out new software or hardware until after its Windows 2000 implementation.

Finally, we'll discuss network and systems management in terms of current and future implementations. These utilities are themselves applications and therefore will be included in the application assessment. The use of some systems management utilities may actually play a role in inventorying the applications currently deployed on the network.

CASE STUDY: DEWEY, CHEATHAM, & HOWE (DCH)— ATTORNEYS AT LAW

BACKGROUND

DCH is a law firm that has been in business for over 100 years. Its primary practice is in real estate law, although it has recently expanded into other practice areas.

PROBLEM STATEMENT

DCH has always been conscious of its competition and has taken measures to combat being put out of business. Ten years ago, DCH implemented its first computer system. In the years since, certain components of the system have been upgraded or replaced, and other areas have remained intact. A result of this piecemeal tactic is a network with no standards, and various proprietary applications that may or may not still work individually, let alone in conjunction with each other.

CURRENT SYSTEM

DCH Partner

"I use the email system to communicate with my clients. Sometimes it works and sometimes it doesn't. It's really becoming a problem because more and more clients are relying on email as the only means of communication."

Jimmy "the Computer Guy"

"I've been taking care of the DCH network for seven years now. I work out of my home on nights and weekends doing computer work because it's my hobby. My real job is in finance. I'm getting to a point where I don't understand some of the enhancements they want to make. I just installed SMS 1.2 on the server so I could help deploy applications—but I can't figure out how to get it to work."

Paralegal

"I use this system more than anyone else in this office. The major programs are email, PCDOCS document management, SQL Server 6.5, Word, Excel, and then all of our monthly CDs. The CDs are basically volumes of books and reference information the attorneys and I use on a day-to-day basis. They also have an accounting program called Peachtree or something like that—I don't ever use it, though."

ENVISIONED SYSTEM

DCH Senior Partner

"We want to do something that will allow us to reinvent ourselves on the technology end. I believe that would help us all do our jobs. I'm pretty much on the Windows 2000 bandwagon. I've read a lot about it and think we can just start over with it. Of course, we'll have to retain all of our critical applications, mainly our CDs, email, Peachtree, and PCDOCS."

continues

CASE STUDY: DEWEY, CHEATHAM, & HOWE (DCH)— ATTORNEYS AT LAW

continued

Attorneys

"Long story short, we need to get a real consultant. Jimmy has been great, but he doesn't have what we need anymore. We need some tools that will help us manage the network and will notify us of any problem that happens—and preferably offer some solutions as well."

PERFORMANCE

Performance is not too much an issue with the DCH network. Because they maintain a single physical location for their 250 practicing attorneys and 50 support staff, the local area speeds are sufficient for them.

SECURITY

Default security measures for the envisioned Windows 2000 system are sufficient for the needs of DCH.

MAINTAINABILITY

Senior Partner

"I don't plan on hiring an IT person. We need to concentrate on our core business, which is real estate law. Therefore, our new systems have to be largely self-maintaining. I have no problems sending a paralegal to the server room daily to change a tape or something, but anything more than that is not a good system in my eyes."

Paralegal

"I sometimes feel like I'm more an IT intern than a paralegal with all the maintenance I have to do on the system. I'd like to concentrate on doing the work I was hired to do instead of worrying over the computers all the time."

AVAILABILITY

Partner

"This system is up maybe 75% of the time, which is really unacceptable. We need the new system to at least be up whenever we're working—typically between 8:00 a.m. and 8:00 p.m. daily and some Saturdays. Other than that, I don't care if it's up or down."

New IT Consultant

"They've asked me to design a new system that will have 99% uptime during the time they are working—which is basically anytime they are not sleeping. I'm working on getting the application lists and everything else I have to become familiar with together for this design."

DO THE LAB

It's a good idea to prepare a lab environment when determining the impact Active Directory will have on existing systems and applications. By this point in the process, you will have probably already set up a testing lab to simulate the current environment, which is a very important part of the lab because it allows you to more accurately test the functionality of applications as they would appear on the envisioned network. For more information on setting up a Windows 2000 testing lab, see "Designing the Test Environment" on the Windows 2000 Server Resource Kit.

OPERATING SYSTEM UPGRADES

As you consider the applications and what may "portable" to Windows 2000, also consider the Windows 2000 upgrade paths. The upgrade paths supported by Windows 2000 are pretty impressive in terms of OS upgrades, but there are still application requirements that must be met. Microsoft provides information to developers on how to write code for previous versions of Windows that will migrate properly; however, this information was not available at the time most applications were written for Windows 95, 98, or NT, so a great deal of the applications out there need to be tested under the new platform.

Table 8.1 lists the upgrade paths for all Windows 2000 platforms.

> NOTE
>
> **Testing Applications** Sections later in the chapter will cover common items to watch out for when testing applications.

EXAM TIP

Upgrade Paths   There will most likely be a question on any Windows 2000 exam that tries to throw you in an upgrade scenario, so you should know where the "gotchas" are in this equation by using the data on supported upgrade paths in Table 8.1.

TABLE 8.1

WINDOWS 2000 SUPPORTED UPGRADE PATHS

Previous Version	Windows 2000 Platform	Release
Windows 95 (all)	Professional	Full (Retail)
	Professional	Upgrade
Windows 98 (all)	Professional	Full (Retail)
	Professional	Upgrade
NT 3.51/4.0 Workstation	Professional	Full (Retail)
	Professional	Upgrade
Windows 2000 Professional	Professional	Full (Retail)
	Professional	Upgrade
NT 3.51/4.0 Server	Server	Full (Retail)
	Server	Upgrade
	Advanced Server	Full (Retail)
NT 3.51 Server with Citrix	None	None
NT 4.0 Terminal Server	Server	Full (Retail)
	Server	Upgrade
	Advanced Server	Full (Retail)
NT 4.0 Server— Enterprise Edition	Advanced Server	Full (Retail)
	Advanced Server	Upgrade
	Datacenter Server	Full
BackOffice Small Business Server	None	None
Windows 2000 Server	Server	Full (Retail)
	Server	Upgrade
Windows 2000 Advanced Server	Advanced Server	Full (Retail)
	Advanced Server	Upgrade
	Datacenter	Full
Windows 2000 Datacenter Server	Datacenter	Full

NEED FOR AN APPLICATION INVENTORY

Analyze the impact of Active Directory on the existing and planned technical environment.

The first step in assessing the impact of Active Directory is to determine what types of software you have running across the enterprise. For large enterprises, it is recommended that you use an inventory tool such as SMS or Tally Systems NetCensus. The use of an inventory tool can save hundreds of hours and can provide somewhat granular details about the applications installed throughout the network. When working with smaller environments, ones under about 100 users, it may not be cost effective to use an inventory utility to collect software installations and configurations. The following sections discuss how you might approach a software inventory.

Size Up the Company

Obviously, the size of the company and the geographical disbursement of its employees play a large role in deciding how to perform a software inventory. The attorneys of DCH are physically located in the same building, so a manual inventory is not out of the question for them if the cost of an application-assisted inventory is an issue. However, even though it may be painless to inventory a server or two manually, consider inventorying 100 or more computers. To make a long story short, if the company can justify the cost, use an inventory collection utility.

Select Your Weapon

No, we're not going to the gun shop! To do an electronic inventory, you must select a package that allows you to collect the data you need. The following list describes the minimal information you should record for each application installed on the network.

◆ Software title and manufacturer

◆ Major version number

◆ Minor version number (if applicable)

◆ Application type (such as client/server [which piece], stand-alone, and so on)

◆ Architecture designed for (such as 16-bit or 32-bit)

The main benefit in using an inventory collection utility aside from the amount of time it saves you, is its ability to collect very rich information about each product it recognizes.

IN THE FIELD

THE YEAR 2000 FIASCO

If you were involved at all in preparation for Year 2000, you likely were engrossed in hardware and software inventories for much of 1999. The same utilities that were instrumental then in helping you collect information about hardware and software may be reused in preparation for Windows 2000. Tally Systems NetCensus was around long before Year 2000, but gained significantly in functionality and popularity in 1999. It is still here today and is an excellent choice for Windows 2000 preparation. Of course, Microsoft's System Management Server also provides a sophisticated inventory mechanism that can be utilized throughout the lifetime of hardware and software, not only to maintain centralized inventory but also to provide sophisticated software "push" installations utilizing rules set up based on that inventory.

NOTE

Recognition of Software Most popular hardware and software inventory tools utilize "recognizers" to detect software. Recognizers are comprised of a set of information about a product that allows the software to "recognize" it in an installed state. Common recognizers include registry entries, directory structures, certain EXE files, and so on.

NOTE

Asset Management The term "asset management" may be used here loosely. It refers to the packaging, distribution, management, analysis, and reporting of applications deployed on a network. We are concerned just with the inventory of applications here, but would certainly recommend you leverage the asset management applications if available. In fact, many tools we describe here are asset management tools.

We mentioned both Microsoft SMS and Tally Systems NetCensus as inventory collection utilities. Other utilities are available on the market today. Table 8.2 describes some of the popular utilities and where to obtain more information about them on the Web.

TABLE 8.2

POPULAR SOFTWARE INVENTORY COLLECTION UTILITY APPLICATIONS

Vendor	Product	Webformation
Tally Systems	NetCensus	http://www.tallysys.com/cenergy/ products/ntc/index.html

Vendor	*Product*	*Webformation*

Asset Technologies	AMS Desktop	`http://www.assettech.com/`
		`Products/AMS_Desktop/ams_`
		`desktop.html`

Attest Systems	GASP Suite	`http://www.attest.com/` `products/default.asp`
Microsoft	Systems Management Server	`http://www.microsoft.com/` `smsmgmt/default.asp`

One final note about an inventory application: Choose the right tool for the right job. You may find that a single application is very appealing in one environment, and then decide it's much too complicated and/or costly for the next. Consider your setup time and any customization time necessary for the inventory tool as well.

Manual Collections

If you do decide to use a manual inventory process, make sure you have the proper resources and a plan. It is very easy to waste time recording information about the same product on different machines, especially if multiple inventory technicians are involved. Create a centralized database and make updates directly to it. If you have the time and resources, write a simple Web-based input system with an Access or Excel back-end "database." By doing this, you can index and report from the data as you go.

IN THE FIELD

USING THE WINDOWS 2000 READINESS ANALYZER

The Windows 2000 Readiness Analyzer tool analyzes your system and reports potentially incompatible hardware devices and software applications. The tool compares the devices and applications on your system against a list of known issues. Although this check also occurs during Windows 2000 Setup, you can download and run the tool before installing Windows 2000 to help ensure that your installation will succeed.

continues

continued

N O T E **Microsoft Readiness Framework** For more information about the MRF and the Skills Manager database, visit `http://www.microsoft.com/ DirectAccess/training/mrf.asp`.

In an organization with standardized desktop configurations, this tool can provide a great deal of insight as to what applications need to be investigated. If standardization is not a high priority for an organization, this tool will be less valuable unless run on every computer. It works on the servers as well.

Additionally, the Microsoft Readiness Framework (MRF) provides a comprehensive set of proven practices, guidance, and learning solutions for technical readiness and sustained customer and partner performance with the Windows 2000 platform. This framework includes a skills manager database application that contains the competencies, learning plans, and resources for Windows 2000 Active Directory planning and design.

Standalone Applications Versus Client/Server Applications

As you know, the software that runs from a desktop may or may not require a server to function. Some applications, such as Microsoft Outlook, can operate with *or* without a server. Make sure you distinguish the standalone applications from the client/server-based applications in your inventory. Client/server applications may require additional research in the areas of how they connect to the server and authentication. The section later in this chapter on removing NetBIOS will discuss these issues in more detail. Server-side applications should be inventoried with the most caution. You need to be very careful to record critical information, such as protocol requirements, directory integration, and redundancy.

There probably should be a column for "other" on your inventory sheet. There are always those applications that insist on off-the-wall configurations that drive you nuts to configure, much less port to Windows 2000. Our wonderful attorneys at DCH have one such application, which just happens to be an application you can use to collect inventories—SMS.

DOS-Based Applications

Some companies still rely on DOS programs that just won't break and it is very difficult to get those companies to understand that they are falling behind. Microsoft has been pretty nice in providing support for these legacy applications, and this support doesn't stop completely with Windows 2000. A majority of the DOS applications that run on Windows NT will run on Windows 2000. So, you must include them on the inventory. If you are using an inventory collection utility, you probably will *not* pick up all of the DOS programs because they won't be recognized by the software, so you must be careful to identify them manually.

A Word About Home-Grown Applications

Be extremely cautious when gathering information about applications that were written for internal use. A majority of these applications do not follow Microsoft's published specifications for best practices in software development, and may therefore cause problems with—or not run properly at all with—Windows 2000. In fact, one of the major reasons applications do not run correctly under Windows 2000 is poor development practices. Identify those applications if possible and find out who developed them. This will help you determine how they may be supported under Windows 2000.

> **NOTE**
>
> **Benefits of MSINFO32.EXE** An excellent source for information about applications is the Microsoft System Information Utility (msinfo32.exe). This utility contains a set of ActiveX controls that are used to gather specific information about a computer, such as installed drivers, system components, and information.

CATEGORIZE THE APPLICATIONS

Once you've compiled your software listing, it's time to identify which applications are absolutely critical on the network and which ones you can drop from the list immediately. The goal here is to dump as much of the list as possible and facilitate standardization. After all, you are migrating to a new dimension—what a great time to reinvent the network standards!

One thing that you should keep in mind as you categorize the applications is that you must somehow get input representative of all the users across the organization. While this is relatively simple for an organization like DCH, it can be rather challenging for worldwide organizations. At the very least, get input from a level of management appropriate for the organization—in other words, based on the organizational chart, determine the appropriate people to speak for entire departments or business units, and give them a chance to do so.

Analyze the Application Inventory

You will be surprised at the amount of software a 50-person company has installed on its network. We are not talking about a few applications; we're talking upwards of 150 on the average! Imagine the software for a 20,000-seat enterprise! Ack! Don't worry too much; after you filter out the different versions of applications the list should collapse quite a bit. Use some sort of filtering process to narrow your list as much as possible. If multiple versions of applications are listed, make sure you consider the need for different versions before you cancel one out. The goal again is to standardize without jeopardizing mission-critical business processes.

Once you've completed the initial tweaking of the inventory listing, you need to spend time with the users of the applications to assign priorities. Prioritizing certain applications is a no-brainer. Prioritizing others is tough. Prioritizing the balance will seem impossible at times. Certainly, differences of opinion about what is critical and what is not will be noticeable.

The next three sections discuss ways you might prioritize an organization's applications. This is not a process mandated by Microsoft, but rather an approach you may choose to follow when preparing your list of applications that need assessment.

Priority-One Applications

Priority-one applications are mission-critical. They are applications that would close the business (or come darn close) if they did not function. For example, a company that provides Web hosting to its clients would definitely consider its Web servers and the application software they run to be priority one applications. That same company would probably consider Microsoft Excel a novelty, whereas an accounting firm would go under without it. The variance between businesses and the people within them will almost always be something you must contend with, so be prepared.

The following list highlights some of the applications you can expect to put on a priority-one list:

◆ Any line of business (LOB) application

◆ Enterprise messaging systems

◆ Data warehousing systems

◆ Departmental applications, such as AutoCAD in the Engineering group, or an ERP implementation

◆ Ecommerce applications

◆ Tape backup applications

◆ Emulation packages (provide access to LOB applications)

◆ Home-grown applications that provide a critical service to the business

Priority-Two Applications

A majority of the applications you keep will be located on the priority-two listing. These are the common everyday applications that a company uses to collaborate, share information, and, in general, do the job. These applications, although very important to the efficiency of the company, are not considered mission-critical.

The following list highlights some of the applications you may conclude are priority two:

◆ Office automation packages, such as Microsoft Office

◆ Management utilities, such as Intel LanDesk or Microsoft System Management Server

◆ Virus-scanning packages

◆ Network-monitoring packages

◆ Reporting applications, such as Crystal Reports

Priority-Three Applications

The final priority level for applications is level three. This will almost certainly be a melting pot of sorts for all the applications that can't or won't fit in the priority-one or -two buckets. These are the applications that may still be a very large part of operations for specific areas of a company, but are simply used as an enhancement or a utility. These applications should be tested last to avoid running out of time on more important applications if the testing period is limited.

The following list highlights some of the applications you may add to a priority-three listing:

◆ Utility programs, such as WinZip or WS_FTP

◆ Home-grown applications (unless written because no other solution was available to provide the required service to the business)

◆ Everything else that doesn't fit in priorities one and two

DETERMINE THE PROBLEM APPLICATIONS

Once you've verified the prioritization of applications, the next step is to determine which ones are going to give you problems.

Why Do Applications Fail?

There are a number of reasons applications may fail under Windows 2000. A majority of reasons are associated with the platform for which the application was developed to run. In general, the larger the application vendor, the better the odds are that the application will run correctly on Windows 2000. This can be attributed to the fact that most established companies have a standard technique they adhere to when developing applications, and part of that technique is to follow the application development guidelines made publicly available by Microsoft. Additionally, if problems are discovered, these established companies will likely issue patches or new versions designed specifically for Windows 2000.

You can loosely compare this concept to the whole Year 2000 mess. Typically the larger, more established companies had Y2K fixes out for their supported application base well before "crunch" time. Conversely, many smaller companies did not release fixes—or required that customers upgrade to a new version.

Where Are the Problems?

Most applications that run under Windows 9x and NT will run under Windows 2000. There are, however, exceptions that you'll read about in the following sections.

OS/2 and POSIX Applications

The Windows 2000 development team did not spend a lot of time beefing up support for OS/2 and POSIX applications. Although these platforms are still supported as they were in Windows NT, they don't take advantage of Windows 2000 features. The general rule of thumb is if an OS/2 or POSIX application runs under Windows NT, it should run under Windows 2000. You'll find that to be a common theme throughout this section.

DOS Applications

DOS applications may continue to run properly under Windows 2000. If they ran under Windows NT, they should work. If they ran under Windows 9x, they may work, although the Windows 9x platforms were written with much more consideration for legacy applications, so the percentage of applications that actually work under Windows 2000 will be less than 100%. When DOS applications are running under protected kernel environments, such as Windows 2000, failures tend to occur in a few well-known areas:

◆ **Direct hardware access.** Any DOS application that requires direct communication with a hardware device will not work. Windows 2000 security will not let any application touch hardware outside the BIOS. Only Kernel mode services in Windows 2000 can directly access hardware.

◆ **FAT.** Plain and simple: DOS applications were written to FAT standards because they had no other file system to write to. If the application attempts to access an NTFS partition, it will probably crash because it doesn't understand NTFS. Furthermore, DOS FAT partitions are limited to 2GB in size, and typically report larger volumes as negative numbers.

◆ **Graphics display.** DOS applications that produce graphics must not be set to run in a window. Windows 2000 cannot send DOS graphics to a window, but can generally display them full-screen.

◆ **Security.** DOS programs do not understand the Windows 2000 security model. They do not understand Active Directory, policies, NTFS, or any of the new features built into Windows 2000. When they crash, it's usually a hard crash with esoteric error messages.

Windows 3.x (16-Bit)Applications

It's surprising how many 16-bit applications are still very much in use in the corporate environment. Most of them, if they run under Windows NT, will run under Windows 2000. Since Windows 3.x was really just a graphical extension to DOS, you can imagine them sharing the same trouble spots that DOS has relative to Windows 2000. The well-known areas that Windows 3.x applications may fail under Windows 2000 are as follows:

◆ **Direct hardware access.** Windows 3.x applications operate according to the expectation that they will be able to directly access hardware when they need to. If a Windows 3.x application, such as a network redirector, needs to access any hardware directly to operate, it will not run under Windows 2000. Windows 3.x applications that use VXDs (Virtual Device Drivers) to access hardware directly will not run under Windows 2000.

◆ **FAT.** Like DOS, Windows 3.x applications expect to be running on a FAT partition. If that partition is greater than 2GB, the application may have difficulty if it needs to check for free disk space, as in DOS. Setup programs that check for free disk space are especially susceptible to this problem, and likely will not install. You can try to fake out the application by installing it to a partition with less than 2GB of available space.

◆ **Security.** Windows 3.x applications are no better at understanding the Windows 2000 security model than DOS
applications. They therefore may crash suddenly due to
security violations, and produce unpredictable error messages.

◆ **Device drivers.** There are specific Windows 3.x applications
that can be written to use a specific Windows 3.x device
driver, such as for a printer or sound card. Because these
device drivers are not compatible with Windows 2000, these
applications will not run correctly. Windows 2000 does
include drivers for a plethora of devices, and a device's manufacturer will probably make what it does not contain available.
These drivers will not help the lowly 16-bit application
written to a 16-bit driver, however.

◆ **CPU utilization.** Remember cooperative and preemptive
multitasking? 16-bit Windows and DOS applications are
written to control the CPU until they are done and then
relinquish it to the next application (cooperative multitasking).
Windows 2000, of course, manages the CPU based on application priority and will ration it out to all applications fairly
(preemptive multitasking). 16-bit applications are run in a
virtual machine under Windows 2000—much the same as
they were under Windows NT. If you have an application
that is particularly hard on the CPU, you can make it run
in a separate shared memory space.

Windows 9x Applications

Windows 9x applications made giant leaps forward with the 32-bit
environment. Still, they may have trouble in many of the same areas
as the 16-bit DOS and Windows 3.x applications. The following list
describes the trouble spots:

◆ **Device drivers.** Windows 95 device drivers are not compatible
with Windows 2000. The good news is that most of these
drivers should contain updated Windows 2000 versions.
However, if an application specifically requires a Windows 95
video or some other driver, it will not function properly under
Windows 2000. Windows 98 introduced a fix to the problem
of every new OS requiring a different type of device driver by

> **NOTE**
>
> **Windows (or Win32) Driver Model**
> The WDM is a standard to which inde-
> pendent hardware vendors (IHVs) may
> write device drivers. This standard is
> supported as a means of writing a
> single driver that works on the
> Windows 9x, NT, and 2000 platforms.

introducing the Windows Driver Model (WDM), which is supported under Windows 2000. Drivers written to the WDM should migrate to Windows 2000.

◆ **Security.** Unless a Windows 9x program was written with Windows 2000 security in mind, it will fail. It may fail with a more decipherable error message thanks to the Win32 API, but it will fail nonetheless. This doesn't mean that all Windows 9x applications will fail—just those that need to make calls to security APIs.

◆ **Win32 API.** Windows 9x and Windows 2000 both use the Win32 API, but as you might imagine, they are not the same. Most differences are due to the new Windows 2000 security model. A majority of the problems you find with Windows 9x applications will involve the Win32 API.

◆ **Registry problems.** One of the major differences between Windows 9x and Windows NT was the notion of user profiles. Windows 2000 builds on Windows NT in this area, so you might imagine that a Windows 9x application that makes specific use of the Windows 9x registry won't run. This is because of the HKEY_LOCAL_MACHINE and HKEY_CURRENT_USER registry hives. Because all Windows 9x users typically share the same profile, some applications wrote common application information to the HKEY_CURRENT_USER\Software hive instead of the HKEY_LOCAL_MACHINE\Software hive where it belongs. Once ported to Windows 2000, the specific application may run fine for one user but not for the next, because Windows 2000 creates a separate registry hive for each user, much like Windows NT does.

Windows NT Applications

You'll have the most luck migrating Windows NT applications to Windows 2000. That "Built on NT Technology" really comes into play here. Very few properly written NT applications will have trouble with Windows 2000. The area of Windows NT applications that have the most trouble migrating to Windows 2000 are services. Most services do migrate well, but here are some common failure areas:

◆ **Services.** Third-party applications that perform some function under Windows NT that is now integrated into Windows 2000 will not function properly. Disk quota packages and administration utilities are examples. In fact, it is recommended that you phase out these third-party utilities and utilize the built-in services. Applications that were built to do just about anything with the SAM, whether it was to provide for granular administration or to manage accounts, will probably not function correctly with Active Directory. Long story short: The utilities that ship with Windows 2000, such as the disk, file and user quotas, and Active Directory administration tools know and understand Windows 2000 and Active Directory better than a third-party utility could, so it is recommended that you use the new stuff and phase out the old.

◆ **System utility software.** If there is one area where we strongly recommend you do not even attempt to migrate, it is this area. Utilities that perform maintenance, for example on the hard disk partitions of Windows NT, will not understand NTFS5, the new version of NTFS that ships with Windows 2000. These utilities can cause damage in the form of data loss if used incorrectly. Other utilities, such as backup utilities, do not understand Active Directory and therefore cannot understand the new permissions structure of Windows 2000. These applications should be upgraded to versions that do understand the new Windows 2000 security model and Active Directory. Virus-scanning utilities are exempt from this and should continue to run fine after migrated to Windows 2000, but of course it's always recommended that you have the latest and greatest version.

◆ **Active Directory.** A general statement about Active Directory: Any application that was written to access the SAM database in Windows NT should be upgraded to a version written for Active Directory. These applications will continue to work on Windows 2000 domain controllers running in mixed mode, but a general goal of a Windows 2000 migration should be to take it to Native mode.

> **NOTE**
>
> **Vendor Web Sites** It is always a good idea to check both vendor Web sites and the Windows 2000 Software Compatibility Web site before embarking on a potentially long and painful application compatibility testing journey. It really stinks to do a week's worth of work to find an answer that might already be published at a vendor Web site with a fix waiting for you to download.

IN THE FIELD

MICROSOFT'S WINDOWS 2000 UPGRADE WEB SITE

An extremely important set of utilities that can be used to help you determine the level of work required for a Windows 2000 upgrade an be found at `C:\MCSE TG\ToPE\983108pe.doc`.

This Web site serves as a home base for information vital to the entire upgrade process. Central to this information is a hardware and software compatibility database. You can search this database by company or product name. The information in this "Directory of Windows 2000 Applications" is provided by independent software vendors, including Microsoft application teams. The database is continually updated, so if you find that an application is currently not listed or is listed as in the process of being tested, checking back a few days, weeks, or months later may yield different results.

Finally, this site includes a link to a comprehensive guide to upgrading to Windows 2000, which walks you through all the required steps. This guide also contains a link to all Windows 2000 Certified applications.

IN THE FIELD

TAKING IT TO THE LAB

One of the more important processes you will endure when examining your existing systems and applications is in the Windows 2000 test lab. Depending on factors such as your available resources, time, and money, your test lab may be used for a very short duration before the production rollout, or may be used alongside a phased production rollout to test applications as they are needed. Whatever the case, you need to at the very least test the priority-one applications, even if they are certified by Microsoft to be Windows 2000 compatible.

Microsoft BackOffice applications, such as Exchange and SQL, are the server-end workhorses of the Microsoft family. They should be tested thoroughly in the test lab, along with other priority-one applications, prior to Windows 2000 production rollout.

Microsoft and other well-established application vendors are making available many white papers and other documentation detailing the use of their products under Windows 2000.

UNDERSTANDING THE SOLUTIONS

We've discussed what might go wrong with an application; it's now time to take some action. When it comes right down to it, there are really only a couple of approaches to addressing problems with applications:

◆ **Lab Testing.** You have Windows 2000 running in the test lab and it should be simulating the production environment as close as it can. Test the application in the lab to determine if it will work appropriately.

◆ **Vendor Support.** It is a good idea to make some sort of contact with the software vendor. These days, just about anything you want to know about an application is available on the vendor's Web site.

It is recommended that you use both approaches, as you will undoubtedly be able to uncover some little issue the vendor missed, or vice versa.

IN THE FIELD

MIGRATION DLLS HELP WINDOWS 9X APPLICATIONS

Many vendors of Windows 9x applications have developed utilities that help ailing applications as they are migrated to Windows 2000. Microsoft has made available an interface that developers can use to write migration DLLs. *Migration DLLs* are primarily for Windows 9x applications that are now compliant with Windows 2000. All migration DLLs on a system are run during the upgrade process, which gives their applications a chance to correct any problem on the fly.

This procedure will work only for Windows 9x applications and is typically needed because of the differences between the Windows 9x registries and Win32 API structure.

By the end of this process, you should end up with a list of applications that for one reason or another will not make it through the migration process. So what are you to do? There are three main options.

Upgrade

The primary reason for upgrading an application is to retain the application data. Additionally, the cost associated with upgrading an application is typically much less than it is to replace that application with another. The users will also benefit from an upgrade since a majority of the features and functions they know should apply to the upgraded version as well.

Obviously, if an upgrade is needed for an application, rigorously test the new version. Also, determine *when* you will perform the upgrade. If you run the upgrade before migrating to Windows 2000, what are the consequences? If you migrate after will the old application run until you can get it upgraded? You must plan this out carefully, because end users will most definitely be affected. Test upgrading both the old OS and old application to Windows 2000 and the new application. Test multiple iterations, such as upgrading the OS first and the application second, then the application first and the OS second. Choose the most effective method to use for your actual production upgrade.

Replace

Another alternative is to replace an existing application with a different product. This option presents a couple of additional challenges in the area of data retention and end-user training. Usually a new application has a new interface and a new way of organizing and representing data. To the user, this could present a major hurdle because she'd have to learn a new product. Additionally, unless there is a predefined import path or conversion mechanism, historical data may be difficult, if not impossible to integrate with the new system.

Of course, in making the decision to replace an application, a good deal of the consideration should be placed on data retention, training, and cost. If, for example, you decide it is time to replace your MS Mail for PC Networks with Exchange Server, you must consider the learning curve the users are going to have in moving from the MS Mail client interface to the Outlook interface. Of course, in this example, retaining the data is accomplished via a fairly simple import process.

Adequate testing of the new system and data import and export procedures should be done in the lab. This is an area, too, where you'll want to involve specific key users of this application in a production pilot. Make sure you keep management up to speed on the decision-making process, as they will be your advocates for getting users to help you test the applications.

Retire

Be careful making the decision to retire software. Make sure you discuss the potential retirement with all stakeholders before making the final decision. You must also decide what to do with any data that is left behind.

In most cases, you'll consider retiring software when the functionality it provides is no longer needed. If a standard application was Rumba for the Mainframe for access to a 3270 that is no longer in service, then it would make sense to retire Rumba. That example is easy, but what about the case where you have an application such as SMS that was deployed to push out applications to users. With the Group Policy functionality built into Windows 2000, you get that specific functionality out of the box. You are then faced with the dilemma that if you remove a fully deployed SMS installation, you might somewhere down the road need remote control capabilities, which are not included in the Group Policy functionality.

Take care in retiring software, make sure you cover all the bases.

REMOVAL OF NETBIOS

Microsoft decided to end Windows' reliance on NetBIOS in Windows 2000, so you can optionally choose to remove support for it. Before you do, however, make sure you have no down-level clients or servers remaining on the network, and also ensure that you have no applications that require NetBIOS remaining on the network. In short, wait a while before you remove it, because unless you are building a company from the ground up on bleeding edge technology, NetBIOS is going to be around for a while.

So why do we want to remove NetBIOS anyway? The main reason is to not only remove the protocol layers required to support it, but also reduce network browser traffic associated with it. NetBIOS over TCP/IP (NBT) and NetBIOS over IPX (NBIPX) are two "overlays" to core protocols that add overhead to the network in general. Removing support for them and standardizing on one core protocol increases performance by reducing overhead and easing management. The following list describes the advantages of removing NetBIOS:

◆ **End reliance on WINS.** Aside from being Microsoft proprietary, WINS is not the most stable database, as you probably well know. The preferred name resolution service will be DNS.

◆ **Single name resolution method.** Instead of using up to seven name resolution methods (discussed in Chapter 5, "Analyzing the Physical Environment"), the removal of NetBIOS and integration of DNS will provide a single uniform method for name resolution.

◆ **Easier network support.** The fewer the protocols to support, the better.

◆ **Increased network performance.** Again, by streamlining the name resolution methods and reducing protocol overhead, over network performance should be faster.

◆ **Increased performance connecting to multihomed computers.** NetBIOS attempts to connect on all transports available at the client. If multiple connections succeed, all but one is cancelled. This is inefficient. By using DNS and TCP/IP only, an efficient and quick connection can be made to the destination computer.

◆ **Enhanced security.** Hackers love NetBIOS because it provides them easy access to computers from the Internet. Removing this functionality decreases the chances of intrusion.

A majority of the "pre-2000 versions" of Microsoft BackOffice products rely on NetBIOS somewhere, as do many others. Additionally, all previous GUI versions of Microsoft operating systems rely on NetBIOS. So how do you tell where NetBIOS is being used?

Finding NetBIOS in the Environment

There are two main areas you can examine to find out how NetBIOS is used throughout your environment, WINS and the client computer. Additionally, you can use a network sniffer to capture all NetBIOS traffic as it travels across the network.

WINS

The first place you should start is in the WINS database. By examining its entries, you can determine a lot about NetBIOS in your environment. If you plan to move all operating systems to Windows 2000, you can ignore the following WINS entries, as they are OS-specific.

- ◆ COMPUTERNAME<00>
- ◆ DOMAIN<00>
- ◆ COMPUTERNAME<01>
- ◆ \\-__MSBROWSE__<01>
- ◆ COMPUTERNAME<03>
- ◆ USERNAME<03>
- ◆ COMPUTERNAME<06>
- ◆ DOMAIN<1B>
- ◆ DOMAIN<1C>
- ◆ DOMAIN<1D>
- ◆ DOMAIN<1E>
- ◆ COMPUTERNAME<1F>
- ◆ COMPUTERNAME<20>
- ◆ COMPUTERNAME<21>
- ◆ COMPUTERNAME<BE>
- ◆ COMPUTERNAME<BF>

NOTE

NetBIOS Service Types Use the Microsoft TechNet article Q163409 for a listing of NetBIOS service types. This list should help you identify the purpose of a WINS entry during your investigation.

After you've removed these entries, you can examine what is remaining. The downfall is the next step. WINS will not come out and tell you why the entry is needed, but you should be able to investigate it and determine what you can do from there.

Clients

If you have client computers that don't register their NetBIOS information to WINS, you need to check their local NetBIOS cache. Don't worry: You won't have to go to each workstation to do this. You can use the NBTSTAT command with the -a <COMPUTERNAME> switch (**NBTSTAT -a RemoteComputerName**). The return from this command will be a listing similar to that in Figure 8.1.

If you have a list of computer names, you can incorporate this command in a batch file and redirect output to a file for examination. Alternatively, you can use NBTSTAT -A <IPADDRESS> to collect the same information.

So now you have all the NetBIOS entries. What do they tell you? Well, not a whole heck of a lot, to be honest. What they do tell you is whether you have NetBIOS happening on the network, which is a starting point. Determining which applications are using NetBIOS is the fun part!

FIGURE 8.1
NetBIOS name cache from the computer named ARCHSERVER2.

Determining Which Applications Use NetBIOS

It's too bad there isn't a utility available that would go out and tell you what applications are using NetBIOS. Unfortunately, you have to be sly about it. The NBTSTAT command will tell you the information you need to know. Step by Step 8.1 explains how it works.

STEP BY STEP

8.1 How to Tell Whether an Application Uses NetBIOS

1. Go to the computer you wish to test.

2. Drop to a DOS window and type **NBTSTAT -s 1** (the "s" is case-sensitive). This will list the NetBIOS sessions table and refresh it every second (see Figure 8.2).

3. While the sessions table is being refreshed, launch the application in question.

4. Switch back to the NetBIOS sessions table. If the application required a NetBIOS session, it will be listed in the NetBIOS sessions table (see Figure 8.3).

FIGURE 8.2
NetBIOS sessions table for the computer named ARCHGAME; no NetBIOS sessions are taking place currently.

continues

continued

FIGURE 8.3
NetBIOS sessions table for the computer named ARCHGAME; this time with a NetBIOS session connection.

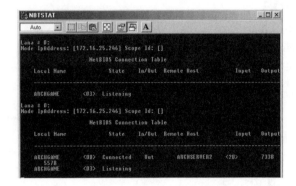

This process sounds like quite an undertaking, but it shouldn't be too bad considering you can use the same computer to test most applications.

Once you figure out which applications are using NetBIOS, you can determine what the impact of turning it off would be. Don't do this in production! Use the test lab to determine the impact of removing NetBIOS. Remember, before you can remove NetBIOS, you must have an alternative name resolution solution in place. Active Directory requires DNS as this replacement. See Chapter 10, "DNS and Active Directory," for more information about DNS and Active Directory.

PLANNED CHANGES TO SYSTEMS AND NETWORK APPLICATIONS

Whether you've just discovered an application that needs to be upgraded or replaced, or you've planned to take that action in the future, Active Directory should be considered in the planning stages. Additionally, any hardware upgrades you have planned, or that need to happen in order to comply with Windows 2000 requirements, should be planned in conjunction with the migration. If you don't pay close attention to the hardware and software and how you want to roll it out, you could end up spending about two or three times the time and money on getting this accomplished. In short, *plan!*

Upgrades to Hardware or Software

How you decide to get the hardware or software into production will affect the bottom line. For example, if you have a need to roll out a new application to every employee in the company, distributing that application before you migrate to Windows 2000 would add significant cost to the migration itself. You would not only have another application to test for compatibility, you'd have the cost of rolling it out now. It would be much more beneficial if you could roll out the application after Windows 2000 migration. This way you could distribute it with a group policy and be done with it. Of course, this is a logistical challenge—as you well know by now, getting to Windows 2000 quickly becomes harder as the company gets bigger and more disperse.

Rollout of New Equipment

Most companies will coordinate the rollout of new hardware with the rollout of Windows 2000. It doesn't make much sense not to, especially with the hardware requirements for Windows 2000. When making selections for new hardware, make sure right away that it is supported; check it against the Hardware Compatibility List (HCL) for Windows 2000, found at **http://www.microsoft.com/ windows2000/upgrade/compat/search/devices.asp**.

The HCL now allows you to search for compatible software as well as hardware. You should also make sure, especially for domain controllers, that you size the hardware correctly. For this, Microsoft provides a utility, simply named Active Directory Sizer, in the Windows 2000 Server Resource Kit. It is available for download from **http://windows.microsoft.com/windows2000/reskit/**.

Active Directory Sizer allows you to estimate the hardware requirements for deploying Active Directory in an organization based on the organization's profile, domain information, and site topology. It takes a number of user inputs and using internal formulas estimates:

◆ Number of domain controllers per domain per site

◆ Number of global catalog servers per domain per site

◆ Number of CPUs per machine and type of CPU

◆ Number of disks needed for Active Directory store

◆ Memory required

◆ Network bandwidth utilization

◆ Estimated domain database size

◆ Estimated global catalog database size

◆ Estimated intersite replication bandwidth required

If used correctly, Active Directory Sizer can produce a list of all hardware needed to support Active Directory throughout the entire organization. This utility does not include information on sizing member servers.

TECHNICAL SUPPORT STRUCTURE

As with any major upgrade, the technical support staff of an organization will play a crucial role with the Windows 2000 migration. Having the right people at the right time in the right spot is a challenge. For this reason, you need to incorporate that into your planning. As we've already discussed, the technical support and administration models will both influence and be influenced by the design of Active Directory.

Administration Models

We discussed in Chapter 4 the three IT administration models: centralized, decentralized, and hybrid. Depending on the current infrastructure and domain model and your plans for Windows 2000 Active Directory design, the technical support staff resource distribution may need to change. For example, if you have an organization that has five sites around the U.S., each with its own server support staff and domain, and your plans for Windows 2000 are to collapse all domains into a single domain and centralize all the administration, you need to look at how that changes the need for technical support in the remote locations areas. Does this mean you have to fire technical support people? No. If you have a team of five in a remote site and you figure with the collapse of administration back to the central office you can drop that number to two, then the other three should be reassigned to different areas of IT. Additionally, you will need to increase the technical support staff at the central office, so if reassignment isn't viable at an employee's current location, then offering a transfer may be.

Technical Support Responsibilities

Additional to the transfer or reduction in administrative bodies is the role of the technical support team. There are various roles these people play within the current environment. You need to identify how those roles may change, whether they'll be needed, and to what extent they'll be needed. You also need to determine what additional technical support responsibilities will be necessary for the organization to support Windows 2000. Finally, you'll want to make sure each technical person with responsibilities in the organization is properly trained on how to support his specific area of the proposed network.

Strong technical support provides a backbone for a successful migration. Several areas of technical support should be filled with appropriately trained technical professionals.

Administrative Level

The technical team that will have administrative control over the network should be the first to go through training. They need to be sharp and able to think clearly on their feet. They will be the ones providing delegated authority once the Windows 2000 Active Directory is in place, so they will need to develop policies and procedures on how to handle those requests.

Domain administrators should be redundant. This means there should be more than one with this level of access in the event something bad happens. They should be involved with, if not charged with, the migration process. This responsibility gives them on-the-job training, which is the most valuable training available.

Platform Support

Because of the sheer vastness of Windows 2000 and Active Directory, it is recommended that technical staff choose focus areas. For example, you might designate one person to be in charge of the namespace design, which would include DNS and domain naming strategies. Another person may be in charge of the physical areas of sites and subnets, and so on. Additionally, for large enterprises, it would be a good idea to separate some groups into platform-specific responsibilities. You may have one group responsible for Server, one for the clustering and WLBS features of Advanced Server, and another group to manage the Datacenter product. This allows for the promotion of pure focus and expert level support.

Hardware Support

The hardware support team would be responsible for sizing the hardware appropriately for its purpose. They would also be responsible for the implementation of hardware monitoring and preventative maintenance. They would use such products as Compaq's Insight Manager and HP's Top Tools to provide alerts if hardware is showing signs of impending failure.

In large enterprises, hardware support teams would be split between the server side and the workstation side. On the server side, hardware support for Server and Advanced Server installed base should be separated from hardware support for the Datacenter product because of the vast differences in the hardware Datacenter is designed to run on (basically a mainframe).

Application-Specific Support

On the application side, most corporations of any size already have teams that support specific applications. These teams are usually separate from the help desk and focus on the server-side products. It is recommended that organizations implement this structure at the core of the network. You may, for example, have a core Exchange team, a core SMS team, and a core ERP team. These teams focus on both providing the services of their core applications to end users, and on the strategic direction of the products in the environment.

Help Desk

The first tier support for many organizations is either an onsite or on phone help desk. The help desk is responsible for diagnosing and alleviating problems with desktop computers. It is essential that the help desk personnel be properly trained on supporting the Windows 2000 Professional platform. Additionally, the help desk should be briefed on the Active Directory design and related services, such as group policies, software distribution, remote installation services, and more.

NETWORK AND SYSTEMS MANAGEMENT

In the past, network and systems management were considered task-based processes. Administrators used an application to manage certain aspects of the network, such as performance and needed additional tools to manage the remaining aspects. Systems management has been constantly evolving as well. Microsoft's SMS 1.2 was not the easiest and most robust product, but it was capable of management services. SMS 2.0 is hundreds of times more "manageable" than its predecessor.

This section describes the impact that Active Directory and directory services in general will have on systems and network management.

Windows Management Services

The foundation of systems and network management looking forward is in the Windows Management Services built into Windows 2000. The goal of these services is to provide a well-managed Windows environment, one designed around management disciplines and roles, and that will operate efficiently within the context of both a homogeneous Windows environment and a heterogeneous enterprise. Microsoft describes three management roles within an organization: desktop management, network management, and data center management.

EXAM TIP

Desktops Can Drive Portions of the Design Current workstation and desktop configurations have a definite impact on your Windows 2000 design. In all scenarios, consider whether clients may need upgrades to utilize Active Directory and Group Policy settings.

Desktop Management

The purpose of the desktop management role is to ensure that all users in the organization have the computing resources that they require to do their jobs.

The challenges of desktop management include centralizing control of thousands of computers, the lack of hardware and software standards, user accounts, remote control, and upgrade or patch requirements.

Network Management

The purpose of the network management role is to ensure that the network is highly available and running properly. Network management must focus on adhering to SLAs.

The challenges of network management are in the area of availability and several points of failure.

Data Center Management

The purpose of data center management is to manage the server computers within an enterprise.

The challenges of data center management are with guaranteeing server and application availability, ensuring that data is both protected and preserved, and providing centralized control of user accounts and network resources.

MANAGEMENT DISCIPLINES

Microsoft has broken the entire management problem into logical groups. Table 8.4 describes these groups.

TABLE 8.4

MICROSOFT WINDOWS MANAGEMENT DISCIPLINES

Disciplines	*Discipline Domain*
Change and configuration management	System administration, state management, and life cycle management
Security management	Authentication, access, and auditing

Disciplines	*Discipline Domain*
Performance management	Tracking, tuning, modeling, and monitoring
Problem management	Error isolation, remote troubleshooting, and trouble ticketing
Event management	Consolidation, aggregation, delivery, and monitoring
Batch and output management	Job control, queueing, scheduling, and printers and plotters
Storage management	Data storage, retrieval, backup, and archiving

Several of these management disciplines and the aforementioned roles overlap, as shown in Figure 8.4. For example, a desktop manager is tasked with ensuring that users have the software they require to perform their jobs. A security manager is tasked with ensuring that users have the software they require to perform their jobs—*and nothing else.*

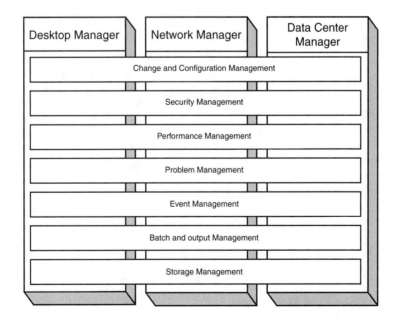

FIGURE 8.4

Some of the Windows 2000 management disciplines overlap roles.

So that's a brief description of the Windows Management Services. Let's now take a look at how Windows 2000 and Active Directory impact these services.

Common Services

Common services represent the necessary building blocks with which Microsoft, as well as other vendors, can build value-added solutions. For example, Microsoft SMS is built on the Windows Management Services as a value-added solution. Windows 2000 provides the following common services:

◆ **Active Directory.** Active Directory provides two key common management services. First, it provides a standardized location service, which is a standard way to locate resources within the computer systems. Second, it provides the basis for applying Group Policy to the objects managed by Active Directory.

◆ **Event notification.** Windows records a large number of system, security, and application events. Developers need to have the ability to deliver event notifications to other services and people.

◆ **COM and DCOM.** COM and DCOM provide object orientation for the management services.

◆ **Windows Management Instrumentation (WMI).** WMI represents a uniform model in which management data from any source can be managed in a standard way. WMI provides this functionality for software, while WMI extensions to the WDM provide this functionality for hardware and drivers.

◆ **Replication.** Services to provide consistent and transacted replication of management information to various points.

◆ **Load balancing.** Services to support the balancing of the various demands placed on the servers being managed.

◆ **Scheduling.** Services to support the scheduling of management and other processing tasks throughout the computer system.

Presentation Services

Presentation services affect how an administrator will interact with the management logic and common services layers. Microsoft provides common presentation services to ensure that people developing management solutions do not have to duplicate the development effort to provide the services. Windows 2000 includes the following presentation services:

◆ **Automation.** Administrators can provide automated management tasks by leveraging the Windows Scripting Host and therefore any COM controls that expose automation interfaces.

◆ **Presentation.** Microsoft provides the Microsoft Management Console (MMC), which provides a unified administrative interface to allow administrators to manage users, computers, networks, services, and other system components.

◆ **XML (Extensible Markup Language).** XML is a subset of the Standard Generalized Markup Language (SGML) that ensures structured data will be uniform and independent of applications, vendors, or platforms. XML data will be delivered over Web-based protocols.

Management Services

The management logic layer of Windows Management Services provides two classes of service. First, it provides a set of standard management tools that are built from the common services. Second, it enables development of high-end, full-functioned, high-valued management solutions, such as SMS. Windows 2000 provides management services in four areas, as described in the following sections.

Change and Configuration Management

The change and configuration management features provided by Windows 2000 are in the areas of the IntelliMirror suite of technologies, and Remote Installation Services (RIS). Desktop change and configuration management will be covered in detail in Chapter 9, "End-User Needs and Desktop Management," but we'll describe these features here as well:

◆ **User data management (IntelliMirror technology).** Windows 2000 supports the mirroring of user data to the network and local hard disk. This technology allows a user's data to follow him.

◆ **Software installation and maintenance (IntelliMirror technology).** Windows 2000 provides a central management facility to control user software installation and management in the areas of applications, service packs, updates, repairs, and removal. This allows a user's applications to follow him.

◆ **User and computer settings management (IntelliMirror technology).** Windows 2000 provides a central management facility to control end user desktop settings, such as display of the Run command on the Start menu, screen savers, and so on. This allows a user's preferences to follow him.

◆ **Remote Installation Services.** Provides for simplified and/or automated setup of client operating systems.

Security Management

The MMC and snap-ins are utilized to control security settings on a policy basis. Administrators can change domain-wide security settings or security settings for particular groups of users with a few mouse clicks. These security settings include Kerberos v5, NTLM, and SSL/TLS authentication, public key security and protocols, distributed password authentication (DPA), and Group Policy.

Network Quality of Service

Windows 2000 provides support for guaranteed Quality of Service (QoS). QoS describes the processes and technology that ensure a certain level of service quality to applications. It also allows administrators and network managers to allocate network resources as needed. A good example of QoS is in the streaming video arena. Suppose you have a T-1 line that is constantly 80% utilized, but you need to stream a training session across it. Without QoS for the training application, the video will no doubt be jumpy and pixilated, and probably not very effective. Administrators can alleviate this problem by specifying a certain amount of bandwidth for the training application, thereby guaranteeing its quality of service.

Storage Management

Based on the ever-growing size of information storage requirements, Microsoft provides several features with Windows 2000 to help administrators manage this information:

◆ Integrated "Windows NT" backup

◆ Disk management

◆ Disk quotas

◆ Distributed File System (DFS)

◆ Hierarchical Storage Management (HSM)

◆ Removable storage management

Summing Up Windows Management Services

What you should be taking from this section is that Windows 2000 provides a well-planned approach for network and systems management—called the Windows Management Services—and it's integrated into the core OS. That is a huge bonus, especially for the small and "in-between" sized companies that can justify the need for enterprise network and systems management utilities, but often cannot justify the cost. Granted, as with most built-in features, there are functions such as asset management, remote control, and diagramming that are not included. This is where the value-added management solutions enter the picture. First, though, let's make a few recommendations for your current environment.

If in your current environment you have an enterprise network and/or systems management utility, such as Microsoft SMS or CA Unicenter, take a good hard look at how and why you use that utility. Do you use it to manage? To assess? To analyze? To report? Who uses it? Where do they use it from? Do they use it to manage heterogeneous environments? If so, how? Does your tool do anything the new tools in Windows 2000 don't? By answering these questions honestly, you should be able to determine whether you need to retain a value-added network and systems management utility after you upgrade to Windows 2000.

Value-Added Management Solutions

As stated earlier, Microsoft developed the Windows Management Services such that third-party or even additional Microsoft applications, may be written to leverage its model. Microsoft has worked with and continues to work with other companies, such as Tivoli, Computer Associates, HP, NetIQ, CompuWare, and BMC Software to develop value-added network and systems management tools that use Windows Management Services. Additionally, companies like Cisco Systems are building Directory Enabled Networks (DENs) by supporting WBEM and Active Directory. DENs will complement Windows Management Services to provide a common set of management services across heterogeneous environments.

CHAPTER SUMMARY

KEY TERMS

- asset management
- Windows 2000 Readiness Analyzer
- Microsoft Readiness Framework
- priority-one applications
- priority-two applications
- priority-three applications
- NBTSTAT
- Active Directory Sizer
- Msinfo32
- Windows management services
- Windows management instrumentation

There are many elements of a network environment to consider when planning a Windows 2000 Active Directory implementation. At the very minimum, you need to consider the following:

- ◆ Your existing systems and applications
- ◆ Planned upgrades and rollouts
- ◆ Your technical support structure
- ◆ Your existing and planned network and systems management

When analyzing your systems and applications, it is best to utilize an inventory utility such as Microsoft SMS or Tally NetCensus. These utilities allow you to collect system and application information to a centralized database for analysis. This method is preferred over a manual inventory because it reduces time and allows you to channel your effort toward the analysis of the systems and applications, not identifying them.

CHAPTER SUMMARY

Once you have a good inventory, you should structure applications by priority. Priority-one applications are mission critical, priority-two applications are necessary for daily operations, and priority-three applications are those that are nice to have, but typically are not a necessity for the company.

The next step is to check with hardware and software vendors and the Windows 2000 hardware and software compatibility Web site for any issues that are already known. For Microsoft applications and all hardware, the HCL is an excellent resource for compatibility information. Any applications for which you cannot find published compatibility information must be tested in a lab environment. It may also be necessary to test proven applications and/or hardware in a lab to verify they function in the particular environment in which you are working. Applications that fail tests or do not comply with Windows 2000/Active Directory requirements should be upgraded, replaced, or retired.

NetBIOS may be removed once you move the entire environment (servers and workstations) to Windows 2000. This likely will not be possible shortly after a migration because many applications require NetBIOS. To test whether an application uses NetBIOS, you can use the NBTSTAT utility.

You must understand a company's technical support environment. Virtually all companies will have some form of technical support, whether it is a formal department or business unit, or Jimmy the computer hobbyist accountant. The existing support structure may not be suited for the Active Directory implementation once it takes place. For example, if your plans are to collapse five resource domains into a single domain and centralize administration, you will not need various levels of support where the existing resource domains used to be.

The foundation of systems and network management looking forward is in the Windows Management Services built into Windows 2000. The goal of these services is to provide a well-managed Windows environment designed around management disciplines and roles, that will operate efficiently within the context of both a homogeneous Windows environment and a heterogeneous enterprise.

CHAPTER SUMMARY

Microsoft has broken the management tasks into desktop, network, and datacenter roles, and each role plays a part in several management disciplines. Each discipline describes a critical area of focus for specific individuals and/or support teams.

The management logic layer of Windows Management Services provides two classes of service. First, it provides a set of standard management tools that are built from the common services. Second, it enables development of high-end full-functioned high-valued management solutions, such as SMS. Windows Management Services is broken into four areas:

◆ Change and configuration management

◆ Security management

◆ Network Quality of Service

◆ Storage management

Microsoft continues to work with companies such as Tivoli, Computer Associates, HP, NetIQ, CompuWare and BMC Software to develop value-added network and systems management tools that use Windows Management Services.

APPLY YOUR KNOWLEDGE

Exercises

8.1   Performing a Manual Software Inventory

In this exercise, you will perform a manual software inventory on a computer in your environment. This exercise will prepare you for the task of manually collecting information about software in your environment. It will also make you appreciate the value of an assisted inventory collection utility!

Estimated Time: 15 Minutes

1. Select a computer on which to perform a manual application inventory. Make sure this computer is running Windows 98, NT, or 2000. (For the purposes of this exercise, you can go through the motions with a Windows 2000 computer, but in actuality you'll likely perform this task before a Windows 2000 migration.)

2. On that system, choose applications you and the company determine are required for migration to Windows 2000.

3. Using Table 8.5, record pertinent information about each application per the sample provided. For the Priority column, categorize each application as Priority One, Priority Two, or Priority Three.

4. To obtain the appropriate information about each application, launch the application and utilize Help, About.

5. At this point you have a prioritized listing of applications. The next logical step is to perform analysis on these applications in a test environment. You should visit the application vendor's Web site and the Windows 2000 hardware and software compatibility Web site before you begin testing, to verify that no published information about compatibility is already available.

TABLE 8.5

Vendor	Application	Major Version	Minor Version	Application Type (Client only, client/ server, server, etc.)	Architecture (DOS, Win16, Win32, etc.)	Priority
Microsoft	Word 2000	9.0	2720	Client	Win32	Two

APPLY YOUR KNOWLEDGE

8.2   Removing NetBIOS Support

In this exercise, you walk through the removal of NetBIOS support for a single network connection. You then attempt to make a NetBIOS connection to a resource on the target server and monitor the connection with the NBTSTAT utility.

You will need two computers for this exercise, one of which must be Windows 2000. The other should be Windows 9x (because of its reliance on NetBIOS), but the exercise will still work with two computers running Windows 2000.

Estimated Time: 10 Minutes

1. On the Windows 2000 computer, verify that NetBIOS is currently enabled for the NIC through which you will connect the Windows 9x computer. Open the properties of the NIC, double-click TCP/IP, click Advanced, and select the WINS tab (see Figure 8.5).

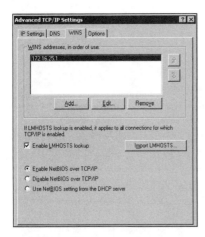

FIGURE 8.5
You can enable or disable NetBIOS at the NIC level in Windows 2000.

2. On the windows 2000 computer, open a command window and start the NBTSTAT utility to query the NetBIOS session cache every second (**NBTSTAT -s 1**). Make note of any NetBIOS sessions currently in use. Let this program look while finishing up the next few steps.

3. On the Windows 9x computer, open a NetBIOS session with the Windows 2000 computer by clicking Start, Run, and entering *servername* (where *servername* is the name of your Windows 2000 computer) in the space provided.

4. On the Windows 2000 computer, notice the additional NetBIOS session established from your Windows 9x computer.

5. Stop the NBTSTAT loop on the Windows 2000 computer and close all open windows on the Windows 9x computer.

6. From the Windows 2000 computer, navigate to the WINS tab of TCP/IP properties (refer to Step 1).

7. Disable NetBIOS over TCP/IP by selecting the appropriate radio button (see Figure 8.6).

8. Commit the removal of NBT support by clicking OK three times to close out the properties window for your NIC.

9. From the Windows 9x computer, attempt to make a NetBIOS connection to the Windows 2000 computer as you did in Step 3. If you are running Windows 9x with TCP/IP as your primary protocol, you should receive an error message that it cannot find the computer. This is a direct result of not having NetBIOS available. (Depending on your configuration, this may succeed under Windows 2000 by using DNS as a name resolution mechanism; otherwise it will fail.)

APPLY YOUR KNOWLEDGE

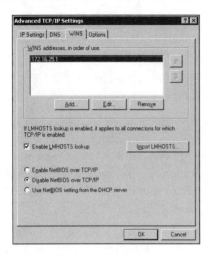

FIGURE 8.6
By disabling NetBIOS over TCP/IP, you will no longer have NetBIOS-based access to the Windows 2000 Server.

10. Return to the Windows 2000 computer and enter **NBTSTAT -s**. It should return No Connections. This confirms that NetBIOS is indeed removed from that connection.

Review Questions

1. What tool does Microsoft provide that allows administrators to test the viability of a Windows 2000 upgrade on a single machine?

2. Name the technology included in Windows 2000 to provide network and systems management.

3. Give five reasons why you might want to remove NetBIOS.

4. What should you check as a precaution before migrating any new or existing system to Windows 2000?

5. List one or more reasons you might perform a manual software inventory instead of automating the process using an inventory utility.

6. What is the primary reason for upgrading an application that is deemed incompatible with Windows 2000?

7. Describe a priority-one application and list two examples.

8. Why is it necessary to partition the technical support areas for Windows 2000?

9. What would be the main advantage of waiting until after Windows 2000 is installed to introduce a new application?

10. Describe the problem some Windows 9x applications have (in assessing the application for Windows 2000) regarding how they use the registry.

Exam Questions

1. The IntelliMirror suite of technologies includes which management features? (Choose three.)

    A. User data management

    B. Software installation and maintenance

    C. User and computer settings management

    D. Storage management

    E. Network Quality of Service management

    F. Security management

2. You are the enterprise network director considering the removal of NetBIOS from your company. Which of the following would *not* be among the advantages you cite to justify NetBIOS removal?

APPLY YOUR KNOWLEDGE

A. A single method of name resolution

B. Enhanced security

C. Reduced memory requirements

D. No more reliance on WINS

3. Suppose the Dewey, Cheatham, and Howe firm implements a technical support structure that may require the help desk personnel to take remote control of a user's desktop. What should you do to implement such a solution?

   A. Let Windows 2000 integrated network and systems management utilities take care of it— remote control of desktops is provided out of the box.

   B. Install terminal services on all the Windows 2000 Professional workstations.

   C. Install pcAnyware in remote host mode on all the Workstations. Install pcAnyware on each of the help desk employees' desktops to allow them to attach via TCP/IP.

   D. Install a system management utility such as Microsoft Systems Management Server and enable the remote control features of the product.

4. The IT consultant for Dewey, Cheatham, and Howe—in preparation for moving them to Windows 2000—has just completed a software inventory using NetCensus. What should he do with this list?

   A. Create lists of priority-one, -two, and -three applications.

   B. Begin to test the applications in the test lab.

C. Begin visiting software vendors' Web sites and making phone calls to determine whether they have a version for Windows 2000.

D. Upgrade each application to a Windows 2000-compatible version, one by one.

5. You find that a software application written for Windows 95 makes use of the HKEY_CURRENT_USER\Software registry key for application-specific data. What may exist to fix this problem during the upgrade of this OS to Windows 2000?

   A. A script to change the use of the Windows 2000 HKEY_CURRENT_USER\Software registry key so the application will work.

   B. A migration DLL provided by the software manufacturer.

   C. A COM script provided by the software manufacturer.

   D. The Windows 2000 upgrade utility will alleviate this problem; there's no need to search for another fix.

6. You're the IT consultant for Dewey, Cheatham, and Howe. You have just completed the migration to Windows 2000. DCH now wishes to remove NetBIOS. Which two processes must you complete before you can determine where you can remove NetBIOS?

   A. Determine where NetBIOS is being used by collecting information from WINS, and the local cache of each machine using the NBTSTAT -a *<COMPUTERNAME>* command.

APPLY YOUR KNOWLEDGE

B. Determine where NetBIOS is being used by collecting information from WINS, and the local cache of each machine using the NETSTAT -a <COMPUTERNAME> command.

C. Determine which applications are using NetBIOS by issuing the NBTSTAT -s 1 command on a workstation or server and launching applications.

D. Determine which applications are using NetBIOS by issuing the NETSTAT -s 1 command on a workstation or server and launching applications.

E. Apply the Microsoft Readiness Framework utilities to the servers on which you wish to remove NetBIOS.

7. Suppose you upgrade a Windows NT primary domain controller to Windows 2000. After you complete the upgrade, the services for a third-party disk quota software will not start. What is most likely causing this problem?

A. This is by design. You must reinstall disk quota software after you upgrade to Windows 2000 before it will function correctly.

B. Since Windows 2000 contains native disk quota management, third-party applications will not function correctly and should be removed.

C. You must stop the quota manager services before upgrading, then restart them after the upgrade is complete.

D. By upgrading to Windows 2000, you have exceeded a quota for the system partition and must remove some data to adhere to the quota policy.

8. You are the consultant for a large manufacturing company. One specific business unit in this company uses an application that is incompatible with Windows 2000. You contacted the vendor and learned that no fix or upgrade is available. Data produced by this application is dynamic and extremely important and is stored as database files and indexes. What would you suggest the business unit do if they needed to retain support for the application under Windows 2000?

A. Migrate the application to another application that supports the same file format. Test this application in the test lab before implementing it in production.

B. Retire the application and import its data into Excel for retention.

C. Retain one computer running the old OS to continue using the old application.

D. Upgrade anyway and hope the old application still functions enough for your needs.

9. Your network consists of Windows NT and UNIX. You wish to provide a single point for network management across both platforms. How do you provide this service?

A. Use the integrated Windows management services shipped with the core Windows 2000 OS.

B. Deploy a third-party management utility, such as Unicenter TNG.

C. Deploy Microsoft Systems Management Server.

D. Deploy Tally Systems NetCensus on all domain controllers.

APPLY YOUR KNOWLEDGE

10. You have just completed the software inventory for XYZ Corp. You find that their line of business application is a 10-year-old DOS application and they do not plan to upgrade that application once they move to Windows 2000. What should you make XYZ Corp. aware of as you complete your assessment? (Choose two.)

    A. DOS applications expect to have direct access to hardware, which violates the Windows 2000 security model.

    B. DOS applications will migrate to Windows and function properly. They have nothing to worry about.

    C. Most DOS applications expect to run on the FAT file system and may operate with unpredictable results under Windows 2000.

    D. If the DOS application produces graphics, it must be set to run in a Windows 2000 command window, not full screen.

    E. The DOS software vendor will likely carry over support for the application even after migration to Windows 2000.

Answers to Review Questions

1. The Windows 2000 Readiness Analyzer tool analyzes your system and reports potentially incompatible hardware devices and software applications. The tool compares the devices and applications on your system against a list of known issues. See the sidebar "Using the Windows 2000 Readiness Analyzer."

2. Microsoft provides the Windows Management Services technology integrated into Windows 2000. This technology is centered in management disciplines and roles that will operate efficiently within the context of both a homogeneous Windows environment and a heterogeneous enterprise. See "Windows Management Services."

3. There are several advantages to removing NetBIOS: no more reliance on WINS, a single method of name resolution, easier network support, increased network performance, and enhanced security. See "Removal of NetBIOS."

4. Before migrating any system to Windows 2000, whether it is new or old, always check the Windows 2000 Hardware Compatibility List to make sure the equipment and its components are certified as compatible for Windows 2000. It is best to check the HCL on Microsoft's Web site to ensure that you are seeing the most up-to-date information. See "Rollout of New Equipment."

5. Manual inventories can be used in a variety of situations. First, if you organization has fewer than 100 (or other number suitable in your opinion) computers, the cost of an automated inventory collection utility often cannot be justified, which leads to the second reason—lack of funding for sophisticated software inventory utilities. In addition, you may have DOS or even some Windows applications that are not recognized by automated utilities and thus require manual collection. See "Manual Collections."

APPLY YOUR KNOWLEDGE

6. The primary reason for upgrading an application is to retain the application data. Additionally, the cost associated with upgrading an application is typically much less than it is to replace that application with another. See "Upgrade."

7. Priority-one applications are mission-critical, the sort that would close the business if they did not function. Priority-one applications are different for different companies, but typically include line-of-business applications for all major business units, messaging systems, data warehousing systems, and ERP applications. See "Priority-One Applications."

8. Because of the vastness of Windows 2000 and Active Directory, it is recommended that technical staff choose focus areas. For example, you might designate one person to be in charge of the namespace design, which would include DDNS and domain-naming strategies. Another person may be in charge of the physical areas of sites and subnets, and so on. See "Platform Support."

9. One advantage of waiting to deploy a new application until you have Windows 2000 and Active Directory in place is Group Policy. You can use Group Policy functionality to roll out applications to specific groups and/or the entire organization. See "Upgrades to Hardware or Software."

10. For some Windows 9x applications, developers wrote common application information to the HKEY_CURRENT_USER\Software hive instead of the HKEY_LOCAL_MACHINE\Software hive where it belongs. See "Windows 9x Applications."

Answers to Exam Questions

1. **A, B, C.** The IntelliMirror suite of technologies is focused on user data Management, software installation and maintenance, and user and computer settings management. Storage management, network Quality of Service management, and security management all refer to Windows Management Services management disciplines and are not addressed under the IntelliMirror technology. See "Change and Configuration Management."

2. **C.** Removing NetBIOS provides for several advantages, such as enhanced security and easier network support. It does not provide for decreased memory requirements. See "Removing NetBIOS."

3. **D.** Windows 2000 provides several great management features and utilities native to the operating system; however, it does not provide remote systems administration services for workstations. For this, Microsoft recommends installing a systems management utility such as SMS and enabling the remote administration capabilities. pcAnyware will work in this situation but is neither cost-effective nor manageable. Terminal services do not apply to Windows 2000 Professional. See "Windows Management Services."

4. **A.** The very first thing you should do after you complete a software inventory is prioritize the applications. In this book, we suggest partitioning the list into priority-one, -two, and -three

APPLY YOUR KNOWLEDGE

applications. The next step would then be to begin testing the applications and searching the vendor websites for Windows 2000 compatibility information. See "Categorize the Applications."

5. **B.** To address some areas of incompatibilities, including the registry problems Windows 9x applications may have when ported to Windows 2000, application developers are making available migration DLLs. Migration DLLs will execute during the upgrade process and will be able to fix an ailing application. As always, you never want to assume a hack to the registry will fix the problem. See "Windows 9x Applications."

6. **A, C.** Before removing NetBIOS, be sure it is no longer needed by any application on the network. All servers and workstations must be Windows 2000. You should also make use of the NBTSTAT utility, which displays NetBIOS-related connection information. The NETSTAT utility displays information about current TCP/IP network connections and will not display NetBIOS-related information. The Microsoft Readiness Framework contains a set of competencies, methodologies, and skills assessments applied to people, not machines. See "Removing NetBIOS."

7. **B.** The NTFS5 file system contains attributes for quota information. Since this native support for quotas exists in Windows 2000, third-party utilities written to do the same thing may not function correctly and should be removed. See "Windows NT Applications."

8. **A.** There will be applications that simply will not migrate to Windows 2000 for one reason or another. These applications require special attention. You will need to make a recommendation to management based on the traffic. In this case, since the application data is dynamic and needs to be retained, it is recommended that you find another application to take its place. Excel may present the data, but is not very good in terms of dynamically changing it based on an intricate business rule. See "Upgrade."

9. **B.** Microsoft recommends using a third-party application to provide unified network management across platform boundaries. Windows Management Services provides a framework for these third-party applications, such as Unicenter, to adhere to. SMS is more geared to systems management. NetCensus is a software inventory utility. The Windows Management Services shipping with Windows 2000 may not be sufficient to accomplish network management in cross-platform situations. See "Windows Management Services."

10. **A, C.** Most DOS applications, especially the ones that run okay under Windows NT, will run just fine under Windows 2000. There are exceptions, such as DOS applications that need to access hardware directly, or DOS applications that need the FAT file system. These applications will give you trouble if not addressed. DOS applications that produce graphics must be run in full-screen mode rather than in a window. Do not expect vendor support for a DOS application running under Windows 2000. See "DOS Applications."

Suggested Readings and Resources

1. *Designing the Test Environment.* Windows 2000 Server Resource Kit

2. Microsoft Readiness Framework. Information available at **http://www.microsoft.com/DirectAccess/training/mrf.asp**.

3. Microsoft TechNet Article Q163409. NetBIOS Suffixes (16th Character of the NetBIOS Name)

4. White Paper. Introduction to Windows 2000 Management Services. Available at **http://www.microsoft.com/windows2000/library/howitworks/management/manageintro.asp**.

5. Web site. Upgrading to Windows 2000. Available at **http://www.microsoft.com/windows2000/upgrade/**.

This chapter covers the following Microsoft-specified objectives for the Designing a Microsoft Windows 2000 Directory Services Infrastructure exam:

Analyze the business requirements for client computer desktop management.

- **Analyze end-user work needs.**

- **Identify technical support needs for end-users.**

- **Establish the required client computer environment.**

▶ One thing is clear—end-users will always let you know if they aren't happy. The focus of this chapter is on gathering the appropriate information from end-users (or representatives for end-users) so you can effectively answer their technical support needs and provide a computing environment sufficient for their various work needs.

CHAPTER 9

End-User Needs and Desktop Management

▶ Understand how to take an end-user's "non-technical" requirement and map that to a Windows 2000 change and configuration management technology, such as IntelliMirror.

▶ Try to work with IntelliMirror, Group Policy, remote OS installation, and SMS in a lab environment. This is by far the best way to get to know these technologies.

▶ Know the current and future technical support needs of your user base. For example, if a department requires support primarily for software installation and removal, be able to forecast the future technical support needs once software installation and maintenance is configured to manage software via group policies.

▶ Implement folder redirection policies in a lab setting and get to know how workstations are affected. Also, experiment with the offline folder (user-invoked) settings.

INTRODUCTION

What really is the purpose of an IT department? It's not to play with the neat and expensive "toys," nor is it there to design really fancy domain structures. When you step back and look at the big picture, IT is there to provide service to end-users and provide a platform to allow them to be productive.

This chapter is dedicated to discovering the needs of the end-user and building the required solutions to fit those needs. We'll focus on end-user desktop management as a means to provide these services. This could be considered an "availability" chapter because a lot of this information is pertinent to making certain things available.

What are those "certain things"? They are whatever the client needs relative to applications, OS functionality, or access to data and technical support. They are the typical services you provide to your clients without even thinking about it.

In this chapter, we'll analyze the end-user work needs. Typical needs always include simplification. "Whatever you can do to make my life easier." Ever heard that before? "I have to log on way too many times—is that really necessary and is it too hard to fix—sounds easy to me!" If I had a quarter... (You get the picture.)

Next we'll discuss the technical support needs of end-users, such as what their expectations are, and what processes they feel are a necessity.

We'll finish up with a change and configuration management plan that will allow us to establish and manage the computer environment for clients based on the information we collect. Of course, we'll focus on the Windows 2000 Server and Professional functionality through the use of Group Policy, IntelliMirror, and RIS.

NOTE

Getting a Grasp on Group Policy It may benefit you to skip ahead and skim the section "Considering Group Policy" in Chapter 12, "Designing an OU and Group Policy Management Structure" that covers Group Policy. This will provide an understanding of what it is and how it works. This chapter is focused on the business aspects of desktop management and will not go into technical detail about Group Policy, IntelliMirror, or Remote Installation Services (RIS).

CASE STUDY: NEEDY NEEDY, INC.

BACKGROUND

Needy Needy, Inc is a health-care organization based in Seattle, WA. They have approximately 1,250 users in three Seattle hospitals. The corporate offices adjoin the Seattle Central Health hospital and house approximately 700 of the 1,250 employees. These 700 employees are responsible for medical records, AR/AP, and several other business functions for the three hospitals.

PROBLEM STATEMENT

The NNI end-users are well adjusted to using computers for their jobs. However, the hospital has been reluctant to standardize on any OS and application set, therefore end-users are not able to exchange information easily. Additionally, no hardware standards exist and the desktop computers are only loosely managed by the IT department. The help desk consists of six over-worked individuals who handle about 50 calls each per day.

CURRENT SYSTEM

Executive Secretary
"My boss is a vice president in this company. He relies on me to do his dirty work, which usually consists of preparing documents, setting up meetings, and preparing presentations. I have a very difficult time doing this work from my desktop because it is very slow, so I go to his office when he's not around and use his computer."

Help Desk Tech
"Fifty percent of the calls I receive have to do with some software the user installed and messed up. We cannot continue to allow standard users to install software they have no business installing. I cannot continue to support it unless I have some standard base from which to start—there are just too many different applications floating around. I'd be very happy to see us come out with a supported software standards list."

ENVISIONED SYSTEM

IT Manager
"We need some way to manage these computers from afar. A great number of help desk calls do *not* require us to visit a desktop, yet we do anyway. Also, we need some way to control what the users can and cannot do so they can't get themselves into trouble."

Executive Secretary
"I just want to be able to open Word without something crashing or corrupting. I think just about every component inside my computer has been replaced at one time or another."

continues

CASE STUDY: NEEDY NEEDY, INC.

continued

Data Center Manager

"We have the facilities to implement server-based storage of data. I said something to the IT manager about that and standardizing our policies with the end-users so that all data is stored on the network, but I don't know what ever came of it."

PERFORMANCE

IT Manager

"Well, the speed of the network is fine, but it takes us five hours to replace a computer for a user. That's about four hours too long. All the hardware and software performs just fine once up and running, but getting there is a time-consuming process."

Help Desk Tech

"He's definitely right, and it takes that long because I have to not only rebuild the entire client computer from scratch, I often have to try and appease the user by making it look like the one they had before. That is painfully slow."

SECURITY

IT Manager

"The security policy we have for desktop computers is really a verbal policy. We ask that employees use common sense when leaving their computers with sensitive data on the screen. We do give our executive secretaries glare screens to make it difficult for others to see over their shoulders. When it comes to software and hardware, there is no written or verbal policy in place that controls what can and cannot be installed. Consequently, we have users with personal financial packages, games, and other non-business related software and hardware installed on their computers."

Help Desk Manager

"I don't really think we have any issues with security. The help desk guys are given administrator access to the domain after they pass their 90-day probationary period. They need that access to effectively do their job."

MAINTAINABILITY

IT Manager

"We are in reactive mode constantly. I have guys working on the servers to fix various problems on a daily basis. The help desk staff is pulling 300 calls a day on average and most have to do with the same things over and over again. Users can't find their data, an OS dies, hardware dies... We just need to do a better job maintaining the systems in general and I think half these problems will disappear."

CASE STUDY: NEEDY NEEDY, INC.

Lead Help Desk Tech

"It would be really nice if we could attach to client computers remotely so we don't have to go to the desktops. Also, it would be awesome if we could centrally manage our software and software update rollouts. That way we wouldn't have to run around this building as much."

AVAILABILITY

Client Care Hotline Manager

"I run a group of about 20 people who field calls to a hotline for patient care information. My staff moves from computer to computer on a daily basis because we are staffed 24×7. Some computers contain different configurations from others. We need to make it so that each user has his own configuration and applications available when he logs on anywhere."

AR/AP Manager

"We generate letters for various reasons and store them on the network. Sometimes our people forget to store them on the network because it defaults to the C: drive. On more than one occasion we've lost critical data because a computer dies. We need this information available to us at all times and we can't worry about PCs that break."

What! The End-User?

Now before you get all bent out of shape, relax a bit and let us explain this concept. The end-user, whether you want to admit it or not, is critical to the perceived success of a computer network design and its implementation. We've all been there. We work our tails off for weeks fine-tuning and testing a solution. We're proud of it. Everyone in IT is patting us on the back. Life is great! Then we roll it out and the end-users hate it! Why? Is it change? Is it that we've made things hard on them? Is it something else? These questions and others, strategically focused at extracting the information we need to satisfy end-users, must be answered before we spend weeks on what *we* think the answers are.

Now let's quantify this a bit. End-users have a lot of needs, wants, and desires, and they won't all fit into this book. To keep in line with the material you need to cover for the exam, we'll focus on the objectives listed with this chapter as we analyze end-user work needs, determine tech support needs, and establish the required environment based on a business's needs.

End-User Discussions

Microsoft classifies just about any end-user who touches a computer as a knowledge worker, and rightfully so. End-users use computers in the business to gain knowledge about their job. They gain knowledge by accessing information presented to them by applications or the Internet.

We use tools and processes to make applications and services available to the end-users. The problem on our end in the past has been the lack of solid desktop management utilities. Microsoft started the *zero administration initiative for Windows* (ZAW) several years ago, and although their intention was great, the management and administration toolset was too cumbersome for easy management. Well, times have changed. The Group Policy, IntelliMirror, and Remote Installation Services provided with Windows 2000 will allow the ZAW now to become more of a reality than ever before.

It all starts with the user. We need to find out what the user needs relative to the business, and then incorporate that into a plan.

Of course, relevance is key here. Users might ask for anything and everything—that is not what we're looking for. We're looking for the business requirements for end-user work and support needs.

Simplify My Job—Please!

Users are all different, yet all the same. They all have a different perception of the same common requirement of IT: "Make my job easier!"

The best way to approach users is not to approach them at all. Approach representatives from each user group or department. These "go-to" people should understand what the needs of their respective departments are. We'll continue to use the term "end-user" throughout this chapter to refer to this go-to person.

However you do it, make sure you don't become the answer to all their problems. That is not your job; you want to simplify both the end-user experience and your own, so do a lot of listening and writing, and clearly set the expectation that a compromise likely will be the end result of your analysis.

Downtime

Users get awfully mad when they can't do their jobs. Several things can take a computer "down" in a user's eyes. IT help desk staff spend a majority of their time going to user desktops to fix software that has quit working, network problems, missing files, and other minor issues, all of which—in the user's eyes—cause his computer to be "down." Generally speaking, any downtime is wasted productivity. As we get deeper into solution development for client desktop management and administration, we'll discuss some methods of addressing broken or limping computers.

Roamers

An interesting group of users you must consider consists of roaming users. Does the business unit or organization have users that must roam from computer to computer, as in the Needy Needy, Inc. (NNI) Client Care Department? Are these users frequently disconnected from the network? Do applications need to follow the users to be available wherever they go? Is there always good network connectivity? These are just a few of the questions you need to address with the end-users.

Conducting the End-User Needs Analysis

Analyze the business requirements for client computer desktop management.

So we set the stage on what to expect from the users. Now let's discuss what you need to do to get the correct information from the user. We'll follow the change and configuration management model, which includes IntelliMirror and RIS, as well as support, because that is what we have to offer. Anything outside of that will require the assistance of an additional utility, such as SMS, as discussed in previous chapters. The following sections represent segments of information you need to address with the users.

Data Management

As discussed in Chapter 8, "Impact of Active Directory," data management refers to the notion that a user's documents "follow" him or her. It is best to divide this segment of the analysis into three sections: accessibility, availability, and protection.

Data Accessibility

The Client Care Department at NNI has a specific requirement that employees of that department be able to access their data from any computer. The Data Accessibility module of User Data Management makes this happen using IntelliMirror technology. Figure 9.1 represents data accessibility.

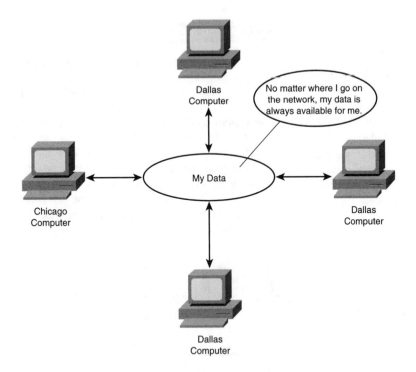

Users will not jump right out and tell you they need this feature. This is something you'll probably have to present to them based upon your knowledge of the department or company and what the users state their needs are. Many IT consultants develop unique skills that enable them to help end-users explain what they want. You will need to help them by asking questions and making observations.

Data Availability

Data availability uses the IntelliMirror technology to ensure the most up-to-date versions of a user's data reside on both the server and the user's local computer. It also provides an intelligent synchronization mechanism, which utilizes local caching of data when users are connected to the network. This way, the user's data is synchronized automatically with the server copy. When a user leaves the network, he simply works on his locally cached copy of the data, which is then synchronized back to the server when he accesses next. This feature is commonly referred to as offline storage. Figure 9.2 illustrates data availability.

FIGURE 9.1
With IntelliMirror features configured, a user's data is accessible from any computer on the network.

> **EXAM TIP**
>
> **Components of IntelliMirror** Latch onto the fact that IntelliMirror is not merely a one-tool option, but rather an aggregate of several Windows 2000 features, including Remote Installation Service, Group Policy Objects (GPOs), software distribution, offline folders, and remote storage.

IN THE FIELD

NOTE

Smart Synchronization The synchro- nization engine utilized here may be configured to prompt a user to synchronize documents across slow wide area network (WAN) links. It's important that such synchronization not take place automatically because of the time it could take to synchro- nize large amounts of data.

THE TRAVELING SALESPERSON

A good example of offline storage usefulness involves the traveling salesperson. She starts out in L.A., her home office, where she has Word and Excel documents saved to the server and synchro- nized to her laptop. She logs off the network and hops on a plane to Chicago, and while on that plane she does some work on three of her documents. She gets to the Chicago office and logs on to the network there. Her documents are resynchronized with the server in L.A. in the background. She can continue to use either the local copy or the server copy of her data.

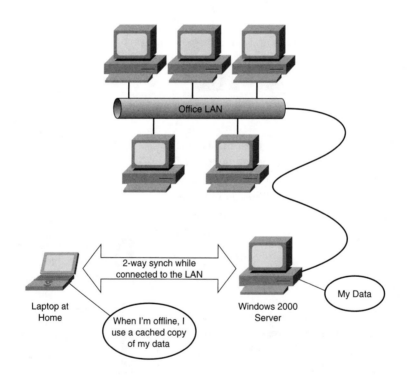

FIGURE 9.2
With IntelliMirror features configured, a user's data is available both online and offline.

This technology is good to push in organizations or departments that employ people who travel frequently or do work from home.

Data Protection

One of the more frustrating service calls a help desk technician makes is one that requires a computer rebuild or replacement. Whenever that happens, it's almost certain that the user is going to lose some data, if not all of it. This problem can be resolved using IntelliMirror's data protection feature. This feature allows administrators to redirect a user's data (via a policy) to a network share. To the user, the data is in My Documents, which is assumed to be local. This is very powerful and ensures that user data is available to back up with the corporate backup rotation.

It is recommended that if you have the opportunity to implement this—do it. This is a feature that's been long-awaited and now we have it, so let's use it. Figure 9.3 illustrates data protection graphically.

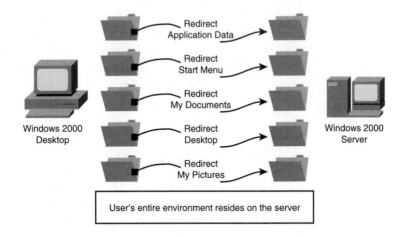

Redirect
Application Data

Redirect
Start Menu

Redirect
My Documents

Redirect
Desktop

Redirect
My Pictures

Windows 2000
Desktop

Windows 2000
Server

User's entire environment resides on the server

FIGURE 9.3

With IntelliMirror features configured, administrators can seamlessly redirect users' folders to a network share.

Software Installation and Maintenance

The goal behind software installation and maintenance is to provide policy-based deployment and management of software throughout the entire software life cycle. The software life cycle includes following a software from "life to death": including planning for the software, deploying the software, maintaining the software, and removing the software. This is a large part of satisfying the user in terms of making software available and up-to-date. It uses the Windows Installer technology to perform just-in-time installations on desktops, and can also be used to provide automatic repair of damaged applications.

There are two ways software can be distributed to the user base—it can be published or assigned. These are the two key areas you need to consider when discussing applications with end-users.

Published Applications

Published applications are made available to users on an as-needed basis. The users can install a published application by selecting it in the Add/Remove Programs Control Panel applet. Additionally, if users attempt to open a document they don't have the software to open, the published application will automatically be installed. The key here is that published applications are made available to users only, not computers, and they are not mandatory, meaning they are not forcibly installed.

Assigned Applications

Assigned applications apply to users *and* computers. This means that an application can be assigned to roam with a user, or may be assigned to a specific computer itself. Assigned applications are mandatory when assigned to a computer. They are installed the next time the computer is booted. If they are assigned to a user, however, they present themselves on the user's desktop or Start menu as shortcuts the next time the user logs on. The software is installed the first time the user attempts to launch it using one of these icons. Figure 9.4 illustrates a software installation and maintenance policy.

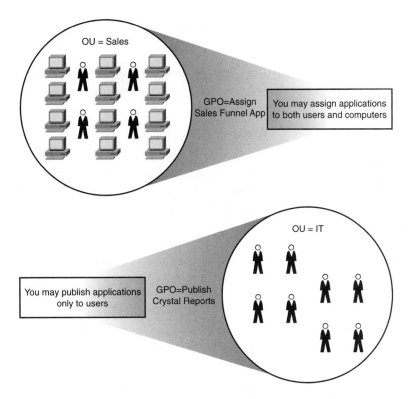

FIGURE 9.4
Using software installation and maintenance, you can publish and assign applications using group policies.

The Windows Installer Service

The key technology behind software installation and maintenance is the Windows Installer service. To be compatible with this service, applications must be authored or repackaged. There are a number of authoring and packaging tools available, including but not limited to tools from the following companies: InstallShield, Seagate, Veritas, and Wyse. If you have SMS 2.0 in the environment, the System Management Server Installer feature supports the repackaging of applications option. When Windows Installer applications are deployed, they have the ability to run in the security context of the

> **NOTE**
>
> **Veritas Repackaging Utility** A limited edition of the Veritas Microsoft Installer File (MSI) repackaging utility shipped with the release version of Windows 2000 Server and Advanced Server.

Windows Installer service, which has the right to install applications on the local computer, even if the logged-on user does not.

The Windows Installer technology brings about several benefits, which are described in the following sections.

Auto-Healing Applications

This is probably the coolest feature of the Windows Installer service. When an assigned application is installed using the Windows Installer, it is protected from accidental (or deliberate) damage. For example, if you install Excel for Suzie ExeHater, and she deletes excel.exe, you don't have to worry about going to her desk anymore to fix the broken application. When she launches Excel, the Windows Installer service checks to ensure that all the required application files and components are available. If it finds a problem, such as a missing excel.exe file, it retrieves that file from a predetermined (at installation time) distribution point and automatically fixes the application. All of this happens right in front of the user, and she never knows the difference!

Custom Installations

The Windows Installer technology also lets you make the best use of your client's computer hard disk space by providing custom installations. Optional application features, such as clip-art or an org-chart plug-in, can be made visible in an application without actually being installed. If a user invokes a menu option for one of these optional components, they are immediately installed from a predetermined distribution point on the network.

Clean Removal of Applications

Ever tried to remove an application that didn't have an uninstall program with it? Ever run an uninstall that actually removed everything? How about those decisions you've made to remove the shared files with which an application is associated, only to find that it broke something else! Windows Installer technology addresses the un-installation process by ensuring that files are not orphaned and that files required by other programs (such as shared files) are not removed.

> **WARNING**
>
> **Published Applications Are Not Resilient**   Only assigned applications will re-install missing files or components. Published applications will not automatically fix themselves. For critical high-maintenance applications, use assignment as the preferred means of distribution.

There are two options for removing software deployed using software installation and maintenance policies in conjunction with Windows Installer packages: forced and optional removal.

Forced removal immediately uninstalls software from users and computers during the next policy invocation period. For software assigned to users, the next invocation period is the next time the user logs on. For computers, the next invocation period is the next time the computer starts up.

Optional removal allows users to continue using an application that has been retired. When the software is lifted from the software installation and maintenance group policy, the administrators specify optional removal so users can continue using the application, but the application will not be deployed to any other users and can be removed using the standard method (Add/Remove Programs) at any time.

ZAP Files

It is important to point out here that not all applications are capable of being repackaged to the Windows Installer format. For this reason, we have the *ZAP file* (.zap). ZAP files are text files that can be analyzed and executed by the software installation technology within Group Policy. Zap files allow you to publish non-Windows Installer applications with some limitations:

◆ They cannot be *assigned* to users or computers. They can only be *published*.

◆ They do not have the resilience that the Windows Installer applications have. This means they cannot heal themselves. Instead they invoke and rerun the setup program from the beginning if a problem is encountered.

◆ They require user intervention during installation because they run the software's original setup program.

◆ They cannot install with elevated privileges. This means they have to use the user's privileges as the security context during installation.

Anatomy of a ZAP File

You can use any standard text editor, such as Notepad, to create a ZAP file. Two sections, Application and Extensions, make up a ZAP file, the layout closely resembles an INI file. Table 9.1 illustrates the ZAP file contents.

TABLE 9.1

ZAP FILE ANATOMY

Section	Tag	Description
[Application]		Includes information about how to install the program as well as information that will be displayed to users during installation and in Add/Remove Programs
	FriendlyName (required)	Name to be used during software installation and in Add/Remove Programs
	SetupCommand (required)	The command used to install the application (such as setup.exe); this .zap file should reside in the same folder as this file
	DisplayVersion (optional)	Version number of the application, which is displayed during installation and in Add/Remove Programs
	Publisher (optional)	Publisher of the application, which is displayed during installation and in Add/Remove Programs
	URL (optional)	Pointer to a Web page containing more information about the application
[Ext](optional)		Use this section to associate the application with the appropriate file extensions saved in Active Directory
	XLS=	Sample association for an Excel workbook
	XLT=	Sample association for an Excel template

The following ZAP file code listing is from Microsoft TechNet Article Q231747, "How to Publish Non-MSI Programs with .zap Files."

```
[Application]
; Only FriendlyName and SetupCommand are required,
; everything else is optional.

; FriendlyName is the name of the program that
; will appear in the software installation snap-in
; and the Add/Remove Programs tool.
; REQUIRED
FriendlyName = "Microsoft Excel 97"

; SetupCommand is the command line used to
; run the program's Setup. If it is a relative
; path, it is assumed to be relative to the
; location of the ZAP file.
; Long file name paths need to be quoted. For example:
; SetupCommand = "long folder\setup.exe" /unattend
; or
; SetupCommand = "\\server\share\long _
; folder\setup.exe" /unattend
; REQUIRED

SetupCommand = "setup.exe"

; Version of the program that will appear
; in the software installation snap-in and the
; Add/Remove Programs tool.
; OPTIONAL
DisplayVersion = 8.0

; Version of the program that will appear
; in the software installation snap-in and the
; Add/Remove Programs tool.
; OPTIONAL
Publisher = Microsoft
```

User and Computer Settings Management

NNI stated they needed to be able to control the desktop settings on user computers so their users could not get themselves into trouble. That wish can be granted by the user and computer settings management function of the IntelliMirror technology.

User and computer settings management does just that; it allows you to manage settings for groups of users and computers. You can manage a variety of configuration settings for both users and computers, which will be detailed in Chapter 12, "Designing an OU and Group Policy Management Structure." For now, we'll just summarize the functionality with a list—a list you should keep handy as you discuss options with end-users or IT management:

◆ Computer settings management

- Control options for NetMeeting and IE

- Configure options for the task scheduler and the Windows Installer

- Control various system settings, such as logon information and disk quota settings

- Control various network settings, such as offline file and folder settings

◆ User settings management

- Control a rich set of Windows components, such as NetMeeting and IE, the MMC, and Windows Installer

- Control numerous settings on the Start menu and taskbar

- Control numerous desktop settings

- Customize and/or prohibit Control Panel objects, such as setting a default Active Directory printer path, or disabling the Display Control Panel applet

- Control various network and system settings

Figure 9.5 illustrates a computer that has been "locked down" using user and computer settings management.

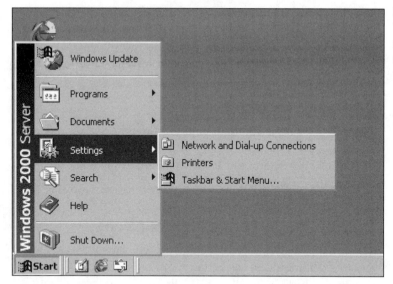

Remote OS Installation

In a large environment, it is impossible to roll out workstations and then spend an additional 3–5 hours configuring each one with the company standard operating software. Because of this, disk-imaging software, such as Symantec's Ghost, added an exceptional amount of speed and efficiency in rolling out computers. In a lot of cases, the use of this cloning software could knock a 3–5 hour installation down to a matter of minutes. Of course, with that gain in speed come inherent problems, such as Security ID (SID) duplication, that are currently causing companies to scramble as the security leaks that come along with SID duplication show their ugly faces.

What does all this have to do with Remote OS installation? Well, nothing really, but it did serve as a sort of first generation of remote OS installation technology.

Remote OS installation uses Pre-boot eXecution Environment (PXE) DHCP-based remote boot technology to initiate the installation of an OS. This means that a client computer with a ROM that supports PXE can be simply placed on to a desktop and turned on. It attaches to the network and finds a remote installation server, which supplies the client with a wizard that initiates an installation of a preconfigured Windows 2000 Professional OS. You can control

> **NOTE**
>
> **Supported PXE Versions**   Windows 2000 supports PXE versions .99c and above, except in some rare situations that require .99L.

how this wizard operates and even what options are available to the user based on that user's placement in Active Directory and his associated GPOs. There are two types of remote OS installations available: CD-based and RIPrep image format.

CD-Based Installations

The CD-based installations are equivalent to initiating a standard Windows 2000 Professional setup with the CD. The main difference with remote installation is that the CD files actually reside on a RIS server across the network.

RIPrep Image Format Installations

This is the next generation of cloning desktop computers. In this scenario, administrators can perfect a desktop, complete with a custom standardized installation of Windows 2000 Professional and all standard applications. Once the desktop is quality-tested, administrators run a wizard (RIPrep.exe) that prepares the installation as an image and replicates it to RIS servers.

Remote Installation Services

RISs runs on a Windows 2000 server. This service was designed to reduce the costs associated with pre-installing or physically visiting each workstation to install the OS. By combining RIS with the IntelliMirror management technologies discussed earlier, companies can benefit from lower total cost of ownership (TCO), as well as better disaster recovery with easier application and OS management. See Figure 9.6.

Requirements for RIS

EXAM TIP

RIS Requirements It is a good idea to learn the requirements for RIS; they are likely to appear on the exam.

First and foremost, NT File System (NTFS) is required for RIS installation. You are also required to install RIS to a partition other than the partition on which Windows 2000 is installed. It is also a disk hog (obviously, because it's holding OS images!) so it requires at least enough room for one Windows 2000 Professional CD, plus room for the RIS service files. Microsoft recommends a minimum of 800MB to 1GB be available, although much more will be needed for multiple images.

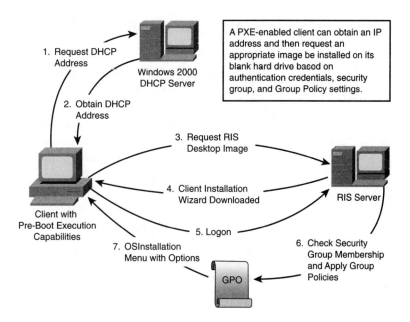

1. Request DHCP Address

Windows 2000 DHCP Server

A PXE-enabled client can obtain an IP address and then request an appropriate image be installed on its blank hard drive based on authentication credentials, security group, and Group Policy settings.

2. Obtain DHCP Address

3. Request RIS Desktop Image

4. Client Installation Wizard Downloaded

RIS Server

Client with Pre-Boot Execution Capabilities

5. Logon

6. Check Security Group Membership and Apply Group Policies

7. OSInstallation Menu with Options

GPO

FIGURE 9.6
The remote OS installation process in a nutshell.

Besides NTFS and significant disk space, RIS requires that the following three services be available (not necessarily on the same computer):

> **NOTE** **Partition for RIS Installation** When you install RIS on a Windows 2000 Server, you will be required to install it to an NTFS5 partition other than the boot partition.

- ◆ **Domain Name System (DNS).** RIS relies on DNS for locating the directory service and client machine accounts. You can run any Windows 2000 compliant DNS server, or you can run the DNS that ships with Windows 2000.

- ◆ **Dynamic Host Configuration Protocol (DHCP).** In order for the PXE-enabled computers to obtain an IP address, DHCP must be enabled on the network.

- ◆ **Active Directory.** RIS relies on Active Directory to locate existing client computers as well as existing RIS servers. It is required that RIS be installed on a Windows 2000-based server that has access to Active Directory. It does not have to be a domain controller; RIS can run from a member server that is part of the domain as well.

With all this in mind, you should have a pretty good idea of how to satisfy the end-user work needs, which will segue into their technical support needs.

Technical Support

The end-users need support—that's for sure. How they get support and what agreements you enter in to are up to you. In discussing the end-user work needs, you are in a sense discussing the technical support needs. If users say they need applications to follow them, you can expect to support that functionality. On the other hand, if you provide them with remote OS installation functionality, you better believe they are going to expect you to support it.

The following list indicates some of the most common technical support needs:

◆ Application installation

◆ Printing problem troubleshooting

◆ System rebuilds

◆ System deployments

◆ Application troubleshooting

◆ General troubleshooting

> **NOTE**
>
> **Net Send** If you need to get a message out to all users quickly because you're taking a server down, you can utilize the **NET SEND** command, which makes use of the Messenger service in Windows NT/2000 to display your message on user desktop screens, provided that the users are logged on.

In addition to the user's traditional technical support needs, which can be termed as "reactive" in the way they are executed, you can also provide value-added support services. For example, consider leveraging the use of an intranet to start a knowledge base, so users can check it for FAQs or Frequent Problems discussions. This could be managed by the help desk. Most companies these days have Internet access, and although some don't let all users browse, those that do can enable access to hotlinks of common vendor support pages. There are numerous other proactive technical support services that you can make available to the user base and manage centrally. In any environment, good communication is the single most proactive approach to effective support. If you *tell* a group of users you are going to bounce a server at a specific time, there shouldn't be any question about the server being down at that time.

Change and Configuration Management

Change and configuration management refers to the management of ongoing changes and configuration issues that arise as administrators try to ensure that people have the platform they need to perform productive work. Figure 9.7 describes the change and configuration management process.

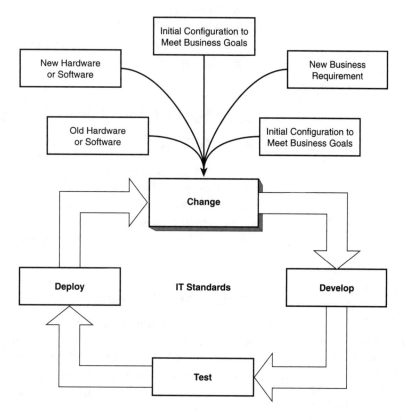

FIGURE 9.7
The desktop Change and Configuration Management Process.

Change is inevitable. How you address it weighs heavily on the by others of success or failure. For example, if a standard software application changes you need to have a plan to get that application rolled out quickly. If you don't, you cost the company time and money and upset the users. That's (unfortunately) just how it is—hence the need for a good change and configuration management policy.

With Windows 2000 and Active Directory deployed in an environment—and with Windows 2000 Professional on the workstations—administrators can use Active Directory and Group Policy objects to create policy-based managed computing environments for users and groups of users. This provides for significantly reduced time at the desktop for issues such as application or OS installations, updates, service packs, and unauthorized configuration changes. The end result of this is a significant reduction in TCO for the desktop services segment of the business.

Establishing the Client Computing Environment

To demonstrate a bit further some areas of change and configuration management, we'll address some of NNI's requirements for desktop computer management. Keep in mind that there are literally thousands of options for configuring desktops using group policies and IntelliMirror. The ones we'll cover here will give you a good overview of their usage.

Setting the Standards

The first key component in establishing the required computer environment for your end-users is to set some standards. NNI has a problem with the lack of both hardware and software standardization. While it is possible to centrally manage non-standard environments, it winds up being a complex maze of GPOs and RIS images specific to hardware or software needs.

So the first critical business decision is standardization on both hardware and software. This can obviously be a phased implementation as current computers come off lease or are due to be replaced. Push for standardization on a specific model of desktop and laptop computer. Each of these models should obviously be listed on the Windows 2000 Professional Hardware Compatibility List (HCL), and should contain a PXE-capable ROM so they can

> **WARNING**
>
> **Need for Compatible HAL** When cloning a system with hardware different from that in the RIPrep image, there is one hardware constraint. The Hardware Abstraction Layer (HAL) must be the same on both systems. The main difference on a workstation's HAL is whether it supports Advanced Configuration Power Interface (ACPI). For ACPI and non-ACPI workstations, you must maintain two separate images.

extract an OS image from an RIS server. Here is a beautiful thing: Past methods of imaging systems expected the hardware to be the same for all computers that received the image. With RIPrep and Windows 2000 Plug and Play, this limitation is gone!

Software Distribution Using the Windows Installer

The NNI helpdesk staff fields occasional calls where the user has either deleted or moved an application system file. To address this problem, we'll create policies that deliver all applications to users via the software configuration and management portion of IntelliMirror. Step by Step 9.1 walks you through configuring a GPO to roll out the Windows 2000 Administration tools.

IN THE FIELD

DEPLOYING SOFTWARE: HOW IT USED TO BE

In the past, deploying software required a considerable amount of time and effort for several reasons:

- A tech had to visit each workstation to perform software installations.

- If an organization changed software policies or standards, a tech had to visit the workstations again to install or remove software.

- If a person's job responsibilities changed, a tech had to visit that person's workstation to install a new set of applications specific to the new role.

- If a user received a file for which they didn't have an associated application, a tech likely would have to come install that application.

- If a user deleted an application system file, rendering the application unusable, a tech had to repair the application.

These are just some of the reasons a tech would visit a user's desktop. Now, in that same environment, the software installation and maintenance technology, coupled with group policies and the Windows Installer technology, would allow administrators to manage all of the above tasks without sending a technician to the desktop.

NOTE

Why the Windows 2000 Admin Tools? To package an application into an MSI file would require more time than you should commit while reading this text. For demonstration purposes, we'll utilize an MSI file that is available by default under Windows 2000 Server.

FIGURE 9.8
Your Windows Installer package must reside on a network share accessible to users.

STEP BY STEP

9.1 Creating a New Package for Distribution

1. Create a test OU and a test user within that OU. Nothing special needs to be done as far as configuration.

2. Create a new GPO for that OU, and open the GPO to edit.

3. Expand Software Settings under User Configuration and right-click Software Installation.

4. Select New, Package.

5. In the Open dialog box, type the Universal Naming Convention (UNC) pathname (even though it may be local) to the MSI file for the Windows 2000 admin tools. This should be comparable to Figure 9.8.

6. Click Open. The MSI file is added to the list of software packages assigned to users of that OU (see Figure 9.9).

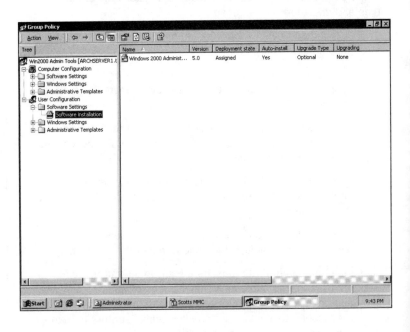

FIGURE 9.9
The completed package is ready for distribution.

The package you created in Step by Step 9.1 inherited the default properties for objects in the Software Installation container (see Figure 9.10), the most significant of which is that the application is going to be *assigned* to the user. To test, log on as that user. The Windows 2000 Administration tools should install.

In effect, what we've done here is made one application available to a subset of users. Now imagine that this subset is a group of sales people, and the application is a sales funnel-tracking program needed by only the sales force. You can see how easy it is to push the applications out to users with this method.

Remote Desktop Management

Another problem communicated by NNI is the lack of remote desktop management. Windows 2000 does not provide remote control out of the box, but our friend SMS 2.0 does! To eliminate several NNI help desk calls, we suggest they implement SMS for remote desktop control. Although we discuss SMS in general throughout this book, we'll highlight its useful features pertinent to this chapter.

SMS 2.0 integrates very well with the Windows 2000 software installation and maintenance mechanism, and for good reason. The SMS developers and the software installation and maintenance development teams at Microsoft overlapped. The outcome of this collaborative effort is two technologies that complement each other, with SMS being the value-added "add-on" to the Windows 2000 native software installation and maintenance technology.

SMS provides several features in addition to remote control capabilities; these are described in the following sections.

Software Distribution and Installation

SMS takes the Windows 2000 software installation and maintenance one step further by adding rules and intelligence to the equation. For example, in native Windows 2000, if a user joins a group, software is automatically sent to them according to the group's policy. With SMS, that application can be distributed immediately based on a sophisticated targeting process, software, and hardware inventory for the client.

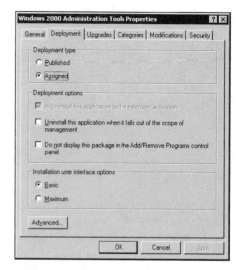

FIGURE 9.10

The deployment properties page of the package displays the deployment options and user interface options.

Software Metering

Software metering is important in hospital environments, such as NNI, as well as any other environment that needs to keep a close eye on licensed software. It gives the administrator the ability to monitor, analyze, and control the use of applications on the network. Software metering assists network administrators in fulfilling the following business objectives:

◆ Ensuring that software usage does not exceed the number of licensed copies you own

◆ Avoiding the purchase of too many licenses

◆ Conforming to the software usage licensing agreements regarding total and concurrent use and expiration dates

◆ Ensuring that illegal or unauthorized software is discovered and not permitted to run

Software metering becomes particularly handy in situations where you want to restrict the use of software, whether it is for licensing or other technical, political, or administrative reasons. Additionally, the software-metering database that is created can be used as a source for historical software usage reporting for trend analysis, which can be helpful when determining the number of licenses to purchase for application upgrades. The Suggested Readings and Resources list at the end of this chapter refers you to additional software metering information.

Diagnostics and Troubleshooting

Among the most important advanced diagnostics tools included with SMS is the full version of Network Monitor. This and other utilities, such as HealthMon, can be utilized to analyze network conditions and server performance.

By implementing SMS throughout the environment, the help desk will have the ability to take control of a user's ailing workstation and perform diagnostic testing on it without being physically present. This will reduce the time required to visit each desk for each trouble ticket.

Implementing Folder Redirection

The AR/AP department at NNI generates various letters and other correspondence and needs to ensure that data is stored on the network at all times, so it is included in the corporate backup every night. One solution to this problem is for the department to implement a document management system, such as iManage or PC DOCS, that forces them to store the documents on a network share. Of course, NNI would never approve such a solution for the AR/AP department, so they are left to simply remember to save the files on the network. For the most part, they do a good job of it, but recently they've lost more than one critical file due to local storage and a dead hard drive.

Windows 2000 addresses this problem by giving administrators an option to redirect specific folders such as My Documents to a network share, all transparent to the user.

In addition to the My Documents folder, you can redirect the following folders:

◆ Application Data

◆ Desktop

◆ My Pictures

◆ Start Menu

Step by Step 9.2 describes the general process by which you can redirect any or all of the aforementioned folders.

STEP BY STEP

9.2 Redirecting Folders to a Network Share

1. Create a network share on a file server to store the redirected folders.

2. Create a new GPO for the appropriate site, domain, or OU for which folders are to be redirected.

3. Edit the GPO, and expand User Configuration, Windows Settings, and Folder Redirection.

4. Right-click the appropriate folder and select Properties.

continues

continued

5. Select Basic Redirection, which redirects all files and folders within the selected folder hierarchy to the network share.

6. Type the network share from step 1 in the Target Folder Redirection field.

7. Repeat steps 4–6 for all folders you wish to redirect.

There are several advantages to implementing folder redirection. If you wish to enforce standard customized Start Menu and Desktop folders, you can redirect these folders to the network and allow only Read permission to a predefined directory structure for each. Additionally, if the user has a roaming user profile that contains the My Documents folder, then by design, the My Documents folder is synched with the network at logon and logoff time. If you relocate the My Documents folder to the network, this synch process does not need to occur. This can significantly reduce the amount of logon time traffic.

Making Files Available Offline

One downfall with folder redirection is that it is folder-rooted and there are only five predefined Windows folders you can redirect using Group Policy.

So, what if you have a subfolder of My Documents and that is all you want to redirect? Suppose a user has created a business-critical folder structure used to organize reports. What if a user simply has a file he needs to store on the network, yet needs to be synchronized on a laptop? In these cases, you must rethink your logic. Instead of redirecting predefined folders to a network share using centrally controlled group policies, you'll reverse the process and leave it up to the user to implement.

If a user has a custom folder structure on her hard drive, that data must first be moved out to a network share, typically to her secure home directory. Once moved, the original folder structure may be removed from the hard drive. Finally, to make the data that is now on the network available again on the local hard drive, right-click the top of the folder structure and select Make Available Offline." A synchronization process will create a cached copy of the data on your computer so that it can still be accessed while the user disconnected from the network. This process is similar to the Windows 9x Briefcase technology, the beauty of which is that it will scale down to the file level or up to an entire root folder and all subfolders and files. Because it is designed to be utilized by standard users, it is front-ended with an easy wizard interface.

IN THE FIELD

PREVENTING SERVER DATA FROM BEING MADE AVAILABLE OFFLINE

In certain situations, you as an administrator may want to prevent users from being able to cache certain data offline. Financial information or company confidential information, for instance, should not leave the company. If you allow users to make these and other types of data available offline, you make it very easy for them to transport this data wherever they and their laptop go.

By disabling caching on a Windows 2000 Server shared directory, you "turn off" the ability for that data to be made available offline. To do this, open the Sharing property page on a shared folder and click the Caching button. Remove the check box from the Allow Caching of Files in This Shared Folder option. Now when a user attempts to make a file or folder available offline when connected through this share, the Make Available Offline option simply does not show up.

This is a share-level operation, so you either allow caching, or you don't.

CHAPTER SUMMARY

KEY TERMS

- IntelliMirror
- remote OS installation
- Remote Installation Services (RIS)
- Change and configuration management
- user data management
- software installation and maintenance
- user computer settings management
- data accessibility
- data availability
- data protection
- published application
- assigned application
- CD-based installation
- RIPrep image format
- Pre-boot eXecution Environment (PXE)
- Windows Installer
- Microsoft Installer File (MSI)
- resilient application
- ZAP file
- file and folder redirection

The end-users of an organization will play a large role in determining the perceived success or failure of a solution. When developing a desktop change and configuration management plan for an organization, you must consider the needs and requirements of the end-users and end-user management. It is best to hold any discussions with end-user management, who will have a good understanding of both the business requirements and general needs of the departments or business units they represent. Corporate application standards must be considered when discussing these needs.

You must understand the technology represented by IntelliMirror, Remote OS Installation, SMS, and Group Policy. Without a good understanding of these overlapping technologies, you will have a difficult time understanding how to map the business requirements to the corresponding technology.

The technical support needs of the end-users must be considered as well, and should be evaluated before and after the desired solution is implemented. The overall goal is to reduce the reactive "problem resolution" needs and transfer them to strategic forward-looking needs.

After you have gathered the required information, utilize the tools discussed in this chapter to carry out the implementation of desktop management.

APPLY YOUR KNOWLEDGE

Exercises

9.1 Implement Folder Redirection

This exercise demonstrates how to implement My Documents folder redirection through the use of Group Policy. This process would be recommended for the NNI AR/AP departments.

Estimated Time: 20 Minutes

1. Create an OU named **Exercise 9.1** and within it create a user named **user91**.

2. If you have a network of more than one computer, create a share named **mydocs_redir** on a computer you are not using for logon. Otherwise, create the share on your local computer. (Make sure you create the directory outside the My Documents folder!) Just use the default permission of Everyone for this exercise, although in a real situation you would want to restrict access to this folder to the necessary users.

3. Log on as **user91** and open the Properties dialog box for My Documents. Notice the location of the folder and that the user has permission to change its location (the Move button is enabled), as shown in Figure 9.11.

4. Close all programs and log off.

5. Log on to your Active Directory domain controller as Administrator.

6. Open the Active Directory Users and Computers and drill down to your Exercise 9.1 OU.

7. Open the properties page for the OU and click the Group Policy tab.

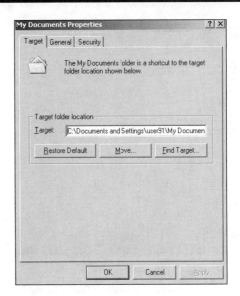

FIGURE 9.11
Properties dialog box for My Documents. Notice the physical location of the folder, and that the logged-on user can change it.

8. Click New to create a new GPO. Name it **MyDocs Redirection 9.1** and click Edit to open the Group Policy editor.

9. Drill down to Folder Redirection by expanding User Configuration then Windows Settings. Your screen should resemble Figure 9.12.

10. Right-click the My Documents folder and select Properties. The properties window opens displaying that no administrative policy has been specified (see Figure 9.13).

APPLY YOUR KNOWLEDGE

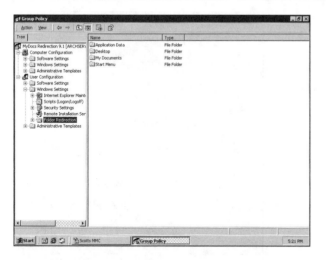

FIGURE 9.12
The folder redirection options within Group Policy.

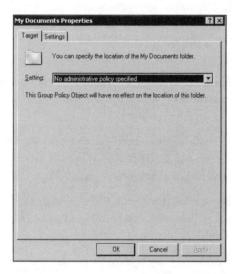

FIGURE 9.13
The general property page of the My Documents Properties folder redirection option specifies that no administrative policy has been defined.

11. In the Setting list box, select Basic—Redirect Everyone's Folder to the Same Location.

12. In the Target Folder Location field, type the complete UNC path to the share you configured in step 2. When complete, your screen should resemble Figure 9.14.

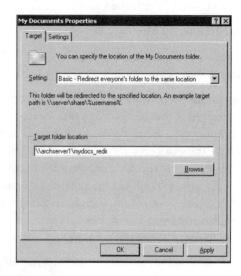

FIGURE 9.14
The general property page of the My Documents Properties folder redirection option after configuration.

13. Click the Settings tab.

14. Deselect the Grant the User Exclusive Rights to My Documents option. This will ensure that no permissions changes on the target folder will occur.

15. In the Policy Removal section, click the option Redirect the Folder Back to the Local User Profile Location When Policy Is Removed. This will ensure that any changes to My Documents are returned once the policy is removed. Your settings should resemble those in Figure 9.15.

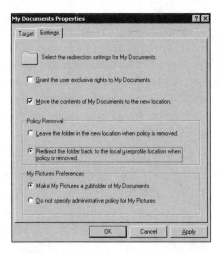

FIGURE 9.15
The Settings property page for the My Documents Properties folder redirection option.

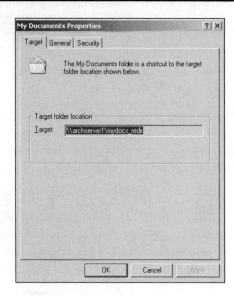

FIGURE 9.16
The location shown here allows you to verify the redirection.

16. Click OK to close the My Documents properties box and then close the Group Policy editor.

17. Return to your workstation and log on as **user91**.

18. Open the properties of the My Documents folder and observe the location of the folder (see Figure 9.16). Also observe that the user can no longer change the location.

19. To return your workstation to a local My Documents, simply remove the policy from the OU.

9.2   Make Files and Folders Available Offline

This exercise demonstrates Windows 2000 Professional's ability to cache network files locally and make them available offline. This process is similar to the Windows 9x Briefcase technology, but a lot more advanced. You will need both Windows 2000 Professional and Server on separate computers to complete this exercise.

Estimated Time: 20 Minutes

APPLY YOUR KNOWLEDGE

1. Log on to Windows 2000 Server as an administrator or its equivalent.

2. Create a folder on the root of a drive. Name and share this folder `Exercise92`.

3. Create a text file named `Ex92data.txt` and open it to edit. Type `I'm going to make this file available to my workstation offline` and save and exit the file.

4. Log on to your workstation as a user with the permission to map a drive.

5. Open Windows Explorer and map a drive to *\\servername*\exercise92 (where *servername* is the name of your server).

6. Click on the drive letter representing the Exercise92 share.

7. Right-click the file ex92data.txt. Select Make Available Offline. A quick synchronization process takes place, during which you see the window shown in Figure 9.17.

8. Remember the drive letter with the data you made available offline.

9. If you happen to be quick enough, click the Details button, then the Setup button to get to the synchronization configuration. Otherwise, you can reinvoke synchronization on the context menu of the data you've just made available offline.

10. Observe the synchronization setup options as shown in Figure 9.18.

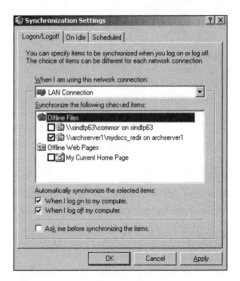

FIGURE 9.18
You can modify the default synchronization options by accessing the Synchronization Settings dialog box.

FIGURE 9.17
When you make your files and folders available offline, they must be synchronized from the server down to your Windows 2000 Professional client.

APPLY YOUR KNOWLEDGE

11. Unplug your network cable and reboot. Do not plug the network cable in again. Log on as if you are logging on to your server, which will use the locally cached user profile.

12. By default, when you make data available offline, it is placed in a special offline folder on your computer. A shortcut to the offline files folder is placed on your desktop.

13. Double-click the Offline Files shortcut to display your files. You should see the file you created previously. Open it to verify that it is truly the file you created.

> **N O T E**
>
> **Long Route to the Offline Files** If you do not have an Offline Files shortcut, you can still navigate to the offline files by accessing My Network Places, Entire Network, Microsoft Windows Network, and so on.

14. Locate the Offline Files icon (a miniature computer) in your system tray. Right-click it and select Settings. This is one place where you can configure your offline folder settings (see Figure 9.19).

15. To remove the offline settings, plug in your network cable and log on again. Navigate to the \\servername\exercise92 share and right-click ex92data.txt again. This time, Make Available Offline should be checked. Selecting it again will remove the synchronization.

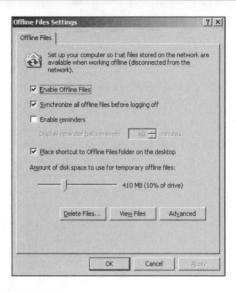

FIGURE 9.19
You can configure advanced offline files settings by accessing the Settings option on the context menu of the offline files icon in the system tray.

Review Questions

1. What is the name of the technology suite that describes user data management, software installation and maintenance, and user and computer settings management?

2. What are the three requirements for a remote installation server?

3. What is the technology that allows workstations to "boot from the network interface card (NIC)" and access a remote installation server?

4. What value-added application would allow an administrator to deploy software based on a set of administrator-defined rules?

APPLY YOUR KNOWLEDGE

5. Name the user data management feature that allows a user's data to follow the user wherever he may be in the enterprise?

6. What are the two installation options for Remote OS installation and what is the difference between the two?

7. What is the technology that enables an application to heal itself if something goes wrong with its system components?

8. What type of file must be created to use the software installation technology within Group Policy to deploy a non-Windows Installer-ready application? What two tags within this file are required?

Exam Questions

1. To which entities can you publish software using group policies?

   A. Users

   B. Computers

   C. Both users and computers

   D. Organizational Units

2. An NNI user logs on one Monday morning and notices something different about her computer. She now has icons on the desktop and Start menu for an application she did not have on Friday. What likely is behind the new icons?

   A. Over the weekend, a passerby sat at her computer and installed that application.

   B. An administrator associated a GPO with the user's OU that automatically published the application to her desktop.

   C. An administrator associated a GPO with the user's OU that automatically assigned the application to the user.

   D. An administrator shared the application from Active Directory, which caused the icons to appear on the user's desktop.

3. Suppose the NNI end-user representatives provide you with a list of applications they would like to have available to them at any point in time so they can install them. You find that one of these applications is somewhat old, and unable to be repackaged. How would you make this application available to the users?

   A. For all applications that can be repackaged, acquire the appropriate packages and create a GPO that publishes the application to the user's Add/Remove Programs Control Panel applet. For the application that cannot be repackaged, create and publish a ZAP file for the application.

   B. Assign all applications using the Group Policy software installation technology. Software installation will take care of distributing all applications using the appropriate installation method.

   C. For the applications capable of repackaging, obtain the appropriate package. Publish or assign those packages using a GPO. For the application that is not capable of repackaging, create a ZAP file and publish the application using a GPO.

APPLY YOUR KNOWLEDGE

D. For the applications capable of repackaging, obtain the appropriate package. Assign those packages using a GPO. For the application that is not capable of repackaging, create a ZAP file and assign the application using a GPO.

4. Suppose NNI standardizes its client OS to Windows 2000 Professional. They also standardize each department's applications (additional to the company standard applications) and wish to decrease the time it takes to set up new users and reinstall complete desktops for existing users. What would you suggest they do to accomplish these goals?

   A. Utilize a RIS server to store the Windows 2000 professional CD and all applications. Create custom software installation policies for each department. Boot computers from a PXE-enabled ROM or from a RIS floppy to run the network version of Windows 2000 installation. As users log on, install all applications based on department group policy settings.

   B. Obtain a standard client computer. Install Windows 2000 Professional and all applications for a specific department. Utilize RIPrep to prepare an image of that computer for an RIS server. Repeat this process for each department. Utilize a PXE-enabled ROM or a RIS boot floppy to invoke cloning.

   C. Obtain a standard client computer. Install Windows 2000 Professional and only applications that are standard for all departments. Utilize RIPrep to prepare an image of that computer for an RIS server. Utilize a PXE-enabled ROM or an RIS boot floppy to

invoke cloning. Create custom software installation GPOs for each department, so the appropriate applications are either installed or made available via publication or assignment as users log on.

   D. Burn copies of your Windows 2000 Professional CD and distribute it to all departments. Share the installation files for all applications listed by NNI. Send a technician to install Windows 2000 and the appropriate applications for all workstations.

5. Suppose NNI wants to allow hospital visitors access to the Internet by setting up pods of computers in designated areas. They organize all pod computers into an Active Directory OU named POD and allow logon rights only to the user poduser. They create a custom security policy that does not allow poduser to access the hospital network. They create another security policy that makes Internet Explorer (IE) the only application available to run. They now want to lock down the Start menu, and provide a custom background and screen saver. Describe how you would approach this task. (Choose two.)

   A. Create a new GPO on the POD OU and modify the computer configuration settings for the Start menu, screen saver, and desktop wallpaper.

   B. Create a new GPO on the POD OU and modify the user configuration settings for the Start menu, screen saver, and desktop wallpaper.

   C. Modify an existing POD OU GPO and add user configuration settings for the Start menu, screen saver, and desktop wallpaper.

APPLY YOUR KNOWLEDGE

D. Modify an existing POD OU GPO and add computer configuration settings for the Start menu, screen saver, and desktop wallpaper.

E. Create a folder redirection GPO for the Start Menu folder and apply it to the POD OU.

6. Marsha Triptaker, the manager of NNI's Critical Care Unit, travels around the country to affiliated hospitals to assist in establishing good business practices. She uses her laptop extensively to compose important Word and Excel documents that contain very large high-quality graphics. She stores them in a subfolder of her My Documents folder, which contains all of her personal and professional data. While she is gone, her secretary needs access to those documents so she can apply formatting and get them prepared to print. How should these documents be stored so they are kept up to date and available to both Marsha and her secretary?

A. The documents should be stored on a network share to which both Marsha and her secretary have access.

B. The documents should be stored on a network share to which both Marsha and her secretary have access. Marsha should select Make Available Offline on the context menu of the network folder to retain a synchronized copy of the files on her laptop.

C. Marsha should store her files on her laptop and share the folder. She should give only her secretary access through the share.

D. An administrator should create a file and folder redirection policy so that Marsha's My Documents folder is physically stored on

the network. It is then automatically cached to her laptop.

7. NNI help desk techs have been playing with Windows 2000 Server with terminal services running in remote administration mode. They've noticed that Windows 2000 Professional did not have this capability, but want to be able to open a remote session on a client computer for troubleshooting purposes. What should they do?

A. Install Windows 2000 Server as the standard desktop OS and enable terminal services in remote administration mode.

B. Purchase and implement a third-party utility such as Microsoft Systems Management Server that enables remote administration of a Windows 2000 Professional workstation.

C. Configure a GPO for OUs that contain computers you wish to control remotely. Change the Allow Remote Control setting under Computer Configuration to Enabled.

D. Install and configure pcAnyware on each workstation you wish to control remotely. Use TCP/IP to connect to these workstations.

8. Which of the following ZAP files is valid?

A. ```
[Application]

SetupCommand=setup.exe

DisplayVersion=

Publisher=

URL=http://www.fictionalsw.com/
➥releasenotes.html

[Ext]
```
```

APPLY YOUR KNOWLEDGE

B. [Application]

FriendlyName=My Fictional Software

SetupCmd=setup.exe

DisplayVersion=2.0

Publisher=Fictional Software, Inc.

URL=**http://www.fictionalsw.com/
➥releasenotes.html**

[Ext]

C. [Application]

FriendlyName=My Fictional Software

SetupCommand=winsetup.exe

DisplayVersion=2.0

Publisher=Fictional Software, Inc.

URL=**http://www.fictionalsw.com/
➥releasenotes.html**

D. [Application]

FriendlyName=My Fictional Software

DisplayVersion=

Publisher=

URL=http://www.fictionalsw.com/
releasenotes.html

[EXT]

FTS=

9. You deploy two applications, one using a Windows Installer MSI file, and the other using a ZAP file. A system dynamic link library (DLL) eater virus is discovered on all client workstations and users begin to complain that the software distributed with the ZAP file is inoperable, but the software distributed with the Windows

Installer is fine. What is likely the reason for this phenomenon?

A. The virus did not "eat" the working applications' DLL files.

B. The ZAP file installation did not specify resilience options, and therefore the application could not heal itself.

C. The Windows Installer application is able to heal itself when a system component such as a DLL becomes corrupt or is deleted. ZAP-installed applications are not able to heal themselves.

D. Applications deployed with the Windows Installer actually run from the server, which was not affected by the virus. ZAP-installed applications run on the workstations and are therefore susceptible to viruses.

10. You are the sole administrator for a growing company of 25 employees. Because you have no help, you create one standard workstation image for all users. This image contains all applications and utilities the users will need. You do not want the users to mess up their Desktop and Start menu environments, but you do want them to have some control over the computer. You wish to store one standard Desktop and Start Menu folder on the network so you can manage one instead of 25. How would you implement this?

A. Copy the Desktop and Start Menu folders from the standard image to a sharepoint on the network. Customize the folders as needed. Create a domain-wide GPO to restrict access to the desktop and start menu as needed. Include in that GPO a folder redirection policy for both the Desktop and Start Menu folders.

B. Copy the Desktop and Start Menu folders from the standard image to a sharepoint on the network. Delete the folders and shortcuts you don't want.

C. Create a domain-wide GPO that redirects all users' Desktop and Start Menu folders to their own subfolder of a sharepoint on the network. Create a GPO for each user that restricts the Desktop and Start Menu folder options.

D. On each computer, right-click the Desktop and Start Menu folders and select Make Available Offline to redirect them to the network. Using a GPO, restrict the Start Menu and Desktop options for each user.

Answers to Review Questions

1. The IntelliMirror suite of technologies describes user data management, software installation and maintenance, and user computer settings management. See "Conducting the End-User Needs Analysis."

2. Windows 2000 RIS can be installed on any Windows 2000 Server product. To properly install RIS, you must have a partition with a recommended minimum of 800MB formatted with NTFS. Additionally, you must have support for Active Directory, DNS, and DHCP services. See "Requirements for RIS."

3. PXE is a technology for bootstrapping a client. PXE is a ROM-based technology that allows a client to boot to the network and, using DHCP and DNS, locate a RIS that can provide the client an OS. See "Remote OS Installation."

4. Microsoft Systems Management Server 2.0 has been designed to make full use of Windows management services and complements the functionality of Windows 2000 in many areas. One such area is with sophisticated targeting of client computers for software distribution based on defined rules, as well as client hardware and software inventory. See "Remote Desktop Management."

5. The Data Accessibility feature of IntelliMirror's User Data Management technology is focused on providing users access to data from any computer in the enterprise. To the user, this equates to "my data follows me everywhere." See "Data Accessibility."

6. There are two options for configuring remote OS installation: CD-based installation and RIPrep image format. The main difference between the two is that the CD-based installation is essentially the Windows 2000 Professional setup program running across the network, and the RIPrep image format actually builds a "clone" image of Windows 2000 and pre-configuration applications and provides a wizard-based setup for client computers. See "Remote OS Installation."

7. Windows Installer technology introduces a higher level of sophistication to software installation and maintenance. It includes several benefits, including the ability to perform JIT installations based on feature or document invocation, clean removal of applications, and application resiliency (the ability for applications to heal themselves by pulling pristine files from a predetermined loca-

tion should something go wrong). See "The Windows Installer Service."

8. Not all software is going to be capable of repackaging to the Windows Installer ready format (the Microsoft Installer [MSI] files). For these applications, you can create a special information file called a ZAP file to provide the Group Policy software installation mechanism with the information it needs to perform the installation. The two required tags within ZAP files fall under the [Application] heading. They are FriendlyName and SetupCommand. See "ZAP Files."

Answers to Exam Questions

1. **A.** You may only publish software to users using group policies. You may assign software to both users and computers. You cannot publish or assign software directly to OUs, although you can attach GPOs that publish or assign software to OUs. See "Software Installation and Maintenance."

2. **C.** Assigned applications are either installed immediately or advertised to the user. In this case, the application was assigned to the users OU and set to advertise. Advertised applications appear as though they are installed by placing shortcuts on the desktop and Start menu, as well as modifying the registry. They are installed when the user invokes one of its icons. Published applications are not advertised to users and only appear in the Add/Remove Programs Control Panel applet. Passersby may well sit at computers overnight and play around; however, it's not

likely that's what happened here because they'd need to know the user's password to log on. See "Software Installation and Maintenance."

3. **C.** The NNI user representatives said they would like the applications available for them to install as they need them. For applications capable of repackaging, you'll need to obtain the Windows Installer package. You can either publish them to Add/Remove Programs, or assign them so they advertise their availability on the desktop—that should be the user's preference. For the older application not compatible with Windows Installer technology, you have no choice but to create a ZAP file and publish it to the client's Add/Remove Programs Control Panel applet. See "ZAP Files" and "Software Installation and Maintenance."

4. **C.** Because NNI has a company standard set of applications, and each department has its own set of standard applications, it would stand to reason that one image with only company standard applications would be most efficient. Administrators could then define GPO for each department that would either assign or publish that department's applications. Using a RIPrep image format will allow the administrators to develop the standard operating and application environment and clone that up to RIS servers for distribution. Client computers that support PXE could attach and download the image, whereas computers that do not support PXE could use an RIS boot disk. Creating multiple images would work, but would be less efficient from an administration standpoint. With today's technology, it

APPLY YOUR KNOWLEDGE

is inconceivable that to perform many manual installations. See "Remote OS Installation," "Remote Installation Services," and "Software Installation and Maintenance."

5. **B, C.** To perform any customizations to the Start menu or any other area of user profile, you must modify the user configuration settings within a GPO. If there's an existing GPO for an object, you can modify additional settings to add the functionality required, although it is recommended that GPOs be created for specific tasks, so as not to confuse them. Computer configuration settings contain settings specific to computers, not users. The GPO you create may well be a GPO to force redirection of the Start Menu folder; however, redirecting the Start Menu folder alone will not accomplish the settings changes needed for the desktop. See "User and Computer Settings Management."

6. **B.** Because Marsha has more data than just the important Word and Excel files in her My Documents folder, it is more practical for her to move that folder to a network share to which she and her secretary have access, and then make it available offline. This will ensure that her data remains synchronized on the network and her laptop, and that she and her secretary have access to it. You could have an administrator redirect her My Documents folder, but that would redirect the entire folder to the network and she needs to redirect only one. See "Implementing Folder Redirection" and "Making Files Available Offline."

7. **B.** Hopefully you won't consider installing a Windows 2000 Server as a desktop OS, which could lead to disaster! The correct answer is to incorporate an additional value-added utility, such as SMS 2.0, which has the capability to allow remote administration. Windows 2000 out of the box does not support remote control services for client computers, so answer C is totally off. pcAnyware may work for a small environment, but should not be considered as an option in the enterprise. See "Remote OS Installation."

8. **C.** ZAP files must contain only two pieces of information (called tags) to be considered functional. Under the [Applications] section, the tags FriendlyName and SetupCommand are required. All other tags in that section, and the entire [Ext] section, are optional. A is missing the FriendlyName tag, B has the SetupCommand tag misspelled, and D is missing the SetupCommand tag altogether. See "ZAP Files."

9. **C.** The Windows Installer enables applications to become resilient to harm by providing a mechanism to deliver pristine system files to the desktop should they be needed. Conversely, because the ZAP files are non-Windows Installer compliant, they are unable to heal themselves should a system file become corrupt. At best, they can be configured to reinstall from scratch if they become inoperable. Although it is possible that the virus did not affect the MSI distributed application, it is not the answer we were looking for. Windows Installer distributed applications do not necessarily run from the server. See "The Windows Installer Service" and "ZAP Files."

APPLY YOUR KNOWLEDGE

10. **A.** To create a basic starting point for folder re-direction, copy a version of the Start Menu and Desktop folders to the sharepoint on the network. Perform any customizations to them, such as adding shortcuts to applications. You'll then create a folder redirection policy so that every user will utilize the network version of the Start Menu and Desktop folders. In this situation, you can implement a domain-wide policy and then block that policy on specific computers, such as the administrator's computer. You cannot right-click the Start menu or desktop and make it available offline. Also, if you redirect each user to his own folder on the network, you are defeating the purpose of standardizing the Start menu and desktop. See "Implementing Folder Redirection."

Suggested Readings and Resources

1. Microsoft Official Curriculum. *Course 1560: Updating Support Skills from Microsoft Windows NT 4.0 to Microsoft Windows 2000.* Module 8, "Using Group Policy to Manage Desktop Environments," and Module 9, "Using Group Policy to Manage Software."

2. White Papers:

   Introduction to Change and Configuration Management

   Group Policy

   Remote Operating System Installation

   Using Group Policy Scenarios

   The Windows Installer Service

   Introduction to Windows 2000 Management Services

3. Microsoft TechNet Articles:

   "Step by Step Guide to User Data and User Settings." Available on the April 2000 and later TechNet CD.

   "Chapter 14 – Metering Software." From *Systems Management Server 2.0 Administrators Guide.* Available on the September 1999 and later TechNet CD.

4. Iseminger, David. *Active Directory Services for Microsoft Windows 2000 Technical Reference.* Microsoft Press, 2000. Chapter 14, "Administratively Leveraging Active Directory Services."

DESIGNING A DIRECTORY SERVICE ARCHITECTURE

This chapter covers the following Microsoft-specified objectives for the Designing a Microsoft Windows 2000 Directory Services Infrastructure exam:

Design an Active Directory naming strategy.

- **Establish the scope of the Active Directory.**

- **Design the namespace.**

- **Plan DNS strategy.**

▶ DNS is the foundation of Active Directory. You use DNS to create a namespace, which typically defines the scope of Active Directory services—although scope can be much bigger than a single namespace.

Design the placement of DNS servers.

- **Considerations include performance, fault tolerance, functionality, and manageability.**

- **Plan for interoperability with the existing DNS.**

▶ This objective focuses on the use and proper placement of DNS servers throughout the enterprise. Emphasis will be on Active Directory integrated zones, but you should know how to create standard primary, standard secondary, caching only, forwarders, and slaves. Your ability to identify which type of DNS server fits a given situation will be key. You also need to know the requirements for non-Microsoft DNS servers used in Windows 2000 implementations.

CHAPTER 10

DNS and Active Directory

▶ Make sure you understand the terminology used throughout this chapter. Some terms that have been around a while have changed in scope, so even if you recognize a term, look over its definition.

▶ Pay close attention to the sections that describe choosing the root DNS namespace.

▶ Further examine the interoperability between WINS, DHCP, and DNS. If you have the chance, implement WINS and DHCP integration with DNS and down-level clients in a lab setting.

▶ Spend the entire time estimated to get through Exercise 10.2. This comprehensive exercise will take you through a case study-like scenario, which will help you relate design strategies to real-world situations. It will also help you learn how DNS resolves names in complex environments.

▶ Allow yourself some extra time to fully grasp the section "Complex Namespace Considerations," which ties in with Exercise 10.2. We highly recommend that you read the additional material suggested in that section.

INTRODUCTION

By now you no doubt have a new appreciation for the considerations in designing a directory services infrastructure. You are now beginning Chapter 10, and it is the first chapter that really hits on the actual directory services infrastructure design. Does that mean Chapters 1–9 are irrelevant? Absolutely not. They form the foundation that gets you to this point. Without understanding the business needs and the technical requirements of the organization, you cannot effectively create an Active Directory architecture that meets and will continue to meet the needs of the company.

Active Directory is big. Its scope can include every single object (user, file, printer, and so on) every server, every domain, and even every WAN within a corporation. It can also be a confined to a single computer. Active Directory follows naming standards, such as DNS and LDAP, for naming and resolving objects throughout the directory. Because it is standards based, a variety of access protocols can be used, which enables integration with many different directory services, such as Exchange and Novell's NDS.

This chapter will focus on the planning and design of the Active Directory namespace. DNS is the foundation that allows Active Directory to be one of the most flexible, scalable, and manageable directory services available. We'll take a detailed look at DNS in this chapter. It is critical that you understand DNS before you attempt an enterprise design, as you'll soon see.

IT ALL BEGINS WITH DNS

You wouldn't begin to build your dream home without first considering its foundation. The foundation must fit just right and provide the proper utilities—such as plumbing and water lines—for your custom home. Once you have the foundation in place, you begin to build on that, leveraging the time you spent to tediously plan and design your foundation by building the rest of the house—the part you'll actually use.

The Domain Name System (DNS) is much like that foundation. It provides core locator services for Active Directory (and many other Windows 2000 components)—your "dream house."

When the house is built and you're all settled in, the role of the foundation turns to a single purpose: stability. Its purpose is to support the house; if it can't do that anymore it is no good to you. DNS has a singular purpose as well: to provide *unambiguous* name resolution services to clients, servers, and the like participating within its namespace. It uses a database of records (called *resource records)* to provide answers to these name resolution queries.

IN THE FIELD

THAT WAS THEN...

In the old days—a whopping 10 years ago in computer terms—name resolution occurred through the use of static, manually created and managed *host files.* You can imagine all the work required to manage these files, especially when considering the Internet. Every time a new computer was added or an old one removed, an entry had to be added to removed from the host file. Additionally, host file administrators had to manually copy this file to all other servers and clients on the network so the new machine could be accessed. Yuck!

The host file was fine for small networks in peer-to-peer configurations, but as the peer-to-peer networks became server centric and grew outside the walls of a single location, it became obvious that this flat file namespace was not going to work; a better name resolution strategy was needed. Enter DNS.

NOTE

Partitioned Namespace   DNS uses domains to partition namespace. The terms "partition" and "domain" are used synonymously within this chapter.

NOTE

Implied Dot/Period   There is an implied period (.) at the end of a DNS FQDN. This period refers to the DNS namespace root, simply named ."

DNS implements a hierarchical, server-based name resolution solution. The hierarchical structure provides for much better scalability than the flat host file, which is evident with today's Internet. In the hierarchical structure, DNS may be *partitioned* into separate *domains* and then distributed to servers that would be responsible for name resolution services only in its partition of the namespace.

DNS servers use a top-down approach for resolving names across partitions. For example, if I needed to resolve `www.in.state.us.gov`, my Internet query would essentially start at . (the Internet root) and work its way down through the .gov partition, then us.gov, and so on until I find the www record in the in.state.us.gov partition. In this example, the in.state.us.gov manages objects only found in that partition (theoretically pertaining to the State of Indiana), such as records for the State of Indiana's Web servers.

This scalability, reliability, and delegated management (ability) *is* the reason we have such a vast and fast Internet today that is cooperatively managed by literally millions of people. Incidentally, Active Directory is built to model DNS. *Hmmm.* Imagine having all the abilities that comprise the Internet in your own private enterprise!

> **EXAM TIP**
>
> **Understanding DNS is Critical** As stated earlier, if you do not understand DNS, you simply should not bother taking this exam. Read this chapter carefully until you have a solid handle on the DNS material.

NAMING CONVENTIONS

Slow down, tiger! Before you jump in and model the enterprise after the Internet you really need to understand a lot more about DNS, Active Directory, and how they integrate. We'll start with an examination of the naming conventions used in both Active Directory and DNS.

Active Directory supports several naming conventions because clients need to be able to reference network resources in several ways. This section discusses the new and the old naming conventions, including the DNS hierarchical naming conventions used in Windows 2000 and Active Directory.

NetBIOS Name

The old days of NetBIOS are just about behind us. For years, Microsoft has relied on this flat namespace model to provide name resolution services for computers, shares, and other network resources. This scenario in the enterprise is quite limiting, as NetBIOS names are limited to 15 characters. The possibility of breaking the rules by duplicating a NetBIOS name somewhere in an enterprise organization is something administrators must contend with.

> **NOTE**
>
> **NetBIOS Character Rules** Both NetBIOS and DNS come complete with a hefty set of legal and illegal character rules, which are explained later, in Table 10.1.

NetBIOS is *broadcast based*, meaning if a computer wanted to find another computer by its NetBIOS name, it would send out a broadcast for that name and hope the other computer would respond. To reduce broadcast traffic, Microsoft introduced the LMHOSTS file. LMHOSTS served as a sort of name resolution mechanism that allowed LMHOSTS-enabled clients to resolve NetBIOS names to IP addresses locally, or through a complicated maze of LMHOSTS server-based includes. This, like the DNS HOSTS files, became tedious and extremely time-intensive to manage. Enter WINS.

NOTE

Directed Broadcast *Directed broadcasts* are just what they sound like. They are broadcast packets directed to a certain place—in this case a WINS server. They alleviate much of the network traffic associated with normal broadcast name resolution.

Microsoft introduced the Windows Internet Name Service (WINS) to again reduce broadcast traffic and this time centralize the repository of NetBIOS names on a network. WINS is a flat-file database repository for all NetBIOS names on a given network. It has the ability to replicate its database via "push" and "pull" relationships with other WINS servers to extend the reach of NetBIOS name resolution. Furthermore, WINS allowed for dynamic name registration and provided a facility for directed broadcasts.

NetBIOS in Windows 2000

Active Directory suggests a pre-Windows 2000 name—a NetBIOS name—as the first 15 bytes of an object's relative distinguished name (discussed shortly). This can be changed at any time but still needs to conform to the NetBIOS guidelines of 15 characters or fewer. Clients running earlier versions of Windows will use this name concatenated with the NetBIOS name of the Windows 2000 domain to logon. For example, if I were running Windows 98 on my desktop, I would log on to my home Windows 2000 domain using TheArchers\sarcher if I wanted to use NetBIOS. In this case, the NetBIOS name of my domain is TheArchers and the NetBIOS version of my username is sarcher.

Fully Qualified Domain Names (FQDNs)

In the recent past we've seen the Internet explode. This explosion has made information available at the click of a button, resulting in a much faster paced business world that we ever could have imagined. We've seen a number of gigantic companies merge in the recent past: Boeing and McDonnell Douglas, Chrysler and Mercedes, AOL and Time Warner—the list goes on and on. These mergers can produce gargantuan companies.

To manage all the computer names and provide name resolution in companies like this with a flat namespace would be a nightmare. This is where you can really start to see the value with DNS. Having the ability to partition the namespace and maintain continuity within the network is a major bonus, and DNS does it well. Of course, with a hierarchical namespace, the way you identify a computer or user on the network must change. You must utilize the *fully qualified domain name* (FQDN) to properly describe a computer on the network. The FQDN has two parts:

◆ **Host name.** In simple terms the host name is the computer name.

◆ **Domain name.** The domain name is the DNS domain name in which the host resides.

The FQDN provides assurance that a host is unambiguously resolvable within the entire namespace. The FQDN for one my servers, for example, is *archserver1*.**home.thearchers.com**. In this example, the host name (or relative distinguished name) is in italic and the domain name is in bold.

Relative Distinguished Name

The FQDN for a computer, as you can imagine, can be pretty difficult to remember. For this reason, there exists the *relative distinguished name*, which is simply the host name of the computer. So why not simply call it a host name? Within a partitioned namespace, it is possible, and perfectly legal, to use the same computer name several times, as long as each computer is in a different namespace partition. So for example, if I had a simple namespace of thearchers.com, and added two subdomains to that, I might have something like east.thearchers.com and west.thearchers.com—as in Figure 10.1. I could legally have three computers named myclient within this namespace—one in each partition.

To properly reference the computer myclient by its host name, I would have to give that host name some context. Sure, I could use the FQDN to describe a single computer in the entire namespace, but as I've stated, the FQDN can be long and difficult to remember. For this reason, you can describe the computer by its relative distinguished name (myclient), which is the host name of the computer within the context of the proper domain, such as east.thearchers.com. See Figure 10.2 for a graphical representation of the FQDN.

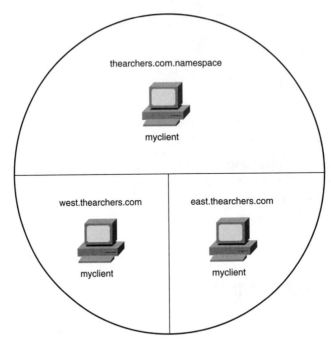

FIGURE 10.1
thearchers.com DNS namespace.

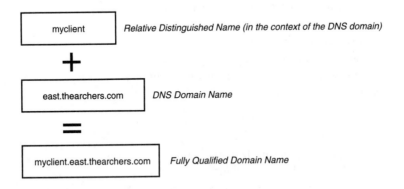

FIGURE 10.2
The decomposition of a FQDN.

An Example—User Principal Name

It is a good practice to get a feel for how Windows 2000 makes use of the DNS hierarchical structures. To do this, we'll discuss the *user principal name (UPN)*, which can be closely associated to the way we use a FQDN and relative distinguished name to describe a computer.

The UPN consists of a user logon name and a domain name identifying the domain in which the user account is located. For example, sarcher@home.thearchers.com would represent my UPN at my home Windows 2000 domain. In this example, my username (relative distinguished name) is sarcher and the domain in which my account resides is home.thearchers.com (which is also known as the UPN *suffix*). It looks a lot like an email address for good reason: it is easy to remember. This is the preferred method for logging on to a Windows 2000 domain.

> **NOTE** **UPN and UPN Suffix**   You can only use the UPN and UPN Suffix designation (sarcher@home.thearchers.com) to log on to a Windows 2000 domain from a Windows 2000 Professional workstation. Down-level clients and servers must continue to use the NetBIOS equivalents.

CONCEPTS IN DNS DESIGN

There are five concepts you must understand wholeheartedly or you absolutely will not get it. The DNS design-planning phase starts here. You will be either introduced to (or, if you're ahead of the game, refreshed on) the fundamental DNS building blocks. Because Active Directory is so tightly integrated with the DNS namespace, understanding these concepts will put you ahead of the game when you begin to design your Active Directory domain structure.

The following five concepts will be discussed in the sections that follow:

◆ DNS namespace

◆ DNS domains

◆ DNS zones

◆ DNS root namespace

◆ Name resolution

DNS Namespace

A *namespace* by definition is a bounded area in which a given name can be resolved. A telephone directory, for example, can be considered a namespace because it forms an area in which names or telephone subscribers can be resolved down to their corresponding telephone numbers. The Internet is also a single namespace: Any network device may be resolved down to its IP address. There are two types of namespaces: flat and hierarchical.

Flat Namespaces

Flat namespaces, such as that of NetBIOS, don't scale well. The drawback is the sheer size of a flat namespace. All objects must be contained in one structure, and all objects must be resolvable with no ambiguity. Therefore, all objects must have a unique name. Couple that requirement with the limitation of 15 character names, and you start running out of meaningful names very quickly.

Hierarchical Namespaces

Hierarchical namespaces, as we've discussed, are divided up into one or more partitions. Objects within a hierarchical namespace are required to be unique only within their partition, and not the entire namespace. With this hierarchy comes scalability of monstrous proportions—I don't have to keep reminding you the Internet is a single hierarchical namespace, right? Enough said.

Character Sets

> **WARNING**
>
> **No White Space** With the advent of long file names in file systems, which include white space, you may be tempted to use them in DNS naming. Don't—it's illegal!

There is additional topic we should bring up here: the topic of names themselves. Organizations with a prior investment in NetBIOS technology may be using names that are not legal with the DNS naming rules set forth in RFC-1123. This industry standard RFC defines legal DNS characters as A–Z, a–z, 0–9, and the hyphen (-).

Because NetBIOS allows special characters in its names, some companies will find themselves in a situation where they must change every computer name to conform to DNS standards. For this reason, the Windows 2000 implementation of Dynamic DNS (DDNS) supports both the ASCII and UniCode character sets. This feature was implemented to ease the transitional period from a pure NetBIOS environment to a pure DNS environment. Of course, the drawback here is, because it is a Microsoft implementation, every DNS server must be pure Windows 2000.

Table 10.1 illustrates the NetBIOS and DNS naming comparison.

TABLE 10.1

COMPARISON OF NETBIOS AND DNS NAMING

Type	NetBIOS (Flat)	DNS (Hierarchical)
Character restrictions	Unicode characters, numbers, white space	Same as for NetBIOS, except you cannot use white spaces and the period (.) has special meaning
	Symbols: ! @ # $ % ^ & ') (. - _ { }	
Maximum length	15 character bytes	63 octets per label
		255 octets per fully qualified domain name (FQDN)
Name service	WINS, broadcast	DNS, DDNS

Because Windows 2000 also supports NetBIOS, the impact of non-DNS RFC-1123 compliant computer names is minimal. Keep in mind that to ever get to a pure DNS environment, these issues will need to be addressed.

The best practice, if you are still in a Windows 9x and Windows NT environment, is to conform to RFC-1123 standards for naming with your NetBIOS computer names. You can then theoretically (if applications will allow it) move away from NetBIOS into a pure DNS environment when the time comes.

DNS Domains

DNS *domains* are partitions of the hierarchical namespace of DNS. Each domain contains objects that it is responsible for resolving names for, which in general significantly reduces the load on name resolution servers—compared to past methods. If you had a domain that looked like *aaa.bbb.ccc.company.com* for example, the domains could be listed separately by picking out each word between the periods, such as *aaa, bbb, ccc, company,* and com. Within each domain, a namespace partition exists, which provides the boundary for name uniqueness requirements, as illustrated in Figure 10.3.

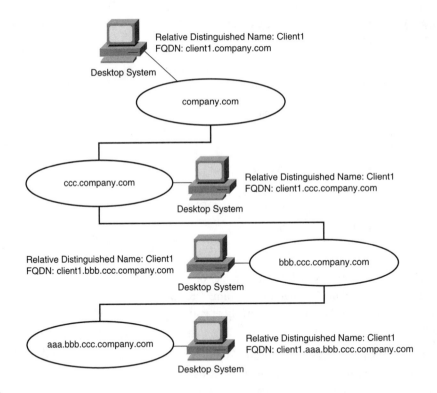

FIGURE 10.3
This figure illustrates the flexibility a hierarchical DNS domain structure yields in computer naming.

DNS Zones

A *DNS zone* is a database file comprised of resource records. These resource records, such as the Start of Authority (SOA) and Name Server (NS) records, make up the data that allow DNS servers to resolve names and services in a specific part of the DNS hierarchical namespace. DNS zones are used to determine which servers are responsible, or *authoritative*, in a given DNS namespace.

It is important that you don't confuse a DNS zone with a DNS domain. Zones differ from domains in that their make-up can consist of one or more partitions in the form of domains, so there is no requirement for a 1:1 relationship between zones and domains. To illustrate, Figure 10.4 uses the `company.com` namespace to illustrate a zone that is authoritative for three domains.

There are two types of DNS zones: forward lookup and reverse lookup.

NOTE

Resource Records Resource records make up the basic unit of information DNS servers use to fulfill queries. They will be discussed in detail later in this chapter.

EXAM TIP

Know Your Zones Understanding how zones work is crucial to Active Directory planning, and quite likely to be tested on the exam.

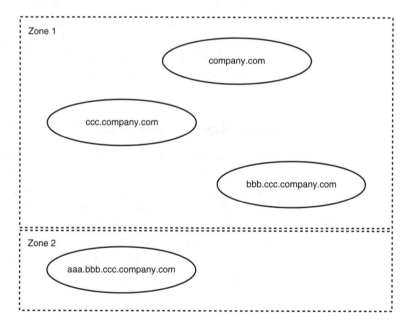

FIGURE 10.4
A single DNS zone can be authoritative over several DNS domains in a single namespace.

NOTE

Service Resource Records We will discuss service resource records later in this chapter.

Forward Lookup Zones

You must create at least one forward lookup zone on a name server before it will function. Each forward lookup zone includes SOA and NS records for that zone, and its primary function is to resolve FQDNs to IP addresses. With Windows 2000, the forward lookup zone will also resolve service resource records to the appropriate domain controller as well.

Reverse Lookup Zones

Unlike the forward lookup zone, reverse lookup zones are not required. When they are created, they require SOA, NS, and PTR (pointer) records; they are responsible for resolving IP addresses to FQDNs and are primarily used when using utilities, such as NSLOOKUP.

The reverse lookup zones incorporate a special domain called in-addr.arpa. This domain uses a notation in which subdomains are formed using the reverse ordering of the numbers in the IP address. The in-addr.arpa domain tree then requires the use of PTR records to provide reverse mappings (IP address to FQDN) of the corresponding host names.

DNS Root Namespace

The DNS root namespace is the top-level DNS domain in a namespace. The root namespace on the Internet, for example, is .'''' (dot). Any Internet-wide search must begin at the root. For example, a name resolution on the Internet commonly starts at the root, then goes to the com, net, or other top-level domains, and on down to your specified domain. All DNS servers contain helpers, called *root hints*, that help them get queries to the root servers expeditiously. Figure 10.5 illustrates the Internet root domain and the first- and second-level domains.

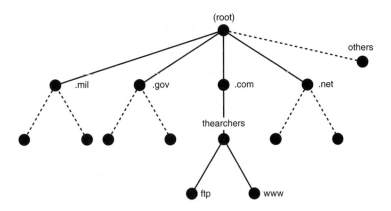

FIGURE 10.5
There are millions of registered domains on the Internet—all under a common root.

Name Resolution

When a client sends a query to a DNS server, it wishes to have that DNS server resolve that query, which typically means returning an IP address that corresponds with the host name. It is important to understand that this process uses zone database resource records to fulfill the query. We'll cover this concept in more detail later in this chapter when we discuss resource records.

THE COMPONENTS OF DNS

You should now have a good understand of DNS at the conceptual level. We're not going to stop there! The major components of DNS are as follows:

◆ Servers

◆ Resolvers

◆ Resource records

◆ Zone database files

As you read through this section, it may help to keep in mind the purpose of DNS: to resolve names.

DNS Servers

DNS runs as a service under Windows 2000 on any server on which Windows 2000 will run. It is based on the client/server model, with the server piece providing a zone database for its clients, known in DNS talk as *resolvers*. The process works like this: A client sends a query to the DNS server, which responds by returning the name or IP related information requested, either returning a pointer to another DNS server, or returning an error indicating it doesn't have the information requested and doesn't know how to get it. That's it. Not a whole lot of action, but definitely useful.

There are two types of DNS servers (well, four types, really, but only two major types): primary and secondary. The other two—caching-only and forwarders—are considered purpose-based and do not manage zone files. The following sections explain these servers.

Primary Servers

In a DNS zone, the *primary* server is the authoritative server. All administrative functions for the zone must be performed on this server. This includes creating, deleting, or modifying resource records, creating DNS subdomains, and more. There is only one primary server in any given zone.

Secondary Servers

Secondary DNS servers contain mirror copies of primary zone database files and are primarily used to balance the load across multiple servers. You can think of a primary DNS server as the PDC in a Windows NT domain, and the secondary DNS servers as BDCs within that domain. They receive all their zone data from the primaries via a process called *zone transfer*, which will be discussed later in this chapter. Secondary DNS servers are not limited to operating in a single zone, so you can "back up" several zones on a single secondary DNS server as illustrated in Figure 10.6.

NOTE

Active Directory Integrated Zones
Windows 2000 allows you to integrate your DNS zone database with Active Directory. This offers several advantages, and also changes the rules regarding primary and secondary serves. This concept will be covered later in this chapter.

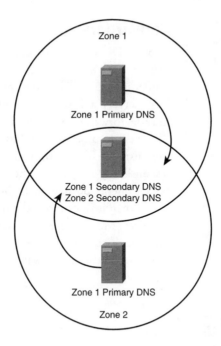

FIGURE 10.6
A secondary DNS server can contain zone database information for multiple DNS zones.

Caching-Only Servers

Caching-only DNS servers are exactly that: DNS servers that resolve queries by utilizing a cache it builds as it queries other DNS servers. These servers do *not* maintain DNS zone information; they use the cache file and other DNS servers to fulfill the submitted queries. The advantage of using caching-only servers is that you don't have the added overhead of zone transfers. Of course, whenever we talk about advantages, there always seem to be disadvantages as well. Caching-only servers are no exception. The disadvantage is the cache itself. If you've been in the computer business for any length of time, you know where we're going with this. If you have to reboot a caching-only server, the volatile cache information is lost and must be rebuilt from scratch. Nonetheless, caching-only DNS servers will be ideal in situations such as small branch offices or even some regional offices where control is centralized.

Forwarders

Another DNS server that doesn't maintain any zone database information is the *forwarder*. Can you guess what the job of the forwarder is? Typically in large organizations with a large distribution of DNS servers, a forwarder is configured to handle all requests that must be forwarded away from the geographical origination point. The thought process behind using a forwarder is to filter all requests for outside resolution through one server, therefore taking that responsibility away from other DNS servers. The time it takes to resolve queries outside the high-bandwidth area is considerably longer than it is for internal requests, so in some situations it may make sense to configure a forwarder. The best example is with communications to the Internet, as illustrated in Figure 10.7. Other DNS servers can use forwarders in two modes: *non-exclusive* and *exclusive*.

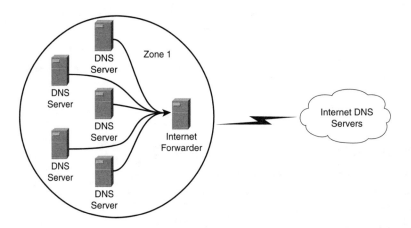

FIGURE 10.7
DNS servers can filter low-bandwidth requests through a forwarder DNS server.

Non-Exclusive Mode

When configured to use a forwarder DNS server in *non-exclusive* mode, a DNS server forwards queries to its forwarder DNS server and receives the results back. If the resulting data is resolved data, the DNS server returns it to the client that originally submitted the query. If not, the DNS server tries to resolve the query using its own zone information.

Exclusive Mode

DNS servers that use forwarders in *exclusive* mode act similarly to those in non-exclusive mode, except that when a query is not resolved by the forwarder or forwarders, the query is considered unresolvable and an error is returned to the requesting client. This brings about another specialization term for DNS servers. Servers set to use a forwarder in exclusive mode are considered *slave* servers because they are totally reliant on the forwarders.

Resolvers

We briefly mentioned *resolvers* during our introduction to DNS servers. Resolvers actually are packaged in with the TCP/IP stack of both clients and servers in Windows 2000. In essence, resolvers give the server or workstation the ability to resolve queries.

Resource Records

Resource records, as discussed previously, are the basic building blocks of a DNS zone. They are the means of providing name resolution services to DNS clients—somewhat important to DNS!

There can be literally millions of resource records in a given zone, but there aren't many different types of them. We'll list, explain, and provide examples of the common resource records (commonly referred to as "RRs") in this section, but will not decompose them in grave detail. If you want that, the Windows 2000 Server help is an excellent resource for that information.

This list describes the common RRs in DNS:

◆ Start of Authority (SOA)

◆ Name Server (NS)

◆ Mail Exchanger (MX)

◆ Address (A)

◆ Pointer (PTR)

◆ Canonical Name (CNAME)

◆ Windows Internet Name Service (WINS)

◆ WINS Reverse (WINS-R)

◆ Service (SRV)

The sections that follow describe the types of resource records and explain their uses and formats.

Start of Authority (SOA)

The *Start of Authority* record is first entry in all forward and reverse zones. DNS zone database files must have a declared authoritative DNS server for the zone. The SOA record includes this information, as well as the server that is authoritative for the domain. The following example describes the SOA record:

```
@         IN  SOA archserver1.thearchers.com.
administrator.thearchers.com. (
                          30           ; serial number
                          900          ; refresh
                          600          ; retry
                          86400        ; expire
                          3600      ) ; minimum TTL
```

> **NOTE**
>
> **<domain name>.dns** The examples provided in this section have been extracted from my DNS zone file: thearchers.com.dns. If you have DNS running on your server, you can find this file in <%systemroot%>\ system32\dns. If you have an Active Directory integrated zone, this file is not available; create a secondary DNS server for your zone to make this file available.

Name Server (NS)

Name server records are responsible for defining the DNS servers that are secondary servers for the zone specified in the SOA. They are also responsible for defining the DNS servers that are primary servers for delegated zones. It is recommended that all zones be serviced by at least two DNS servers, all of which will be listed as NS records in the parent zone. The following example illustrates NS record entries:

```
@                           NS    archserver1.thearchers.com.
@                           NS    archserver2.thearchers.com.
```

> **NOTE**
>
> **The "@" in a DNS Record Entry** The @ symbol in a DNS record specifies the owner of the record. Use of a free-standing @ symbol specifies that the owner is the current origin—typically the server on which the file resides.

Mail Exchanger (MX)

One of the more familiar DNS resource records for you messaging types is the *MX* record. The Mail Exchanger is used to specify where mail should be routed for users within this DNS domain. Multiple MX records can be specified and be given a weight (a priority of sorts) that specifies the preferred method of getting mail to the destination. The following example highlights the weight in bold.

```
thearchers.com  IN      MX      10
archmail.thearchers.com.
thearchers.com  IN      MX      5
archmail2.thearchers.com.
```

Address (A)

The *address* record is extremely straightforward; it maps a host name to an IP address. It is the most common record used throughout DNS and is one of the two records Windows 2000 Professional and/or Windows 2000's implementation of DHCP can handle dynamically. The address record is illustrated in the following example:

```
ARCHCPQ              900   A     172.16.25.100

ARCHSERVER1                A     172.16.25.1

ARCHSERVER2          1200  A     172.16.25.2

ARCHWORK             1200  A     172.16.25.114
```

Pointer (PTR)

You will recall that we mentioned reverse lookups briefly earlier in this chapter. A traditional address record provides a host name to IP address resolution path, but not the reverse. The *PTR* record provides the reverse lookup by mapping IP addresses to host names. An example follows:

```
1                    1200  PTR
archserver1.thearchers.com.
100                  900   PTR
archcpq.thearchers.com.
114                  900   PTR
archwork.thearchers.com.
2                    1200  PTR
archserver2.thearchers.com.
```

Canonical Name (CNAME)

A canonical name is nothing more than an alias. Using the CNAME, you can create user-friendly names that reference a specific DNS host (A) record. Be cautious when using CNAME records, because they add an extra step in the name-resolution process. When a CNAME alias is used in a query, the DNS server must query the CNAME record for the "owner" field, which references the A record the DNS server must read. The following example illustrates a CNAME alias record:

```
mylaptop                    CNAME  archcpq.thearchers.com.
```

Windows Internet Name Service (WINS)

WINS records are used to query WINS when DNS cannot resolve a record. It's important to note that WINS and WINS-R records are only available in Microsoft's implementation of DNS. The format of the record follows:

```
@                           0    WINS   L2 C900 (
                                 172.16.25.2 )
```

WINS Reverse (WINS-R)

The *WINS-R* record provides capabilities similar to those of a PTR record for providing reverse lookup—the only difference being (obviously) that the WINS-R record does send an IP address to WINS to find a corresponding NetBIOS name. The format of the WINS-R record is similar, as you would expect, to the PTR record (see the following example):

```
@                           0    WINSR  L2 C900
(thearchers.com. )
```

Service (SRV)

The final resource record we'll discuss in this section is the *service resource* record. This is the most abundant record in a Windows 2000 DNS, as is evident in our example. The SRV record provides a method by which (among other things) servers advertise their services. This is the convergence point of sorts for clients participating in an Active Directory domain; servers register their services here and clients send requests for those services here. The following example illustrates a collection of SRV records:

```
_gc._tcp              600     SRV    0 100 3268
archserver1.thearchers.com.
_kerberos._tcp        600     SRV    0 100 88
archserver1.thearchers.com.
_kpasswd._tcp         600     SRV    0 100 464
archserver1.thearchers.com.
_ldap._tcp            600     SRV    0 100 389
archserver1.thearchers.com.
_kerberos._udp        600     SRV    0 100 88
archserver1.thearchers.com.
_kpasswd._udp         600     SRV    0 100 464
archserver1.thearchers.com.
```

> **NOTE**
>
> **Other DNS Platforms** Keep in mind that you *can* use DNS platforms other than Microsoft Windows 2000 DNS. If you do, however, they at a minimum must support SRV records.

Zone Database Files

As previously discussed, the zone database is a repository of all resource records for a given zone. By utilizing these resource records, DNS servers fulfill client requests for computers, services, and the like. Recall from our earlier discussion that the primary server in a zone—the "PDC" of the zone—is the only server on which changes to the zone database can take place. Secondary zones then poll their respective primaries when they are ready to update their zone file. This update occurs via a zone transfer process, of which there are three:

> **NOTE**
>
> **Active Directory Integrated Zones** If using an Active Directory integrated zone, then zone transfers are not needed, as the zone information takes part in Active Directory replication.

◆ Full (AXFR)

◆ Incremental (IXFR)

◆ DNS Notify

The following sections describe these zone transfer processes.

Full Zone Transfers

You might have guessed that in a full zone transfer (AXFR), the entire zone file is replicated from the primary to all secondary servers in a particular zone. Figure 10.8 describes the full zone transfer process.

As you can imagine, very large zone database files can create quite a bit of network traffic during full zone transfers, especially over WAN links.

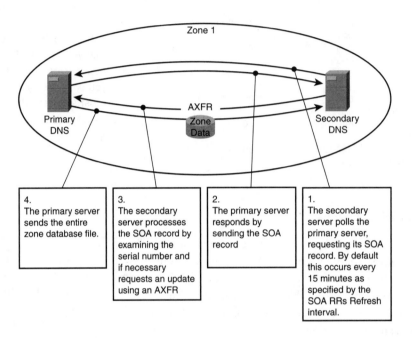

4.
The primary server sends the entire zone database file.

3.
The secondary server processes the SOA record by examining the serial number and if necessary requests an update using an AXFR

2.
The primary server responds by sending the SOA record

1.
The secondary server polls the primary server, requesting its SOA record. By default this occurs every 15 minutes as specified by the SOA RRs Refresh interval.

FIGURE 10.8
The secondary servers in a zone poll the primary to initiate a full zone transfer.

> **NOTE**
>
> **Backward Compatibility** To remain compatible with DNS servers that do not support incremental transfers, Windows 2000 DNS servers transfer entire zone files even if set for incremental.

Incremental Zone Transfers

To remove the large zone database size problems caused by performing a full zone transfer, an industry standard (RFC-1995) process was developed. This process involves the transmission of only changed zone database records, resulting in an *incremental zone transfer* (IXFR). The process is similar to that of full zone transfers, the only difference being what is transferred to the requesting server.

Primary servers that support the aforementioned RFC have the ability to track changes to their records since the most recent update. When secondary servers request an IXFR transfer, the primary is able to check its log of changes and send only those changes that have occurred since the last update. These changes are sent in order of oldest first.

Transfers Using DNS Notify

In the previous two types of zone transfers, the secondary servers polled the primary to determine whether they needed updates. The *DNS Notify* process reverses that methodology by allowing a primary server in a zone to notify its list of secondary servers that a change has occurred. Each of the secondary servers then requests the primary SOA record to determine whether it needs updates, and the process ends up similarly to the others; the only difference is that both AXFR and IXFR processes can be initiated by different secondary servers, as illustrated in Figure 10.9.

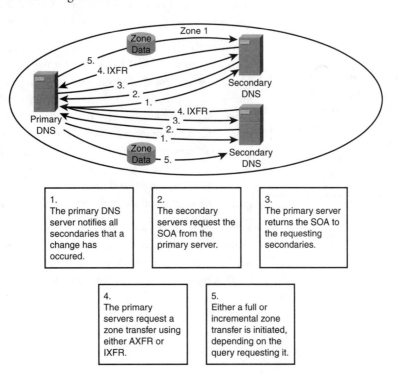

1.
The primary DNS server notifies all secondaries that a change has occured.

2.
The secondary servers request the SOA from the primary server.

3.
The primary server returns the SOA to the requesting secondaries.

4.
The primary servers request a zone transfer using either AXFR or IXFR.

5.
Either a full or incremental zone transfer is initiated, depending on the query requesting it.

FIGURE 10.9
A primary server can notify all of its secondaries immediately as changes occur to its zone database.

Zone Transfer Best Practices

Because zone transfers are such an integral part of DNS, they warrant their own "best practice" section.

With the addition of Active Directory integrated zones, Microsoft has taken the bulk of the guesswork out of DNS planning. If you can get away with it, always use Active Directory integrated zones— one per Active Directory domain. The rest of this section will focus on the standard DNS text database file replication practices.

As we've discussed, Windows 2000 Active Directory domain trees have a contiguous namespace. They can exist in a single DNS zone, in one zone per domain, or in any other fashion you deem required. The way you structure your zones should take into consideration the Active Directory domains, the geographical layout of the company, and the number of DNS name servers you can afford within a zone, not to mention the administration of the zones.

If you establish different zones per physical location, you can be somewhat comfortable that zone data will remain close to the users who access it from those locations, resulting in the best possible performance. In this scenario, you may end up with a large number of zones, each of which produce replication traffic and by nature are more difficult to manage. Just the opposite is true for large centralized organizations that use a single DNS zone. In this case, it's the size of the zone file being replicated that may cause issues. This is where the incremental zone transfer gets the spotlight. By incorporating IXFR, you reduce replication of large amounts of data down to next to nothing.

In summary, choosing the right zone and replication strategy is a delicate balance between the number of zones, the number of DNS servers per zone, and the need for fault tolerance and/or load

> **NOTE**
>
> **Load Balancing** Load balancing in DNS is achieved by creating multiple A resource records for the same host in a single zone. DNS servers that are RFC-1794 compliant will then rotate name resolution between all of the entries for a given host in round-robin fashion.

balancing. As long as these practices are addressed during the planning of DNS, there really is no wrong way to set it up, just a wrong way for a specific scenario.

DNS NAME RESOLUTION

All things aside, the primary purpose of DNS is to resolve names. It does so using one or both of the following options:

- ◆ Recursion
- ◆ Iteration

Both of these processes are noteworthy and you should have a thorough understanding of how each works before you move into the design stages of DNS. Recursion and iteration are discussed in the sections that follow.

Recursive Queries

When a client submits a query to a DNS server, it expects to get a response. That response can come in one of three forms: a resolved name, a failure notice, or a pointer to another DNS server. Clients set to use *recursive* queries basically won't allow their DNS server to pass the buck—or the query, in this case. The client expects the DNS server to take the responsibility to either resolve the name, or fail.

DNS servers in essence become clients to one another while fulfilling a recursive query for a client, as illustrated in Figure 10.10. DNS clients use recursive queries quite often, but DNS servers—in their role as clients to one another—rarely use recursion.

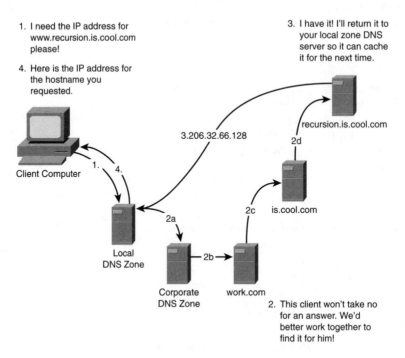

FIGURE 10.10
The recursive query process.

Iterative Queries

Clients can use *iterative* queries in addition to recursion. When a client submits an iterative query to a DNS server, it has no expectations of the server. It allows the server to return the best answer it can, based on its zone file and cache. If that answer is a pointer to another DNS server, the client resubmits the query to that server and the process starts all over again—hence iteration. The iterative query process is illustrated in Figure 10.11.

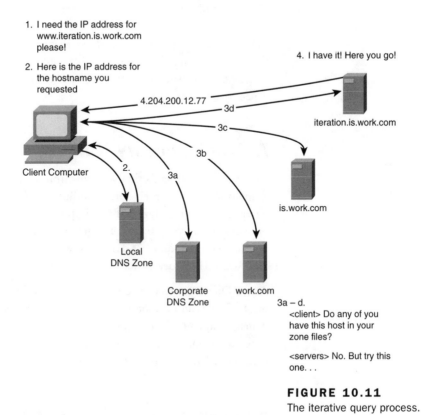

1. I need the IP address for www.iteration.is.work.com please!

2. Here is the IP address for the hostname you requested

4. I have it! Here you go!

4.204.200.12.77

Client Computer

Local DNS Zone

Corporate DNS Zone

work.com

is.work.com

iteration.is.work.com

3a – d.
 <client> Do any of you have this host in your zone files?

 <servers> No. But try this one. . .

FIGURE 10.11
The iterative query process.

NAMING AND NAME SERVICES

In the sections that follow, we will discuss how Active Directory uses DNS. We'll begin with a bit of review.

DNS Naming

DNS is a hierarchical database used to store and manage resource records within a zone. A DNS zone database can contain resource records that describe a single DNS domain, or a discreet portion of a DNS domain tree (one or more domains). For example, a primary

DNS zone file could manage `thearchers.com` DNS zone information, while another primary zone database file could be implemented to manage only records in the `office.thearchers.com` DNS domain. Conversely, a single zone database file could be authoritative over the entire domain structure, including both `thearchers.com` and `office.thearchers.com`.

Active Directory Naming

Microsoft recommends that you synchronize Active Directory domain names with their corresponding DNS zone names. It is not a requirement, but suggested for simplicity. Also, if you use the recommended Active Directory integrated DNS zones, it is highly recommended that you use a 1:1 mapping between these DNS zones and Active Directory domains.

Active Directory stores and manages information different than that of DNS. Instead of resources records, Active Directory stores and manages domain objects. All domain objects are stored in the Active Directory database and are managed by the Microsoft Management Console (MMC) snap-ins or via custom scripts.

Selecting the DNS Service

We've discussed the requirements and recommendations for selecting a DNS server service, but have not formally presented them until this point. This is a very important step as you consider the available products on the market. Microsoft's DNS Server in Windows 2000 makes a very strong statement—as it should—of being the best available server to host DNS and integrate with Active Directory. The decisions made here will influence the entire implementation of Windows 2000 and Active Directory throughout its entire life cycle, so be careful to make the right ones. If you are a Microsoft junkie, the decision is a no-brainer. However, other DNS platforms—such as the Berkeley Internet Name Daemon (BIND)—have been around a very long time and are tried-and-true many times over. They should be considered as you try to choose the best solution for the environment.

Regardless of your selection, the rules you need to consider are as follows:

◆ **Support for SRV records is essential.** Service resource records map to the name of a server offering a service requested by a client. This is how Active Directory operates, and it *cannot* do without.

◆ **Support for dynamic update protocol is recommended.** This might as well be mandatory, because the functionality the dynamic update protocol provides is probably not something you would want to handle manually. Each time an Active Directory service is added, a corresponding SRV resource record for that service is added to DNS by the domain controller. Imagine having to manage this manually!

◆ **Support for incremental zone transfers is optional.** Incremental zone transfers allow changes *only* to a DNS zone file to be replicated to other DNS servers, dramatically decreasing the amount of data to be transferred when compared to the traditional fill zone file transfers.

Of course, the Windows 2000 version of DNS supports all three of these services, and integrates WINS and DHCP in with them to provide even greater value from the client workstation end.

If there is an existing DNS server in the environment that is destined to be used with Windows 2000, it must support SRV records at a very minimum. It is recommended that you find a DNS that supports all three of the previous items.

> **NOTE**
>
> **BIND 8.1.1** The Berkeley Internet Name Domain (BIND) DNS server version 8.1.1 is the earliest version that has both SRV and dynamic update support.

DNS Zone Data Storage Options

Microsoft makes its DNS server very difficult to beat when considering Windows 2000 and Active Directory. Aside from satisfying all the aforementioned requirements and recommendations, it also has the ability to store its zone database file in Active Directory. The benefit of this, as discussed earlier in this book, is replication; the DNS server uses the Active Directory replication topology.

New and Improved DHCP
Knowing and understanding the new DHCP will greatly enhance your ability to design a DHCP plan in Active Directory. Pay close attention to the new functionality given to DHCP in Active Directory.

NOTE

Be Careful with the Use of DDNS
You may be questioning the difference between DNS and DDNS. In this book, when discussing the DNS server provided by Microsoft with Windows 2000, we choose to refer to it as Dynamic DNS (DDNS). Be careful when considering DNS in general; to be considered dynamic, the DNS server must support dynamic updates.

NOTE

WINS Lookup When you have two name-resolution services in use on the network, it would be wise (except for specific reasons) to allow them to refer unresolved queries to one another to ensure that all hosts are being found. Configure the DNS server to query WINS in the event that a name is not resolved.

Additionally, unlike the traditional text data file options for primary and secondary DNS zones, Active Directory integrated DNS servers all act as primary zones, which means changes can be made on any server without regard to what is primary (read/write) and what is secondary (read only).

WINS and DHCP Integration

WINS and DHCP both provide critical roles in the overall Active Directory. When considering DNS servers, it is important you consider these two value added services—especially during a long and drawn-out migration from a previous installation of Windows NT.

Both WINS and DHCP have been somewhat overhauled in Windows 2000 to provide some additional functionality. This functionality is mainly to help down-level clients dynamically register with DDNS. It is very important to consider this functionality in your overall design.

It is unlikely that companies will immediately move all client operating systems to the Windows 2000 Professional platform. Because pre-Windows 2000 client operating systems do not understand how to speak DDNS, a NetBIOS name server—WINS—may, and probably will be required.

DHCP provides functionality such that if a down-level client can lease an IP address, it can then register its hostname and IP address with DDNS. So, in a sense, DHCP acts as a proxy between the client and DDNS by managing these updates. Down-level clients should continue to register with WINS for general network services, which make use of the NetBIOS name retained by Windows 2000 just for this reason.

Microsoft has also implemented the functionality to register and keep all clients up to date in the appropriate DDNS zone. To do this, clients register their hostnames and IP addresses for DDNS via DHCP. This way, DHCP can manage updating DDNS as a client's IP address changes, as sometimes occurs in DHCP environments.

DDNS and DHCP Modes of Interaction

The interoperation of DDNS and DHCP is Microsoft proprietary. Because no IETF standards were in place at the time of development, Microsoft was forced to create its own—hence, it is unlikely that this interoperability will be available with DNS systems other than Microsoft's.

The DDNS and DHCP interaction was developed to dynamically support two modes of operation, as described in the following sections.

NOTE   **IETF Submission**   Microsoft has submitted its specification for DDNS and DHCP interoperability to the IETF for review. At the time of this writing, you could access it at **http://www. ietf.org/html.charters/dhc- charter.html**.

Down-Level Client Mode

Because down-level clients cannot register directly with DDNS, they need a little help. Down-level client mode allows down-level clients to register their address (A) and pointer (PTR) resource records with a Windows 2000 DHCP server. The DHCP server in turn registers *both* the A and PTR resource records with DDNS. This mode is *not* recommended for multi-homed computers (see Figure 10.12).

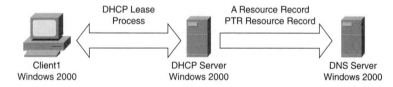

FIGURE 10.12
Down-level clients can register their A and PTR resource records with a Windows 2000 DHCP server, which in turn updates DDNS.

Active Directory Mode

The Active Directory mode is used by Windows 2000 Active Directory-enabled client computers. These DHCP client computers track names and addresses themselves, and send A resource records directly to the DDNS server. They ask the DHCP server to register the corresponding PTR resource record. The DHCP server is also responsible for removing PTR resource records when a lease expires, and can be configured to remove the A resource records as well.

This mode is the default for Active Directory-aware clients. For multi-homed clients, it is the required mode (see Figure 10.13).

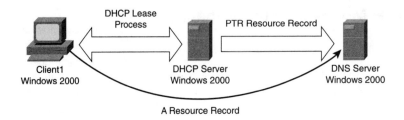

FIGURE 10.13
Active Directory clients can register their A resource record directly with DDNS, while DHCP handles the PTR resource record registration.

How Active Directory Uses DNS

We've been discussing DNS and Active Directory on various levels throughout this chapter. We're now going to take a look at the core integration of the two.

When an Active Directory domain controller is brought online, it uses DNS dynamic update functionality to register all of its services with DNS. This process is known as *domain controller registration*. Once registered with DNS, a domain controller's resources are made available to client computers. These client computers query the nearest DNS server to locate a domain controller providing the service they require. These services are represented in DNS as SRV resource records (SRV RRs).

The following sections cover Active Directory and DNS core integration.

Registration of Domain Controllers

As previously stated, Windows 2000 domain controllers register their host names with DNS. If configured, they will also register their NetBIOS computer names with WINS servers to enable down-level clients to locate them using NetBIOS. You may recall from "NetBIOS school" that domain controllers register using a "1C" designation to a WINS server.

SRV Resource Record Registration

Additional to registering a host name with DNS, Active Directory domain controllers register a slew of SRV resource records to DNS. For each network service a domain controller provides, an associated SRV resource record is registered with DNS to provide a means for clients to locate that service.

SRV records provide the service, protocol, and domain in which the service is available. The format template is as follows:

```
<service>.<protocol>.<domain>
```

For example, a domain controller in the thearchers.com domain that is offering the TCP-based LDAP service will register its SRV resource record for this service as follows:

```
_ldap._tcp.thearchers.com
```

SRV RR Naming

There are three conventions that are utilized within DNS and Active Directory relating to resource records. They are as follows:

◆ **Service and protocol specifications.** To protect against duplication of names in the namespace, the service (ldap) and protocol (tcp) strings are registered with DNS using a leading underscore (as seen in previous example).

◆ **_msdcs Subdomain.** This special subdomain (under each DNS domain) is implemented to ensure that clients can find pure Windows 2000 domain controllers. There are a number of reasons why this subdomain is used, but protection against rogue LDAP servers is one of the top reasons. Because of this reason, you should not use the _msdcs subdomain for any other purposes, nor should you modify it in any way.

◆ **Clients choose server.** DNS has the ability to return multiple resource records to a client that matches its request. NetLogon is a good example of this, since every domain controller in a given DNS zone can provide this service. It is the responsibility of the client to determine which server to choose.

Server Types

The Active Directory NetLogon service registers the following four well-known server types when it registers its SRV resource records with DNS.

◆ **dc.** Domain controller

◆ **domains.** A domain GUID (globally unique identifier)

◆ **gc.** Global Catalog Server

◆ **pdc.** Primary Domain Controller

By including the special subdomains, DDNS can group servers together according to their roles and allow clients to query for a specific server type.

Locating Domain Controllers

Clients use a special service, called the *locator* service, that runs in the context of their NetLogon service. This service can find a domain controller using either the NetBIOS name or the DNS name. The actual processes are long and drawn out for both and are out of scope here. It will be sufficient (for this exam) to understand that clients use the locater service within the context of NetLogon to locate domain controllers.

NAMESPACE PLANNING

Now that you have a good understanding of the elements that go into developing a naming strategy and have seen how the structures are used, we'll put them to work. We'll move a bit closer to Active Directory in this section because of its tight integration with DNS—and, after all, it's the focus of this book!

To design a namespace that fits the needs of the company, you need to couple the naming standards of DNS with your naming strategy for Active Directory. Active Directory is tightly integrated with DNS, so decisions you make here will directly affect its overall design.

This chapter focused heavily on DNS for a reason: You cannot effectively strategize the structure of Active Directory, DNS, or the namespace in general without thoroughly understanding how it operates.

You should keep the following in mind as you prepare your namespace design:

◆ Do you currently have a registered DNS namespace on the Internet?

◆ Do you plan to set up private DNS servers on your network or the Internet?

◆ How will you use DNS to support Active Directory?

◆ What naming requirements do you need to follow in determining DNS domain names for computers?

◆ Do you currently have NetBIOS computer names that don't conform to DNS standards in naming?

These questions, and more like them, will be answered in the sections that follow. Keep in mind that there are several scenarios that affect the DNS name you choose to represent your organization, the most influential being your Internet presence and your plans to continue or break away from that namespace.

One other note: Your DNS strategy weighs heavily on your plans for the structure of Active Directory. In fact, Microsoft recommends that you have your Active Directory domain structure planned and ready to go before you develop your DNS domain, zone, and zone replication topology. For that reason, we strongly suggest that you read this chapter and Chapter 11, which will focus on the Active Directory domain design, before solidifying your overall namespace design.

Scope of Active Directory

The rule of thumb about the scope of Active Directory is to keep it as large and wide as possible to prevent the necessity of any future restructuring. It is important to be outside that proverbial box when considering scope, especially in this Internet era.

Most companies today have an Internet presence already, and many large companies have more than one registered DNS domain name to support that presence. Part of the planning of the DNS and Active Directory namespace involves a crucial decision regarding the internal root namespace: Will it or will it not overlap with registered Internet namespace?

Best to Have a Single Root Domain

While we're on the subject, we should point out that each Active Directory domain tree accommodates only one root domain. For this reason, it is highly recommended that you choose a domain name that represents the entire company. This ensures that all users throughout the enterprise will have access to all resources no matter where they are—if they have the permission. This can prove to be a major challenge within organizations that traditionally operate as separate entities with separate goals and objectives, but all under the same holdings company. For those companies that cannot justify a single domain tree with a single root domain, multiple domain trees may be combined to form an Active Directory forest.

Active Directory and the Internet Namespace

In most cases, companies moving to Windows 2000 that host Internet sites internally are going to want to integrate Active Directory with their Internet namespace. There are several ways in which a company could choose to handle this and similar situations:

◆ Use a registered DNS domain name for the Active Directory root domain.

◆ Use a delegated DNS subdomain for the Active Directory root domain.

◆ Use different DNS domains for Public and Private.

Each of these options will be discussed in detail later in this chapter. Figure 10.14 represents a simple Active Directory domain structure illustrating root (parent) and subdomains (child domains).

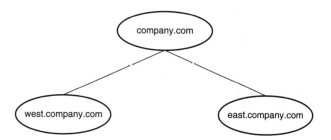

FIGURE 10.14
The parent–child, or root–subdomain, relationship.

Naming Hierarchy

Active Directory domains are arranged in a hierarchical structure, which defines the relationship between domains. For simplicity sake, DNS zones should map 1:1 to Active Directory domains, although it is not required. The goal in designing a naming hierarchy is to represent the organization in a logical format for ease of use. The fictional company represented in Figure 10.14 is a good example.

First DNS Domain Name

The first DNS domain name is special. It defines the root of your Active Directory—the top of the food chain. All other domains will be derived from this name.

Only one name should be chosen as the root DNS name of your organization, and it should be a name based on the company or the company's business. One thing you might find surprising here is that once you choose the root DNS name, you should immediately register it with an official domain name registrar—whether you plan to use it on the Internet or not—to avoid headaches in the future. In other words, if you ever plan to take the namespace public, you'll be assured that you already own it on the public side.

The following list suggests things you need to consider when selecting a DNS root namespace:

> **WARNING**
>
> **Root Domain Not Easily Altered**
> Once created, the root domain name cannot be changed without uninstalling Active Directory. If this is done, the namespace is lost and must be re-created by reinstalling Active Directory.

NOTE

Accredited Domain Name Registrars
For a list of all accredited domain
name registrars, visit the ICANN Web
site at `http://www.icann.org/`
`registrars/accredited-list.html`.

◆ Choose a name that is easy to remember, easily recognizable, and acceptable to use within your organization.

◆ Choose a name that will remain static, due to the implications involved in changing it.

◆ Choose a name that is available on the Internet and register it immediately with an accredited domain name registrar.

CHOOSING THE ROOT DNS NAMESPACE

NOTE

Use WHOIS for Uniqueness   To
determine whether your chosen DNS
namespace is available, you can
utilize the free InterNIC WHOIS search
at `http://www.internic.net/whois.`
`html`.

Additional to choosing an appropriate name for your root domain, you must consider your current configuration and whether you plan to have an Internet presence in the future. If you already have an Internet presence, which is likely in this day and age, you must consider the separation of internal assets from the Internet. There are three scenarios that most commonly describe how organizations should approach this daunting task, all of which have benefits and drawbacks. The one you choose must meet both the current and future business and technical requirements of the organization. Security is of utmost importance during this stage of the design, as mistakes can easily lead to the unwanted publishing of Active Directory services to Internet DNS servers.

In the sections that follow, we'll discuss three popular options for configuring the root namespace.

Using a Registered DNS for Public and Private

If you already have an Internet presence, such as mycompany.com, you may consider using the same namespace for your internal DNS and Active Directory structure. This would require setting up two DNS servers—one publicly and one privately—and configuring them with the same DNS domain name. You would then have to ensure that the public DNS zone contained only records to be made publicly available on the Internet, and that the private DNS zone contained all records for internal use, as well as the records for the company's external servers, such as Web and ftp.

By using the Internet registered domain namespace, you create additional complexity and put a critical focus on your security team, or the team responsible for the firewall. You also must do some planning regarding which records you want published in which DNS zone (public and private). In most cases, www.mycompany.com would reside on the public side of the firewall. This means anyone on the Internet could get to it; but what if someone from inside the company needs access to it? The answer comes in some manual upkeep of the Internal zone file. You must manually add records to the internal DNS that references the *internal* IP addresses of the *external* Web servers. The upkeep of this "superset" of zone database records increases TCO due to the manual administration.

One useful piece of technology available to throw into this mix is a proxy server. By configuring the proxy server to treat *.mycompany.com as internal resources, you ensure that the clients wanting access to the public Web (or other) servers utilize the internal DNS to resolve the internal IP address of the external servers. A useful side effect of this configuration is the assurance that clients will be able to access the external servers efficiently, rather than relying on the Internet to resolve them back to the external interface of the corporate Web servers. See the section "Overlapping Internal and External Namespaces" later in this chapter for more details on the complexity of this configuration.

Table 10.2 lists some of the pros and cons of using a single namespace for both public and private use. Figure 10.15 illustrates how a company using this scenario might be configured.

NOTE

Headache Avoidance Option!   One way to avoid the potential publishing of internal services to Internet DNS servers is to use a public DNS server that does not support SRV records.

TABLE 10.2

PROS AND CONS OF USING A SINGLE NAMESPACE FOR BOTH PUBLIC AND PRIVATE DNS

Pros	Cons
No additional domain name registration with a domain name registrar.	Existing DNS servers must support Active Directory SRV RRs at minimum.
No modifications are necessary to existing DNS domain names or host names on client computers.	Time saved by using the public name space will be consumed with the complex firewall configurations to make sure no inbound/outbound ports are open that may provide Internet users access to your corporate data.
Same logon and email names can be used.	Requires the use of proxy autoconfiguration files.
Can make use of existing DNS zones.	

> **NOTE**
>
> **Start of Authority (SOA)** The first record in each DNS zone is the Start of Authority resource record (SOA RR), which identifies a primary DNS name server for the zone as the best source for information within that zone and as the entity for processing updates within that zone.

> **NOTE**
>
> **Delegation** *Delegation* is the process of assigning responsibility of a portion of DNS namespace to another entity, which is represented by the DNS NS (name server) record.

Using a Delegated DNS Subdomain as AD Root

Microsoft recommends that, if at all possible, you use a delegated DNS subdomain of your registered public domain as your Active Directory root. For example, if your public DNS is mycompany.com you could use ad.mycompany.com on the inside. This subdomain would be created on a separate server as a separate zone, and would not be exposed to the Internet. Only the public DNS domain (mycompany.com) would be exposed to the Internet.

This would entail adding a *delegation* record to the server that is authoritative for the mycompany.com domain. The delegation record would then assign authority over the specific portion of the mycompany.com namespace described by the delegation record—in this case, to ad.mycompany.com.

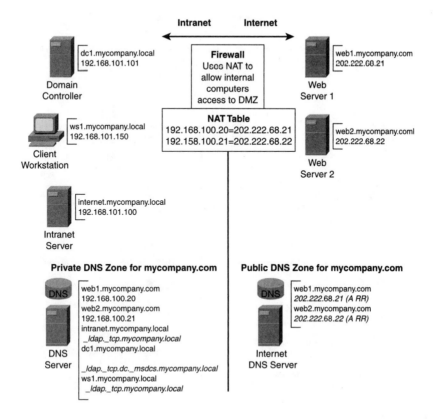

FIGURE 10.15

This is how a company using a common public and private namespace might look.

Such a configuration allows the internal network to be isolated from all outside traffic. Your Active Directory domain namespace would then be rooted at ad.mycompany.com, so child domains—such as one for Asia—would take the form asia.ad.mycompany.com. Pay close attention to how deep you allow subdomain creation because the FQDN can get quite long.

Figure 10.16 illustrates how a company using a delegated DNS subdomain as the Active Directory root domain might look.

Table 10.3 describes some of the pros and cons associated with this configuration.

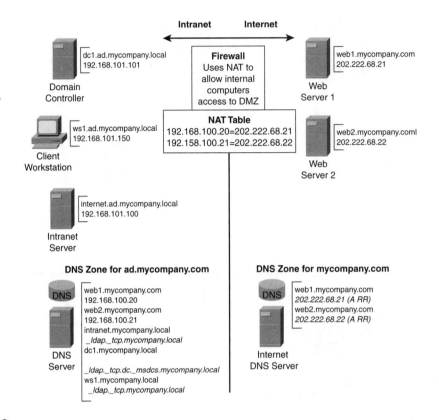

FIGURE 10.16
MyCompany, Inc. is able to protect its internal
integrity by using a delegated subdomain of its
public DNS.

TABLE 10.3

DELEGATED SUBDOMAIN PROS AND CONS

Pros	Cons
Isolates all Active Directory objects from the Internet.	Delegated Active Directory root domain requires an additional DNS server.
Internet DNS domain servers do not require updating, with the exception of the added NS record.	Since we introduced an additional level in the domain name hierarchy, the internal Active Directory structure will produce longer FQDNs.

Using Different DNS Domains for Public and Private

The InterNIC reserves a special domain for companies that do not have an Internet presence and do not foresee themselves having one in the near future: *.local*. Companies with an established public DNS name that want the utmost in segregation of public and private resources can also use this private DNS name. .local is similar in concept to the private IP address schemes, such as 192.168/16 (192.168.0.0 mask 255.255.0.0). Domains that end in .local will not and cannot be resolved on the Internet, because there are no root .local servers allowed.

Continuing on with our previous example, myCompany may choose to utilize this private namespace, which would root its Active Directory namespace at mycompany.local. Their corresponding public namespace could be mycompany.com. The Active Directory structure falls under the mycompany.local structure. Figure 10.17 illustrates how a company might be configured to use this approach.

Using the .local namespace internally also puts to rest a risk of potential DNS domain overlap. For example, mycompany.com, which is registered on the public Internet, could choose to utilize mycomp.com as its internal private DNS namespace. Problems could occur if down the road another company publicly registers mycomp.com on the Internet. Because there is only one "true" DNS root—the Internet root—the two companies could end up with problems should the first want to take the name public. This is an example of why it is important to always register your internal DNS on the Internet, even if you don't think it will ever be used.

Table 10.4 describes the pros and cons of the .local domain.

> **NOTE**
>
> **Different Internal and External DNS Names**   Having different internal and external names is essentially the same as having a disjointed namespace that has been obtained by an acquisition. Both can be handled by having separate DNS zones.

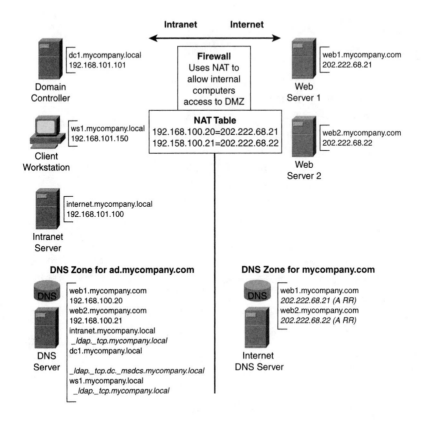

FIGURE 10.17
Many companies will elect to use the .local
namespace to segregate the private and public
namespaces.

| TABLE 10.4 |

THE PROS AND CONS OF USING THE .LOCAL DNS DOMAIN

Pros	*Cons*
Only required to register the .com side with the InterNIC.	Hosts configured with .local will not be resolvable from the Internet.
Does not expose the Internet naming hierarchy to the private network.	Users may become confused by the difference in namespaces.

Pros	*Cons*
No need to mirror servers internally.	If change is desired to conform to valid registered DNS on the inside, Active Directory must be uninstalled and reinstalled.

COMPLEX NAMESPACE CONSIDERATIONS

In this section, we shift focus from the namespace itself to the process of resolving names both internal and external to the organization. You know now that Windows 2000 uses DNS to resolve names, and you've examined the methods for creating an internal namespace and observed its relationship with the external registered namespace. You know that generally the approach to configuring DNS is to expose on the Internet your external DNS records with an external DNS server, and to locate DNS servers used to resolve internal queries behind the corporate firewall. All this is fine and dandy when you have a nice uniform singular namespace, but what happens if your namespace becomes more complicated, perhaps with a merger?

Your internal DNS namespace can include a private root. A private root looks just like the Internet root (.), but resides on the internal DNS servers. Your client computers' capabilities will determine whether you can utilize a private root. There are four types of clients that may be in use in an organization and require DNS name resolution:

◆ Proxy-unaware clients

◆ Clients that support local address table (LAT)

◆ Clients that support name exclusion list (NEL)

◆ Clients that support proxy autoconfiguration file (PAC)

NOTE

Why a Private Root? You would want to use a private root in your DNS namespace if you were merging two or more companies together and needed to provide uniform DNS name resolution between the two companies with a disjoint namespace. Exercise 10.2 helps explain this concept.

Clients That Allow an Internal DNS Root

Only two of these types of clients will allow you to utilize a private root. Clients that support either *name exclusion list* (NEL) or *proxy autoconfiguration file* (PAC) can be configured to resolve DNS names in this type of environment. Both PAC and NEL provide a sort of filtering process that allows administrators to configure the names of DNS domains. Both by default, attempt to resolve all names through the proxy server (the Internet) with the exception of those domains configured in the filter. For example, if companies One and Two, one.com and two.com, respectively, merge and wish to retain their two separate namespaces, a private DNS root can be configured to sit atop both one.com and two.com. Filters on PAC- and NEL-enabled workstations can be configured to exclude *.one.com and *.two.com from going to a proxy server, and instead direct them to the private root DNS, which in turn directs them to the appropriate subdomain for internal name resolution.

Clients That Do Not Support an Internal DNS Root

The two remaining client types, those that do not support proxy and those that support only a local address table (LAT), must be considered separately from the others. To provide these clients with name resolution, you must dedicate one or more DNS servers to maintain zones that contain every name from the internal namespace. Additionally, these servers must be configured to forward requests they cannot satisfy through the firewall to the Internet DNS servers.

Overlapping Internal and External Namespaces

You might think that using the same DNS name internally and externally would make things easier to manage, since it makes for a single namespace. In actuality, it complicates things. Consider the company BigSmooth, whose registered external DNS name is bigsmooth.com. If they were to use *bigsmooth.com* internally as well, how would their clients understand the difference between `www.bigsmooth.com`, the external Web server, and `client15.bigsmooth.com`, an internal client? They would need to manage the complexity in the following ways:

◆ Clients must use PAC files to resolve the name of an external server unless all external server DNS records are cloned on the internal DNS servers, which increases TCO.

◆ All PAC files must be configured to differentiate between internal and external hosts, such as in our `bigsmooth.com` example, which also increases TCO.

BEST PRACTICES

We've discussed a lot of material in this chapter—material that warrants a "best practice" summary. We'll start with best practices for designing a namespace:

◆ You should use Active Directory integrated DNS zones if at all possible. Each Active Directory domain should have a DNS zone that corresponds (exactly) to the name of the domain.

◆ DNS should be running on at least two domain controllers per Active Directory domain. If using Active Directory sites, at least one domain controller should be running in each site and, if at all possible, a secondary zone for this DNS server should be created on an existing DNS server outside the site.

◆ Considerable time should be spent in designing the zone replication (transfer) topology according to the layout of the network. If using Active Directory integrated zones, this is a non-issue. Otherwise, the use of primary, secondary, caching-only, and forwarder DNS servers should be considered with delicate attention to the layout of the network and the namespace.

◆ Considerable time should also be spent analyzing the client computer capabilities in preparation for an internal DNS root, if required in a complex namespace.

Table 10.5 describes the best practices in naming.

TABLE 10.5

BEST PRACTICES IN NAMING

Practice	*Process*
Migrating non-DNS compliant naming schemes to DNS	If you cannot afford to change all NetBIOS names that don't comply with RFD-1123 standards in DNS naming, utilize the Windows 2000 DNS and the ANSII and/or Unicode character sets during the transition.
Deciding on a public or private domain	You must mitigate the risk of using a public DNS for your Active Directory root. There are pros and cons either way. Microsoft recommends using a delegated subdomain of your public registered domain, which provides separation from public and private and allows you to maintain a contiguous namespace.
Naming the root domain	The name of the root domain should describe your organization as a whole. It should be easy to remember for your users, and should have something to do with the company. Avoid using names that are cryptic.
Designing DNS zones	DNS zones should strictly adhere to Active Directory domains (which we will discuss in Chapter 11, "Designing the Active Directory Structure").
DNS replication	If using standard DNS, you need to consider redundancy in servers by introducing primary and secondary zones. Consider the traffic load and the volume of hits the DNS servers are taking. This may lead to the need for load balancing. If Active Directory integrated zones are used, this is a non-issue because it uses the Active Directory replication topology.
DNS servers	The DNS servers you choose to use must support SRV records, and should support incremental zone transfer and dynamic update. These standards are outlined in RFC-2052, RFC-1995, and RFC-2136, respectively.

CASE STUDY: ALLBOOKS, INC.

BACKGROUND

Allbooks, Inc., a bookstore that has been in business for 25 years, is considering a Windows 2000 rollout as part of its five-year business plan. Allbooks has offices in five locations across the United States and operates as a single large company with five business units that drive the sales of five different types of books.

PROBLEM STATEMENT

Allbooks realizes the impact technology can have on its business. It does not have any technology professionals experienced in the planning stages that it knows has to happen before a Windows 2000 design. It wants an outside consulting company, WayFront, Inc., to prepare a preliminary high-level infrastructure services design that will support its Windows 2000 deployment.

CURRENT SYSTEM

The current networking infrastructure within and between each of the five Allbooks facilities is antiquated. Cat III cabling and old ACC infrastructure equipment provide connectivity to its Windows 3.11 peer-to-peer networks. Each peer-to-peer network stands alone and is able to communicate across the slow WAN links if necessary. They have absolutely no email, name resolution, or servers.

ENVISIONED SYSTEM

Allbooks CIO

"I was just hired by this company and given the task of updating it to current technology. I had no idea what I was up against. My vision is a "rip and replace" with the current equipment. It would be too difficult for us to try and retain anything."

WayFront Infrastructure Architect

"This company must have been operating in the dark ages before this new initiative. The CIO contracted me to design the Windows 2000 services infrastructure, which consists first of designing the namespace, which consists of Active Directory and DNS and their associated services. Looks like we'll be able to leave out WINS!"

PERFORMANCE

Allbooks CIO

"I've gotten the approval to run fiber to the desktop! This is a long-term decision that was very difficult to make because of the associated cost."

continues

CASE STUDY: ALLBOOKS, INC.

continued

WayFront Infrastructure Architect

"We've performed an initial assessment of the five geographic locations and have recommended T-3 leased-line connections between all of them—with the Indianapolis facility as the hub. This, along with the fiber to the desktop, should give them a good and fast physical infrastructure. By the way, we are going with all top-of-the-line Cisco gear to make this happen."

SECURITY

Allbooks CIO

"As we design our DNS namespace, it is critical that we keep our internal network separated from the Internet. We've invested quite a bit of money in our new firewall solution, so I want to make very good use of it."

MAINTAINABILITY

WayFront Network Consultant

"I've been tasked with developing a management policy for the DNS and Active Directory infrastructure services. They want to be able to manage the entire network from a single location."

Allbooks CIO

"I know we probably won't even get to the stage where we install Windows 2000 for a while because we'll be planning it. I just want to make sure we don't make mistakes during the planning phase that will hurt us in the future. Our requirement is that all name servers be maintainable from both here at corporate (Indianapolis) and every other site."

AVAILABILITY

Allbooks CIO

"It will be very important that all name servers and Active Directory domain controllers provide some kind of redundancy. We will be totally reliant upon these services in the new environment and want to make sure they are always available to us."

CHAPTER SUMMARY

Choosing the namespace for your Active Directory implementation is one of the more critical decisions you'll make during a Windows 2000 project. To change the namespace in the future, you have to remove and reinstall Active Directory—not a good thing. It is highly recommended that you take considerable time to effectively plan the namespace design before touching a computer. The namespace should represent the company as a whole, and should be kept as simple as possible.

Because most companies are already registered on the Internet, another level of complexity must be factored into the namespace selection. Companies must decide whether they will continue the use of a registered DNS domain name internally, use a delegated subdomain of that registered domain, or use a completely different namespace altogether. There are pros and cons with each method, and much of the decision relies on the current and future business and technology initiatives of the company.

DNS servers in Active Directory environments must support Service Resource Records at a minimum. Both the Windows 2000 DNS and BIND version 8.1.1 provide support for these records. Additionally, to provide the best service, Active Directory DNS servers should support all three of the following:

◆ **Support for SRV Records is essential.** Service resource records map to the name of a server offering a service requested by a client. This is how Active Directory operates; it *cannot* do without.

◆ **Support for dynamic update protocol is recommended.** This might as well be mandatory, because the functionality the dynamic update protocol provides is probably not something you would want to handle manually. Each time an Active Directory service is added, a corresponding SRV resource record for that service is added to DNS by the domain controller. Imagine having to manage this manually!

KEY TERMS

- namespace
- scope
- relative distinguished name
- user principal name (UPN)
- user principal name (UPN) suffix
- DNS domain
- DNS zone
- Primary DNS server
- Secondary DNS server
- caching-only server
- forwarder
- name resolution
- resolver
- zone transfer
- full zone transfer
- incremental zone transfer
- recursive queries
- iterative queries
- SRV resource record
- A resource record
- PTR resource record
- Start of Authority

Chapter Summary

- local
- WHOIS
- root DNS namespace

◆ **Support for incremental zone transfers is optional.**
Incremental zone transfers allow changes *only* to a DNS zone file to be replicated to other DNS servers, dramatically decreasing the amount of data to be transferred when compared to the traditional fill zone file transfers.

Active Directory is tightly integrated with DNS. Because of this, it is highly recommended that you stick to DNS naming standards when designing the Active Directory naming strategy. You should make the scope of Active Directory—the name resolution boundary—as broad as possible.

In complex configurations, such as those born of two merged companies with separate namespaces, you should consider utilizing a private DNS root. You can use a private DNS root if your client computers support name exclusion lists and/or proxy autoconfiguration files.

To complete the requirements for designing a DNS strategy, it is recommended you first read Chapter 11.

APPLY YOUR KNOWLEDGE

Exercises

10.1 Understand Your Options

The purpose of this exercise is to reiterate the pros and cons for each of the three options for creating the root namespace. This is an extremely important decision that relies heavily on how the pros and cons match up to the company requirements.

Estimated Time: 5 minutes

Match the Root DNS namespace design option in the *Namespace Option* in Table 10.6 to two advantages on the left, and two disadvantages on the right.

TABLE 10.6

ADVANTAGES AND DISADVANTAGES OF ROOT DNS NAMESPACE OPTIONS

Advantages	*Namespace Option*	*Disadvantages*
Isolates all Active Directory objects from the Internet.	Private and public share same namespace	Hosts configured with local will not be resolbable on the Internet.
No need to mirror public servers internally.		Existing DNS servers must support SRV RRs.
No additional public domain name registration is required.	Private is delegated subdomain of public	Private Active Directory root domain requires an additional DNS server.
Does not expose the Internet naming hierarchy to the private network.		Requires complex firewall configurations.
The same logon and email names can be used.	Private and public are disjoint namespaces	Larger FQDNs will be produced throughout the domain tree internally.
Only required update to public DNS is the addition of a NS record.		If a valid registered DNS is one day required on the private side, a total reconfiguration of DNS and Active Directory will occur.

APPLY YOUR KNOWLEDGE

10.2 Trace DNS Queries

This exercise presents a diagram of a fictional company that has just merged with another company. Both companies will retain their individual namespace and will need to be able to resolve DNS names in their own namespace, on the Internet, and in the namespace of the other company. It will present scenarios for which you must provide a DNS query resolution path. You will draw in your book during this exercise; it would help to use different ink colors so you can keep query resolution paths apart from one another.

Be sure to read the background information before attempting to conquer this exercise!

Estimated Time: 80 minutes

Scenario

The DNS scenarios presented in this exercise represent the most complicated case: two companies that have merged but must retain separate namespaces. Make sure you read the following instructions carefully and refer to them as much as you need to during the exercise.

You can assume that the namespaces of both companies—LOA, Corp., and WT, Corp.—consist only of names within the registered DNS domains loa.com and wt.com.

All loa.com client computers are configured to use the proxy server with proxy autoconfiguration (PAC) files.

None of the computers in wt.com utilize PAC files.

The goal of this exercise is to demonstrate the appropriate configuration of DNS servers, zones, and clients. The given configuration satisfies the following requirements:

◆ Expose only the public portion of the namespace to the Internet.

◆ Enable a computer from one company to resolve both internal and external names within its company.

◆ Enable a computer from either company to resolve any name from the Internet.

◆ Enable a computer from either company to resolve both internal and external names in the other company.

You must now trace query hops from the originating client, through the DNS maze to the destination, then back to the client using the solution design provided to you.

> **N O T E**   **Detailed Scenario Information**   This exercise was derived from a scenario presented in the Microsoft white paper "Windows 2000 DNS." This 70-page white paper contains very detailed information regarding this scenario, and we highly recommend that you read through it.

Solution Concept

The figure presented repeatedly in this exercise represents a solution to the requirements. The paragraphs in this section describe the solution concept so you have a clear picture of the design.

APPLY YOUR KNOWLEDGE

Each company, LOA and WT, has exposed one DNS server to the Internet that is authoritative for the respective zones, loa.com and wt.com. Each zone contains records pertaining only to external names and delegations that each company wishes to expose to the world.

The two companies are joined via a VPN connection. These are the only similarities between the two companies.

WT Namespace Design

WT's internal client computers are not proxy clients. This means they must dedicate one or more DNS servers to host zones containing all the names from the company namespace.

Every client must send its DNS queries to these servers.

Each of these servers must forward queries to a forwarder. If the forwarding DNS server contains the top-level namespace (wt.com), then the forwarder is a DNS server exposed to the Internet that must be accessed through the company firewall. All other DNS servers forward unresolved queries to the DNS server at the top of the company namespace.

All WT DNS servers hosting its top-level namespace zone file (wt.com) must also host the top-level zone file from LOA (loa.com). This is to enable cross-company name resolution.

LOA Namespace Design

The private namespace for LOA includes a private root, because its clients are capable of using PAC or NEL files.

LOA must devote one or more internal DNS servers to manage zone files containing internal names from its namespace.

Every DNS client submits a query to some internal DNS server, or to the proxy server according to the client's PAC file.

Every internal DNS server contains in its root hints the address(es) of the private root DNS server.

To allow LOA clients to resolve names from the WT namespace, and vice versa, the private root zone must contain a delegation record to the top-level zones of each company (loa.com and wt.com).

1. Study the figure before each question. Then read each scenario carefully and draw a path representing DNS query hops from the originating computer all the way through until name resolution occurs, and then back to the originating computer. Every two scenarios you'll see another picture like Figure 10.18, so you'll only have to draw an "A" and "B" scenario on each figure.

2. (A) A computer in LOA Corporation needs to connect to www.third.loa.com. Starting with the first.loa.com client computer, draw the appropriate DNS name resolution path.

3. (B) A computer in WT Corporation needs to connect to www.third.wt.com. Starting with the first.wt.com client computer, draw the appropriate DNS name resolution path.

APPLY YOUR KNOWLEDGE

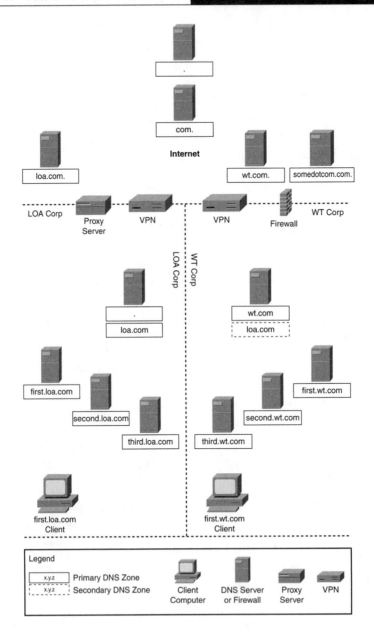

FIGURE 10.18
This figure represents the DNS network that supports
companies LOA and WT after their recent merger.

APPLY YOUR KNOWLEDGE

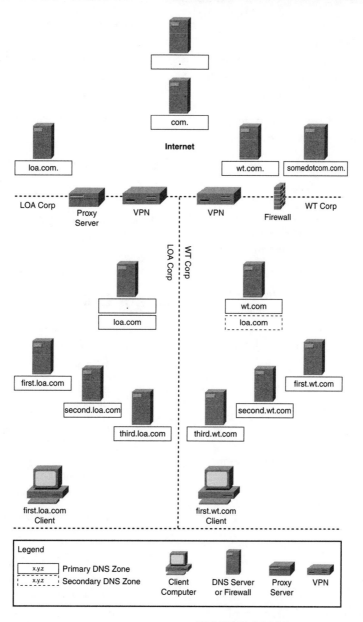

FIGURE 10.19
This figure represents the DNS network that supports companies LOA and WT after their recent merger.

APPLY YOUR KNOWLEDGE

4. (A) A computer in LOA Corporation needs to open the Web page www.somedotcom.com. Starting with the first.loa.com client computer, draw the appropriate DNS name resolution path.

5. (B) A computer in WT Corporation needs to the Web page www.somedotcom.com. Starting with the first.wt.com client computer, draw the appropriate DNS name resolution path.

6. (A) A computer in the LOA Corporation needs go to the WT Corporation to contact a computer named xcomputer.wt.com. Starting with the first.loa.com client computer, draw the appropriate DNS name resolution path.

7. (B) A computer in the WT Corporation needs to resolve a DNS query for xcomputer.loa.com. Starting with the first.wt.com client computer, draw the appropriate DNS name resolution path.

Review Questions

1. Describe a namespace.

2. Describe the difference between a DNS domain and a DNS zone.

3. What two names comprise a fully qualified domain name?

4. Name and describe the three types of DNS zone transfers.

5. Describe the recursive query process.

6. List the legal characters for DNS, as described by RFC-1123.

7. What special record is added to the authoritative DNS parent domain of a child that enables the child DNS domain to have authority over that segment of namespace?

8. Describe the two modes DHCP server works in to assist in the client name registration process.

9. Aside from the required (SRV RR) and recommended (dynamic update and incremental zone transfer) options, what else does a Windows 2000 DNS server provide that makes it hard to beat?

10. In what situation would you likely see the use of WINS and WINS-R resource records in DNS?

Exam Questions

1. Which of the following is *not* a true statement concerning the DNS namespace planning process?

   A. The namespace must be as simple as possible and describe the organization as a whole.

   B. The namespace should remain as static as possible.

   C. Choose a name that is available on the Internet and register it immediately.

   D. The namespace can be anything you want it to be, since it can be easily changed.

2. You are the CIO for a new company. You have a registered DNS namespace on the Internet, but want to be absolutely sure your Active Directory-based DNS internal namespace is unresolvable from the Internet. Which namespace should you use?

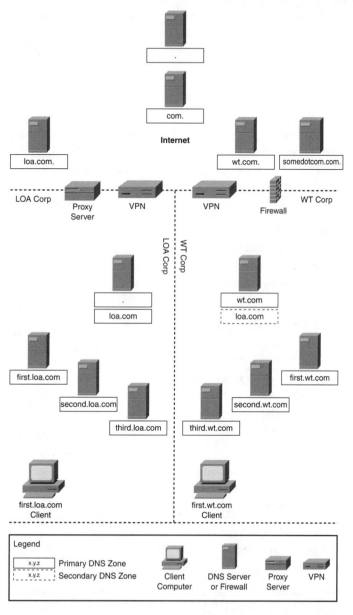

FIGURE 10.20
This figure represents the DNS network that supports companies LOA and WT after their recent merger.

APPLY YOUR KNOWLEDGE

A. .local

B. .private

C. 192.168.0.0

D. .internal

3. Suppose you were tasked with designing the DNS structure for Allbooks. You are given the namespace allbooks.com as the registered and internal namespace. Based on what you know about Allbooks, how would you design the DNS zone replication topology?

  A. Create a separate zone for each physical location. Integrate one primary and two secondary DNS servers per zone. Configure the secondary servers within each site to poll the primary within their site.

  B. Configure one zone with five DNS domains corresponding to the assumed Active Directory domains for each geographical location. Place the primary server at the corporate headquarters and a secondary server in each of the five remote offices. Configure the secondary servers to request incremental zone transfers from the primary.

  C. Utilize Active Directory integrated zones and let the replication occur according to the Active Directory replication topology.

  D. Create one DNS zone and five DNS domains within that zone. Configure caching servers at each of the five remote offices.

4. You are a design engineer working with Allbooks, Inc., on the DNS structure. The Allbooks CIO explains his concerns about its external DNS servers not supporting SRV records. Which of the following Allbooks external DNS servers must support SRV records?

A. All external servers.

B. Only servers with authoritative zones.

C. Only servers with nonauthoritative zones.

D. External servers need not support SRV records.

5. Suppose Allbooks had been running Windows 98 instead of Windows 3.11 and wished to retain desktop computers until they came off lease. How would this change your DNS services infrastructure planning?

  A. Nothing would need to change.

  B. You would want to incorporate WINS for NetBIOS name resolution into the environment, rather than implementing pure DNS.

  C. You would not install DNS on the Windows 2000 servers, but rather install WINS and build Active Directory around it.

  D. To incorporate Windows 98 computers into the Windows 2000 environment, you'll need to remove NetBIOS by turning off NBT.

6. Suppose you are the administrator of a Windows 2000 domain. Your domain is a subdomain of the parent, and uses a DNS subdomain to partition the namespace. Your subdomain is in a zone of its own. You have a group of programmers that must frequently connect to a server in another DNS domain two domains deeper than yours, but in the same zone. Your programmers want to be able to easily connect to this server (intranet1.manufacturing.eastcoast.ad.company.com) via a simple name. What can you do to provide this service to your users?

APPLY YOUR KNOWLEDGE

A. Write a DOS batch file that contains the connection string for the intranet1 server. Name the batch file the name the programmers would like to refer to the server.

B. Create a CNAME record in DNS and fill in the Alias field with the name the programmers want to use.

C. Create a DNS PTR record in the reverse lookup zone. Name the PTR record the name the programmers would like to use.

D. Create a host file on each of the programmer's computers. Create a host name to IP address mapping to the IP address of the intranet server. Use the name the programmers want to use as the host name.

7. You have three DNS zones: zoneA, zoneB, and zoneC. Each zone contains resource records for separate Active Directory domains within contiguous namespace. ZoneA sits at the top of the domain structure. You wish for all Internet queries to be channeled through a server in zoneA. How should you configure each of the other DNS servers?

A. Configure each server in zoneB and zoneC as caching only servers. Configure a server in zoneA to forward requests from all caching only servers to the Internet.

B. Configure a single server in zoneA with a forwarder to an appropriate Internet DNS server.

C. Configure one server in zoneB and one server in zoneC to forward to the authoritative server in zoneA. Configure zoneA to forward to the Internet.

D. Configure servers in zoneA with forwarders to zoneB and zoneC. Configure servers in zoneB with forwarders to zoneA and zoneC. Configure servers in zoneC with forwarders to zoneA and zoneB. Configure the primary server in zoneA to forward all unanswered queries to the Internet.

8. Which of the following host names are *not* valid in a DNS-centric environment? Choose two.

A. MYCOMPUTER

B. MyComputer-12345

C. My_Computer

D. MyComputer.com

E. My-com-puter

9. You are the DNS administrator for a corporation that utilizes single DNS zone for all resource records on the network. You have one standard primary server and nine standard secondary servers, and have users evenly distributed among the secondary servers. After logging bandwidth performance data on your network, you chart the results and find that the utilization spikes every 15 minutes. What do you suspect is causing the utilization spikes?

A. The SOA record for the primary server in the zone is configured for a 15-minute refresh interval. Secondary servers are configured to request a full zone transfer according to the primary servers refresh interval.

B. The SOA record for the primary server in the zone is configured for a 15-minute refresh interval. It therefore replicates its zone file to all secondary, caching-only, and forwarder servers every 15 minutes.

C. The NS record for the secondary zone servers is set at a refresh interval of 15 minutes. Consequently, they replicate their zone database file among themselves every 15 minutes.

D. The NS record for the primary server in the zone is configured for a 15-minute refresh interval. Secondary servers are configured to request a full zone transfer according to the primary servers refresh interval.

10. You are in charge of designing the namespace to be used by your company when it moves to Windows 2000. Your company has a registered the abc.com DNS domain on the Internet, and maintains a Web site hosted at an ISP. You want to come up with the best namespace design possible for your users, who are not accustomed to DNS naming. You want to isolate all of the Active Directory data from the outside world, but want to provide a clear and easy access path to the Internet for internal employees. What would you name the DNS root domain internally?

A. abc.com

B. ad.abc.com

C. abc.local

D. abcinternal.com

11. You are a consultant overseeing the merger of CorpA and CorpB, whose namespaces are corpa.com and corpb.com, respectively. You wish to configure DNS in both organizations with a private root. At a minimum, what must each client in each company support before incorporating a private root would be a viable option?

A. BIND version 8.1.1

B. Local address tables (LAT)

C. Proxy autoconfiguration (PAC) files

D. Service resource records

APPLY YOUR KNOWLEDGE

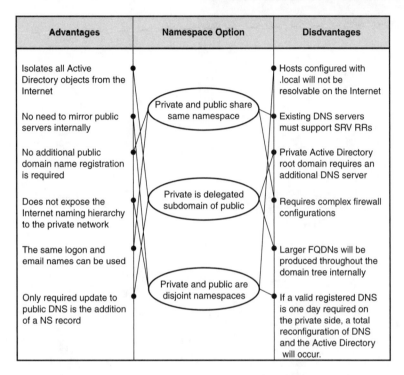

Advantages	Namespace Option	Disdvantages
Isolates all Active Directory objects from the Internet	Private and public share same namespace	Hosts configured with .local will not be resolvable on the Internet
No need to mirror public servers internally		Existing DNS servers must support SRV RRs
No additional public domain name registration is required	Private is delegated subdomain of public	Private Active Directory root domain requires an additional DNS server
Does not expose the Internet naming hierarchy to the private network		Requires complex firewall configurations
The same logon and email names can be used	Private and public are disjoint namespaces	Larger FQDNs will be produced throughout the domain tree internally
Only required update to public DNS is the addition of a NS record		If a valid registered DNS is one day required on the private side, a total reconfiguration of DNS and the Active Directory will occur.

FIGURE 10.21
Answers to Exercise 10.1.

Answers to Exercises

Exercise 10.1

The answers to Exercise 10.1 are displayed in Figure 10.21.

The following illustrations and explanations provide the answers to each part of Exercise 10.2.

The following list contains the explanation of each hop illustrated in Figure 10.22.

APPLY YOUR KNOWLEDGE

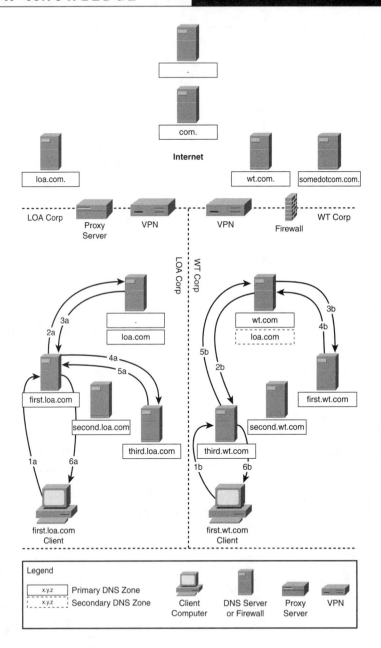

FIGURE 10.22
Answers to Exercise 10.2 Questions 2 and 3.

APPLY YOUR KNOWLEDGE

1a. Because first.loa.com is configured with the proxy autoconfiguration file, it is able determine that www.third.loa.com is an internal host. It therefore sends the DNS query to its assigned DNS server.

2a. Because the DNS server first.loa.com is not authoritative over third.loa.com, it needs to query a root server. This root server is internal to the LOA network.

3a. The root server returns a pointer to the authoritative server in third.loa.com.

4a. The first.loa.com server sends a query to third.loa.com, the server specified by the root server.

5a. third.loa.com is able to resolve www and returns that data back to first.loa.com.

6a. first.loa.com returns the resolved query to the client.

1b. The computer in first.wt.com must send its query to its configured DNS server, first.wt.com. This server is not authoritative for the third.wt.com zone.

2b. first.wt.com forwards the query to the wt.com zone.

3b. The wt.com zone contains a delegation record for the third.wt.com zone and sends the query to the server that is authoritative over that zone.

4b. The server in third.wt.com zone resolves the query and return the response to the wt.com server.

5b. The wb.com server returns the resolved query to the first.wt.com server.

6b. The first.wt.com server returns the resolved query to the client.

The following list contains the explanation of each hop illustrated in Figure 10.23.

1a. Because the client in first.loa.com is a proxy client, it determines that www.somedotcom.com is an Internet resource and sends the request to the proxy server.

2a. The proxy server sends a DNS query to its assigned DNS server, loa.com (public).

3a. loa.com sends the query to the Internet root.

4a. The Internet root returns a pointer to the .com zone.

5a. The server in loa.com sends the query to the .com zone.

6a. The .com server returns a pointer to the somedotcom.com zone server.

7a. loa.com sends the query to the somedotcom.com zone.

8a. The servers in somedotcom.com resolve the query for www and return it to loa.com.

9a. loa.com returns the resolved query to the proxy server. (At this time, the proxy server actually contacts www.somedotcom.com on behalf of the client)

10a. The proxy server returns the data to the client in the form of a Web page.

1b. The client in first.wt.com forwards the request to its configured DNS server.

2b. first.wt.com cannot resolve the query, so it forwards it to the wt.com zone.

APPLY YOUR KNOWLEDGE

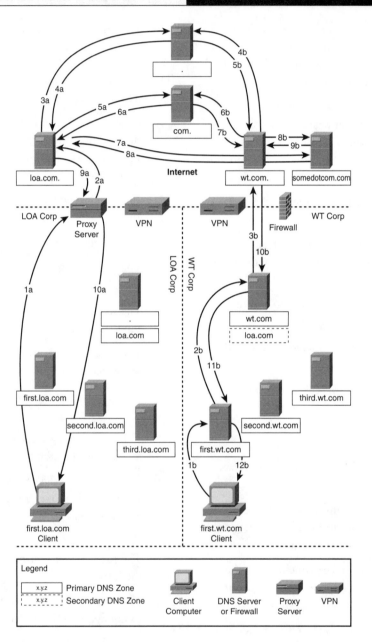

FIGURE 10.23
Answers to Exercise 10.2 Questions 4 and 5.

APPLY YOUR KNOWLEDGE

3b. The internal wt.com zone is unable to resolve the query, so it must be external. It forwards the query to the Internet wt.com zone.

4b. The Internet wt.com server cannot resolve the query, so it sends it to the Internet Root.

5b. The Internet root returns a pointer to the .com zone.

6b. wt.com forwards the query to the Internet .com zone.

7b. The .com servers return a pointer to the somedotcom.com zone.

8b. The wt.com server forwards the query to the somedotcom.com zone.

9b. Because somedotcom.com was able to resolve the query, it returns the resolved data to wt.com.

10b. wt.com returns the resolved data through the firewall back to the internal wt.com zone server.

11b. The internal wt.com server returns the data to first.wt.com.

12b. first.wt.com returns the data to the client. (At this point, the client sends out a request for the Web page using the IP address.)

The following list contains the explanation of each hop illustrated in Figure 10.24.

1a. Because the computer in first.loa.com is a proxy client, it is able to determine that xcomputer.wt.com is internal, even though it is not within the contiguous namespace of loa.com. It therefore sends the query to its configured DNS server in the first.loa.com zone.

2a. first.loa.com is unable to resolve xcomputer.wt.com, so it sends the query to the Internal root server.

3a. The internal root server for LOA Corp. contains a delegation record for the wt.com zone, and returns a pointer to the authoritative sever within that zone.

4a. first.loa.com forwards the query through the Virtual Private Network (VPN) that has been established between the two companies, and onto the authoritative server in the wt.com zone.

5a. wt.com is able to resolve xcomputer.wt.com and returns the answer back through the VPN to the first.loa.com zone server.

6a. first.loa.com returns the answer to the client.

1b. The computer in first.wt.com forwards its query for xcomputer.loa.com to its DNS server.

2b. The first.wt.com cannot resolve the name, so it forwards the query to a server containing the wt.com zone. This server is also configured with a secondary copy of the loa.com zone database. Therefore, xcomputer.loa.com can be resolved right here.

3b. The answer to the query is returned to first.wt.com.

4b. The answer to the query is returned to the client.

APPLY YOUR KNOWLEDGE

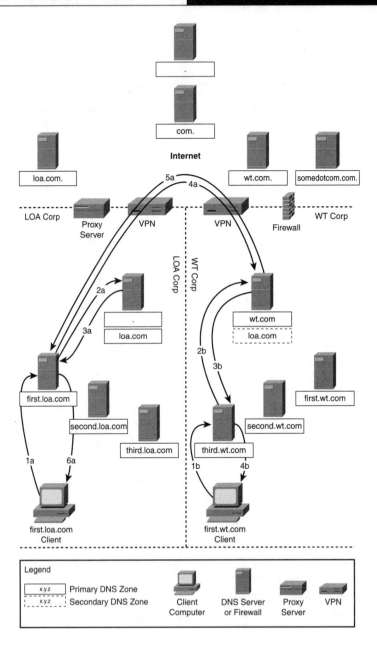

FIGURE 10.24
Answers to Exercise 10.2 Questions 6 and 7.

APPLY YOUR KNOWLEDGE

Answers to Review Questions

1. A namespace is a bounded region in which any name can be resolved. Domains and domain trees in Active Directory form namespaces. See "DNS Namespace."

2. DNS domains are partitions of DNS namespace. In aaa.bbb.com, "aaa," "bbb," and "com" all represent DNS domains. A DNS zone contains a database of resource records and delineates which DNS server is authoritative for that zone. Zones can contain one or more domains. See "DNS Domains" and "DNS Zones."

3. The FQDN is comprised of a host name with context, known as a *relative distinguished* name, and the domain in which the object resides. See "Fully Qualified Domain Names (FQDNs)."

4. The three types of zone transfers in DNS are full, incremental, and notify. Full zone transfers consist of a transfer of the entire DNS zone database file from a primary DNS server to a secondary DNS server. Incremental zone transfers follow the same process as a full zone transfer, but only transfer changes since the last transfer. Notify transfers occur periodically as primary servers are updated. They notify a list of secondary servers that changes have occurred, and then a full or incremental zone transfer is requested. See "Zone Database Files."

5. The recursive query process is typically initiated by the client when it queries DNS. When using recursion, the client will not accept a pointer to another DNS server for an answer from its primary DNS server. Instead, it requires the server to do all the work—that is, send the query on

behalf of the client through DNS namespace until it is resolved, and then return it to the client. See "Name Resolution."

6. RFC-1123 states that the legal character set for a DNS domain are A–Z, a–z, 0–9, and the hyphen (-). See "Character Sets."

7. For a DNS child domain (zone), such as aa.bbb.com in the DNS parent domain bbb.com to be authorized to manage that zone, a special NS "delegation" record that points to the child zone must be placed in the authoritative parent zone. See "Using a Delegated DNS Subdomain as AD Root."

8. DHCP assists both down-level clients and Active Directory clients with the registration of A and PTR records in DNS. In "down-level client mode," the DHCP server registers both the A and PTR records in DNS on behalf of down-level (pre-Windows 2000) clients. In Active Directory mode, DHCP can register and manage the PTR record for the client. The client is able to track changes and register its own A record with DNS. See "WINS and DHCP Integration."

9. The major push for the Windows 2000 version of Active Directory is that it has the ability to store its zone information in Active Directory, allowing participation in Active Directory replication, as well as the distributive nature of Active Directory. See "DNS Zone Data Storage Options."

10. First, you will see these DNS RRs implemented only under Microsoft's DNS service. The DNS WINS resource record is used to allow DNS to attempt to resolve a query using WINS if it fails

to do so in DNS. WINS-R is much the same as a PTR record, and is used to allow reverse lookups via WINS; essentially, if the reverse lookup DNS zone cannot produce a name for an IP address, DNS will send the request to WINS to see if it can. See "Resource Records."

Answers to Exam Questions

1. **D.** A DNS namespace absolutely cannot be changed without impacting every single solitary object in the directory. You should carefully plan the namespace design and choose a name that reflects answers A, B, and C. See "First DNS Domain Name."

2. **A.** The special namespace reserved by the InterNIC for companies that don't plan to have an Internet presence is the .local domain. This domain can be used by Active Directory for companies that do have an Internet presence, but do not want an internal namespace that can be seen on the Internet. See "Using Different DNS Domains for Public and Private."

3. **C.** Because you can treat Allbooks as a new company in a sense, you have the ability to utilize all Windows 2000 DNS servers and take advantage of Active directory integrated zones. A, B, and D all could work theoretically, but would be much more inefficient than Active Directory integrated zones. See "Zone Database Files."

4. **D.** SRV resource records are not required for DNS servers on the Internet. Whether or not a zone is authoritative is immaterial. See "SRV Resource Records Registration."

5. **B.** If you wanted to retain Windows 98 on the network, you would need to retain a NetBIOS name resolution system—WINS—and potentially even integrate it with DHCP and DNS. Removing NetBIOS by turning off NBT would effectively destroy a network with Windows 98 on it because it communicates using NetBIOS. You cannot design Active Directory around WINS. See "NetBIOS Name."

6. **B.** If you need to create an alias to a host in DNS, you use the CNAME resource record. The CNAME record can abstract the fully qualified domain name by associating an alias to the actual A resource record of the host. Answers A and D would work, but neither would be the preferred method. Answer C would not work; a PTR resource record provides IP address to host name resolution in a given zone. See "Canonical Name (CNAME)."

7. **B.** In this scenario we have a contiguous namespace and a zone for each Active Directory domain. By default, when a query is unresolvable in a subdomain, such as the ones represented by zoneB and zoneC, it is forwarded to its parent domain, which is represented by zoneA. A server in zoneA could then be configured to forward requests out to the Internet. See "DNS Servers."

8. **C, D.** These are not valid host names. The legal character set, as defined in RFC-1123, is a–z, A–Z, 0–9, and the hyphen (-). All other characters are illegal in DNS. Choices A, B, and E *do* meet the required character set requirements. See "Character Sets."

9. **A.** The Start of Authority resource record for the zone contains a refresh interval setting to govern the replication of the zone file between primary

APPLY YOUR KNOWLEDGE

and secondary servers. Secondary servers in this case are set up to request a full zone transfer instead of an incremental zone transfer at this refresh interval, which may be causing the performance spikes. The NS (Name Server) resource record describes a name server in a zone, and does not contain a refresh interval setting. Secondary servers poll primaries for zone transfers, primaries do not force the zone file onto the secondary servers without their request. See "Zone Database Files."

10. **B.** Namespace planning is wide open; any of the available answers could be made to work. However, to satisfy the requirements, a delegated subdomain of the public registered domain would be most efficient. You can then create the Active Directory root domain in the ad.abc.com

domain internally. This configuration isolates the internal and external data, since the Active Directory scope begins at the ad.abc.com level. See "Choosing the Root DNS Namespace."

11. **C.** To make use of a private root in your namespace, all DNS-enabled client computers must support either proxy autoconfiguation (PAC) files, or name exclusion lists. BIND version 8.1.1 is a UNIX-based DNS server, and local address tables are tables of both internal and external IP addresses, which do not assist in name resolution. Service resource records are actual DNS records used for a variety of functions by both DNS servers and clients, but do not assist in private root implementations. See "Clients That Allow an Internal DNS Root."

Suggested Readings and Resources

1. TechNet Article. "Windows 2000: Designing and Deploying Active Directory Service for the Microsoft Internal Corpnet."

2. TechNet Article. "Designing the Active Directory Structure." From the Windows 2000 Server Resource Kit.

3. Microsoft Corporation. *Windows 2000 Server Resource Kit.* Microsoft Press, 2000. Chapter 6.

4. White Paper. Active Directory DNS

5. White Paper. Configuring Windows 2000 DNS to Support Active Directory

6. Iseminger, David. *Active Directory Services for Microsoft Windows 2000 Technical Reference.* Microsoft Press, 2000. Chapter 6.

7. Nielsen, Morten Strunge. *Windows 2000 Server Architecture and Planning.* Chapters 7, 10, 12, and 13.

This chapter covers the following Microsoft-specified objectives for the Designing a Microsoft Windows 2000 Directory Services Infrastructure exam:

Design an Active Directory forest and domain structure.

- **Design a forest and schema structure.**
- **Design a domain structure.**
- **Analyze and optimize trust relationships.**

▶ The Windows 2000 Active Directory service encompasses four major areas: forests, domains, OUs, and sites. This objective list focuses on forests and domains. The first domain is also a forest, and hence introduces the forest root and the schema, the database behind Active Directory. Active Directory uses transitive trusts within a forest of domains. These trusts are created automatically, but may need to be optimized. This objective covers the crucial elements of Active Directory.

Design an Active Directory site topology.

- **Design a replication strategy.**
- **Define site boundaries.**

▶ Sites enable you to incorporate the physical characteristics of the network into your design. They work at the physical IP subnet level and allow for the compression and control of replication traffic. Sites, site links, site link bridges, and replication are a huge part in the design of Active Directory as a whole.

CHAPTER 11

Designing the Active Directory Structure

Design the placement of operations masters.

- **Considerations include performance, fault tolerance, functionality, and manageability.**

Design the placement of global catalog servers.

- **Considerations include performance, fault tolerance, functionality, and manageability.**

Design the placement of domain controllers.

- **Considerations include performance, fault tolerance, functionality, and manageability.**

▶ The proper placement of domain controllers may seem petty in today's well-connected world. When it comes to servicing Windows 2000 clients, however, it is all about location, location, location. This chapter discusses some scenario-based placement recommendations for domain controllers, both "plain" and with the additional responsibilities of global catalog servers and operations masters.

STUDY STRATEGIES

▶ Treat Chapter 10 and Chapters 12 through 14 as extensions of this chapter. Read each chapter very carefully in conjunction with the other chapters to get the most from this part of the book, which covers arguably the most critical objectives for this exam.

▶ Concentrate first on the business and technical assessments you have done in previous chapters. Then take that information and apply it to a domain design.

▶ Focus a good deal of attention on the "rules" for domain controller, global catalog server, and operations masters placement throughout the network.

▶ Make sure you thoroughly understand the relationship between DNS and Active Directory. If you feel unsure of the relationship between the two, take another look at Chapter 10, "DNS and Active Directory," or other resource material on DNS and Active Directory.

▶ Concentrate on matching real-world situations with the use of a single domain, multiple domains in a single tree, multiple domain trees, or multi-domain forests.

▶ Know and understand the implications of implementing multiple forests.

▶ Don't just read. Get into a lab and implement some complex domain designs, DNS strategies, and site layouts. Move objects between domains, try to remove or rename a domain and see what happens, relocate operations masters roles, and use some utilities such as NTDSUTIL and Replication Monitor.

INTRODUCTION

Now it is time to get down to business. You have endured the nontechnical, business-oriented (yet critical) stages of the directory services design, you have gotten through the grueling physical infrastructure assessment, and now you know what DNS is all about. This chapter covers the technology you're going to use that makes the aforementioned all worthwhile: Active Directory services. In particular, this chapter focuses on the four main elements of the Active Directory design: domains, forests, *organizational units* (OUs), and sites.

This chapter begins by introducing several terms that appear throughout this chapter. Several terms have changed meaning under Windows 2000, *domain* being just one of them. The discussion then moves into domains, trees, forests, schema, trusts, OUs, and sites, and introduces each briefly. Finally, the focus turns to planning and design concepts crucial in making the Active Directory implementation a success. Where appropriate, this examination cross-references Chapter 10 for DNS-related integration because it is crucial to understand that component well.

Your forest design will represent your entire organization. The term *forest* describes the aggregate of all domains and domain trees throughout Active Directory. This includes both contiguous and noncontiguous namespaces, because a forest can be a single domain as well as several trees of domains of disjoint namespaces.

An often-underemphasized part of Active Directory is the use of groups. The concept remains the same from Windows NT to Windows 2000, but the way groups are utilized and replicated throughout the environment must be addressed, and is addressed here!

CASE STUDY: WAYFRONT CONSULTING

BACKGROUND

WayFront Consulting, a large national consulting firm specializing in Network and eBusiness strategic solutions, is planning a migration to Windows 2000. The network topology at WayFront, highlighted in Figure 11.1, is the result of an internal year-long project that has just completed. WayFront uses a decentralized regional management system at its offices in five regions of the United States. The central head-quarters is located in Denver, the north region headquarters in Minneapolis, the south in Dallas, the east in Boston, and the west in L.A. Each of the four regional offices employs about 2,500 people and has at least two remote offices under its responsibility. The central headquarters employs about 4,000 people and supports connectivity to the regional offices. Each regional office maintains its own connection to the Internet for *virtual private network* (VPN) connectivity with remote locations in their region only. All Internet access is funneled through the corporate T-3. All remote offices connect to the Internet using ADSL, and then connect to their regional office using a VPN. Each remote office employs fewer than 100 people.

> **NOTE** **Internet Clouds** In an attempt to keep Figure 11.1 neat, four separate Internet clouds were used. You should consider them all to represent a single Internet when working through this chapter.

PROBLEM STATEMENT

WayFront wants to plan the design of the Windows 2000 Active Directory. It wants to determine where to create sites, how to create its forest of domains, how to manage replication, and how to effectively use groups and OUs throughout its environment. Because the network infrastructure upgrade was such a success, it decided to create a team and run the project internally. The team consists of individuals from each of the regional offices. Each regional office representative will communicate design plans to offices within the region, so as to get adequate input.

Project Sponsor

"We realize the value IT can have on an organization, and we want to 'eat our own dog food' in a sense by putting our processes and methodologies to work before we go out and really start selling the product. I think this will be the best hands-on training we can offer. Microsoft follows that methodology and look what it has done for them!"

Project Manager

"We've taken the results of the physical infra-structure analysis and generated reports, charts, and graphics pertaining to our environment. I want to make sure we leverage the countless hours that went into creating these documents."

CASE STUDY: WAYFRONT CONSULTING

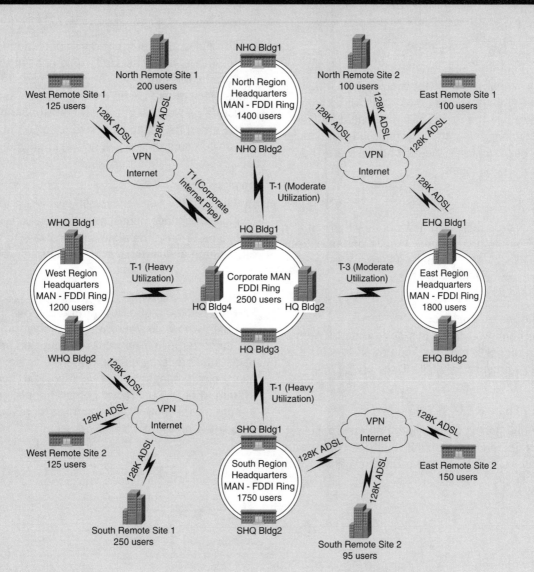

FIGURE 11.1

The enterprise network at WayFront Consulting.

continues

CASE STUDY: WAYFRONT CONSULTING

continued

CURRENT SYSTEM

The current network operating system is exclusively Windows NT 4.0. WayFront, however, wants to design a Windows 2000 Active Directory structure to suit the needs of the business without considering the current system. After the design has been finalized, they will address the "how" factor for migration.

CIO

"We have a rock-solid network now that our infrastructure is up to speed. I really kind of hate to see Windows NT go, but we know we're replacing it with something better."

Lead Design Engineer

"I've been waiting for this since Beta 1! We have such a cool enterprise; I can't wait to start the design process for Active Directory."

ENVISIONED SYSTEM

The end goal is to implement an enterprise *network operating system* (NOS) infrastructure with Windows 2000 and Active Directory. This system must employ a decentralized (regional) administration model and must be flexible enough to easily integrate additional remote offices. It must make efficient use of the existing network infrastructure as well. All users from all workstations in the enterprise should be able to log on from any office using their email address.

CIO

"My expectations are that we'll gain in the simplification of management for our regional offices. I'd like us to have the ability at corporate to manage remote and regional office assets as well."

Lead Design Engineer

"We have somewhat a decentralized administration model now, but there is not synergy throughout the enterprise. The trust relationships are a pain, and I can't log on somewhere else and get all my own settings. I think we're going to see a system where all users will benefit from the new features, especially when searching for resources across the enterprise."

FIRST THINGS FIRST

As mentioned in the introduction, it is important to cover some of the key terms and concepts used throughout this section of the book. The domain design process demands you know these (and without a doubt, some additional concepts as well); so make sure you understand the concepts first before you dive into the rest of this chapter. They are short and to the point here—well, as close to the point as possible!

Object

In Active Directory, everything is an *object*—users, printers, groups, and even policy settings are stored as objects. An object is any distinct, named set of attributes that represents something unique and concrete. Attributes hold data that define the object. For example, a user object may have name, phone number, and extension attributes that define its subject matter (the user). You will notice that *object* throughout this book really scales to mean just about anything with *attributes*. So consider an object anything you can right-click and access a properties page.

Container

A *container* is a special kind of object. It has attributes that define its subject matter and is part of Active Directory, but does not represent something concrete. Containers can contain objects and other containers.

Figure 11.2 describes containers as well as scope, namespace, objects, trees, domains, domain trees, forests, and sites (as discussed in this section).

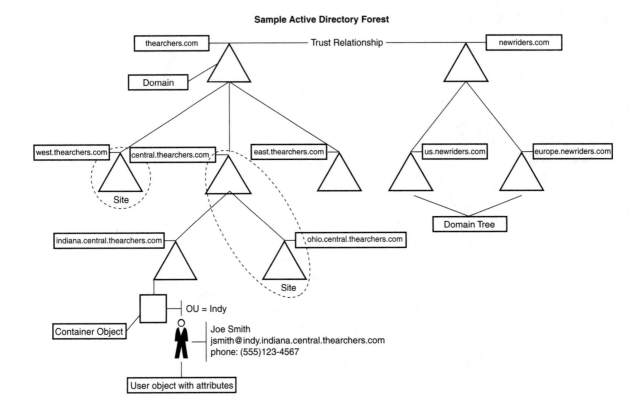

FIGURE 11.2

Active Directory consists of scope, namespace, objects and attributes, containers, trees, domains, domain trees, forests, and sites.

Tree

Trees describe a hierarchy of objects and containers. The "leaf" objects of a tree (the endpoints) are usually objects, and the "nodes" of a tree (the points of the tree that contain branches) are usually containers. Trees are very helpful in describing how objects are connected and how to get from one object to the next. In the Windows Explorer, a directory folder that contains files is a container, and the files are objects. Likewise an Active Directory domain is a container that includes several subcontainers and objects. You can form entire trees of domains within Active Directory, as described in the next few sections.

Domains

A *domain* is a security boundary, the basic partitioning unit of Active Directory. Active Directory is made up of one or more domains, each of which may contain millions of objects and containers. A domain is a special kind of container, and can be considered an abstract object as well because it has its own attributes. In Active Directory, you can span several domains and share a common schema, configuration, and *global catalog* (GC) to form domain trees. It is best to design domains around something that is not volatile in the organization, something that can endure change. In general, this means to structure domains around the geopolitical boundaries of the organization. In other words, design domains based on cities, states, regions, and countries.

EXAM TIP

Be Able to See the Forest *and* the Trees Know the difference between a forest and a tree, but more importantly, know when they can be the same.

Organizational Units

One shortcoming of Windows NT is its inability to allow certain groups of employees (not necessarily administrators) to manage subsets of users, computers, or groups within a given domain. To do this in Windows NT means creating a new domain or giving Betty Jo User sweeping Domain Admin permissions, neither of which properly addressed the seemingly simple issue of allowing Betty Jo to do specific functions such as changing passwords for her group of users. Organizational units enable Windows 2000 administrators to subdivide a domain according to the IT administrative model. With OUs, Betty Jo can be *delegated* the fine-grained permission to *only* reset passwords *only* for her group of users.

Domain Trees

As the name suggests, domain trees are one or more domains that share a common schema, configuration, and global catalog and form a contiguous namespace. Because they share these elements, automatic Kerberos trust relationships between domains are created. These trusts, unlike the trust relationships in Windows NT, are automatic and transitive. This means that if domain A trusts domain B and domain B trusts domain C, domain A trusts domain C! Domain trees furthermore enable administrators to logically divide up the organization's namespace in a way that coincides with the structure of DNS.

Forest

A *forest* can be a single domain, a single domain tree, or a set of domain trees that do not share a common namespace, which is referred to as having a *disjoint* namespace. Even though these domain trees may not share a contiguous namespace, they continue to share a common schema, configuration, and global catalog. All domain trees within a given forest trust each other via automatic Kerberos trust relationships. The same does not hold true in the scenario where two established companies merge, each with its own forest. In this case a manual Windows NT 4.0 style trust relationship between forest root domains must be established.

Site

The *site* terminology with Active Directory is stolen from Exchange terminology. Well, for that matter, so is the basis for Active Directory!

NOTE **Exchange Directory** The X.500 and LDAP basis for Active Directory was originally introduced as the Exchange directory in Microsoft Exchange 4.0.

NOTE **What Is Well-Connected?** Microsoft defines well-connected IP subnets as anything with greater than 512KB total bandwidth. You may determine that your organization is such that 128KB or 256KB is plenty and can deem those "well-connected." This is not set in stone, but rather is a preference.

A site is a way to create your replication boundaries within Active Directory. They are comprised of one or more "well-connected" physical IP subnets.

The beauty is, sites work at the physical layer and are independent of the logical layer where domains operate. This means that a site can consist of multiple domains, and domains can operate in multiple sites. Of course, where the domains reside relative to site boundaries does make a difference, as explained later in this chapter.

Another advantage of sites is the capability to control and compress replication data based on physical limitations of the bandwidth between the data origination points. Also, when a user logs on, he is authenticated by a computer within his site (based on subnet site membership) and is therefore authenticated on a fast and reliable connection.

Domains, domain trees, forests, and sites are discussed in more detail later in this chapter.

> **EXAM TIP**
>
> **And the Bandwidth Played On**
> Although there may be real-world exceptions, the 512KB WAN link is the recommended minimum bandwidth that should be used in a site planning scenario, and you can anticipate IP subnets that are "well-connected" during the exam.

Trusts

Trusts in Windows 2000 differ drastically when compared to Windows NT. We now have automatic Kerberos trusts that are transitive across the domain tree structure. This means you need on the order of n times less actual trusts to be established to establish a *complete trust* model. The variable n in this statement is derived from the following equations used to determine the number of trust relationships needed to deploy a complete trust model:

Windows NT   *(n*[n − 1])*

Windows 2000   *n − 1*

Figure 11.2 shows nine domains. In Windows NT it would take a whopping 72 manual trusts to create a complete trust model. This is because each domain must individually trust all other domains. In Windows 2000, the concept of a trust is still the same: to allow communications between domains. The difference? Transitivity. You have probably already done the math. It would take only eight trust relationships in Active Directory to support this same environment. And now for the icing on the cake: The administrator has to do absolutely nothing for this to happen; it is automatic.

Schema

Objects and attributes have been mentioned several times. Where they come from is something you need to both know and understand. The schema is yet another database that if messed with by the wrong person in the wrong place and the wrong time can be devastating to the entire organization. To you Windows NT gurus, it sounds like a registry of sorts. It is, but with a different purpose and name. The *schema* is a repository that holds the namespace definition through the use of objects and attributes in a forest. It contains the definitions for all object types legal to use within Active Directory and contains definitions that may be *extended* for each object type.

Directory Partitioning and Distribution

The domain is the basic unit of partitioning in Active Directory. The term *partitioning* here means that a forest of domains is split up and distributed to domain controllers on a per-domain basis. Each domain controller then is responsible only for its partition (domain) of the directory. It is clearer if you reverse this and envision the entire directory as the aggregate of each domain's directory partitions, as in Figure 11.3. The main reasons for partitioning the directory are scalability and performance. Within a domain, each of the domain controllers must replicate the contents of the directory to stay in sync—by replicating only one partition of the directory (their domain's), they can keep replication traffic to a minimum. The next section contains more on replication.

The aggregation of directory partitions is commonly referred to as the Active Directory *catalog*. There is exactly one Active Directory catalog per forest. As you can imagine, if that catalog were not partitioned, replication traffic alone would degrade performance and reduce scalability.

It is important to mention here that each domain controller maintains at least three naming contexts: the directory partition, the configuration container, and the schema. We've covered the directory partition and will cover the schema at length; but it is important you quickly come to understand the configuration container.

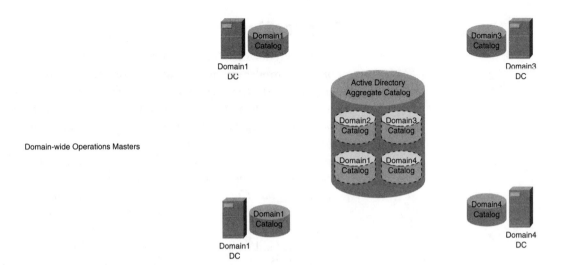

Domain1
DC

Domain1
Catalog

Domain3
Catalog

Domain3
DC

Active Directory
Aggregate Catalog

Domain-wide Operations Masters

Domain2
Catalog

Domain3
Catalog

Domain1
Catalog

Domain4
Catalog

Domain1
Catalog

Domain1
DC

Domain4
Catalog

Domain4
DC

FIGURE 11.3
The entire Active Directory consists of each of
its domains' directory partitions.

Configuration Container

When you think of the configuration container, think of the sites
and subnets, the physical structure of Active Directory. The
configuration container is a naming context that contains physical
network topology information and uses site information to make the
appropriate connections to domain controllers during client/server
activities and even server/server activities. In the case study, for
example, WayFront is divided into five distinct regions. Suppose
these regions are connected with very slow and data-saturated WAN
links, and are therefore broken into five different sites. When a user
in the east region attempts to log on, she is directed to a domain
controller that exists in her site first, because the definition of site is
high-speed connectivity. If a domain controller isn't available in her
site, she is then directed to the next least-expensive site, and so on.
The Active Directory makes use of the configuration container to
make these determinations.

Replication

Because Windows 2000 uses a multi-master replication model (every domain controller contains a read/write version of the directory [catalog] database), replication of changed data is a major concern. As just discussed, the unit of replication is the domain, but the replication model incorporated with Active Directory is much more granular than that. Microsoft incorporated an extremely granular replication model based not on object comparisons, but on object *attribute* comparisons using a trigger. This trigger, known as the *Update Sequence Number* (USN), is incremented for an object whenever an attribute for that object is changed. When domain controllers need to replicate, they examine the values of their USNs for each object, and replicate only the attributes whose objects contain differing USNs. Figure 11.4 illustrates a simple replication process. Replication is discussed in more detail later in this chapter.

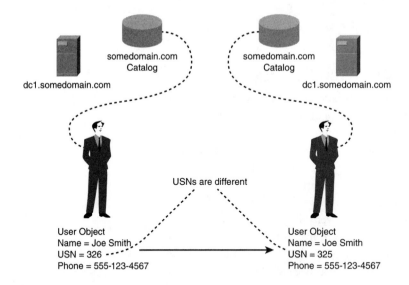

FIGURE 11.4
Domain controllers dc1 and dc2, which happen to be replication partners, exchange USNs for the user object Joe Smith, and replicate his phone number.

Global Catalog

You may be wondering how, with all this partitioning, a user request for information from another domain is handled. If that user is looking for a specific service, DNS handles the query (as you learned in Chapter 10) by forwarding it on throughout the DNS space until the query is resolved. But what if that user is searching for another user in the organization? *Global catalog servers* take care of these situations. Global catalog servers are normal Active Directory domain controllers with some additional responsibility. They are tasked with storing information from all other domains in the forest, information about each and every object in each and every directory partition in the entire forest of domains. To preserve as much disk space as possible and keep replication times down for this information, global catalog servers store only a subset of the attributes about each object, as illustrated in Figure 11.5.

> **N O T E**
>
> **Global Catalog Attributes** A fair estimation for the number of attributes a normal Active Directory object uses is about 15. The GC will utilize about 7 or 8 of these attributes by default.

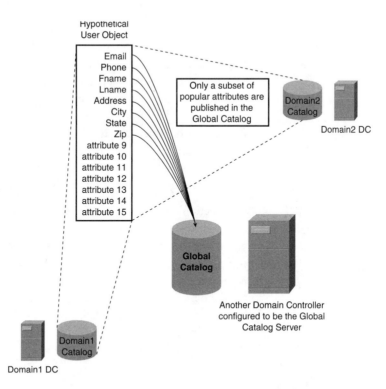

FIGURE 11.5

Global catalog servers store every object in every domain in the forest, but only store a subset of attributes about each object.

Of course, one side effect of not publishing all object attributes to the GC is a limit on what information can be resolved. That is why Microsoft took great care to publish (by default) the most popular attributes to a global catalog. Members of the Schema Admins group can modify this by using the Active Directory Schema MMC snap-in; keep in mind, however, that doing so increases the disk space required to host the GC, as well as adds performance-related overhead.

In summary, global catalog servers store a full copy of their own domain partition and *partial replicas* of all other domain partitions throughout the forest.

Setting the Stage for Active Directory

The stage has pretty much been set for Active Directory by getting a good grip on DNS. Now we need to concentrate on how to use that stage to get the lights set up and wired, and position the other equipment so that it will be just perfect for its users. That stage serves as a solid foundation on which you can build something very flexible, yet durable enough to support your user base. Designing Active Directory is much like setting up the equipment and lights on stage; they all need to be solid, yet flexible enough to be added to and removed from without much disturbance.

This section and the rest of this chapter focuses on the planning and design of the overall domain structure and leverages all that work you did earlier, including the business analysis, operational and organizational structure assessment, physical assessment, and IT administration model analysis. This section then sets the stage for the design. Keep in mind that in the real world, the material covered in this part of the book will likely take weeks, months, or in the rare extreme case, a year or more to properly plan, design, and implement.

Business and Technology Assessment

Remember all that work you did earlier? It is time to use it! The basic design process for a Windows 2000 network differs significantly from that of past networks. We've been saying that all along, but we will now prove it by discussing the design process for Windows 2000.

You establish your domain design by first understanding the business. Where does the company operate geographically? How does it distribute its resources within that geographical model? What is the size of the company? Are international operations involved? How many people work in each location? How does the company expect to grow over the next three to five years? Answering these questions and more like them will give you a good understanding of how the company conducts its day-to-day business. Be patient: This process will not be quick, especially for a large organization. It is important, however, that you do have this information before you start the design process. Not doing so will severely impact the success of your design.

Coupled with the business aspects of the organization are its physical characteristics—what the underlying support infrastructure looks like. Is there a current WAN topology diagram available? Where are the WAN links and what are their speeds and current utilization? What is the TCP/IP structure? Does it even exist?

You are fast approaching the climax of the project. You have spent about 50% of your time picking up the supporting information and formulating a plan to get to this point. You will spend another 30% or more of your time putting together the design based on the plans, and the rest of the time implementing (only 20% or even less time). When you go to create your Active Directory implementation plan, discussed in Chapter 15, "Designing an AD Implementation Plan," you will see how these "rule-of-thumb" numbers work out.

The following sections describe the three areas we've been discussing: operational, physical, and administrative. We provide only a refresher on these areas because they are discussed in other chapters of this book.

Operational Environment

The operational environment for an organization defines how it distributes and manages its resources. You should classify the company based on its size, because size alone typically dictates how a company operates within its geography. Recall that you can classify companies in the following ways:

◆ Local

◆ Regional

◆ National

◆ International

◆ Subsidiary

◆ Conglomerate

Most companies operate within one of these models, although you will find a company here and there that breaks all the rules and is difficult to classify. You just have to adapt, improvise, and overcome in those situations.

If you start by looking at where geographically a company does business, you will be able to classify it pretty easily. WayFront, the consulting company case study, is pretty easy to narrow down because they have five distinct regional offices throughout the United States. We can immediately rule out local, international, subsidiary, and conglomerate because they don't fit any of these models. We now are left with a choice between regional and national. To decide this, we need more information.

The distinction between regional and national (in this case) depends on how the company runs its business. For that, we will look into the physical and administrative layout of the organization.

Physical Environment

It is a relatively basic step to determine the company's overall operational structure, but that will get you only so far. To really get down to the level of detail you need to pull off a good design, you need to get physical. Relax; you don't have to hit the gym or dig out that Olivia Newton-John single, you just have to determine how everything fits together in the organization in terms of physical infrastructure. The physical assessment you did in Chapter 5, "Analyzing the Physical Environment," really defines this part of the plan, and you should use that to your advantage.

The physical assessment of the company helps define its technical requirements and will help you determine how to structure Active Directory sites and subnets to control replication traffic. Aside from the sizing aspect—the number of users in each location, growth plans, and so on—you need to focus here on the physical network infrastructure that forms the company topology. WayFront, for example, has provided us with a network topology diagram (a must in this stage of the game), so we can visualize the company layout. A good network diagram labels each WAN connection clearly and describe its capacity and general utilization. WayFront consists of five major physical sites, each connected with point-to-point T-1s or T-3s to form a hub-and-spoke topology. Four of the five major sites have remote offices in their region that connect to the regional office via a 128K ADSL Internet connection to form a VPN. From this information alone, you can start to visualize the physical components, sites and subnets, of Active Directory.

Administrative Environment

The final and most critical element that makes up your design plan is the company's IT administration model. Recall from Chapter 4, "Analyzing the IT Administration Model," the three models:

◆ **Centralized.** Single point of administration for the entire corporation

◆ **Decentralized.** Multiple points of administration that service specific parts or disciplines within the organization

◆ **Hybrid.** A combination of centralized and decentralized administration

Your OU design should focus primarily (if not solely) on the IT administration model. This chapter includes a bit of OU work, but Chapter 12, "Designing an OU and Group Policy Management Structure," provides the in-depth look at OUs and their function within Active Directory.

It is important during the design process to understand the IT administration model so that you can determine where to break domains into domain trees, use OUs rather than domains, or use security groups rather than either of the other two. Knowing how and when to make this distinction could make a huge difference in the complexity of your design. As with life, work, or anything else in this world, the design should be kept as simple and as manageable as possible. So, the old saying "Keep it simple, stupid" really applies here.

In examining the WayFront case study a little more, we were able to find out the following additional information:

◆ WayFront focuses on five lines of business: networking, eBusiness, collaboration, hosted solutions, and infrastructure. Each of the five lines of business exists at every WayFront location.

◆ The IT staff at WayFront exists in each of the regional offices and in the main campus. They are responsible for integrating technology with the strategic business initiatives of the company and are responsible for representing the five lines of business internal to the company.

◆ The help desk employs WayFront technical resources on their way up the ladder. They exist in each location with more than 100 users and use the company intranet as a knowledge store.

We can safely deduce after finding out this information that WayFront operates as a national company with regional offices.

Are they always going to be this easy? Of course not; the process will be the same, however, and with practice and repetition, the process of turning a company's operational, physical, and administrative practices into something usable for the Active Directory design will become more streamlined and comfortable. Make sure you leverage the previous chapters in this book during this process; you may not always use all the information covered in these chapters, but will need to know more than the technical aspects (as we've shown).

RULES OF DOMAIN CREATION

Domains are the basic unit of partitioning, replication, and security in Windows 2000, so it makes sense that there are some rules that should be adhered to as you plan your domain design. Remember that a single domain is also considered a domain tree and a forest because of the schema, configuration and global catalog; in essence, therefore, you can have all the functionality of a forest with a single domain at a fraction of the management cost. The message here is one of simplicity: Don't create multiple domains if you don't have to. The following are the justifications for creating additional domains:

◆ You need to support decentralized administration and OUs will not suffice. Some regional offices will not accept a domain design that does not give them complete control over the assets they paid for or support. They therefore require the creation of a new domain to retain complete control, and often do not allow the corporate office administrative access.

◆ You need to isolate or balance replication traffic. If your user base is large and you expect a million or more objects in a domain, you should consider creating additional domains to balance the intra-domain replication traffic. By doing this, you can isolate this replication traffic to domain controllers within the new domain.

◆ You need to support international differences. If the organization operates in more than one country, you will need to create a separate domain to support the currency and language differences, and most likely decentralized administration.

◆ You need to support more than one domain policy. Chapter 7, "Analyzing Security Requirements," discussed the domain security policy as a policy that affects every user in the domain. If you have a need for multiple domain security policies, by definition you need multiple domains.

◆ Existing Windows NT domain structures must be retained. You may have a compelling reason to keep an existing domain or domains in place. You should mitigate all risk involved in doing so and try to replace existing domains with OUs where appropriate.

◆ Company politics dictate it. If company executives demand additional domains be created for security or autonomy, you may have no choice but to comply. You should, however, argue your case and push for the use of OUs where appropriate.

If you think you cannot do with a single domain, check against these justifications to be sure.

Integration of Organizational Units

OUs offer a structuring mechanism that enables you to subdivide a domain and place domain objects—users, groups, computers, other OUs, and other domain objects—into a more structured hierarchy. Windows NT domains are flat and don't offer a way to delegate administration, which forces many companies to create resource domains to accomplish this task. OUs provide a means by which administrators can grant a user or group of users fine-grained administrative control over objects in that OU.

> **NOTE**
>
> **OUs and Delegation** As stated previously, Chapter 12 is dedicated to the use of organizational units; therefore, this chapter just concentrates on design concepts with OUs.

Through the effective use of OUs, administrators can model the IT administrative structure of the network and get darn close to perfectly modeling the organization of the business. During the Active Directory design, you might find it compelling to create OUs under the following circumstances:

◆ You need to delegate administration.

◆ You have existing Windows NT resource domains.

◆ You need an application point for *Group Policy Objects* (GPOs).

◆ You need to control access to resources. You can publish shares to Active Directory, place those share publications under an OU, and apply permissions through the OU to all shares instead of applying permissions on each share individually.

◆ You want to group objects with common properties.

This is not an exhaustive list, but does describe the most common applications of OUs.

OUs Versus Domains

The biggest advantage OUs have over domains is flexibility. You can change the structure of your OU model a lot easier than you can that of the domain model. Overall, the addition of OUs in the domain structure enables you to reduce the number of domains needed to support an organization, which in turn reduces administration cost, as well as hardware cost because you don't need additional domain controllers to support OUs.

When you get to a point where a choice between OUs and additional domains is needed, consider Table 11.1.

TABLE 11.1

A COMPARISON OF DOMAINS AND OUs

Required Feature	Domains	OUs
Organizational business units must have separate DNS names.	Yes	No
Decentralized administration by completely separate administrative personnel.	Yes	No
Decentralized administrative control.	No	Yes
High-level Domain Admins must not have access to parts of the network under another group's authority.	Yes	No
Two parts of the network are separated by an extremely slow link and you don't want any replication traffic to cross it.	Yes	No
You need to hierarchically structure the company based on its administrative and organizational needs.	No	Yes
Delegation of administrative control.	No	Yes
Structure is likely to change.	No	Yes
Implement different security policies.	Yes	No
Reduce the number of objects in each domain	Yes	No

You have a good deal of flexibility in creating an OU structure (covered in Chapter 12). It is important to point out some of the more typical OU models that fit well within most companies. These typical OU models are as follows:

◆ Based on the geographical structure of the company

◆ Based on the company's business units or departments

◆ Based on the IT administrative model

Because you can nest OUs, you can build a relatively structured OU model. Consider yourself warned, however; nesting OUs, and in particular GPOs linked to OUs, can impact performance and bring unnecessary complexity into your environment (as discussed in more detail in Chapter 12).

Making Smart Use of Groups

With all this talk about domains and OUs, it is easy to overlook the groups within Windows 2000. There are two types of groups, which are used primarily for security purposes: security groups and distribution groups.

Security groups can contain users, computers, and other groups and can be used to grant object permissions and individual object attribute permissions.

Distribution groups are used for nonsecurity purposes and cannot be used to grant permissions. They exist primarily because of Active Directory integration of email, such as Exchange 2000. Security groups may be added to distribution groups, but distribution groups may not be added to security groups.

This section discusses security groups, because at this point we don't really care about email integration! Windows 2000 has four types of groups: local, global, domain local, and universal. Each of the groups is named for the scope in which it can be used, as illustrated in Table 11.2.

NOTE

Group Availability Not all Windows 2000 groups are available all the time. The domain mode setting dictates the availability of certain groups.

TABLE 11.2

WINDOWS 2000 SECURITY GROUPS

Type	Legal Members	Scope of Usage	Domain Mode
Local	• Users from its own forest	Local computer only	Native, mixed
	• Global groups from its own forest		
Global	• Users from its own domain	Entire forest and any trusted domains	Native, mixed
	• Global groups from its own domain		
Domain local	• Users from anywhere in the forest	Their own domain only	Native only
	• Global groups from anywhere in the forest		
	• Universal groups from anywhere in the forest		
	• Domain local groups from its own domain		
Universal	• Users from anywhere in the forest	World. Entire forest and any trusted forest	Native only
	• Computers from anywhere in the forest		
	• Global groups from anywhere in the forest		
	• Universal groups from anywhere in the forest		

This section belongs in this chapter for a couple of reasons. First, all domain local, global, and universal groups are published in the global catalog. However, all universal groups' members are also published to the GC. This means you need to carefully watch your use of universal groups because of the potential performance hit. Wonder why universal group membership is published to the global catalog? The proper use of a universal group is to provide access to resources for users, computers, and so forth on a forest-wide basis. By publishing membership to global catalog servers, users are able to pick up their universal group membership locally (if best practices are used in placement of global catalog servers) at logon time. During the logon process, the *Local Security Authority* (LSA) queries the global catalog server for a user's universal group membership and adds it to his security token. With that in mind, you can probably imagine the implications slow or scheduled replication of the global catalog can have on universal group membership.

Second, groups are used to organize user and computer objects into manageable lists that can be granted permission to resources across the entire forest. With that understanding, you need not consider the user or group needs when designing the Active Directory domain and OU structure, but instead, create a simple and manageable design and the integration of groups will sit on top of it.

Two groups have a significant amount of control over an Active Directory environment and are highlighted in the following sections.

Enterprise Admins

Because domains are by definition a unit of security, a member of the Domain Admins group in a parent domain does not have inherited domain administrator power in any of its child domains. There is, however, one group that does, and in fact has sweeping power throughout the entire forest. The *Enterprise Admins* universal group has such power and its membership should be carefully considered. Because it is a universal group, the Enterprise Admins group is only available after Active Directory has been switched to native mode.

Schema Admins

The *Schema Admins* group is the most dangerous in the entire Active Directory. Only members of this group can make modifications to the schema, which affects every object and attribute throughout the entire forest. This chapter uses words such as *extreme, urgent, critical, crucial,* and *vastly* to describe the importance of controlling this group's membership.

THE DESIGN PROCESS

Just to reiterate, you must have a good understanding of all the pieces that go into creating the Active Directory domain structure before you proceed with the design process. Improper design plans virtually anywhere can lead to serious problems down the road, especially with the underlying support infrastructure of DNS and that all-important root domain. My advice (as well as the advice of every other person whose material I've read): Keep it simple! It is possible to over-design Active Directory and attempt to make too much use of the hierarchical structure and have it backfire on you. Stick to simplicity and best practices and you will be fine.

To be honest, there is no cookie-cutter approach to this. The remainder of this chapter represents how I would approach this task given an organization such as WayFront (and given the Microsoft exam objectives). This is definitely not the approach you would take in every design effort for every company; too many variables are involved. This discussion focuses on the material covered on the exam, and supplies you with enough knowledge to go out there in the future and do what works for you and for the particular project on which you are working.

Determining the Number of Forests

You have the information you gathered during the business analysis. You have categorized and sized the company. You have the physical structure and network topology diagram. You have the planned IT administration model. You have spent the time to do a Gap Analysis. You have determined the average bandwidth utilization on all segments of the LAN and WAN. To sum it all up, you have done the legwork and it is time to put that information to use.

One logical starting point is with the number of forests. This 100,000-foot level view helps define the amount of work you have ahead of you. In most cases, you can get away with using a single forest, which is optimal. Several downfalls are associated with creating multiple forests:

◆ You have multiple schema and configuration containers and have to manually maintain synchronicity between them. This equates to added administrative cost and overhead.

◆ You need to create explicit one-way Windows NT 4.0–style trust relationships between domains from different forests. There are no automatic transitive trusts between forests.

◆ The search scope for users is *Entire Directory*. This equates to a single forest. Users therefore would need to learn how to locate resources in other forests.

◆ Users logging on outside their "home forest" would need to remember their entire UPN, which could be something like sarcher@in.state.us.country.thearchers.com, because their abstracted username would not be present in forests other than their own.

◆ You cannot move accounts from one forest to another. To do so requires that the accounts be removed from one forest and re-created in the other.

You can see that creating multiple forests is not going to enable you to reap the full benefit of Active Directory. Because of this, you might expect the reasons to create multiple forests to be almost nonexistent. If you search really hard, you may be able to come up with a few.

If you find in your IT administration model assessment that there are serious political goings-on, you may have the need to create multiple forests. If more than one group insists on having complete control over forest-wide elements such as the schema, and are unwilling to compromise, the only alternative is to create multiple forests.

One scenario you will face down the road is in the mergers and acquisitions arena. If two companies have well-established Active Directory forests and decide to merge and share resources across, you wind up with multiple forests. This extreme case should be only a temporary solution, because IT professionals should begin working an integration strategy to roll one company into the other's namespace as a separate tree rather than a forest.

There is no way of automatically synchronizing information between forests, so to create multiple forests is to create administrative overhead. If at all possible, use a single forest.

> **NOTE**
>
> **Company Politics** It is a sad day in the IT world when we have to start designing the network around company political pressures. Try your utmost to resolve these types of situations so that they don't complicate the design.

Planning Your Domain Design

The next logical step is to determine the number of domains you need throughout your (single, assumedly) forest. Remember the previous discussion on domain creation criteria and also the use of OUs. You should create a domain plan based on the information you collected throughout this book and the domain creation criteria in this chapter. You need to carefully consider the first domain because of its purpose as the Active Directory root domain that

defines the namespace for the organization. One exception to this
rule is the case in which multiple root level domain trees are needed,
as in Figure 11.6. The strongest validation for using multiple
domain trees is with a company that has multiple registered namespaces on the Internet and needs to maintain consistency throughout the enterprise. You will see this scenario with conglomerates and
other company categorizations that operate as separate entities.

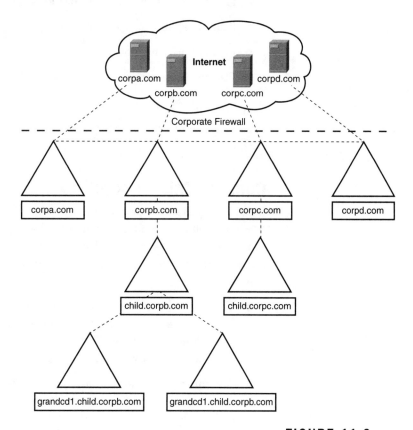

FIGURE 11.6
Having more than one registered DNS domain
on the Internet is the primary reason for creating multiple domain trees.

The remainder of this chapter discusses each element of your domain design plan, which should include the following:

◆ Put together a site plan.

◆ Plan the number of domains needed per forest.

◆ Plan the root domain for each forest.

◆ Plan for parent/child domain relationships.

◆ Plan the DNS namespace integration with domains.

◆ Plan the placement of domain controllers.

◆ Plan the placement of operations masters.

Before getting into the domain plan, it is important to point out some common misconceptions that can greatly affect the design of the domain hierarchy.

Common Misconceptions

Because there is such a drastic difference between NT domains and Windows 2000 domain trees, there is no doubt going to be some confusion in terms of domain planning. The following list points out some issues and suggests how you should handle them should they come up:

◆ There is no longer a reason to create additional domains because of space limitations on the number of objects in a given domain. Windows 2000 domains can support millions of objects per Active Directory partition.

◆ Administrators no longer have to create resource domains to delegate administrative authority because the domain is no longer the smallest unit of administrative delegation. Administrators can now create OUs within a domain and use a wizard to delegate granular control.

◆ The requirement for a PDC is no longer needed. Windows 2000 implements the Active Directory as a distributed database to all domain controllers, which are all created equal. All domain controllers maintain a read/write copy of the Active Directory database for their respective domains.

◆ The purpose of a Windows 2000 domain is to reflect administrative efficiency, partition Active Directory into manageable units, and control replication. Administrators from child domains do not necessarily have to fall below administrators in parent domains in the organizational chart. Do not concern yourself with space limitations in an Active Directory partition. Microsoft has tested single domains with more than a million objects and expects they will scale to upward of 10 million. This does not mean you should use only one domain all the time. It means that in cases where you may consider using an additional domain, make sure you qualify that decision by referencing the domain creation criteria earlier in this chapter. The single domain model is much easier to manage than a domain tree model in some cases.

> **N O T E** **Domains and Objects** Carefully weigh the pros and cons of partitioning Active Directory into additional domains when you expect more than a million objects.

In cases where you need to grant administrative control somewhere outside the central IT group, you no longer have to automatically create additional domains to do so. You may find that another domain would work best in some situations; but always weigh the pros and cons of using OUs instead.

Windows NT domains called for one PDC and one or more BDCs to distribute the domain controller workload. With this model, the PDC contained the only read/write copy of the SAM and was responsible for replicating it out to all BDCs, which contained a read-only copy. The entire domain therefore depended on the availability of the PDC. Windows 2000 domains remove that requirement by making all domain controllers equal and giving them a read/write copy of the Active Directory partition for their domain. If one goes down, the others continue to function and allow changes to Active Directory data. You will find that some operations are not conducive to a multi-master distributed database model such as Active Directory. For this reason, Windows 2000 implements special responsibilities on specific domain controllers, known as *operations masters*. These special roles are discussed shortly.

One of the most costly misunderstandings organizations have when they look at a domain tree is "pecking order." They see that root domain and its subordinates (child domains) and assume that administrators in the top-level domains automatically have administrative power over their child domains. This couldn't be further from the truth. Once again, the domain is a security boundary, and this security boundary *can* prevent Domain Admins from parent domains from having administrative control in these child domains. This is where the Enterprise Admins group comes into play. Members of the Enterprise Admins group do have sweeping administrative control in all domains; remember, however, that even administrators of the domain at the bottom of the tree can be added to the Enterprise Admins group. Make it clear that domain tree hierarchies are not created to melt the egos of administration teams, but rather to create an administrative efficiency and a logical structure to the organization.

PUT TOGETHER A SITE PLAN

This may seem like an odd place to start when planning your domain structure; but when you think about it, you really need to have your physical network mapped out before you design you logical network, right? Honestly, it depends on your thought process and how you prefer to begin the design; we'll start in this book with the site structure.

Testing of Site Layouts   New testing conventions include drag-and-drop type exam questions in which you assemble answer items in a specific order based on a given scenario. Site layout seems like a logical possibility for this new type of testing.

EXAM TIP

The logic behind starting with a site plan is this. If you take a look at your physical network topology, you will automatically know where you are going to need to split into sites to control replication traffic. It makes sense then to create an initial sketch (yes, a pencil-and-paper sketch) of a site plan and start hashing it out from there. Your limiting factor throughout the entire physical network is the bandwidth that connects them. If this is not going to change prior to the Windows 2000 rollout, you must work with it.

After you have a site plan put together, you then start planning how to incorporate a domain structure. You must keep in mind the replication strategies (discussed in a minute) and what information is replicated at what time and how. This important factor could play a large role in the domain structure you come up with. Let's stop there and get into site planning. We'll pick up with domains in the subsequent sections.

The Facts About Sites

As discussed previously, sites are used to help define the physical structure (topology) of your network. Once again, the definition of a site is one or more well-connected TCP/IP subnet(s). This typically means a LAN or high-speed MAN, but depending on your tolerance for latency, can expand to include certain high-speed WAN links as well. Sites can be used to control the following:

◆ **Replication traffic.** When sites are defined between two or more networks, the Active Directory replication traffic is manually scheduled to occur at specific time intervals, usually equating to "off-peak" hours.

◆ **Logon authentication traffic.** When a client workstation requests logon authentication, Windows 2000 attempts to find a domain controller in the same site as the workstation, which ensures the logon process occurs locally and not over WAN links.

Sites operate at the physical level in the Active Directory architecture. They therefore operate independently of domains and domain controllers. Consequently, the following operations are perfectly legal:

◆ You can add all domain controllers from a single domain to a site.

◆ You can add only some of a domain's domain controllers to a site.

◆ You can add several domain controllers from different domains to a single site.

Sites contain two types of objects: server objects and connection objects. The *Knowledge Consistency Checker* (KCC) generates connection objects. The purpose of the KCC is to generate a replication topology for both intra-site and inter-site replication. Server objects are created for a computer when the Active Directory installation code (dcpromo.exe) is executed. Server objects are placed into the appropriate sites based on the server's TCP/IP configuration.

> **NOTE**
> **KCC** The network topology information generated by the KCC is placed on the configuration partition on each domain controller in the forest.

Making Use of TCP/IP Subnets

A site is composed of one or more physical IP subnets that make up the LAN, MAN, or WAN; these subnets can be physically in the same building, across the street from each other, or in two separate cities.

The following simple example shows the relationship between sites and subnets:

```
Site-1
Subnet: 172.16.25.0/24
Subnet: 172.16.26.0/24
Subnet: 172.16.27.0/24

Site-2
Subnet: 192.168.0.0/16
Subnet: 172.16.28.0/24
```

NOTE

Default-first-site-name All servers and workstations must exist in a site. By default, when you install Active Directory for the first time, a generic site named Default-first-site-name is created. You can change this site name at any time.

How you group the subnets into sites depends on how you view well-connected networks. How you view well-connected networks depends largely on how much uncompressed replication traffic traveling across a WAN link can be tolerated. In some situations, a rarely used 256K frame connection suffices, whereas in others, a T-3 is not enough.

You use the Active Directory Sites and Services utility to define the subnets that comprise a site. After the subnets have been created, you associate each subnet with a site by just selecting the site from a drop-down list.

IN THE FIELD

TAKE SOME LEGWORK OUT OF SITES AND SUBNETS

Suppose you have a multi-site enterprise to be brought onto Windows 2000. Each physical site consists of one or more IP subnets. By default, Active Directory creates a single site and deposits all domain controllers (regardless of domain) into that single site. If you wait to configure your site and subnet structure until later, you will have to move the server objects between sites in Active Directory Sites and Services, adding time, complexity, and overhead, and increasing your chances for error.

On the other hand, if you create your site and subnet structure beforehand, each domain controller added to the enterprise is automatically placed in the site represented by the IP subnet on which the server resides. This can significantly reduce the amount of administrative overhead required to complete the site implementation.

Now that you know the lowdown on sites and subnets, we need to spend a bit of time discussing the processes for both intra-site (within one site) and inter-site (between sites) replication.

Intra-Site Replication

Intra-site replication describes the replication operations that occur within one site. Remember that each domain needs to keep the Active Directory partition in sync with all other domain controllers in that domain; for those domain controllers within a single site, therefore, replication occurs automatically. The goal with intra-site replication is to use as few CPU cycles as possible to get the job done. Because sites define well-connected networks, bandwidth preservation is not considered, so replication data is not compressed. Domain controllers utilize a notify process to let other domain controllers know they have a change to replicate. Specifically, when a change occurs on a domain controller, that domain controller waits a configurable amount of time (five minutes by default) before notifying all the other domain controllers within the site. The other domain controllers then pull the changes from the originator. If no changes occur during a configurable amount of time (six hours by default), the domain controllers replicate anyway just to be sure. Replication within a site uses *Remote Procedure Calls* (RPCs).

As stated previously, the KCC is responsible for creating the replication topology, a pathway between replication partners. When new domain controllers are brought online, they are automatically entered into the calculations made by the KCC.

One final thing to understand about replication in general is that each directory partition (schema, configuration, and directory) has its own replication topology. Because the schema and configuration are both forest-wide, they can share a topology. The directory partition is replicated only to domain controllers within its domain. The only time the directory partition shares a topology with the schema and configuration is if all domain controllers in a site are in the same domain.

Figure 11.7 illustrates replication within a site.

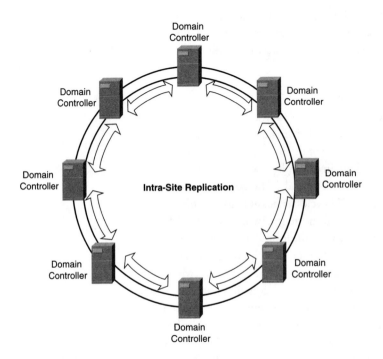

FIGURE 11.7
Replication within a site occurs automatically based on notifications. A replication "ring" is used to illustrate replication partners.

Inter-Site Replication

Inter-site replication describes replication between two sites. The process assumes bandwidth to be precious, and therefore compresses data before sending it across. Unlike intra-site replication, inter-site replication is scheduled manually and does not use a notification process. You can therefore schedule replication to occur during off-peak hours or even over lunch. The obvious trade-off here is latency; a change made in another site will not be realized until the scheduled replication occurs.

Inter-site replication can occur using a combination of the following protocols:

◆ **RPC over TCP/IP.** This appears as IP in the interface and is a synchronous transport.

◆ **SMTP.** Simple Mail Transfer Protocol requires CDO v2 interface and the SMTP component from IIS v5 (both ship with Windows 2000).

Microsoft has been somewhat vague about why it included SMTP support for inter-site replication, but some believe it is in preparation for supporting heterogeneous directory replication somewhere down the road. It is important to point out that the SMTP protocol is limited at this point to replicating only the schema, configuration, and global catalog—which means it cannot replicate the directory partition. This is because some domain operations, such as global policy, require use of the *File Replication Service* (FRS), which doesn't support asynchronous transport.

One final note. You will hear the term *bridgehead* come up in the case of inter-site replication. You Exchange buffs might be smiling; yes, it is a carry-over term from Exchange used to describe the server or servers within a site used as "gateways" to adjacent sites for replication data. These servers have the added responsibility of sending and receiving the replication data and getting it incorporated into their respective sites.

NOTE

Inter-Site Replication Data Compression Most replication data is compressed to 10–15% of its original size.

Setting Up the Site Links and Bridges

So, you have created two different sites so that you can control replication traffic. Now you need a way to get replication data from site A to site B. *Site links* represent a connection between sites to be used for replication. They consist of the following:

- ◆ **Membership.** There must be two or more sites in the site link.

- ◆ **Cost.** Value that determines which site link will be used for replication should multiple site links be configured.

- ◆ **Transport.** IP (RPC) or SMTP.

- ◆ **Schedule.** The times that replication is allowed to occur.

- ◆ **Frequency.** How often replication is attempted. Default is every 180 minutes.

Each site within a multiple site environment must be connected by at least one site link; otherwise, it will have no way of replicating with domain controllers from any other site. Also, keep in mind that a site link is not a one-to-one mapping of sites. Instead, a site link defines a set of replication parameters that can be shared by two or more sites. Figure 11.8 describes inter-site replication using a site link.

Site link bridges are used to connect sites and model the routing behavior of a network. Because most networks today are fully routed, you shouldn't have to configure site link bridges. This is because all site links by default are transitive, meaning they implicitly belong to a single site link bridge and can therefore "see" all other sites. If you have a network that is not fully routed, you lose the transitivity of the site link and will therefore need to create additional site link bridges. These are explained here so that you have an understanding for the exam; but again, you probably won't see much of this in the real world.

Imagine you have a site and site link structure similar to that in Figure 11.9. Sites A and B are linked using the site link AB. Sites B and C are linked using the site link BC. No route exists between sites A and C, so those domain controllers cannot replicate data directly.

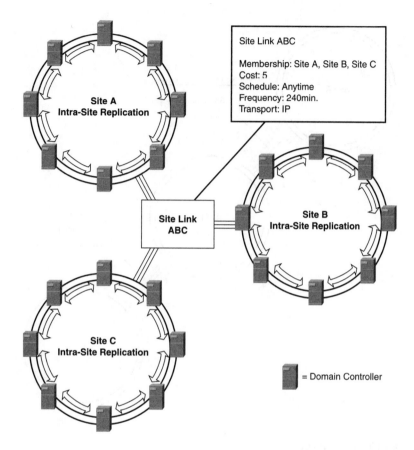

Site Link ABC

Membership: Site A, Site B, Site C
Cost: 5
Schedule: Anytime
Frequency: 240min.
Transport: IP

= Domain Controller

FIGURE 11.8
Sites A, B, and C all contain domain controllers
from mycompany.com and all replicate between
sites based on the parameters configured in
the site link.

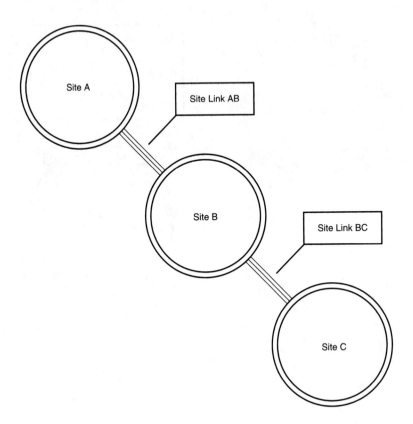

FIGURE 11.9
A site and site link configuration in an IP network that is not fully routed.

Site link bridge ABC could be configured to "attach" site links AB and BC to allow for transitivity between the sites. Figure 11.10 illustrates the configuration with the site link bridges added.

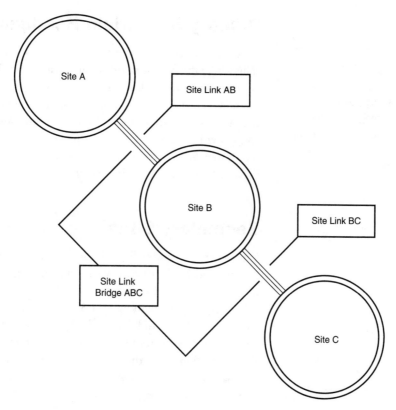

FIGURE 11.10
Site link bridge ABC provides transitivity between sites A, B, and C.

PLANNING A SITE STRUCTURE FOR WAYFRONT

Are you ready to put your site knowledge to use? Grab some paper and a pencil and let's design a preliminary site structure for WayFront. This process is meant to be iterative, so be open to suggestions when you design a site plan. Let's review WayFront.

Refer to Figure 11.1 to get a refresher on the physical layout of the company. We will design the preliminary site layout based on information we know, and build on this layout as we move closer to the final domain design.

NOTE

Corporate Site (Primary) There is nothing special about this site other than that it is a starting point. The "primary" means nothing technical here; it is just a way to distinguish the main headquarters from the rest of the sites you are about to draw.

Primary Site: Main Headquarters

Most companies have some sort of main headquarters and it is typically where the corporate offices are located. For WayFront, the corporate office is neatly labeled on the diagram for you, smack-dab in the middle. Notice that four buildings make up the main headquarters, all of which are connected on an FDDI-based MAN. Because you know FDDI is high speed, it makes sense to stick all four buildings into a single site. Draw a square in the middle of your paper. Label it **Corporate Site (Primary)**.

Secondary Sites

Your secondary sites will be all the regional offices or branches of significant size. In the case of WayFront, four regional offices are connected either by T-1 or T-3. You will recall that a well-connected IP subnet equates to anything over 512KB by definition, so you may be wondering why we didn't include these sites in the primary. The answer is that we certainly could have, but the total bandwidth of the connection is not the factor here; rather, it is the average *available* bandwidth, which *may* be significantly less than the total. The network topology diagram even labels the utilization classification on each high-speed WAN connection. A T-1 or T-3 that's even moderately used on the average probably has a peak utilization near full capacity. All this must be considered in your decision to break the network into sites. Additionally, you cannot forget about the type of work and hours of operation for potential sites, because that information affects the replication schedule you will set up after the sites have been defined.

Therefore, draw four more boxes, one at the farthest reaches of every side of your paper, which now should look something like Figure 11.11. Label your boxes according to the figure. The dotted lines in the figure represent the actual physical WAN connections running between sites.

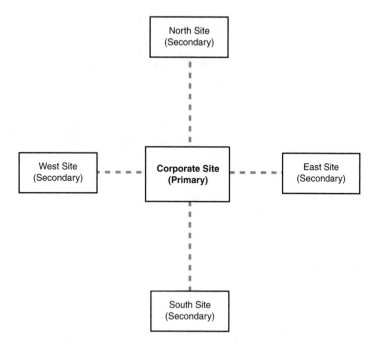

FIGURE 11.11
Preliminary site sketch including primary and secondary sites.

Tertiary Sites

The final sites we will add to this preliminary diagram are what we call tertiary sites. *Tertiary sites* are all additional sites that are somewhat less significant in size, but just as important as all the other sites. WayFront connects satellite offices in each region to the regional headquarters using a VPN. The VPN is supported by 128K ADSL connections in each satellite office that connect through the Internet to another 128K link in the regional office. Because of the relatively slow speeds that support these offices, they definitely need to be placed in a site of their own. You just about have to stick each remote office in its own site, so the number of tertiary sites will probably reflect the number of offices 1:1.

> **NOTE**
>
> **Sites Require Domain Controllers**
> Because sites are created to control directory replication, it stands to reason that a site requires at least one domain controller to make it useful.

Add a tertiary site square to your sketch for each satellite office. Go ahead and draw a dotted line that represents the VPN connection to the regional office as if it were a real point-to-point connection. When all is said and done, your sketch should resemble that of Figure 11.12.

The next step is to determine how you should connect the sites using site links or site link bridges. You must take into consideration the available bandwidth, the replication schedule, cost, and tolerance for latency as you determine the site link plan.

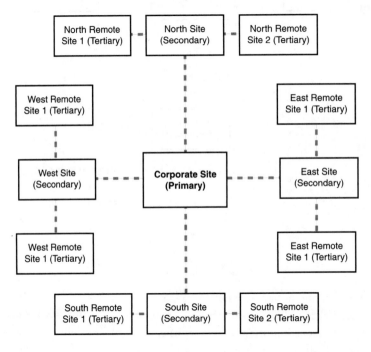

FIGURE 11.12
Your "completed" preliminary site sketch.

Site Link Plan for WayFront

This section may be a bit premature because we have not yet gotten to the meat of the domain design portion of this chapter, but it keeps with the flow of sites. We discussed site links previously as a means to replicate data between two or more sites. When designing the replication strategy, consider all sites first. By this I mean, because a site link is transitive and can be created to control replication between multiple sites, it wouldn't hurt to see whether you could take care of all replication with one site link, right?

As it turns out, if you can get all locations to agree on the schedule, cost, frequency, and protocol, you can create a single site link and life is good. WayFront agrees that the five major offices (the primary and secondary sites) can be included in a single site link, but the remote offices should have site links of their own. Draw a light circle around the five major sites and label the circle something like "Primary and Secondary Sites Site Link."

Each of the remote offices should be configured to replicate with its regional office, so it in a sense would get changes initiated by the corporate office third hand (corporate replicates with region, region replicates with branch offices). They could be configured to replicate directly with the corporate office if necessary, but that could prove to be too costly, especially during the day because there is not a direct physical connection with the corporate office. The only thing you would have to keep up on once this site link is configured is the replication schedule between the regional office and its local offices. If the primary site link was configured to replicate at noon and 6 p.m., and the regional site link was configured to replicate at 11 a.m. and 5 p.m., for example, the remote sites would not get the noon update until 5 p.m.. Of course, because the remote offices are connected by such little bandwidth, the better schedule for replication for them would be after hours (around midnight, for example). This way, the updates are fresh each morning; however, changes made that day do not get replicated out until midnight.

You must make a decision here: Do you replicate more often during the day and sacrifice bandwidth, or do you set the expectation with users that changes made at the corporate and regional offices will not be available until the next day. In WayFront's case, changes are more important, so it chooses to replicate at 1 p.m. and 7 p.m. Draw light circles around each set of regional office and remote office combinations. Label this "Regional/Remote Office Site Link."

Your final preliminary sketch should resemble that of Figure 11.13.

Now you have a preliminary site and site link diagram that should resemble the physical topology of the network. We used the word *preliminary* throughout this section because we may want to make some changes to the site plan based on information discussed in the following section.

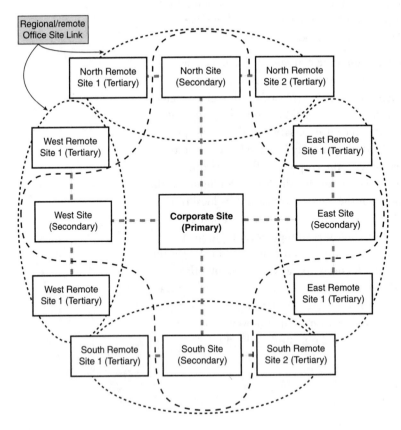

FIGURE 11.13
Final preliminary site and site link draft for WayFront.

DOMAIN PLANNING

Now take the preliminary site plan and move it aside for the time being; we're going to talk about domains. Don't forget what you have designed so far, because it will be important as you start thinking about incorporating domains (and domain controllers) into your site structure. This may be coming across like you must have a site structure put in place before you design your domains. Although it helps a great deal in defining your network in terms of strong and weak connections, it is not required. Again, there are a million iterations involved in designing the Active Directory structure, I chose to create the site structure first because it is something relatively static and a good starting point.

Determining the Number of Domains

Remember once again, the simpler the domain plan is, the better. If you can pull off a single domain design with efficiency, do it. It will be much easier to manage in the long run and if there is ever the need for an additional domain, it may be easily added.

The following list summarizes the earlier bullets considering domain creation criteria, and represents the main reasons you will consider creating a new domain:

- ◆ Security
- ◆ Administration
- ◆ Replication
- ◆ Domain retention

If during the design process you feel the need to create a new domain, compare that need against this list. Chances are it will fall under one of these categories. If not, you should highly consider creating an OU to address this need. Chapter 12 provides an in-depth look at OUs.

The rest of this chapter explores each of these criteria as we design the domain structure for WayFront. Before we do so, however, we must address the special first domain: the forest root.

> **NOTE**
>
> **Political Pressure**   Political pressure has been omitted from the list this time because that's typically not something you would see in testing scenarios on a Microsoft exam.

PLANNING THE ROOT DOMAIN

You soaked up a great deal of information about creating the DNS root in the preceding chapter. The DNS root internally doesn't necessarily have to be your Active Directory root, but the criteria for creating the two are very similar. Active Directory is based on DNS. I think that is clear. DNS forms a namespace. I think that is clear as well. The Active Directory root domain integrates with DNS to create the first domain in a given forest of domain trees. Is that clear? In the best-case scenario, you should have only one Active Directory root for only one forest. Although as previously discussed, company politics, two or more groups of administrators wanting control over the schema, requirements to retain separate namespaces, or mergers and acquisitions make a good argument for the creation of additional forests or domain trees, which may require additional root domains. Before you decide to go that direction, make sure you consider the pros and cons (cons are listed earlier in this chapter).

Using a Registered DNS Namespace

Remember the options for creating DNS root (internal) domains from Chapter 10? The same concept holds true of the Active Directory root, except it does not have to fit at the top of the namespace created by DNS. For example, WayFront's registered Internet DNS domain is wayfront.com. Internally, they decided to utilize the same DNS name for simplicity. When they go to install the Active Directory on the first domain controller, they can choose to "root" it in a DNS subdomain, such as ad.wayfront.com, as illustrated in Figure 11.14.

In this case, because the internal and external DNS names are the same, there must be some distinction between what is internal and what is external. We discussed using some manual updates of DNS zone files on the inside to make external Web servers "locally" available to users. We additionally discussed the use of a proxy server with an autoconfiguration (PAC) file to determine whether the internal or external DNS servers were contacted. For more on this, refer to Chapter 10.

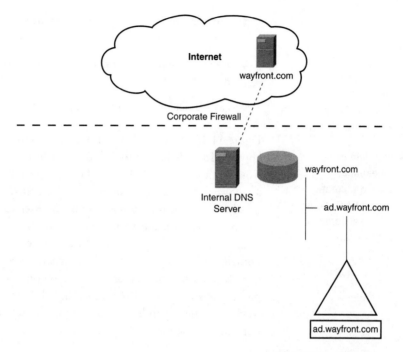

FIGURE 11.14
WayFront's decision to implement the Active Directory root domain in a DNS subdomain maintains continuity with the Internet namespace.

You could of course root your Active Directory at wayfront.com, or start your internal DNS at ad.wayfront.com, or use the .local designation, or probably a slew of other options. The important thing is that you try to keep things as simple as possible both for the administration team and for the user base.

Creating a Dedicated Root Domain

One suggestion that yields a couple of advantages throughout the enterprise is to create a dedicated root domain. Dedicated root domains do require additional hardware, but do not cost a lot to maintain. They essentially are there as a namespace placeholder, as well as to provide a couple additional advantages:

◆ Provides for "same-level" administration hierarchies across a domain tree with a contiguous namespace

◆ Provides for a true top-down administration model if one is so desired

◆ Avoids obsolescence in naming if done correctly

NOTE

Recommended Subdomain of Registered DNS Namespace
Microsoft recommends you create your Active Directory and DNS roots as a subdomain of the registered DNS namespace, such as ad. wayfront.com.

Figure 11.15 illustrates how an Active Directory for WayFront might appear with a dedicated root domain. A likely iteration of this figure would be to root the AD in a subdomain of DNS namespace, such as ad.wayfront.com. Be warned with this scenario, however: Because using a dedicated root domain means no user accounts and very few computer accounts are actually created in the domain, they must then reside in a subdomain. If ad.wayfront.com is the root, the first domain with users in it would be four levels deep, generating a UPN of johndoe@sub1.ad.wayfront.com. If you only have one forest root, you can abstract this UPN by creating a UPN suffix, such as wayfront.com. If you have multiple forests, each user would need to remember his complete UPN to log on in a forest other than his own.

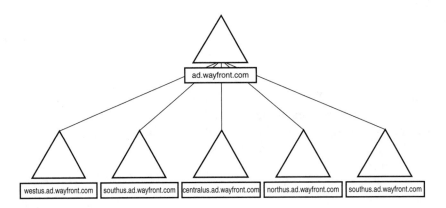

FIGURE 11.15
If your design goal is to have a single namespace that provides for multiple domain trees, you can create a dedicated, or "phantom," root Active Directory domain.

Whatever you decide, remember that the DNS and Active Directory names should represent your entire company and should conform to DNS standards in naming.

Let's start with a dedicated root domain for a single forest in the WayFront case study. Take out a clean sheet of paper and add a triangle to the very top of the page. Label this triangle **ad.wayfront.com** and put an asterisk next to it to designate it the Active Directory forest root domain.

Planning for Parent/Child Domain Relationships

Now that we have our root domain created (and presumably you created the corresponding DNS root), we need to determine how to incorporate additional domains. As stated previously, you need to weigh the pros and cons between creating new domains and creating OUs. OUs as you will recall are new to the domain language and are used to further subdivide domains for organizational as well as administrative purposes.

You should consider four main reasons in your decision to create a new domain. The first reason is administration. We know that WayFront wants to implement a decentralized administration model so that they can operate autonomously at the regional level. Because the regional offices are large and already have IT administration staff, it makes sense to split them out into another domain.

The second reason is security. As you learned in Chapter 7, Windows 2000 implements a domain-wide security policy in which settings for the Kerberos authentication protocol, password policy, and domain-wide account lockout policies are implemented. If any of the three items must differ for one reason or another between sites or even departments, you have no choice but to create another domain. This situation could arise internal to WayFront in the HR or Payroll department. These departments may have significant reason to more strictly enforce security policies due to the nature of the data they work with (for example, salaries and HR files).

EXAM TIP

Parent/Child Domains During Upgrade Scenarios Bear in mind that upgrading a Windows NT 4.0 multi-master or complete trust domain to a Windows 2000 domain often results in the creation of parent and child domains. Once the upgrade is complete, the extra domains can be consolidated into a single Windows 2000 domain or can be left in a parent-child relationship.

NOTE

Global Catalog Server Placement We'll hit the topic of global catalog server placement and replication at the end of this chapter.

NOTE

Functional First-Level Domains WayFront is actually working with second-level domains because of the "phantom" root domain. You can go ahead and treat these as first-level domains, however, because they are the first level to have users.

The third reason is to further control replication traffic. You learned that the main purpose of a site is to control replication traffic; so why create additional domains? The answer lies in just how much replication traffic your site links can handle. If you have a domain that spans multiple sites with slow (you define slow) physical links between them, those links may not be able to endure even the compressed inter-site replication traffic. This is typically a judgment call, and usually screams for that net available bandwidth assessment. As a rule of thumb, if your utilization on that WAN link is constantly above 50–75% (depending on the total throughput), create another domain. By doing this, you no longer have to replicate intra-domain information (the directory partition), you just need to replicate global catalog information. WayFront fits this equation because of those heavily used T-1 and T-3 lines.

The final reason for creating additional domains is when you need to retain an existing NT domain. Some companies will want to retain all or part of their domain design when moving to Windows 2000. They will just not want to endure a drastic restructuring and will most likely end up collapsing these domains down the road. These are cases we just have to live with if we can't talk them into a redesign. We shouldn't have this problem with WayFront because we are doing a from-scratch redesign of the network, the Windows 2000 way!

So, to get into what this section is all about, let's discuss the WayFront domain tree and forest to illustrate parent/child domain relationships.

WayFront Domain Tree

We have determined that we need at least five more domains in the WayFront organization. We determined this because we fit two of the reasons (administration and replication) for which you would typically create additional domains. So how are we going to lay these domains out? We have a dedicated root domain that we want to use as a placeholder for our namespace. This actually gives us a good opportunity to put all regional headquarters on the same domain level, level one. We can be somewhat assured that no IT administrative egos get squashed in doing this, because everyone is on equal footing. Take out your paper with the root domain on it, and draw five more triangles a couple of inches under the root domain. Do not label these domains yet, because we need to discuss how they should be named.

Microsoft recommends that first-level domains be modeled (and named) after geopolitical or continental boundaries (that is, continents or countries). Why? Domains are extremely difficult to restructure should the organization pull a major shift on you. For this reason, you should name first-level domains after something that will remain static for a long time. Because WayFront is not multinational in scope, it rules out both of these recommendations. That's okay, however. East, west, north, and south aren't going to change anytime soon. If you choose this path, however, and have future expansion plans, you may be digging yourself a hole. Consider the eastern region of the United States is east.ad.wayfront.com and a new office in London opens up. You could add it as England.ad.wayfront.com, but that would fall out of the "directional" theme you had going. Be keenly aware of situations such as this. A better convention would be to incorporate the country, such as eastus.ad.wayfront.com; that way there is no confusion where east is to the user base.

Go ahead and write in the appropriate names for the domains. From left to right, label them as follows: **westus**, **southus**, **centralus**, **northus**, and **eastus**. The centralus domain is the corporate headquarters. You can draw lines connecting the tips of the five triangles to the base of the dedicated root. When you complete the lines, your drawing should resemble Figure 11.16.

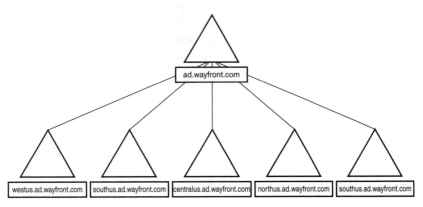

FIGURE 11.16
The WayFront domain structure.

Making the Connection

The lines you just drew represent transitive trust relationships between parent domains and their children. Transitive trusts are bidirectional in nature and are created automatically by the KCC as a domain is added to the tree (more about trusts shortly).

Completing the Tree

So we have given the WayFront organization the ability to offer decentralized administration by creating child domains. We now need to address any second- or third-level domains. The second-level domains should still be named after something relatively static, although with a more focused scope. They use the state as an example, but in many cases that is still too large in scope. In WayFront's case, the winner for a second-level domain name would probably be the city name. In reality, WayFront doesn't need another level of domains to handle the remote-branch-level sites. The utilization on the WAN lines is small, the user base is small, and we have already got each remote office split into its own site. For remote offices with IT staff, we can create an OU and delegate administrative control.

PLANNING THE USE OF TRUST RELATIONSHIPS

Trust relationships are relationships established between domains that allow users from one domain to be recognized by a domain controller in another domain. This technology of course is what enables users to access resources outside of their own domain.

Windows NT trusts were one-way manual trusts, meaning only the trusted domain users had access to the trusting domain resources. As previously discussed, the number of trust relationships it took to establish a complete trust between *n* domains was $n*(n - 1)$. These trusts had to be manually managed and were quite burdensome in large environments.

Windows 2000 trusts are bidirectional and transitive and can be summed up by the expression: *If A and B and B and C, then A and C.* In addition to the two-way and transitive (*implicit*) trusts offered automatically throughout a Windows 2000 forest, you can create one-way transitive *shortcut trusts.* You can also create the old Windows NT style one-way manual trusts for situations in which you need to authenticate across Windows NT or non-Windows operating systems, or between forests. These types of trusts have been labeled *external trusts.* All Windows 2000 trusts are listed here:

◆ **Two-way transitive trusts.** These trusts are created by the KCC when new domains are added to a forest. The goal of the transitive trust is to allow users to log on to any domain in the forest with a single user logon and password and be granted access to their appropriate resources.

◆ **Shortcut trusts.** Shortcut trusts are manually created between two adjacent Windows 2000 domains; they are either one-way or coupled with another shortcut trust to form a two-way. They are one- or two-way transitive trusts. The shortcut trust is used to provide a shorter *trust path* from one domain to another domain in the same forest but different domain tree. This new path can be given a lower cost than the automatic trust, which may require tree-walking (see Figure 11.17) to allow access to resources in the target domain more quickly.

◆ **External trusts.** External trusts are implemented in the same way as shortcut trusts, with the difference being the target domain is a domain in a different Windows 2000 domain tree. Additionally, external trusts can now be made to Kerberos realms outside the Windows 2000 operating system. A *realm* is the Kerberos equivalent of a Windows 2000 domain.

EXAM TIP

Trusts, Trusts, Trusts Know exactly what the different kinds of trusts are and when they are appropriately used. Do not be fooled by mixed mode versus native mode trust questions.

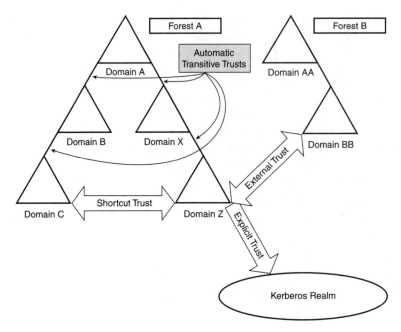

FIGURE 11.17
Sample domain structure illustrating the three
different types of trust relationships.

Shortcut Trusts

If a user in domain C needed access to a resource in domain Z, to
get there using the transitive trusts, that user's request would *walk
the tree* up through domains B, A, X, and then to Z. Although this
model is guaranteed to work for any all-connected tree within a forest, the *trust path*—that is, the direction the user has to follow to get
there—may cause latency in making the connection. To speed up
the connection, you can create a *shortcut trust* to enable that user to
go directly from her domain to the domain in which the resource
resides.

This process can be associated with Murphy's Law at the airport:
We've all been through it. You arrive at Gate A50, which is all the
way down the end of one wing of the terminal. Your connecting
flight, which leaves in 15 minutes, is at Gate B50, which you can see
right out the window across the tarmac from A50. Of course, to get

there, you have to walk all the way down and then all the way back, all the time scheming how you could make some money off creating a shortcut for yourself and others!

External Trusts

External trusts exist to give you the connectivity you need in today's heterogeneous environment. How many organizations you know of operate solely on Microsoft platforms? Although Windows NT and Windows 2000 have a lot of the market share, you rarely find an organization that doesn't have NetWare, AS/400, UNIX, Linux, or some other platform as part of its line of business. With the Kerberos authentication protocol, you can now create cross-platform trust relationships between Windows 2000 and any other platform that supports the MIT Kerberos V5 authentication protocol.

External trusts are also used to connect two Windows 2000 forests and Windows 2000 domains to Windows NT domains. These trusts are nontransitive, meaning only the domains for which they exist may utilize them. Keep in mind that these trusts are meant for backward compatibility with Windows NT as well as heterogeneous connectivity to support single sign-on. They should be used only in the situations previously described.

> NOTE
>
> **Kerberos and Single Sign-On** For more information about the Kerberos authentication protocol and Windows 2000 Single Sign-On, see the security section on Microsoft's Web site at `http://www.microsoft.com/windows2000/library/technologies/security/default.asp`.

PLACING DCS AND GCS IN THE RIGHT SPOT

Although the automatic and transitive trusts throughout the forest are all well and good, the efficiency of the network depends on the location of the domain controllers throughout the network. A location without a domain controller will be able to log on over a WAN connection and work just fine, but the lack of local authentication and search capability would likely degrade the performance to an unacceptable level.

Placing Domain Controllers

By placing a domain controller at each physical location throughout the network, users will have a local computer that can service query requests without requiring that WAN link, which is typically slower than LAN speed. Windows 2000 replication can then take over and ensure each and every domain controller is updated at the appropriate time, whether that be overnight during off-peak hours (inter-site) or based on notification and polling (intra-site).

You should adhere to the following guidelines when designing the placement of domain controllers:

◆ Domain controllers must be able to respond to a client request in an acceptable time period. This is especially important for the logon process.

◆ At least one domain controller per Windows 2000 site should be a global catalog server. The global catalog would then provide users with way to resolve queries for domain objects throughout the forest, locally.

Placing Global Catalog Servers

The requirement for global catalog servers is one per forest. By default, the first domain controller you install in the forest is automatically made a global catalog server. You may recall the implications the absence of a global catalog server presents during logon in native mode: No GC, no logon.

The following guidelines should be adhered to as you design the placement of global catalog servers:

◆ You should place at least one global catalog server in each site in each Active Directory forest.

◆ In native mode, a client must contact a global catalog server at logon to determine universal group membership. Because of the potential security breach presented by not having this information available, users cannot log on without contacting a global catalog server.

> **NOTE**
>
> **Making a DC a GC** To make a domain controller a global catalog server, open the Active Directory Sites and Services configuration utility. Expand your site name, expand Servers, expand the *<servername>* object, and right-click NTDS Settings. Select the Global Catalog check box.

◆ If you use UPNs (for example, sarcher@thearchers.com) for logon, you should place more global catalog servers in each location so that you can spread the load of UPN lookups. These lookups involve a global catalog server for direction to the user's home domain for authentication.

We'll save the WayFront DC and GC design to do as an exercise at the end of this chapter.

> **WARNING**
>
> **Capacity Requirements for Global Catalog Servers** Because global catalog servers maintain directory partitions from each and every domain within the forest, a considerable amount of disk space is required to store the collective database.

OPERATIONS MASTERS

In addition to just being a domain controller and/or a global catalog server, a given server could also act as an operations master. Operations masters, which are also known as *flexible* (or *floating*) *single-master operations* (FSMOs), are special servers designated to be the "single master" of some operation.

Active Directory is implemented as a multi-master distributed database. This model is very cool, and is quantum leaps above the old Windows NT single-master model. With progress, however, also come a few speed bumps. In this case, they are in the form of specific operations not conducive to a multi-master implementation. These operations require a single-master copy of the database to which they write. To allow these operations to take place under Windows 2000, Microsoft introduced the operations masters.

The primary reason these special network operations don't work well in a distributed environment is that they don't take well to collisions. In normal Active Directory replication, if the same attribute on the same object is modified in two different locations at the same time, a collision will likely occur. To resolve this collision, Windows 2000 examines the following in order:

◆ The version number on each object attribute

◆ The time stamps

◆ The IP address

> **NOTE**
>
> **FSMO Versus Operations Masters** The terms *FSMO* and *operations masters* are used interchangeably in just about every publication I've seen. I recall from a meeting with Microsoft that they were "changing the terminology" from FSMO to operations masters. Just be aware that "fizz-mo" is still alive and well in several publications.

This method is very good at solving collisions that are easily and logically solved.

For the handful of network operations that don't take well to collisions, an operations master server is assigned to be the single-master server for that operation, thus eliminating the chance for a collision. These single-master servers can change or offload these roles to other domain controllers in the event of shutdown or failure; hence the terms *flexible* and *floating*.

Operations Master Roles

Without further ado, the five operations master roles are listed and explained here:

- ◆ Forest-wide operations master roles
  - Domain naming master
  - Schema Master
- ◆ Domain-wide operations master roles
  - Infrastructure master
  - PDC emulator
  - RID master

As you can see, some roles are needed only on an enterprise (forest)-wide basis, and some on a per-domain basis. As each role is discussed in the following sections, you learn the "why" in terms of its scope.

Domain Naming Master

The server holding the domain naming master role controls the addition, deletion, and some of the modifications of all domains to the forest. It should be pretty obvious why this is a forest-wide operation—because a domain can be added to the forest from any point in any domain tree. The primary function on this server role is to ensure that new domain names don't conflict within their relative namespace. An additional role this server takes on is the management (adds and removes) of cross-references to domains and external directories.

EXAM TIP

Operations Master Roles
Understanding the operations master roles is not optional—this knowledge is absolutely required to successfully challenge the exam! Know also how native versus mixed mode affects them.

Schema Master

The Schema Master server is the only server from which changes to the schema can be made. We discussed briefly the risks of changing the schema, and therefore Microsoft makes it quite difficult to even get to the point where you can modify the schema. Of course, the schema is a forest-wide partition of Active Directory and is therefore grouped with the forest-wide operations master servers. This means there is only one Schema Master server throughout the forest at a given time. When changes are made to the schema, the Schema Master is responsible for replicating all the changes out to the other domain controllers.

Infrastructure Master

The infrastructure master is responsible for maintaining GUIDs, SIDs, and distinguished names of objects referenced in domains other than the one in which it resides. If a user's name is changed in the current domain, for example, the infrastructure master is responsible for ensuring that change is reflected in each group to which the user belongs. Microsoft recommends the infrastructure master not reside on a global catalog server if at all possible. If you have more than one domain, and you host the infrastructure master on a global catalog server, cross-domain references in that domain are not updated.

PDC Emulator

The PDC emulator provides support for down-level clients, such as Windows 9x clients, that need to log on to a Windows 2000 domain. It also acts as the PDC for Windows NT BDCs that may still exist in the domain and retains the master browse list. There should be no question why this is a domain-level operation; just consider a Windows NT network and the domain-level role of a PDC. After Windows 2000 has been migrated to native mode, you might think the PDC emulator goes away. In fact it does not; it maintains a critical role as the preferential domain controller to which other domain controllers in the domain replicate password changes. This way, a failed password authentication request can be passed to the PDC emulator for a "second-chance" logon. The PDC emulator is also responsible for processing account lockouts.

RID Master

Windows 2000 RID masters are responsible for allocating pools of 512 *relative identifiers* (RIDs) to each domain controller in their domain. The RIDs are used by domain controllers during the creation of a new security principle. *Security principles* are users, groups, or computers and are represented by a *security ID* (SID), which is comprised of a RID and a SID unique to the domain. By ensuring that only one server per domain allocates RID pools for all domain controllers within that domain, you ensure that all objects are identified uniquely throughout the domain. The RID master is also responsible for moving objects from one domain to another. By tasking the RID master with this role, Windows 2000 ensures the uniqueness of object SIDs throughout the forest.

PLACING THE OPERATIONS MASTERS

All the operations master roles are capable of running on a single domain controller, which is the case when a single domain controller in a single domain is brought online. Then, as domains are added to the forest, the domain-wide roles (RID master, PDC emulator, infrastructure master) are assigned to the first domain controller in each new domain. Figure 11.18 illustrates this process.

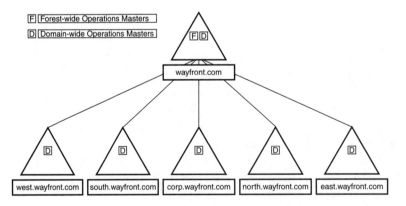

FIGURE 11.18
Who owns the operations masters roles by default?

In this figure, the wayfront.com domain was created first, so it by default gets all forest and all domain roles—because the first domain is a forest as well, right? Each subsequent domain added to the forest gets only the domain-wide operations masters roles. To get to the bottom line, therefore, each domain has three and only three domain-wide operations master roles. Each forest contains two and only two forest-wide operations master roles.

Domain-Based Role Assignment

Most organizations will design Active Directory domains with at least two, if not more domain controllers in each. When considering the operations masters roles in multi-domain controller domains, the default assignments do not take into consideration performance or fault tolerance. Microsoft recommends the following approach for addressing these situations:

◆ On a per-domain basis, select local primary and *standby* operations masters domain controllers in the event of a primary failure. The standby domain controller may be in the same site and should be a direct replication partner with the primary for faster replication convergence consistency among a large group of computers.

◆ Select an off-site standby domain controller in the event of a site-specific disaster. Ensure the connection between sites is configured for continuous replication over a persistent link.

For large enterprise environments (such as WayFront), you should plan the placement of operations master roles to match the replication topology. The following are general recommendations for the placement of operations masters:

◆ You should place both the RID master and the PDC emulator roles on the same domain controller if it is not overloaded. Otherwise, you can place the PDC emulator and RID master on separate primary operations master domain controllers, but you should ensure they both have direct connection objects to the standby PDC emulator and RID master servers.

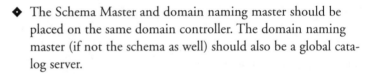

NOTE

Using Replication Monitor You can use the Active Directory Replication Monitor utility to view connection objects between domain controllers.

◆ The Schema Master and domain naming master should be placed on the same domain controller. The domain naming master (if not the schema as well) should also be a global catalog server.

◆ The domain controller hosting the Schema Master and domain naming master should be in close physical proximity to the person or team responsible for these types of updates.

◆ The infrastructure master should be placed on a domain controller that has a direct connection object with a global catalog server, but not on the same server as a GC.

Managing the Operations Masters

For you to be able to manage the operations masters roles, you must first understand how to determine which domain controllers have operations masters roles. To show you how to do so, this section discusses a couple of different methods, beginning with the Microsoft Management Console utilities. Use the MMC Active Directory Users and Computers utility (dsa.msc) to determine "who" owns the domain-specific operations masters roles. Step by Step 11.1 shows you how.

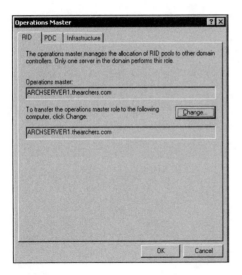

FIGURE 11.19
The domain-wide Operations Master dialog box enables administrators to navigate through the RID, PDC emulator, and infrastructure masters for the domain.

STEP BY STEP

11.1 Viewing the Domain-Specific Operations Masters Roles

1. Open the Active Directory Users and Computers MMC utility.

2. In the left pane, right-click the Active Directory Users and Computers object, and select Operations Masters.

3. A dialog box similar to that in Figure 11.19 displays, enabling you to navigate through the RID, PDC Emulator, and Infrastructure tabs.

4. Click Cancel to close the dialog.

To identify the forest-wide operations masters role holders, you must use a couple of different utilities. To view the domain naming master, follow Step by Step 11.2.

STEP BY STEP

11.2 Viewing the Domain Naming Master Role Holder

1. Open the Active Directory Domains and Trusts MMC utility.

2. In the left pane, right-click the Active Directory Domains and Trusts object, and select Operations Master.

3. A window similar to Figure 11.20 displays, illustrating the current domain naming master.

4. Click Cancel to close the dialog box.

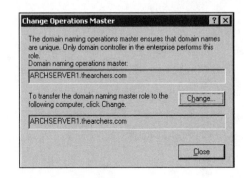

FIGURE 11.20
The Domain Naming Master dialog box illustrates the current domain naming master and enables an Administrator to change it if necessary.

Getting to the Schema Master is a bit more involved, because the Active Directory Schema MMC utility is not installed by default. To install it, run the Windows 2000 Administration Tools setup from the Add/Remove Programs Control Panel group. After you do this, you must create a custom MMC and add the Active Directory Schema snap-in. Step by Step 11.3 then shows you how to view the schema master role owner.

STEP BY STEP

11.3 Viewing the Forest-Wide Schema Master

1. Open your custom Schema Manager MMC.

2. In the left pane, right-click Active Directory Schema and select Operations Master.

3. A window similar to Figure 11.21 displays, illustrating the current Schema Master.

4. Click Cancel to close the dialog box.

FIGURE 11.21
The Schema Master dialog box illustrates the current Schema Master and enables an Administrator to change it if necessary.

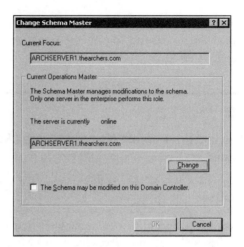

You can use some additional utilities that are a bit quicker than the aforementioned methods to determine whom the operations masters are. The first is the Active Directory Replication Monitor (replmon.exe), which is installed during the Windows 2000 Administration Tools installation. You can only view and query the role holders using this utility. Figure 11.22 illustrates the streamlined output from this utility.

Finally, you can use the NTDSUTIL utility to not only view, but *seize* and/or change the operations masters role holders.

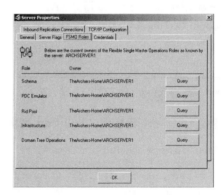

FIGURE 11.22
The FSMO Roles tab of the Replication Monitor Server Properties dialog box lists all five operations master roles.

Transferring the Operations Masters Roles

You may have noticed the Change button on Figures 11.19 through 11.21. If you want to transfer the responsibility for one or more of the operations masters roles from one domain controller to another, you initiate the process by clicking this Change button. This is the preferred way to relocate the operations master role to a new domain controller.

This process is *not* initiated automatically, so you must be very careful when shutting down servers for maintenance or for other purposes.

NOTE

Relocating Operations Masters Roles You can transfer the three domain-wide operations masters roles to any domain controller in the same domain. You can transfer the forest-wide operations masters roles to any domain controller in the forest. Make sure you pay close attention to the rules for locating operations masters before relocating them.

Implications of Losing an Operations Master

In the event of a catastrophe, you may be faced with a server that crashes and becomes damaged beyond both hard and soft repair. What if this server was responsible for one or more operations masters roles? The answer depends on which role or roles the domain controller was responsible for. Some roles are critical to the operation of the network, and some are not. You may not even know you have lost one of these roles until you perform an action that requires it.

In the event of a failure, you have the option to *seize* the role. By seizing the role, you are forcefully taking that role away from the original (presumably dead) server, and handing it off to another server.

WARNING

Think Before You Seize! You must be absolutely certain that a domain controller whose RID master, Schema Master, or PDC emulator roles have been seized never comes back online. They must be reformatted and the OS must be reinstalled otherwise.

Seizing Operations Masters Roles

Seizing operations master roles is an extreme step. It should be your last-ditch effort to reestablish these roles in the environment. If at all possible, fix the ailing domain controller so that you can bring it back online in the same capacity, with the same registry and configuration as before the problem.

To seize an operations master role, use the NTDSUTIL utility.

Table 11.3 describes briefly the impact failure of the various operations master roles has on the network.

NOTE

Usefulness of NTDSUTIL You can use the NTDSUTIL utility to perform many low-level Active Directory administration tasks. For more information, enter **NTDSUTIL ?** at the command prompt. This utility is available with Windows 2000 Professional as well as the Server line.

TABLE 11.3

Operations Master Role	Impact of Failure to Users	Impact of Failure to Administrators	What to Do with Failed Server
Schema Master	None	None until they try to modify the schema.	If seized role to standby, old server must not return to network without a fresh format and reinstall.
Domain naming master	None	None until they try to add, modify, or delete domains in the forest.	If seized role to standby, old server must not return to network without a fresh format and reinstall.
Infrastructure master	None	None unless they have recently moved a large number of objects from one domain to another.	Even if role was seized, when the original infrastructure returns to production, the role may be transferred back.
RID master	None	None until they need a reallocation of RIDs for creating domain objects.	If seized role to standby, old server must not return to network without a fresh format and reinstall.
PDC emulator	Down-level clients may not be able to log on	Windows NT BDCs will not get replicated information.	Must seize the role fast if you still have Windows NT and down-level clients on the network. Original server can be returned and given back the role without reinstallation.

MIGRATION CONCEPTS

Until now, this chapter has been highly focused on Active Directory design concepts, as dictated by the exam objectives. One thing we thought was missing was a brief focus on the actual design decisions you would certainly have to endure when considering a Windows 2000 Active Directory implementation. This final section discusses some prominent migration concepts and best practices.

Methods of Migration

You can get your Windows NT domain to the final state in two different ways (Windows 2000 Active Directory):

◆ In-place upgrade

◆ Partial or complete domain restructure (domain collapse and/or consolidation)

As you might imagine, these two options are not mutually exclusive. Some organizations choose to upgrade first and then restructure, others choose to restructure first then upgrade, and still others just upgrade their existing domain structure in place.

In-Place Upgrade

The in-place upgrade is by far the easier and less risky option of the two. To perform an in-place upgrade, you "simply" run the Active Directory Installation Wizard (DCpromo.exe) on the PDC in each domain. Because Windows 2000 by default installs in mixed mode, it can interoperate with the remaining BDCs during the upgrade process. The main benefit to this upgrade is that all users, groups, shares, and security remain intact. The biggest distinction between the in-place upgrade and a restructuring is that the in-place upgrade maintains the existing domain structure. That could be good or bad, depending on how well fit your current domain structure is to the desired Active Directory structure.

IN THE FIELD

COVER YOUR BDC!

When you perform an in-place upgrade, you need to make absolutely sure you have a back-out plan. Since you must upgrade the PDC first, you're at high risk of causing significant network problems should something go wrong with the upgrade. For this reason, it's highly recommended that before you start the upgrade process, you take a fully synchronized BDC offline by literally unplugging the network cable and turning off the machine (after a safe shutdown, of course). By doing so, you ensure that you have a good copy of your NT SAM database. If something happens during the upgrade process and you lose the PDC, you then can bring the BDC back online and promote it to be the PDC, thus restoring your original NT 4.0 network.

Additionally—and this should be automatic—make sure you have a good registry and NT system file backup before you start this sort of upgrade.

Domain Restructuring

The three common restructuring scenarios are as follows:

◆ **Post upgrade.** Most companies will follow the easier in-place upgrade path to get to Windows 2000, and then will restructure their domains as a second phase.

◆ **Restructure rather than upgrade.** If an organization considers its existing domain model implementation substandard, it may choose to do a pristine Windows 2000 implementation with a completely new domain structure using the design concepts discussed in this chapter. Typically in such a case the pristine Windows 2000 environment is rolled into production over time.

◆ **Post migration.** After an organization has been up and is running under the initial Active Directory design, it discovers whether the design was optimal. In those cases where it is not, a restructuring of the Active Directory structure might be necessary. This case is usually not considered in the initial migration, because it assumes Windows 2000 has been implemented for some time.

An organization might restructure its domains for a number of reasons, but the most overwhelming reason is to design the domain structure around features that allow the business to operate more efficiently—in other words, for reasons discussed since the beginning of this book, including the following three main reasons:

◆ **Scalability.** Windows NT domain designs must consider things such as SAM database size and administrative limitations. Active Directory enables you to design fewer, larger domains, thus reducing administration costs.

◆ **Fine-grained administration.** Windows NT does not allow for granular administration, and consequently many resource domains may have been conceived for delegation of administration. Active Directory uses OUs to further subdivide a domain, providing for more granular administration.

◆ **Simple administration.** Trusts are automatic. Delegation of administration down to the attribute level is simple and wizard driven. This allows a company to structure Active Directory easily around its business and IT administration model.

A number of implications go along with domain restructuring. These implications often drive whether organizations initially restructure their domains. The major implication by far is the fact that changing a user's account domain changes that user's SID, which affects his access to resources throughout the enterprise. For such a user to retain access to his resources, the ACLs on those resources must be updated to reflect his new SID. Microsoft recommends that all SIDs added to the ACLs on resources be group SIDs, because it is far easier to "re-ACL" a resource using a few groups than it is using many users. This process becomes less prominent when using basic move utilities to relocate security principals. During a move process, the task of relocating a security principal updates a special attribute, SIDhistory, which retains the old SID as it generates a new one.

> NOTE
>
> **SIDhistory** SIDhistory is an attribute of Active Directory security principals, and is used to store the former SIDs of moved objects, such as users, groups, and computers. SIDhistory makes it possible to delay the inevitable resource ACL updates by maintaining multiple SIDs for security principals.

You must watch out for a known situation when migrating from Windows NT 3.51. During Windows NT 3.51 authentication, a user's access token is built using only SIDs relative to the user's account domain and local groups from the domain controller where authentication is taking place. The result is that Windows NT 3.51 access tokens cannot contain universal groups from outside the user's account domain. Entries from the user's SIDhistory, or the SIDhistory of any groups of which the user is a member, will be from domains other than the user's account domain. This means they will be excluded from the user's access token, which will result in access being denied to resources that rely on SIDhistory to grant access.

Upgrade and Restructuring Decisions

As you prepare for Windows 2000 and Active Directory, you should answer some questions to determine just how to approach the process. First and foremost, you must determine whether an in-place upgrade is the right thing to do. If some or all of the following conditions are true, an upgrade is right for you:

◆ You are content with your current domain structure.

◆ Your domain structure is adequate to carry through to Windows 2000, at which time you can perform some restructuring.

◆ You think you can manage the migration without impacting your production environment.

If you do plan to upgrade, you will benefit from the following best practices:

◆ You should upgrade all account domains first to begin leveraging the benefits of Windows 2000 administration tools.

◆ You must upgrade the PDC first and then BDCs. You must follow this rule for each domain.

◆ Make sure you have a complete backup of your SAM before attempting to migrate. In some cases, taking a fully synchronized BDC offline (unplugging the NIC cable) ensures that you can recover from disaster should something go wrong.

◆ Upgrade member servers and workstations at your leisure, because they are not reliant on Windows 2000 infrastructure.

◆ If you are using LanMan Replication to replicate scripts within the domain, migrate the server hosting the export directory last (because of conflicts between the LMRepl process of Windows NT and File Replication Service of Windows 2000.

◆ Switch to native mode as soon as possible to begin leveraging the full functionality of Windows 2000. All domain controllers (both PDCs and BDCs) in the domain must be upgraded.

If some or all of the following conditions are true, you should consider restructuring:

◆ You are not satisfied with the current domain structure.

◆ Your domain structure is inadequate to carry through to Windows 2000.

◆ You think you cannot manage the migration without adversely affecting the production environment.

There are two ways to restructure your domains: after an in-place upgrade, or from the get-go. When you decide to do so really depends on how comfortable you are with the current environment. Because restructuring can become complicated, Microsoft provides a utility to help both perform and manage the migration to a new domain structure. The *Active Directory Migration Tool* (ADMT) is a utility that simplifies the process of migrating users, computers, and groups to new domains. It provides various benefits through a wizard-based interface, including pre- and post-migration reporting, robust options, and a "trial-run" mechanism.

In addition to the Microsoft ADMT, third-party ISVs will likely play a large role throughout the restructuring process. FastLane, BindView, and Mission Critical are just some of the ISVs that provide Active Directory migration utilities.

CHAPTER SUMMARY

KEY TERMS

- object
- container
- domain
- domain tree
- forest
- site
- trust
- schema
- catalog
- domain controller
- configuration container
- replication
- update sequence number
- Global catalog
- partial replica
- security group
- distribution group
- local group
- domain local group
- global group
- universal group
- Group scope
- Local Security Authority (LSA)
- Enterprise Admins
- Schema Admins

This chapter covered a lot of material regarding the Active Directory structure. It focused on the following four design elements:

◆ Domains

◆ Forests

◆ Organizational units

◆ Sites

The design of the Active Directory structure is a highly iterative process. If this book were a novel, this chapter would be the climax. Everything you have read so far in this book has been background information for the content of this chapter.

To begin the design process, you can start wherever you feel comfortable starting, whether it is with sites and the physical design, domains, and the logical design or with a combination. The underlying implicit requirement is that you have "done your homework" by collecting all the preliminary information about the current and

CHAPTER SUMMARY

future plans for the business and the technology side of the company. A requirement before starting the site planning for an enterprise is a network topology diagram. This isn't required for those one- and two-location shops.

It is a good idea to read this chapter along with Chapter 10, which serves as a foundation for Active Directory. The two complement as well as intermingle with one another. Chapter 12 covers OUs and Group Policy management in depth, and Chapter 13 covers the schema. These four chapters make up the core of this book and will no doubt be the basis for several exam questions.

This chapter covers quite a bit of additional information you should look for on the exam. Designing the placement of global catalog servers, domain controllers, and operations master servers to achieve optimum performance, fault tolerance, and manageability are concepts that *will* appear on the exam.

KEY TERMS

- operations masters
- FSMOs
- parent domain
- child domain
- transitive trust
- shortcut trust
- explicit trust
- network topology
- latency
- Knowledge Consistency Checker (KCC)
- intra-site replication
- inter-site replication
- RPC-based replication
- SMTP-based replication
- site link
- site link bridge
- Schema Master
- domain naming master
- infrastructure master
- RID master
- PDC emulator

APPLY YOUR KNOWLEDGE

Exercises

11.1 Designing the Placement of Domain Controllers

In this exercise, you design the placement of domain controllers within the WayFront enterprise. You then designate specific domain controllers as global catalog servers, as well as determine the optimal placement for operations masters.

Estimated Time: 30 minutes

1. Retrieve your latest two drawings of the WayFront enterprise, or refer to Figures 11.12 and 11.15.

2. Analyze the drawings (figures) and, if necessary, overlay the domain structure on the site layout structure so that you have everything on one page.

3. Based on the recommendations for domain controller placement, draw a square with a "DC" inside it to represent the location for each domain controller. Assume only one building in each of the regional offices contains the servers for the MAN.

4. Based on the recommendations for global catalog server placement, draw a square with a "GC" inside it adjacent to the "DC" square on which a global catalog should reside.

5. Based on the recommendations for domain naming master and Schema Master, draw circles with "DNM" and "SCH," respectively, adjacent to the domain controller(s) on which they should reside.

6. Based on the recommendations for RID master, PDC emulator, and infrastructure master placement, draw small circles with "RID," "PDC," and "INF" next to each domain controller on which they should reside.

11.2 Utilizing NTDSUTIL.EXE

In this exercise, you get familiar with the NTDSUTIL.EXE command-line utility by browsing through the Help menus. By doing this, you learn the available functions that can be performed using this utility.

Estimated Time: 10 minutes

1. Drop to a DOS window (on Server or Professional) and type **NTDSUTIL <enter>**.

2. Type **?** to bring up a list of commands.

3. Read the descriptions for each of the subcommands and navigate through them. For each subcommand, bring up its Help menu and read the available options.

4. If you haven't already, from the ntdsutil: prompt, type **authoritative restore <enter>**.

5. Notice that you receive an error stating you must boot to DOS repair mode before you can run this utility. Notice also, however, the workaround option: set SAFEMODE_OPTION=DSREPAIR. If there are problems with the Active Directory database, this utility can assist.

6. To exit the utility, type **Q** or **quit <enter>**.

APPLY YOUR KNOWLEDGE

11.3 Creating the Initial Site Structure

In this exercise, you use the Sites and Services MMC snap-in to design the initial site and subnet structure according to the physical information presented in Table 11.4.

Estimated Time: 15 minutes

> **NOTE**
> **Subnet Syntax** Subnet syntax in Table 11.4 is presented in the form of network ID/number of subnet mask bits. For example, 10.100.2.0/24 is the 10.100.2.0 network with a subnet mask of 255.255.255.0.

TABLE 11.4

AUTOOFFICE SITE AND SUBNET STRUCTURE

Site Name	Subnet(s)
Great-Lakes	10.100.2.0/24
	10.100.3.0/24
	172.16.12.0/24
Silicon-Valley	10.100.50.0/24
	10.100.51.0/24
South-Atlantic	10.100.75.0/24
South-Pacific	10.100.76.0/24
New-England	172.16.13.0/24

1. Open the Active Directory Sites and Services MMC snap-in on a domain controller by selecting it from the Administrative Tools Programs menu option.

2. Expand sites. If you have not customized your sites previously, you will have only one site, named Default-First-Site-Name.

3. Rename Default-First-Site-Name to **Great-Lakes**.

> **NOTE**
> **Sites with No DCs** During this exercise, you will be prompted to move domain controllers into sites and have each site join a site link for replication. Because you are running (presumably) with limited resources, you need not be concerned with finding DCs to move into sites. You can complete this site design exercise without doing that.

4. Create each of the additional sites by following Steps 5–7.

5. Right-click Sites and select New Site (see Figure 11.23). Type the name of the site from Table 11.4. You cannot use spaces in site names, so make sure you type the name exactly as it appears.

APPLY YOUR KNOWLEDGE

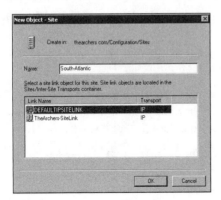

FIGURE 11.23
You not only must give the site a legal name, but also must select a site link for replication.

6. Include the site in the DEFAULTIPSITELINK site link object. This is for replication purposes and must be selected. Click OK to continue.

7. Click OK in the ensuing reminder window (see Figure 11.24). This is a good information box that reminds you of the additional items that should be completed.

FIGURE 11.24
This message box reminds you that you should add subnets to your sites, link the site to other sites, and install or move domain controllers into the site.

8. To associate one or more subnets with each site, follow Steps 9–10 for each subnet in Table 11.4.

9. Right-click Subnets and select New Subnet (see Figure 11.25). Type the IP subnet address in the Address line, and the mask reflecting the number of mask bits in the table in the mask line (**24=255.255.255.0**).

APPLY YOUR KNOWLEDGE

FIGURE 11.25
Add the subnet ID (address) and subnet mask for each sub-net, and associate it with a site.

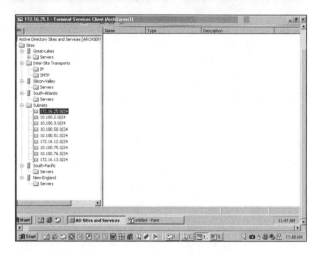

FIGURE 11.26
The Sites and Services MMC utility after all sites and subnets have been created.

10. Select a site with which to associate the subnet. Each subnet can be associated with only one site. Click OK.

11. If you by chance have a routed network, you can actually set up a subnet for each segment and then install a domain controller on each segment. The result is that domain controller objects are

automatically placed in the correct site. This is very powerful for enterprise organizations with hundreds of domain controllers.

12. When complete, your Active Directory Sites and Services MMC utility should resemble Figure 11.26.

APPLY YOUR KNOWLEDGE

Review Questions

1. Describe the purpose of operations master roles.

2. List three of the four primary reasons for creating more than one Active Directory domain.

3. Which replication protocols can be used for intra-site replication? Inter-site replication?

4. Where would you control the replication between two or more Windows 2000 sites?

5. What is the name of the Windows 2000 security group that has sweeping control over all domains in the forest? Which mode must you be in to utilize its full benefits?

6. What is the purpose of the global catalog?

7. For what reason it is recommended you have a current network topology diagram?

8. Describe the three types of trust relationships and explain where each type is used.

9. Describe three of the downfalls associated with creating multiple forests.

10. Which tool would you use to configure additional attributes to be replicated to the global catalog?

Exam Questions

1. You work for a company that has three offices across the United States. You want to design a domain structure that allows each office to act autonomously with its own administrative structure, yet still be able to manage the entire network from a central location. Your company has only one registered DNS name. How would you design this network?

A. Create three domains, domain1.com, domain2.com, and domain3.com. Let Windows 2000 manage transitive trusts between them. Each domain will have local administration. Add selected members to the Enterprise Admins group for sweeping control over the entire network.

B. Create three domains, topdomain.com, sub1.topdomain.com, and sub2.topdomain.com. Let Windows 2000 manage transitive trusts between them. Each domain will have local administration. Add selected members to the Enterprise Admins group for sweeping control over the entire network.

C. Create one domain, domain1.com. Create two OUs, Remote Office 1 and Remote Office 2, within domain1.com. Delegate administrative control to the IT group within each remote office. Add selected members to the Enterprise Admins group for sweeping control over the entire network.

D. Create three domains, domain1.com, domain2.com, and domain3.com. Create two-way trust relationships between each domain (for a total of six). Each domain's administration staff will have sweeping control over that domain only. Control administrative control over other domains through the trust relationships.

APPLY YOUR KNOWLEDGE

2. What factor greatly influenced the decision to split the WayFront regional offices into four different sites rather than one large site?

  A. The moderate to heavy utilization of the T-1 and T-3 lines that connect them.

  B. Each regional office required its own administrative hierarchy.

  C. Each office already had Internet connections.

  D. The relatively high number of users in each location.

3. How could WayFront reduce the global catalog replication latency between the tertiary sites (the regional remote offices) and the rest of the network? (Choose the best answer.)

  A. Decrease the replication frequency between the primary site and the regional offices.

  B. Decrease the replication frequency between the remote sites and the regional offices.

  C. Move the VPN connection to the central office rather than at each regional office and add the remote sites to the site link for the central and regional offices.

  D. Redo the site structure so that all offices are members of the same site. Train administrators not to make unnecessary changes that cause replication during the day.

4. Suppose you complete the implementation of Windows 2000 for WayFront as you designed in this chapter. Shortly thereafter, users from one of the east region remote offices begin to complain that entire directory searches take painfully long to return data. What might be the cause of this problem?

  A. The global catalog in that region is out of date due to the replication schedule.

  B. Users in that east region remote office are running on old computers that need to be upgraded for increased performance.

  C. There is no domain controller configured to be a RID master in that site.

  D. There is no domain controller configured to maintain a global catalog in that site.

5. You are the administrator for XYZ Corporation, which has two distinct divisions, Sales and Engineering. These divisions have the Internet registered namespaces xyzSales.com and xyzEngr.com, respectively. The internal Windows 2000 domain forest was designed as two distinct trees, ad.xyzsales.com and ad.xyzengr.com, each with domains four levels deep. A user in the michigan.midwest.us.namerica.ad.xyzsales.com domain frequently accesses resources in the california.west.us.namerica.ad.xyzengr.com domain and has requested a new computer because her application (running from the other domain) is too slow. What might you as an administrator do that may help her?

  A. Run fiber-optic cabling directly to her desktop and replace her NIC rather than the entire computer.

  B. Create a manual one-way shortcut trust relationship so that the michigan.midwest.us.namerica.ad.xyzsales.com domain is trusted by the california.west.us.namerica.ad.xyzengr.com domain.

APPLY YOUR KNOWLEDGE

C. Update the bandwidth between the two domains.

D. Update the automatic transitive trust relationships created by the Windows 2000 KCC so that a trust exists between the user's domain and the domain containing the resources she needs.

6. You are the administrator for a small company and have just completed the rollout of a simple Windows 2000 network. The network consists of one domain and five domain controllers. One of these domain controllers goes down and you remove it from your network as you wait for a part to repair it. Everything is fine for a week, and then suddenly you can no longer create any type of security principal (user, group, and so on). What is likely the cause of this problem?

A. The domain controller that went down was the infrastructure master for the domain.

B. The domain controller that went down was the RID master for the domain.

C. The domain controller that went down was the domain naming master for the domain.

D. The domain controller that went down was the Schema Master for the domain.

7. Your company's development staff has just completed work on an ERP application and now wants to roll it out to users in your Windows 2000 domain. The application is Active Directory–aware and makes use of a new object class with custom attributes. You must prepare Active Directory with this new object class. How should you proceed?

A. Logged on as a member of the Enterprise Admins group, attach to the Schema Master server and extend the schema.

B. Logged on as a Schema Admin, open the Active Directory domains and trusts and create a new object class and attributes under the domain in which the application will reside.

C. Create a domain in a new forest so that you can extend the schema for the application.

D. Logged on as a member of the Schema Admins group, attach to the Schema Master server and extend the schema via the Active Directory Schema MMC snap-in.

8. Your international company has tasked you with designing the domain structure for its Windows 2000 initiative. The company operates in three countries: the United States, Mexico, and France. Each country requires the use of its native language, character set, currency, and so on. Assuming each of the offices in each country are well-connected within the country, select the domain structure, global catalog placement, and operations master placement that will best service your company.

A. Create one domain and place domain controllers in each country. Create OUs at the country level and place objects by country in each OU. Install the Spanish and French character sets on the appropriate DCs. Place one GC per physical site in each country. Split the operations master roles among five DCs in the United States.

APPLY YOUR KNOWLEDGE

B. Create three domains: one for the United States with the English language, one for France with the French language, and one for Mexico with the Spanish language. Place one GC per physical site across the board. For each domain, place the Schema Master and domain naming master roles on the same GC domain controller in the central site. Place the RID master and PDC emulator roles on the same server in each domain, and place the infrastructure master role on a server that is a direct replication partner with a GC server.

C. Create three domains: one for the United States with the English language, one for France with the French language, and one for Mexico with the Spanish language. Place one GC in the central U.S. corporate headquarters site. For each domain, place the Schema Master and domain naming master roles on a single domain controller in the central site. Place the RID master and PDC emulator roles on the same server in each domain, and place the infrastructure master role on a server that is a direct replication partner with a GC server.

D. Create three domains: one for the United States with the English language, one for France with the French language, and one for Mexico with the Spanish language. Place one GC per physical site across the board. For each domain, place the Schema Master and domain naming master roles on a single domain controller in the central site. Place the RID master and PDC emulator roles on the same server in each domain, and place the infrastructure master role on a GC server in each domain.

9. WayFront decides to create a new division, WayBack, which is focused on providing backward compatibility and regression testing for its clients. WayFront wants WayBack to have its own registered Internet namespace, and would like the division to be treated as a separate entity, but wants to provide seamless network integration between the two divisions and wants the capability to assist in managing WayBack's network. Assuming WayFront's internal Active Directory root begins with ad.wayfront.com, how would you suggest they address the integration of the new division?

A. Create a new forest for WayBack because the network administration is much simpler when there are two separate forests. Create the top-level domain as ad.wayback.com.

B. Rename the root domain for WayFront to adwayfront.wayfront.com, and then integrate a new domain named adwayback.wayfront.com for the new division.

C. Create a new domain tree with a root name of ad.wayback.com. Make this domain tree part of the existing forest. Build the WayBack domain tree structure under ad.wayback.com and continue to build the WayFront domain structure under ad.wayfront.com.

D. Create an entirely new domain structure for the two divisions. Create two top-level domains: wayfront.com and wayback.com, and create a two-way transitive trust between them. Build each division's domain structure under the respective domains.

APPLY YOUR KNOWLEDGE

10. ManageMe Corp. has just completed a bare-bones Windows 2000 implementation. They now want to integrate a new decentralized IT administration model into the Active Directory structure. Choose the best method for approaching this task.

    A. Create new domains to reflect the structure of the IT administration model.

    B. Create new forests to reflect the structure of the IT administration model.

    C. Create new global and universal groups to reflect the structure of the IT administration model.

    D. Create new organizational units to reflect the structure of the IT administration model.

Answers to Exercises

Exercise 11.1

Figure 11.27 represents one possible solution to the exercise. The number of domain controllers per domain is not restricted, but should be at least two for primary or secondary sites and one per remote site office. The following rules are illustrated here:

1. Domain controllers should be positioned such that they can provide adequate response time for user queries and logon requests.

   At least one domain controller per physical location satisfies this requirement.

2. The domain naming master and Schema Master should be located on the same global catalog domain controller and physically located in the vicinity of the administrator with schema responsibilities.

   It makes sense to leave these operations master roles at the top of the domain tree, where no user accounts should reside (except for the schema administrator). That way, you are assured a higher level of security than if in another domain. Only one of each of these roles must exist in the forest.

3. The RID master and PDC emulator master should exist on the same domain controller in each domain.

   Be sure you remember to assign these roles to other domain controllers in the domain if you do not want them to reside on the first domain controller for that domain.

4. The infrastructure master should reside on a non-global catalog server that is a direct replication partner with a global catalog server.

   Use the Active Directory Replication Monitor to determine who a specific domain controller's replication partners are. Don't forget that the infrastructure master will not function properly if placed on a global catalog server.

5. Global catalog servers should exist in every physical site to provide quick search capability for the entire directory.

6. Where appropriate, use more than one domain controller for redundancy. Within each domain, you should have at least two domain controllers to reduce the chances of catastrophe. This is especially important at the root level of the domain tree.

APPLY YOUR KNOWLEDGE

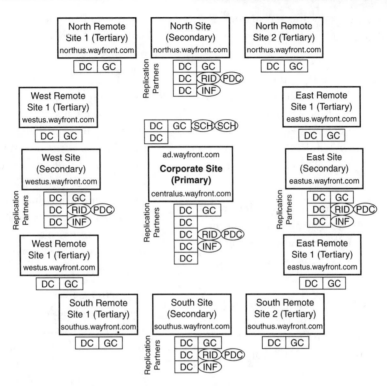

FIGURE 11.27
WayFront enterprise network with domain controller, global catalog server, and operations masters placement.

Answers to Review Questions

1. In the Windows 2000 distributed multi-master environment, certain network operations don't adapt to this model well. These are operations that require a single-master copy of the database to which they write. To allow these operations to take place under Windows 2000, Microsoft introduced the operations masters. See "Operations Masters."

2. The four main reasons for creating multiple domains are security, replication, administration, and domain retention. See "Determining the Number of Domains."

3. For intra-site replication, only RPC over IP can be used. For inter-site replication, both IP (RPC) and SMTP can be used. Remember, however, that SMTP can be used only to replicate the schema and configuration partitions. IP (RPC)

APPLY YOUR KNOWLEDGE

must be used for the domain directory partition. See "Intra-Site Replication" and "Inter-Site Replication."

4. You can configure inter-site replication properties between two or more Windows 2000 sites by changing the properties of the site link(s) between the sites. The site links enable you to control the replication schedule, the replication frequency, cost, and protocol. See "Setting Up the Site Links."

5. The Enterprise Admins group has sweeping control over the entire Active Directory when run in native mode. While in mixed mode, this group is implemented as a global group. See "Enterprise Admins."

6. Global catalog servers are tasked with storing partial replicas of all domains in the entire forest. Global catalog servers store only a subset of the attributes about each object. See "Global Catalog."

7. To visualize your site structure, you need to have a network topology diagram available. This diagram visually helps you determine where the replication boundaries should be located so that you can properly plan your site structure. See "Designing the Site Structure."

8. The three types of trust relationships are implicit (automatic) transitive trusts, shortcut trusts, and external trusts. The KCC generates the transitive trusts between a child domain and its parent. You can manually create one-way or two-way (two one-way) shortcut trusts between two domains in two distinct Windows 2000 trees to quicken access to specific resources by eliminating tree-walking. You can create external (nontransitive) trusts between Windows 2000 and Windows NT,

a domain in another Windows 2000 forest, or with any other MIT Kerberos v5–implemented realm. See "Planning the Use of Trust Relationships."

9. Aside from losing the transitive trust relationships between domains, you will also run into several other downfalls, including the following: different schemas; entire directory searches for users will not return all hits because entire directory searches search only one forest at a time; users logging on outside their "home forest" need to remember their entire UPN; and finally, you lose the ability to move accounts to domains within another forest. See "Determining the Number of Forests."

10. The Active Directory Schema utility may be used from the Schema Master domain controller by a member of the Schema Admins universal group to configure additional (or remove existing) object attributes to be replicated to global catalog servers. See "Global Catalog."

Answers to Exam Questions

1. **B.** Because each office needs to act autonomously, you should create three domains. Because there is only one Internet-registered domain name, you should create these domains with only one top-level root domain so that you can have a uniform namespace throughout the network. Administrators chosen to have the ability to manage all domains should be added to the Enterprise Admins universal group (native mode only). Answer A would work, but would present a noncontiguous namespace throughout the forest. Answer C would not allow for complete

autonomy in the decentralized administration requirements, and Answer D is something from the Windows NT 4 era. See "Rules of Domain Creation."

2. **A.** The decision to split the WayFront regional offices into their own sites weighed heavily on the *available* bandwidth between them. Because each of the T-1 and T-3 circuits were between moderate and heavy utilization, the replication traffic would have only degraded the connections. Answer B has nothing to do with the physical structure of Active Directory, Answer C does not apply to the regional sites, but does apply to the regional remote office sites. If you answered D, give yourself partial credit; the number of users at each site contributes to the heavy utilization on the WAN circuits. See "Planning a Site Structure for WayFront."

3. **C.** Using the current model, all WayFront remote sites in all regions receive global catalog replication data from the secondary sites, which receive it from the primary site (refer to Figure 11.12). Because of this, the tertiary sites may have to wait for two replication frequencies (primary to secondary, secondary to tertiary). A better configuration would be to move the VPN to the corporate office and allow the tertiary sites to replicate using the same schedule as the primary and secondary sites. Answers A and B would work, but would allow for too much replication across the already saturated bandwidth. Answer D would cause serious congestion problems and is not a good way to manage a network. See "Planning a Site Structure for WayFront."

4. **D.** For users in one domain to perform entire directory searches, they must have quick access to the entire directory. Best practice says to place a global catalog server at each physical site to provide this service. If entire directory searches are taking extraordinarily long, most likely a domain controller is not configured to maintain a global catalog local to that user. Answer A would still yield quick search results, albeit out of date. Answer B won't help, and Answer C is irrelevant because the RID master has nothing to do with entire directory searches. See "Placing Global Catalog Servers."

5. **B.** By creating a shortcut trust so that the "resource" domain (california...) trusts the "user" domain (michigan...), you enable the user to avoid having to tree-walk to the root and back down the other domain tree. Answer A may make local network communication faster, but she will still have to tree-walk to the next domain tree, Answer C is not practical because the two domains are likely not even physically connected, and Answer D is illegal; you cannot modify the autogenerated trust relationships. See "Shortcut Trusts"

6. **B.** The RID master operations master role provides pools of relative IDs to each domain controller for the domain. DCs then use these RIDs and the domain SID to create unique identifiers for domain security principles. If the RID master goes down, administrators may be unaware of this loss until the domain controllers need an additional allotment of RIDs. It is recommended that if the server hosting the RID master service will be operational again, you wait until it is back online because seizing the RID master role could cause serious implications, such as the possibility of creating duplicate RID pools. Answers A, C, and D all discuss the wrong operations master role for this problem. See "RID Master."

APPLY YOUR KNOWLEDGE

7. **D.** To make any modifications to the schema, you must (1) be a member of the Schema Admins universal group and (2) install and run the Active Directory Schema MMC snap-in focused on the Schema Master domain controller. Answer A is incorrect because the user is presumably not a member of the Schema Admins group. Answer B is incorrect because you cannot use the Active Directory Domains and Trusts utility to extend the schema. Answer C could be considered correct if there were some compelling reason to create an additional forest, but it is much more reasonable to extend the existing schema; so in this case, Answer C is incorrect. See "Schema Master."

8. **B.** Because of the international language constraints, you must create at least one domain for each language. Microsoft best practices state to place a global catalog server at each physical site. Microsoft best practices also state that the RID master and PDC emulator operations master roles should reside on the same domain controller, one per domain. The domain naming master and the Schema Master should go on a single global catalog server in the corporate site in close proximity to the administrator in charge of the schema. Finally, the infrastructure master role should be placed on a domain controller in each domain that is a direct replication partner with a global catalog server. Answer A is incorrect because of the number of domains required. Answer C is incorrect because of the number of global catalog servers. Answer D is incorrect because the infrastructure master will not function properly if placed on a global catalog server. See "Rules of Domain Creation," "Placing Global Catalog Servers," and "Placing the Operations Masters."

9. **C.** The recommended method of designing Active Directory to preserve synergy between the internal namespace and the Internet namespace is to create either separate forests or separate domain trees. Because a requirement of seamless network integration is required, the creation of an additional domain tree within the same forest is preferred. Answer A is incorrect because it is a flat-out lie; the more forests to administer, the more complexity needed. Answer B is incorrect because of the implications involved with renaming domains. Answer D is incorrect because it is not practical to start completely from scratch. See "Planning for Parent/Child Domain Relationships."

10. **D.** The design goal for organizational units was to provide a means of partitioning domains into manageable units so that administrative control could be delegated if needed. Answer A reflects the old way of accomplishing this task and is therefore incorrect. Answer B is way off; you should have only one forest for optimum efficiency. Answer C may come into play down the road, but is not correct in this case because you cannot use groups to accurately define your IT administration model. See "Integration of Organizational Units."

Suggested Readings and Resources

1. Iseminger, David. *Active Directory Services for Microsoft Windows 2000 Technical Reference.* Microsoft Press, 2000.

2. Nielsen, Morten Strunge. *Windows 2000 Server Architecture and Planning.* Coriolis, 1999.

3. TechNet articles

   - "Active Directory Migration Tool Overview."
   - "Flexible Single-Master Operation Transfer and Seizure Process."
   - "How to Find FSMO Role Holders."
   - "FSMO Placement and Optimization on Windows 2000 Domain Controllers."
   - "Active Directory Architecture."
   - "Designing the Active Directory Structure."

4. White papers

   - "Active Directory Site and Services Manager."
   - "Active Directory Technical Summary."
   - "Planning Migration from Windows NT to Windows 2000."

5. Web sites

   - Mission Critical Software. "Windows 2000 Migration Solutions." `http://www.missioncritical.com/Solutions/solMigration.htm`.
   - FastLane Technologies. "Windows 2000 Migration Solutions." `http://www.fastlane.com/products`.
   - BindView. "Windows 2000 Migration Solutions." `http://www.bindview.com/solutions/migration/index.html`.

This chapter covers the following Microsoft-specified objectives for the Designing a Microsoft Windows 2000 Directory Services Infrastructure exam:

Design and plan the structure of organizational units (OU). Considerations include administration control, existing resource domains, administrative policy, and geographic and company structure.

- **Develop an OU delegation plan.**

- **Plan Group Policy object management.**

- **Plan policy management for client computers.**

▶ An integral part of designing an Active Directory Services infrastructure is the design and use of organizational units. OUs were designed to be flexible enough to allow organizations to mold them to specific structures, such as IT administration, organizational structures, or even to take the place of existing resource domains. Additionally, OUs are an integral part of the management of client computers through Group Policy.

CHAPTER 12

Designing an OU and Group Policy Management Structure

OUTLINE

▶ Don't concern yourself so much with the gory details and the internal technical workings of OUs and GPOs. You need to focus on the big picture—the design of each of these structures for different organizations. Before you take the exam, consider a few companies you know well and design a hypothetical OU and GPO strategy for them. Go as far as to interview a few key people about how they run the network and divvy up administrative tasks.

▶ Make sure you do the exercises at the end of this chapter. They do a good job of walking you through different delegation strategies.

▶ In your test environment, create multiple GPOs that cause something different and visible to happen, such as removing the Run menu option or changing the background. Apply these at different levels of the SDOU hierarchy. Turn on and off blocking and no override and see how that affects users within the hierarchy. Look at the security properties of the GPOs and modify the ACL and see how that affects its application.

▶ Soak up as much additional information about OU and GPO design strategies as possible. The outside resources suggested at the end of this chapter will give you a good starting point for additional information. The Microsoft TechNet Web site is full of additional readings, as is the Windows 2000 Web site. This is one of the core chapters for the exam, so spend quite a bit of additional time here making sure you understand the concepts.

INTRODUCTION

As we discussed previously, a well-known shortcoming of Windows NT was its inability to grant specific levels of administrative control to non-administrators. For example, large organizations that outsource specific areas of IT find themselves in a dilemma when deciding how to allow that outsourced company enough administrative power to perform their service, and still maintain control over the network. With Windows NT, the choices were to add the outsourced company employees to the Domain Admins group, or do the work for them. Neither accomplished the business goals.

The *organizational unit* (OU) in Windows 2000 not only fixes that problem, but also provides a method of partitioning the domain namespace into a manageable hierarchy of users, computers, groups, shares, printers, and other objects. With such a functional hierarchy, companies now have a structure through which they can delegate a very granular form of administration to a security principle. For example, an administrator can grant Joe Smith—a regular user—the ability only to create new UserID's in a specific OU.

This chapter focuses on the planning and design of the organizational unit structure. We'll highlight the flexibility of OU design by discussing the various OU models, by geographic location, company structure, and operational structure. OUs are primarily used to delegate administrative control, so we'll spend some time discussing how to develop an OU delegation plan. Finally, since Group Policy objects are typically associated with OUs in an organization, we'll discuss some aspects of Group Policy management.

ORGANIZATIONAL UNITS

Design and plan the structure of organizational units (OU). Considerations include administration control, existing resource domains, administrative policy, and geographic and company structure.

After you have your domain structure designed, you must consider how to implement the OU structure. OUs are container objects in a domain that can hold other container objects or leaf objects, such as users, groups, and printers. There are several benefits in using OUs, such as the ability to organize directory objects, delegation of administrative authority, and anchoring Group Policy objects. We will discuss each of these benefits, as well as additional planning, design, and management features associated with OUs, throughout this chapter.

Because of the granularity of Windows 2000 security, administrative control can be granted on a per-user, per-object, per-attribute basis. Using a combination of OUs and Access Control Lists (ACLs), you can create an environment that mirrors the way the network is administered. To go even further, you can now extend the administrative control outside the boundary of the domain administrator, allowing the core IT administration team to focus on strategy and network health rather than resetting passwords.

There are several important OU-related facts you must understand before you begin to organize your OU structure:

◆ **OUs are *not* security principals.** You cannot treat OUs like security principals and try to base access control off of them. NetWare folks: This is drastically different from NDS OUs! In Windows 2000, access control is the job of *Security Groups*, such as Domain Local, Global, and Universal groups.

◆ **Users do *not* navigate the OU structure.** The structure of OUs will be transparent to users. You should create the OU structure with administration in mind—not users.

◆ **OUs have less effect on performance than Group Policy.** There is very little processing overhead related to nested OU structures. Microsoft does, however, recommend that you not exceed 12–15 OUs levels in your hierarchy. If you find you need more than that, rethink your design!

NOTE

Physical Limitations on OUs
Microsoft suggests your OU hierarchy not go deeper than 12–15 levels; however, there is no true limitation to its depth.

◆ **GPOs attached to OUs may degrade performance.** If you find degrading performance, check the number of GPOs you have within your OU structure; they require much more processing overhead than do OUs.

◆ **DNS namespace does not reveal your OUs.** OUs are not used to partition the DNS namespace, and therefore are not exposed to the DNS community. OUs can be addressed only by one of the query methods for the directory: ADSI, LDAP, or MAPI.

◆ **OUs cannot span domains.** OUs are contained entirely within one domain and cannot contain objects from other domains.

The following sections focus on planning the OU structure for an organization.

Plan Your OU Strategy

To effectively plan an OU structure, you must examine the company's organizational structure and its administrative model. You might recall that this sounds very similar to the elements you considered with domain design. It is. The difference lies with the rules you followed with domain design—mainly, if you didn't have a reason to create a domain, you likely have a reason to create an OU. Remember also that OUs are created within each domain, so even if you did have a reason to create a domain, you may still have a reason to create additional partitions within its structure.

The following list highlights some of the reasons you'll likely create OUs:

◆ To delegate administrative control

◆ To group like objects

◆ To control the application of group policies

◆ To replace existing Windows NT resource domains

◆ To create an administrative hierarchy of OUs

◆ To simplify the administration of resources

All of these are valid reasons for creating OUs; however, the four highlighted in the following sections represent the best reasons.

Delegation of Administration

In Windows NT, to delegate administrative tasks you likely created resource domains. To do the same thing in Windows 2000, you simply create an OU and delegate specific (*granular*) administrative tasks within that OU. You group users, groups, printers, shares, and so on together so a single administrator may control them. By creating a tree of OUs within your organization and delegating the administrative control for parts of it, you can delegate authority even down to the average end-user level.

The scope of delegated administration is very flexible. Generally speaking, though, you can delegate permission to do the following:

- ◆ Reset passwords only.

- ◆ Create and delete child objects—users, groups, printers, and so on.

- ◆ Change attributes on a particular object, such as the first and last name on a user.

Of course, you can delegate many more tasks, but these are the most common.

Application of Policies

Because Group Policy objects can be assigned at the site, domain, and OU levels, users or other directory objects that have like policies can be organized into OUs. Group policies allow you to do the following:

- ◆ Control security options.

- ◆ Assign or publish software.

- ◆ Assign logon/logoff (user) and startup/shutdown (computer) scripts.

As you work with the IT administrative structure within the organization, Group Policy must be considered and probably should be considered close to the top of the list. The fact that software can be distributed via these GPOs to the OUs to which the GPOs are attached can significantly reduce the management and administration of software standards throughout the organization.

Grouping of Objects with Like Properties

OUs are very good for controlling how objects in the directory partition are organized. A good example is with printers. To give users an easy way to find printers, you could create a domain-wide Printers OU. Because the OU itself contains an ACL to control access to it and its objects, you can control which users see the contents of a particular OU when they perform searches. So for example, it is possible to control which users can view specific types of printers (such as color printers) through OU nesting and permissions.

> **NOTE**
>
> **Permissions and Rights** A design decision made by Microsoft confuses a lot of people, especially professionals moving from the NetWare and NDS world. OUs cannot be used to administer rights to objects. Conversely, they can be used to control access to their contents during queries.

Replacement of Existing Resource Domains

The use of resource domains to delegate administrative authority within a Windows NT network was an expensive but necessary evil. Because that is no longer a necessity, companies moving to Windows 2000 need to determine what to do with existing resource domains. One (not-so-trivial) option is to collapse resource domains into OUs. Although this task is not easy and may require the assistance of a Microsoft or third-party migration utility, the end result is at least one fewer domain to manage, which means fewer trusts to manage, which means more sleep for administrators!

Understanding the Impact of Change

You should understand a couple of things before you begin the OU structure. First, because objects within an OU structure are configured by default to inherit Access Control Entries (ACEs, the specific security entries that make up an ACL) from their parent object, moving an object from one OU to another may cause changes to the ACL of the object and result in certain accessibility issues. Second, since GPOs are assigned at the OU level and apply by default to every object within that OU, moving an object from one to another may change the group policies applied to it and therefore cause security problems and other unexpected changes.

> **NOTE**
>
> **ACEs and ACLs** Access Control Lists (ACLs) are structures attached to objects to control access to them. They consist of Access Control Entries (ACEs), which are the individual users or groups permitted access to that object and the associated permissions. Both ACEs and ACLs will be covered throughout this chapter.

It is recommended that you examine both the inherited ACEs and GPOs associated with each OU before you attempt to move objects between them.

General OU Guidelines

Keep in mind that as with everything else with Windows 2000, there are several useful ways to create your OU structure. Because of this, we are going to stick with the general guidelines and let you fill in the specifics based on any given situation.

To build a meaningful OU structure, you must consider the current domain structure of the organization and how the IT group is structured within the domains. These very high-level guidelines set the stage for more specific guidelines, as included in the following sections.

Nesting and Naming

As mentioned previously, your OU structure can be as deeply nested as you see fit—there are no physical limitations on this. However, realistically the structure should not exceed 15 levels, and LDAP queries begin to degrade at a depth of five levels. If you find your OU structure is consistently exceeding these soft boundaries, you need to reconsider your domain structure and take another look at the administrative structure of the organization.

You should name OUs with descriptive names that reflect the structure that they represent. For example, if in the domain eastus.wayfront.com the WayFront organization has Sales, Services, and Administration departments, they might form their OU structure according to those departments, and name them Sales, Services, and Administration. These names are relatively static, which is the key to naming OUs. OUs that represent structures within the organization that are likely to change—such as OUs for special projects—become an issue when a particular project comes to an end and you are faced with deleting the OU and restructuring its objects.

To make a long story short, model OUs after something that is not likely to change. The following two sections illustrate how and where to discover these areas of business.

Organizational Structure

The way the company is organized represents its organizational structure. If you've seen an organizational chart for the company, you've gained insight as to how the company is organized and how it operates within its geographic scope. Remember the previous chapters on this stuff?

It is best to begin with the organizational chart because it typically defines the functional divisions of the company and says something about how its employees work. Figure 12.1 illustrates a hypothetical organizational chart for a WayFront domain.

Depending on the administrative requirements within each of these functional areas, they may be represented by one or more OUs each.

Administrative Structure

There are three types of administrative models within an IT organization: centralized, decentralized, and hybrid. We discussed each of these models at length previously in this book. This is where you need them. Within each division (or region or branch or other unit)

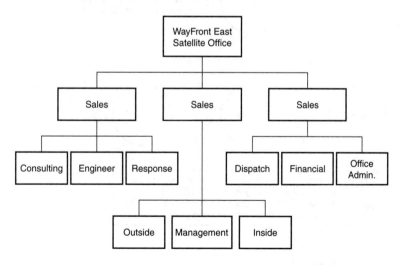

FIGURE 12.1
The eastern remote office high-level organizational chart.

of a company, IT resources must be managed in some way, shape, or form. In the case of WayFront, the remote satellite offices are managed by their corresponding regional office. Close scrutiny of the administration model for this office will help you understand how the OUs need to be structured. Keep in mind that you not only must consider how resources are managed, but also need to consider Group Policy.

In this case, the east region headquarters IT staff manages all of the remote satellite office resources from the east region headquarters. They do, however, grant delegation of control to specific users and allow them to do password resets for all users in the site. Based on this model, they could use the OU structure illustrated in Figure 12.2.

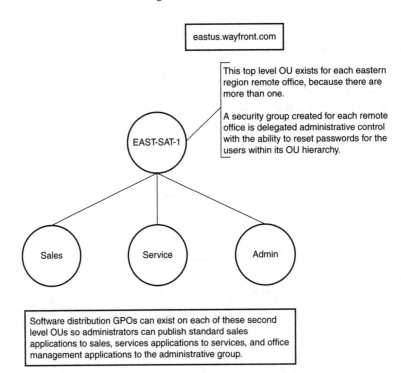

FIGURE 12.2
The east satellite office OU structure within the
`eastus.wayfront.com` domain.

Figure 12.2 points out the most significant influences to its design, which are the following:

◆ Overall administrative control resides with the IT administrative group at the east region headquarters.

◆ Specific applications for each functional group need to be published via Group Policy.

◆ A special group of users is delegated the administrative ability to reset passwords for the entire remote office.

FLEXIBILITY IN OU DESIGN

By creating an OU hierarchy within domains within domain trees within a forest, you really have a ton of flexibility and are able to closely mirror the organizational and administrative structure of a company. By using OUs rather than domains where possible, you are also able to eliminate a lot of the complexity associated with managing multiple domains.

Because Windows 2000 and Active Directory remove the 40MB SAM database limitation, organizations that introduced additional resource domains can now be implemented as a single domain with geopolitical boundaries—such as continents, countries, regions, states, and cities—set up as OUs. Appropriate administrative control can then be handed back to appropriate individuals or groups as a delegation. You must consider the rules for creating a domain before you decide you want to use exclusively OUs.

Reasons for Creating Domains and OUs

Reasons for Creating Domains	Reasons for Creating OUs
You need to isolate or balance replication traffic.	To delegate administrative control
You need to define and implement different domain-wide security policies.	To group like objects together
Existing NT domain structures must be retained.	To control the application of group policies
You need to support decentralized administration and OUs will not suffice.	To replace existing Windows NT resource domains
You need to support international differences.	To create an administrative hierarchy of OUs
Company politics dictate the need for additional domains.	To simplify the administration of resources

The following sections expand upon the flexibility of Windows 2000 OUs.

Organize by Geography

Any company—large and geographically dispersed, or small and centralized—can choose to implement a single Windows 2000 domain. Large companies that may have a presence across the United States can partition that domain using OUs based on geographic location. A company that fits this model is Components Galore, Inc. (CGI), a national company with offices in several cities in several states. Figure 12.3 illustrates just one way CGI could implement OUs.

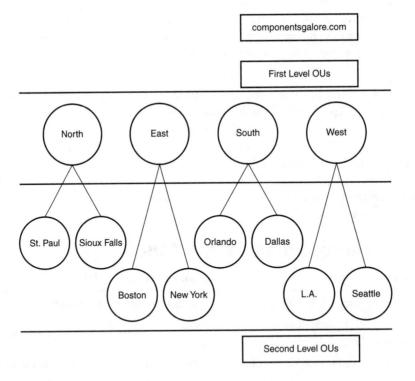

FIGURE 12.3

Components Galore designed its first- and second-level OU structure according to geographic location.

Using this model, CGI can simply add a second-level OU when a new office is opened up in a specific region. The first-level OUs can be used to assign regional group policies or even delegate control over an entire region. They may also be used for nothing but a placeholder in the hierarchy.

Keep in mind that this model can be used for multinational models as well. However, there often is a difference in preferred languages to contend with from one country to the next. When this situation arises, you must create additional domains because (as discussed in Chapter 11, "Designing the Active Directory Structure") character sets, currency, and so on, are focused at the domain level.

Geographic-Based OU Structure Advantages

Countries, cities, states, regions, and other geographic disciplines tend not to move or change, so your first-level OUs remain static. This is one of the general recommendations in developing the OU structure. Another advantage is the fact that administrators have a good idea where an OU's objects are physically located if they are broken down by location. This is important now and again when a physical computer may need to be located or a user calls in with a question.

Geographic-Based OU Structure Disadvantages

Sometimes the geography of a company doesn't match the organizational diagram and therefore may be difficult for administrators and users to comprehend. In this case, what typically ends up happening is confusion concerning to which business function a user, printer, or other resource actually belongs.

Organize by Function or Department

Some companies are organized more by business function or department. In cases like this, the OU structure should be focused on these areas more than on geographic boundaries. Such a company typically categorizes its business as functional practices or divisions, and each of these practices or divisions likely has one or more subcomponents, typically in the form of departments. eMagic operates in this fashion, and organizes its single-domain OU structure as in Figure 12.4.

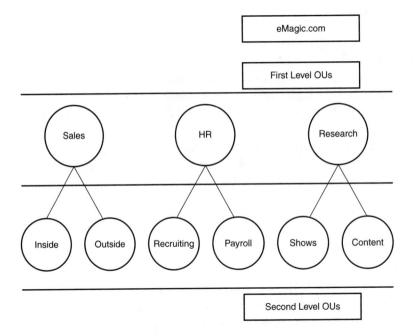

FIGURE 12.4
The eMagic company organizes itself by functional practice. Each functional practice has one or more subpractices.

eMagic can expand its business by adding more functional practice areas and by adding departments or subpractices within each of these practice areas.

Function- or Department-Based OU Structure Advantages

Well-established business functions typically do not change, so the first-level OU structure should remain static.

Function- or Department-Based OU Structure Disadvantages

Administrators may have difficulty identifying where an object within an OU is physically located. Also, for businesses that change frequently to stay atop their market, this structure may do more harm than good. This is probably not a good model for companies in the technology industry!

Organize by Administration

Many companies will use the first two levels of the OU structure to reflect the IT administration model itself. For example, a company that uses decentralized IT administration throughout the country might structure its OU model to reflect the IT hierarchy, as in Figure 12.5.

You may have noticed in Figure 12.5 that SpeedThought uses an IT model that is focused on specific departments—in this case, Sales and Services. Under the second-level OUs then could be further divisions within each department that break out of the IT administration model. For example, the IT Sales OU could be further divided into Outside Sales and Inside Sales, and the IT Services OU could be further divided into Professional Services and Technical Services.

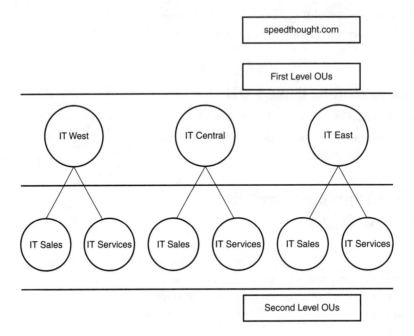

FIGURE 12.5
The SpeedThought organization uses the first-
and second-level OUs to reflect its IT administrative hierarchy throughout the company.

IT Administration-Based OU Structure Advantages

This model is by far the best for IT (and OU) administrators because it is tailored to the way they run the network. OU administrators can easily identify where resources are administered from, and the delegation of administrative control is a cinch.

IT Administration-Based OU Structure Disadvantages

Administrative delegation outside the IT department becomes a bit more challenging in this model. Because users are grouped according to how IT manages them, they may not be adequately organized for Group Policy assignments.

Organize by Business Unit

Some of the larger corporations organize by cost centers, which typically represent separate business units. The OU structure is flexible enough to accommodate this model as well. The giant MG Motor Corporation (MGMC) is just such a company. They have literally hundreds of business units to accommodate several different lines of business in the auto market. Their OU structure (scaled down for this illustration) might resemble Figure 12.6.

Business Unit-Based OU Structure Advantages

This model would work well in a conglomerate where each business unit is treated separately from the rest of the organization.

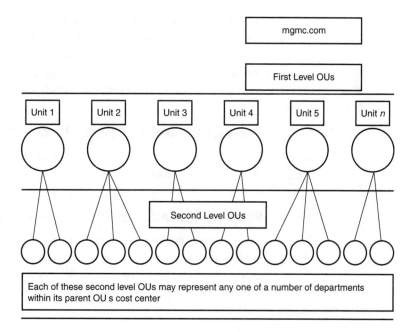

FIGURE 12.6

The MG Motor Company operates under several business units—each with its own "bottom line."

Business Unit-Based OU Structure Disadvantages

There are more disadvantages to using this model, even if each business unit is managed autonomously. Administrators run into the same issues as with other models, such as not knowing where resources physically reside. There is also a good chance that users from different departments or different functional units may be grouped into one OU but require different software or have different desktop restrictions that make Group Policy assignment complex. Finally, the names of business units often change in today's business environment.

Organize by Project

Similar to the cost center model represented as a business unit model, organizations whose business revolves around project-based work, such as a building contractor or a consulting company, may choose to structure their OUs accordingly. Figure 12.7 represents the NewStrategy Consulting Company, which uses this OU approach.

Project-Based OU Structure Advantages

The only advantage to organizing by project is the logical grouping of resources per project.

Project-Based OU Structure Disadvantages

Using project-based OU structures breaks a major recommendation in OU design—that OUs should remain relatively static. The definition of a project states that it has a definite start and end time. What happens to the resources when a project ends? They must be reassigned to other OUs. What happens if a consultant is part of many projects at the same time? Just about all the other disadvantages related to OU structures apply here as well, such as administrators having no idea where geographically or departmentally a resource exists. To make a long story short, don't use project-based OUs at the top level. They can be used as a lower-level structure if the company is organized in such a way, but keep in mind that they will require a lot of administration.

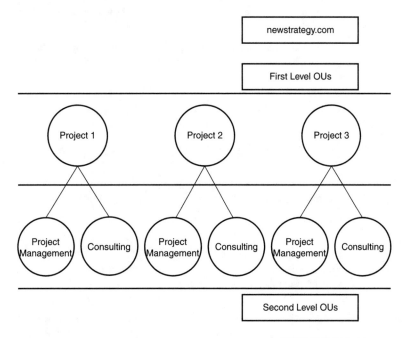

FIGURE 12.7
NewStrategy is a consulting firm whose business revolves around project-based work.

R E V I E W   B R E A K

REVIEW OF POPULAR OU DESIGN OPTIONS

Design Option	Advantages	Disadvantages
Organize by geography	Your first-level OUs remain static, which is a best practice in OU design. Also, administrators have a good idea where an OU's objects are physically located.	If the geography of a company doesn't match the way an organization is managed, it may be difficult to comprehend. This may cause confusion about to which business unit or function a user or object actually belongs.
Organize by function or department	Well-established business functions typically do not change, so the first-level OU structure should remain static.	Administrators may have difficulty identifying where an object within an OU is physically located.
		For businesses that change frequently to stay atop their market, this structure may do more harm than good.
Organize by administration	Tailored to the way administrators run the network.	Administrative delegation outside the IT department becomes a bit more challenging in this model.
	OU administrators can easily identify where resources are administered from.	Users may not be adequately organized for Group Policy assignments.
	Provides for easy delegation of administrative control.	
Organize by business unit	This model would work well in a conglomerate where each business unit is treated separately from the rest of the organization.	Administrators may have difficulty determining where resources physically reside.
		Users from different departments or different functional units may be grouped into one OU but require different software or have different desktop restrictions that make Group Policy assignment complex.
		The names of business units often change.
Organize by project	The only advantage to organizing by project is the logical grouping of resources per project.	Project-based OUs are *not* relatively static.
		Project resources are typically a part of many projects at once, which would be structurally impossible to reproduce with OUs.
		Just about all the other disadvantages related to OU structures apply here as well.

Use the Plan

The best approach you can take at planning the OU structure is to determine exactly how the company runs its business through the administrative eyes of IT. You will most likely create a hybrid of two or more of these models according to the company. Look at the organizational chart. Is there a separate chart for each location? If so you may consider using geographic locations for the top level or two. The most important thing to remember, though, is that the OU structure should be developed according to how the company administers and delegates control of IT resources within the operational and organizational structures. Don't just start creating OUs. You must sit down with the IT administrative staff and plan it out. What is the administrative model? How many locations are there? What are the core business units? Do they exist at each location? Is there IT staff at each location? In each region? These questions and more like them are the ones you need to answer during the planning process.

Don't forget about the Group Policy thing either. If you plan to use Group Policy to distribute software or lock down user workstations, you must consider how you plan to do that through the OU structure.

The OU structuring options we discussed in this section are popular options for beginning the overall OU design, but are not exhaustive by a long shot. Again, the flexibility is tremendous, which gives you the ability to mold the OU structure as tightly as you want around the business and IT administration model of the company.

IN THE FIELD

OU DESIGN USES A COMBINATION OF THE SUGGESTED MODELS

We've discussed several possible OU design models, including geographic based, administrative based, and business unit based. We've discussed the advantages and disadvantages of each. But what if your organization would benefit from more than one model? The truth of the matter is that when you set out to design the OU structure, if you *don't* use a combination of two or more models, you probably are not doing justice to the OU design.

continues

continued

In many companies, the logical breakdown of administration is first divided by geographic boundaries, then divided by department or business unit. In almost all cases, your first-level OUs will resemble some physical element of the company, whether at a high level—such as a continent name—or a bit lower, such as a city or state name. It all depends on your domain structure. Your second-level OUs then begin to drill into functional areas of the business, such as business units or departments. From about the third level on, you focus on administrative delegation, desktop control, and software distribution. This is where the design becomes critical because it begins to affect the user population.

DESIGNING AN OU STRUCTURE

You create an OU structure to do a lot of things: organize objects with like requirements, apply group policies, delegate administrative control, logically structure the directory to reflect the organization, and so on. Deciding what OUs to create, how to create them, and what you should associate with each OU itself can be a daunting and time-consuming task. The following sections discuss the OU itself and what you should include in your design specifications to ensure a smooth implementation.

OU Associations

By the time you sit down to actually design the OU structure, you should have a high-level plan in your head. You should have the company IT administrative organizational chart in hand, along with other organizational charts for each division or segment of the company. For each OU you create, you must be able to answer the following three questions:

◆ Why are you creating the OU?

◆ Who will perform administration on the OU?

◆ What permissions will the OU administrator require?

The following sections explain why these questions are important.

Why Are You Creating the OU?

You must have a good reason for creating the OU. Remember, OUs at the first few levels should remain relatively static. If someone asks you why you are creating a specific OU at a specific level, you should be able to explain, right? For example, you create an OU named Midwest Region at the top level. Chances are you created this OU as a placeholder for the second and third (and deeper) levels of OUs to create a logical structure. You probably didn't create it to delegate administration or distribute software to specific sales employees.

Who Will Manage the OU?

Each OU should have a manager associated with it. The OU configuration window contains a Managed By tab on which you can select an administrator from the directory to be "in charge" of that OU. As you (presumably the domain administrator) delegate the administration of the OU structure throughout the domain, you must determine what level of access the OU managers will have over that OU. The OU manager is responsible for performing the following OU-level tasks:

◆ Performing additions, deletions, and modifications to all objects within the OU

◆ Determining whether OU permissions should be inherited from parent OUs

◆ Determining whether OU permissions should be propagated to next-level OUs

◆ Delegating next-level OU authority to other administrators

The domain administrator can always take ownership of any OU in the domain.

What Permissions Will the OU Manager Require?

Each OU manager must have a certain level of control over that OU. When you delegate the administration to the next-level administrator, you control the level of administrative power he or she has over that OU. You do this by using the Delegation of Control

Wizard to modify the ACL on the target OU. This process is handled by granting a user or group permissions for the OU. You cannot grant another user OU permissions because the OU is not a security principal.

Keep in mind that whatever permissions you grant the OU administrator apply for all objects within that OU and will also apply for any additional OUs produced under that one.

You must consider delegating to OU administrators the ability to perform the following tasks:

◆ Create, delete, and manage user accounts

◆ Reset passwords on user accounts

◆ Read all user information

◆ Create, delete, and manage groups

◆ Modify the membership of a group

◆ Manage Group Policy links

◆ A plethora of custom, granular, single-task options, such as adding users to the OU

It is important that you understand here that delegation, although a powerful concept, can turn around and bite you. Be careful that too much delegated authority doesn't wind up in the wrong hands.

CREATING THE OU HIERARCHY

The following sections discuss the OU hierarchy and specifically what should exist at each level. Some of this may be a bit repetitive from the previous sections, but repetition of this kind of information can do you nothing but good!

First-Level OUs

Let's start from the very top. In an international company, the first-level OUs will likely end up as continent names. If you follow best practices, however, these divisions of the namespace should be handled by domains. Domains, as you should recall, should be used when multinational character sets or languages need to be implemented. Also, domains are a security and replication boundary, and networks between countries are usually not fast enough to sustain intra-domain replication.

Whether your first-level partitioning is a domain or an OU, the same primary rule still applies—that is, the name should be static and stable. This means it should not change and should be able to withstand a company reorganization.

It is also important that you keep in mind that first-level OUs do not have to represent the physical geography of the company. For example, if a company has two locations, one in Indiana and one in Washington, but the administration for both is done from Indiana, there is no need to create separate OUs. This will be a very difficult concept to grasp because your first instinct is to separate by physical geography. Remember, the OU structure is there for you to model the administrative structure of the organization. If you want to use geographic-based OUs, you can certainly do so; just keep in mind the purpose of OUs.

Second-Level OUs

In a large company, the second-level OUs often end up being countries if that company operates internationally, or cities if that company operates in one country only.

Of course, each of the second-layer OUs must be a child of a first-layer parent, as you saw in some of the previous figures. One additional thing about second-layer OUs when using the country as a name: It is recommended that you use the ISO 3166 standard two-character country code to name the OU. This is just a recommendation, not a requirement.

If you choose to integrate individual U.S. states at this level (because most states are as large as some foreign countries), you should follow the U.S. Postal Code two-character format because individual states are not represented in ISO 3166. If you do this, be keenly aware of potential ISO 3166 / U.S. Postal Code conflicts, such as Canada and California (CA), Columbia and Colorado (CO), Albania and Alabama (AL), and so on.

> **NOTE**
>
> **Why Not States for Second-Level OUs?**   States aren't prohibited from being used at the second level, of course—it just works out most often that states are not used at this level. For a multinational company, often the first layer OU ends up being the continent and the second layer the country. In a national company, often the first layer OU ends up being the state or region, and the second layer the city.

> **NOTE**
>
> **ISO 3166 Country Codes**   For more information and a complete listing of the ISO 3166 country codes, please visit **http://www.din.de/ gremien/nas/nabd/iso3166ma/ codlstp1.html**.

Remaining-Level OUs

It is likely that you won't place any or many resources in the first two levels of OUs because you'll want to drill down a few more layers to integrate the business model. The remaining levels of OUs should be defined according to the company model within the second-level OU. For example, an international company whose first-level OU is based on continent and second-level OU is based on country may look like Figure 12.8. TrainingKit Incorporated is a multinational company with decentralized IT administration. Within each region, TrainingKit operates in a centralized administration model and uses Group Policies to publish software for each department. They have a need to allow departmental administrators the ability to reset passwords for that department's users only. The subsequent OUs may look something like Figure 12.9.

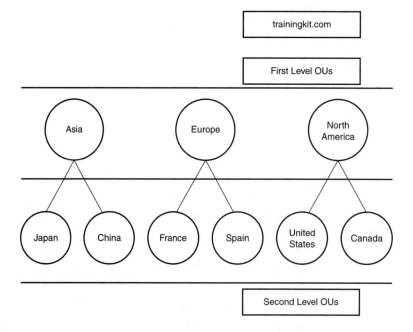

FIGURE 12.8

TrainingKit Incorporated is an international company with a hybrid administration model. The corporate office is in Paris, France.

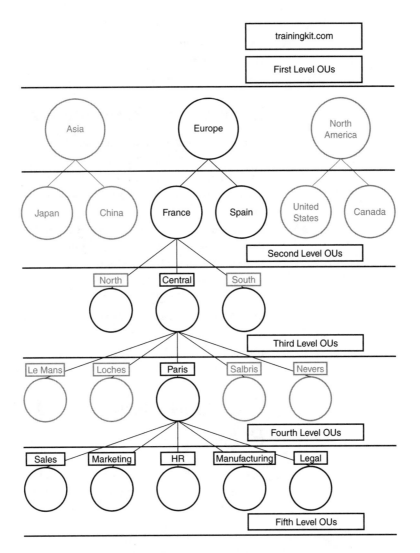

FIGURE 12.9
TrainingKit needs the ability to publish department-specific applications to its users and to allow departmental based representatives the ability to reset passwords.

Again (I can't say this enough), OUs are flexible! You can implement them in any of a thousand different ways to reflect your organization.

Nesting and Performance

It is important after looking at Figure 12.9 to reiterate that OUs carry very little overhead in terms of performance. In fact, there is no theoretical limit as to the number of nested OUs you can create. Microsoft does recommend that you keep the number of nested OUs to 15 or fewer, and there is no reason you shouldn't be able to do so. The best OU design involves fewer levels and more OUs per level (breadth rather than depth). Group Policy objects that are associated with OUs do cause some administrative overhead, however, so you should take that into consideration during the design process. Also, LDAP searches for objects within a domain (or forest for that matter) begin to degrade at about five levels deep. According to Microsoft, this degradation increases exponentially the deeper you go.

PREPARING FOR AN OU DELEGATION PLAN

So you now have somewhat of an idea how to design the OU structure for an organization. Now let's focus our attention of the development of an OU delegation plan.

Before jumping right in, though, it is that important you completely understand the Active Directory security model.

Getting the Security Model Straight

We've been discussing delegation of administrative authority throughout this chapter, but what does it really mean? Active Directory provides a method for secure access down to the object attribute level. This means you can expose this granular level of security through OU delegation. We used the example about allowing a specific user or user group the ability to reset passwords only within a specific OU. That is a perfect example of object *attribute* level security. Those users are only able to modify the password attribute for the user accounts within the OU. Before we get into the delegation of authority, we'll review the security aspects necessary to make it happen.

AD Security Components

Active Directory is composed of three main security components: Security principals, security identifiers, and security descriptors. Each of these components plays a key and very specific role in Active Directory security. Table 12.1 explains each of these security components.

TABLE 12.1

ACTIVE DIRECTORY SECURITY COMPONENTS

Security Component	Purpose	Description
Security principals	Receive permissions	Composed of users, groups, and computers. Security principals are the only objects to which you can apply access control permissions.
Security identifiers (SIDs)	Uniquely identify security principals	SIDs are alphanumeric structures assigned to uniquely identify security principals. The first part of the SID is unique to the issuing domain; the second part, the relative identifier (RID), is unique for all objects within the domain. SIDs are never reused and are transparent to users.
Security descriptors	Protect objects	The security descriptor defines the access permissions for objects. See the following section for details.

Security Descriptors

The security descriptor structure for each object contains the parts illustrated in Figure 12.10, which are explained in the following list:

◆ **Owner SID.** The SID of the owner of the object. The owner is responsible for granting access permissions and rights for the object. By default, the SID owner is the creator of the object.

◆ **Group SID.** Used to integrate Windows 2000 with non-Microsoft operating systems.

◆ **Discretionary ACL (DACL).** The DACL contains the access control permissions for an object and its attributes. It also contains the SIDs that determine who can access the object. These permissions and rights are represented as ACEs, which are explained in the following section.

◆ **System ACL (SACL).** The SACL contains a list of events that can be audited for an object.

A client will be able to view objects only in the directory that he has the ability to view. For example, if an administrator wishes to hide the objects in an OU from all users, he can remove the Authenticated Users and Everyone groups from the ACL on the OU. Because the ACL of an object is published with the object in the Global Catalog, only users with permission to view the object can do so.

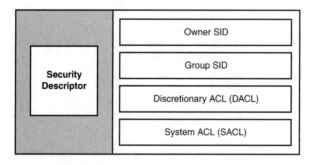

FIGURE 12.10
The security descriptor structure is attached to each object within Active Directory.

Access Control Entries

ACEs are part of both the DACL and the SACL on the security descriptor. They define the "line items" that have specific permissions or rights to an object. Access is controlled through the ACEs and can be either granted or denied. When access is denied, the ACE used to deny access is at the top of the DACL and takes precedence over all other ACEs that grant access to the same object, attribute, or set of attributes. ACEs that both grant and deny access to objects contain the following components:

◆ **Globally Unique Identifier (GUID).** Identifies the type of object or attribute.

◆ **SID.** Identifies the Active Directory security principal of the ACE.

◆ **A set of access rights.** Can be at the object, object attribute, or set of object attributes levels.

◆ **Flags.** Control inheritance of the ACE by its child objects.

Ownership

Every object in the directory has one and only one owner. The user who creates the object is by default the owner of that object, and has the authority to control how the object is accessed and by whom. The owner does *not* have to be represented in the object's DACL.

The important thing to consider about object ownership is that the owner has full control of the object. She can also delegate the ability to grant permissions to other (presumably administrators) to conserve administrative effort. One such delegation is the *take ownership* right. The user who is granted the take ownership right can then "seize control" of the object and have full control over its permissions. Once ownership is taken from the original owner, the original owner can perform operations on the object only as allowed by the DACL on that object.

Domain administrators always have the take ownership right over any object in Active Directory.

Inheritance

One of the more important processes to consider during the OU structuring process is inheritance. Objects that are created in OUs inherit the permissions that are granted (via ACEs) to the parent object. Because OUs can be nested inside other OUs, child OUs inherit permissions from parent OUs. By carefully considering this process during design, you can eliminate the need to grant permissions to individual objects within the directory.

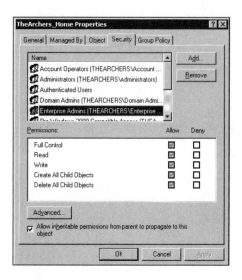

FIGURE 12.11
Right-click an OU and click on the Security tab to view the ACL, ACEs, and Inheritance options. Inherited permissions appear with a grayed check box, as in this figure.

When a permission is assigned to an OU (or any other container in Active Directory), it can be applied to the container object only, to the object and all of its children, to its children only, or only to specific children.

Permissions are determined at the time of creation and are composed of a combination of the schema definition for that object type and that object's parent's permissions. You can choose to block inheritable permissions on a specific object or OU by deselecting a check box on that object. Once you do this, changes to the parent permissions that normally would be inherited by the object would be blocked.

Figure 12.11 illustrates the DACL, ACEs, and inheritance-blocking elements for an Active Directory object.

NOTE

Security Tab You must select Advanced Features from the View tab in the Active Directory Users and Computers utility before you can view the Security tab on objects.

DEVELOPING AN OU DELEGATION PLAN

Okay. You now have enough information to begin delegating administrative control through OUs. You should now have an idea of how the security features work, and should understand how to design an OU structure. Planning the delegation portion uses both of these principles.

As stated previously, delegation of administration is the process of decentralizing administrative responsibility to other administrators or specific and trusted end-users. The ability to grant attribute-level control through individual OUs is a powerful security concept in Active Directory, and it eliminates the need to create multiple domains for the sake of administration.

As you develop the OU delegation plan, you need to do the following:

◆ Define the type of access administrators will have to OUs.

◆ Understand how you can delegate administrative control.

◆ Understand the tools for delegation.

Each of these tasks will be addressed in the sections that follow.

Common Delegation Tasks

To form an effective delegation plan, you need to understand what it is you can delegate. Table 12.2 describes the options for delegating administrative tasks.

TABLE 12.2

COMMON OPTIONS FOR OU-LEVEL DELEGATION OF ADMINISTRATION

Delegate	Description
Complete administrative control over an OU	The user or group of users receiving the delegated control can change properties on the OU itself, as well as create, update, and delete objects within that OU.
Control over specific objects, such as users, groups, printers, shares, and so on	The user or group of users receiving the delegation can manage only the objects specified in the delegation.
Create or delete only	The user or group of users receiving the delegation can create new or delete existing objects within the OU.
Create or delete objects of a specific type	The user or group of users receiving the delegation can create new or delete existing objects of the type specified in the delegation.
Administrative control over certain object attributes	The user or group of users receiving the delegation can manage only the specific object attributes—such as user passwords—specified by the delegation.

Keep in mind that since you can delegate down to object attribute-level permissions, there are literally thousands of delegation options in Active Directory. The ones listed in Table 12.2 are general and common and should serve as enough of an example for you to grasp the concept.

Define OU Administrator Access

A critical part of defining the OU structure is defining the delegation plan. This section falls after the section on designing the OU structure in this book only because it made sense to break out delegation so we could focus on it. In the real world, you will put this section to use as you design the OU structure, not afterward.

Crucial to the success of your OU design is defining the type of access and actions that can be performed on objects in every OU. This process will not be easy if your OU structure does not cascade nicely, which is why it is so important to plan and scrutinize it. The goal of your design is to have the ability to delegate control at the OU level.

The following list builds on a previous listing of questions an administrator should be able to answer regarding an OU design. This list takes those questions and converts them to requirements. To define the type of access administrators will have on OUs, you must do the following:

◆ **Determine the level of administration IT should retain.**
   You must also decide at what level you will delegate administration to other administrators or users.

◆ **Determine to whom to delegate what.** This information will help form the roadmap for OU ownership and level of authority granted to administrators and non-administrators.

◆ **Determine the owner of each OU.** Each OU has an owner that is responsible for its upkeep. By default, the owner is whoever creates the object.

◆ **Determine how to handle inheritance.** By default, all objects within an OU inherit the permission from the parent object. This may be "turned off" if inheritance is not required.

◆ **Build a flexible delegation model.** Because each unique object exists only once in the directory, you must build flexibility into your OU structure so you can, for example, grant to a user who may administer one OU the proper permission, while denying that same user access to two other OUs.

◆ **Map administrative roles to authority.** Always make use of the built-in Windows 2000 security groups before creating additional groups.

Delegation Methods

Ideally, domain administrators should be responsible only for the following:

◆ Developing the initial OU structure

◆ Repairing mistakes (this is where that take ownership right comes in real handy)

If you follow these recommendations, you can keep the Domain Admins membership to a minimum. Additional OU creation can be handled by "down-level" administrators or even specified end-users. Of course, you never want to stick an end-user who doesn't understand what he is doing in a position of power, controlled or not.

Top-level OUs should be created by delegating full control. Bottom-level OUs should be created for delegating per object-class control. If you have divisions of your company that require their own OU structure, you can perform Step by Step 12.1 to allow delegated creation of the OUs below the top level.

STEP BY STEP

12.1 Allowing Delegated Groups to Control OU Creation

1. Create an OU for each division that requires its own OU structure.

2. Create a local group for each division.

3. Populate this local group with the highest-level administrators for that division.

4. Assign the local group full control over its OU.

5. If the division's administrative group requires the ability to set its own membership, add it to the OU's ACL; otherwise, leave it out.

If your organization doesn't have divisions or business units that require full control of additional OUs, the domain administrators can complete the OU structure and retain full control—and administrative responsibility—for the entire organization.

Determine Whether Additional OUs Are Necessary

Groups with full control can decide whether additional OUs are required to further refine the administrative control within each division, business unit, or other logical partition within the company. To do this, they need to examine the object classes that will be created in the directory. Common object classes include users, group, printers, OUs, and shares.

For each object class, you should consider the following:

◆ Which groups need full control over a specific object class? Groups with full control can create, delete, and modify objects and object attributes of that class.

◆ Which groups need to be able to create objects of a specific class? By default, the creator of an object is the owner of the object.

◆ Which groups should be only allowed to modify specific attributes of existing objects of a specific object class?

For each case where you decide to delegate control, you will need to create a local group that will be allowed to perform the desired function, add the pertinent user objects to that group, and grant that group the specific right on the highest OU possible. Typically, that OU will be the OU that contains objects the users are granted permission to manage.

> **NOTE**
>
> **Creating Computer Accounts** To reduce administrative overhead, you can modify the ACL on the default computer's container and allow all users the right to add computer accounts to the domain.

Delegation Tools

There are three tools you can use to delegate control on objects in Active Directory:

◆ Delegation of Control Wizard

◆ Security tab of the Object Properties window

◆ DSACLS.EXE command-line utility

The following sections describe these utilities in more detail.

Delegation of Control Wizard

You can launch the Delegation of Control Wizard by right-clicking an object and selecting Delegate Control from the context menu. The wizard walks you through the following straightforward process:

1. Select the user or group to which you want to delegate administrative control.

2. Select the tasks to delegate. You can select from a predefined list of common tasks, or choose to create a customized task list.

3. If you select from the list of common tasks, you are done.

4. If you selected to customize the task list, you must indicate the scope of the task you wish to delegate. You can choose to delegate control of the object itself, including all objects within the object and creation of new objects, or you can choose from a list of available objects in the folder.

5. Finally, you must select the permissions you wish to delegate. You can display general permissions, object specific permissions, and create/delete child object permissions.

The Delegation of Control Wizard essentially provides a step-by-step approach to modifying the ACL on the object. You can choose to directly modify the ACL as well.

Object Security Tab

To open the Security tab (refer to Figure 12.11), you must have selected to view Advanced Features from the MMC's View menu. This provides a more advanced method of performing the job the Delegation of Control Wizard performs. Additionally, you have the ability to control inheritance of access rights from the parent object.

DSACLS.EXE

The DSACLS.EXE resource kit utility is a command-line interface that allows you to control ACLs on objects. DSACLS has the ability to either edit or replace the ACEs on an object or tree of objects.

CONSIDERING GROUP POLICY

So far we've really not considered the inner workings of Group Policy as a deciding factor in the OU design. The truth of the matter is that there are two key design influences that affect the structure of OUs: delegation of administration and GPO placement. Group Policy Object (GPO) management can be delegated in much the same way as OU management, and consideration of it is vital to the success of your entire site, domain, and OU hierarchy. The remainder of this chapter will focus on the structure and components of Group Policy and how it influences the design of the OU structure.

HOW GPOs WORK

Windows 2000 Group Policies are conceptually very simple to understand. You modify a setting and apply that setting to a user or computer, which inherits it. Unfortunately, it is not the concept you will be tested on. Instead, you will be tested on your knowledge of how GPOs work relative to the rest of the Active Directory installation. The GPO concepts are quite simple, but how they are used can be extremely complicated and difficult to follow. They can be inherited from site, domain, and OU (SDOU) levels within the Directory, can be blocked at some levels and filtered through security groups and ACLs at others, and can be managed by several groups of administrators throughout the organization. In short, there is a lot to know and understand about them.

As you continue through the rest of this chapter, keep in mind the following information about GPOs:

◆ A GPO is a standalone object. Even if you right-click an OU and create a new GPO through the properties context menu, you are still creating an object that may stand on its own.

◆ GPOs are linked to one or more SDOU objects within Active Directory. This process occurs automatically when you create a new GPO using the process described in the previous bullet.

◆ GPOs by default affect all users and computers within the SDOU objects to which they are applied.

◆ User and computer objects by default may inherit GPO data from each OU level of the SDOU object hierarchy, but only one site's and one domain object's GPOs may apply to any user or computer object.

◆ GPOs physically reside at a domain level, except for when they are focused at the site level. In this case, they are physically located on the domain controller hosting the forest root domain.

> **NOTE**
>
> **Do You SDOU?** Microsoft uses the terminology SDOU to represent Sites, Domains, and Organizational Units. When you see this terminology throughout this chapter, it refers to one or more sites, domains, or OUs in Active Directory. GPOs can be applied to only these types of objects.

Group Policy Objects contain the Group Policy settings that you create using a Group Policy editor. They store policy information in the following two locations:

◆ **Group Policy Container (GPC).** Used for policy data that is small in size and does not change frequently. GPCs are Active Directory objects that contain sub-containers for machine and user Group Policy information. GPCs have version properties, which are used to ensure that its information is synchronized with the GPT, and status information, which is used to determine whether the GPO is enabled or disabled.

◆ **Group Policy Template (GPT).** Used for policy data that is large in size and may change frequently. GPTs are implemented as file and folder structures in the system volume (SYSVOL) of domain controllers.

GPO data storage is split into two different locations because of the amount of information that must be stored. You do not want to store logon scripts, registry settings or software installation options in Active Directory because to do so would fill it with a large amount of data, the application of which could bring the system to its knees. Instead, that data is stored in the SYSVOL, which is replicated to all domain controllers throughout the domain, and SDOU objects to which the GPO is linked and references to the GPT location are stored in Active Directory as GPC objects.

Viewing the Group Policy Container (GPC)

To view information in the GPC, use the Active Directory Services Interface Editor (ADSIedit) and expand the Policies object (see Figure 12.12). Each of the GUID's listed under this object represent GPC's for the GPOs defined throughout the environment. If you have not defined any GPOs in your environment, there will still be two entries listed here, one for the default domain policy, and one for the default domain controller policy.

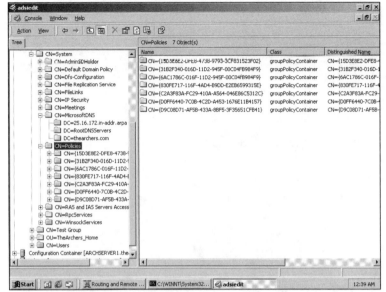

FIGURE 12.12
A view of Active Directory-based GPO and GPC data using ADSIedit.

Viewing the Group Policy Templates (GPT)

To view the GPT information, navigate to the drive hosting the SYSVOL data on a domain controller in a domain. Change to the <sysvolroot>\sysvol\sysvol\<domain name> folder. When you create GPOs, the 128-bit GUID generated to that GPO is used to create a directory under the preceding path to represent that GPO's GPT. Navigate through this directory structure and you will find policy information for administrative templates, scripts, user-specific settings, machine-specific settings, and more. See Figure 12.13.

FIGURE 12.13
A view of the GPT information stored on the SYSVOL of domain controllers.

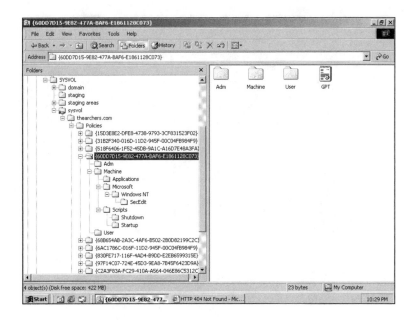

CREATING AND LINKING GPOs

To create a GPO, you use the Group Policy Editor (GPE). You can launch this application in a number of ways, but the most popular is to invoke it when linking a GPO to a site, domain, or OU. Remember, to link a new or existing GPO to a SDOU, you select the Group Policy tab on the properties dialog box of the object you wish to link it to. From this interface, you can do the following:

♦ **Create a new GPO and link it to this object.** By selecting the New button, you invoke the GPE and may define new policy settings. This option automatically links the new GPO with the SDOU object you are focused on.

♦ **Edit an existing GPO.** By selecting a GPO and clicking the Edit button, you launch the GPE to edit an existing GPO.

♦ **Link an existing GPO to this object.** By clicking the Add button, you can choose from domain/OU level GPOs, Site level GPOs, or all GPOs to link to the SDOU object.

◆ **Remove a GPO from the SDOU object and/or remove the GPO from existence.** By clicking on the Delete key, you can either remove the GPO from the SDOU object, or remove it for good from all objects.

◆ **Display GPO options.** By clicking the Options button, you can force the GPO to be applied to all children, even if the children explicitly block policy inheritance, and you can disable the policy from being applied.

◆ **Display the GPO properties.** By clicking on Properties, you can choose to disable the user policies or the computer policies from being processed. You can also modify the GPO ACL, and display which OUs are using (linked to) the GPO throughout the site.

There is also a customizable Group Policy MMC snap-in available in the MMC. When you add this snap-in to an MMC, you focus it on a particular GPO.

THE APPLICATION OF GROUP POLICIES

Suppose you have a group of users that requires a specific Windows desktop setting, such as a screensaver and desktop wallpaper combination. Rather than going to each desktop and manually configuring the settings, you could group the user objects into an OU and apply a Group Policy object. All users within the OU receive the policy by default, and that's that—or is it?

What happens when there are multiple conflicting policies applied to the same object? What happens in the case where one or two or ten of the users within an SDOU object shouldn't get the policy? What happens when that almighty administrator with delegated authority decides users don't need locked-down desktops and undoes a corporate-wide policy? Thankfully, Microsoft asked these questions during development of the Group Policy technology! We'll address situations representative of these questions in the sections that follow. First, let's take a closer look at inheritance.

Rules of Inheritance

Like Group Policy, inheritance is conceptually very simple to understand. If a parent has something, then all of its children, its children's children, and so on, implicitly have that something as well. It's much like heredity where human traits are passed on from generation to generation. In Group Policy, only configured settings are inherited by child objects; all other settings are ignored. There are three standard scenarios:

◆ A parent object has a value set, and one or more of its children does not.

◆ A parent has a value set, and one or more of its children has a nonconflicting value set for that same object.

◆ A parent has a value set, and one or more of its children has a conflicting value set for that same object.

In the first scenario, a child that does not have configured values for a setting will inherit its parent's values. There are exceptions to this rule that will be discussed shortly.

In the second scenario, a child that has nonconflicting values for a setting will inherit its parent's values *and* apply its own. Consider user logon scripts a good example here. Administrators may associate logon scripts with top-level OUs to map standard drive letters, and with child OUs to map departmental drive letters. In this case, the same setting is configured in each GPO and applies sequentially (in hierarchical order) on the client.

Finally, a child that has conflicting settings will not inherit its parent's settings. In this case, the child OU settings prevail and are applied to all of its children. A good example here would be disabling the Run menu item. If the Run menu item is set to "on" on the parent, but an administrator with delegated authority wishes to disable it, the two settings will conflict, and by virtue of being the closest to the user or computer object, the child OU setting wins.

NOTE

DENY Always Wins…Still   Just as the "No Access" NTFS permission always takes precedence on file and folder security, a parent GPO that denies access to something—such as the Run Menu command—will always be applied.

Blocking

So what happens if in your OU structure you have entire child OUs that don't need a policy assigned to its parent, grandparent, or other higher-level structure? Administrators can block policy inheritance by selecting a check box on the Group Policy properties page of an SDOU object. Policy inheritance stops at the point of blockage. In Figure 12.14, you see the logical flow of inheritance through the SDOU structure. If you were to block inheritance at the middle OU level, then your inheritance path would resemble that shown in Figure 12.15.

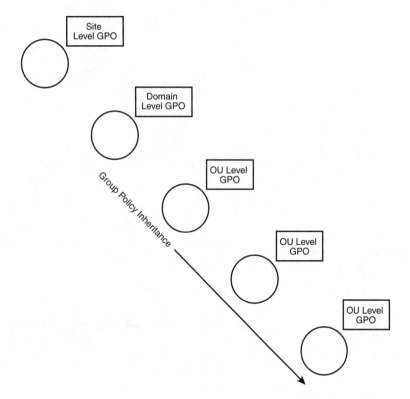

FIGURE 12.14

Group Policy inheritance begins at the site level and flows down through a single domain and that domain's OU structure.

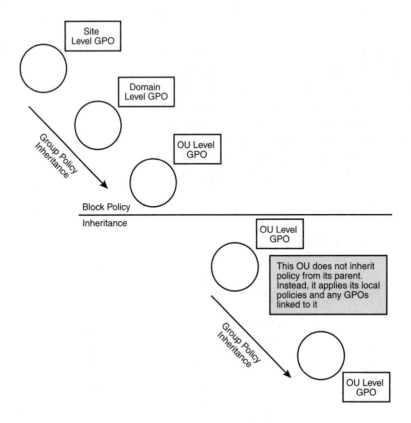

FIGURE 12.15
When inheritance is blocked, GPOs linked
to SDOUs above the blockage point are not
inherited. GPOs linked at the blockage SDOU
and below are inherited.

There is one thing to remember here: If you choose to block policy inheritance, you block inheritance of all GPOs linked to objects above the one with blocking enabled.

No Override

The problem, of course, with allowing administrators to block policy inheritance at a child level is that you run the chance of corporate standard high-level policies being disregarded. Because you can delegate the ability to manage and manipulate GPOs to OU administrators, you give them the authority to "overrule" you when it comes to applying policy. Suppose, for example, you create a GPO to remove the Run menu option and link it to the mytoys.com domain. By doing this, you effectively remove the Run menu from every computer in that domain. Because you have a lot of users with differing requirements, you need to have a well-established OU structure based on varying levels of IT administration and geographic location. An OU administrator for the Sales OU four layers deep can block policy inheritance, create a GPO that allows the Run menu, and just like that—your security is compromised.

Do you honestly think Microsoft would allow such a thing to happen? Of course not. Administrators can check the No Override option on a GPO to force its application regardless of blockage or conflicting policies, as illustrated in Figure 12.16.

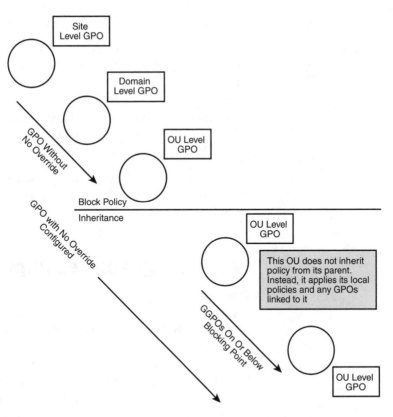

FIGURE 12.16
GPOs configured with the No Override option will be inherited by child SDOUs regardless of whether the child has block policy inheritance or has a conflicting policy setting.

Using Security Groups to Filter Policy Settings

The problem with what we have discussed so far is that a given GPO applies to all users and/or computers within the SDOU to which the GPO is linked. To combat this problem, we get to the real reason these policies are called "Group" Policies.

Because all objects in Active Directory have an ACL associated with them, there must be a way to allow or deny access to a GPO, which is itself an object. In fact, there is.

In the rare cases where you have members of a SDOU that require different policy settings, you can use Windows 2000 security groups to control the application of GPOs. Figure 12.17 displays the ACL with ACEs for a particular GPO. By default, the security group Authenticated Users is allowed the Apply Group Policy permission. This permission permits the group and its members to receive GPO settings. If you have a subset of users that should not get the settings of a policy, you can simply create a security group for them, and add the security group as an ACE with Deny Apply Group Policy to the GPOs ACL. This group's membership will not be permitted to receive that particular GPOs settings.

You can conceivably take this approach right down to the user and/or computer level, although adding individual user accounts to ACLs is not recommended.

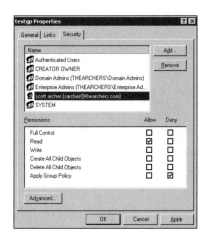

FIGURE 12.17
The Access Control Entries for a GPO.

When Group Policies Apply

One thing you may assume is that group policies only apply at logon time. In fact there are several different occasions when GPOs apply themselves to the objects they are linked to. For starters, remember that there are two types of GPOs: those that are linked to computers, and those that are linked to users. These two types can be included in a single GPO, which can make things quite confusing. We will discuss how to make them less confusing in a bit. Regardless of where they are defined, Group Policies are applied at the following times:

◆ Computer GPOs can be applied at startup time before the user is logged on, and at shutdown after the user is logged off.

◆ User GPOs can be applied during user logon and logoff.

There is an additional configurable Refresh setting that GPO administrators can choose to enable. There are several issues that need to be considered before this option is implemented, but it will actually refresh policies while a user is logged on and going about his business.

By default, both user and computer policies are refreshed every 90 minutes. You must take this into consideration now when making radical changes to GPOs that are in use on the network. Such changes may cause client computers to function differently and cause confusion and help desk calls, which is contrary to the Group Policy goal.

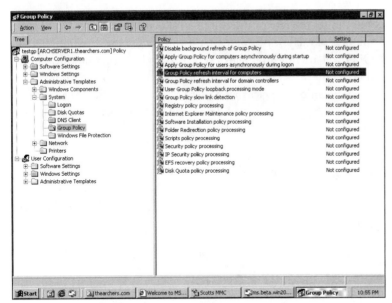

FIGURE 12.18
The Group Policy object configuration area for the computer section of a policy.

Figure 12.18 illustrates the Group Policy computer configuration area of the default Group Policy administrative template. Notice all the other settings you can make per GPO on this screen, some of which are explained in the following list:

◆ **Disable Background Refresh of Group Policy.** You can enable this option to completely disable the automatic refresh of the GPO. By doing this, computer policies will apply only at startup/shutdown, and user policies will apply only at logon/logoff.

◆ **Group Policy Refresh Interval for Domain Controllers.** You can use a separate value for the refresh setting on domain controllers.

◆ **Group Policy Slow Link Detection.** You can choose not to apply Group Policies over slow WAN links: This area allows you to define what a slow WAN link is.

You can set the refresh interval to a value between 0 and 64,800 minutes (45 days). Be aware that if you choose the 0 setting, the GPO will attempt to update every 7 seconds. This is not ideal in a production situation because of the amount of traffic it would cause, not to mention the fact that a user's screen might flicker every 7 seconds as the policy refreshes! Because of this, Microsoft recommends not refreshing GPOs more frequently than the default value of 90 minutes.

It is highly recommended that you devise some sort of method of notifying the users when a significant policy update is occurring. You could, for example, create a script that opens a window on the client to explain the update.

Local Group Policies

GPOs are not limited to Active Directory. Local computers have a scaled-down version of a GPO that is applied before any other GPO—it is called the Local Group Policy Object (LGPO). LGPOs can contain only security settings, scripts, and software policies. You cannot deploy applications using LGPOs. LGPOs consist only of the GPT section since they are not contained within Active Directory. They are not stored on the SYSVOL either, but rather in %systemroot%\system32\grouppolicy. LGPOs are processed even if the block policy inheritance on the parent SDOU is checked, and, if there is a conflict between an Active Directory GPO and an LGPO, the Active Directory GPO will prevail.

You might see the terminology LSDOU; it refers to the order in which policy objects are applied and includes the LGPO, which is always first. In the next section, we introduce the 4LSDOU terminology, which includes Windows NT 4.0 system policies, which are applied even before LGPOs.

Mixing Windows 2000 and Windows NT Policies

You can't really mix GPOs with Windows NT system policies—they are two different animals. You can, however, place Windows NT system policies on the SYSVOL to allow your down-level policies to be applied to down-level clients. This is especially useful during an upgrade.

Remember these two things when dealing with Windows NT system policies:

◆ If you have any older Windows NT 4.0-style system policies and need to implement their functionality once their target clients are upgraded to Windows 2000, you must convert them (manually) to GPOs; the upgrade process will not do it for you.

◆ You cannot use the GPE to modify Windows NT 4.0 style system policies. You must use the native tools.

Order of Application

We've been hinting at it all along, but haven't really laid it out for you. The following describes how policies—old and new—are applied according to a couple of scenarios.

If you have a standalone Windows 2000 client or member server, policies are applied as follows:

◆ Windows NT 4.0 policy file (ntconfig.pol)

◆ LGPOs

If you have a Windows 2000 client or member server operating in a mixed-mode environment, policies are applied as follows:

◆ Windows NT 4.0 policy file (ntconfig.pol)

◆ LGPOs

◆ Site GPOs

◆ Domain GPOs

◆ OU GPOs applied hierarchically until the user or computer object is reached.

Finally, if you are operating in a pristine Windows 2000 native-mode environment, policies are applied as follows:

◆ LGPOs

◆ Site GPOs

◆ Domain GPOs

◆ OU GPOs applied hierarchically until the user or computer object is reached.

> **NOTE**
>
> **Proper Use of LGPOs** LGPOs should be rarely used in a domain-centric environment. They're recommended use is for standalone computers or for highly specialized computers on a LAN.

CREATING A GROUP POLICY MANAGEMENT PLAN

As you can imagine, keeping track of everything that goes on within the SDOU structure can be quite challenging. The fact that you can delegate control of OUs and GPOs and at varying levels makes it that much more difficult. That is why planning is so incredibly important to the successful implementation of Active Directory.

Group Policy is a very powerful tool, and as such should be used with restraint. The more you use GPOs, the more apt you are to turn what seemingly may be a good solid plan into complete and total chaos. As with DNS and domain design, OU design and delegation, and site and subnet structuring, you need to sit and thoroughly plan out your use of Group Policy. When you do the plan (you must consider all of the above together) to ignore the integration of each would spell almost certain doom!

To reiterate, the following are the things you must understand at the very least as you begin to plan the structure and management of Group Policies:

▶ Group Policies can be used to configure just about everything about a user's computer and/or working environment.

▶ Policies are contained in a GPO, which is comprised of an Active Directory based GPC and a file and folder (SYSVOL) based GPT. GPOs are then linked to SDOUs throughout the directory.

▶ When a GPO is applied to an SDOU, it applies to all SDOUs and leaf objects within it.

▶ You can block policy inheritance on a SDOU, and can configure individual GPOs to forcefully apply by specifying no override.

▶ You can control access to GPOs through the use of security groups (and security principals). If a subset of users should not get a policy they would otherwise get, you can Deny the Apply Group Policy permission in an ACE on the GPO ACL.

▶ GPOs are processed first at the local machine (LGPO), then at the site level, then at the domain level, and finally throughout the OU hierarchy.

▶ OUs are anchored at the domain level, and are not inherited throughout the domain hierarchy. GPOs from one domain, however, can be linked to OUs in another domain.

▶ Policies that don't conflict are cumulative. If policies do conflict, the one that is applied closest to the object prevails.

▶ Computer GPOs are applied at computer startup and shutdown, whereas user GPOs are applied at user logon and logoff.

▶ The default refresh rate is 90 minutes for both user and computer-based GPOs. This can be changed to a number of minutes between 0 and 64,800 (45 days).

▶ Computer policies always take precedence over user policies.

▶ GPOs are *not* applied to security groups. Security groups can be used only to configure who has access to have a GPO apply to them. By default, the Authenticated Users group allows all GPOs to apply to all users and computer to which it is applied.

To configure a Group Policy, you need the following:

▶ A Windows 2000 domain controller

▶ Read/Write permissions to the SYSVOL on a domain controller

▶ Read/Write/Modify permissions to the SDOU to which your GPO will apply

SCOPE OF GROUP POLICY MANAGEMENT

As mentioned previously, there are two elements that greatly influence the OU design structure: the delegation of control and GPO placement. We discussed delegation of control earlier in this chapter when we designed the OU structure. Now to add to that, we need to look at how different GPO strategies influence that design. In reality, you would look at both of these at the same time.

There are several design factors again that apply here with GPO placement and design. You need to consider how to handle each of these, as you'll see in the next several sections. The design factors that influence the scope of Group Policy management are as follows:

◆ The IT Administration type (centralized, decentralized, or hybrid)

◆ Delegation of administrative control

◆ Performance

◆ Structure of policy types

The sections that follow detail each of these design factors.

Administration Type

So what do we mean when we say administration type? What does it represent? It represents a hierarchy of administration in most cases. You might have a central corporate IT staff with smaller IT staffs around the country responsible over those locations, one large IT staff responsible for all facets of administration, or a unique derivation of both. Whatever the case may be, the OU structure is focused at providing a hierarchical structure for IT administration and delegation and it always fits into one of the three types of administration.

Group policies are used for a number of reasons. They are used to define client desktop and user specific settings, to roll out and manage software applications, to configure logon/logoff and startup/ shutdown scripts, and more. The one thing all these features have in common is they are all IT administrative functions. It would make sense then that they would be created and applied according to how the IT administrative staff operates.

There are two common ways to structure your GPO design: monolithic or layered. Each has pros and cons and each maps to a type of administration.

> **NOTE**
>
> **Two Structures? Why Not Three?**
> You can consider the hybrid type administration a form of decentralized administration.

Monolithic Design

In a *monolithic* design, the goal is to place all the policy settings for a group of users or computers in an SDOU object into a single GPO for that object. The problem with this approach is twofold: first, you don't have much flexibility in your administrative delegations, and second, the nature of these GPOs makes them general—and there would no doubt end up being an onslaught of GPOs at deeper OU levels to either block or change policies for special cases. The advantage of this design, though, is very quick logon processing time. During the logon process, all GPOs to be applied are applied in order of precedence, one at a time. For example, if a user logs on and must apply seven GPOs, she would have to wait while Active Directory opened a GPO, read its contents, applied its settings, and closed it, seven synchronous times. The advantage, then, with the monolithic design is that there is (conceivably) only one GPO to open and process. Figure 12.19 illustrates the monolithic design.

This approach would be best for a centrally controlled IT infrastructure.

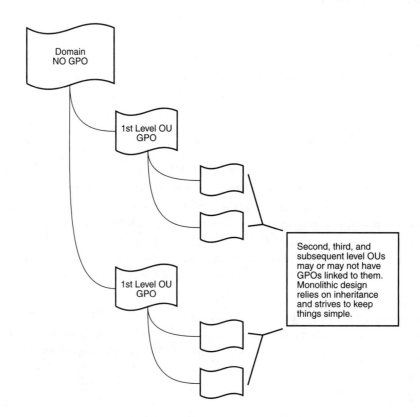

FIGURE 12.19
The monolithic approach focuses on speed
more than it does administration or flexibility.

Layered Design

The *layered* design uses a top-down approach and should be the model implemented in a distributed IT environment. You place purpose-based OUs at each level of the SDOU hierarchy and rely on both inheritance (implicit) and explicit settings for each object. Using a layered design provides administrators with the flexibility to delegate certain parts of administrative control to other areas. They could, for example, create the top-level base GPOs that apply throughout the organization and then delegate the control of OU-based GPOs and leave their design in the hands of a next-level administrator, who could tailor GPOs to fit the functional needs of his users.

The primary advantage to using a layered approach is that changes to GPOs generally will have to be done only on one or a few GPOs and can be inherited by the rest of the organization. The disadvantage is the logon performance hit. Figure 12.20 illustrates the layered design.

Delegation of Control

Each of the preceding models is definitely something you can implement. The monolithic model, however, does not play well in a distributed environment because of its inherent lack of flexibility in terms of administrative delegation. It's pretty safe to assume that most companies will implement their OUs and GPOs in a layered approach. This approach allows centrally controlled organizations to force policy down from the top level using the No Override option, but it also allows them to loosen their grip and entrust confidants down the OU structure to perform anything from a single, simple task such as resetting user passwords for a specific OU to creating an elaborate substructure of OUs and GPOs to suit their needs.

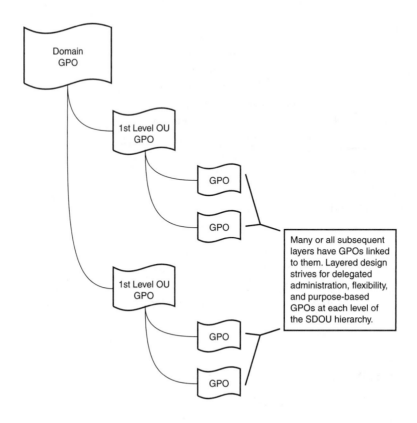

FIGURE 12.20
The layered approach focuses on flexibility and
delegation of administration more than it does
on speed.

The amount of control the central "governing" IT body decides to
relinquish to the subordinate administration staff is dependent upon
its comfort level with the administration staff—not limitations with
technology. This is an important concept to remember.

It may be necessary to enforce critical GPOs created and managed at
the top of the Active Directory hierarchy upon all subordinate
SDOUs throughout the environment. To do this, you check the No
Override Group Policy option. Microsoft recommends that you
limit the use of this function and its counterpart—Block Policy
Inheritance—because overuse of these options could have an adverse
affect on the overall Group Policy process.

Performance

Your OU design could be 400 levels deep and your logon performance wouldn't be affected as much as it would if you had to process 10 GPOs. There is no scientific proof of these numbers, but it is true that GPOs are responsible for causing the most lag in logon time. As discussed earlier, each GPO must be processed synchronously, which means they stack up. If a user account resides in an OU 10 levels deep and eight of those SDOU structures have associated GPOs, that client must wait while eight GPO files are opened, processed, applied, and closed—one at a time. The moral of this story is that you should keep a watchful eye on user logon performance as your GPO depth grows.

In some cases, you can use security groups to filter the effect of GPOs. Remember that GPOs are objects and hence have an associated ACL. By adding users who don't need specific policies to a security group, and then disallowing the application of that GPO to that security group, you can eliminate some overhead.

GPOs are rooted at the domain level. This means they are stored on domain controllers in a specific domain. GPO links are replicated to global catalog servers and thus can be applied to any computer or user in the forest. That said, you should be aware of the performance hit you'll take in retrieving the GPO from another domain—especially if that domain is separated by a slow WAN link.

Another strategy you can use to increase performance is to disable the unused portion of all GPOs. Each GPO consists of two distinct sections: the user configuration section and the computer configuration section. One of the best design practices is to create GPOs according to function—that is, to create separate GPOs for user and computer settings. You can break down this even further, as we'll discuss in the next section. To disable a section of a GPO, access its properties page and select the appropriate check box. Figure 12.21 displays the properties box for sitegpo.

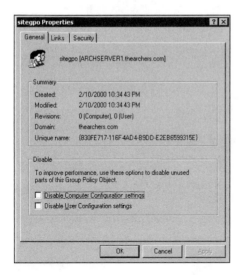

FIGURE 12.21

The properties window for a GPO named sitegpo. You can choose to disable either the unused portions of the computer or user configuration settings on this page.

The result of disabling the appropriate section is that it takes approximately half the time to process only half the GPO—in other words, the disabled part is totally ignored.

Structure of Policy Types

The final area we need to discuss regarding the scope of Group Policy management is in the structure of the policy types within a GPO. GPOs can contain a single or multiple policy types, such as software installation policies, logon scripts, user settings policies, computer settings policies, and so on.

In a single policy-type structure, many GPOs may be generated to provide the same functionality as a single GPO using a multiple policy type structure. Figure 12.22, for example, illustrates how multiple policy-focused GPOs can be associated with a single GPO. One of the benefits of this model is the organization of GPOs. With a good standard naming convention, similar policies can appear together in the GPO listing. That doesn't sound like too big a benefit until you have 30 or 40 of them to manage. The downfall of the single policy structure is the performance hit your users are likely to take.

The policies in Figure 12.22 are not necessarily linked directly to the Accounting OU object, but apply nonetheless.

In a multiple policy structure, you attempt to place all policies in a single GPO and apply it to an appropriate SDOU object. Figure 12.23 illustrates the Accounting OU with this scenario in mind. Although it looks simpler to manage, consider who is managing it. This is a good configuration for a small, centrally managed company, but not for a distributed company because all administrators would need to access and potentially modify the same GPO.

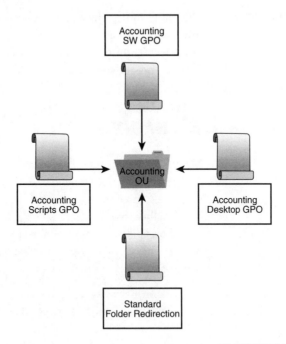

FIGURE 12.22
The Accounting OU contains several single policy-focused GPOs.

FIGURE 12.23
The Accounting OU now contains only one directly linked OU that contains all settings for its users and computers.

One thing to keep in mind here is the recommendation that you split policy settings by user and computer. This would increase the number of required accounting GPOs to two: one for the computer settings and one for the user settings.

MANAGING CLIENT COMPUTERS

Many Group Policy functions are focused at managing desktop computer environments. Using GPOs, administrators are able to configure a desktop computer once and have that configuration continually enforced. The following key Group Policy settings enable organizations to work toward reduced cost of ownership in the areas of both desktop and server administration. They are the cornerstones to Group Policy:

◆ **Administrative Templates.** Administrative templates are a set of registry-based interfaces that allow administrators to configure the application settings, desktop appearances, and behavior of services on all desktop computers that get the policy.

◆ **Security.** Administrators can configure security options on the local computer, clients on the network, and on the network itself.

◆ **Software Installation.** Through the use of Windows Installer and Group Policy, administrators can deploy, maintain, and remove software throughout the entire network.

◆ **Scripts.** Administrators can specify startup and shutdown computer scripts as well as logon and logoff scripts for users and apply them to few or many computers throughout the environment.

◆ **Folder Redirection.** Administrators can force client computers to store specific folders, such as My Documents, on a network share.

CASE STUDY: SPEEDWAY MANAGEMENT CORP. (SMC)

BACKGROUND

SMC is in the process of implementing Windows 2000 across its corporate network. The site, DNS, and domain designs have been completed and it wishes to continue the design process with OUs and Group Policy.

SMC currently runs on Windows NT in a single-domain environment and maintains high-speed WAN links between the three racetracks it manages. The Windows 2000 domain design consists of a single-domain structure with three sites. DNS servers exist in each site and manage a single Active Directory integrated zone.

PROBLEM STATEMENT

Throughout the implementation of Windows NT at SMC, administration was controlled centrally by the corporate IT staff. Although this process was effective, SMC employees began to become frustrated because the IT staff could not provide services in the required amount of time.

CURRENT SYSTEM

The current system is a Windows NT network with a single domain. All administration is controlled centrally by the SMC IT administration staff. External offices do not have the capability to manage any of their local resources.

Network Manager

"We don't want to give administrators at other offices full domain administrative permissions because we have standards in place here and are concerned that they will deviate from standards."

Network Engineer

"There are several initiatives we have coming up that I could use some help on, such as locking down client computers and distributing standard software from a centralized location. I don't know how to handle the remote locations."

ENVISIONED SYSTEM

The envisioned system is one that will allow for centralized administration with delegated control for certain business areas. It will also allow us to incorporate our standard hardware, software, and security settings and enforce those among the network.

Network Manager

"I would like to extend our administrative capabilities to our other offices, but I still want to maintain ultimate control over the network. I'd like them to be able to manage certain areas of and have flexibility with their environments, but not impact the rest of us."

CIO

"I travel a lot and always have some sort of problem plugging into the network in a remote office and having access to everything I need. I want to be able to sit in a remote office and have it feel like I am right here."

continues

CASE STUDY: SPEEDWAY MANAGEMENT CORP. (SMC)

continued

MAINTAINABILITY

Centralized management with delegation is key. All objects in the directory must be easy to understand and manage.

Network Manager

"We must be able to maintain the entire network from our corporate data center. That means there should not be a thing I don't have access to. I also want to be able to drive corporate standards throughout the organization."

Help Desk Manager

"I have support staff in every building we occupy. Right now, their hands are tied when they need to make even a simple change on a server because they have to wait for someone here to make the change for them and replicate it out. I would like for them to be able to at the very minimum be able to reset passwords for users they assist."

PERFORMANCE

User logon performance is a problem currently, so that is high on the priority list to fix. Network bandwidth between locations is adequate for most operations; however, use of the expensive links should be kept to a minimum unless necessary.

Network Manager

"Our remote users sometimes complain of logon lag time. We have servers at every location so it's hard to diagnose where the problem lies. That problem needs to be addressed during our upgrade."

CIO

"When I dial up now and log on to the network, my logon script runs and it takes forever to exit. I would really like to address that problem with this new system."

CHAPTER SUMMARY

We discussed a lot of concepts in this chapter, but the most important one to take with you is this: The OU and Group Policy structure should be designed according to the IT administration type first, and the company organizational model second. Before you touch a server, you need to have an OU and GPO plan in place, preferably on paper, and approved by all administrative parties involved in the process. For each level of the OU hierarchy, you need to associate an administrator who will have ultimate control over that section of administration.

You should consider the development of both the OU and GPO structure at the same time to avoid any restructuring or less than optimal implementation of either.

Table 12.3 provides some best practice recommendations in designing both the OU and GPO structure for an organization.

One final note: In case you didn't get it yet—planning is crucial. The domain structure must be correct the first time because it is next to impossible to restructure domains without adversely affecting your users. With OUs and GPOs you have a bit more breathing room because it is fairly easy to restructure; however, getting it right the first time will save you a lot of time and save your company money to say the least!

KEY TERMS
- ISO 3166 country codes
- nesting
- Access Control Entry (ACE)
- Access Control List (ACL)
- Security descriptor
- Group Policy Object (GPO)
- Group Policy Template (GPT)
- Group Policy Container (GPC)
- Group Policy Editor (GPE)
- delegation of control
- inheritance
- block policy inheritance
- no override
- SDOU
- LSDOU
- 4LSDOU

CHAPTER SUMMARY

TABLE 12.3

BEST PRACTICES IN OU AND GPO DESIGN

Task	Description
Choose the right OU model.	Take caution in choosing the OU model you implement and make sure it accurately reflects the IT administration model as well as the operational structure of the organization.
Keep OU design simple.	Reasons to create OUs are as follows: • To enhance administrative control and accurately reflect the organizational structure of the company • To provide a structure for Group Policy • To replace existing Windows NT resource domains • To hold other OUs in the top or middle tier of the OU hierarchy
Delegate administration.	Keep the following in mind as you develop the delegation of administration plan: • For each OU created in the directory, you should associate a responsible party who will administer the OU, define the reason for its being, and the extent of the permissions the delegated parties will have. • The central IT group should retain full administration for the first, second, and in deep hierarchies, even the third level of OUs. • Minimize the delegation of attribute-level permissions. These are very difficult to keep track of and could potentially open security holes.
Remain consistent in your design.	Consistency is key to keeping things simple. If you have an environment with multiple domains, consider using the same OU model throughout.
Plan the location of user and computer objects within the OU structure.	This has a huge impact on the overall OU and Group Policy structure.
Plan the Group Policy structure.	The Group Policy structure should be considered all the way through the domain and OU design process. The best-case scenario for the Group Policy structure is to have it flow with your domain and OU structure.
Determine GPO management scope.	Determine whether to use single policy-focused GPOs or GPOs that include multiple policies. Determine how to delegate administration over GPOs, and determine whether to use a layered or monolithic design.
Keep an eye on performance.	GPOs can degrade performance because they must be processed one at a time. Optimize performance by disabling unused portions of GPOs, using security groups to filter the effects of GPOs, and limit cross-domain references to GPOs.

APPLY YOUR KNOWLEDGE

Exercises

12.1 Creating an OU Structure

In this exercise, you will utilize the Active Directory Users and Computers utility to create a small organizational unit structure and create and apply customized Group Policy objects to specific containers.

You will create an OU structure to model the administrative needs of a fictional company. This company has a centralized headquarters and four offices, one in each quadrant of the U.S. Each office requires its own administration. Each office has several departments that require specific desktop settings and software.

Estimated Time: 45 Minutes

1. Open the Active Directory Users and Computers MMC utility and expand the domain tree in the left console pane.

2. With the domain name highlighted, right-click anywhere in the right console pane and select New, Organizational Unit.

3. Type **East** as the name of the OU.

4. Repeat Steps 2 and 3 for the North, South, and West OUs. Each should be a child of your domain object.

> **NOTE**
> **North and South**   The North and South OU structure is not required throughout this exercise. It is there simply to get you comfortable through repetition at creating the OU and GPO structures.

5. In the left console pane, right-click the East OU and select New, Organizational Unit.

6. Name the OU **Department 1** and click OK.

7. Repeat Steps 5 and 6 so that each top-level OU contains two departments: Department 1 and Department 2. When complete, your left console pane (fully expanded) should be similar to that of Figure 12.24.

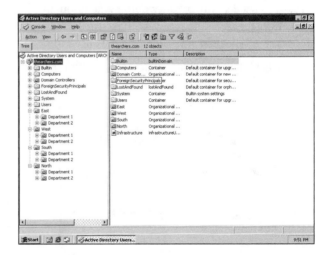

FIGURE 12.24
Your top-level OUs are typically controlled by the central IT group. For this exercise, your structure should resemble this.

8. Right-click the Department 1 OU under the East OU and select New, User. Name the user **EastDept1** and assign it a password of **password**.

9. Repeat Step 8 until you have a single user account in each of the second-level department-based OUs.

APPLY YOUR KNOWLEDGE

At this point, you have an environment that simulates a real company with decentralized IT administration across four regions of the United States. Each of these regions contains two departments. You have no user accounts in the top-level OUs, and all user accounts in the bottom-level OUs. Realistically, you may have users strewn about the entire structure, but for this demonstration that is not necessary.

10. To create a Group Policy object and automatically link it to the East OU, right-click East and select Properties, then the Group Policy tab.

11. Click New to create and link a new GPO. Name the GPO **East and West Base User Policy**, as in Figure 12.25.

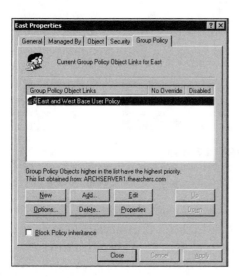

FIGURE 12.25
Group Policy tab for the East OU when configuring the East and West Base Policies.

> **NOTE**
>
> **Base Policies** In this exercise, both the East and West offices require the same base settings, and both the North and South offices require the same settings, but different than those of East and West. Remember too that you should split the user and computer settings into different GPOs.

12. Click the Edit button to launch the Group Policy Editor.

13. Right-click the GPO container at the top of the left console pane and select properties.

14. Disable the Computer portion of the policy by enabling the appropriate check box, as illustrated in Figure 12.26. Click Yes to confirm the pop-up message. Click OK to close the Properties dialog box.

FIGURE 12.26
Disabling the unused portion of the base user policy will optimize the processing of this GPO.

APPLY YOUR KNOWLEDGE

15. The users in both East and West offices are not allowed to have the Run menu on their computers. To disable the Run menu, drill down the User Configuration, Administrative Templates, and Start Menu & Task Bar hierarchy.

16. In the right console pane, double-click Remove Run Menu from Start Menu.

17. Click Enabled and then click OK. Notice the updated Setting column entry for this option.

18. Close the Group Policy Editor.

19. While still on the Group Policy tab for the East OU, click New to create an additional GPO. Name this one **East and West Base Computer Policy.**

20. Click the Properties button while this GPO is highlighted. Disable the User configuration settings by selecting the appropriate check box and clicking OK. (Click Yes in response to the ensuing message.) Click OK.

21. Click Edit to launch the Group Policy editor.

22. Under the Computer Configuration, drill down through Windows Settings, Security Settings, and Event Log, and select Settings for Event Log.

23. In the right console pane, double-click Retain System Log.

24. Enable this policy setting and increase the number of days to 10 (see Figure 12.27). Click OK. This setting is dependent on the retention method for system log, so you are presented with a window (see Figure 12.28) to let you know of the additional setting. Accept by clicking OK.

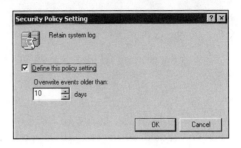

FIGURE 12.27
Increasing the retention time for system event logs ensures that events will not be overwritten until 10 days after they occurred.

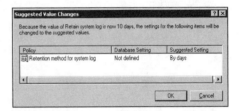

FIGURE 12.28
As a result of increasing the retention time for the system log, you must set the retention method to By Days.

> **NOTE** **Verifying the Changed System Log Setting** The default system log setting is 7 days, so you will be able to tell the GPO was applied by checking to see if it is set to 10 after you log on.

25. Close the Group Policy Editor.

26. Close the Group Policy properties page.

APPLY YOUR KNOWLEDGE

27. Right-click the West OU and select properties. Click on the Group Policy tab.

28. To link to the existing GPOs, click the Add button.

29. Navigate to the east.<yourdomain> object using the drop-down list (see Figure 12.29). Once there, you should see the two GPOs you just created.

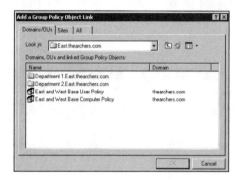

FIGURE 12.29
The two GPOs you created are populated in the directory so you can link them to additional OUs with like requirements.

30. Add both of them to your West OU. You cannot multiple select here, so you'll have to add one, then repeat the process to add the other.

31. If you wish, repeat Steps 10–30 to create two additional GPOs for the North and South OUs. Replace East and West with North and South where appropriate. This will not be required for the additional exercises.

32. To test the functionality of the OUs, log on to the Windows 2000 domain using one of the user accounts you created. You can use the same workstation to test all accounts. East and West should have no Run menu under Start, and a 10-day retention time on the system event log.

12.2 Delegation of Administrative Authority

In this exercise, you will use the Delegation of Control Wizard to delegate the ability to reset passwords on user accounts in an OU. This is a continuation of Exercise 12.1.

Estimated Time: 30 Minutes

1. In the Active Directory Users and Computers MMC utility, right-click the East OU and select New, Group.

2. Change the group scope to Domain Local and type to Security by selecting the appropriate radio buttons.

3. Name the group `East Department 1 OU Managers` and click OK.

4. Right-click the East OU's Department 1 OU and select New, User.

5. Name the user `Eastadmin` and give a password of `password`.

6. Right-click the Eastadmin user and select Add Members to Group. Select the group you created in Steps 2 and 3 and click OK. Close the results box.

> **NOTE**
>
> **Use of the Security Group**   You created the security group so you can delegate administration to a group and not a lone user. You placed the security group in an OU structure you manage so you can keep track of who is a member.

7. To delegate the ability to allow members of the new security group to reset passwords only in East Department 1, right-click the East's Department 1 OU.

8. Select Delegate Control to launch the Delegation of Control Wizard. The wizard starts (see Figure 12.30).

FIGURE 12.30
The Delegation of Control Wizard.

9. Click Next to begin the delegation process. Click Add and select the East Department 1 OU Managers security group to the bottom pane (see Figure 12.31).

10. Click OK and then Next.

11. Enable the radio button to create a custom task to delegate (see Figure 12.32). Click Next.

12. Select the option for Only the Following Objects in the Folder. Scroll to the bottom of the list and check User Objects (see Figure 12.33). Click Next.

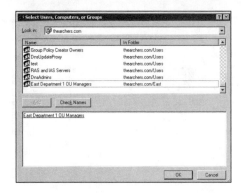

FIGURE 12.31
The first step is to select the group that will have administrative control delegated to it.

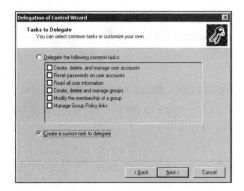

FIGURE 12.32
Because we want to delegate granular control, we need to create a custom task.

APPLY YOUR KNOWLEDGE

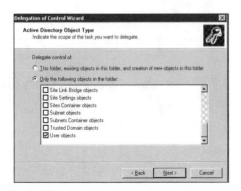

FIGURE 12.33
You want to give permissions only over attributes on user objects.

13. Scroll down the permissions options until you find Reset Password and enable it (see Figure 12.34). Click Next.

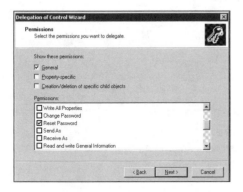

FIGURE 12.34
The attribute level control we've been discussing.

14. You have successfully delegated fine-grained administrative control! Notice the nice summary on this window (see Figure 12.35). Click Finish.

FIGURE 12.35
The summary window lets you know what you just did.

15. The user EastAdmin now has the authority to reset passwords in the East's Department 1 OU only (which equates to his own and that of east-dept1). To test, log on to a server or workstation with the administration tools, navigate to a user object in the East, Department 1 OU, right-click the user and select "Reset Password." Type a new password and click OK. You should be able to do this.

16. Navigate to the West's Department 1 OU and try the same thing with the westdept1 user. You should get an error when you attempt to complete the process.

Review Questions

1. What is the purpose of an organizational unit?

2. Which three questions must you be able to answer about each OU you create?

3. List three options for delegating administrative authority.

APPLY YOUR KNOWLEDGE

4. List three tools you can use to delegate administrative authority.

5. List the contents of a security descriptor.

6. Describe a Group Policy Object (GPO) and then describe the contents of a GPO.

7. When do computer based Group Policy settings apply? List all possible conditions.

8. What is the limit of OU structure depth (nested OUs)?

9. Where are Group Policy Templates (GPT) stored?

10. Where are Group Policy Containers (GPC) stored?

Exam Questions

1. What is the best way the SMC corporate IT staff could enforce its standard OS and security across the network with Windows 2000?

   A. Develop standards documentation and post it to the intranet. Each administrator, help desk associate, and employee would be responsible for conforming to it.

   B. Create a GPO structure for the network. Apply base OUs at the top level and select the No Override option to force them upon child objects.

   C. Create an OU structure for the network. Apply Base GPOs at the top level and select the No Override option to force them upon child objects.

   D. Create the GPOs at the top level and then select the option to Block Policy Inheritance.

2. How could SMC provide the administrators in the other offices with administrative authority over a subset of objects? (Choose two.)

   A. Create an OU called delegation of control. Add the objects that need to be administered to the new OU. Modify the DACL on the OU.

   B. Add the administrators-to-be to a security group. Use the Delegation of Control Wizard to assign the security group the appropriate level of permission on the OUs for their offices.

   C. Add the administrators-to-be to a security group. Navigate to the OU you want to the group to administer, and make the appropriate changes on its DACL.

   D. Add the administrators-to-be to a security group. Navigate to the OU to which you want to the group to administer, and make the appropriate changes on its SACL.

   E. Add the administrators-to-be to a security group. Navigate to the OU for which you want the group to administer, and make the appropriate changes on its GPO.

3. Suppose all three SMC locations required special settings to be configured during the startup process and the logon process. Which two Group Policy settings would you create?

   A. Create GPO settings in the User Configuration section for the logon process settings.

   B. Create GPO settings in the Computer Configuration section for the startup process settings.

   C. Create GPO settings in the User Configuration section for the startup process settings.

   D. Create GPO settings in the Computer Configuration section for the logon process settings.

   E. Create GPO settings in the User Configuration section for the user GPO refresh interval settings.

   F. Create GPO settings in the Computer Configuration section for the computer GPO refresh interval settings.

4. What could SMC do with the Windows 2000 OU and GPO design to optimize performance while processing them? (Choose four.)

   A. Limit the use of cross-domain GPO links.

   B. Limit the OU nesting depth to no more than 15 levels.

   C. Limit the OU nesting depth to no more than 5 levels.

   D. Limit the GPO application depth to no more than 5 levels.

   E. Limit the GPO application depth to no more than 15 levels.

   F. Disable unused portions of all GPOs.

5. Suppose the SMC CIO travels to each racetrack on a daily basis, but does not have a laptop. How can you ensure that he always has access to his files and software? Assume that all software is readily available in Microsoft Installer format (MSI).

   A. Create an OU for the CIO and place his computer account in it. Create a single GPO for software distribution and a single GPO for Windows settings management. Create a scripts GPO for both logon and logoff drive letter mappings. Apply all GPOs to the CIO's OU.

   B. Create an OU for the CIO and place his user account in it. Create a single GPO for software distribution and a single GPO for Windows settings management. Create a scripts GPO for both logon and logoff drive letter mappings. Apply all GPOs to the CIO's OU.

   C. Create a security group for the CIO and place his user account in it. Place the MSI based software packages in a central place and instruct the CIO to map a drive to that location and install the software he needs.

   D. Create a distribution group for the CIO and place his computer account in it. Place the MSI-based software packages in a central place and instruct each location's help desk on how to install the packages.

6. How can you ensure that there are no conflicting policies that override the GPO settings attached to the CIO's user account OU?

   A. For all GPOs attached to the CIO's OU, specify the Block Policy Inheritance option.

   B. For all GPOs attached to the CIO's OU, specify the No Override option.

   C. Top level GPOs automatically override subordinate GPOs, so no action is required to ensure that there are no conflicting policies.

   D. Modify the DACL of the OU that contains the CIO's user account by creating an ACE that specifies the No Override permission.

APPLY YOUR KNOWLEDGE

7. A department within your company wants its managers to have the ability to modify the properties of only its users in Active Directory. Your company's security policy states that only the User Admins security group can create new user accounts throughout the domain. How can you delegate administrative authority to achieve the desired results?

   A. Create an OU for the department's users. Create security groups for the User Admins and the department's managers. Add an ACE to the department's OU that allows the User Admins to create user objects and its managers to modify the properties of user objects.

   B. Add an ACE to the domain object ACL that allows the User Admins group to create user accounts. Create an OU for the department's users. Create a security group for the department's managers. Add an ACE to the department's OU that allows its managers to modify properties of user objects.

   C. Use the Delegation of Control Wizard to add the User Admins security group to a Security group that contains the department's users. Give the User Admins group the right to create user accounts within the department's group. Give the department's managers the right to modify permissions within the department's security group.

   D. Add an ACE to the domain object ACL that allows the User Admins group to create user accounts. Create an OU for the department's users. Add individual ACEs to the department's OU ACL for each of its managers that allows them to modify properties of user objects.

8. Which of the following is *not* created when specifying Group Policy settings?

   A. Group Policy Template

   B. Group Policy Container

   C. Group Policy Script

   D. Group Policy Object

9. Select the answer that represents the proper order of precedence of Group Policy Object application.

   A. Local Policy, Site, Domain, OU Hierarchy

   B. OU Hierarchy, Site, Domain, Local Policy

   C. Domain, Site, OU Hierarchy, Local Policy

   D. Local Policy, Domain, Site, OU Hierarchy

10. Your small startup organization consists of three departments: Sales, Engineering, and Recruiting. You wish to create a directory structure that can be centrally administered by a group of IT administrators. You want at some point to split the administrative duties among specific individuals in each department. Each of these departments requires unique desktop and software configurations. Select the most optimal, scalable, and maintainable design.

    A. Create a single domain that reflects the name of the company. Use the default site with no modifications. Create three OUs, one for each department. Place all users in the appropriate OU. Add all IT administrative user accounts to the Domain Admins group.

B. Create a single domain for each department. Use the default site with no modifications. Place all users in the appropriate domain. Add all IT administrative user accounts to the Domain Admins group for each domain.

C. Create a single domain that reflects the name of the company. Use the default site with no modifications. Create three OUs, one for each department. Create an IT Admins security group and add the appropriate IT administrators to that group. Delegate full control permissions to the IT Admins group on each of the three OUs.

D. Create a single domain that reflects the name of the company. Use the default site with no modifications. Create three OUs under the users container, one for each department. Place all users in the appropriate OU. Add all IT administrative user accounts to the Domain Admins group.

Answers to Review Questions

1. The purpose of organizational units is to partition the domain namespace into a manageable hierarchy of users, computers, groups, shares, printers, and other objects. With this partitioning and its nested capabilities, administrators no longer have to create additional domains or add users who need to perform minor administrative functions to the Domain Admins group. See "Introduction."

2. When you create an OU, you should be able to answer why you are creating the OU, who will perform administration on the OU, and what permissions the OU administrator will require. See "OU Associations."

3. There are various options for creating OUs. You can create OUs to delegate complete administration over a specific partition of domain namespace, delegate control over specific objects in the OU, delegate permissions to create or delete specific objects only, and more. See Table 12.2, "Common Options for OU-Level Delegation of Administration," for a complete description.

4. There are three methods available for delegating administrative authority: the Delegation of Control Wizard, the Security tab on the target object, and the DSACLS.EXE command-line utility. See "Delegation Tools."

5. The security descriptor is comprised of the following four objects: the owner SID (security identifier of the owner of the object); the group SID (used to integrate Windows 2000 with non-Microsoft operating systems); the discretionary access control list (DACL), which contains ACEs that describe permissions to that object; and the system Access Control List, which contains a list of events that can be audited for the object. See "Security Descriptors."

6. A GPO contains the Group Policy settings that you specify for application on a site, domain, or OU. It is a virtual container that stores its data in the Group Policy Container (GPC) and the Group Policy Template (GPT). See "Considering Group Policy."

APPLY YOUR KNOWLEDGE

7. Computer GPOs apply when a computer starts up (before a user logs on) and when it shuts down. User GPOs apply at user logon and logoff time. Both GPOs are set to refresh automatically every 90 minutes by default. This refresh time is controllable on a per-GPO basis. See "When Group Policies Apply."

8. Although there is no physical limitation, Microsoft recommends that your OU nesting hierarchy not exceed 15 levels. OUs create very little processing overhead, but if they have GPOs attached to them they degrade exponentially in performance. Additionally, if your OU structure ends up being more than 15 levels, you need to rethink your design. See "Organizational Units."

9. Group Policy Templates (GPTs) are file and folder structures that include all Group Policy information for a GPO. They are stored on the SYSVOL of the domain controllers in the domain in which the GPO is anchored. They are replicated to all domain controllers in the domain. See "Group Policy Objects."

10. Group Policy Containers (GPCs) are Active Directory-based objects that store a subset of GPO information. They include subcontainers for Machine and User Group Policy information and have the following properties: version information and status information. See "Group Policy Objects."

Answers to Exam Questions

1. **C.** To force your baseline GPOs on all objects in the environment, create an OU structure and then apply your base GPOs to the domain object or top-level OU. Specify the No Override option

so that no other conflicting or policy inheritance blocking OUs will overwrite the base GPO. See "No Override."

> **NOTE**
>
> **Applying GPOs to the Domain Level**
> The Domain Admins and Enterprise Admins groups by default contain an ACE in every GPO DACL that does not allow them to partake in GPO processing. This is why you can get away with domain-wide mandatory policies, and not restrict your administrative capabilities.

2. **B, C.** To delegate administrative authority, create a security group for each administrative team requiring the same level of permissions. You can then either use the Delegation of Control Wizard to give the security group the appropriate permissions over the object, or navigate directly to that object and add the security group and appropriate permissions as an ACE to the object's DACL. An object's SACL is used for auditing and not permissions, and a GPO is used to deliver Group Policy settings for users and/or computers. See "Delegation of Control."

3. **A, B.** The GPO structure is split into two parts: user configuration and computer configuration. Startup and logon processes (scripts) are configured for computers and users, respectively. So you would create a GPO for a logon script in the user configuration section, and a GPO for a startup script in the computer configuration section. You could create both of these scripts using the same GPO; however, that goes against best

APPLY YOUR KNOWLEDGE

practices in keeping the user settings and computer settings in separate GPOs. You should modify policy refresh settings only when you need policies to refresh more or less frequently during the time a user or computer is operational. This will not affect startup/logon settings. See "Structure of Policy Types."

4. **A, B, D, F.** To optimize the performance of your OU and GPO structure, you should conform to some rules. Specifically, limit the use of cross-domain GPO links. GPOs are anchored at the domain level, so any links to objects in another domain require a connection to the global catalog server. You should also limit your OU nesting to fewer than 15 levels and 5 levels if GPOs are attached to those OUs. GPOs cause the degradation in performance, whereas OU nesting has very little effect on performance. Finally, you should split your GPOs into user GPOs and computer GPOs; take advantage of disabling the user settings on computer GPOs, and computer settings on user GPOs to optimize processing time. See "Performance."

5. **B.** Because the CIO will be using multiple computers, that automatically rules out options A and D. To allow him access to his files from anywhere on the network, you should create an OU for him and add his user account to it. You then associate the appropriate GPOs with that OU. The GPOs would connect him to his data, display his Windows settings, and make his software available. Option C is incorrect because it does nothing about his data and Windows settings. See "Application of Group Policy and the corresponding Case Study."

6. **B.** By default, GPOs applied closest to the user object that conflict with other GPOs will prevail.

To force a policy upon child objects, you must specify the No Override option. By doing this, administrators can force that policy on child objects even if they are configured to block policy inheritance or have a conflicting setting. See "No Override."

7. **B.** Because the User Admins are the only group with the clearance to create user accounts in the domain, they must have that permission throughout the domain and should be added to the domain objects ACL accordingly. To allow the departments managers to modify the user account properties only for its users, you should create an OU for that department and delegate permission to modify user properties to a security group you create for the department's managers. You can use the Delegation of Control Wizard for this, or you can manually modify the ACL of the OU. See "Delegation of Control."

8. **C.** When a Group Policy setting is created, it is stored in a virtual container called a Group Policy Object (GPO). The GPO actually stores its data in two other containers: the Group Policy Container (GPC) and the Group Policy Template (GPT). The Group Policy scripts refer to the logon/logoff and startup/shutdown scripts that are defined within GPOs but are not created at the time of GPO creation. See "How GPOs Work."

9. **A.** The machine local policy is applied immediately and is followed by the site, domain, and OU hierarchy. Using this model, the settings applied closest to the client computer are the final settings if there is a conflict. The easiest way to remember this ordering is the term LSDOU (local, site, domain, OU). See "Local Group Policies."

APPLY YOUR KNOWLEDGE

10. **A.** The domain should reflect the name of the company, and you should assume that because there was no mention of multiple sites that the default site was sufficient. The OU structure for this organization needs to be one top-level OU per department because of the varying needs of each. This way, you can associate GPOs with each OU to address the needs of individual departments. Since there are plans to further delegate control in each department, this model is flexible enough to handle that change or addition. The Domain Admins will, by virtue of being Domain Admins, have administrative power over all OUs in the domain. There is no need to add the IT administrators to another group, unless you don't want them to have domain administration permissions. See "Flexibility in OU Design," and refer to Chapter 11 for detailed information on domain design.

Suggested Readings and Resources

1. White Paper. Windows 2000 Group Policy.

2. White Paper. Introduction to Windows 2000 Change and Configuration Management.

3. Microsoft TechNet Articles:

    - "Windows 2000: Designing and Deploying Active Directory Service for the Microsoft Internal Corpnet." Available on March 2000 and later TechNet CDs.

    - "Designing the Active Directory Structure." Available on July 1999 and later TechNet CDs.

    - "Using the Delegation of Control Wizard." Available on June 1999 and later TechNet CDs.

    - "Designing the Active Directory." Available on August 1999 and later TechNet CDs.

4. Nielsen, Morten Strunge. *Windows 2000 Server Architecture and Planning.* Coriolis, 1999. Chapters 8 and 9.

5. Cone, Boggs, Perez. *Planning for Windows 2000.* New Riders, 1999. Chapter 6.

6. Lowe-Norris, Allistar G. *Windows 2000 Active Directory.* O'Reilly and Associates, 2000. Chapter 9. (This chapter is also available on Microsoft TechNet.)

7. *Microsoft Windows 2000 Server Resource Kit.* Microsoft Press, 2000. Chapter 9.

OBJECTIVES

This chapter covers the following Microsoft-specified objective for the Designing a Microsoft Windows 2000 Directory Services Infrastructure exam:

Design a schema modification policy.

▶ Managing the Active Directory schema has network-wide implications. One aspect of management involves deciding when and how to modify the schema. "Extending" the schema is a powerful feature that requires a well-thought-out and tightly managed policy.

CHAPTER 13

Developing a Schema Modification Plan

▶ Open the Active Directory schema using the MMC and traverse both classes and attributes to get a feel for the types of information defined in each.

▶ Do both exercises at the end of this chapter and pay special attention to the processes discussed in each.

▶ In your test lab, create new attributes; structural, abstract, and auxiliary classes; and attribute syntax rules—and examine how each is represented in the directory.

▶ Discuss schemas in general with programming and database gurus.

INTRODUCTION

As you become increasingly comfortable with the Active Directory structure and begin to see the value of an enterprise-wide directory service, you'll no doubt want to start exploring how to further extend the directory and its associated objects and attributes. To do this, though, you'll need to have a thorough understanding of the schema.

In this chapter we'll focus on developing a schema modification policy. In doing so, we'll take a relatively detailed look at the schema itself. Understanding how it is implemented will go a long way as you consider extending it to further grow with your organization.

SCHEMA OVERVIEW

The Active Directory schema is stored in a database, which indicates the following:

- ◆ It is dynamically extensible.

- ◆ It is dynamically available to user applications.

- ◆ It can use DACLs to protect or filter access to all classes and attributes.

Through use of its classes, attributes, and attribute syntax, the schema defines every object that can be stored in the directory. It additionally contains a set of rules that manage the hierarchical structure and content of Active Directory.

There is only one schema per Windows 2000 forest. It is stored on every domain controller and maintained forest-wide. The advantage to this is that all objects—such as users, computers, and groups— conform to the same set of rules and contain the same types of data. You may recall from a previous discussion that the schema is one of the areas that doesn't implement well in a distributed environment. Because of this, there is only one writable copy of the schema— held by the Schema Operations Master—at any given time within a forest.

WARNING

Don't Take Schema Modification Lightly   This chapter discusses modifying the Active Directory schema, an irreversible process. Consider this warning as one of those constant and familiar "You are about to modify the registry" warnings you're probably familiar with. Modifying the registry in Windows NT or 2000 has system-wide implications. Modifying the schema has *enterprise*-wide implications. Thus, don't carelessly or casually perform modifications to the schema.

Locating the Schema

The *schema* is a naming context—a tree of directory objects that forms a unit of replication. It is a child of the configuration container yet is implemented as a unique unit of replication (see Figure 13.1). Because the schema defines a naming context (a configuration), it is a child of the configuration container. You will recall that the configuration container itself is a unit of replication. The schema container however does not participate in "normal" replication with the configuration container because of its single-master implementation. Instead, it is its own unit of replication, which is the reason for the dotted line in Figure 13.1. The later section "Implications of Schema Modification" further describes the schema replication process.

You can reference the schema container by its distinguished name (DN), as you can any and all other Active Directory objects. The DN for the Active Directory schema is as follows:

```
cn=schema,cn=configuration,DC=<your_root_domain>,
➡DC=<your-namespace-root>
```

The DN of course represents the logical location of the schema, but it is physically stored in the Active Directory database, which is a file named ntds.dit. This file is stored in the <systemroot>\ntds directory and is created when the very first domain controller in a forest is installed.

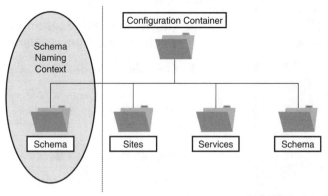

FIGURE 13.1
The Active Directory schema container is a child of the configuration container.

The Schema Container

The schema container holds all the class and attribute definitions required to view the objects in the directory. It does not appear under the configuration container as you might expect but is instead viewable using the Active Directory Schema MMC snap-in. Additionally, you can use the ADSIedit MMC utility to bind to the schema naming context and view its contents.

The RootDSE represents the top of a domain namespace. It holds special attributes that refer to the naming contexts of a single domain controller. These contexts again are the directory (domain), schema, and configuration. Additionally, it refers to the forest root naming context. The RootDSE contains the attribute schemaNamingContext, which provides the location of the schema so that applications connecting to any domain controller in the forest have a standard and uniform place to request the location of the schema. Figure 13.2 illustrates the property page of the RootDSE in ADSIedit focused on naming context. The attribute displayed is schemaNamingContext, and the value is the DN of the schema.

To view the schemaNamingContext attribute in RootDSE, follow Step by Step 13.1.

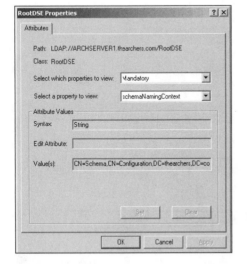

FIGURE 13.2
Applications can determine the location of the schema by querying the RootDSE entry at the top of the namespace.

STEP BY STEP

13.1 Retrieving the Location of the Schema Without Knowing the Domain Name

1. Open the ADSIedit MMC snap-in.

2. Within the ADSIedit MMC, right-click ADSIedit in the left console pane. Choose Connect To.

3. Select the Naming Context radio button, and from the drop-down list select RootDSE. Click OK.

4. Expand the RootDSE entry under ADSIedit in the left console pane.

5. Right-click the RootDSE folder and select Properties.

6. In the Select a Property to View drop-down list, select schemaNamingContext.

7. The value you are looking for (the logical location of the schema) is displayed in the Value(s) field.

ACTIVE DIRECTORY SCHEMA OBJECTS

The objects in Active Directory are defined by schema classes and attributes. These classes and attributes are stored in Active Directory as schema objects. The schema container itself is even represented in the directory as an instance of a special object called the dMD (Directory Management Domain) class. This X.500 class is for data that pertains to the authoritative domain for an enterprise.

Classes are defined by classSchema objects and are therefore instances of the classSchema class. Attributes are defined by attibuteSchema objects and are therefore instances of the attributeSchema class.

The following sections describe classes and attributes in detail.

What Is the Schema Class?

A *class* is a formal description of a discrete, identifiable type of object that is stored in Active Directory. Users, computers, printers, and groups are all instances of classes. When you create a user in the directory, you are essentially creating an instance of the user class, which is defined and governed by the classSchema object.

Out of the box, Active Directory defines 142 schema class objects. There are four types of classes that make up the entire directory, which will be discussed in the following sections. But first, we need to discuss a bit more about classes in general.

> **NOTE**
>
> **classSchema and attributeSchema**
> For more information on the classSchema and attributeSchema classes, refer to the white paper "Active Directory Schema," which is available on the Windows 2000 Web site (**http://www.microsoft.com/ windows2000**).

> **NOTE**
>
> **Possibility for Multiple Superclasses**
> A subclass can be derived by more
> than one class—hence the use of the
> plural "superclasses."

Classes contain either mandatory or optional attributes. Classes may also be derived from other classes, creating a class hierarchy. You need to remember that subclasses—classes derived from other classes—inherit the mandatory and optional attributes from their parent classes (which are known as superclasses). If another class is derived from a class that was derived from another class, then that class will inherit the mandatory and optional attributes from both superclasses. Any subclass can define its own attributes as well. If your head is spinning right now, don't worry—it's only temporary!

The following sections describe the four types of classes.

Structural Classes

Structural classes are the only classes that can have instances in the directory. Structural classes are used to create the structure of Active Directory and are derived from other structural classes or abstract classes.

> **NOTE**
>
> **The "Top" Class**   Every class is
> derived from a special class called
> top that sits atop the class hierarchy.
> Each class then inherits the manda-
> tory attributes from top.

Abstract Classes

Abstract classes are used only to derive structural or other abstract classes. They are essentially used as templates. Abstract classes cannot contain objects whose superclasses are made only of abstract classes. This means that every object in the directory must have at least one superclass that is nonabstract. Abstract classes themselves cannot be instantiated in the directory.

Auxiliary Classes

Like abstract classes, *auxiliary* classes cannot be instantiated in the directory. Instead, the purpose of the auxiliary class is to simply provide a list of attributes. The class may then be added to the definition of a structural subclass. Auxiliary classes can be used to derive additional auxiliary classes.

A good example of the use of auxiliary classes comes with security principals. The class securityPrincipal is an auxiliary class. The user structural class is derived by many classes, one of which being the securityPrincipal class. Instances of the user class—such as domain users—inherit all the attributes of all of its superclasses, therefore making every user a security principal in the directory. Figure 13.3 illustrates how the structural class user is defined. Notice the use of both abstract and auxiliary classes in its definition.

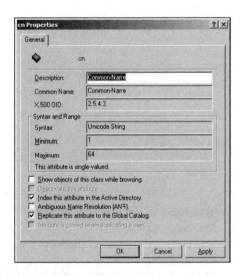

FIGURE 13.3
The user class is derived from several abstract and auxiliary classes.

88 Classes

The original 1988 implementation of X.500 did not require class categorization. The updated 1993 version recognized structural, abstract, and auxiliary classes. Because of this, any pre-1993 classes defined that don't fall into one of these three categories are placed into another class called the *88* class. You should not create new instances of this class.

What Is the Schema Attribute?

Attributes are used to define the classes within the schema. They are themselves defined in the schema, but separately from the classes. This allows a single attribute definition to be applied to many classes. A class definition can contain mandatory and optional attributes. All attributes are objects of the attributeSchema class.

Mandatory Attributes

Mandatory attributes are just what they sound like: object attributes that must be specified before an object can be created. For example, the *cn* (common name) of an instance of the user class is required before that instance can be created.

Optional Attributes

Optional attributes are just what they sound like as well: object attributes that may or may not be specified when an instance of an object is created. For example, the userPassword attribute is optional for instances of the user class (user accounts). Of course, it is always recommended that you set a password for users.

Single- or Multi-Valued Attributes

Both types of attributes may be single-valued or multi-valued. This means they may hold a single value, or a list of values. The values in a multi-valued attribute must all conform to the syntax rule governing that attribute.

Attribute Syntax

Attribute syntax refers to a set of rules that govern the legal values an attribute can hold. One attribute might be set to require integers only, another a date, and still another a string. The syntax attached to an attribute force that attribute to store and present data in a standard and uniform format throughout the entire schema. Each attribute can be associated with exactly one syntax.

Attribute Indexing and Replication

Attributes can be indexed to make searches in Active Directory for or on that attribute more efficient. They may be replicated to the Global Catalog to make entire directory searches more efficient.

Indexing a Schema Attribute

To index a schema attribute, you simply navigate to that attribute property page and enable the Index This Attribute in the Active Directory check box. By doing this, you are telling Active Directory that it can sort and group by that attribute, which is useful for queries and reports. There are a few rules you should follow when determining whether to index an attribute:

◆ Select only single-valued attributes. If you select multi-valued attributes, you increase the cost of storage, update time, and search time.

◆ Select attributes whose values are most likely to be unique. You don't need to index attributes that hold information, such as country if you already know all objects share that country.

◆ The more indexed attributes a schema class has, the longer it takes to create an instance of that class.

◆ All instances of the attribute are added to the index, not just the instances that are members of a particular class.

Figure 13.4 displays the attribute property page containing the indexing and replication options for the attribute.

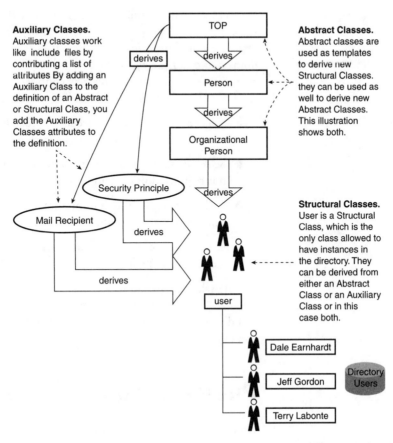

Auxiliary Classes.
Auxiliary classes work like include files by contributing a list of attributes By adding an Auxiliary Class to the definition of an Abstract or Structural Class, you add the Auxiliary Classes attributes to the definition.

Abstract Classes.
Abstract classes are used as templates to derive new Structural Classes. they can be used as well to derive new Abstract Classes. This illustration shows both.

Structural Classes.
User is a Structural Class, which is the only class allowed to have instances in the directory. They can be derived from either an Abstract Class or an Auxiliary Class or in this case both.

FIGURE 13.4
The cn attribute property page.

Replicating a Schema Attribute to the Global Catalog

Only a subset of attributes that define each class are populated in the Global Catalog (GC) by default. If every attribute were to be replicated to the GC, the strain on DCs and bandwidth in general would likely wind up being overbearing.

Your user base may utilize a specific attribute that is not replicated to the Global Catalog by default. Full directory searches on that attribute would turn up only those attributes located in the local domain and not the entire directory, therefore producing incomplete results. In these situations, you may consider adding an attribute to the GC. The following rules should be considered in this situation:

◆ Select attributes that are needed for locating objects that may occur anywhere in the Active Directory forest.

◆ Select attributes that need to be read quickly, but may or may not require additional attention.

◆ To keep replication to a minimum, select attributes whose values are relatively stable.

◆ Keep an eye on the size of the attribute. Choose attributes that are relatively small in size.

You are relatively free to replicate any attribute to the Global Catalog. Just keep in mind that to do so increases replication time and disk storage requirements and may or may not yield the benefits you expected.

Preparing to Modify the Schema

Now that you have a bit of schema background, we'll start moving toward developing a schema modification policy. First, however, we will take a look at how you can prepare for schema modification.

There are a few instances in which you will be faced with no choice but to extend the schema. When Microsoft Exchange 2000 is released, for example, the first step in its installation will be to add its class and attribute definitions to the schema. Installing software is one process that can extend the schema. Other ways to do it include using the Active Directory Schema MMC, ADSIedit, and writing (and running) custom ADSI scripts.

It should be mentioned here that software installations involving schema extensions will likely need to be done in two stages: one to extend the schema and one to install the software.

Remember, the schema can be extended only by a member of the Schema Adminis group. Additionally, the only extensible copy of the schema resides on the Schema Master domain controller.

EXAM TIP

Extending the Schema Although modification of the schema is not very prevalent, it is possible that this activity will be the subject of certain exam questions. Some applications (like Microsoft Exchange 2000) need the schema extended to be installed properly. It's important to understand that often the installer (such as Exchange Installer) handles the schema extension, and in such cases there should not need to be any extension performed manually.

When to Modify the Schema

You should modify the schema only when you have exhausted every other means of accomplishing whatever it is you want to accomplish. This means examine every single object class and attribute definition to make absolutely sure you cannot use a combination of one or more of them to accomplish your goal. There are over 140 classes and over 850 attributes that make up the schema, which makes for literally thousands of possible combinations.

Modifying the schema is an irreversible operation with directory-wide implications. You cannot "un-extend" the schema. You can only disable portions of it. When and if you do so, you run the risk of creating inconsistencies in the directory schema. Inconsistencies in the schema can cause significant Active Directory problems that may not be immediately noticeable. With that said, you can see why there is such emphasis on planning and mitigating risks associated with extending the schema.

Table 13.1 lists some common situations and suggests resolutions regarding schema modifications.

TABLE 13.1

SOME COMMON SITUATIONS REQUIRING MODIFICATION OF THE SCHEMA

Situation	*Suggestion*
You cannot find an existing class to fit your needs.	Create a new class.
You find an existing class that would fit your needs with the addition of some attributes.	Either create new attributes and associate them with the existing class, or derive a new subclass and add additional attributes as needed.
You only need a set of unique attributes—not a class.	Create a new auxiliary class and attach it to the appropriate class.
Existing classes and/or attributes are no longer relevant.	Deactivate the class(es) or attribute(s).

What Can I Modify?

If you come to the conclusion that extending the schema is your only choice, you must understand what you can and cannot modify. As Table 13.1 suggests, the following are the types of modifications you *can* make in the schema.

◆ Create a new class or subclass.

◆ Modify an existing class or subclass.

◆ Create new attributes.

◆ Modify existing attributes.

◆ Deactivate a class and/or attribute.

What Can I Not Modify?

Not all schema objects can be modified. Some aspects of the *classSchema* and *attributeSchema* object (hence all classes and attributes) are defined as pairs in which one of these attributes can be modified, and the other can never be modified or deactivated, by anyone. Table 13.2 describes these pairs.

> **NOTE**
>
> **Class-Definition Objects** Some text uses the terminology *class-definition* and *attribute-definition* to describe the classSchema and attributeSchema objects.

TABLE 13.2

CLASS-DEFINITION ATTRIBUTE PAIRS

Modifiable Attribute	System Only (No Modification Allowed)
Must-Contain	System-Must-Contain
May-Contain	System-May-Contain
Poss-Superiors	System-Poss-Superiors
Auxiliary Class	System-Auxiliary-Class

Anything that begins with *System-* cannot be modified under any circumstances.

Finally, the attribute-definition object specifies the syntax of an attribute and whether the attribute is single- or multi-valued. This information is hard-coded and cannot be changed.

Relevance of Data

As you investigate further what is going to be involved in making a schema modification, you should also consider the relevance of the change. Remember that the schema is global across the entire forest. Although the schema will be updated globally, that doesn't mean objects must be instantiated globally. If you are making schema modifications for an application that will be installed in only one domain, for example, you must verify that instances of the object or attribute you are creating are relevant across the domain in which you create them.

How to Modify the Schema

Once you determine modification of the schema is inevitable, you must understand how to do it. The first step is to remove Microsoft's built-in "safety locks," which are there to prevent inadvertent modifications from taking place.

Remove the Safety Locks

Microsoft uses the following safety locks to secure the schema:

◆ By default, schema modification is disabled on all domain controllers.

◆ The schema object is protected by the Windows 2000 security model. Only members of the Schema Admins (forest root administrator by default) group can write changes to the schema.

◆ Only one domain controller in the forest contains a copy of the schema with write access. This is the domain controller holding the Schema Master FSMO role.

◆ By default, modification of the schema is disabled even on the Schema Master server. It must be enabled using the Active Directory Schema MMC before any modification can take place.

◆ By default, modification of the schema is disabled even on the Schema Master server. It must be enabled using the Active Directory Schema MMC before any modification can take place.

The following sections describe how to remove these safety locks.

Locate the Schema Master and Enable Write Access

You can use a variety of methods to determine which domain controller in the forest holds the Schema Master role. Some we have discussed in this book are NTDSUTIL and Replication Monitor. Once you determine the Schema Master role holder, you must enable that instance of the schema for modification by checking the The Schema May Be Modified on This Server check box on the Change Operations Master property window. You get to this by selecting Operations Master from the context menu of the Active Directory Schema MMC object (see Figure 13.5). When you enable the Schema Master for schema modification, the following registry key is set:

```
HKEY_LOCAL_MACHINE\SYSTEM\CurrentControlSet\Services\NTDS\
➥Parameters\ Schema Update Allowed REG_DWORD 0x00000001
```

If changes to the schema are made at a domain controller that is not a schema writable domain controller (the Schema Master), the settings do not apply and the following message is generated in the Active Directory Schema MMC:

```
The displayable status could not be changed.
```

So, in summary, you can make changes to the schema from any domain controller, but you must be connected to (or, more appropriately, your utility must be focused on) the domain controller that contains the writable copy of the schema—the Schema Flexible Single Master of Operations.

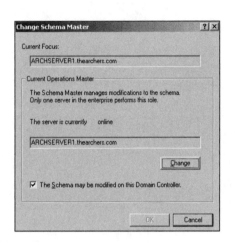

FIGURE 13.5
The Schema can be modified only if it is allowed!

Add Appropriate Administrators to Schema Admins

Once you enable the schema for modification, the only other thing you need to do is verify that the administrator making the changes either logs on as an account in the Schema Admins group, or is added to it. Again, by default, the only member of this group is the administrator in the first domain created.

Obtain an Object Identifier (OID)

The next step in creating a Schema object—whether it be a class or attribute, or some derivation thereof—is to obtain an *object identifier (OID)* for it. Each schema object must be represented by a globally unique number, which is referred to as the OID.

OIDs are referenced in dotted-decimal notation—the same idea behind a TCP/IP address. They take the form *1.2.840.x.w.y.z.* The ISO controls the distribution of high-level OIDs to Name Registration Authorities (NRAs), which in turn distribute OID braches to requesting companies or individuals. The American National Standards Institute (ANSI) issues root OIDs in the United States using the high-level OID 1.2.840. Microsoft, for example, was issued the root OID of 1.2.840.113556. They can in turn issue anything below this OID to resources that require OIDs, such as the Active Directory Schema, SNMP, OSI Applications, and other X.500 directories.

Table 13.3 dissects an OID Microsoft uses for the schema class builtin-domain.

TABLE 13.3

OID DISSECTION OF THE SCHEMA CLASS BUILTIN-DOMAIN

Value of the OID (1.2.840.113556.1.5.4)	Issued To	Sequence of Events
1	ISO ("root")	Issues 1.2 to ANSI
2	ANSI	Issues 1.2.840 to the United States
840	USA	Issues 1.2.840.113556 to Microsoft
113556	Microsoft	Internally manages several OID branches under 1.2.840.113556, which includes a branch called Active Directory (see next row).
1	Active Directory	A branch called Active Directory, which includes a branch called Classes (see next row).
5	Classes	A branch called classes, which includes a branch called builtinDomain (see next row).
4	Built-In Domain	A branch called builtinDomain.

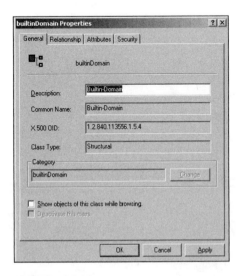

FIGURE 13.6
The properties window of Builtin-Domain displays its X.500 OID.

Figure 13.6 displays the properties of the Active Directory schema class Builtin-Domain. Notice the X.500 OID.

Most countries in the world have their own NRA responsible for the issuance of OIDs. They do cost, but you should only have to register once per company.

When you go to create a class or attribute in the schema (you will need to provide an OID before you can continue) it is a mandatory attribute.

After obtaining an OID for your new schema object, you are ready to create it. We will save the creation process for the exercises at the end of this chapter, but we will discuss the implications of schema modification here.

Implications of Schema Modification

As we've discussed, schema modification impacts the entire network because it exists on and is replicated to each and every domain controller in the forest. Active Directory uses a multi-master replication model, but a single master—the domain controller holding the Schema Master operations master role controls changes to the schema. Additionally, when modified in a large environment, it is almost inevitable that multiple versions of the schema will exist for a limited period of time.

In this section, we will discuss how the schema avoids write conflicts and will take a look at replication and recovery.

Write Conflicts

Active Directory avoids schema write conflicts by utilizing a single-master model. That is easy to understand—the way the schema is actually implemented is a bit more challenging to grasp.

There is a minimum of two copies of the schema in existence at a single point in time; a read-only schema cache, and a writable schema database. During cache updates, the "old" version of the cache is not removed until all connections to it are closed. When the new cache is updated, all new threads connect to it.

When a modification is done to the schema, it waits five minutes before updating the cache and starting the replication cycle. During this five minutes, none of the new classes or attributes, or modifications to classes or attributes, can be used. This must happen to ensure the cache remains consistent.

You can force an update to the schema cache, but it is highly recommended you do so only once per editing session. Failing to heed this warning may produce multiple instances of the schema cache and temporarily drain memory.

NOTE

No Reboots!   One of the design challenges Microsoft was able to overcome was allowing schema modifications without the need to reboot. The multiple-cache scenario is how they accomplished this task. In fact, they claim that Windows 2000 reboots are a mere 10% of what they were in Windows NT 4!

Replication Latency

Because schema modifications take place on a single domain controller, they must be replicated out to all other domain controllers, which introduces latency. To ensure integrity and expedite convergence, Microsoft uses a model different and independent of the multi-master replication model to update schemas.

Because schema replication and directory replication do not occur at the same time, it is conceivable that an object instantiated from a newly created schema class or attribute be replicated to a domain whose schema has not yet received that update. In this case, the replication of the object will fail because there is no defined schema class for it.

If this situation occurs, a schema update is automatically sent from the Schema Master domain controller. That in turn triggers a schema cache update on the target domain controller. Active Directory then re-replicates objects that failed to the target domain controller.

Concurrency Control

So what happens if two schema admins attempt to make conflicting changes to the same schema object? To prevent this from happening, the thread requesting update to the schema also (transparently) writes a value to the schema container as part of the write transaction. Only one thread can write to this container at once, therefore ensuring that schema updates occur serially. Chances of you running into this situation manually (with humans making schema changes) are slim; however, if you happen to be installing two directory-enabled applications simultaneously, your chances increase. This is because Active Directory uses one thread per schema object creation. While you are assured that schema object modifications occur serially, you are not guaranteed which application will "win" if two try to write conflicting versions of the same object at the same time.

The resolution for this comes in the management of the schema. You should *never* install two directory-aware applications at the same time.

DEVELOPING A SCHEMA MODIFICATION POLICY

Design a schema modification policy.

Now that you have a good understanding of the characteristics of the schema, its location, the objects involved, and when and how the schema can be modified, it's essential to be able to devise and implement a sound policy that will help you govern the process by which the schema is modified.

As part of your migration to Windows 2000, you need to create a formal team of schema managers that govern the modifications to the schema. This team need not necessarily be all members of the Schema Admins group, but should have a complete and thorough understanding of how the schema works, how to effectively plan for schema modifications, how to mitigate risk, and in general how to avoid problems.

> **IN THE FIELD**
>
> ### LOOK TO THE DATABASE GURUS
>
> When developing a schema management team, you want to have representation from schema experts. Who better fits that bill than a database developer? The schema is a database, and although it can only loosely be compared with the popular database systems (such as SQL, Oracle, Informix, and Sybase), the same key structural ideas are shared.
>
> Look at database developers, or even developers in general, as a form of subject matter experts to make up the core technical side of the schema management team.

The schema management team should be responsible for the development of a Schema Modification Policy. This policy should be added to the standard operating procedures for the company and should be a required reading for all network administrators considering the installation of a directory aware application.

At the very minimum, the policy should include the following sections:

◆ **Initiation.** How schema modifications are submitted and approved and by whom

◆ **Planning.** Verifying that the requested changes fit the needs of the company, how they will be implemented, and by whom, and what the risks are

◆ **Lab-based testing.** Proof of concept

◆ **Implementation.** The update of the production servers

The following sections detail each portion of the process.

Initiating Schema Modifications

One of the first sections documented in the Schema Modification Policy should be the process by which a schema modification request must be initiated. Ideally, your schema management team will hold the key to the locked schema (in the default case, this "key" is the Administrator password for the forest root domain) and will be responsible for both managing it and assisting the domain administrators during implementation.

The implementation section should include the following three functional areas:

◆ **Submitting requests to modify the schema.** This section should include the procedure by which schema modification requests should be submitted. This day and age would probably dictate that a custom intranet page be prepared for this.

◆ **Validating the need for the requested change.** This is the bulk of the work required by the schema management team because they must determine what, if anything, the change could affect. In doing so, the team must mitigate the risk of making such a change.

◆ **Approving or denying the requested changes.** Based on evidence collected so far, the schema management team must determine whether to allow the change. If they decide to allow the change, the next stage of the policy is executed.

Planning Schema Modifications

As with all other aspects of Windows 2000, planning is essential. The same goes for making schema modifications. Once approved, the schema management team (in a joint planning effort with the requesting party) should create a plan to implement the changes.

The schema modification planning session should consist, at a minimum, of the following two elements:

◆ Ensuring once again that the requested modifications fit the needs of the requested modifications

◆ Creating a recovery plan

Testing Schema Modifications

Each and every schema modification request that is approved should be tested in a simulated lab environment prior to implementation. This way, any failures or warnings can be properly addressed before production implementation.

The schema management team should be jointly involved in this process as well and should be documenting its results for some kind of a knowledgebase.

Executing Schema Modifications

The final stage is the actual modification of production schema. Although this task might ultimately be performed by the network administrator (or other network-related individual) the schema management team should be present to oversee the operation.

CASE STUDY: PROFESSIONAL SALES FORCE (PSF)

BACKGROUND

PSF is a new professional services sales company specializing in the highly competitive eBusiness market. It has a staff of 600, which is evenly dispersed in three offices around the country. These offices are in Denver (headquarters), Orlando, and Atlanta. PSF runs Windows 2000 and uses a phantom top-level domain (psf.com) with three domains (Denver.psf.com, Orlando.psf.com, and Atlanta.psf.com) residing at the second level. Each domain is administered autonomously and the root domain is in Denver.

PROBLEM STATEMENT

In Orlando, the sales staff has decided to attempt innovation to address its problems. Because of the complex and ever-changing sales cycle, is it very difficult for the financial analyst to maintain his sales pipeline. The sales staff is constantly changing prospect, funnel, and close totals (three totals the pipeline must include and must include accurately enough to prepare a forecast for the months to come).

CURRENT SYSTEM

Sales Manager

"Each week, we have a two-hour meeting with our entire sales staff to discuss the pipeline. Each rep is responsible for updating his prospect—potential sales, his funnel—sales that are committed to but not yet closed, and his closed—sales that have been inked—figures with the financial analyst before the meeting is over."

Financial Analyst

"Each week after the sales meeting, I take the updated numbers and update my pipeline and forecast. It takes me the entire week because I have to revisit the sales staff and acquire their full account list to determine what money belongs to what account."

ENVISIONED SYSTEM

Sales Manager

"It would be really nice if we had a single place for our reps to both update and manage their sales universe. We found such a system written for Windows 2000; it says something about directory integration so I assume I'll have to let our IT people install it."

Financial Analyst

"With this new system, I should be able to open up the database that sales uses to manage its accounts and get the information I need in real time."

IT Administrator

"This new sales funnel manager application integrates with Active Directory. It needs to modify the schema to store some additional information about sales users. This information includes the salesperson's sales certification ID (each salesperson must be professionally certified), and the primary sales certification he holds. The funnel manager application uses the certification ID as a database key for security."

CASE STUDY: PROFESSIONAL SALES FORCE (PSF)

MAINTAINABILITY

Sales Manager
"Each sales rep should be able to manage his account list, including the creation of new accounts and the deletion of old accounts—but only his own. I should be able to see all accounts."

AVAILABILITY

Biff the Salesman
"I use whatever computer is available at the office because I move around a lot—I want to make sure I have access to my accounts wherever I am."

CHAPTER SUMMARY

Active Directory schema is stored in a database, which indicates the following:

◆ It is dynamically extensible.

◆ It is dynamically available to user applications.

◆ It can use DACLs to protect or filter access to all classes and attributes.

The schema is composed of classes, attributes, and attribute syntax. Structural classes are used to form the structure of Active Directory; for example, you derive a user object from the user schema class, an OU object from an organizationalUnit class, or a group object from a group class. *Deriving* objects means you "instantiate," or create an instance of, an existing Active Directory class. Two other classes, abstract and auxiliary, are used as templates to derive structural classes, or as attribute containers, respectively.

Attributes are used to define schema classes. They come in many shapes, forms, and sizes. For example, a mandatory attribute that is applied to a class must be specified before an object derived from that class can be instantiated. Conversely, optional attributes may or may not be specified at the time of instantiation.

Attributes can be associated with exactly one *attribute syntax*, which is a set of rules that preside over the type of data that is acceptable for that attribute.

KEY TERMS

- structural class
- abstract class
- auxiliary class
- 88 class
- mandatory attribute
- optional attribute
- attribute syntax
- Object identifier (OID)
- classSchema object
- attributeSchema object

CHAPTER SUMMARY

Modifying the schema is a task that has forest-wide implications. Therefore, great caution must be taken when extending the schema. You should extend the schema if you need to do the following:

◆ Create a new class or subclass.

◆ Modify an existing class or subclass.

◆ Create new attributes.

◆ Modify existing attributes.

◆ Deactivate a class and/or attribute.

The schema can be modified only by a member of the Schema Admins group, and all modifications can be applied only to the domain controller holding the Schema Master FSMO role. Additionally, schema modifications must be enabled before the database is opened for write.

As you implement Windows 2000 and Active Directory, you should create a schema management team. This team will be responsible for approving all modifications to the schema and will control access to the schema. They should also be responsible for publishing a Schema Modification Policy, which contains the following sections:

◆ **Initiation.** How schema modifications are submitted and approved and by whom

◆ **Planning.** Verifying that the requested changes fit the needs of the company, how they will be implemented, and by whom, and what are the risks

◆ **Lab-based testing.** Proof of concept

◆ **Implementation.** The update of the production servers

APPLY YOUR KNOWLEDGE

Exercises

WARNING

Watch Your Schema! These exercises walk you through schema modifications. Please don't do this on a production domain controller!

13.1 Creating Schema Attributes

In this exercise, you will create a few new schema attributes in preparation for Exercise 13.2. We will use the schema attributes referenced in the case study, although an application may or may not implement the schema objects in this fashion.

Estimated Time: 10 Minutes

1. Verify that you are logged on as a member of the Schema Admins group and that the schema has been enabled for modification.

2. Open the Active Directory Schema MMC.

3. Expand the Active Directory Schema in the left console pane.

4. Right-click Attributes in the left console pane and select New, then Attribute. Pay close attention to the ensuing warning shown in Figure 13.7.

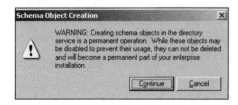

FIGURE 13.7
Heed this warning!

5. Click Continue to continue the attribute creation process.

6. Refer to Figure 13.8 to fill in the attribute properties.

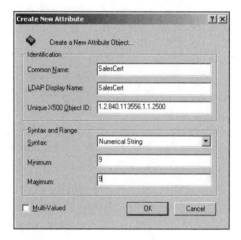

FIGURE 13.8
The Create New Attribute window.

7. Click OK to add the object to the schema attributes.

8. Scroll down the right console pane to your new SalesCert object and open its properties context window.

9. Use Figure 13.9 to give it a description, index it in Active Directory, and add it to the Global Catalog.

APPLY YOUR KNOWLEDGE

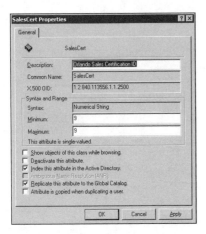

FIGURE 13.9
Use the SalesCert attribute general properties window to add it to the Global Catalog and index it in the directory.

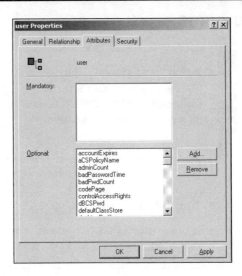

FIGURE 13.10
The user schema class attribute window before modification. Notice that you cannot add mandatory attributes to this structural class.

10. Repeat steps 4 through 9 to add an attribute to store the most recent sales certification date. Use OID 1.2.840.113556.1.1.2501 and name the attribute SalesCertProgram.

13.2 Extending a Schema Class

In this exercise, you will extend the *user* class and add the attributes from Exercise 13.1 in the appropriate places.

Estimated Time: 10 Minutes

1. While still in the Active Directory Schema MMC, click Classes in the left console pane.

2. In the right console pane, scroll down to the user schema class.

3. Open the user properties context window, and select the Attributes tab. See Figure 13.10.

4. To add the two Sales optional attributes, click the Add button.

5. Scroll down and select both attributes you created in Exercise 13.1. You will have to do this one at a time. Figure 13.11 shows the added attributes.

   The user schema class attribute window after modification displays the attributes added to the user class.

6. Click the OK button. You have just extended the user class schema object to support two additional user attributes!

APPLY YOUR KNOWLEDGE

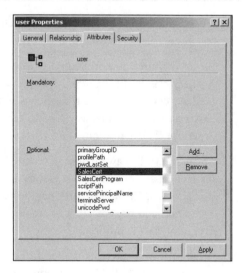

FIGURE 13.11
The optional attributes are visible here.

Review Questions

1. Describe the four types of schema classes.

2. Describe the two common types of schema attributes and the primary difference between them.

3. Describe how Windows 2000 prevents schema write conflicts.

4. What is the scope of a schema extension?

5. What is the purpose of an Object Identifier?

6. List three types of schema modifications that can be performed.

7. Describe the difference between a single-valued and multi-valued attribute and then describe the attribute syntax rules.

8. Describe how applications determine the location of the schema.

Exam Questions

1. You are in charge of coordinating the installation for the Sales Funnel Manager application for PSF. You want to determine how the application should be installed. Which of these answers best describes how the installation process should occur?

   A. The application must be installed in two separate phases; an administrator in Orlando must first install the application itself, then an administrator in Denver must extend the schema.

   B. The application must be installed in two separate phases; a domain administrator must install the application in Denver, then after replication, a schema administrator must extend the schema on the domain controller on which the software will reside in Orlando.

   C. The application must be installed in two separate phases; a schema administrator must update the schema on the Schema Master in Denver, then after schema replication, a domain administrator must install the application in Orlando.

   D. A domain administrator in Orlando must simply run the application's setup program and it will extend the schema and install the application immediately.

2. Suppose the IT administrator in the Orlando domain is new and doesn't know where the Schema Master FSMO role holder is located. How could she locate this information?

APPLY YOUR KNOWLEDGE

A. Utilize the ADSIedit utility, connect to dMD, and view the value of schemaNamingContext attribute.

B. Utilize the NTDSUTIL to view the RootDSEs of the current operations masters.

C. Utilize the Schema Manager by selecting Operations Master from the context menu of the Active Directory Schema object.

D. Utilize the Active Directory Replication Monitor and view the Schema Roles tab on the properties page of a server.

3. To which group must the administrator who runs the schema extension portion of the application installation belong?

A. Local Domain Administrators

B. Schema Admins

C. Enterprise Administrators

D. Enterprise Administrators and Local Domain Administrators

4. You want to create three new structural classes using the least number of administrative steps possible. Each class must be derived from different existing classes. Each new class requires three new attributes be added to its definition. Which answer requires the least administrative steps to complete the task?

A. Derive your three new structural classes. Create the three new attributes. Add each new attribute to the class definition for each structural class.

B. Create an auxiliary class. Create the three new attributes. Add the three attributes to the auxiliary class. Derive the three new structural classes and add the auxiliary class to each structural class definition.

C. Create the three new attributes. Create an auxiliary class. Add the new attributes to the auxiliary class. Create the three new structural classes and add the auxiliary class to each structural class definition.

D. Create the three new attributes. Create a new abstract class. Add the new attributes to the abstract class. Create the three new structural classes and add the abstract class to each structural class definition.

5. You attempt to run the schema modification portion of the Sales Funnel Manager setup and receive an error message stating that modification of the schema is not enabled on this domain controller. Where must you enable the schema for modification?

A. Using the Active Directory Schema MMC utility, select Operations Master from the context menu of the Active Directory Schema object and enable the domain controller for schema modifications.

B. Using the NTDSUTIL, type the command **enable schema write** from the domain fsmo prompt.

C. Using the Active Directory Replication monitor, right-click the Schema Master domain controller and select Enable for Write.

D. Using the ADSIedit utility, connect to the RootDSE and enable the Schema Master for modifications.

APPLY YOUR KNOWLEDGE

6. Members of the Denver corporate sales team would like the ability to query an Orlando salesperson by certification number. What actions must/should occur to make this operation possible/efficient. (Choose two.)

   A. The attribute should be added to SYSVOL.

   B. The attribute should be indexed.

   C. The attribute must be indexed.

   D. The attribute must be added to the Global Catalog.

   E. The attribute should be added to the Global Catalog.

   F. The attribute must be added to SYSVOL.

7. Suppose you add a new attribute to store a Social Security number in the schema. What must you do to ensure that only numbers are accepted as input for this attribute's value?

   A. Add an attribute mask.

   B. Create a class that allows only numbers for input and add the attribute to the class.

   C. Select a number-only attribute type when creating the attribute.

   D. Apply an attribute syntax rule to the attribute.

8. During normal operations on the Schema Master domain controller, how many copies of the schema are utilized by Windows 2000?

   A. 1

   B. 2

   C. 3

   D. 4

Answers to Review Questions

1. The schema consists of the following four types of classes:

   - **Abstract classes.** A superclass from which other classes can be derived. It cannot be instantiated as an object in the directory.

   - **Auxiliary classes.** A superclass that other classes can include in their definition. It cannot be instantiated as an object in the directory.

   - **Structural classes.** The only type of schema class that can be instantiated as an object in the directory.

   - **88 classes.** Class created solely to hold all pre-1993 implementations of class objects that do not fall into one of the previous categories. These classes are rarely, if ever, used.

   For more information, see "What Is the Schema Class?"

2. The schema contains the following two main types of attributes:

   - **Mandatory attributes.** attributeSchema objects that, when part of a structural class, must be specified before the object may be instantiated.

   - **Optional attributes.** attributeSchema objects that, when part of a structural class, may or may not be specified when an object is instantiated.

   For more information, see "What Is the Schema Attribute?"

3. The Active Directory avoids schema write conflicts by utilizing a single-master model. The Schema Master operations master role is assigned

APPLY YOUR KNOWLEDGE

to the first domain controller in the forest by default. By default, all modifications to the schema must occur on the copy of the schema database hosted by the Schema Master. See "Write Conflicts."

4. The scope of a schema extension is the entire Active Directory forest. Although a schema object may not be instantiated throughout the forest, its definition is replicated to each and every domain controller in the forest. For more information, see "Schema Overview."

5. An OID is a globally unique identifier required to reference schema objects, which need be unique throughout the world. The OID takes the form of 1.2.840.w.x.y.z in the U.S., where *w* is an OID level assigned to a company, and *x.y.z* are arbitrarily assigned to objects within the directory. *1.* is controlled by the ISO, *1.2* is controlled by ANSI, and *1.2.840* is assigned to the United States by ANSI, which is the name registration authority for the U.S. For more information, see "Obtain an Object Identifier (OID)."

6. There are several types of schema modifications you can make, including the following:

   • Create a new class or subclass.

   • Modify an existing class or subclass.

   • Create new attributes.

   • Modify existing attributes.

   • Deactivate a class and/or attribute.

   There are some instances in which you cannot perform modifications; for example, you cannot modify the system portion of any schema object, nor can you modify any portion of the schema that defines the Active Directory structure. See "What Can I Modify?"

7. Attributes can be defined to contain a single value or a list of values. It is recommended that you minimize the use of multi-valued attributes because of their added overhead. When you apply an attribute syntax rule to an attribute, whether it is a single or multiple valued attribute, that rule governs each value within that attribute. See "Single- or Multi-Valued Attributes."

8. When you install a directory-enabled application, chances are it will need to extend the schema in some way. To do this, it must locate the schema. The RootDSE refers to the top of the namespace, which holds the domain, schema, and configuration containers. It contains the special attribute schemaNamingContext, which provides the location of the schema so that applications connecting to any domain controller in the forest have a standard and uniform place to request the location of the schema. See "The Schema Container."

Answers to Exam Questions

1. **C.** Applications that extend the schema generally need to be run in two distinct phases. This is especially true when there are multiple domains in the forest. A schema administrator must first extend the schema on the domain controller holding the Schema Master role. Changes to the schema must then replicate out to the other domains, or at minimum the domain in which the application is to be installed. After that completes, the application can be installed by a local domain administrator. See "Preparing to Modify the Schema."

2. **C.** Each of the utilities presented in A, B, C, and D are valid ways to determine the Schema Master. Only answer C is correct, however. In Answer A, you would use ADSIedit to connect to RootDSE, not dMD. In Answer B, you would use NTDSUTIL to view the DNs of the operations masters, not the RootDSEs. In Answer D, you could use replication to view the FSMO Roles property page, not the Schema Roles property page. See "Locate the Schema Master and Enable Write Access."

3. **B.** To have the correct permission to extend the schema, an administrator must be a member of the Schema Admins group. See "Preparing to Modify the Schema."

4. **C.** Answers A, B, and C all allow you to perform the task, but all require more administrative steps than Answer C. Because you add attributes to classes, it stands that attributes must be created first. Whenever you have more than one attribute that could potentially be included in a class definition, you should create an auxiliary class. The auxiliary class allows you to make use of inheritance to define classes. Abstract classes can only be used to derive other abstract and structural classes. See Exercise 13.1, "Creating Schema Attributes," and Exercise 13.2, "Extending a Schema Class."

5. **A.** The only way to enable the schema for write (unless you directly edit the registry) is to enable the check box that allows for schema modifications on the Schema Master domain controller. You do this by selecting Operations Master from the Active Directory Schema context menu. See "Locate the Schema Master and Enable Write Access."

6. **B, D.** To give the Denver office the ability to query by the SalesCert number, it must be added to the Global Catalog. It may optionally be indexed so that it can be sorted by and grouped by, but does not have to be. Replicated data exists on SYSVOL, but you do not explicitly add data to it. See "Replicating a Schema Attribute to the Global Catalog."

7. **D.** You can force an attribute to a certain type of data, such as an integer or numerical string, by applying an attribute syntax to it. Attribute syntax rules are applied to attributes at the time of creation. See "Attribute Syntax."

8. **B.** During normal operations, there are typically two copies of the schema in use on the Schema Master domain controller. The writable schema database is used to apply modifications to the schema, and to create a read-only schema cache. The read-only schema cache is used for all other operations. When a modification is made to the schema, the schema cache is re-created and added to memory in addition to the old schema cache, which is slowly phased out online. By doing this, schema modifications are dynamic and do not require a reboot. See "Write Conflicts."

Suggested Readings and Resources

1. White Paper. Step-by-Step Guide to Using Active Directory Schema and Display Specifiers.

2. White Paper. Advanced Management of the Active Directory Using the Schema and Display Specifiers.

3. White Paper. Active Directory Architecture.

4. White Paper. Microsoft Active Directory Service Interfaces: ADSI Open Interfaces for Managing and Using Directory Services

5. White Paper. Windows 2000 Active Directory Display Specifiers.

6. TechNet Article. The Active Directory Schema. Available on July 1999 and later TechNet CDs.

7. Nielsen, Morton Strunge. *Windows 2000 Server Architecture and Planning*. Coriolis, 1999. Chapter 15.

8. Iseminger, David. *Active Directory Services for Microsoft Windows 2000 Technical Reference*. Microsoft Press, 2000. Chapter 10.

This chapter covers the following Microsoft-specified objective for the Designing a Microsoft Windows 2000 Directory Services Infrastructure exam:

Plan for the coexistence of Active Directory and other directory services.

▶ A directory service must have the capability to interoperate with other platform-independent directory services. Effective planning and coexistence testing is essential here, as with any other area of Active Directory.

CHAPTER 14

Planning for Coexistence

▶ Make sure that you run through each of the exercises in this chapter. If you do not have the resources available to walk through them, read them and refer to the abundant figures included in the exercises.

▶ You should not need a thorough and detailed understanding of Services for UNIX; however, you should understand how it provides interoperability services with Active Directory. Make use of the SFU Web site (listed in the suggested readings at the end of this chapter).

▶ Set up an Exchange 5.5 Server and an Active Directory domain. Install and configure the ADC and create various connection objects. Examine how different CA configurations react during synchronization.

▶ Set up a NetWare server (preferably with NDS 8) and configure it and a Windows 2000 domain controller to synchronize OU objects with Active Directory. Examine the different options for synchronization.

▶ Altogether, you should have general knowledge of other directory services and how Active Directory can integrate with them. You should not have to know this information in gross detail for this exam, but you should still spend time with the utilities in a lab setting.

INTRODUCTION

Unless your Windows 2000 install is confined to a single office and a small group of users, it will likely be requested to integrate with an existing directory service. As pointed out frequently in this book, directory services are not new. Novell's NDS, for example, has been around for several years already and is a tried and true directory service. Consequently, you will rarely find an organization looking (at least initially) for a pure Active Directory environment.

Microsoft's interoperability strategy is based on a four-layer framework that covers the integration of the following:

◆ Network

◆ Data

◆ Applications

◆ Management

Their philosophy is simple: By supporting key standards, Windows 2000 can interoperate with virtually any other standards-based operating platform.

The migration of Windows NT to Windows 2000 may involve the integration and coexistence of Active Directory with Windows NT. This chapter opens with a short discussion of that, and then moves into the non-Microsoft platform integration and coexistence. After that, the discussion turns to Active Directory and Exchange 5.5/2000 coexistence, as your Exchange customers are bound to be interested in integrating the Exchange Directory and Active Directory. The chapter wraps up with a discussion of the Services for UNIX interoperability features.

> **NOTE**
>
> **Integration of ...**   This chapter does not cover the integration of operating systems at all these levels. If you want to read additional material, refer to the *Interoperability Capabilities* guide posted on TechNet.

> **EXAM TIP**
>
> **Coverage of Coexistence**
> Although there is an incredible amount of detail in real-world coexistence scenarios, it's important to keep in mind that when taking a Microsoft exam, the answer will most likely include a Microsoft-based solution. Also, because of the granularity of this topic, coexistence scenarios will probably remain very high-level ones.

COEXISTENCE WITH WINDOWS NT

Plan for the coexistence of Active Directory and other directory services.

As you migrate from Windows NT to Active Directory, you might need to coexist for an extended period of time (depending on domain structure). Because of this, and because Microsoft wrote both Windows NT and Windows 2000, the interoperability of Windows NT and Windows 2000 is seamless. Provided that you follow the best practices for upgrading Windows NT to Windows 2000, you should not endure any networking-related problems.

This does not mean you won't have some application compatibility problems, however, which is usually the case whenever you upgrade from one platform to another.

Bottom line: Be sure to follow Microsoft's directions for migrating Windows NT to Windows 2000.

PLANNING COEXISTENCE WITH NETWARE NDS

Microsoft's fleet of NetWare migration, interoperability, and coexistence utilities has increased dramatically with Windows 2000. *Services for NetWare 5.0* (SFN 5) provides customers with a complete set of new operability services for integrating NetWare servers and environments with Active Directory. Previous versions of SFN just provided file and print services and a Bindery-based directory service manager application. The new version ships with those utilities, as well as the following:

◆ Microsoft Directory Synchronization Services (MSDSS)

◆ File Migration Utility (FMU)

◆ File and Print Services for NetWare v.5

The remainder of this section describes these and other interoperability utilities and services available with Active Directory.

MSDSS Benefits

MSDSS provides several benefits to organizations looking to simplify directory management or ease the transition from NDS to Active Directory. Table 14.1 lists highlights of those benefits.

TABLE 14.1

BENEFITS TO IMPLEMENTING MSDSS

Benefit	Description
Creates a single point of administration	By creating one-way synchronization sessions, organizations can manage both Active Directory and NDS simultaneously through a single interface.
Ensures integrity across multiple directories	MSDSS makes great strides in solving the problem with maintaining multiple directories and keeping them in sync. Active Directory and NDS can be kept as perfect mirror images of one another with the appropriate setup.
Synchronizes several object types and changes	MSDSS is aware of the most common types of changes performed on the most common types of objects, and can therefore synchronize nearly everything about many objects.
Supports the single sign-on initiative	When accounts are administered centrally in Active Directory, the same password can be used to log on to both Active Directory and NDS.
Preserves NDS investment	For companies with an initial investment in NDS that want to migrate to Active Directory, a reverse synchronization can occur using MSDSS, which populates Active Directory with the NDS objects. You should be careful to use Active Directory design rules when creating an OU structure.
Supports different tree structures	Because synchronization sessions are rooted at the tree level, Active Directory and NDS can have completely different tree structures but still remain in sync.
Simplifies NDS-to-Active Directory migrations	Obviously, after NDS information has been populated in Active Directory, users can just be configured to log on to Active Directory, while still maintaining access to resources as they are migrated across.

Working with MSDSS

MSDSS makes synchronization with both NDS and NetWare Binderies possible. It is a scalable service focused on helping Novell customers simplify the challenge of implementing Active Directory in an existing NetWare environment. MSDSS can provide bi-directional synchronization support in NDS environments, and unidirectional support in Bindery-only environments.

Microsoft defines *synchronization* as the capability to *replicate* changes made in one directory to another directory, so that both directories contain the same information. Make sure that you don't mistake synchronization for replication. A good way to remember this is through the following saying: "To sync is to make the same; to replicate is to duplicate."

To accomplish this task between Active Directory and Novell NDS/Bindery, the MSDSS is made up of the following components:

◆ Sessions

◆ Object-level synchronization

◆ Directional synchronization

The following sections describe these components in detail.

MSDSS Sessions

The unit of synchronization between NDS and Active Directory is the *organizational unit* (OU). To keep an Active Directory OU in sync with a NetWare OU, you create a session. A session can keep one set of OUs in sync, and each MSDSS server can support up to 50 sessions.

Figure 14.1 illustrates MSDSS in the environment and how a session might be configured. You can schedule sessions to synchronize OUs periodically according to a specific schedule or you can call on them manually.

NOTE **50-Session Limit** At the time of this writing, only the second Release Candidate for SFN was available. This limit, as well as others throughout this chapter, is subject to change. To check the latest information, go to **http://www.microsoft.com/ indows2000/guide/server/ solutions/NetWare.asp**.

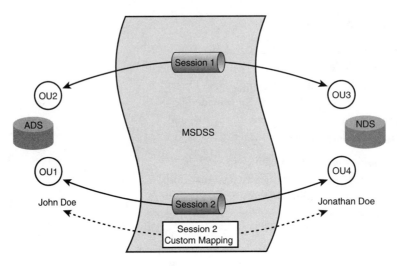

FIGURE 14.1
MSDSS sits between Active Directory and
NetWare NDS (or Bindery) to facilitate OU
synchronization.

Object Mapping

To make sure that objects from each directory are accurately represented in the MSDSS session, the session configuration includes an object-mapping section where you can actually map specific Active Directory OU objects, such as users, to their NDS counterparts and vice versa. This makes it very intuitive to synchronize objects that may not necessarily have the same display representation. For example, NDS user Jim Smith needs to stay synchronized with Active Directory user James Smith. Because the names don't match, you must create an object mapping for these two.

Object-Level Synchronization

As mentioned before, the MSDSS synchronization process occurs at the object level. Therefore, it would stand that during a session synchronization, only objects within the specified OU would be asked to synchronize, and only then if they had changed since the last synchronization. In other words, only objects (users, groups, and so on) that have changed since the last synchronization are synchronized.

You may be wondering how synchronization occurs, right? Who is the originator and who is the recipient? Can I sync two ways? Funny you were wondering, because the next sections happen to describe just that!

Directional Synchronization

Depending on your needs and the technology you are working with, you can opt to create either a one- or two-way synchronization process between NDS/Bindery and Active Directory.

One-Way Synchronization

Some organizations planning a move to Active Directory in the future might opt to create a one-way synchronization session. The one-way session pushes changes made in Active Directory to NDS but does not synchronize changes that originate in NDS. This method should be chosen to centralize administration to Active Directory.

One-way synchronization is called *forward* synchronization and is incremental and granular, meaning only changed *object attributes* are synchronized with NDS. This is different from the two-way synchronization (described next). One-way synchronization does not require any NDS schema modification.

One-way session synchronization is supported for all versions of NDS, as well as versions 3.x and 4.x running in Bindery or Bindery-Emulation mode.

Two-Way Synchronization

Organizations that truly need to interoperate Active Directory with NDS should consider creating two-way synchronization sessions. The two-way synchronization process reads and synchronizes changes made in both NDS and Active Directory. That means a *forward* and *reverse* synchronization takes place. Reverse synchronization is granular only at the object level, and filters out objects that have not changed before synchronization.

Two-way synchronization does require that a single attribute be added to the NDS schema to track the Active Directory object *globally unique identifier* (GUID). This is a very fast and safe operation and does not require a reboot.

NOTE

Bindery Mode Two-way synchronization sessions are not supported for Bindery mode NetWare servers. Bindery is the processor to NDS and essentially is a flat-file directory database, much like the Windows NT SAM.

Two-way synchronization sessions are recommended for customers who must maintain both Active Directory and NDS directories but who must have changes in one reflected in the other.

Interoperability Features of SFN

Some additional features of SFN are worth mentioning here—in particular, the *File Migration Utility* (FMU) and *File and Print Services for NetWare v.5* (FPNW v.5). These services are either new (FMU) or rewritten (FPNW v.5) from previous versions.

File Migration Utility

The FMU is integrated with MSDSS and provides for a transparent and seamless migration experience for end-users. It can not only migrate files from NetWare to Windows 2000, but also can retain the directory structure and security permissions on each file and enable the user to maintain access to his files all the way through a migration.

All this makes it easy for an administrator to gradually migrate users documents through a wizard-based, migration-management interface.

File and Print Services for NetWare v.5

FPNW v.5 allows a Windows 2000 server to act as a NetWare server to NetWare clients in a Bindery-mode environment. Windows 2000 actually performs as well or better than NetWare servers in the file and print arena, which has always been NetWare's strong suit. Because FPNW v.5 effectively emulates NetWare servers, the transition from NetWare to Windows 2000 becomes somewhat simplified because of the seamless integration on the server side and the absence of any client-side modification requirements.

Additional NetWare Interoperability Features

You should at least have an understanding of several more features when looking at interoperating or migrating from NetWare, including the following:

◆ **Directory Service Manager for NetWare (DSMN).**
Companies that manage Bindery versions of NetWare face a
huge challenge today because they have to manage each server
separately. The DSMN utility helps organizations manage
Bindery-mode users from several servers in a common
interface.

◆ **Gateway Services for NetWare (GSNW).** GSNW is largely
unchanged from previous versions of NetWare utilities. It provides Microsoft client computers access to a NetWare volume
on the server end, thus eliminating the need for clients to run
NetX or VLM code on workstations.

◆ **ADSI.** ADSI provides a common LDAP programming interface that enables you to create custom scripts to pull LDAP-
accessible information from both NDS and Active Directory.

◆ **Directory Service Migration Utility (DSMU).** The DSMU
makes it possible for administrators to migrate NDS and
Bindery-mode data to Active Directory. This utility enables
you to model user, group, file, and permission information in
Active Directory before committing it to migrate.

Keep in mind these utilities do not ship on the Windows 2000
media CD.

PLANNING COEXISTENCE WITH UNIX

Finally! Microsoft broke down and wrote a set of utilities that better
allow Active Directory and one or more flavors of UNIX to talk to
one another. More and more UNIX environments are now moving
to Windows-based computers on the desktop (simply due to price
and TCO). Although "desktop"-based UNIX platforms may be
diminishing, UNIX is not going away. Several corporations that
have UNIX platforms rely on those operating systems to deliver
stable and efficient service to requesting clients. What happens,
therefore, when a requesting client is of the Intel architecture? The
following sections answer this question.

Why Services for UNIX?

The primary business goal behind creating *Services for UNIX* (SFU) was to provide a comprehensive set of tools to help bridge the gap between UNIX and Windows for users and administrators. The goal is to create a logical network where resources are shared seamlessly between the two platforms and access to it controlled by shared enterprise policies rather than either platform.

Some of the specific design goals include the following:

◆ Transparent sharing of data between UNIX and Windows using *Network File System* (NFS)

◆ Remote command-line access from a Windows or UNIX computer to another Windows or UNIX computer using Telnet

◆ Providing UNIX Korn shell and commands such as ls, pwd, and so on

◆ Heterogeneous network administration, including integrated directory management via NIS server functionality

◆ User password synchronization

◆ Simple administration and installation of SFU components

◆ Management of SFU components using *Windows Management Instrumentation* (WMI)

The following sections describe the core SFU capabilities.

File Sharing with NFS

For Windows and UNIX computers to share information, they must speak the same language, which in this case is NFS. Windows 2000 Services for UNIX includes the following NFS components:

◆ Server for NFS

◆ Client for NFS

◆ Gateway for NFS

◆ User Name Mapping

EXAM TIP

UNIX Coexistence Because Windows NT and UNIX have always coexisted very well, scenario questions relating to Windows 2000 and UNIX are likely to revolve around Kerberos, Single Sign On, and DNS.

NOTE

SFU Web Site For additional information on Services for UNIX, visit `http://www.microsoft.com/windows2000/sfu/`.

EXAM TIP

SFU-Related Questions If you encounter SFU-related questions on the exam, they will likely come from one the four core capabilities: Server, Client, Gateway for NFS, and User Name Mapping.

Each of these components, as well as Windows Authentication and other Windows services, plays a necessary role in providing access between UNIX and Windows.

Like most Windows 2000 utilities, SFU management and configuration utilities are accessed through the MMC. To access them, install SFU, and then select Windows Services for UNIX from the Administrative Tools. You can also administer most NFS options from the command line. For more information, type the following at a command line:

```
nfsadmin [client ¦ server ¦ gw] /?
```

Server for NFS

The Server for NFS is nothing more than a Windows-based server hosting NFS to allow UNIX-based clients to access its files. UNIX client users will not know the server they are accessing is a Windows 2000 server; it is that transparent. Server for NFS supports NFS on all Windows file systems, including FAT, CDFS, and NTFS. The following list describes the Server for NFS in more detail:

◆ **Support for NFS 2 and 3.** Server for NFS provides complete support for versions 2 and 3 of the NFS protocol and supports file locking as specified by the *Network Lock Manager* (NLM) protocol.

◆ **Simple sharing.** Provides a way to share NFS directories (NFS Sharing tab) and set NFS security on Windows-based computers. NFS access permissions can be restricted to read, read/write, and root (based on each computer).

◆ **Access control and authentication.** UNIX *user IDs* (UIDs) and *group IDs* (GIDs) are used in conjunction with Windows security via a mapping to a user account. This ensures that users get expected file access permissions from Windows and/or UNIX computers. A component called User Name Mapping does just that (and on the UNIX side). A component called Server for NFS Authentication handles authentication. Each of these is described in detail later in this chapter.

◆ **Simple administration.** Provides both GUI and command-line utilities for administering the server for NFS.

> **NOTE**
>
> **NFS** NFS is the standard file-sharing protocol for UNIX environments.

> **NOTE**
>
> **PCNFSD** The server version of SFU supports only PCNFSD, a PC-compatible version of the NFS Daemon (the UNIX equivalent of a service).

Through your Windows NFS server, you can share UNIX folders by using the NFS Sharing Properties tab. You can share out individual directories or entire drives, but you cannot share directories below directories that are already shared. For that reason, all drive letters are treated as separate root directories. You can alternatively use the nfsshare command-line utility to share out a UNIX directory in much the same way as you can the native Windows Net Share command.

The server for NFS uses *discretionary access control lists* (DACLs) to simulate the permissions that UNIX uses. It is important to understand that UNIX and Windows have two *different* security models and that there isn't always a one-to-one mapping between permissions. The UNIX and NFS world does not have a take ownership permission, for example, but the superuser (root) can take ownership of any file and give ownership to any user. Default permissions throughout are read/write for everyone. You can change permissions on the NFS Sharing tab by clicking the Permissions button.

Client for NFS

Client for NFS allows Windows-based computers access to NFS files and directories stored on UNIX file servers. In other words, it provides Windows clients access to UNIX files and directories using NFS. Additionally, to the Windows user, it looks as if he is accessing files on his own computer or another network share; the fact that he's actually getting files from UNIX is transparent to him.

The Windows client for NFS supports both NFS versions 2 and 3 and has the following features:

◆ **Simple access to files and directories.** Because it is transparent, users access UNIX files and directories like they do any other file or directory.

◆ **Authentication.** The Windows Client for NFS provides access to NFS data by passing through authentication credentials using a mapping file. Each Windows user is mapped to a UNIX user. When a Windows user wants to access NFS data, Windows passes UNIX the OID or GID of the user and thus provides the user his real UNIX permissions to the resource.

NOTE **NIS and PCNFSD** The Client for NFS supports both PCNFSD authentication and *Network Information Services* (NIS) authentication.

◆ **Performance.** Administrators can tune the performance of the NFS mount using AutoTune and other administrative tools. Some of the performance factors are defaulted as follows:

Prefer TCP	No
Mount type	Soft
Retries	5
Timeout	0.8 seconds
Read buffer size	32KB
Write buffer size	32KB

◆ **Default file-access permissions.** Defaults are rwxr-xr-x.

You can connect to an NFS export in several ways. You can use either the traditional Windows Net commands or the traditional UNIX Mount commands and can use either command with both the standard Windows and standard UNIX share syntax. To connect to a directory called home on a server called unix1, for example:

```
Net use * \\unix1\home
Net use * unix1:/home
Mount \\unix1\home *
Mount unix1:/home *
```

If you are connecting to a UNIX NFS directory from Windows, you will get better performance using the mount *server:/share* syntax.

> **NOTE** **UNIX Permission Format** UNIX permissions such as rwxr-xr-x are read as follows: read/write/execute (rwxr) for the owner, read/execute (xr) for the group, and read/execute (x) for the user.

Gateway for NFS

Gateway for NFS allows NFS shares to be accessed by computers that do not have NFS client software installed. It does this by mounting NFS shares and then exporting them as Windows shares, which can be accessed using the standard network redirector.

Each gateway share you export consumes a drive letter from the gateway computer, so you are limited to the number of free drive letters you have available.

To configure a gateway share, you actually run a utility separate from the rest of the SFU utilities, Gwconfig.exe.

User Name Mapping

The User Name Mapping service is critical to the success of SFU because it provides the Windows-to-UNIX and UNIX-to-Windows account mappings. Additionally, it maps Windows DACLs to UNIX UID/GID pairs and vice versa. With this information, Client for NFS or Gateway for NFS enables Windows users access to NFS resources without explicit UNIX authentication. The Server for NFS uses this mapping to provide the authentication on behalf of the UNIX server by using the Server for NFS authentication component of SFU.

The User Name Mapping can be maintained centrally on a single server, which simplifies administration and provides a consistent way for users to gain access to the UNIX resources they need. Also, because it can retrieve UNIX usernames from *Network Information Service* (NIS) or by using PCNFS files, it causes very little (if any) disruption to the NIS infrastructure.

Simplification of Administration

To enhance and simplify the administration of the network, SFU provides the following tools:

◆ Telnet Client

◆ Telnet Server

◆ MMC snap-in

◆ ActivePerl

The following sections describe each of these tools in more detail.

Telnet Client

SFU provides a character-mode Telnet Client to replace the graphical-mode client that shipped with Windows NT. This new client is actually integrated with Windows 2000 and is much faster than its predecessors. The Telnet Client that ships with SFU comes with additional support and features. For example, it supports both Stream mode and Console mode and provides support for logging an entire Telnet session to a file.

Telnet Server

The Telnet Server that ships with SFU enables UNIX users to connect to Windows computers and run programs or perform administrative tasks. It accepts logons from a variety of sources, including Windows 2000, Window NT, Windows 9x, and many character-mode terminal clients.

The new Telnet Server supports both Stream mode and Console mode. Console mode is useful for running screen-oriented programs, such as the vi editor. Stream mode, on the other hand, is more like a UNIX dumb terminal and is not suited for applications such as vi.

Users can authenticate to the Telnet Server using NTLM authentication. This enables Telnet users to be authenticated in the background by passing through their Windows credentials. Both Telnet Client and Telnet Server must support NTLM authentication for it to work.

> **WARNING**
>
> **Beware of NTLM** If you use NTLM authentication only on your Telnet Server, you effectively lock out UNIX users because they don't have NTLM support. If you are in a mixed environment, you need to use username/password authentication as well.

Services for UNIX MMC

SFU provides a single MMC interface through which all facets of SFU can be managed with the exception of gateway for NFS. For all other configurations, a single MMC instance can be used to manage one or multiple SFU servers throughout the enterprise. Because SFU supports the WMI, management can be fully scripted from the command line. And speaking of scripting, the entire MMC is written in JavaScript (see Figure 14.2).

Support for Perl and Perl Scripting

SFU version 2.0 provides support for ActiveState's ActivePerl 5.6, which is a full-featured version of ActivePerl and PerlScript for Windows 2000! This version of ActivePerl includes support for the fork() multiprocessing command, as well as support for the Windows Scripting Host, which makes it another tool available to script administrative tasks.

FIGURE 14.2

The Services for UNIX MMC looks a bit different from other consoles, mainly because it is written in JavaScript.

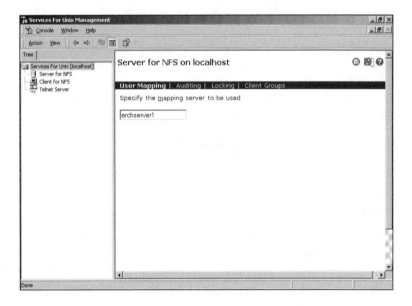

Simplified Account Administration Using NIS

SFU version 2.0 provides some very important tools that help simplify the account management in a mixed environment, including the following

◆ NIS Migration Wizard

◆ Server for NIS

◆ Password synchronization

The following sections describe each of these tools in more detail.

NIS Migration Wizard

The NIS Migration Wizard enables you to migrate NIS (a UNIX directory) domain environments to Active Directory. It takes your UNIX NIS source files and migrates them into Active Directory.

In preparation for migration, you can make the NIS source files available to the Windows 2000 domain controller that will be running the migration wizard in one of two ways: via NFS or copying them locally using FTP. Regardless of which method you choose, all the map source files should reside in the same directory.

If required, you can run the migration wizard multiple times in a phased migration; you will find the process much smoother, however, if you run all your migrations as a single step. During a phased migration, you need to migrate all password files before attempting to migrate group or shadow files, which depend on the password files.

Server for NIS

SFU implements NIS server functionality on Windows 2000. Server for NIS installed on a Windows 2000 domain controller can be implemented as a master NIS server or a slave NIS server. If a slave is selected, the master NIS server must be a Windows 2000 server.

Server for NIS stores NIS objects in Active Directory and integrates UNIX users, groups, and hosts into their Windows-based equivalents. This enables UNIX users and groups to be managed the same way normal Active Directory users and groups are managed—through the Active Directory Users and Computers MMC.

Password Synchronization

SFU version 2.0 provides a password synchronization utility that you can use to provide two-way password synchronization between UNIX and Active Directory. This utility installs a *Single Sign-On Daemon* (SSOD) that is compiled for each of the following UNIX platforms:

◆ HP-UX 10.3 and newer

◆ Sun Solaris 2.6 and newer

◆ IBM AIX 4.3 and newer

◆ Digital True64 UNIX

◆ Linux RedHat 5.2 and newer

If your UNIX platform is not listed here, you can compile the SSOD on your platform to enable the two-way password synchronization features.

For detailed information regarding password synchronization, refer to the white paper "Password Synchronization in Windows Services for UNIX."

UNIX Shell and Utilities

SFU version 2.0 includes a full-featured, Posix-compliant UNIX Korn Shell for Windows with an initial toolset of about 60 commands. Many of these commands (vi, pwd, ls, ln, mv, and so on) have been around since the inception of UNIX, and the rest for a very long time. The goal of bringing them over to the Windows 2000 side is to ease the transition from UNIX to Windows for programmers and administrators who are used to the UNIX environment.

This implementation of the Korn shell is not case sensitive and supports drive letters as file system mount points rather than a single "root" to which everything mounts. This provides enough flexibility to make the Korn shell practical on the Windows 2000 end.

A Bit About the SFU Environment

The UNIX Korn shell (sh.exe) implements two startup files to set the user environment. These files are the .profile and the .kshrc. The .profile is customizable for each user and is read every time the user logs in or opens a new window. The .kshrc is read every time a process opens a subshell that requires its own environment settings.

Implementation of .profile and .kshrc

SFU version 2.0 implements both the .profile and the .kshrc almost exactly the same way they are implemented on UNIX. The only changes are the names of the files and a slight modification required to get one of the files read. The names of the files are profile.ksh and environ.ksh, respectively. The profile.ksh should be stored in the user's home directory. If you want the environ.ksh to execute when a new subprocess is opened, you must add a line to the profile.ksh file that specifies the location of the environ.ksh file.

Command-Line Editing

Windows users migrating to the Korn shell can accomplish standard Windows command-line editing by using the arrow keys and ASCII editors such as edit. Conversely, you can set an environment variable for UNIX users moving to Windows to use the Korn shell. This enables rich UNIX editors such as vi and emacs.

Common Usage Scenarios

This section is included because the discussion of SFU so far has been largely fact and even a little "salesy."

There are four basic types of heterogeneous networks to which you will likely install SFU. This does not mean there are only four environments in which it works. It just means that there are four basic and definable combinations of UNIX and Windows resources.

The type of custom installation of SFU you perform depends largely on the type of environment to which you are installing. The following four scenarios are the most common:

◆ Primarily Windows 2000, some UNIX

◆ Substantial mix of UNIX, Windows NT, and Windows 2000

◆ Existing UNIX with new Windows 2000 and/or Windows NT

◆ Large UNIX environment with existing NIS domain

The following sections describe these scenarios in more detail.

Primarily Windows 2000, Some UNIX

In this situation, you want to make sure to install the full SFU, including the Server for NIS, on a domain controller. If client use of NFS resources is minimal, you should install Gateway for NFS and export UNIX directories to be accessed by standard Windows clients using standard Windows commands. If your clients will all hit the UNIX server(s) heavily, you should consider installing the Client for NFS, because heavy use of the Gateway for NFS will become a bottleneck.

Substantial Mix of UNIX, Windows NT and Windows 2000

When you have a good mix of UNIX and Windows, it really depends on the direction you are trying to go and where your resources reside as to what you install and how you configure it. At the very least, you should install both Client and Server for NFS and Gateway for NFS, as appropriate. You should also install NFS User Name Mapping if you need to provide full access to the existing UNIX file system resources.

Existing UNIX with New Windows 2000 and/or Windows NT

In organizations that are traditionally UNIX on the back end and in which Windows is just being introduced, you want to leverage as much of the UNIX administration and management as possible. One of the easiest ways to do so is to install the password-synchronization services to facilitate password synchronization between the two environments. Obviously, the User Name Mapping is required here as well. Create all Windows usernames to be a mirror image of what you see on the UNIX side. You must also remember that password-synchronization services must be installed on each domain controller in Active Directory, as well as on each UNIX server on which a user has permission to change his password.

Large UNIX Environment with Existing NIS Domain

In this case, it may make sense to install the full Server for NIS on the new domain controller. After you do this, you can use the NIS Migration Wizard to populate Active Directory and provide a fully redundant and replicated master NIS server for the directory. There can only be one master NIS server. Any domain controller in Active Directory can be a subordinate NIS server to an Active Directory–based master. Windows domain controllers cannot be slaves to the UNIX environment.

What About Kerberos?

In some cases, you can use the MIT Kerberos version 5 authentication protocol to create trust relationships between Active Directory domains and UNIX Kerberos realms. By doing this, it may be possible for Active Directory *Key Distribution Centers* (KDCs) to refer user *ticket-granting-tickets* (TGTs) to UNIX KDCs for resources in a UNIX realm, and for UNIX KDCs to refer UNIX clients to Active Directory KDCs for access to resources in Active Directory. For more information about Kerberos interoperability, see the white paper "Windows 2000 Kerberos Interoperability" at **http://www.microsoft.com/windows2000/library/howitworks/security/kerbint.asp**.

SYNCHRONIZING EXCHANGE 5.5 AND ACTIVE DIRECTORY

As organizations begin to adopt and implement Windows 2000, you should begin to see some that want to integrate their existing Exchange 5.5 with Active Directory. This section is focuses on providing you the high-level drilldown of the *Active Directory Connector* (ADC) and additional reference material (if you are interested in reading more about it).

The basic building blocks for Active Directory and Exchange integration are as follows:

◆ Windows 2000 Server/Advanced Server/DataCenter

◆ Active Directory Connector

◆ Exchange Server

◆ LDAP version 3.0

The exam will have general questions regarding Exchange and Active Directory integration, all of which should be adequately covered by this section. You should go to **http://www.microsoft.com/exchange**, however, and take a look at the ADC white papers.

EXAM TIP

Exchange Interoperability
Because Active Directory grew from Exchange and greatly leverages LDAP, there *are* likely to be exam questions related to Exchange. The Active Directory Connector for Exchange not only allows users to leverage Active Directory for mail users lookup, but also prepares for a smooth transition to Exchange 2000.

About the ADC

The ADC is the only directory-synchronization utility Microsoft shipped on the Windows 2000 CD. The ADC is the component that synchronizes Windows 2000 Active Directory with the Exchange directory. It is expected that many companies will use this technology to help build their initial Active Directory databases.

The ADC provides the following functionality:

◆ Uses the LDAP API to perform fast replication between the Exchange and Active Directories

◆ Hosts all active replication components on Active Directory, not Exchange

◆ Replicates only changes between Exchange and Active Directory whenever possible

◆ Maintains object mappings through replication (for example, Active Directory groups are replicated to Exchange Distribution Lists)

◆ Hosts multiple connections on a single Active Directory server and manages them via *connection agreements* (CAs)

ADC Versioning

ADC comes in two versions: one on the Windows 2000 Server CD, and one that ships with Exchange 2000. The first to ship was the one on the Windows 2000 CD. It provides replication of objects from the Exchange site-naming context and provides a good method for companies to "upload" data from Exchange to Active Directory in bulk.

The second version ships with Exchange 2000. This new and improved version of the ADC provides the capability to synchronize information from the configuration-naming context, which provides support for old (5.x) and new (2000) Exchange sites and down-level routing.

WARNING

Avoiding a Conflict on LDAP Port 389 If you install the ADC on a domain controller, you will likely need to change the LDAP port ADC uses to communicate with Exchange. Active Directory internally uses LDAP port 389 and locks it upon startup. Because port 389 is standard for LDAP, the ADC attempts to use it as well upon startup only to find it in use. To get around this potential conflict, you should configure your Exchange environment to use a port number other than 389 and higher than 1024, such as 3890. You would then configure your ADC Connection Agreements to use the same port.

Connection Agreements

To configure synchronization between the Exchange Directory and Active Directory, you configure one or more CAs.

CAs hold synchronization information, such as servers to replicate between, objects to replicate, target replication containers, and the replication schedule. You can create multiple CAs per ADC server. You can create unidirectional or bi-directional CAs to suit your needs. Microsoft recommends that no more than 50–75 CAs be created per ADC installation.

You can configure each CA to synchronize multiple object types or a single object type. For example, you can create a single CA to synchronize only the user objects in an Exchange container that consists of both users and distribution lists. You can then configure a second CA to synchronize the groups. Of course, you can create a single CA to synchronize all objects if the destination for each object type is the same (for example, the same Active Directory OU).

> **NOTE** **MSADC Service** The ADC is a Windows 2000 service (MSADC in Task Manager) that can be started or stopped like any other service. Additionally, you can configure it using the MMC Active Directory Connection Management snap-in.

Configuring Connection Agreements

CAs define a relationship between Active Directory and Exchange. You configure a CA using a wizard, which walks you through configuring the following:

◆ **Synchronization direction.** Configure either one-way or two-way connections.

◆ **Bridgehead server configuration.** Bridgehead servers are the servers that reside at each end of the CA.

◆ **Creating a synchronization schedule.** Define when synchronization is allowed to occur.

◆ **Selecting source and destination containers.** Select the containers from both Exchange and Active Directory to synchronize.

◆ **Determining how deletions will be processed.** You can choose to store deletion records in a file or actually perform the deletion in both directories.

◆ **Optimizing the CA.** Configure advanced options.

The following sections explain each of these items in more detail. This process is core to defining the relationship between Active Directory and Exchange. For this reason, this discussion focuses on the CA and the why and how. Again, there is a lot more to this that is beyond the scope of this book; therefore, you should read the recommended material.

Configuring the CA Direction

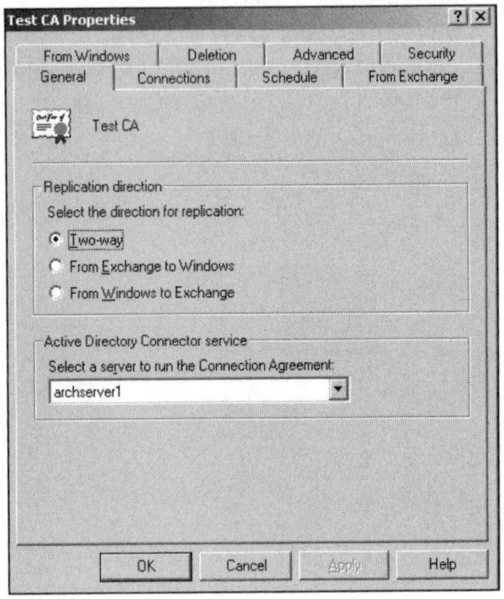

Directory synchronization can be either one-way or two-way. If you want to populate Active Directory with Exchange data, but still manage all objects from Exchange, for example, you could create a one-way CA from *Exchange to Windows*.

In other words, you can set the synchronization direction to be one of the following:

◆ **Two-way.** Allows changes to originate from either Active Directory or Exchange and to be replicated to the other directory. Use this type of CA when you need to manage objects from both Active Directory and Exchange.

◆ **One-way (Exchange to Windows).** Allows changes that originate in Exchange to replicate over to Active Directory. Use this type of CA when you need to manage objects from Exchange only. Changes to an Active Directory object will *not* be synchronized with the corresponding Exchange object under this CA.

◆ **One-way (Windows to Exchange).** Allows changes that originate in Active Directory to replicate over to Exchange. Use this type of CA when you need to manage objects from Active Directory only. Changes to an Exchange object will *not* be synchronized with the corresponding Active Directory object under this CA.

FIGURE 14.3
You configure the synchronization direction on the CA General Properties page.

Figure 14.3 shows the General Properties page for a new CA.

Configuring CA Bridgehead Servers

CAs require bridgehead servers to be configured on each end of the agreement. The only requirement for a bridgehead is with the Active Directory server: It must be a domain controller. The Exchange bridgehead can be any Exchange server. The ADC service uses the directories on each of these bridgehead servers for synchronization.

NOTE

Bridgehead Servers You will not find a setting on a server that says Make This Server a Bridgehead. The term *bridgehead* is used to describe servers with a defined connection to other servers.

When you define the bridgehead servers in each directory, you need to provide an account to establish the connection. This account must have at least write permissions for its directory.

Figure 14.4 shows the connection Properties page for a new CA.

Creating the Synchronization Schedule

Like many other synchronization or replication tasks, you can create a schedule to control when CA synchronization takes place.

CAs keep the servers and objects they define synchronized by using a polling interval to probe each directory to determine whether there are changes to synchronize. By default, polling occurs every five seconds during the times you configure.

Figure 14.5 shows the CA Schedule tab.

Selecting Objects and Containers to Synchronize

You must tell the CA what to synchronize with what. You typically synchronize the objects of a recipient container in Exchange with the objects in an OU in Active Directory (and vice versa). Table 14.2 lists the object relationships between Active Directory and Exchange.

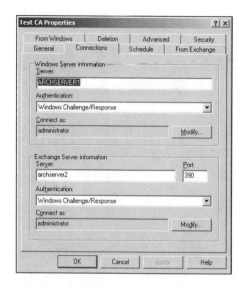

FIGURE 14.4
You configure the bridgehead servers and connect an account for each directory you will be writing to on the Connections tab.

TABLE 14.2

HOW THE EXCHANGE OBJECTS MATCH UP WITH ACTIVE DIRECTORY OBJECTS

Exchange Object	Active Directory Object
Mailbox	User
Distribution List	Group
Custom Recipient	Contact

You use the From Windows and From Exchange property pages on the CA to configure your object synchronization. Notice in Figure 14.6 that you do have the opportunity to synchronize some or all of the objects listed in Table 14.2. Notice also that for any CA, you can

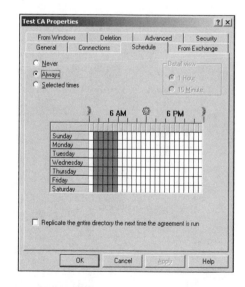

FIGURE 14.5
Polling occurs automatically every five seconds. You can control when an action is taken based on polling results on the Schedule tab.

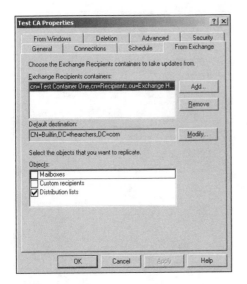

FIGURE 14.6
You must configure some parts of the From Exchange and From Windows tabs for every one- or two-way CA you create.

have multiple sources that synchronize to a common destination. This proves useful, for example, if you want to collapse a structured hierarchy of Exchange users from various recipient containers to a single Active Directory OU. This does not enable you to go the other way, however, and split users from a single source container or OU to numerous destinations.

How to Handle Object Deletions

You do not always want to delete a user account when a mailbox is deleted, nor do you want to delete a mailbox when a user account associated with it is deleted. For this reason, the default setting for all CAs regarding object deletions is not to replicate the deletion to the other directory. Instead, the server hosting the ADC maintains the following two files:

◆ **Ex55.csv.** Stores the deletions originating from the Exchange server

◆ **NT5.ldf.** Stores the deletions originating from Active Directory

Both files are stored at <%SystemRoot%>\program files\msadc\ msadc\<CA Name>\.

Optimizing CA Settings with Advanced Properties

The Advanced Properties page of the CA has some important check boxes. This is a multipurpose property page, meaning that you can configure various things here regarding your CA, including paged results and designation as a primary CA. The *paged results* area configures the maximum number of objects per page for synchronization. The larger the number, the fewer LDAP queries required, but the more memory required. Microsoft recommends this number not be set higher than the LDAP search results number in Exchange. Figure 14.7 shows the Advanced Properties page and Figure 14.8 shows the Exchange LDAP search setting.

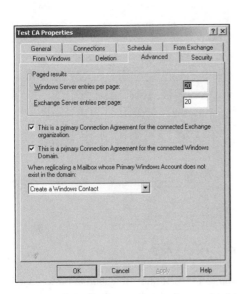

FIGURE 14.7
The CA Advanced Properties window.

The two primary CA check boxes in the middle of the Advanced Properties page are key when you have more than one CA defined in your environment, and work as explained here:

◆ **This is a primary Connection Agreement for the connected Exchange organization.** When you create a new "non-homed" (no associated mailbox) mail-enabled object in Active Directory, such as a contact or group, only the primary CA can create the new Exchange objects. If this is not specified, any CA replicating objects from that Active Directory OU can create the Exchange object (potentially creating duplicate objects).

◆ **This is a primary Connection Agreement for the connected Windows Domain.** This setting is used in the exact same way as the preceding one, but instead of working from Active Directory to Exchange, it governs new object synchronization from Exchange to Active Directory.

One final setting worth mentioning is the action to take when replicating a mailbox whose primary user account does not exist in the directory. The default action is to create a mail-enabled contact in the directory. Depending on your situation, however, you can create enabled or disabled user accounts as well.

EXCHANGE 2000 AND ACTIVE DIRECTORY INTEGRATION

Exchange 2000 integration with Active Directory is a topic for an entirely different (and pretty thick) book. It is important, however, to mention a couple very high-level things here while on the subject.

Exchange 2000 integrates with Active Directory and therefore does not include its own directory service. This is a very important concept to grasp. It uses Active Directory for object browsing, security, and name resolution. Because it does use Active Directory for its database, it requires a schema extension to be performed before installation. By doing this, Exchange 2000 can associate a mailbox, mail server, and so on with a standard user account in Active Directory.

FIGURE 14.8
The LDAP Properties page in Exchange Server enables you to configure the maximum number of objects to be returned by LDAP queries.

EXAM TIP

Exchange 2000 on the Exam You may see Exchange 2000 on the exam. If so, you will likely see it as a choice in answering the question "What installations require schema modifications?" or something along those lines. Exchange 2000 definitely requires a schema extension.

NOTE

Preparing for Exchange 2000 The coexistence of Exchange 2000 and Exchange 5.5 will be a necessity for the Exchange 2000 upgrade process, so keep that in mind as you integrate Active Directory with Exchange 5.5 now.

CASE STUDY: SYNCHRONICITY

BACKGROUND

Synchronicity is a company that has been through a lot in the past year. They started out as a small NetWare shop that employed about 30 people. The focus of business was developing *data representation technology* (DRT), a competing technology to XML. DRT was a success and the company was consumed by a larger firm that took over development and introduced UNIX as the core operating platform. That company has just recently decided to implement Active Directory as its core.

PROBLEM STATEMENT

Owner

"Like many other companies in our shoes, we've grown at a phenomenal rate. With the acquisition last year, we introduced IBM AIX into the environment and that now runs our HR, Accounting, and Payroll ERP applications. We still have quite an investment in NetWare and have just completed upgrading to 5.1 and NDS 8. The problem we face now is the lack of synchronization between all these systems. Besides NDS and AIX, we have Windows NT 4.0 and Exchange 5.5 in the mix, and it's a hassle and costs us money to keep these systems in sync."

CURRENT SYSTEM

UNIX Manager

"Right now I run all the UNIX administration. That is, anything on the AIX side of the house, I get. Anything having to do with our ERP implementation, I get. Lately, 90% of what I get has to do with passwords not being in sync, users leaving the company who need to be deleted, and other things like that. When I get those notices, I have to handle them all myself because our staff was reassigned to do e-commerce development.

NetWare Manager

"I lost a lot of my staff too after we were acquired; they all wanted to become developers ... go figure. That has left me and only me to keep this place in order and try and manage 45 people. Not easy, especially because now we have Windows NT users and UNIX users integrated with the NetWare NDS, and we just weren't prepared for it. I have to do a lot of manual administration."

ENVISIONED SYSTEM

NetWare Manager

"We've all been looking at ways to make our issues better and have all agreed that Microsoft has the leg up on utilities. I will become one of the Active Directory managers because we are going to stick Active Directory in this environment and synchronize NDS with it and take over management from the Active Directory side."

UNIX Manager

"I've been a UNIX man all my life, so I'm not too keen about the advent of Active Directory as the central repository for directory information. I am a team player, however, so I'm relinquishing my responsibilities as UNIX manager and will move over to the development team for the UNIX commerce services."

CASE STUDY: SYNCHRONICITY

Exchange Manager

"The Exchange directory is the closest thing we have to a logical organization partitioned out like Active Directory should be. We need to choose whether we'll manage the Exchange directory or Active Directory when the time comes."

MAINTAINABILITY

Active Directory Manager

"Changes made to Active Directory should be replicated out to each of the other directories within 30 minutes of the change."

UNIX Manager

"I should not have to mess with UNIX administration anymore. That is, I should not have to open the AIX utilities to manage users, groups, or anything else after we move to the new system."

NetWare Manager

"I have the same outlook as the UNIX people. If you are going to take management 'away from me,' please take it all; I'll find something else to do. I don't want to have to touch Nwadmin32

again for this company, but I'll continue to work over on the DRT side."

Exchange Manager

"I don't think I'm doing to get away with hands-free administration, but I think managing the Exchange directory from Active Directory is a great step. I will be joining the Active Directory team and will also be maintaining Exchange in the process. Users are the most important here; we don't want to lose anybody's confidence during this process."

PERFORMANCE

Global IT Manager

"It is essential that all directories are updated in a timely manner. Because we are a local company with a single office, we don't have to worry about crossing WAN lines for replication. Administrators must be able to jump directly to a configuration interface and make an appropriate change, force replication, and so on to make this a success in my eyes."

CHAPTER SUMMARY

This chapter covered the high-level Active Directory integration with NetWare, UNIX, and Exchange—the three most likely coexistence initiatives you will be up against.

Each of these interoperability initiatives comes complete with its own toolset, as described in Table 14.3.

TABLE 14.3

WHAT YOU NEED WHEN INTEGRATING ACTIVE DIRECTORY WITH OTHER DIRECTORY SERVICES

To Interoperate With	*You Need*
NetWare	Services for NetWare 5.0
UNIX	Services for UNIX 2.0
Exchange	Active Directory Connector

Services for NetWare 5.0 contains the MSDSS utility, which allows for one-way or two-way synchronization between NDS and Active Directory or for one-way synchronization between the Novell Bindery and Active Directory. Additionally, SFN contains migration utilities, file and print utilities, and other services that make NetWare and Active Directory interoperability possible.

Services for UNIX 2.0 contains several utilities and services that allow Active Directory and a number of the popular UNIX (and Linux) platforms to coexist and interoperate. Some of these utilities include the following:

CHAPTER SUMMARY

◆ Client for NFS

◆ Server for NFS

◆ Gateway for NFS

◆ User Name Mapping

◆ NIS support and migration

◆ Kerberos interoperability

◆ Telnet Client and Server

◆ UNIX Korn Shell

SFU 2.0 works out of the box with a variety of popular UNIX platforms, and may be recompiled to work with additional platforms.

Exchange integration with Active Directory has received quite a bit of attention at Microsoft. The ADC shipped with Windows 2000 and a newer version ships with Exchange 2000. The goal of the ADC is to synchronize the Exchange and Active Directory directories and provide a mechanism for unified management.

CAs connect the two directories and may be configured for two-way synchronization or one-way synchronization focused on either Active Directory or Exchange.

APPLY YOUR KNOWLEDGE

Exercises

14.1 Create a Two-Way MSDSS Session

In this exercise, you create a two-way MSDSS session and prepare to synchronize a NetWare NDS OU with an Active Directory OU. You need both Active Directory and NetWare NDS installed in a test environment to complete this exercise.

Estimated Time: 45 minutes

1. On your Active Directory domain controller, create an OU named West. Create five or six users and place them in this OU.

2. On your NetWare NDS server, create an OU named West. Create five or six different users than those created in step 1, and place them in this OU.

3. Install SFN, referring to the SFN documentation for necessary installation instructions.

4. Launch the Directory Synchronization utility from the Administrative Tools of your domain controller. This launches the MSDSS MMC utility.

5. To start the process that creates a two-way synchronization bridge between the West OUs, right-click the MSDSS *(domain name)* icon in the left console pane and select New Session. The wizard in Figure 14.9 appears.

6. Click Next to begin. Select your publishing and subscribing directories. Publishing directories act as the *master* directory and make information available to one or more subscribers. Select two-way synchronization to allow changes to flow both ways after completed (see Figure 14.10).

FIGURE 14.9
Welcome to the New Session Wizard window.

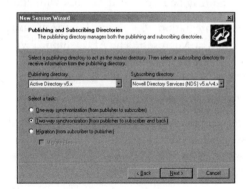

FIGURE 14.10
The publishing directory makes its directory information available to subscribers.

7. Click Next. On the Container and Domain Controller window, browse to the West OU you created previously. The domain controller should be the one you are on (see Figure 14.11).

APPLY YOUR KNOWLEDGE

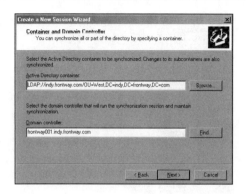

FIGURE 14.11
Select the OU to synchronize and the domain controller that will manage that synchronization session.

8. Click Next. On the Subscribing Container window, browse to the West OU you created on NDS previously. Then type in your NDS username and password. Beware that you may have to type in your entire user context (see Figure 14.12).

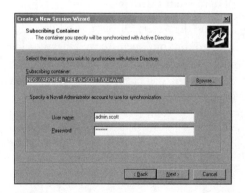

FIGURE 14.12
Select the NDS OU to synchronize with your Active Directory OU.

9. Click Next. Because you have user objects in NDS that you need to transfer to Active Directory, you need to perform an initial reverse synchronization. Check only that box. Leave the password settings at default; do browse the password setting options, however (see Figure 14.13).

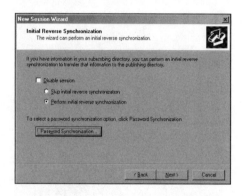

FIGURE 14.13
To move objects from a subscribing directory into a publishing directory, you must perform an initial reverse synchronization.

10. Click Next. If your OU structure contained sub OUs that were not the same on each side, you could create a custom mapping to make sure objects from each directory are synchronized to the correct location. Because you have a simple OU structure, choose the default mapping (see Figure 14.14).

APPLY YOUR KNOWLEDGE

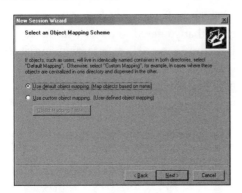

FIGURE 14.14
You can choose either the default or a custom object mapping.

11. Click Next. Give the session a friendly name. This name will appear in the MSDSS right MMC console pane (see Figure 14.15).

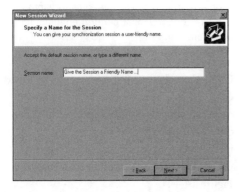

FIGURE 14.15
You can give the synchronization session a user-friendly name.

12. Click Next. Review the summary information and click Finish (see Figure 14.16).

FIGURE 14.16
You have the opportunity to review your synchronization settings before you commit them.

13. Click Finish. The initial reverse synchronization begins. Depending on the speed of your servers, this may take a few minutes. When complete, close the status window.

14. To view the Active Directory OU you chose for synchronization, open Active Directory Users and Computers and drill down to the West OU. Do the users you created in NDS appear (see Figure 14.17)?

APPLY YOUR KNOWLEDGE

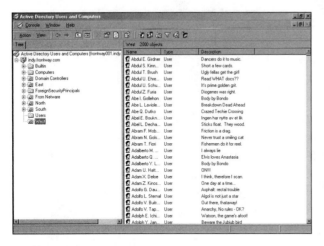

FIGURE 14.17
Active Directory users. Compare this screen capture to that of Figure 14.18.

FIGURE 14.18
NetWare ConsoleOne view of NDS users.

15. On your NetWare server, open ConsoleOne (if you have NetWare 5.1) or nwAdmin (all other versions). Drill down to the West OU you created and observe the users. Do the users you created in Active Directory appear (see Figure 14.18)?

16. Try making changes to objects on one directory and see whether they replicate to the other directory. You may need to use MSDSS to force replication to have the objects synchronize in a timely manner.

14.2 Creating an ADC Connection Agreement

In this exercise, you create a two-way Connection Agreement between Active Directory and Exchange and examine its synchronization. For this exercise, you must have an Active Directory domain controller and an Exchange 5.5 Server.

Estimated Time: 45 minutes

1. On your Exchange server, create a new recipient container and name it Sync with AD.

2. On your Active Directory domain controller, create an OU named Sync with Exchange.

> **NOTE**
> **LDAP** Make sure you don't forget to change the Exchange Server LDAP port number. Drill down to Protocols under Configuration under your Site.

3. Create two Active Directory users in the Sync with Exchange OU. Do *not* give these users an email address, and make sure you leave a few common fields open to test synchronization (that is, only fill in the name and alias).

APPLY YOUR KNOWLEDGE

4. Create two Exchange users in the Sync with AD recipients container. Have Exchange create new domain accounts for these users.

5. Return to Active Directory Users and Computers. Open the users container and move the new accounts you just created (from Exchange) to the Sync with Exchange OU. These accounts must reside in this OU to partake in synchronization (in this exercise).

6. Verify you have everything as it should be so far. You should have two Exchange mailboxes in the Sync with AD recipients container. You should have four objects in the Active Directory Users and Computers OU: two standard users you created and two Exchange-created users corresponding to the Exchange mailboxes.

7. To create a two-way Active Directory Connector CA, open a custom MMC and add the Active Directory Connection Management snap-in.

8. Expand the Active Directory Connection Management icon to reveal the ADC. Right-click the ADC and select New Connection Agreement.

9. On the General Properties page, name the CA Sync Exchange and AD and select two-way for the direction for replication (see Figure 14.19).

10. On the Connections page, select your Active Directory domain controller and provide authentication information. Use the Administrator account for now. Type in the name of the Exchange server and make sure you change the LDAP port to match that of your Exchange server. Provide it with authentication information as well; Administrator works just fine for this exercise (see Figure 14.20).

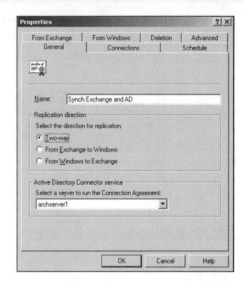

FIGURE 14.19
The direction of replication controls where changes can originate.

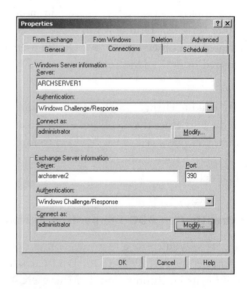

FIGURE 14.20
You must configure the Windows and Exchange servers, authentication methods, ports, and so on.

11. On the Schedule tab, select Always. Also make sure you choose to replicate the entire directory next time the CA is run. This ensures the immediate sync of all objects (see Figure 14.21).

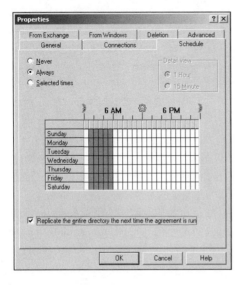

FIGURE 14.21
If you select Always on the schedule, you have the assurance that the CA will not have schedule restrictions that would cause directories to become out of sync.

12. Click the From Exchange tab. Click Add, and drill down to the Sync with AD recipient container and add it. Click Modify to select the default Active Directory to which OU Exchange objects will be replicated. Choose Sync with Exchange and add it (see Figure 14.22).

13. Click the From Windows tab. Click Add, and drill down to the Sync with Exchange OU and add it. Click Modify to select the default Exchange recipient container to which Active Directory objects will be replicated. Choose Sync with AD and add it (see Figure 14.23).

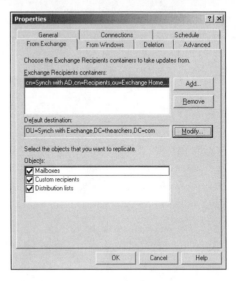

FIGURE 14.22
You can select multiple "from Exchange" containers and synchronize them with a common "to Active Directory" container.

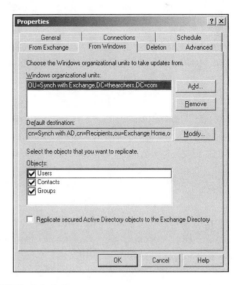

FIGURE 14.23
You can select multiple "from Active Directory" containers and synchronize them with a common "to Exchange" container.

APPLY YOUR KNOWLEDGE

14. Click the Deletion tab and in both areas select Delete The to force object deletion in the "remote" directory when an object is deleted in the "local" directory (see Figure 14.24).

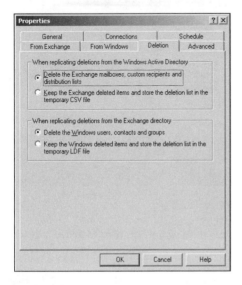

FIGURE 14.24
You can choose to delete objects during synchronization or you can maintain a file that contains references to deleted objects.

15. Accept the defaults on the Advanced tab and click OK to save the CA. Figure 14.25 shows the Advanced tab settings.

16. To ensure full synchronization, right-click your CA and select Replicate Now.

17. Refresh your Exchange Sync with AD container. What objects do you see? You should initially see only your two Exchange mailboxes because you did not "mail enable" the Active Directory test users you created.

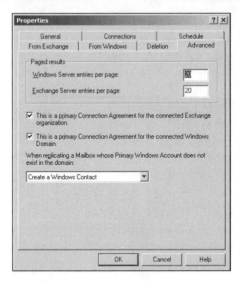

FIGURE 14.25
Make sure you make this the primary Connection Agreement; otherwise, new objects will not be created.

18. Refresh your Active Directory Sync with Exchange OU. What objects do you see? You should initially see all four of the objects, the two you created there and the two accounts you had Exchange create for you.

19. In your Active Directory OU, open the properties of your native Active Directory users and enter an SMTP email address for them in the Email field. Save each record.

20. Still in Active Directory, open the properties of your Exchange users (the accounts Exchange created for you) and enter an arbitrary office number.

21. Select Replicate Now from the CA context menu.

APPLY YOUR KNOWLEDGE

22. Observe the new Exchange custom recipients. These were created as a result of filling in SMTP email addresses for your Active Directory users.

23. Create a new custom (Internet address) recipient in your Exchange Sync with AD container. Give it an arbitrary email address and name.

24. Replicate now.

25. In Active Directory, observe the Mail Enabled Contact. This was triggered by creating an Exchange custom recipient.

26. Create a new user in your Active Directory Sync with Exchange OU. After the password screen, you get an extra window in which you can create an Exchange mailbox (see Figure 14.26). This is made possible by having the ADC installed with a CA configured for that OU. You would not get this extra window in another OU without a CA configured.

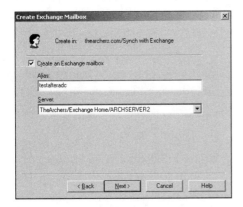

FIGURE 14.26
You now have the option to create an Exchange mailbox, just as if the Exchange Administrator program or Exchange itself were installed on this computer.

27. Replicate now.

28. Verify the new Exchange mailbox was created in the proper Exchange recipient container.

29. Delete an Exchange mailbox.

30. Replicate now.

31. Verify the associated Active Directory account is deleted.

Review Questions

1. Name the three components that make up Microsoft Directory Synchronization Services.

2. Describe the capabilities of the File Migration Utility included in Services for NetWare 5.0.

3. What is another name for one-way synchronization?

4. Name the four NFS components that ship with Services for UNIX.

5. Describe the two ways a Windows computer can connect to an NFS UNIX directory.

6. Describe the use of a User Name Mapping service under Services for UNIX 2.0.

7. Name some of the elements that make up a CA.

8. By default, how are object deletions handled by ADC CAs?

9. How many CAs can a single Active Directory Connector bridgehead manage?

10. How many sessions can one MSDSS server manage?

APPLY YOUR KNOWLEDGE

Exam Questions

1. Which of the following are benefits to implementing MSDSS? (Choose two.)

   A. Preserves the existing NDS tree structure

   B. Synchronizes only one object type

   C. Provides two-way attribute-level synchronization

   D. Supports the Single Sign-On Initiative

   E. Supports two-way synchronization between Active Directory and Bindery-based NetWare servers

2. You are an administrator in a Windows 2000 and UNIX-based environment. You want to provide your Windows clients access to UNIX shares using Gateway for NFS. Which of the following describes a limitation when using this technology?

   A. 50 sessions per Gateway for NFS Server

   B. Number of available drive letters on your Gateway for NFS Server

   C. Client computers must be running Client for NFS.

   D. 50–75 simultaneous users

3. Which two Korn shell files are used to set the user environment? Choose the SFU (Windows) names for these files.

   A. profile

   B. profile.ksh

   C. kshrc

   D. environ.ksh

4. You configure an ADC Connection Agreement between your Exchange server and an Active Directory domain controller. You cannot get synchronization to work at all. You verify all the server names and object names are correct and that you specified an LDAP port on the CA other than 389; but still nothing works, even if you choose Replicate Now. What else could cause this problem?

   A. The CA replication schedule is set to Never.

   B. The CA replication schedule is set to Always.

   C. The Exchange LDAP protocol is disabled.

   D. The Exchange LDAP port is set to 389.

5. How should Synchronicity implement Services for NetWare to accomplish the administrative goals?

   A. Utilize MSDSS to create a single two-way synchronization session between each Active Directory OU and NDS OU that needs to be synchronized.

   B. Utilize MSDSS to create a single two-way synchronization session between each pair of OUs that need to be synchronized.

   C. Utilize the FMU to migrate all NDS users and groups over to Active Directory.

   D. Utilize MSDSS to create a one-way synchronization session going from Active Directory to NDS. Select the option to populate Active Directory with NDS data once, and then manage all changes from Active Directory.

6. How should Synchronicity implement Services for UNIX to accomplish the administrative goals? (Choose the best possible answer.)

APPLY YOUR KNOWLEDGE

A. Run the NIS Migration utility, implement Active Directory as a master NIS server, and incorporate NIS users and groups with Active Directory users and groups using a mapping file. Incorporate password synchronization between Active Directory and IBM AIX.

B. Install Client for NFS on all workstations and incorporate Single Sign-On and User Name Mapping.

C. Install Gateway for NFS on a single Windows 2000 server. Share each UNIX directory that clients will access. Incorporate User Name Mapping so that Windows users can have native UNIX permissions within the shared directory.

D. Utilize a Kerberos trust between the IBM AIX realm and Active Directory domain. Synchronize user accounts and passwords between Active Directory and AIX.

7. Synchronicity wants to populate Active Directory with Exchange data and then continue to manage the Exchange directory via Active Directory. How would you suggest they do so? (Choose two.)

A. Create a two-way CA between the OU in Active Directory and the recipient container in Exchange.

B. Create a one-way CA from Windows to Exchange to initially populate Active Directory. Once populated, change the direction of the CA to go from Exchange to Windows.

C. Export the Exchange directory and incorporate it with an ADSI script to populate Active Directory.

D. Create a one-way CA from Exchange to Windows to initially populate Active Directory. Once populated, change the direction of the CA to go from Windows to Exchange.

E. Create a one-way CA from Windows to Exchange to initially populate Active Directory. Once populated, change the direction of the CA to go from Exchange to Windows.

8. Suppose Synchronicity uses Corel's version of Linux as its core platform and wants to provide for single sign-on between that and Active Directory. How could this be accomplished?

A. You must install the Single Sign-On Daemon and select the Corel Linux platform from the list of possible UNIX operating systems.

B. You cannot use the Single Sign-On Daemon, but you can use a password-mapping file between the two systems.

C. You must compile the Single Sign-On Daemon on the Linux platform.

D. You must compile the Single Sign-On Daemon under Active Directory and select the appropriate Linux platform to compile for.

9. You implement Services for UNIX (SFU) on your network. Which of the following UNIX shells are available as a result?

A. C shell

B. Bourne shell

C. Korn shell

D. ORIX shell

APPLY YOUR KNOWLEDGE

Answers to Review Questions

1. MSDSS is made up of sessions, object-level synchronization, and directional synchronization. A session is what keeps an Active Directory OU and an NDS OU in sync. Each MSDSS server can support up to 50 sessions. In most cases, entire objects (users, groups, and so on) are synchronized according to the session schedule. Sessions can be two-way between NDS and Active Directory, or one-way with either Active Directory or NDS originating changes. See "MSDSS Sessions."

2. The FMU provides for a near transparent file and folder migration process from NetWare to Windows 2000. The FMU process migrates files, retains the existing directory structure, retains security settings, and enables the user to access files all the way through the process. See "File Migration Utility."

3. Another name for one-way synchronization is forward synchronization. Forward synchronization is incremental and granular, which means only changed object attributes are synchronized with the remote directory. See "One-Way Synchronization."

4. The four NFS components are Server for NFS, Client for NFS, Gateway for NFS, and User Name Mapping. Server for NFS is a Windows 2000 server with the NFS file system installed so that UNIX users can access its resources. Client for NFS is client-side software that enables Windows 2000 clients to access UNIX NFS-based information transparently. Gateway for NFS is installed on a server to provide a UNIX volume to multiple Windows users who do not have NFS client software. Finally, the User Name Mapping maps Windows- to-UNIX and UNIX-to-Windows accounts and handles security and authentication. See "File Sharing with NFS."

5. With Client for NFS software installed, Windows client computers can access information on UNIX computers by mapping a drive using one of the following syntaxes: `net use * \\unixserver\share`, or `mount unixserver:/share`. The latter is more efficient for NFS and the UNIX world. You can also interchange these commands. See "Client for NFS."

6. User Name Mapping provides the Windows-to-UNIX and UNIX-to-Windows account mappings. Additionally, it maps Windows DACLs to UNIX UID/GID pairs and vice versa so that the native system can use native security clearance to authenticate users to resources. See "User Name Mapping."

7. Connection Agreements hold synchronization information, such as servers to replicate between, objects to replicate, target replication containers, and the replication schedule. See "Connection Agreements."

8. The default setting for all CAs regarding object deletions is not to replicate the deletion to the other directory. There are several reasons for this, but the most relevant one is that objects deleted in Active Directory may still have a mailbox in Exchange. See "How to Handle Object Deletions."

9. The rule of thumb is 50–75 CAs per ADC server before performance degradation starts becoming an issue. If you reach this limit, you should consider splitting the load across at least two or three servers. See "Connection Agreements."

10. The hard limit is 50 sessions for SFN RC1. Because this is pre-release software, this limit may change and is something you should keep an eye on. See "Sessions."

Answers to Exam Questions

1. **A, D.** MSDSS brings several benefits to a heterogeneous environment. It provides for single sign-on, preserves existing NDS structure, provides a single point of administration, synchronizes several object types, and greatly simplifies NDS migrations. It provides for attribute-level synchronization only with one-way configurations, and can only synchronize Bindery-mode NetWare servers in one-way configurations as well. See "MSDSS Benefits."

2. **B.** When using Gateway for NFS, you are limited only by the number of drive letters you have available. Each directory you make available for clients requires a drive letter. Client computers accessing Gateway for NFS shares do not have to be NFS aware and may access the data like it resides on a Windows computer. See "Gateway for NFS".

3. **B, D.** The .profile and .kshrc are used on UNIX platforms implementing the Korn shell to set the user environment. To fit into the *<filename>*. *<extension>* model, SFU implements these files as profile.ksh and environ.ksh. See "SFU Implementation of .profile and .kshrc."

4. **D.** Because Active Directory domain controllers constantly use LDAP, the operating system locks LDAP port 389 at startup. For this reason, you must change the LDAP port number on Exchange and specify the new port number in

   each CA you create. A and C are possible answers, but are unlikely to occur. B would not cause the CA not to synchronize. See "Connection Agreements."

5. **D.** Synchronicity requires centralized directory administration, so you can rule out A and B because they present a two-way session that allows changes in NDS to synchronize across. You cannot accomplish this task using the FMU, so the correct answer must be D. A one-way forward synchronization session using Active Directory as the originator is what Synchronicity is looking for. You could do a single reverse synchronization when you initially set up the session (which populates Active Directory with NDS objects). See "Working with MSDSS."

6. **A.** The best answer is to migrate Network Information Service (NIS) account information to Active Directory and utilize Active Directory Users and Computers to manage those accounts as well as native Windows 2000 accounts. You must keep all passwords synchronized and must maintain a User Name Mapping to properly map native UNIX UID/GID permissions. B, C, and D do not take into consideration a single point of administration for account information. See "Simplified Account Administration Using NIS."

7. **A, D.** To initially populate Active Directory, you must create a Connection Agreement that allows Exchange directory data to populate Active Directory. You can do this by creating a two-way Connection Agreement and then changing it to a one-way from Windows to Exchange. You can also accomplish this by creating an initial one-way CA from Exchange to Windows to allow Exchange to populate Active Directory. Once complete, you change the direction of the CA to

APPLY YOUR KNOWLEDGE

point from Windows to Exchange. You can utilize a script to populate Active Directory, but would not be able to manage the Exchange directory once completed without additional steps. See "Connection Agreements."

8. **C.** Because there are so many flavors of UNIX, Linux, and so on, the SSOD may need to be recompiled under the platform for which you want to provide single sign-on. It works out of the box for many of the major UNIX platforms.

You cannot compile it on Active Directory, so D is incorrect. There is no such thing as a password-mapping file. See "Password Synchronization."

9. **C.** SFU version 2.0 includes a full-featured, Posix-compliant UNIX Korn shell for Windows with an initial toolset of about 60 commands. Neither the C shell nor the Borne shell is supported under SFN, and the ORIX shell is made up.
See "UNIX Shell and Utilities."

Suggested Readings and Resources

1. Microsoft TechNet Online. `http://www.microsoft.com/technet/`.

   - "Services for NetWare v.5: The Resource for Microsoft Windows 2000 Interoperability with NetWare."
   - "Synchronizing Windows 2000 Active Directory with Novell Directories."
   - "Windows Services for UNIX version 2."

2. *The Microsoft Windows 2000 Server Resource Kit Deployment Planning Guide.* Chapter 20. Microsoft Corporation, 2000.

3. Web Sites.

   - Windows 2000 Server Interoperability Capabilities Guide. `http://www.microsoft.com/windows2000/guide/server/features/interop.asp`.

   - Services for UNIX. `http://www.microsoft.com/windows2000/sfu/`.

4. White Papers. `http://www.microsoft.com/windows2000/library/howitworks/`.

   - "Password Synchronization in Windows Services for UNIX."
   - "Windows 2000 Kerberos Interoperability."
   - "Introduction to Services for UNIX."
   - "Directory Integration with the Windows 2000 Active Directory."

PREPARING FOR IMPLEMENTATION

This chapter covers the following Microsoft-specified objective for the Designing a Microsoft Windows 2000 Directory Services Infrastructure exam:

Design an Active Directory implementation plan.

▶ This objective is not to test your ability to write a project plan, but rather to test your knowledge and understanding of the planning process. It is to test your ability to organize and architect a Windows 2000 solution. If you were to look at the exam objectives, you would see this objective is strategically placed at the end of the third major unit, so it acts as the ultimate task in designing the Active Directory architecture.

CHAPTER 15

Designing an AD Implementation Plan

OUTLINE

▶ Don't worry a whole lot about the detail of this chapter. Do concern yourself, however, with the logical progression of the implementation plan.

▶ Use this chapter to get an understanding of how to approach an Active Directory implementation. Use the earlier chapters of this book to understand the ins and outs of how to implement Active Directory.

▶ Exercise 15.2 is an open-ended exercise, and you may be inclined to skip right over it. If you can afford the time, spend 30 minutes or so and work through a high-level implementation plan for the company represented in the case study.

INTRODUCTION

By now you should appreciate the complexity of a Windows 2000 implementation. This book focuses on designing Active Directory, and therefore concentrates full-time on those topics directly related with designing directory services—and yet it still screams for a detailed and methodical planning process.

You should spend about 80% of the entire duration of a Windows 2000 project in the planning and design phase. This means if you estimate a rollout to take a week, you need to precede that week with four weeks of planning and design. The thought behind this is if you plan and design a solution, you should be able to test that solution in a lab, mitigate risk, and then roll out that solution in production with confidence that it is the right solution and will work as expected.

IN THE FIELD

THE 80/20 "RULE OF THUMB"

You will likely find many different estimations on the 80% plan and 20% execute rule of thumb as you read additional publications. This is at best an educated guess based on Microsoft publications, the technology itself, and the collective experience of IT professionals who have been heavily involved with implementations since the early days of Windows 2000.

In some cases you will find this estimate to be right-on. In others, it will be skewed a bit, and in still others it may be way off. Several factors influence the amount of time you actually spend planning, designing, testing, and executing. Probably the most influential is the company corporate culture—what value they put on thoroughly planning technology implementations will definitely play a crucial role in just how long they give you to plan. Other influences will likely be the industry the company is in (insurance, manufacturing, and so on) as well as budget, resources, from-scratch versus upgrade, and so forth.

In summary, don't take this as a hard-and-fast rule, but more as a general rule of thumb based on the collective experience of IT professionals.

Although there is not one required method for creating an Active Directory implementation plan, there are tried-and-true methodologies, such as *Microsoft Solutions Framework* (MSF) and *Project Management Institute* (PMI). This chapter uses a mix of both MSF milestone-driven implementation planning and PMI's phased project approach. Keep in mind that your implementation plans should be tailored to uniquely fit the business and technical requirements of your customers. However specific you get with each customer, the implementation plan on average should contain about 50% "templated" information and 50% custom information.

The Active Directory implementation plan you construct will likely be only a part—albeit a large part—of the entire project plan for Windows 2000.

> **NOTE**
>
> **Details on the MSF Methodology**
> For more information on Microsoft Solutions Framework project methodology, visit the MSF Web site at `http://www.microsoft.com/msf/`.
>
> **Details on the PMI Methodology**
> For more information on Project Management Institute's project methodology, visit the PMI Web site at `http://www.pmi.org/`.

IN THE FIELD

ACTIVE DIRECTORY'S LEVEL OF IMPORTANCE

It is true that Active Directory will be only a part of an overall Windows 2000 Implementation, but by far the largest and most critical part. There will always be exceptions, but in most cases the Active Directory implementation plan, which includes Active Directory services, should get a large percentage of the overall focus.

A close second in large implementations will likely be client configurations—how you plan to upgrade client computers from the existing OS to Windows 2000 Professional, without disrupting end-users. Additionally, if you are migrating from another NOS, such as NetWare, you spend a high percentage of time developing an appropriate plan.

WHY AN IMPLEMENTATION PLAN?

When used effectively, an implementation plan clearly identifies a roadmap for your implementation. You should not follow an infrastructure implementation plan, such as one you create for Active Directory, step by step as you might think. In actuality, it serves as a conceptual framework for the deployment and makes it easier for the various teams to determine progress.

You may be part of an organization that has adopted its own project delivery framework. If so, you would be smart to port what you find valuable in this chapter to that methodology because you are likely comfortable with it.

Again, the information you find in this chapter is one way of developing an implementation plan. Do *not* consider this the only way; several possible derivations exist for each step within the plan.

A PHASED APPROACH WORKS WELL

All deployment projects go through a lifecycle, phases of existence that start at the start and end at the end. Typically, products are envisioned, planned, deployed, maintained, and retired. These five phases make up a lifecycle for a product. Similarly, an implementation plan may consist of different phases that take a project from start to finish (and beyond). When you use a phased approach, it provides a clear-cut mechanism for the hierarchical breakdown of tasks and subtasks that make up a phase. You should develop your implementation plan using this phased approach and, at most, four levels of tasks. If you do this, you can assign resources, time, and cost to subtasks and roll that up to determine task, phase, and project costs and durations. This process was utilized in creating Figure 15.1.

ID	Task Name	Duration	Pred	Cost	Resource Names
1	**Sample Implementation Plan**	**7.5 days**		**$9,000,00**	
2	**Phase One**	**7.5 days**		**$9,000.00**	
3	**Task 1**	**4 days**		**$4,800.00**	
4	Subtask 1	4 days		$4,800.00	Resource 1
5	**Task 2**	**3.5 days**		**$4,200.00**	
6	Subtask 1	2 days	4	$2,400.00	Resource 1
7	**Subtask 2**	**1.5 days**		**$1,800.00**	
8	Subtask a	6 hrs	6	$900.00	Resource 1
9	Subtask b	2 hrs	8	$300.00	Resource 1
10	Subtask c	4 hrs	9	$600.00	Resource 1

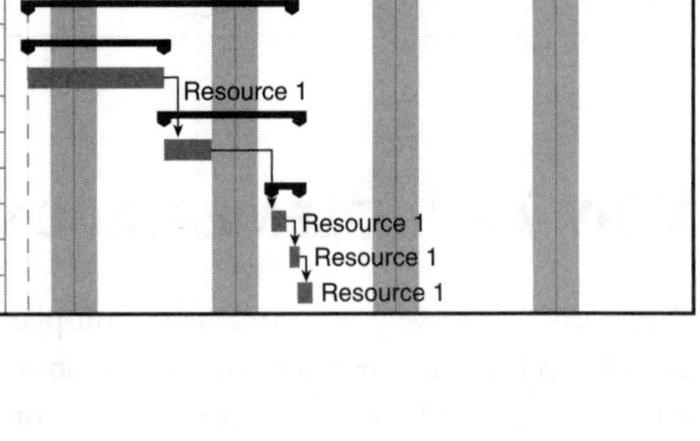

FIGURE 15.1
Assign resources, time, and cost to leaf-level subtasks.

Microsoft Project is an excellent tool to assist in creating your implementation plan.

PROJECT PHASES DEFINED

Before you start drilling down to task- and subtask-level detail, you should have a base understanding of what you want to accomplish in each project phase. The five phases for the implementation plan are as follows:

◆ **Goals and Objectives.** You must have an understanding of the business needs before you begin this phase. This is the logical first phase of Active Directory implementation planning in which you evaluate the features and benefits of Active Directory and supporting technology according to the business and technology needs of the organization.

◆ **Planning and Design.** Perform a business and technology assessment to produce Gap Analysis. Feature selection and solution design. Prepare functional specification and proof of concept.

◆ **Pilot.** Test, train, and deploy according to your project implementation plan in a lab and pseudo-production setting.

◆ **Execution.** Phased production rollout and testing.

◆ **Closure.** Post-project review, knowledge transfer, as well as transfer of operations and support services.

It is important that you do not intermingle the objectives of one phase with another. It is okay to have one phase's *deliverables* feed the next phase, but to split a task across two phases is generally not recommended.

That said, take a look at the first phase.

PHASE ONE: GOALS AND OBJECTIVES

The first phase of a Windows 2000 project is actually an initiation-type phase during which the vision for the project as well as the company for the next three to five years is discussed at length.

From that, a clear direction for the Windows 2000, and more specifically Active Directory, project is achieved and that feeds the first logical Active Directory design phase: Goals and Objectives.

Determine Goals and Objectives

Projects do not have goals and objectives. People do. You should have a good idea where the business is heading at this point because theoretically the heads of business have already met to discuss strategy and the future of the company and how technology will be used to get them from where they are today to where they want to be.

Your job at this juncture is to begin assembling Active Directory goals and objectives. You need to find out the *Why* and that will help you present the *How*. Having a clearly defined set of goals and a clearly defined list of objectives that will enable you to accomplish those goals is a critical step in deploying Active Directory. If you don't know what you're working for, what's the point?

Figure 15.2 presents a high-level outline you may choose to use during this phase. When actually completed, this outline would contain task- and subtask-level action items and would have resources, cost, and duration associated with it at the very minimum. This chapter presents these illustrations to give you a starting point for your implementations.

Make Sure You Have the Budget

You should not continue from this point forward without securing the proper funding. You should know at this point what you need because you presumably created a Statement of Work and Project Plan/Schedule before you got to this point—both of which should include preliminary budgetary numbers. There is nothing worse than finding out halfway through a project that you have lost funding and must quit.

EXAM TIP

Read Scenario Requirements Thoroughly Carefully read and understand all scenarios on the exam to determine what kind of implementation approach to use.

ID	ℹ	Task Name	Pred
1		**Phase One: Goals and Objectives**	
2		Secure Executive Support	
3		Determine Business Goals and Objectives	
4		Determine IT Goals and Objectives	
5		**Determine Critical Success**	
6		List Assumptions	
7		List Constraints	
8		High-Level Risk Assessment	
9		Impact Analysis	
10		Secure Funding	
11		Begin Team Building Process	
12		**Prepare a Test Lab**	
13		Evaluate Windows 2000 Feature Sets	
14		Finalize Project Plan and Statement of Work	
15		*Statement of Work Approved (Milestone)*	
16		*Project Schedule/Plan Approved (Milestone)*	

FIGURE 15.2
The Goals and Objectives high-level phase tasks.

Feature Selection and Testing

One thing many people overlook is the necessity of a training and testing lab. You need to have this lab available to you *throughout* the Windows 2000 project, not just at the end when you want to test something. This is extremely important up front as you select Windows 2000 and Active Directory features to implement because you may need to test something before adding it to the "implement" list.

IN THE FIELD

MAKE SURE THE LAB MAKES SENSE

Anyone can build a simple lab and install Active Directory—well, at least anyone with a bit of Windows 2000 experience. The thing you must accomplish in the lab portion of your implementation is to mirror the production environment as closely as possible. In fact, if in a large enterprise you can't possibly accomplish this task, focus on building the lab to mirror the most complex specific configuration you will face during implementation. This may be

continues

continued

some intense multiserver configuration, a complex DNS or interoperability scenario, or something totally different depending on your situation.

You never want to set up a lab that doesn't at least somewhat accurately represent the production environment. Also, if you will be doing an in-place upgrade, don't do a pristine Windows 2000 installation in the lab, because that won't serve its purpose. Instead, start with the preceding version of Windows NT. If you will be using managed migration utilities, such as FastLane's suite of directory management utilities, to do a migration to new servers, collapse domains, or some other complicated process, make sure you mirror that in the lab as well. That is where the value of the lab experience really comes into play.

Table 15.1 lists some of the Windows 2000 Active Directory features you may select to address business or technology goals.

If you find you need to implement a technology you don't feel comfortable with or need to test thoroughly before implementation, the test lab is the place to do so.

TABLE 15.1

WINDOWS 2000 ACTIVE DIRECTORY–RELATED FEATURES

Feature	Description
IIS 5.0	Integrated Web services enable users to easily host and manage Web sites to share information, create Web-based business applications, and extend file, print, media, and communication services to the Web.
Kerberos Authentication	Full support for Kerberos 5 protocol provides fast, single sign-on to Windows resources, as well as other environments that support this protocol.
Public Key Infrastructure (PKI)	The Certificate Server is a critical part of a public key infrastructure that enables customers to issue their own X.509 certificates to their users for PKI functionality, such as certificate-based authentication, IPsec, secure email, and so on. Integration with Active Directory simplifies user enrollment.
Routing and Remote Access Service (RRAS)	Connects remote workers, telecommuters, and branch offices to the corporate network through dial-up, leased-line, and Internet links.
Virtual Private Networking (VPN)	A full-featured gateway that encrypts communications to securely connect remote users and satellite offices over the Internet. Now with an updated PPTP support and advanced security with Layer 2 Tunneling Protocol encrypted by IPsec.
Distributed File System (DFS)	Build a single, hierarchical view of multiple file servers and file server shares on a network. DFS makes files easier for users to locate, and increases availability by maintaining multiple file copies across distributed servers.

Feature	*Description*
System Preparation Tool	Save deployment time by using SysPrep to create an image of a computer's hard drive, including the OS and applications, that you can then duplicate onto other computers.
Windows Installer	Windows Installer monitors application installations and cleanly performs uninstall/removal tasks.
Dynamic DNS	The Active Directory–integrated, Internet standards-based *Domain Name System* (DNS) service simplifies object naming and location through Internet protocols, and improves scalability, performance, and interoperability. Systems that receive addresses from a *Dynamic Host Configuration Protocol* (DHCP) server are automatically registered in DNS. Replication options with legacy DNS systems and through Active Directory can simplify and strengthen name-replication infrastructure.
Delegated Administration	Active Directory enables administrators to delegate a selected set of administrative privileges to appropriate individuals within the organization to distribute the management and improve accuracy of administration. Delegation also helps companies reduce the number of domains needed to support a large organization with multiple geographical locations.
Microsoft Management Console	Unify and simplify system management tasks through a central, customizable console that allows control, monitoring, and administration of widespread network resources. All management functions in Windows 2000 are available through the *Microsoft Management Console* (MMC).
Group Policy	Group Policy allows central management of collections of users, computers, applications, and network resources instead of managing entities on a one-by-one basis. Integration with Active Directory delivers more granular and flexible control.
Centralized Desktop Management	Manage users' desktop resources by applying policies based on the business needs and location of users. IntelliMirror management technologies install and maintain software, apply correct computer and user settings, and ensure that users' data is always available.
Security Configuration Toolset (SCTS)	Reduce costs associated with security configuration and analysis of Windows-based networks. In Windows 2000, use Group Policy to set and periodically update security configurations of computers.
Windows NT 4.0 Domain Migration Tools (ADMT)	Simplify the upgrade process to a Windows 2000 domain.
Directory Synchronization Tools	Maintain and synchronize data between Active Directory and Microsoft Exchange and Novell NDS directories.

Questions to Answer About Goals and Objectives

As you work through this phase, you need to be keenly aware of the questions you see in this section (and others like them). You don't necessarily need to sit down and ask the questions outright, although to do so would not hurt in the least.

Answering these questions will certainly provide you with information you need to move forward with the project and, in many cases, to produce this phase's deliverables. The following list asks these questions, but in no particular order.

◆ Why is your organization deploying Windows 2000?

◆ What is your time schedule for the deployment?

◆ What do you consider in scope and out of scope?

◆ What business and IT benefits do you expect to realize as a result of this deployment?

◆ What do you consider your top five inhibitors?

◆ Who will be involved in the project, what will be their roles, and will they dedicate 100% of their time to the project?

◆ Who is the executive sponsor?

◆ Who is the financial contact?

◆ How will the general user population be affected by this project?

◆ What are your critical success factors?

◆ What are the risks, assumptions, and constraints involved with this project?

As you may well have noticed, not all questions are directed at the client; some are directed at the project team and/or third-party consulting company that may actually be planning and designing the solution.

Potential Deliverables

At the end of this project phase, you need to meet a couple of milestones (see Figure 15.2). First and foremost, and required if you want to continue the project, you must complete the Statement of Work, Project Plan, and Schedule (if not already completed). It is likely that even if it were already completed, you would now need to revise the schedule because you made some pretty big decisions during this phase that drive the timeline of the overall project.

Other documents you may produce as deliverables out of this phase include the following:

◆ Goals and objectives listing

◆ Risk assessment

◆ Active Directory features to implement

◆ Feature to business goal/objective mapping

Phase Two: Planning and Design

The heart and soul of your implementation plan—and consequently the project itself—is the Planning and Design phase. This is where you take the feature selections made in the preceding phase and plan for and design their implementation. The primary deliverable of this phase is the functional specification. The functional specification is the roadmap to which the implementation teams will conform.

This phase requires a high degree of collaboration to be considered successful. In larger organizations in which there are disparate deployment teams, this becomes even more important. Each deployment team (that is, the DNS team, Active Directory domain design team, Group Policy team, desktop standards team, and so on) will work on individual feature designs under their responsibility and will then collaborate with the rest of the project team and synchronize their designs into one common "master" functional specification to be approved by the customer.

It is perfectly fine to have 2 or 3 or 10 or a number of design scenarios included in the functional specification, with the expectation that one design will be eventually agreed upon.

Assess the Business Environment

One of the first things you need to do in the planning portion of this phase is expand on the business vision. You need to determine how the business operates today and, along with key decision-makers, determine how the business *should* operate. You should at a minimum be looking at the following areas:

◆ Operational structure

◆ Organizational structure

◆ Business inhibitors

◆ Competition

◆ Customer relationships

◆ Human resources

◆ Geographical scope and company model

In this book, Chapter 2, "Planning and Conducting Your Business Assessment," and Chapter 3, "Analyzing the Results of the Business Assessment," really go into depth about conducting a business assessment. Keep in mind that as you assess the business, you are assembling information to include in your Gap Analysis—an analysis of the "gaps" between where the business is now and where it needs to be.

Questions to Answer About the Business Environment

You could ask literally thousands of questions at this level. The following list asks a few of the big ones to give you an idea about where to start. The good thing about these types of questions is that they always lead to more questions that become more and more detailed.

◆ What is your organization's general market? Niche or specialty market?

◆ What is your organization's geographical presence?

◆ How many physical locations do you have and where specifically are they?

◆ What is your distribution of employees throughout your geographical presence?

◆ Who are your competitors and what is your greatest competitive concern?

◆ How many customers do you have?

◆ Does 80% of your business come from 20% of your customers? (80/20 rule)

- What is your customer sales cycle?

- How are employee policies and procedures published and distributed? Are they adhered to? Why or why not?

- How are your employees trained?

- How would you rate the success of internal projects?

- Do you have any high-profile operational issues you are dealing with right now? If so, please elaborate.

You can imagine how these questions probably could go on all day. This is one of the primary reasons you should leave a considerable percentage of time (25% of the planning process) for the business and technology assessment. Answers to these questions drive initiatives—which then drive feature selection, design, and implementation.

Don't forget you want to get a current state picture of the business as well as a desired state picture. You also want to document your findings so that you can refer to them at a later date during the Gap Analysis.

Assess the Technical Environment

In much the same way you go after the business state, you need to determine the current and desired technical state. You should at a minimum focus on the following technology areas:

- Project teams/human resources

- Hardware and software

- Infrastructure (LAN/WAN/MAN/SAN)

- Internet

- Administration

- Security

- Standards

- Processes

- Desktop

As with the business state assessment, you may it find necessary to assess several other areas. Feel free to add them. Remember, this is more a roadmap than anything.

Figure 15.3 shows the high-level Planning and Design implementation plan layout. Of course, the real thing will include hundreds of tasks and subtasks with cost, duration, and resources associated with them.

ID	❶	Task Name	Pred
17		**Phase Two: Planning and Design**	
18		Discovery	
19		**Assess the Business**	
20		Current Business State	
21		Desired Business State	
22		**Assess the Technology**	
23		Current Technology State	
24		Desired Technology State	
25		Assess Human Resource Elements	
26		User Impact	
27		Staff Impact	
28		Staff Skills Assessment	
29		**Assess Company Culture**	
30		**Assess Organizational Requirements**	
31		**Assess Standards**	
32		**GAP Analysis**	
33		**Core Solution Design**	
34		Infrastructure Planning and Design	
35		Active Directory Planning and Design	
36		**Feature Design**	
37		Security Features	
38		Policy Features	
39		Additional Selected Features. . .	
40		Prepare Functional Specification	
41		**Project Documents**	
42		Finalize All Project Documents	
43		*Project Documents Approved (Milestone)*	
44		*Core Design Approved (Milestone)*	
45		*Feature Design(s) Approved (Milestone)*	

FIGURE 15.3

The Planning and Design high-level phase tasks.

Questions to Answer About the Technical Environment

You potentially face probably 100 times more questions for a technology assessment than for the business assessment, so this discussion just highlights some good general questions to give you someplace to start. Remember, you don't physically have to ask these questions to the customer; you could just as easily find them out during a detailed discovery phase.

◆ How is IT managed throughout your organization (that is, what is your IT administration model)?

◆ Who provides support at the server, desktop, LAN/WAN, and applications areas in your organization?

◆ Do you have a staff skills database?

◆ What is your network topology? How fast are WAN links? Is there any redundancy?

◆ How many desktop computers do you have and what is their geographical disbursement?

◆ What network protocols are utilized throughout the enterprise?

◆ What is the net available bandwidth on all WAN connections? When does utilization peak?

◆ Do you have published standards listing your server, workstation, router, switch, and so forth (that is, on standard hardware)?

◆ Do you have a standardized server, desktop, router, switch, and so on configuration image?

◆ What collaboration tools do you currently utilize throughout the organization?

◆ Do you have a recent inventory of all hardware, software, and infrastructure devices currently on the network?

◆ Is there a "business critical" use of the Internet in your organization?

◆ How do you protect your information and systems from external sources?

◆ How do you protect your information and systems from internal sources?

Again, this is not nearly an exhaustive list of questions. Remember that you need to collect both current state and desired state information for use in the Gap Analysis. Chapters 4–9 of this book cover these topics in detail. Therefore if you need more information about a particular topic, chances are you will find it in one of those chapters.

Prepare Gap Analysis

Preparing a Gap Analysis is really quite simple if you are adequately prepared for it. Gap Analyses are best written based on current state versus desired state of a single objective. For example, you might have an objective to provide better interaction between your employees and your customers. Your current state might list *how* your employees and customers presently communicate—via email, telephone, and handwritten letters. Your desired state may be to incorporate a collaborative solution that enables the employees to communicate in real-time via the Web when needed. The Gap, of course, would then focus on providing that collaborative solution.

The Gap Analysis is an important deliverable in this phase because it is used to determine the level of effort required to accomplish the project, staffing requirements, cost, the schedule, and more.

Core Solution Design

The core Active Directory design consists really of an infrastructure design and an Active Directory physical and logical design. Chapters 10–14 and higher in this book describe the core solution design as well as certain key Active Directory features, such as Group Policy and IntelliMirror. Refer to these chapters for a more detailed explanation of Active Directory solution features.

You could approach the core solution design in one of several ways. If you have a very large project team divided into several subteams with focus on a single area or set of objectives, you might want to bring them all together for the initial core solutions design concept. By doing so, you get everyone's input regarding namespace design—something that cannot be easily changed and needs the approval of all key players.

Alternatively, you could create a smaller team of subject-matter experts, such as those people who specifically focus on DNS design and who know the current environment. Additionally, this team would need Active Directory design experts (which will include you after reading this book, right?) to design the physical (sites and subnets) and logical (domains, OUs, and so forth) elements of Active Directory.

However you do it, the end result must be a design or design options that meet the business and technology needs of the organization.

> **EXAM TIP**
>
> **The Best Solution** Remember that when reading exam questions, the best solution for a scenario is not always the one that is given as a solution. Understand what the proposed solution is actually addressing and answer with the best available solution.

Feature Design

Feature design components are components such as Group Policy, security, Kerberos authentication, synchronization with disparate directories, Remote Installation Services, and so forth. Each of these areas may or may not require subject-matter expert attention. If you can create a team of experts for each feature you choose to implement, chances are you will not come in on budget! Realistically, you may find you assign one team to develop security, PKI, and Kerberos designs, and another team to focus on Group Policy and software installations.

You can design each feature independently of other systems; however, the dependencies should be documented in the functional specification. If you were designing the software distribution mechanism of Group Policy, for example, you would not necessarily need to include in that design the design of Active Directory OU structure, nor would you design Windows 2000 Professional desktop requirements. You would, however, list each of these dependencies in the functional specification.

Functional Specification Layout

The functional specification serves as a contract between all the team members and the customer. It is developed according to the business objectives, technology objectives, and many other factors relative to the business. It serves as the final roadmap for deployment. It should be detailed enough to hand to peer professionals who were not involved in the planning process at all for implementation.

This document should be managed by the project manager and kept up to date with all other project documents.

Potential Deliverables

At the end of this Project phase, you need to meet a couple of milestones (see Figure 15.3). You must have any and all project documents approved and entered into change control. After all, the next phase is the Pilot. You must also have the functional specification (core and feature design) approved. You may or may not produce some additional deliverables during this phase, including the following:

◆ Updated risk assessment

◆ Gap Analysis

◆ Functional specification

◆ Individual feature design

◆ Statement of scope

◆ Master project plan and schedule

PHASE THREE: PILOT

The purpose of the Pilot phase is to test your design. You need to identify the business, technical, and management issues that must be addressed *before* implementation.

Parallel to the solution testing, you must train your implementation team. It is very important that you involve as many support individuals in the pilot as possible to give them "near real-world" exposure to your solution before it is rolled out. You do not have to do training in a classroom environment; in fact, hands-on experience is arguably the best way to effectively learn technology. You may even try breaking something in the lab to let the help desk staff try and resolve it. You may also at this time begin to train end-users. You should definitely bring in additional training staff so that you don't take away from the implementation team.

Additionally, you need to document everything you can in the lab, especially those areas where something unexpected comes up. You should document flaws in the design, challenges in its implementation, and (in all cases) a resolution. Documenting issues will do you and your team absolutely no good if you cannot provide a resolution.

Figure 15.4 describes the Pilot phase of the project.

ID	❶	Task Name	Pred
46		**Phase Three: Pilot**	
47		**Proof of Concept**	
48		Lab-based pilot	
49		Production pilot	
50		Testing	
51		**Analysis and Reporting**	
52		All challenges documented	
53		All problems documented and resolved	
54		*Proof of Concept Complete (Milestone)*	
55		*Technology Validation Complete (Milestone)*	
56		*Risk Mitigated and Pilot Report Complete (Milestone)*	
57		*Pilot Complete (Milestone)*	
58		**Training**	
59		Deployment Teams	
60		Users	
61		Managers	
62		*All deployment teams are properly trained (Milestone)*	
63		*Users, managers, and other company resources are trained (Milestone)*	

FIGURE 15.4

During the Pilot phase, you roll out your solution into a test lab and pseudo-production environment. Then you thoroughly test it!

Lab-Based Pilot

The first thing you need to do with the final project team (which is probably a bit thinner than the planning team) is prepare the lab to prove your solution design concept. The goal should be to simulate the most complex area of the production environment in the lab and execute the project plan according to the functional specification.

The purpose of doing this in a lab obviously is to mitigate risk and to fix any problems that need fixing before the production rollover. You will save countless hours, dollars, and grief if you first do this in a lab. Period.

Production Pilot

The next step you should take is one you won't see in many other implementation plans. If you can, roll out your solution to a low-risk area of the production network. Obviously with Windows 2000, you must have a namespace, DNS, Active Directory, and other services in place before you can really do this with any success. If that is possible, you really should do so because it gives you a second layer of testing and "real-live people" using the solution, which is incredibly more valuable than a test lab. Whenever you can use users as "guinea pigs" (with their approval of course), you should do so. They will definitely let you know where the flaws are.

Analysis and Reporting

The more records you keep, and the more organized those records are, the more they will mean when you go and interpret them. As you install Windows 2000 and create the namespace, record how you are doing it. When you test legacy applications, record what issues you face and what you do to get around them. If you recommend retiring an application, write it down. You will return to the project sponsor with a pilot report. This report needs to be as all-inclusive as possible.

You will additionally adjust your project plan and other project documents based on your findings during the Pilot phase. Never think your design is 100% accurate before you test it; too many influences could make a seemingly simple application or hardware device operate erratically.

Milestones and Potential Deliverables

Several milestones need to be met during this phase. Because it is the phase just before the production rollout, everything must be in order—including project documents, software configuration, risk management, and so on. Some of the milestones you should reach include the following:

◆ Proof of concept complete

◆ Technology validation complete

◆ Risk management plan updated and approved

◆ Pilot program complete

◆ All deployment teams trained and ready

◆ All users, managers, and so on requiring training have been trained

Compensatory to the milestones are the deliverable documents. Several documents are either produced or updated during this phase, including the following:

◆ Updated functional specification

◆ Updated risk management plan

◆ Pilot report

◆ Training plans

◆ Help desk support plan

◆ Knowledge transfer plan

◆ Disaster recovery plan

◆ List of Windows 2000 tools and utilities required

NOTE **Lab Building and Rebuilding** Expect to spend some time in the lab during the Pilot phase. You really should completely start over in the lab at least twice if not three times. Practice makes perfect!

EXAM TIP **Project Plan** When presented with an exam scenario that addresses a phased approach, remember that this is in reference to project management. Pay attention to what the deliverables are for each associated phase. The project management piece is there to keep the cart properly behind the horse, because some real-world projects tend to accidentally reverse this.

The list of deliverables could go on and on and you could opt to deliver some of these documents at different phases. The important thing again is that required documentation be delivered at some time.

PHASE FOUR: EXECUTION

The climax phase of your implementation plan is Execution. This is what you've been working for since project inception. You perform an incremental implementation throughout the organization. You may choose to utilize your production pilot as the first increment of your production deployment. You may also choose to completely start from scratch to create a pristine Windows 2000 environment. (We recommend the latter.)

During the production rollout, you don't stop testing and documenting. In fact, the production rollout is itself a cycle of deploy, test, validate (and document), and support. One of the secondary focuses during deployment should be knowledge transfer. The support and operations staff, server and infrastructure teams, security team, and so forth should all be integrated into the deployment team for hands-on knowledge transfer.

All of this happens according to the project plan you took 80% of your project lifetime to develop, so it should be well-thought-out already. Logistics, travel, security, and so on should all have been addressed and planned so that you have one thing and one thing only to worry about: getting that solution deployed to production.

Remember the 80% planning and 20% deployment statement? Keep that in mind when you start deployment so that you can see how close it is. You will be surprised.

Figure 15.5 describes a generic Execution phase.

Milestones and Potential Deliverables

Your milestone is pretty clear-cut here: deployment complete. You can break this milestone into several pieces and have smaller increment-based milestones (for example, HR deployment complete or accounting deployment complete) if that is how you structure your rollout.

ID	ⓘ	Task Name	Pred
64		**Phase Four: Execution**	
65		**Location 1**	
66		Deploy	
67		Test	
68		Validate	
69		Support	
70		**Location 2**	
71		Deploy	
72		Test	
73		Validate	
74		Support	
75		**Location n**	
76		Deploy	
77		Test	
78		Validate	
79		Support	

FIGURE 15.5
The Execution phase is the incremental production rollout. This example breaks the increments by location.

Not much deliverable documentation is produced during the production rollout, mainly because you spend so much time up front preparing all the documentation you need for this phase. Because you constantly test and validate your solution, you likely will update some documentation during deployment, but your primary goal is to get the solution deployed.

PHASE FIVE: CLOSURE

The final phase to the project is Closure. This phase occurs when the "implementation complete" milestone has been reached. It is the shortest duration project phase, but carries significant importance.

In the Closure phase, you conduct your post-project analysis and review and deliver any documentation or deliverable knowledge material to the customer.

Figure 15.6 describes a high-level Closure phase.

ID	ⓘ	Task Name	Pred
80		**Phase Five: Closure**	
81		**Post Project Review**	
82		Project closeout report	
83		Project feedback	
84		**Knowledge Transfer**	
85		Documentation delivery	
86		Script/Image/Policy/etc documentation turnover	
87		*Project Closed by Executive Sponsor (Milestone)*	

FIGURE 15.6
In the Closure phase, you and the project stakeholders objectively assess the project and assign it a grade.

Post-Project Analysis

The post-project analysis is a meeting. The project leads and the project sponsor and other key stakeholders objectively discuss the project. They discuss strengths, weaknesses, unforeseen inhibitors, and so forth, and give the project an overall grade. This type of discussion proves extremely valuable for consulting companies, enabling them to leverage from their experience and the feedback of their customers. It is good for companies who use internal resources to perform the migration as well.

During this meeting, the agreed-upon deliverable documentation is handed over, and any digital material is released. Some companies may go as far as to develop intranet sites to store documentation, collect feedback, and publish information pertaining to the rollout project for the general user base.

Milestones and Potential Deliverables

The objective of the project closeout meeting is to obtain signoff from the project sponsor to signify project completion. That is the major milestone for this phase. Your deliverable documentation may vary, but should include at a minimum the following:

◆ All project management documents

◆ Functional specification

◆ Training material

◆ Release notes from Microsoft pertinent to Windows 2000

◆ Project closeout report

Don't forget to celebrate. As you most definitely know by now, Windows 2000 deployments are not simple and easy; they require an extraordinary amount of time, attention, and dedication. When you complete these projects, it is a bigger deal than with previous versions of Windows and deserves a celebration!

CASE STUDY: LANDSCAPES INC.

BACKGROUND

LandScapes Inc. is a small, five-office company that specializes in the design of corporate office park techno-theme landscaping. Its clients include large corporate players from the technology industry. It is known for its ingenuity and creativity in designing some of the most exquisite landscapes in the world.

PROBLEM STATEMENT

As an organization, LandScapes Inc. experiences significant distress in the area of its own technology. Although it is up and running on Windows NT in each of its five geographically dispersed offices, there is no synergy in the company. Each office is its own domain with no trusts established. Employees share information via their Hotmail accounts.

LandScapes Inc. has decided to implement Windows 2000 and Active Directory to alleviate its problems.

KEY BUSINESS OBJECTIVES

The executives at LandScapes Inc. have identified the following key business objectives for an Active Directory implementation:

· Increase communication between offices

· Share information between offices

· Extend the capabilities of the office to client sites

· Reduce costs associated with every aspect of the business

continues

CASE STUDY: LANDSCAPES INC.

continued

KEY TECHNOLOGY OBJECTIVES

Additionally, these key technology objectives are on the table:

- Provide a common directory between all offices

- Enable users from any office to log on at any other office from any computer

- Provide a messaging and collaboration backbone for all employees at all locations

NEXT STEP

The LandScapes executives have hired you, an Active Directory expert, to design an implementation plan for this project.

CHAPTER SUMMARY

You can use this entire book to help you develop an Active Directory implementation plan. This chapter describes how an implementation plan should be configured, but not specifically what the details of each phase should be. It is assumed you can deduce those details from the previous 14 chapters of this book.

Active Directory implementation plans may or may not be a part of a larger master Windows 2000 implementation plan. Certainly it *requires* Windows 2000 to be in place, but Windows 2000 implementation may or may not involve Active Directory initially, because DCPROMO.exe is run after a server is configured. Regardless, the implementation plan should involve the following phases:

- ◆ **Goals and Objectives.** You must have an understanding of the business needs before you begin this phase. This is the logical first phase of Active Directory implementation planning, in which you evaluate the features and benefits of Active Directory and supporting technology according to the business and technology needs of the organization.

- ◆ **Planning and Design.** Perform a business and technology assessment to produce analysis. Complete feature selection and solution design. Prepare functional specification and proof of concept.

| **CHAPTER SUMMARY** |

◆ **Pilot.** Testing, training, and deployment according to the project implementation plan in a lab and pseudo-production setting.

◆ **Execution.** Phased production rollout and testing.

◆ **Closure.** Post-project review, knowledge transfer, transfer of operations, and support services.

By following these phases and the guidelines that go along with each, you should increase your chances for a successful implementation.

APPLY YOUR KNOWLEDGE

Exercises

15.1 Determine Where to Spend the Time

In this exercise, you look at several project timelines and map out exactly where you can expect to spend time on planning and design, assessments, and execution. This is not meant to be rocket-science math, but rather to give you a feel for the amount of time you can expect to spend on certain critical implementation phases.

Estimated Time: 10 minutes

Given the following general formulas

- 80% of the project is spent on planning.

- 25% of the planning is spent on the business assessment.

- 20% of the project is spent on execution.

Determine the length of time you will likely spend during these three phases based on the following scenarios:

1. Your Active Directory implementation project will take 12 months from start to finish.

2. Your Active Directory implementation planning phase will take 6 weeks from start to finish.

3. Your Active Directory implementation business assessment of the planning phase will take 3 weeks.

Answers to Exercise 15.1

1. If the overall project will take 12 months, that means the planning phase will take (*converting months to weeks* 52 * .8) 41.6 weeks, or approximately 291 days. That means the execution phase should take about (365 − 291) 74 days. The business assessment of the planning phase should take about (291 * .25) 73 days. This is obviously an extremely large project.

2. If the planning phase will take 6 weeks, that means the overall project will take (6 / .8) 7.5 weeks or about 52.5 days. The business assessment of the planning phase should take about (6 * .25) 1.5 weeks or 10.5 days. Finally, the execution phase should take about (7.5 * .2) 1.5 weeks or 10.5 days.

3. If the business assessment will take 3 weeks, that means the planning phase should take (3 / .25) or 12 weeks. If the planning phase takes 12 weeks, that means the execution phase will likely last ([12 / .8] * .2) 3 weeks.

15.2 Develop an Implementation Plan for LandScapes Inc.

In this exercise, you examine the LandScapes Inc. case study and come up with an implementation plan for a specific area of the business. You can choose to go very deep and create a detailed plan, or scratch the surface and create a high-level template. That choice is yours. The purpose of this exercise is to get you thinking about implementation pertaining to a given scenario. There is no incorrect solution per se to this exercise. Use what you have learned not only in this chapter, but also throughout this entire book.

Estimated Time: 30 minutes

Focus on the design goals set forth by LandScapes Inc. in the case study, which are listed here:

APPLY YOUR KNOWLEDGE

Key Business Objectives

- Increase communication between offices

- Share information between offices

- Extend the capabilities of the office out to client sites

- Reduce costs associated with every aspect of the business

Key Technology Objectives

- Provide a common directory between all offices

- Enable users from any office to log on at any other office from any computer

- Provide a messaging and collaboration backbone for all employees at all locations

Remember to use the content of this chapter as a template, and the content of this book as your knowledge.

Review Questions

1. Name the five recommended phases of an Active Directory implementation plan.

2. During which phase should you secure funding?

3. During which phase should you mitigate risk?

4. Why is it important that you conduct a post-project review meeting?

5. Name the two project management bodies that provide project management methodologies.

6. What document should be produced to serve as a deployment roadmap?

7. Name three areas of business you should analyze when determining the business requirements.

8. Name three areas of technology you should analyze when determining the technical requirements.

Exam Questions

1. Which of the following Active Directory "supporting" technologies will provide LandScapes Inc. with the capability to address the "Allow users from any office to log on at any other office from any computer" business objective?

   A. A unified namespace

   B. Remote Installation Services (RIS)

   C. Active Directory sites

   D. IntelliMirror

2. Which of the following Active Directory "supporting" technologies address the technology objectives of LandScapes Inc.? (Choose two.)

   A. Exchange 2000

   B. RIS

   C. Group Policy/IntelliMirror

   D. ADSI

3. LandScapes Inc. employs 1,000 people. They predict that a full Windows 2000 Active Directory rollout to all employees will take five weeks to execute, one week per location. How long should the Planning and Design phase of the project be?

APPLY YOUR KNOWLEDGE

A. 25 weeks

B. 20 weeks

C. 15 weeks

D. 20 days

4. You have just completed the business and technology reviews for LandScapes Inc. What deliverable document should you produce that shows the objective-based current state versus future state mapping?

A. Risk management plan

B. Functional specification

C. Gap Analysis

D. Project implementation plan

5. Put the following tasks in the order in which you should complete them.

A. Finalize functional specification

B. Create project teams

C. Active Directory feature design

D. Active Directory core design

Answers to Review Questions

1. The five recommended implementation plan phases are Goals and Objectives, Planning and Design, Pilot, Execution, and Closure. See "Project Phases Defined."

2. You should secure funding for the project during the Goals and Objectives phase. You do not want to get too much further into it and find out you

don't have the financial backing to continue. See "Phase One: Goals and Objectives."

3. Risk management should be something you keep in check all the time. You really begin to focus on mitigating risk during the pilot phase, where you can document your actions according to what occurs during the pilot. See "Phase Three: Pilot."

4. It is important to receive feedback from the project sponsor and other key project stakeholders so that you might learn from your mistakes. This is especially useful for a consulting company that may turn around and begin a brand new project the following week. See "Post-Project Analysis."

5. The two project management methodologies are Microsoft Solutions Framework (MSF) and Project Management Institute (PMI). See the "Introduction."

6. The functional specification serves as a contract between all the team members and the customer. It is developed according to the business objectives, technology objectives, and many other factors relative to the business. It serves as the final roadmap for deployment. See "Functional Specification Layout."

7. The following areas are just some of the general business-oriented areas you need to address:

- Operational structure
- Organizational structure
- Business inhibitors
- Competition
- Customer relationships
- Human resources
- Geographical scope and company model

See "Business Assessment." Chapters 2 and 3 in this book go over the business assessment in more detail.

8. The following areas are just some of the general technology-oriented areas you need to address:

- Hardware and software
- Infrastructure (LAN/WAN/MAN/SAN)
- Internet
- Administration
- Security
- Standards
- Processes
- Desktop

See "Assess the Technical Environment." Chapters 4–9 of this book take these areas into more detail.

Answers to Exam Questions

1. **D.** The IntelliMirror suite of technologies can be configured to provide users with the capability of logging on from any computer throughout the enterprise and accessing his data, applications, and settings. A unified namespace provides the support infrastructure required to make this possible, but doesn't itself address the objective. RIS provides network-based installation of operating systems, and Active Directory sites define the physical topology of the company.

2. **A, C.** Group Policies and IntelliMirror address the need to enable users to roam from one computer to another across the company. Exchange

2000 is a messaging and collaboration platform that utilizes Active Directory as its directory service. RIS and ADSI do not address the technical objectives. None of the available answers addresses the need for a common directory between all offices, which of course is provided by Active Directory.

3. **B.** It is estimated that your Planning and Design phase should be 80% of the overall project. If a project should take 5 weeks to implement, it should take approximately 20 weeks to plan and design. (5 / .2 = 25 weeks total duration; 5 weeks to implement = 20 weeks for planning and design.)

4. **C.** As you assess the current business and technology state and the desired business and technology state, you create a Gap Analysis that explains the "gap" between the current implementation and the desired implementation. You can then use this analysis to help determine project schedule, resources required, and expected level of effort. See "Gap Analysis."

5. **B, C, D, A.** To design anything, you must have your team members in place. For projects of any size, you assemble feature-based project teams. The next option is the Active Directory core design, which must be completed before the next option (the feature design) is completed. The core design includes the namespace, DNS, and domains; and the feature design is Group Policy, IntelliMirror, and other features required to meet business and technical objectives. Lastly, the functional specification, which contains the overall design, is finalized.

Suggested Readings and Resources

1. *The Windows 2000 Server Resource Kit.* Microsoft Press, 2000. Chapters 2–3.

2. Microsoft TechNet Articles

   - "Creating the Windows 2000 Vision/Scope Document and Risk Management Plan."

   - "The MS TCO Model: Applying the MS Solutions Framework to Reduce TCO"

   - "MS Solutions Framework: Managing Organizational Change"

3. The Project Management Institute's online version of the *Project Management Body of Knowledge (PMBOK)* at `http://www.pmi.org/publictn/pmboktoc.htm`.

FINAL REVIEW

Fast Facts

Study and Exam Preparation Tips

Practice Exam

Now that you have finished reading this book and working through its many exercises, you are ready for the Microsoft certification exam. This chapter is intended to be your "final cram in the parking lot."

Organized by chapter, this section is not actually a topical summary, but rather a concentrated review of the most important points, key tables of information, and so on. If you make sure that you are comfortable with the content and concepts presented here, the odds are good that you are prepared for the certification exam.

CHAPTER 1: UNDERSTANDING ACTIVE DIRECTORY

Microsoft Active Directory is a directory service completely integrated with Windows 2000 and consists of essentially two parts:

- ◆ **A directory.** A physical storage container that contains anywhere from a few objects up to millions of various types of objects

- ◆ **Services.** These make the information in the directory useful.

Active Directory incorporates the Internet concept of a *namespace* with the operating system's core directory services. It uses the Internet standard *Lightweight Directory Access Protocol* (LDAP), based on X.500, as its core protocol, and can manage other *network operating system* (NOS) directories.

An LDAP URL takes the following form:

```
LDAP://a_server.mycompany.com/CN=joesmith,OU=wh
➥itepapers,OU=OpSys,OU=Windows2000,DC=
➥Microsoft,DC=com.
```

Most LDAP URLs are kept out of site and are handled by the LDAP-enabled application program.

Fast Facts

DESIGNING WINDOWS 2000 DIRECOTRY SERVICES INFRASTRUCTURE

Active Directory includes three major API sets:

- ◆ **ADSI.** The Active Directory Services Interface is a set of *Component Object Model* (COM) interfaces that give developers the ability to query and manipulate directory services.

- ◆ **MAPI.** The Messaging Application Programming Interface is included in the Active Directory API set for backward compatibility with legacy applications.

- ◆ **LDAP C API.** A solution for developers tasked with developing applications or toolsets required to work across many types of clients.

The schema defines classes of objects, attributes, and attribute syntax (rules) for all Active Directory objects. Global catalog servers maintain directory information from all the source domains in a tree.

Active Directory is a distributed database that implements its Active Directory domain controllers as equals. The Windows 2000 implementation of DNS includes enhancements over the traditional DNS, and these enable it to become the core name resolution backbone on both sides of the corporate firewall. The following list outlines these major enhancements:

- ◆ **Service resource records (SRV RR).** SRV records are used to specify the location of a server for a specific protocol, service, and domain.

- ◆ **Dynamic Update Protocol.** Dynamic Update Protocol provides a means of automatically updating the zone data on a zone's primary DNS server.

- ◆ **Incremental zone transfer.** Incremental zone transfer allows for the partial transfer of a DNS zone file to its replication partners. This partial replication sends only modifications to the requesting server, and therefore drastically decreases the overhead involved in transferring an entire zone file.

- ◆ **Active Directory integrated zones.** If you opt to use the Microsoft implementation of Dynamic DNS, you can store your DNS zone files in Active Directory and take advantage of its replication topology.

Windows Internet Naming Service (WINS) and *Dynamic Host Configuration Protocol* (DHCP) have both been slightly revised to provide support for Dynamic DNS.

LEGACY WINDOWS NT SERVER TO WINDOWS 2000 SERVER UPGRADE PATH

Legacy Version of Windows NT	Upgrade to Windows 2000 ...
Windows NT 3.51 or 4.0 PDC	Domain controller
Windows NT 3.51 or 4.0 BDC	Domain controller or member server
Windows NT 3.51 or 4.0 Member Server	Member server

CHAPTER 2: PLANNING AND CONDUCTING YOUR BUSINESS ASSESSMENT

Think of your strategy as a strategy to better understand your client's strategy for taking its business to the next level. The following list defines the areas of business from which you must extract information:

- ◆ Business vision
- ◆ Business goals and problems
- ◆ Organization of the company
- ◆ Geographic scope and company model
- ◆ Company processes
- ◆ Influences that affect company strategy

WINDOWS 2000 ACTIVE DIRECTORY FEATURE SET

Feature/Service	Description	Benefit(s)
Digital nervous system	A system that represents a person digitally within an organization.	Highly structured information and communication flow, knowledge management, and business processes.
Built on DNS	DNS is the most widely used locator service in the world, used exclusively on the Internet. DNS maps a fully qualified domain name to an IP address.	Scalability. Windows 2000 Active Directory is designed around DNS, which scales from a single entry to supporting the entire Internet.
Active Directory Services Interface (ADSI)	ADSI abstracts the capabilities of several disparate directory services and unites them into a single set of directory service interfaces for easy management.	Greatly simplifies the development of directory-enabled applications. Greatly reduces the complexity of distributed systems management.
Global catalog	Global catalog servers hold a partial replica of all domains in the tree and a subset of all object properties.	Performance. Enables users to quickly search for objects, wherever they are.
Extensible schema	Ability to customize the "built-in" objects and attributes to fit the needs of your organization.	Important information, outside that of default Windows 2000 fields can be published for users to access.
Multi-master replication	Changes can be made on any domain controller in the domain and be automatically replicated to other domain controllers.	Allows for extremely high availability of the directory for changes at any time. Scales to meet enterprise domains.
Kerberos 5 authentication	Replaces NTLM as the primary authentication protocol across all of Windows 2000.	Fast, single logon to Windows 2000 Server environments and to disparate systems that support Kerberos 5.
Microsoft Management Console	Common console for administrators to view network functions and perform management tasks.	Better organization for administrators and their toolsets. Lower cost of ownership for the desktop.
Group Policy	Application deployment, scripts, and policy options from an MMC snap-in.	Automate such tasks as application installation, user profiles, and desktop system updates.
Remote Installation Services	A remote workstation can boot using *Pre-Boot eXecution* (PXE) and attach to a Windows 2000 server to install Windows 2000 Professional.	Remote OS installation services can be set to provide an array of host installation and configuration services.
IntelliMirror technologies	Users can go to any PC on the corporate network and always have access to their files, applications, and settings. An administrator can assign, publish, or remove software to the directory to be picked up by specific users. Administrators can centrally administrate desktop settings and have the ability to lock down computers.	User data is always available, and the user view of the network is always consistent. Administrators can deploy software without ever leaving their seat. Administrators can lock down computers and force users to store data on the server, minimizing the chances of data loss.

continues

WINDOWS 2000 ACTIVE DIRECTORY FEATURE SET *continued*

Feature/Service	Description	Benefit(s)
Distributed File System (DFS)	DFS implements a single name for disparate file system resources at a site.	Makes it easy for users to find and manage data on the network. To the user it looks like he is storing data in one location, whereas behind the scenes, DFS may have it routed to several different areas.
Dynamic DNS	DDNS is a standard for dynamically updating records in the DNS database. DDNS integrates with the Active Directory, or may use flat-text files.	Reduces DNS administration costs by removing the need to statically add and replicate DNS zone data. Will allow for the removal of NetBIOS in the future.
Connectors	Connectors, such as the Active Directory Connector, allow the Active Directory to communicate with disparate directory services, such as Exchange, NDS, and Windows NT.	Fewer directories to manage. Simplified administration using new MMC tools.

The typical company models are as follows:

◆ Regional

◆ National

◆ International

◆ Subsidiary

◆ Branch office

CHAPTER 3: ANALYZING THE RESULTS OF THE BUSINESS ASSESSMENT

The first step required to perform business problem analysis is to map the business problem to a project objective. Following that, you should start to think about the scope of your project. For most projects of any magnitude, you will create more than one project team.

The existing and planned management models of the organization play a key role in the design of the Active Directory security groups, *organizational units* (OUs), sites, and potentially in the delegation of administrative control. When performing an analysis, you want to ask the following:

◆ Does the management model coincide with the geographical scope of the company?

◆ What roles do different levels of management perform and does this impact the design concept for Active Directory?

◆ What role does the management model play in Active Directory security policies? Will there be a need for delegated control to management?

◆ How will changing the management model impact the design of Active Directory?

◆ What special considerations must be given to the executive management and board of directors?

◆ How does the IT management model integrate with the rest of the company? What special considerations will IT management need?

The following suggestions relate to Active Directory design:

◆ Create Windows 2000 domains when you need to support international differences.

◆ Create Windows 2000 domains when you need to isolate domain replication traffic.

◆ For regional operational models, create Windows 2000 domains at the headquarter (root) level as well as at the regional level. Use organizational units for branch locations.

◆ Stay with a single domain if the size of the organization allows it, and centralized administration is desired.

◆ Use Active Directory sites to control replication traffic within or between domains.

SOFTWARE INSTALLATION AND MAINTENANCE IN THE SERVICE AND PRODUCT LIFE CYCLE

Life Cycle Phase	Software Installation and Maintenance Function	Description
Planning	Package acquisition	You must have an MSI (package) file before you can deploy. You have three options with regard to package acquisition. (1) You obtain the package from a vendor. (2) You can create your own (repackaging). (3) You can use a ZAP file. ZAP files are loosely related to Windows INI files.
	Package modifications	Similar to installer (MSI) files, but with an .MST extension. A modified package file enables you to create custom installations of applications for specific-use scenarios.
Deployment	Application assignments	When administrators use Group Policy to assign applications, they appear (to the client) as if they were installed on the computer. They are not installed, however, until the user attempts to open an associated file or invokes the program through the desktop or Start menu shortcuts.
	Application publishing	When administrators use Group Policy to publish applications, those applications are transparent to the user. Users can install published applications through add/remove programs (they shows up as available software) or by document invocation.
Maintenance	Maintenance (general)	Upgrades and redeployments of software are simplified greatly for published or assigned applications. Administrators can use the application assignments or publications to apply service packs upgrades, and so on.
Removal	Forced removal	Software is removed from a computer automatically. Forced removal is mandatory.
	Optional removal	Gives the users the ability to uninstall an assigned or published application for their computers.

CHAPTER 4: ANALYZING THE IT ADMINISTRATION MODEL

In business today, three types of IT administration models are present: centralized, decentralized, and hybrid.

Centralized administration refers to the dependency on a single individual or team in a single location for administration of the network and network resources. Most small companies and some medium and large companies use a centralized administration model.

Decentralized administration models are used when IT administrative resources are spread throughout the organization and are responsible for managing a specific part or resource set (such as printers) of the organization's network.

The hybrid administration model is a combination of both centralized and decentralized administration In large enterprises with vast resource and technology distribution, the hybrid model is most likely what you will encounter.

A domain is both an administrative boundary and a security boundary. Administrative privileges do not extend past domain boundaries, and each domain has its own security policy that applies to all security accounts within the domain.

An organizational unit is a container that organizes objects within a domain into logical subgroups. These subgroups define your administrative model. The design of the organizational units is key to your successful re-creation of a company's administrative model.

A funding model is a broad topic that covers a vast area of economics in the business.

Total Cost of Ownership (TCO) in its most basic form is based on the following principles:

◆ Baseline metrics

◆ Problem recognition

◆ Change validation

The Microsoft (and Interpose) TCO model uses seven categories to group budgeted costs:

◆ Hardware and software costs

◆ Management costs

◆ Development costs

◆ Support costs

◆ Communication costs

◆ End-user costs

◆ Downtime costs

THE COST-BENEFIT EQUATION

Step	*Scope*	*Approach*
Analysis	Well-known categories that provide credibility	TCO, value creation, and ROI processes
Profiling	All project-associated benefits	4×7 benefit matrix
Quantification	Speaks in terms of dollars	Quantification tools such as Expected Monetary Value, 5 Steps to Productivity, and so on

CHAPTER 5: ANALYZING THE PHYSICAL ENVIRONMENT

Assessing the physical size of the company within its geographical scope of operations will have an impact on the physical sizing relative to the networking infrastructure. Additionally, the available bandwidth between physical locations will govern the way you design the Active Directory physical structures, such as sites and subnets.

The following key elements affect a network topology:

♦ Network type

♦ Inter-network links

♦ Network size

♦ Bandwidth

♦ Traffic patterns

♦ Protocols

As a general rule, you should create Active Directory sites for every segment of the business not connected by a well-connected WAN link. Bandwidth managers utilize *Quality of Service* (QoS)-type technology to aggregate and prioritize network bandwidth by analyzing packets that pass through them—the technology that enables administrators to specify bandwidth for priority services (such as mission-critical, line-of-business application services).

Whereas WINS and DNS make up the core IP name resolution services in a Windows NT/2000 environment, SAP and RIP broadcasts are abundant in a Novell environment. Alternatives to WINS and DNS include LMHOSTS and HOSTS files, respectively.

Whereas DHCP is used to issue IP addresses to DHCP-capable clients, QIP servers offer standards-based many-to-one DHCP fail-over, IP address "check-before-assign" capabilities, as well as the ability to assign IP addresses to older BOOTP clients and the ability to update Dynamic DNS servers with client information.

CHAPTER 6: ANALYZING PERFORMANCE-RELATED REQUIREMENTS

You should follow this six-step approach to successfully monitor performance:

♦ Determine a baseline

♦ Quantify measurement information

♦ Determine bottlenecks

♦ Determine feasible response time

♦ Project future needs

♦ Implement a performance analysis and trending standard

By following these six steps, you can ensure that performance-related bottlenecks are detected and reduced or eliminated.

NETWORKING SUBSYSTEM AND ASSOCIATED SYSTEM MONITOR OBJECTS

Network Subsystem Component	Role	System Monitor Counters
Network interface cards	The network interface cards provide throughput between the server resources and physical network.	Server Network interface
Number of users	The number of users relates to network load factor.	Server
Network infrastructure hardware	The network infrastructure hardware is made up of outers, bridges, switches, hubs, and so on, and provides intelligent data transport.	Network segment Network interface
Network protocols	The network protocols provide a common means of transporting data from computer to computer.	TCP, UDP, IP, NBT, NetBEUI, NetBEUI Resource, Nwlink IPX, Nwlink SPX, Nwlink NetBIOS
Network services	The network services serve specific functions on the network, such as name resolution.	Network interface Network segment Objects specific to network services (WINS, DNS, DHCP, RAS, and so on)
Network applications	The network applications are the software that resides on the servers that provide services to clients and other servers.	Application-specific objects
Directory services	The directory services provide network identity, security, authentication, and several other network services.	Server

DISK SUBSYSTEM AND ASSOCIATED SYSTEM MONITOR OBJECTS

Disk Subsystem Component	Role	System Monitor Counters
Controllers	Controllers provide a means for reading and writing data to disk.	Physical disk
Caching	Caching improves disk performance by temporarily storing information on the controller.	Physical disk
RAID controllers (hardware based)	RAID controllers provide options for significant improvement of disk I/O.	Logical disk
		Physical disk
Type of work	Type of work relates to applications, and defines whether processes are disk bound (I/O intensive).	Logical disk
		Physical disk
Type of drives	Type of drives describes disk access time, latency, and so on.	Physical disk

MEMORY OBJECT COUNTERS THAT COULD INDICATE A MEMORY BOTTLENECK

Counter	Threshold	What to Look For
Pages/sec	0–20	Consistently over 5.
Available bytes	Minimum of 4MB	If consistently under 4MB, this could indicate excessive paging.
Committed bytes	Less than physical RAM	Consistently larger than physical RAM
Pool non-paged bytes	No increase; remain steady	If steadily increases without ever decreasing, could indicate a memory leak.

PROCESSOR-RELATED COUNTERS THAT COULD INDICATE A PROCESSOR BOTTLENECK

Counter	Threshold	What to Look For
%processor time	Below 75%	Consistently over 75%
%privileged time	Below 75%	Consistently over 75%
%user time	Below 75%	Consistently over 75%
System: processor queue length	Less than 2	Consistently over 2
Server: queue length	Less than 2	Consistently over 2

NETWORK-RELATED SYSTEM MONITOR COUNTERS

Counter	Threshold	What to Look For
Bytes total/sec (server)	High, but not extreme	If the number is extremely high, and network utilization is low, add a NIC and split the load between the two.
Logons/sec (server)	High, but not extreme	If the number is extremely high and processor utilization is high, add an additional domain controller.
Logons/total (server)	High, but not extreme	If the number is more than 200, add a domain controller.
%Network Utilization (network segment)	Up to 50% on switched networks, 30% otherwise	Analyze with a Network Monitor trace and compare network traffic with utilization. Determine what network traffic can be reduced.
Bytes sent/sec (network interface)	Depends on NIC and protocols; should be a high number	If the number is extremely high, add a NIC or remove unnecessary protocols.
Bytes total/sec (network interface)	Depends on NIC and protocols; should be a high number	If the number is extremely high, add a NIC or remove unnecessary protocols.

DISK OBJECT SYSTEM MONITOR COUNTERS

Counter	Threshold	What to Look For
% Disk Time	Keep under 50%	If disk utilization is consistently over 50%, the disk is being punished.
Disk Queue Length	Keep under 2	If queue length is consistently over 2, it indicates disk congestion.
Avg. disk bytes/transfer	Higher the better	If number is steadily decreasing, it could indicate the impending failure of a hard disk or increased requirement for data processing.
Disk bytes/sec	Higher the better	If number is steadily decreasing, it could indicate impending failure of a hard disk or increased requirement for data processing.

WINDOWS NT/2000 SERVER SERVICE CONFIGURATION OPTIONS

Server Service Setting	Description	Useful For
Minimize Memory Used	Meant to accommodate up to 10 simultaneous users.	Very small environments with fewer than 10 users
Balance	Meant to accommodate up to 64 simultaneous users.	Small organizations in which there exists a single server
Maximize Throughput for File Sharing	File cache access has priority over user application access. Optimized for 64 or more connections.	File servers
Maximize Throughput for Network Applications	User application access has priority over file cache access. Optimized for 64 or more connections.	Application servers

CHAPTER 7: ANALYZING SECURITY REQUIREMENTS

A security principal is any entity that can initiate action. Users are considered security principals, therefore, and so are computers and services.

Windows 2000 authentication supports three core protocols: *Windows NT LAN Manager* (NTLM), Kerberos, and *Secure Sockets Layer/Transport Layer Security* (SSL/TLS).

NTLM was used in Windows NT Server 4.0 and previous versions. MIT Kerberos 5 replaces NTLM as the default authentication protocol for Windows 2000. Kerberos defines the interactions between clients and its authentication service, the *Key Distribution Center* (KDC), which uses Active Directory as its accounts database.

Windows 2000 uses SSL/TLS and X.509 certificates to provide mutual authentication, message integrity, and confidentiality. The Windows 2000 implementation of SSL/TLS supports logon through the use of smart cards, and is used to protect connections on unsecured networks.

CONSIDERATIONS FOR REMOVING NTLM

Environment	Action
Current network still has Windows NT and/or 95/98 computers on it.	NTLM is required to continue supporting previous versions of Windows.
UNIX clients, not configured or the Kerberos protocol, use the existing Windows NT/ Windows 2000 servers.	If UNIX computers are configured to use *Server Message Block* (SMB), you must continue to support NTLM. If UNIX computers are configured to use TCP/IP standard applications, such as FTP and Telnet, NTLM may be eliminated.
Several UNIX clients are configured to use Kerberos. All of them use SMB to connect to Windows NT/ 2000 servers.	You can eliminate NTLM if you configure the UNIX servers to authenticate to Windows 2000 using Kerberos.
Current Windows NT/2000 clients connect to a UNIX server using SMB.	If you continue to use SMB, you must continue to support NTLM. You can replace SMB with the *Network File System* (NFS), which will free you to remove NTLM support.

WINDOWS 2000 SUPPORT FOR PKI STANDARDS

PKI Standard	Definition	Justification
X.509 v.3	Defines content and format for digital certificates	Standard is needed for the exchange of certificates between vendors.
CRL v.2	Defines content and format for digital certificate revocation lists	Standard is needed for the exchange of certificate revocation information between vendors.
PKCS family	Defines behavior and format for the exchange and delivery of public keys	Provides the ability for different vendors to request and move certificates using a standardized process.
PKIX	Defines behavior and format for the exchange and delivery of public keys	Emerging PKI standard positioned to replace the PKCS standard.
SSL v.3	Defines encryption for Web sessions	Most widely implemented security protocol on the Internet. Downfall: it is subject to export controls.
SGC	Defines security similar to SSL without export complications	Allows 128-bit security and, in certain cases, is fully exportable.
IPsec	Defines IP packet encryption for network sessions	Offers transparent and automatic encryption of network transmissions.
PKINIT	Defines standard for using public keys for authenticating to networks that use Kerberos	Allows Kerberos to use digital certificates on smart cards as security credentials for authentication.
PC/SC	Defines a standard for the integration of smart cards and computers	Open standard to which many smart card vendors' specifications adhere.

IPsec is made up of the following four components:

◆ Encryption and encapsulation

◆ Authentication and anti-replay

◆ Key management and digital certificates

◆ Support for unique digital certificates

Security policy defines a security configuration file stored as part of a Group Policy object. You create these files using the Security Configuration Toolset. Local Policy, which is defined on the computer itself, carries the least precedence when a computer is a part of a domain. The domain policy sits in the middle, and the OU policy carries the most weight. The domain policy is applied to all computers in a given domain, and then any specific OU policies are applied for computers that exist in OUs with defined policies.

CHAPTER 8: IMPACT OF ACTIVE DIRECTORY

WINDOWS 2000 SUPPORTED UPGRADE PATHS

Previous Version	Windows 2000 Platform	Release
Windows 95 (all)	Professional	Full (retail)
	Professional	Upgrade
Windows 98 (all)	Professional	Full (retail)
	Professional	Upgrade
Windows NT 3.51/4.0 Workstation	Professional	Full (retail)
	Professional	Upgrade

Previous Version	Windows 2000 Platform	Release
Windows 2000 Professional	Professional	Full (retail)
	Professional	Upgrade
Windows NT 3.51/4.0 Server	Server	Full (retail)
	Server	Upgrade
	Advanced Server	Full (retail)
Windows NT 3.51 Server with Citrix	None	None
Windows NT 4.0 Terminal Server	Server	Full (retail)
	Server	Upgrade
	Advanced Server	Full (retail)
Windows NT 4.0 Server – Enterprise Edition	Advanced Server	Full (retail)
	Advanced Server	Upgrade
	DataCenter Server	Full
BackOffice Small Business Server	None	None
Windows 2000 Server	Server	Full (retail)
	Server	Upgrade
Windows 2000 Advanced Server	Advanced Server	Full (retail)
	Advanced Server	Upgrade
	DataCenter	Full
Windows 2000 DataCenter Server	DataCenter	Full

You should record the following minimal information for each application installed on the network:

◆ Software title and manufacturer

◆ Major version number

◆ Minor version number (if applicable)

◆ Application type (client/server [which piece], standalone, and so on)

◆ Architecture design (for 16-bit, 32-bit, or so forth)

You can expect to put some of these applications on a priority-one list:

◆ Any line-of-business (LOB) application

◆ Enterprise messaging systems

◆ Data warehousing systems

◆ Departmental applications, such as AutoCAD in the Engineering group, or an ERP implementation

◆ E-Commerce applications

◆ Tape backup applications

◆ Emulation packages, which provide access to LOB applications

REASONS WHY APPLICATIONS FAIL WHEN MOVED TO WINDOWS 2000

Reason	DOS	Windows 3.x	Windows 9x	Windows NT 4.0
Need direct hardware access	X	X		
Reliance on FAT	X	X		
Inability to display graphics	X			
More secure environment	X	X	X	
Incompatible device drivers		X	X	
Excessive CPU utilization		X		
Incompatible with Win32 API			X	
Registry problems			X	
Third-party services				X
System utility software				X
Active Directory				X

The Windows 2000 Upgrade Web site (`http://www.microsoft.com/windows2000/upgrade/`) houses helpful information such as a hardware and software compatibility database that is continually updated. The site also includes a link to a comprehensive guide to upgrading to Windows 2000, which links to all Windows 2000 certified applications.

The Windows 2000 Readiness Analyzer tool analyzes your system and compares the devices and applications on your system against a list of known issues. The *Microsoft Readiness Framework* (MRF) includes a skills manager database application that contains the competencies, learning plans, and resources for Windows 2000 Active Directory planning and design.

Microsoft has broken management into the logical groups, as the following table shows:

MICROSOFT WINDOWS MANAGEMENT DISCIPLINES

Disciplines	Discipline Domain
Change and configuration management	System administration, state management, and life cycle management
Security management	Authentication, access, and auditing
Performance management	Tracking, tuning, modeling, and monitoring
Problem management	Error isolation, remote trouble-shooting, and trouble ticketing
Event management	Consolidation, aggregation, delivery, and monitoring
Batch and output management	Job control, queuing, scheduling, and printers and plotters
Storage management	Data storage, retrieval, backup, and archiving

CHAPTER 9: END-USER NEEDS AND DESKTOP MANAGEMENT

Just about any end-user who touches a computer is classified as a knowledge worker. Knowledge workers by definition need access to data and information so that they can convert it into knowledge. Data management, which refers to the capability for a user's documents to follow him from location to location, can be divided into three components: accessibility, availability, and protection.

The goal behind any software installation and maintenance is to provide policy-based deployment and management of that software throughout the entire software life cycle.

Software can be distributed to the user base in two ways: published or assigned. Published applications are made available to users for use on an as-needed basis. The users can install a published application by selecting it in the Add/Remove Programs Control Panel applet. Assigned applications apply to users *and* computers. This means that an application may be assigned to roam with a user, or may be assigned to a specific computer itself. Assigned applications are mandatory when assigned to a computer, which means they are installed the next time the computer starts up.

The key technology behind software installation and maintenance is the Windows Installer Service. To be compatible with this service, applications must be authored or repackaged. Not all applications can be repackaged to the Windows Installer format; ZAP files are text files that can be analyzed and executed by the software installation technology within Group Policy. They enable you to publish non-Windows Installer applications with some limitations:

◆ They cannot be assigned. (They must be published.)

◆ They do not have the resilience that the Windows Installer applications have.

◆ They require user intervention during installation because they run the software's original setup program.

◆ They cannot install with elevated privileges.

During remote OS installation, a client computer with a ROM that supports PXE attaches to the network and finds a *Remote Installation Server* (RIS), which supplies the client with a wizard that initiates an installation of a preconfigured Windows 2000 Professional OS. Non-PXE-enabled clients can be booted from disk to attach to RIS servers. There are two types of remote OS installations available: CD based and RIPrep image format custom images.

CHAPTER 10: DNS AND ACTIVE DIRECTORY

DNS is the foundation of Active Directory. You use DNS to create a namespace for Active Directory; that namespace typically defines the scope of Active Directory services—although scope can be much bigger than a single namespace.

DNS servers use a top-down approach for resolving *fully qualified domain names* (FQDNs) across partitions; Active Directory is built to model DNS. The FQDN has two parts:

◆ **Host name.** In simple terms, the host name is the computer name.

◆ **Domain name.** The domain name is the DNS domain name in which the host resides.

The *Relative Distinguished Name* (RDN) is the host name of the computer within the context of the proper domain, whereas the *User Principal Name* (UPN) consists of a user logon name and a domain name identifying the domain in which the user account is located. Active Directory also suggests a pre-Windows 2000 name—a NetBIOS name—as the first 15 bytes of an object's RDN. The following table compares NetBIOS and DNS names.

COMPARISON OF NETBIOS AND DNS NAMING

Type	NetBIOS (flat)	DNS (hierarchical)
Character Restrictions	Unicode characters, numbers, white	Same as NetBIOS, except you cannot use white space and the period (.) has special meaning
	Symbols: ! @ # $ % ^ & ') (. - _ { }	
Maximum Length	15-character bytes	63 octets per label 255 octets per FQDN
Name Service	WINS, broadcast	DNS, DDNS

The major components of DNS are as follows:

- **Servers.** Primary, secondary, caching only, or forwarders.

- **Resolvers.** Clients

- **Resource records.** The basic unit of information DNS servers use to fulfill queries. The SRV record provides a method by which servers advertise their services and is needed for Active Directory

- **Zone database files.** Repositories of all resource records for a given zone.

With zone transfers, secondary zones poll primaries when they are ready to update their zone file. The three types of transfers are as follows:

- Full (AXFR)

- Incremental (IXFR)

- DNS Notify

Dynamic DNS (DDNS) is implemented via DNS servers that support dynamic updates and SRV records. In an Active Directory integrated zone, zone transfers are not needed, because the zone information takes part in Active Directory replication.

BEST PRACTICES IN NAMING

Practice	Process
Migrating non-DNS-compliant naming schemes to DNS	If you cannot afford to change all NetBIOS names that don't comply with RFC-1123 standards in DNS naming, use the Windows 2000 DNS and the ANSII and/or Unicode character sets during the transition.
Deciding on a public or private domain	You must mitigate the risk of using a public DNS for your Active Directory root. Microsoft recommends using a delegated subdomain of your public registered domain, which provides separation from public and private and enables you to maintain a contiguous name space.
Naming the root domain	The name of the root domain should describe your organization as a whole.
Designing DNS zones	DNS zones should strictly adhere to Active Directory domains.
DNS replication	If using standard DNS, you need to consider redundancy in servers by introducing primary and secondary zones.
DNS servers	DNS servers you choose to use must support SRV records, and should support incremental zone transfer and dynamic update.

CHAPTER 11: DESIGNING THE ACTIVE DIRECTORY STRUCTURE

Windows 2000 Active Directory service encompasses four major areas: forests, domains, organizational units, and sites. The first domain is also a forest root and introduces the schema, the database behind Active Directory. Active Directory uses transitive trusts within a forest of domains. These trusts are created automatically, but may need to be optimized.

Sites enable you to incorporate the physical characteristics of the network into your design. They work at the physical IP subnet level and allow for the compression and control of replication traffic. Sites, site links, site link bridges, and replication are a huge part in the design of Active Directory as a whole.

In Active Directory, everything is an object—users, printers, groups, and even policy settings are stored as objects. An object defined is any distinct, named set of attributes that represents something unique and concrete. Attributes hold data that define the object.

A container is a special kind of object. It has attributes that define its subject matter and is part of Active Directory, but does not represent something concrete. Containers can contain objects and other containers.

Trees describe a hierarchy of objects and containers. The "leaf" objects of a tree (the endpoints) are usually objects, and the "nodes" of a tree (the points of the tree that contain branches) are usually containers.

A domain is a security boundary, the basic unit of Active Directory. Active Directory is made up of one or more domains, each of which may contain millions of objects and containers. A domain is a special kind of container, and can be considered an abstract object as well because it has its own attributes. In Active Directory, you can span several domains together and share a common schema, configuration, and global catalog to form domain trees. Organizational units enable Windows 2000 administrators to subdivide a domain according to the type of IT administration.

Domain trees are one or more domains that share a common schema, configuration, and global catalog and form a contiguous namespace. Because they share these elements, automatic Kerberos trust relationships between domains are created.

A forest is a set of domain trees that do not share a common namespace. Even though these domain trees do not share a contiguous namespace, they continue to share a common schema, configuration, and global catalog. All domain trees within a given forest trust each other via automatic Kerberos trust relationships.

A site is a way to create your replication boundaries within Active Directory. It is comprised of one or more "well-connected" physical IP subnet. Sites work at the physical layer and are independent of the logical layer where domains operate. This means that a site can consist of multiple domains, and domains can operate in multiple sites. Sites contain two types of objects: server objects and connection objects. Connection objects are generated by the *Knowledge Consistency Checker* (KCC). The purpose of the KCC is to generate a replication topology for both intra-site and inter-site replication. Site link bridges are used to connect sites together and model the routing behavior of a network.

Windows 2000 uses a multi-master replication model wherein every domain controller contains a read/write version of the directory (catalog) database. The primary unit of replication is the domain, but the replication model incorporated with Active Directory is more granular—based not on object comparisons, but on object attribute comparisons using a trigger. This trigger, known as the *Update Sequence Number* (USN), is incremented for an object whenever an attribute for that object is changed. When domain controllers need to replicate, they examine the values of their USNs for each object, and only replicate the attributes whose objects contain differing USNs.

A single domain is also considered a domain tree and a forest because of the schema, configuration, and global catalog; you can have all the functionality of a forest with a single domain. Justifications for creating additional domains include the following:

◆ You need to support decentralized administration and OUs will not suffice.

◆ You need to isolate or balance replication traffic.

◆ You need to support international differences.

◆ You need to support more than one domain policy.

◆ Existing Windows NT domain structures must be retained.

◆ Company politics dictate it.

Justification for creating OUs include the following:

◆ You need to delegate administration.

◆ You have existing Windows NT resource domains.

◆ You need an application point for Group Policy objects.

◆ You need to control access to resources.

◆ You want to group objects that have common properties.

COMPARISON OF DOMAINS AND OUs

Required Feature	Domains	OUs
Organizational business units must have separate DNS names.	Yes	No
Decentralized administration by completely separate administrative personnel.	Yes	No
Decentralized administrative control.	No	Yes
High-level domain administrators must not have access to parts of the network under another group's authority.	Yes	No
Two parts of the network are separated by an extremely slow link and you don't want any replication traffic to cross it.	Yes	No
You need to hierarchically structure the company based on its administrative and organizational needs.	No	Yes
Delegation of administrative control.	No	Yes
Structure is likely to change.	No	Yes
Implement different security policies.	Yes	No
Reduce the number of objects in each domain.	Yes	No

WINDOWS 2000 SECURITY GROUPS

Type	Legal Members	Scope of Usage	Domain Mode
Local	• Users from its own forest • Global groups from its own forest	Local computer only	Native, Mixed
Global	• Users from its own domain • Global groups from its own domain	Entire forest and any trusted domains	Native, Mixed
Domain local	• Users from anywhere in the forest • Global groups from anywhere in the forest • Universal groups from anywhere in the forest • Domain local groups from its own domain	Their own domain only	Native only
Universal	• Users from anywhere in the forest • Computers from anywhere in the forest • Global groups from anywhere in the forest • Universal groups from anywhere in the forest	World. Entire forest and any trusted forest	Native only

Several downfalls are associated with creating multiple forests:

◆ You will have multiple schema and configuration containers and will have to manually maintain synchronicity between them.

◆ You will need to create explicit one-way Windows NT 4.0–style trust relationships between domains from different forests.

◆ The search scope for users is the entire directory.

◆ Users logging on outside their forest need to remember their entire UPN.

◆ You cannot move accounts from one forest to another.

THE OPERATIONS MASTER ROLES AND IMPACT OF THEIR FAILURE

Operations Master Role	Impact of Failure on Users	Impact of Failure on Administrators
Schema Master	None	None until they try to modify the schema.
Domain naming master	None	None until they try to add, modify, or delete domains in the forest.
Infrastructure master	None	None unless they have recently moved a large number of objects from one domain to another.
RID master	None	None until they need a reallocation of RIDs for creating domain objects.
PDC emulator	Down-level clients may not be able to log on	Windows NT BDCs will not get replicated information.

You can use the NTDSUTIL utility to perform many low-level Active Directory administration tasks.

CHAPTER 12: DESIGNING AN OU AND GROUP POLICY MANAGEMENT STRUCTURE

Access control lists (ACLs) are structures attached to objects to control access to them. They consist of *access control entries* (ACEs), which are the individual users or groups permitted access to that object and the associated permissions.

Because of the granularity of Windows 2000 security, administrative control can be granted on a per-user, per-object, or per-attribute basis. Using a combination of OUs and ACLs, you can create an environment that mirrors the way the network is administered.

OU realities include the following:

◆ OUs are *not* security principals.

◆ Users do *not* navigate the OU structure.

◆ OUs have less effect on performance than Group Policy.

◆ GPOs attached to OUs may degrade performance.

◆ DNS namespace does not reveal your OUs.

◆ OUs cannot span domains.

Reasons you should create OUs include the following

◆ To delegate administrative control. You can delegate the right to (1) reset passwords only, (2) create and delete child objects—such as users, groups, printers, and so on, (3) change attributes on a particular object, such as the first and last name on a user.

◆ To group like objects together and control the application of Group Policy. This enables you to (1) control security options, (2) assign or publish software, (3) assign logon/logoff (user) and startup/shutdown (computer) scripts.

◆ To replace existing Windows NT resource domains.

◆ To create an administrative hierarchy of OUs.

◆ To simplify the administration of resources.

REASONS FOR CREATING DOMAINS AND OUs

Reasons for Creating Domains	Reasons for Creating OUs
To isolate or balance replication traffic	To delegate administrative control
To define and implement different domain-wide security policies	To group similar objects
To retain existing Windows NT domain structures	To control the application of Group Policy
To support decentralized administration in cases where OUs will not suffice	To replace existing Windows NT resource domains
To support international differences	To create an administrative hierarchy of OUs
Company politics dictate a need for additional domains	To simplify the administration of resources

The OU manager is responsible for performing the following OU-level tasks:

- Performing additions, deletions, and modifications to all objects within the OU

- Determining whether OU permissions should be inherited from parent OUs

- Determining whether OU permissions should be propagated to next-level OUs

- Delegating next-level OU authority to other administrators

Permissions granted the OU administrator apply for all objects within that OU and also will apply for any additional OUs produced under that one. You must consider delegating the ability to perform the following tasks to OU administrators:

- Create, delete, and manage user accounts

- Reset passwords on user accounts

- Read all user information

- Create, delete, and manage groups

- Modify the membership of a group

- Manage Group Policy links

- Single-task options such as adding users to the OU

THREE MAIN ACTIVE DIRECTORY SECURITY COMPONENTS

Security Component	Purpose	Description
Security principals	Receive permissions	Comprised of users, groups, and computers.
Security identifiers (SID)	Uniquely identify security principals	Alphanumeric structures assigned to uniquely identify security principals. The first part of the SID is unique to the issuing domain, the second part, the *relative identifier* (RID), is unique for all objects within the domain.
Security descriptors	Protect objects	Defines the access permissions for the object.

The domain administrator can always take ownership of any OU in the domain. Domain administrators should, however, be responsible only for the following:

◆ Developing the initial OU structure

◆ Repairing mistakes

You can use three tools to delegate control on objects in Active Directory:

◆ Delegation of Control Wizard

◆ Security tab of the object's Properties window

◆ DSACLS.EXE command-line utility

If you have a Windows 2000 client or member server operating in a mixed-mode environment, policies are applied in the following order:

◆ Windows NT 4.0 policy file (ntconfig.pol)

◆ LGPOs

◆ Site GPOs

◆ Domain GPOs

◆ OU GPOs applied hierarchically until the user or computer object is reached

You must understand the following items as you begin to plan the structure and management of Group Policies:

◆ You can block policy inheritance, and can configure individual GPOs to forcefully apply by specifying No Override.

◆ You can control access to GPOs through the use of security groups (and security principals).

◆ GPOs are processed first at the local machine (LGPO), then at the site level, then at the domain level, and finally throughout the OU hierarchy.

◆ OUs are anchored at the domain level, and are not inherited throughout the domain hierarchy. GPOs, however, from one domain can be linked to OUs in another domain.

◆ Policies that don't conflict are cumulative.

◆ Computer GPOs are applied at computer startup and shutdown; user GPOs are applied at user logon and logoff.

◆ The default refresh rate is 90 minutes for both user- and computer-based GPOs.

◆ Computer policies always take precedence over user policies.

◆ GPOs are *not* applied to security groups.

BEST PRACTICES IN OU AND GPO DESIGN

Task	*Description*
Choose the right OU model.	Take caution in choosing the OU model you implement and make sure it accurately reflects the IT administration model as well as the operational structure of the organization.
Keep OU design simple.	Reasons to create OUs are as follows: • To enhance administrative control and accurately reflect the organizational structure of the company • To provide a structure for Group Policy • To replace existing Windows NT resource domains • To hold other OUs in the top or middle tier of the OU hierarchy
Delegate administration.	Keep the following in mind as youdevelop the delegation of administration plan: • For each OU created in the directory, you should associate a responsible party who will administer the OU, define the reason for its being, and the extent of the permissions the delegated parties will have. • The central IT group should retain full administration for the first, second, and in deep hierarchies, even the third level of OUs. • Minimize the delegation of attribute-level permissions. These are very difficult to keep track of and could potentially open security holes.
Remain consistent in your design.	Consistency is key to keeping things simple. If you have an environment with multiple domains, consider using the same OU model throughout.
Plan the location of user and computer objects within the OU structure.	This has a huge impact on the overall OU and Group Policy structure.
Plan the Group Policy structure.	The Group Policy structure should be considered all the way through the domain and OU design process. The best-case scenario for the Group Policy structure is to have it flow with your domain and OU structure.
Determine GPO management scope.	Determine whether to use single policy-focused GPOs or GPOs that include multiple policies. Determine how to delegate administration over GPOs, and determine whether to use a layered or monolithic design.
Keep an eye on performance.	GPOs can degrade performance because they must be processed one at a time. Optimize performance by disabling unused portions of GPOs, using security groups to filter the effects of GPOs, and limit cross-domain references to GPOs.

REVIEW OF POPULAR **OU** DESIGN OPTIONS

Design Option	Advantages	Disadvantages
Organize by geography	Your first-level OUs remain static, which is a best practice in OU design. Also, administrators have a good idea where an OU's objects are physically located.	If the geography of a company doesn't match the way an organization is managed, it may be difficult to comprehend. This may cause confusion as to which business unit or function a user or object actually belongs.
Organize by function or department	Well-established business functions typically do not change, so the first-level OU structure should remain static.	Administrators may have difficulty identifying where an object within an OU is physically located. For businesses that change frequently to stay atop their market, this structure may do more harm than good.
Organize by administration	Tailored to the way administrators run the network. OU administrators can easily identify from where resources are administered. Provides for easy delegation of administrative control.	Administrative delegation outside the IT department becomes a bit more challenging in this model. Users may not be adequately organized for Group Policy assignments.
Organize by business unit	This model works well in a conglomerate in which each business unit is treated separately from the rest of the organization.	Administrators have difficulty determining where resources physically reside. Users from different departments or different functional units may be grouped into one OU but may require different software or have different desktop restrictions that make Group Policy assignment complex. The names of business units often change.
Organize by project	The only advantage to organizing by project is the logical grouping of resources per project.	Project-based OUs are *not* relatively static. Project resources are typically a part of many projects at once, which can be structurally impossible to reproduce with OUs. Just about all the other disadvantages related to OU structures apply here as well.

CHAPTER 13: DEVELOPING A SCHEMA MODIFICATION PLAN

The Active Directory schema is stored in a database, which means the following:

◆ It is dynamically extensible.

◆ It is dynamically available to user applications.

◆ It can use DACLs to protect or filter access to all classes and attributes.

There is only one schema per Windows 2000 forest. It is stored on every domain controller and maintained forest wide. The advantage to this is that all objects conform to the same set of rules and contain the same types of data. There is only one writable copy of the schema—held by the Schema Operations Master—at any given time within a forest.

The schema container holds all the class and attribute definitions required to view the objects in the directory. You can view its contents by using the Active Directory Schema MMC snap-in, or by using the ADSIedit MMC utility to bind to the schema naming context and view its contents.

Within Active Directory, classes contain either mandatory or optional attributes. Classes may also be derived from other classes, creating a hierarchy of classes. Classes are defined by classSchema objects and are therefore instances of the classSchema class. Attributes are defined by atibuteSchema objects, and are therefore instances of the attributeSchema class.

The following four types of classes make up the entire directory:

◆ Structural classes

◆ Abstract classes

◆ Auxiliary classes

◆ 88 classes

To index a schema attribute, you just navigate to that attribute property page and enable the Index This Attribute in the Active Directory check box. By doing this, you are telling Active Directory that it can sort and group by that attribute, which is useful for queries and reports.

> **WARNING**
>
> **Don't Take Schema Modification Lightly**   Modifying the schema is an irreversible operation with directory-wide implications. You cannot "un-extend" the schema. You can only disable portions of it; and when you do so, you run the risk of creating inconsistencies in the directory schema. Inconsistencies in the schema can cause significant Active Directory problems that may not be immediately or easily noticeable. Microsoft specifically recommends that you modify the schema only when absolutely necessary; it should be done very infrequently because of the far-reaching impact schema changes can have.

The following table lists common situations and suggests resolutions regarding schema modifications.

Some Situations That Might Require Schema Modification

Situation	Suggestion
You cannot find an existing class to fit your needs.	Create a new class.
You find an existing class that would fit your needs with the addition of some attributes.	Either create new attributes and associate them with the existing class, or derive a new subclass and add additional attributes as needed.
You need only a set of unique attributes, not a class.	Create a new auxiliary class and attach it to the appropriate class.
Existing classes and/or attributes are no longer relevant.	Deactivate the class(es) or attribute(s).

Microsoft uses the following safety locks to secure the schema:

◆ By default, schema modification is disabled on all domain controllers. You must modify a registry key to enable schema modification. You can find more information at **http://www.microsoft.com/ windows2000/library/planning/activedirectory/ adschemasteps.asp**.

◆ The schema object is protected by the Windows 2000 security model. By default, only members of the Schema Admins (forest root administrator by default) group may write changes to the schema.

◆ Only one domain controller in the forest contains a copy of the schema with write access. This is the domain controller holding the Schema Master FSMO role.

◆ Each schema object must be represented by a globally unique number, which is referred to as the *object identifier* (OID).

Chapter 14: Planning for Coexistence

A directory service must have the capability to interoperate with other platform-independent directory services. Effective planning and coexistence testing is essential here, as it is with any other area of Active Directory.

Microsoft's interoperability strategy is based on a four-layer framework that covers the integration of the following:

◆ Network

◆ Data

◆ Applications

◆ Management

Whereas previous versions of *Services for NetWare* (SFNW) just provided file and print services and a Bindery-based directory service manager application, SFNW 5 provides the following:

◆ Microsoft Directory Synchronization Services (MSDSS)

◆ File Migration Utility (FMU)

◆ File and Print Services for NetWare v.5

MSDSS makes synchronization with both NDS and NetWare Binderies possible. It is a scalable service focused on implementing Active Directory in an existing NetWare environment. MSDSS can provide bidirectional synchronization support in NDS environments, and unidirectional support in Bindery-only environments. MSDSS is made up of the following components:

◆ Sessions

◆ Object-level synchronization

◆ Directional synchronization

Benefits to implementing MSDSS include the following:

- ◆ It creates a single point of administration.

- ◆ It ensures integrity across multiple directories.

- ◆ It synchronizes several object types and changes.

- ◆ It supports the single sign-on initiative.

- ◆ It preserves NDS investment.

- ◆ It supports different tree structures.

- ◆ It simplifies NDS-to-Active Directory migrations.

The File Migration Utility is integrated with MSDSS and can migrate files from NetWare to Windows 2000 and retain the directory structure and security permissions on each file, while enabling the user to maintain access to his files through the migration.

File and Print Services for NetWare (FPNW) v.5 allows a Windows 2000 server to act as a NetWare server to NetWare clients in a Bindery-mode environment. SFNW also includes these utilities:

- ◆ **Directory Service Manager for NetWare (DSMN).** This utility helps organizations manage Bindery-mode users from several servers in a common interface.

- ◆ **Gateway Services for NetWare (GSNW).** This utility is unchanged from previous versions of NetWare utilities.

- ◆ **ADSI.** This common LDAP programming interface enables you to create custom scripts to pull LDAP-accessible information from both NDS and Active Directory.

- ◆ **Directory Service Migration Utility (DSMU).** This utility provides the ability to migrate NDS and Bindery-mode data to Active Directory.

Services for UNIX (SFU) provides a set of tools to help bridge the gap between UNIX and Windows for users and administrators, including the following specific features:

- ◆ Transparent sharing of data between UNIX and Windows using Network File System. Windows 2000 Services for UNIX includes the following NFS components: Server for NFS, Client for NFS, Gateway for NFS, and User Name Mapping.

- ◆ Remote command-line access from a Windows or UNIX computer to another Windows or UNIX computer using Telnet.

- ◆ A full-featured, Posix-compliant UNIX Korn shell for Windows with an initial toolset of about 60 commands (such as ls, pwd, and so on).

- ◆ Heterogeneous network administration, including integrated directory management via NIS server functionality.

- ◆ User password synchronization. A *Single Sign-On Daemon* (SSOD) provides two-way password synchronization between UNIX and Active Directory. It must be compiled for each of the following UNIX platforms: HP-UX 10.3 and newer, Sun Solaris 2.6 and newer, IBM AIX 4.3 and newer, Digital True64 UNIX, Linux RedHat 5.2 and newer.

- ◆ Simple administration and installation of SFU components. Administrative tools include a Telnet client, Telnet server, MMC snap-in, and ActivePerl.

- ◆ Management of Services for UNIX components using *Windows Management Instrumentation* (WMI).

As organizations begin to adopt and implement Windows 2000, integration will be necessary between their existing Exchange 5.5 with Active Directory. The basic building blocks for Active Directory and Exchange integration are as follows:

◆ Windows 2000 Server/Advanced Server/DataCenter

◆ Active Directory Connector

◆ Exchange Server

◆ LDAP version 3.0

The key to the integration is the *Active Directory Connector* (ADC). The ADC provides the following functionality:

◆ Uses the LDAP API to perform fast replication between the Exchange and Active Directories.

◆ Hosts all active replication components on Active Directory, not Exchange.

◆ Replicates only changes between Exchange and Active Directory whenever possible.

◆ Maintains object mappings through replication. For example, Active Directory groups are replicated to Exchange distribution lists.

◆ Hosts multiple connections on a single Active Directory server and manages them via *Connection Agreements* (CAs).

You configure a CA by using a wizard, which walks you through configuration of the following:

◆ Synchronization direction. (which can be two-way or one-way, in either direction)

◆ Bridgehead server configuration

◆ Creating a synchronization schedule

◆ Selecting source and destination containers

◆ Determine how deletions will be processed

◆ Optimize the CA (configure advanced options)

HOW EXCHANGE OBJECTS MATCH UP WITH ACTIVE DIRECTORY OBJECTS

Exchange Object	*Active Directory Object*
Mailbox	User
Distribution list	Group
Custom recipient	Contact

Exchange 2000 integrates with Active Directory and therefore does not include its own directory service anymore.

CHAPTER 15: DESIGNING AN AD IMPLEMENTATION PLAN

An implementation plan identifies a roadmap for your implementation and serves as a conceptual framework for the deployment, making it easier for the various teams to determine progress. Although there is not one single required method for creating an Active Directory implementation plan, there are tried-and-true methodologies, such as *Microsoft Solutions Framework* (MSF) and *Project Management Institute* (PMI) project methodologies.

An implementation plan can consist of different phases that take a project from start to finish (and beyond). When you use a phased approach, it provides a mechanism for the hierarchical breakdown of tasks and subtasks that make up a phase. You can assign resources, time, and cost to subtasks and roll that up to determine task, phase, and project costs and duration.

The five phases for the implementation plan are as follows:

◆ Goals and Objectives

◆ Planning and Design

◆ Pilot. Testing, training, deployment according to project implementation plan in a lab and pseudo-production setting

◆ Execution

◆ Closure. Post-project review, knowledge transfer, transfer of operations, and support services

You should also ask and answer the following subset of questions during the planning phase:

◆ Why is your organization deploying Windows 2000?

◆ What is your time schedule for the deployment?

◆ How will the general user population be affected by this project?

◆ What are the risks, assumptions, and constraints involved with this project?

A Gap Analysis is an analysis of the gaps between where the business is now and where it needs or wants to be.

This element of the book provides you with some general guidelines for preparing for a certification exam. It is organized into four sections. The first section addresses your learning style and how it affects your preparation for the exam. The second section covers your exam preparation activities and general study tips. This is followed by an extended look at the Microsoft Certification exams, including a number of specific tips that apply to the various Microsoft exam formats and question types. Finally, changes in Microsoft's testing policies, and how these might affect you, are discussed.

LEARNING STYLES

To better understand the nature of preparation for the test, it is important to understand learning as a process. You probably are aware of how you best learn new material. You may find that outlining works best for you, or, as a visual learner, you may need to "see" things. Whatever your learning style, test preparation takes place over time. Obviously, you shouldn't start studying for these exams the night before you take them; it is very important to understand that learning is a developmental process. Understanding it as a process helps you focus on what you know and what you have yet to learn.

Thinking about how you learn should help you recognize that learning takes place when you are able to match new information to old. You have some previous experience with computers and networking. Now you are preparing for this certification exam. Using this book, software, and supplementary materials will not just add incrementally to what you know; as you study, the organization of your knowledge actually restructures as you integrate new information into your existing knowledge base. This will lead you to a more comprehensive understanding of the tasks and concepts

Study and Exam Prep Tips

outlined in the objectives and of computing in general. Again, this happens as a result of a repetitive process rather than a singular event. Keep this model of learning in mind as you prepare for the exam, and you will make better decisions concerning what to study and how much more studying you need to do.

STUDY TIPS

There are many ways to approach studying just as there are many different types of material to study. However, the tips that follow should work well for the type of material covered on the certification exams.

Study Strategies

Although individuals vary in the ways they learn information, some basic principles of learning apply to everyone. You should adopt some study strategies that take advantage of these principles. One of these principles is that learning can be broken into various depths. Recognition (of terms, for example) exemplifies a more surface level of learning in which you rely on a prompt of some sort to elicit recall. Comprehension or understanding (of the concepts behind the terms, for example) represents a deeper level of learning. The ability to analyze a concept and apply your understanding of it in a new way represents a further depth of learning.

Your learning strategy should enable you to know the material at a level or two deeper than mere recognition. This will help you perform well on the exams. You will know the material so thoroughly that you can easily handle the recognition-level types of questions used in multiple-choice testing. You will also be able to apply your knowledge to solve new problems.

Macro and Micro Study Strategies

One strategy that can lead to this deeper learning includes preparing an outline that covers all the objectives and subobjectives for the particular exam you are working on. You should delve a bit further into the material and include a level or two of detail beyond the stated objectives and subobjectives for the exam. Then expand the outline by coming up with a statement of definition or a summary for each point in the outline.

An outline provides two approaches to studying. First, you can study the outline by focusing on the organization of the material. Work your way through the points and sub-points of your outline with the goal of learning how they relate to one another. For example, be sure you understand how each of the main objective areas is similar to and different from another. Then, do the same thing with the subobjectives; be sure you know which subobjectives pertain to each objective area and how they relate to one another.

Next, you can work through the outline, focusing on learning the details. Memorize and understand terms and their definitions, facts, rules and strategies, advantages and disadvantages, and so on. In this pass through the outline, attempt to learn detail rather than the big picture (the organizational information that you worked on in the first pass through the outline).

Research has shown that attempting to assimilate both types of information at the same time seems to interfere with the overall learning process. Separate your studying into these two approaches, and you will perform better on the exam.

Active Study Strategies

The process of writing down and defining objectives, subobjectives, terms, facts, and definitions promotes a more active learning strategy than merely reading the material. In human information-processing terms, writing forces you to engage in more active encoding of the information. Simply reading over it exemplifies more passive processing.

Next, determine whether you can apply the information you have learned by attempting to create examples and scenarios on your own. Think about how or where you could apply the concepts you are learning. Again, write down this information to process the facts and concepts in a more active fashion.

The hands-on nature of the step-by-step tutorials and exercises at the ends of the chapters provide further active learning opportunities that will reinforce concepts as well.

Common-Sense Strategies

Finally, you should also follow common-sense practices when studying. Study when you are alert, reduce or eliminate distractions, and take breaks when you become fatigued.

Pre-Testing Yourself

Pre-testing allows you to assess how well you are learning. One of the most important aspects of learning is what has been called "meta-learning." Meta-learning has to do with realizing when you know something well or when you need to study some more. In other words, you recognize how well or how poorly you have learned the material you are studying.

For most people, this can be difficult to assess objectively on their own. Practice tests are useful in that they reveal more objectively what you have learned and what you have not learned. You should use this information to guide review and further studying. Developmental learning takes place as you cycle through studying, assessing how well you have learned, then reviewing, and then assessing again until you feel you are ready to take the exam.

You may have noticed the Practice Exam included in this book. Use it as part of the learning process. The *ExamGear, Training Guide Edition* test simulation software included on the CD also provides you with an excellent opportunity to assess your knowledge.

You should set a goal for your pre-testing. A reasonable goal would be to score consistently in the 90-percent range.

See Appendix D, "Using the ExamGear, Training Guide Edition Software," for more explanation of the test simulation software.

EXAM PREP TIPS

Having mastered the subject matter, the final preparatory step is to understand how the exam will be presented. Make no mistake: A Microsoft Certified Professional (MCP) exam will challenge both your knowledge and your test-taking skills. This section starts with the basics of exam design, reviews a new type of exam format, and concludes with hints targeted to each of the exam formats.

The MCP Exam

Every MCP exam is released in one of three basic formats. What's being called exam format here is really little more than a combination of the overall exam structure and the presentation method for exam questions.

Understanding the exam formats is key to good preparation because the format determines the number of questions presented, the difficulty of those questions, and the amount of time allowed to complete the exam.

Each exam format uses many of the same types of questions. These types or styles of questions include several types of traditional multiple-choice questions, multiple-rating (or scenario-based) questions, and simulation-based questions. Some exams include other types of questions that ask you to drag and drop objects on the screen, reorder a list, or categorize things. Still other exams ask you to answer these types of questions in response to a case study you have read. It's important that you understand the types of questions you will be asked and the actions required to properly answer them.

The rest of this section addresses the exam formats and then tackles the question types. Understanding the formats and question types will help you feel much more comfortable when you take the exam.

Exam Format

As mentioned above, there are three basic formats for the MCP exams: the traditional fixed-form exam, the adaptive form, and the case study form. As its name implies, the fixed-form exam presents a fixed set of questions during the exam session. The adaptive form, however, uses only a subset of questions drawn from a larger pool during any given exam session. The case study form includes case studies that serve as the basis for answering the various types of questions.

Fixed-Form

A fixed-form computerized exam is based on a fixed set of exam questions. The individual questions are presented in random order during a test session. If you take the same exam more than once, you won't necessarily see the exact same questions. This is because two or three final forms are typically assembled for every fixed-form exam Microsoft releases. These are usually labeled Forms A, B, and C.

The final forms of a fixed-form exam are identical in terms of content coverage, number of questions, and allotted time, but the questions are different. You may notice, however, that some of the same questions appear on, or rather are shared among, different final forms. When questions are shared among multiple final forms of an exam, the percentage of sharing is generally small. Many final forms share no questions, but some older exams may have a 10–15 percent duplication of exam questions on the final exam forms.

Fixed-form exams also have a fixed time limit in which you must complete the exam. The *ExamGear, Training Guide Edition* software on the CD-ROM that accompanies this book provides fixed-form exams.

Finally, the score you achieve on a fixed-form exam, which is always reported for MCP exams on a scale of 0 to 1,000, is based on the number of questions you answer correctly. The passing score is the same for all final forms of a given fixed-form exam.

The typical format for the fixed-form exam is as follows:

◆ 50–60 questions.

◆ 75–90 minute testing time.

◆ Question review is allowed, including the opportunity to change your answers.

Adaptive Form

An adaptive-form exam has the same appearance as a fixed-form exam, but its questions differ in quantity and process of selection. Although the statistics of adaptive testing are fairly complex, the process is concerned with determining your level of skill or ability with the exam subject matter. This ability assessment begins with the presentation of questions of varying levels of difficulty and ascertaining at what difficulty level you can reliably answer them. Finally, the ability assessment determines whether that ability level is above or below the level required to pass that exam.

Examinees at different levels of ability will see quite different sets of questions. Examinees who demonstrate little expertise with the subject matter will continue to be presented with relatively easy questions. Examinees who demonstrate a high level of expertise will be presented progressively more difficult questions. Individuals of both levels of expertise may answer the same number of questions correctly, but because the higher-expertise examinee can correctly answer more difficult questions, he or she will receive a higher score and is more likely to pass the exam.

The typical design for the adaptive form exam is as follows:

◆ 20–25 questions.

◆ 90 minute testing time (although this is likely to be reduced to 45–60 minutes in the near future).

◆ Question review is not allowed, providing no opportunity for you to change your answers.

The Adaptive-Exam Process

Your first adaptive exam will be unlike any other testing experience you have had. In fact, many examinees have difficulty accepting the adaptive testing process because they feel that they were not provided the opportunity to adequately demonstrate their full expertise.

You can take consolation in the fact that adaptive exams are painstakingly put together after months of data gathering and analysis and that adaptive exams are just as valid as fixed-form exams. The rigor introduced through the adaptive testing methodology means that there is nothing arbitrary about the exam items you'll see. It is also a more efficient means of testing, requiring less time to conduct and complete than traditional fixed-form exams.

As you can see in Figure 1, a number of statistical measures drive the adaptive examination process. The measure most immediately relevant to you is the ability estimate. Accompanying this test statistic are the standard error of measurement, the item characteristic curve, and the test information curve.

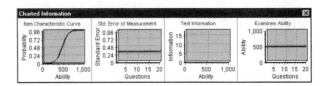

FIGURE 1
Microsoft's adaptive testing demonstration program.

The standard error, which is the key factor in determining when an adaptive exam will terminate, reflects the degree of error in the exam ability estimate. The item characteristic curve reflects the probability of a correct response relative to examinee ability. Finally, the test information statistic provides a measure of the information contained in the set of questions the examinee has answered, again relative to the ability level of the individual examinee.

When you begin an adaptive exam, the standard error has already been assigned a target value below which it must drop for the exam to conclude. This target value reflects a particular level of statistical confidence in the process. The examinee ability is initially set to the mean possible exam score (500 for MCP exams).

As the adaptive exam progresses, questions of varying difficulty are presented. Based on your pattern of responses to these questions, the ability estimate is recalculated. At the same time, the standard error estimate is refined from its first estimated value of one toward the target value. When the standard error reaches its target value, the exam is terminated. Thus, the more consistently you answer questions of the same degree of difficulty, the more quickly the standard error estimate drops, and the fewer questions you will end up seeing during the exam session. This situation is depicted in Figure 2.

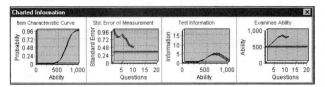

FIGURE 2
The changing statistics in an adaptive exam.

As you might suspect, one good piece of advice for taking an adaptive exam is to treat every exam question as if it were the most important. The adaptive scoring algorithm attempts to discover a pattern of responses that reflects some level of proficiency with the subject matter. Incorrect responses almost guarantee that additional questions must be answered (unless, of course, you get every question wrong). This is because the scoring algorithm must adjust to information that is not consistent with the emerging pattern.

Case Study Form

The case study-based format first appeared with the advent of the 70-100 exam (Solution Architectures). The questions in the case study format are not the independent entities that they are in the fixed and adaptive formats. Instead, questions are tied to a case study, a long scenario-like description of an information technology situation. As the test taker, your job is to extract from the case study the information that needs to be integrated with your understanding of Microsoft technology. The idea is that a case study will provide you with a situation that is more like a "real life" problem situation than the other formats provide.

The case studies are presented as "testlets." These are sections within the exam in which you read the case study, then answer 10 to 15 questions that apply to the case study. When you finish that section, you move onto another testlet with another case study and its associated questions. There may be as many as five of these testlets that compose the overall exam. You will be given more time to complete such an exam because it takes time to read through the cases and analyze them. You may have as much as three hours to complete the exam—and you may need all of it. The case studies are always available through a linking button while you are in a testlet. However, once you leave a testlet, you cannot come back to it.

Figure 3 provides an illustration of part of a case study.

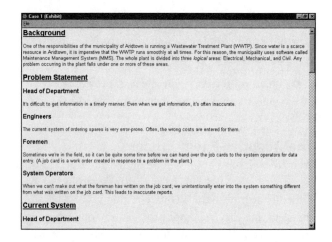

FIGURE 3
An example of a case study

Question Types

A variety of question types can appear on MCP exams. Examples of many of the various types appear in this book and the *ExamGear, Training Guide Edition* software. We have attempted to cover all the types that were available at the time of this writing. Most of the question types discussed in the following sections can appear in each of the three exam formats.

The typical MCP exam question is based on the idea of measuring skills or the ability to complete tasks. Therefore, most of the questions are written so as to present you with a situation that includes a role (such as a system administrator or technician), a technology environment (100 computers running Windows 98 on a Windows 2000 Server network), and a problem to be solved (the user can connect to services on the LAN, but not the intranet). The answers indicate actions that you might take to solve the problem or create setups or environments that would function correctly from the start. Keep this in mind as you read the questions on the exam. You may encounter some questions that just call for you to regurgitate facts, but these will be relatively few and far between.

In the following sections we will look at the different question types.

Multiple-Choice Questions

Despite the variety of question types that now appear in various MCP exams, the multiple-choice question is still the basic building block of the exams. The multiple-choice question comes in three varieties:

◆ **Regular multiple-choice.** Also referred to as an alphabetic question, it asks you to choose one answer as correct.

◆ **Multiple-answer multiple-choice.** Also referred to as a multi-alphabetic question, this version of a multiple-choice question requires you to choose two or more answers as correct. Typically, you are told precisely the number of correct answers to choose.

◆ **Enhanced multiple-choice.** This is simply a regular or multiple-answer question that includes a graphic or table to which you must refer to answer the question correctly.

Examples of such questions appear at the end of each chapter.

Multiple-Rating Questions

These questions are often referred to as scenario questions. Similar to multiple-choice questions, they offer more extended descriptions of the computing environment and a problem that needs to be solved. Required and desired optional results of the problem-solving are specified, as well as a solution. You are then asked to judge whether the actions taken in the solution are likely to bring about all or part of the required and desired optional results. There is, typically, only one correct answer.

You may be asking yourself, "What is multiple about multiple-rating questions?" The answer is that rather than having multiple answers, the question itself may be repeated in the exam with only minor variations in the required results, optional results, or solution introduced to create "new" questions. Read these different versions very carefully; the differences can be subtle.

Examples of these types of questions appear at the end of the chapters.

Simulation Questions

Simulation-based questions reproduce the look and feel of key Microsoft product features for the purpose of testing. The simulation software used in MCP exams has been designed to look and act, as much as possible, just like the actual product. Consequently, answering simulation questions in an MCP exam entails completing one or more tasks just as if you were using the product itself.

The format of a typical Microsoft simulation question consists of a brief scenario or problem statement, along with one or more tasks that you must complete to solve the problem. An example of a simulation question for MCP exams is shown in the following section.

A Typical Simulation Question

It sounds obvious, but your first step when you encounter a simulation question is to carefully read the question (see Figure 4). Do not go straight to the simulation application! You must assess the problem that's presented and identify the conditions that make up the problem scenario. Note the tasks that must be performed or outcomes that must be achieved to answer the question, and then review any instructions you're given on how to proceed.

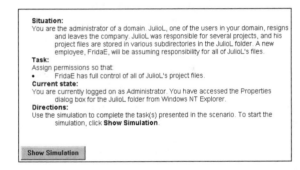

FIGURE 4
A typical MCP exam simulation question with directions.

The next step is to launch the simulator by using the button provided. After clicking the Show Simulation button, you will see a feature of the product, as shown in the dialog box in Figure 5. The simulation application will partially obscure the question text on many test center machines. Feel free to reposition the simulator and to move between the question text screen and

the simulator by using hotkeys or point-and-click navigation, or even by clicking the simulator's launch button again.

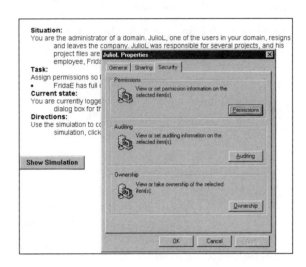

FIGURE 5
Launching the simulation application.

It is important for you to understand that your answer to the simulation question will not be recorded until you move on to the next exam question. This gives you the added capability of closing and reopening the simulation application (using the launch button) on the same question without losing any partial answer you may have made.

The third step is to use the simulator as you would the actual product to solve the problem or perform the defined tasks. Again, the simulation software is designed to function—within reason—just as the product does. But don't expect the simulator to reproduce product behavior perfectly. Most importantly, do not allow yourself to become flustered if the simulator does not look or act exactly like the product.

Figure 6 shows the solution to the example simulation problem.

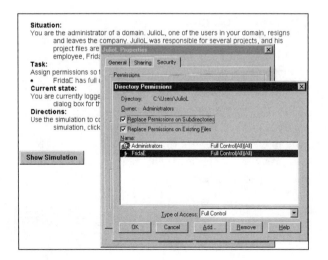

FIGURE 6
The solution to the simulation example.

Two final points will help you tackle simulation questions. First, respond only to what is being asked in the question; do not solve problems that you are not asked to solve. Second, accept what is being asked of you. You may not entirely agree with conditions in the problem statement, the quality of the desired solution, or the sufficiency of defined tasks to adequately solve the problem. Always remember that you are being tested on your ability to solve the problem as it is presented.

The solution to the simulation problem shown in Figure 6 perfectly illustrates both of those points. As you'll recall from the question scenario (refer to Figure 4), you were asked to assign appropriate permissions to a new user, Frida E. You were not instructed to make any other changes in permissions. Thus, if you were to modify or remove the administrator's permissions, this item would be scored wrong on an MCP exam.

Hot Area Question

Hot area questions call for you to click on a graphic or diagram in order to complete some task. You are asked a question that is similar to any other, but rather than clicking an option button or check box next to an answer, you click the relevant item in a screen shot or on a part of a diagram. An example of such an item is shown in Figure 7.

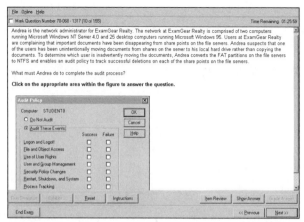

FIGURE 7
A typical hot area question.

Drag and Drop Style Questions

Microsoft has utilized two different types of drag and drop questions in exams. The first is a Select and Place question. The other is a Drop and Connect question. Both are covered in the following sections.

Select and Place

Select and Place questions typically require you to drag and drop labels on images in a diagram so as to correctly label or identify some portion of a network. Figure 8 shows you the actual question portion of a Select and Place item.

FIGURE 8
A Select and Place question.

Figure 9 shows the window you would see after you chose Select and Place. It contains the actual diagram in which you would select and drag the various server roles and match them with the appropriate computers.

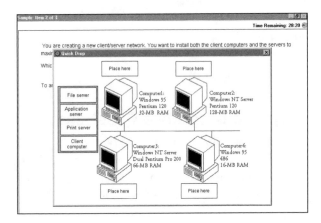

FIGURE 9
The window containing the diagram.

Drop and Connect

Drop and Connect questions provide a different spin on the drag and drop question. The question provides you with the opportunity to create boxes that you can label, as well as connectors of various types with which to link them. In essence, you are creating a model or diagram in order to answer the question. You might have to create a network diagram or a data model for a database system. Figure 10 illustrates the idea of a Drop and Connect question.

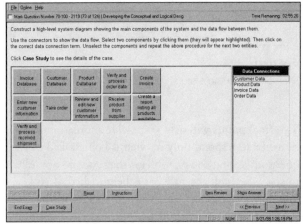

FIGURE 10
A Drop and Connect question.

Ordered List Questions

Ordered list questions simply require you to consider a list of items and place them in the proper order. You select items and then use a button to add them to a new list in the correct order. You have another button that you can use to remove the items in the new list in case you change your mind and want to reorder things. Figure 11 shows an ordered list item.

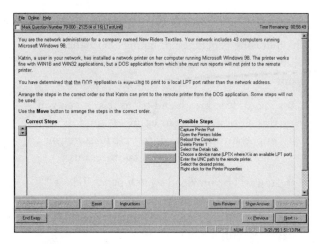

FIGURE 11
An ordered list question.

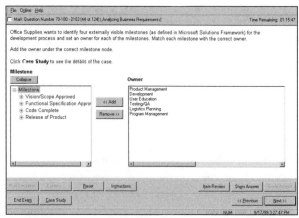

FIGURE 12
A tree question.

Tree Questions

Tree questions require you to think hierarchically and categorically. You are asked to place items from a list into categories that are displayed as nodes in a tree structure. Such questions might ask you to identify parent-child relationships in processes or the structure of keys in a database. You might also be required to show order within the categories, much as you would in an ordered list question. Figure 12 shows a typical tree question.

As you can see, Microsoft is making an effort to utilize question types that go beyond asking you to simply memorize facts. These question types force you to know how to accomplish tasks and understand concepts and relationships. Study so that you can answer these types of questions rather than those that simply ask you to recall facts.

Putting It All Together

Given all these different pieces of information, the task now is to assemble a set of tips that will help you successfully tackle the different types of MCP exams.

More Exam Preparation Tips

Generic exam-preparation advice is always useful. Tips include the following:

◆ Become familiar with the product. Hands-on experience is one of the keys to success on any MCP exam. Review the exercises and the Step by Steps in the book.

◆ Review the current exam-preparation guide on the Microsoft MCP Web site (www.microsoft.com/mcp/examinfo/exams.htm). The documentation Microsoft makes available over the Web identifies the skills every exam is intended to test.

◆ Memorize foundational technical detail, but remember that MCP exams are generally heavier on problem solving and application of knowledge than on questions that require only rote memorization.

◆ Take any of the available practice tests. We recommend the one included in this book and the ones you can create using the *ExamGear* software on the CD-ROM. As a supplement to the material bound with this book, try the free practice tests available on the Microsoft MCP Web site.

◆ Look on the Microsoft MCP Web site for samples and demonstration items. These tend to be particularly valuable for one significant reason: They help you become familiar with new testing technologies before you encounter them on MCP exams.

During the Exam Session

The following generic exam-taking advice that you've heard for years also applies when you're taking an MCP exam:

◆ Take a deep breath and try to relax when you first sit down for your exam session. It is very important that you control the pressure you may (naturally) feel when taking exams.

◆ You will be provided scratch paper. Take a moment to write down any factual information and technical detail that you committed to short-term memory.

◆ Carefully read all information and instruction screens. These displays have been put together to give you information relevant to the exam you are taking.

◆ Accept the non-disclosure agreement and preliminary survey as part of the examination process. Complete them accurately and quickly move on.

◆ Read the exam questions carefully. Reread each question to identify all relevant detail.

◆ Tackle the questions in the order in which they are presented. Skipping around won't build your confidence; the clock is always counting down (at least in the fixed form exams).

◆ Don't rush, but also don't linger on difficult questions. The questions vary in degree of difficulty. Don't let yourself be flustered by a particularly difficult or wordy question.

Fixed-Form Exams

Building from this basic preparation and test-taking advice, you also need to consider the challenges presented by the different exam designs. Because a fixed-form exam is composed of a fixed, finite set of questions, add these tips to your strategy for taking a fixed-form exam:

◆ Note the time allotted and the number of questions on the exam you are taking. Make a rough calculation of how many minutes you can spend on each question, and use this figure to pace yourself through the exam.

◆ Take advantage of the fact that you can return to and review skipped or previously answered questions. Record the questions you can't answer confidently on the scratch paper provided, noting the relative difficulty of each question. When you reach the end of the exam, return to the more difficult questions.

◆ If you have session time remaining after you complete all the questions (and if you aren't too fatigued!), review your answers. Pay particular attention to questions that seem to have a lot of detail or that require graphics.

◆ As for changing your answers, the general rule of thumb here is *don't*! If you read the question carefully and completely and you felt like you knew the right answer, you probably did. Don't second-guess yourself. If, as you check your answers, one clearly stands out as incorrect, however, of course you should change it. But if you are at all unsure, go with your first impression.

Adaptive Exams

If you are planning to take an adaptive exam, keep these additional tips in mind:

◆ Read and answer every question with great care. When you're reading a question, identify every relevant detail, requirement, or task you must perform and double-check your answer to be sure you have addressed every one of them.

◆ If you cannot answer a question, use the process of elimination to reduce the set of potential answers, and then take your best guess. Stupid mistakes invariably mean that additional questions will be presented.

◆ You cannot review questions and change answers. When you leave a question, whether you've answered it or not, you cannot return to it. Do not skip any question, either; if you do, it's counted as incorrect.

Case Study Exams

This new exam format calls for unique study and exam-taking strategies. When you take this type of exam, remember that you have more time than in a typical exam. Take your time and read the case study thoroughly. Use the scrap paper or whatever medium is provided to you to take notes, diagram processes, and actively seek out the important information. Work through each testlet as if each were an independent exam. Remember, you cannot go back after you have left a testlet. Refer to the case study as often as you need to, but do not use that as a substitute for reading it carefully initially and for taking notes.

FINAL CONSIDERATIONS

Finally, a number of changes in the MCP program will impact how frequently you can repeat an exam and what you will see when you do.

◆ Microsoft has instituted a new exam retake policy. The new rule is "two and two, then one and two." That is, you can attempt any exam twice with no restrictions on the time between attempts. But after the second attempt, you must wait two weeks before you can attempt that exam again. After that, you will be required to wait two weeks between subsequent attempts. Plan to pass the exam in two attempts or plan to increase your time horizon for receiving the MCP credential.

◆ New questions are being seeded into the MCP exams. After performance data is gathered on new questions, the examiners will replace older questions on all exam forms. This means that the questions appearing on exams will regularly change.

◆ Many of the current MCP exams will be republished in adaptive form. Prepare yourself for this significant change in testing; it is entirely likely that this will become the preferred MCP exam format for most exams. The exception to this may be the case study exams because the adaptive approach may not work with that format.

These changes mean that the brute-force strategies for passing MCP exams may soon completely lose their viability. So if you don't pass an exam on the first or second attempt, it is likely that the exam's form will change significantly by the next time you take it. It could be updated from fixed-form to adaptive, or it could have a different set of questions or question types.

Microsoft's intention is not to make the exams more difficult by introducing unwanted change, but to create and maintain valid measures of the technical skills and knowledge associated with the different MCP credentials. Preparing for an MCP exam has always involved not only studying the subject matter, but also planning for the testing experience itself. With the recent changes, this is now more true than ever.

This exam consists of 64 questions that reflect the material you have covered in the chapters and that are representative of the types that you should expect to see on the actual exam.

The answers to all questions appear in their own section following the exam. It is stongly suggested that when you take this exam, you treat it just as you would the actual exam at the text center. Time yourself, read carefully, and answer all the questions to the best of your ability.

Most of the questions do not simply require you to recall facts, but require deduction on your part to come up with the best answer. Most questions require you to identify the best course of action to take in a given situation. Many of the questions are verbose, requiring you to read them carefully and thoroughly before you attempt to answer them. Run through the exam; for questions you miss, review any material associated with them.

Practice Exam

1. Martin is configuring the firewall after the company has finished converting to Windows 2000. He wants to ensure that Active Directory traffic will be able to access resources on both sides of the firewall. In order to do so, he must allow which access protocol through the firewall?

   A. X.500

   B. LDAP

   C. DNS

   D. DHCP

2. Karen is in charge of programming at DS Technical Solutions. Her department has been tasked with building new directory-enabled applications that will give the users the ability to work with objects in Windows 2000 as well as NetWare 5. What API should Karen suggest her team use?

   A. ADSI

   B. MAPI

   C. LDAP VB

   D. SAPI

3. At CertificationCorner.com, the schema must be extended. What is the domain controller on which the schema can be found known as?

   A. Root

   B. Global Catalog Server

   C. PDC Emulator

   D. Schema Master

4. Spencer is converting his domain from mixed-mode to native-mode. During the conversion of such, he will have the ability to reduce network traffic by eliminating one form of name resolution. Which name resolution method will he have the ability to remove?

   A. ARP

   B. IP

   C. NetBIOS

   D. SMB

5. Evan is planning to migrate his company from NetWare 5 to Windows 2000. After a short trial run, he wants to migrate all users over to the new domain as efficiently as possible and model the directory data before the migration. Which tool should Evan use to perform this?

   A. NetWare Migration Tool

   B. Directory Service Migration Tool

   C. ADSI

   D. NDS

6. Which of the following features of Windows 2000 offers the ability to customize the "built-in" objects and attributes to fit the needs of your organization?

   A. Extensible Schema

   B. Multi-Master Replication

   C. Kerberos

   D. IntelliMirror

7. Which areas of the business analysis refer to the company model and management model? (Choose two.)

   A. Operational Structure

   B. Goals and Problems

   C. Organizational Structure

   D. Company Processes

   E. Tiered Architecture

8. What are the four phases, given in correct order, of the service and product life cycle?

    A. Preparation, Vision, Deployment, Maintenance

    B. Planning, Coding, Shipment, Installation

    C. Vision, Planning, Preparation, Support

    D. Planning, Deployment, Maintenance, Removal

9. Kristin is preparing for the conversion of DMC to Windows 2000. What is the first step in performing the business problem analysis?

    A. Map the business problem to a project objective.

    B. Deploy the operating system and document the procedure.

    C. Clarify a vision for the maintenance and support.

    D. Install a model of the proposed solution in an isolated network.

10. Jocelyn is creating installation packages that will be deployed to Windows 2000 Professional workstations via Group Policy. What is the extension that will be on the installation packages?

    A. .EXE

    B. .COM

    C. .MSI

    D. .CAB

11. Jeanette works with supporting applications that predate Windows 2000. Given this, it is not possible for her to create true installation packages for deployment. Jeanette follows a procedure that allows her to create a publishable installation package for the legacy application. What extension should be associated with this application package?

    A. .bat

    B. .zap

    C. .srv

    D. .mx

12. At ACME, Inc., they have decided to stop using the ABC Word Processor in favor of Microsoft Word. Previously, ABC was published to all users, and Word will now be assigned. ACME wishes to remove ABC, but allow any users who may still need to use it for old files to do so. Which removal method should ACME use with regard to ABC?

    A. Forced

    B. Optional

    C. Limited

    D. Voluntary

13. Which of the following represent the types of IT administration models present in business today? (Choose three.)

    A. Decentralized

    B. International

    C. Centralized

    D. Hybrid

    E. Mixed

    F. Universal

14. Kliebold Hospitals is planning an Active Directory structure for their numerous hospitals. They want individualized security policies per hospital and do not want security policies to be the same at each hospital. Given this, each hospital should constitute what entity?

    A. Forest

    B. Tree

C. Domain

D. Site

15. Which of the following represents a container that organizes objects within a domain into logical subgroupings?

A. Forests

B. Trees

C. Domains

D. OUs

16. DS Technical is attempting to reduce its Total Cost of Ownership (TCO) to as minimal an amount as possible. What factors should be used in their TCO equation? (Choose three.)

A. Baseline Metrics

B. Problem Recognition

C. Change Validation

D. Return on Investment

E. Parkinson's Law

F. Supply versus Demand

17. In the analysis step of the Cost-Benefit equation, what approaches are used? (Choose three.)

A. ROI

B. TCO

C. 4×7 benefit matrix

D. Value Creation

E. SAP

F. SQL

18. According to Microsoft, a "well-connected" WAN connection must have as its slowest connection a speed equal to or greater than what speed?

A. 256K

B. 384K

C. 512K

D. 1024K

19. Which of the following represent the speeds commonly associated with Ethernet? (Choose two.)

A. 10M

B. 16M

C. 100M

D. 1.544M

E. 45M

20. GB Corporation has several locations within their WAN where the speed is below what Microsoft considers "well-connected". As a network designer, what would you recommend they make those locations?

A. Domains

B. Sites

C. OUs

D. Forests

21. Kristin is in charge of the IT department for IB Industries. IB has two hosts that are constantly communicating and would benefit from a dedicated path, or virtual circuit, between the two hosts. What hardware device will allow this virtual circuit to be created?

A. Switch

B. Router

C. Bridge

D. Hub

22. What is the technology utilized by bandwidth managers to prioritize network bandwidth?

    A. SAP

    B. WINS

    C. RIP

    D. QoS

23. Karen is attempting to troubleshoot entries in her HOSTS file. Which of the following entries are not valid for name resolution? (Choose two.)

    A. `192.16.18.12  Mary #fourth floor`

    B. `Martin  192.16.18.11`

    C. `#192.16.18.10  Steve`

    D. `192.16.18.9  Walter  Michael  DMC`

    E. `192 16 18 12  Harvest Market`

24. CompUall is dividing their domain into sites for administrative reasons. In terms of network addresses, they should define their sites via what component?

    A. IP addresses

    B. Subnets

    C. Gateways

    D. Host names

25. Evan is the administrator for a network that is quickly growing in size. He plans to move from Windows NT 4.0 to Windows 2000 and also wants to incorporate a server that will automatically issue IP addresses, and free him from doing so manually. What type of server does he need to add to the network?

    A. DNS

    B. WINS

    C. IPCONFIG

    D. DHCP

26. Spencer is in charge of a number of servers, one of which is experiencing excessive paging. What can Spencer do to alleviate some of the paging on this server?

    A. Add more memory.

    B. Add another processor.

    C. Install a faster network card.

    D. Install a faster hard drive.

27. Which Control Panel applet must be used to reach the following configuration dialog box?

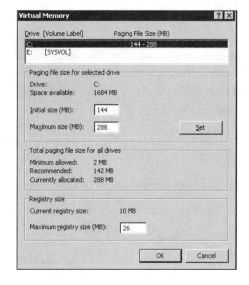

FIGURE PE.1
Figure for Question 27.

    A. Server

    B. System

    C. Administrative Tools

    D. Folder Options

28. For Network Monitor to gather true information about network load, in what mode must the NIC operate?

   A. Common

   B. Protected

   C. Promiscuous

   D. Real

29. Kerby must turn on disk counters to gather a baseline of activity on her system. What command prompt must she give to do this operation?

   A. `diskperf`

   B. `perfdisk`

   C. `perfdisk -a`

   D. `diskperf -y`

30. Allan has determined that his processor is the bottleneck in his server. Which of the following options will help alleviate the bottleneck? (Choose three.)

   A. Add another processor.

   B. Replace the processor.

   C. Move the system files to an unused drive.

   D. Move some applications to a different server.

   E. Add more video RAM.

   F. Increase the speed of the network card.

31. Madonna has been told that prior to the migration to Windows 2000, it is her responsibility to collect a list of all security principals. Within Windows 2000, which of the following can be security principals? (Choose three.)

   A. Domains

   B. Services

   C. Computers

   D. Users

   E. Tasks

   F. Threads

32. Which authentication protocol exists in Windows 2000 for authentication with Windows NT 3.51?

   A. Kerberos

   B. CHAP

   C. NTLM

   D. PAP

33. Certificate servers that sign digital certificates they issue are known as what?

   A. Certificate Authorities

   B. Root Distributors

   C. PKI

   D. Certificate Publishers

34. Chris is trying to determine where the Access Control List for a printer is maintained. The printer is considered an object in Active Directory. Given this, in what location is the ACL for the printer maintained?

   A. In the SAM file

   B. In the HKEY_CLASSES_ROOT portion of the registry

   C. In the Security Descriptor

   D. In the ACE

35. Samantha has been told to upgrade all client machines at FDR Resources to Windows 2000 Professional. She is creating a list of current operating systems in use, and mapping migration strategies. From which of the following operating systems can she use the upgrade version of Windows 2000 Professional? (Choose four.)

A. Windows 95

B. Windows 98

C. Windows NT Workstation 3.1

D. Windows NT Workstation 3.5

E. Windows NT Workstation 3.51

F. Windows NT Workstation 4.0

36. Tony is currently running Windows NT 4.0 Terminal Server. To which of the following operating systems can he upgrade?

A. Windows 2000 Professional

B. Windows 2000 Server

C. Windows 2000 Advanced Server

D. Windows 2000 Datacenter Server

37. Sara and Zuzu have just migrated some old DOS applications over to Windows 2000 to do away with all standalone DOS machines at their site. Most of the migrated applications work well, but one that sends AT-based commands to a modem continues to fail. What is the most likely cause of this problem?

A. The program requires FAT.

B. The program needs direct hardware access.

C. The program cannot work in the graphic environment.

D. The program does not understand Active Directory.

38. Which of the following provides management functionality for software?

A. WMI

B. COM

C. DCOM

D. WDM

39. In the following exhibit, when will the software be installed on the user's machine?

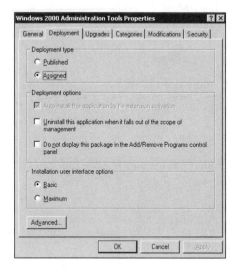

FIGURE PE.2
Figure for Question 39.

A. When the computer starts

B. When the user logs on

C. When the user attempts to launch the program

D. Immediately

40. Megan is planning to implement Remote OS Installation. Which of the following choices must the client computer support to utilize Remote OS Installation?

A. PXE

B. DHCP

C. RIS

D. TOC

41. To which of the following entities can folder redirection apply? (Choose three.)

    A. Start Menu

    B. Desktop

    C. My Network Places

    D. Application Data

    E. Recycle Bin

    F. Taskbar

42. Edna is creating .zap files for software distribution. Which of the following tags are required within the files?

    A. Publisher

    B. SetupCommand

    C. DisplayVersion

    D. URL

43. What is the maximum number of characters that can be used in a NetBIOS name?

    A. 8

    B. 10

    C. 15

    D. 16

    E. 20

44. Susan is setting up a network from scratch. She needs to map out the Fully Qualified Domain Names (FQDNs) for the new network. If the host name is system1 and the domain name is new.office.com, what will the FQDN be?

    A. new.office.system1.com

    B. new.system1.office.com

    C. new.office.com.system1

    D. system1.new.office.com

45. Mary wants to continue to use her UNIX DNS servers with her Windows 2000 network. For Active Directory resolution to take place, what resource records must the UNIX servers support?

    A. SRV

    B. RR

    C. MX

    D. PTR

46. The first record in any DNS zone is which of the following?

    A. CNAME

    B. SOA

    C. MX

    D. SRV

47. Cody is comparing trusts between Windows 2000 and Windows NT 4.0. In Windows 2000, trusts are automatic, and symptomatic of which trust model used in Windows NT 4.0?

    A. Complete

    B. Multi-master domain

    C. Single domain

    D. Single-master domain

48. Jenna needs to modify the Active Directory schema and wants to do so through the MMC snap-in. At the minimum, what group must Jenna be a member of to perform this action through the Active Directory Schema snap-in?

    A. Domain Admins

    B. Enterprise Admins

    C. Schema Admins

    D. Administrators

49. Mary Kay is designing the OU layout for her insurance company. Which IT model should be the primary focus for the OU design?

    A. Technical

    B. Administrative

    C. Supervisory

    D. Regional

50. Ray needs to estimate the amount of replication traffic that will occur between and within sites. What utility generates the replication topology?

    A. NTDSUTIL

    B. DCPROMO

    C. REPLMON

    D. KCC

51. —Access Control Entries—(ACEs) contain which of the following components? (Choose two.)

    A. SID

    B. GUID

    C. Owner

    D. Inheritance

    E. Legacy

52. Which of the following can be used to delegate control on objects in Active Directory? (Choose three.)

    A. NTDSUTIL

    B. DSACLS

    C. Delegation of Control Wizard

    D. Security tab of the Object Properties window

    E. Active Directory Sites and Services

    F. DNS Manager

53. David is planning the implementation of group policies on his network. To which of the following entities can group policies be applied? (Choose three.)

    A. Forests

    B. Domains

    C. Sites

    D. Organizational Units

    E. Attributes

    F. ACEs

54. Alfred needs to support Windows NT 4.0 Workstation and Windows 2000 Professional clients on his Windows 2000 network. For the Windows NT clients, where should the system policies be placed on the Windows 2000 server?

    A. PUBLIC

    B. NETLOGON

    C. SYSVOL

    D. MAIL

55. A formal description of a discrete, identifiable type of object that is stored in Active Directory is known as what?

    A. Attribute

    B. Class

    C. Schema

    D. Property

56. Rod is the administrator for a domain consisting of four domain controllers. How many of those domain controllers contain a copy of the schema that has write access?

    A. 0

    B. 1

C. 2

D. 3

E. 4

57. Hannah has been handed a printout of what she believes are object identifiers (OIDs). OIDs are globally unique numbers using notation that would resemble which of the following?

A. 1:2:3:4

B. 1.2.3.4

C. 1234

D. 1-2-3-4

58. The administrators at Certification Corner are planning to modify their schema. The modifications to the schema will have implications at what level?

A. Forest-wide

B. Tree-wide

C. Domain-wide

D. Site-wide

59. Stephanie needs a tool to allow for synchronization between Active Directory and NDS. Which tool should she consider for this operation?

A. File Migration Utility

B. File and Print Services for NetWare

C. Synchronization Tool

D. Microsoft Directory Synchronization Services

60. Karen is implementing Services for UNIX (SFU) on her network. Which of the following will this offer to her? (Choose three.)

A. C shell functionality

B. Remote command-line access from one computer to another

C. Password synchronization

D. Sharing of files using NFS

E. BASH services

F. Offline file access

61. Spencer is looking for the synchronization utility to go between Windows 2000 Active Directory and the Exchange Directory. The tool that Spencer needs is which of the following?

A. Exchange.msc

B. Active Directory Connector

C. LDAP API

D. MSDC Service

62. Walter has been charged with allowing LDAP traffic through the firewall. What is the default port number at which LDAP functions?

A. 21

B. 80

C. 119

D. 389

63. Aldrich is beginning to prepare for the implementation of Windows 2000 and Active Directory. What is the first phase of the five steps in the recommended implementation plan?

A. Goals and objectives

B. Planning and design

C. Pilot

D. Execution

64. Glenn wants to save deployment time by creating images of the ideal computer's hard drive and rolling it out to other systems. Which Windows 2000 utility will assist with the creation of this image?

A. Ghost

B. DiskImage

C. Sysprep

D. DFS

65. During which of the five steps in the recommended implementation plan would you perform a Gap Analysis?

A. Goals and objectives

B. Planning and design

C. Pilot

D. Execution

E. Closure

ANSWERS TO THE PRACTICE EXAM

1. **B.** The LDAP protocol is used to access resources in Active Directory. LDAP is based on X.500 (Answer A), but is a lightweight version that does not carry all of the additional overhead. DNS (Answer C) is not associated with *accessing* a directory, but rather *locating* it. LDAP is then used to access it and its data. WINS (Answer D) is a service and not a protocol, and thus an invalid selection.

2. **A.** ADSI (Active Directory Services Interface) offers the ability to create objects that are supported by Windows 2000, Windows NT 4.0, NetWare 3.x to 5.x, and other LDAP-supporting directory services. Answer B, MAPI, is the Messaging API included only for backward compatibility, and its use is discouraged for newer development. Answer C, LDAP VB, is not a valid option—LDAP C, on the other hand, is

an API used for developing applications and toolsets that work across the LDAP-supported client spectrum. Choice D, SAPI, is the Speech API, and not a valid choice for the question.

3. **D.** The Schema Master is the server holding the schema. Answer A, the root server, is the one that creates the domain, and is the first installed server within the domain by default. It may be the Schema Master, but need not be. The Schema Master is by default on the root server in the forest, but it may be moved. The Global Catalog Server, Answer B, hosts the Global Catalog, and need not be the same server hosting the Schema. The PDC Emulator, Answer C, is used only for compatibility with NT 4.0 networks.

4. **C.** NetBIOS name resolution is necessary in mixed-mode, but not always needed in native-mode. If Spencer eliminates NetBIOS resolution, dedicated SMB ports (Answer D) will be used instead. Answer A, ARP (Address Resolution Protocol) resolution is always needed to transform MAC (physical) addresses into IP addresses. IP address resolution (Answer B) is a necessary component in Windows 2000, and accomplished through DNS.

5. **B.** The Directory Service Migration Tool allows you to migrate from NetWare 3.x or later versions of NetWare to Windows 2000, and model the directory data prior to the migration. Answer A, NetWare Migration Tool, existed in Windows NT Server 4.0, but does not exist in Windows 2000. Answer C, ADSI (Active Directory Services Interface), offers the ability to create objects that are supported by LDAP-supporting directory services. Answer D, NDS, is the directory platform in NetWare 4.x and later (the bindery exited in 3.x and earlier versions) from which you will be migrating to Active Directory.

6. **A.** The Extensible Schema offers the ability to customize the "built-in" objects and attributes to fit the needs of your organization. Answer B, Multi-Master Replication, allows Windows 2000 the ability to scale to meet the needs of enterprise domains. Answer C, Kerberos, replaces NTLM as the primary authentication protocol across all of Windows 2000. Answer D, IntelliMirror, provides users with the capability to go to any PC on the corporate network and always have access to their files, applications, and settings.

7. **A, C**. Organization and Operational structures refer to the company model and management model. Answer B, goals and problems, involves understanding why the company is considering a solution to a problem. Answer D, company processes, refers to information and communication flow and decision-making.

8. **D**. Planning, followed by Deployment, then Maintenance and Removal, constitute the service and product life cycle. The other choices are invalid for this question, or appear in the incorrect order.

9. **A.** The first step in performing the business problem analysis is to map the business problem to a project objective. It is only after this step has been undertaken that other issues and steps come into play, making the other options invalid.

10. **C.** The installation packages have an extension of .MSI. Individual executable files can have extensions of either .EXE (answer A), or .COM (answer B); .CAB files (answer D) are cabinet files, compressed for space, used for earlier operating systems.

11. **B.** The .zap file format allows you to create packages for older applications. Answer A, .bat, is used for batch files that can automate commands, but not used for packaging. Answers C and D

represent types of records available with DNS and not application packages.

12. **B.** The Optional removal will allow users to remove the program, but will not require it. Answer A, Forced, requires the removal of the program. Answers C and D are not legitimate removal types.

13. **A, C, D**. There are three types of IT administration models present in business today: centralized, decentralized, and hybrid. Choices B (International), E (Mixed), and F (Universal), are not valid administration models.

14. **C.** Each domain has its own security policy that applies to all security accounts within the domain and administrative privileges may not extend past domain boundaries. Creating separate forests and trees represent overkill, whereas separate sites would not perform the required limitation.

15. **D**. An Organizational Unit (OU) is a container that organizes objects within a domain into logical subgroupings. These subgroupings define your administrative model. OUs belong to domains (Answer C), which belong to trees (Answer B) within a Forest (Answer A).

16. **A, B, C**. Total Cost of Ownership (TCO) is based on Baseline Metrics, Problem Recognition, and Change Validation. ROI (Return on Investment) does not factor into TCO. Choices E (Parkinson's Law) and F (Supply and Demand) factor into economic equations, but not TCO.

17. **A, B, D**. In the analysis step, TCO, Value Creation, and ROI are all used. The 4×7 benefit matrix is not used until the Profiling step of the cost-benefit equation. SAP (Service Advertising Protocol) and SQL (Structured Query Language) are technologies that do not factor into this equation.

18. **C.** Each connection in a "well-connected" WAN should be equal to, or greater, than 512KB—Microsoft's suggestion for a well-connected WAN.

19. **A, C.** Ethernet traditionally runs at 10MBps or 100MBps. Answer B, 16MB, is not a common speed on Ethernet networks (used for Token Ring), whereas Answer D—1.544MB is the speed of a T-1 connection, and 45MB is close to the speed of a T-3.

20. **B.** Active Directory sites should be created for every segment of the WAN that is not connected by a link equal to or greater than 512KB. None of the other entries apply—there is no need to create additional domains or forests; OUs will exist within the domain.

21. **A.** A switch allows two computers to establish a virtual connection. A router is used to send data between multiple networks, while a bridge can send data between two networks. A hub can be thought of as a predecessor to a switch, and it forwards data to all computers it is connected to, rather than to the selected one.

22. **D.** Bandwidth managers use Quality of Service technology to prioritize network bandwidth. SAP (Service Advertising Protocol) is used by NetWare. WINS is used for name resolution between NetBIOS names and IP addresses, and RIP is a protocol for routing.

23. **B, C.** Answer A uses the correct syntax and translates the IP address to the host name; it also includes a comment that the computer is on the fourth floor. Answer B is incorrect because the host name is given first, and the IP address second. Answer C is incorrect because the comment character as the first character causes the whole line to be ignored. With Answer D, the IP address can be translated from any of three host names. With answer E, spaces are used between the octets, where periods must be used—thus the name "dotted decimal" to signify the way it is written out.

24. **B.** Sites should be created with subnets. IP addressees are unique entries per host and differ from machine to machine, whereas all at one site should share the same subnet mask value. The address of the gateway is simply the address of the router, and not valid. The host name is purely a text value that can be easily changed and should not be considered when configuring sites.

25. **D.** A DHCP (Dynamic Host Configuration Protocol) server can issue IP addresses to clients. DNS and WINS are means of name resolution between IP addresses and host or NetBIOS names, respectively. IPCONFIG is a utility to see the current IP values on a client or host.

26. **A.** Adding more RAM to the system will allow more of the page file to exist in memory and reduce the need to write to the hard drive. None of the other possibilities presented will impact paging as much as adding more memory.

27. **B.** The System applet allows you to change virtual memory. After selecting the applet, you must next choose the Advanced tab, followed by the Performance Options button, and then the Change button. There is no such applet as Server. The Administrative Tools entry is merely a folder holding individual tools, and the Folder Options applet allows you to configure views and other values when working with folders.

28. **C.** The NIC must operate in promiscuous mode for network traffic other than that of its own to be analyzed. The other answers are invalid mode choices for a NIC.

29. **D**. The `diskperf -y` command will turn the counters on, while `diskperf -n` will turn them off. `Diskperf`, by itself (Answer A), will show the available options for the command, but nothing more. Answers B and C are invalid command choices.

30. **A, B, D**. If the processor is a bottleneck, you can upgrade it, or add another to the system. If, for some reason, these are not feasible, you can move some of the CPU-intensive applications to another server. Moving the system files will have no effect on the bottlenecking of the processor. Adding more video RAM will not help the network speed, and adding a faster network card does not alleviate the bottleneck on the processor.

31. **B, C, D**. Security Principals are any entities that can initiate an action. This would include users, computers, and services only.

32. **C**. The NTLM protocol is used for authentication with previous versions of Windows NT. Answer A, Kerberos, is used with Windows 2000. Answers B and D represent authentication protocols used with dialup networking.

33. **A**. The servers that issue the certificates and sign them digitally are known as Certificate Authorities. All other answers are invalid terms.

34. **C**. The Security Descriptor (SD) maintains the ACL. The SAM file was used to hold user and group information in earlier versions of Windows NT (in the absence of Active Directory). HKEY_CLASSES_ROOT holds information mapping applications to file extensions, and Access Control Entries (ACEs) are entries maintained in the ACL.

35. **A, B, E, F**. The upgrade can be done from Windows 95, Windows 98, Windows NT Workstation 3.51, or Windows NT Workstation 4.0. On all other operating systems, you must

purchase the full version and do a clean installation.

36. **B**. With an upgrade, you can migrate Terminal Server only to Windows 2000 Server. Windows 2000 Workstation is a step down, and not possible. You can install Windows 2000 Advanced Server over Terminal Server, but must use the full version and not an upgrade—the same would be true of Datacenter Server as well.

37. **B**. All of the reasons stated are legitimate ones why DOS applications fail to run in Windows 2000. Given that the described program interacts directly with a modem, however, the most likely cause is that Windows 2000 isolates hardware and will not let applications access hardware directly.

38. **A**. The Windows Management Instrumentation (WMI) provides the uniform model for software, whereas Windows Driver Model (WDM) extensions (Answer D) offer the same for hardware. COM and DCOM provide object orientation abilities.

39. **C**. When the application is assigned to a user, it appears as a shortcut on the desktop or Start menu. When the user clicks on the shortcut, the application is installed.

40. **A**. Pre-boot EXecution Environment (PXE) is required for the client to support Remote OS Installation. DHCP issues IP addresses automatically. RIS—Remote Installation Server—is used to supply the files needed for the installation. TOC is a nonexistent acronym for installation. If the machine does not support PXE, you can use boot disks.

41. **A, B, D**. Folder redirection can be used for Application Data, Desktop, My Pictures, Start Menu, and My Documents. It cannot be used for other entities.

42. **B**. The SetupCommand and FriendlyName tags are required. All other tags are optional.

43. **C**. A NetBIOS name can be up to 15 characters long, and must be unique within the network. All characters are converted to uppercase, and there are limitations on the characters that can be used. In actuality, there are 16 characters within the field, but the last is reserved.

44. **D**. The host name appears at the beginning of the entry, and the Fully Qualified Domain Name (FQDN) would be system1.new.office.com.

45. **A**. Service Resource Records (SRV) must be supported on the DNS servers. RR is the generic Resource Records, which include MX (for Mail Exchange Records) and PTR (for pointers).

46. **B**. The Start of Authority (SOA) resource record is at the start of any DNS zone.

47. **A**. The automatic trusts created in Windows 2000 resemble the complete-trust model that existed in Windows NT 4.0.

48. **C**. Any user wishing to modify the schema must be a member of the Schema Admins group to do so. Schema Admins, therefore, is not only the minimal group Jenna must be a member of to do this action, but the only group she need be a member of as well.

49. **B**. The IT administration model should be the focus for the OU design. All other choices are not used for OU design.

50. **D**. The Knowledge Consistency Checker (KCC) is used for this function. Answer A, NTDSUTIL, is used to change operations masters roles. Answer B, DCPROMO, is used to create objects during installation. Answer C, REPLMON, shows current roles.

51. **A, B**. ACE entries hold SID and GUID information, as well as access rights and property flags.

The ACE entries do not hold the ownership or inheritance information. Legacy is a nonexistent term in relation to ACEs.

52. **B, C, D**. You can delegate control with the Delegation of Control Wizard, the Security tab of the object properties window, or DSACLS.EXE. NTDSUTIL (Answer A) is used to change Operations Masters roles. Neither the DNS Manager (Answer F) nor Active Directory Sites and Services (Answer E) will allow you to make the delegation.

53. **B, C, D**. Group Polices are applied at SDOUs {Sites, Domains, and Organization Units). Group Policies cannot be applied to forests, but only to the entities within them. Attributes and ACEs do not factor into the question.

54. **C**. The system policies should be placed in SYSVOL for the down-level clients. NETLOGON is where they were placed on the NT 4.0 servers. PUBLIC and MAIL are locations for such entities to appear on NetWare servers.

55. **B**. A class is a formal description of a discrete, identifiable type of object that is stored in Active Directory. An attribute is used to define the class within a schema, and could also be considered a property.

56. **B**. Within any domain, only one domain controller will hold a writable copy of the schema. This domain controller is known as the FSMO role.

57. **B**. Object Identifiers (OIDs) use dotted-decimal syntax resembling that used for IP addresses.

58. **A**. The schema is over the forest, and modifications to the schema have forest-wide implications.

59. **D**. The Microsoft Directory Synchronization Services (MSDSS) is used to allow for synchronization between Active Directory and either

NetWare binderies, or NDS. The File Migration Utility (Answer A) is used to migrate from one to the other. Answer B, File and Print Services for NetWare, does not offer synchronization, but only the named services. Answer C is not a valid tool.

60. **B, C, D**. SFU offers remote command-line access between the different computer systems, password synchronization, file sharing via NFS, and simplified administration and Korn shell functionality (not C shell, as listed in Answer A). BASH (Bourne Again Shell) functionality (answer E) is not included, and offline file access (answer F) is nonexistent with SFU.

61. **B**. The Active Directory Connector (ADC) is used to synchronize Active Directory with Exchange. There are no such entities as Exchange.msc (the extension for MMC snap-ins) or MSDC Service (although there is an MSADC Service used for starting and stopping the connector). Choice C, the LDAP API, is but one feature that the ADC provides.

62. **D**. LDAP, by default, uses port 389. Port 21 is used by FTP, and port 80 is used by WWW. Port 119 is used by the NNTP service.

63. **A**. The first of the five steps of the recommended implementation plan is Goals and Objectives. This is followed by Planning and Design. Third comes the Pilot, followed by Execution, then Closure.

64. **C**. The SysPrep utility assists with the creation of the disk image and is included with Windows 2000. RIPrep may also be used in conjunction with Remote Installation Services to clone either vanilla network-based CD installs of Win2000 Pro, or customized images of Win2000 Pro. Ghost and DiskImage are third-party utilities used for creating images that are not included with Windows 2000. DFS (Distributed File System) makes locating files easier, but has nothing to do with imaging.

65. **B**. In the Planning and Design step, a Gap Analysis is performed—an analysis of the "gaps" between where the business is now and where it needs, or wants, to be.

PART

VII

APPENDICES

Glossary

4LSDOU   Term used within this text (and others) meaning Windows NT 4 policy, local policy, site, domain, or organizational unit.

4×7 benefit matrix   A way of expressing the benefits of a project relative to the needs of business. This matrix exposes benefits by using seven systems and business areas plotted against four cost metrics.

88 class   The original 1988 implementation of X.500 did not require class categorization. The updated 1993 version recognized *structural, abstract,* and *auxiliary classes.* Because of this, any pre-1993 classes defined that don't fall into one of these three categories are placed into another class called the 88 class.

A

A resource record   DNS resource record that maps the host name of a client to its associated IP address.

abstract class   Used only to derive *structural* or other abstract classes.

access control entry (ACE)   One of the line-by-line entries in either a DACL or SACL. Can apply to an object class, object, or object property and can be inherited by a specific object type. Access to an object is either allowed or denied through ACEs. See *discretionary access control list* and *system access control list.*

access control list (ACL)   List of users or security groups with access permissions to a particular object. There are two types of ACLs, *discretionary access control list* and *system access control list.*

acquisition   Purchasing, inheriting, or adding to what is already there. In business, acquisitions typically occur when one company buys another one.

Active Directory   Microsoft directory service store that is responsible for storing, managing, and replicating objects and servicing queries from directory-aware computers and applications.

Active Directory Connector (ADC)   Software that provides for synchronization of the Microsoft Exchange 5.5 directory with Active Directory.

Active Directory Integrated Zone   The Active Directory can serve as a storage location for DDNS zone data. This configuration allows DDNS to reap the benefits of multi-master replication and also serves as a fault-tolerance mechanism.

Active Directory Services Interface (ADSI)   A set of *Component Object Model* (COM) objects that provide a focal point for programmatic entry to Active Directory.

Active Directory Sizer   Utility that enables you to estimate the hardware requirements for deploying Active Directory in an organization based on the organization's profile, domain information, and site topology.

Application Programming Interface (API)   Provides developers a rich set of functions that they can use over and over again to retrieve information.

asset management   Process whereby a large organization collects and maintains a comprehensive list of items it owns, such as hardware and software.

Assigned Application A feature of *Software Installation and Maintenance* that enables administrators to advertise application availability to users and computers; also makes it possible to provide mandatory software to users.

attributeSchema object Special schema definition object used to define an attribute.

attribute syntax Rules applied to a schema attribute that restrict the type of information it may contain.

authentication A verification process usually coupled with an *authorization* process so that the latter can grant people specific access to resources.

authenticator In secret key cryptography, an authenticator refers to some type of data, such as time, that is unique and different every time it is used. Kerberos uses time as a means to represent a user's authenticity.

authorization Process that uses a person's identity and context to grant specific permission to resources.

Authorization Data Field within a *session ticket* used to carry SIDs for user and group membership.

auxiliary class Can be used to derive additional auxiliary classes; meant to store attributes and be applied to *structural class* definitions.

B

bandwidth Size of the network connection in terms of capacity.

baseline A base set of performance data captured during normal business operation to be used as a basis for comparison in the future.

Block Policy Inheritance Option on the OU Properties page that if enabled will exclude that OU and its children from Group Policy inheritance.

Administrators may configure GPOs to be forcefully installed, which overrides the Block Policy Inheritance option.

bottleneck Area on a network or server where a slowdown of transmission, accessibility, or other performance-related metric occurs.

bridge Device that sits between two network topologies and enables the transfer of data from one topology to another.

business centric Categorizes a company relative to the way its IT organization is viewed within the company. Business-centric companies typically do not include IT in strategic business decisions.

business model Describes a business in terms of *geographical scope* and company model, company processes, management model, and so on.

business problem An inhibitor, ailment, or other type of issue (usually negative) that businesses face.

business process A clearly defined set of steps required to complete a particular action.

C

caching-only server DNS servers that provide name resolution using only a cache of previously resolved names. Caching-only servers do not maintain a zone database.

CD-based installation Function of *Remote OS Installation* that makes Windows 2000 Professional installation files available across the network for installation.

centralized administration IT administration model that refers to a dependency on a single individual or team in a single location for administration of the network and network resources. Contrast with *decentralized administration*.

Certificate Authority (CA)   An entity (typically a company) that issues digital certificates to other entities (organizations or individuals) to allow them to prove their identity to others.

certificate publication points   These make certificates and CRLs publicly available inside or outside of an organization. They allow widespread availability of the critical material needed to support the entire *PKI*.

certificate revocation list (CRL)   List created and managed by a *Certificate Authority* that stores certificates whose keys either have been compromised or don't belong to the trusted CA anymore.

change and configuration management
Management of ongoing change and configuration issues that arise as administrators try to ensure that people are productive when they use their computers.

change management   Process by which companies strategically and proactively plan to cope with changing business and IT metrics.

child domain   One or more domains located in DNS namespace directly below the domain with the current focus.

classSchema object   Special schema definition object used to define a class.

client (respond only)   IPsec mode preferred for client computers who may need to respond appropriately if a server (or other client) requests a secure connection.

collision zone   Area of convergence for network packets, usually found in Ethernet hubs. Data traveling through hubs must contend for access to a "single road out" of the hub.

community management   A module within the *digital nervous system* initiative that focuses on the

authentication, collaboration (*rendezvous*), and *authorization* of people in a collaborative environment.

company model   Describes how a company operates, usually across *geographical scope*. Typical company models are national, international, regional, and branch office.

Component Object Model (COM)   A standard software architecture based on interfaces and designed to have code separated into self-contained objects.

Connection Agreement (CA)   Software configuration that establishes and maintains synchronization between containers within Active Directory domains and Exchange site recipient containers.

connection type   In the context of a physical infrastructure device, refers to the type of physical link between two devices, such as ATM, *Frame Relay*, ISDN, *Ethernet*, *FastEthernet*, and others.

context   A function within the *Identity Administration* module of the *digital nervous system* that refers to the management of a *digital identity*.

cost-benefit analysis   A justifying aspect of the *Rapid Economic Justification* framework that will be incorporated with financial metrics and risk analysis, and then presented to the key stakeholders of the project.

cost-benefit equation   A tool used within Microsoft's *Rapid Economic Justification* framework to define the step, approach, and scope of a *cost-benefit analysis*.

cryptography   The practice and study of *encryption* and *decryption*—encoding data so that it can be decoded only by specific individuals. Usually involves an algorithm and a secret key.

current state   The current operating, organizational, IT, and other environments within the company. It is used in conjunction with the company vision, goals, and project objectives when conducting a *Gap Analysis*.

D

Data Accessibility   Feature of *User Data Management* that allows a user's data to follow him from computer to computer throughout the network.

Data Availability   Feature of *User Data Management* that ensures that the most up-to-date versions of a user's data resides on both the local computer and on the server.

Data Protection   Feature of *User Data Management* that ensures data, although apparently local, is also redirected to a network share.

decentralized administration   IT administration model that refers to a regional, multiple-site setup with multiple points of administration of all network resources. Contrast with *centralized administration*.

decryption   The practice of decoding data that has been encrypted. Usually involves an algorithm and a key to unlock the data.

delegation of administrative authority   Process by which administrators may systematically relinquish control over specific portions of the network to other administrators. A wizard facilitates this process.

deliverable   Item(s) to be delivered at a particular project stage. In a business analysis, a deliverable is usually a series of documents that explain the findings of the analysis to a given point.

DHCP server   Server hosting *Dynamic Host Configuration Protocol* services. Server that allows administrators to configure *TCP/IP* services for clients. Client computers lease IP configurations from DHCP servers automatically.

digital certificate   Digital package that is part of the *PKI* and contains a public key and a set of attributes, such as the keyholder's name.

digital identity   Represents a person in a *digital nervous system.*

digital nervous system   Microsoft's initiative that digital processes will allow a company to perceive and react better to its environment, sense competitive challenges, and organize timely responses.

digital signature   A way to prove the origin of a piece of data.

directory   A physical storage container that contains anywhere from a few up to millions of various types of objects.

Directory Access Protocol (DAP)   An OSI-standard protocol for accessing an *X.500* directory. DAP is extremely feature rich and carries a lot of overhead.

discretionary access control list (DACL)   Contains the access control permissions for an object and its attributes, and the SIDs which determine who can use the object.

distribution group   Type of group used only by directory-enabled messaging applications, such as Microsoft Exchange 2000. These programs use distribution groups to facilitate message distribution to groups of users. Permissions cannot be assigned through distribution groups.

DNS   See *Domain Naming System.*

DNS domain   Partitions of *DNS* hierarchical *namespace*, which can be further divided into subdomains.

DNS zone   A database file containing resource records that delineates which DNS servers are authoritative for name resolution within a given partition of DNS namespace. Zones can contain one or more DNS domains.

domain   The basic atomic unit of Active Directory. A domain represents an administrative, security, and replication boundary, and forms a *namespace*.

domain controller   A Windows 2000 server running Active Directory.

domain controller security policy   Common to all domain controllers in a given domain, the domain controller security policy defines security settings such as user rights, auditing, and additional security options.

domain naming master   Domain controller given the responsibility to control and manage the additions to and deletions from an Active Directory forest. At any given time, there can be only one domain naming master in the entire Active Directory forest.

Domain Naming System (DNS)   Servers that implement an Internet-standard name resolution technology in which a *fully qualified domain name* (FQDN) is translated to its corresponding IP address.

domain security policy   Common to all Windows 2000 computers in the entire domain, the domain security policy defines account policy settings such as Kerberos policy, account lockout policy, and password policy. This policy is applied to all domain controllers, member servers, and member workstations.

domain tree   One of more domains joined together in parent/child relationships to form a contiguous namespace.

Dynamic DNS (DDNS)   A Microsoft-specific update to the original *Domain Name System* (DNS) specification that permits DNS servers to receive dynamic updates from a variety of clients and services.

Dynamic Inheritance   Uses an algorithm to define the implicit and explicit permissions on an object. Explicit permissions are those assigned directly to that object. Implicit permissions are assigned to parent containers of the object and apply to the object through inheritance.

Dynamic Update Protocol   A protocol that allows DDNS servers to dynamically update records in a DDNS zone database.

E

encryption   The practice of encoding data so that it cannot be deciphered by anyone without a key to decode it. Usually involves an algorithm and a key to lock the data.

Enterprise Admins   Universal group that has sweeping administrative power throughout Active Directory. This group is only available in native mode.

enterprise identity management   A vision that represents the future of how a business processes knowledge, information, and communication, and identity data within a unified directory system.

enterprise infrastructure assessment   Process of examining a corporation's current and planned physical infrastructure components as part of a strategic business and technology analysis.

Enterprise Memory Architecture (EMA)   New memory architecture in Windows 2000 Advanced Server and DataCenter server that allows applications to take advantage of RAM greater than 4GB.

envisioning   How the company foresees the future in strategic areas of business.

Ethernet   A contention-based *LAN* originally developed by Xerox Corporation that can carry digital signals at up to 10Mbps.

existence   A function within the *Identity Administration* module of the *digital nervous system* that specifies a single point of entry into the digital nervous system.

external trust   A one-way nontransitive trust between two domains. Because the trust is nontransitive, only the two participating domains (or Kerberos "realms") are permitted to utilize it.

F

FastEthernet   A contention-based LAN evolved from Ethernet, with the capacity to carry digital signals at 100Mbps.

file and folder redirection   Process by which administrators can control, via Group Policy, alternative storage locations for a user's Application Data, Desktop, My Documents, My Pictures, and Start Menu folders.

flexible single master of operations (FSMO)   See *operations masters.*

flexibility   Refers to planning and deploying technology that will support future growth. See *value creation.*

forest   One or more contiguous domain tree namespaces that form a given enterprise.

forwarder   DNS server that has been chosen to handle communications with other DNS servers that are physically off-site, such as with Internet DNS servers.

Frame Relay   A type of WAN connection in which full or partial increments of a leased line may be utilized. Allows for "bursts" of bandwidth to be allocated when needed.

full zone transfer   Process by which a *primary DNS server*, in response to an AXFR request from a *secondary DNS server*, transfers the entire contents of its zone file to that secondary server. See also *zone transfer* and *incremental zone transfer.*

funding model   A broad term that describes the financial model a company might utilize to justify expenditures, report profit and loss, and in general disseminate economic information.

G

Gap Analysis   Process to pin down the gap that exists between a company's existing business and/or IT environment, and where the company needs or wants to be according to its future vision and goals.

geographical scope   The physical geographical layout of an organization; the boundary in which a company operates.

Global Catalog   A *partial replica* of all domain partitions in an Active Directory tree containing the objects and object attributes most frequently accessed during searches or other Active Directory query operations.

Global Catalog server   A *domain controller* with the added responsibility of storing *partial replicas* of all other domains in the forest.

Group Policy   Windows 2000 technology that enables an administrator to manage desktop environments across a network by applying configuration settings to computer and user accounts. Group Policy settings are contained in *Group Policy objects.*

Group Policy Container (GPC)   An Active Directory object that stores *Group Policy Object* attributes, and includes subcontainers for Group Policy information about computers and users.

Group Policy Editor (GPE)   Editor that uses an administrative template to enable administrators to configure *Group Policy Object* settings.

Group Policy Object (GPO)   A virtual container that holds Group Policy settings that you specify and is attached to a specific object at the site, domain, or OU level in Active Directory; is commonly used to refer to the GPC and GPT (*Group Policy Container* and *Group Policy Template*) as one object.

Group Policy Template (GPT)   A file and folder structure that includes all the *Group Policy Object* information for a particular GPO.

group scope   Determines where in Active Directory you are able to use the group to assign permissions. The scope of a group is dictated by its name: domain local, global, or universal.

growth   In business, growth is measured in terms of mergers, acquisitions, and internal hiring.

H

hashing   Typically an algorithm that provides rapid access to some data items that can be distinguished with a key.

hub   Network device that enables communication between two or more computers or network devices. The entire hub is a *collision zone.*

hybrid administration   IT administration model that is a combination of *centralized administration* and *decentralized administration.*

I-J

identity administration   A module within the digital nervous system that focuses on managing each *digital identity* in terms of *existence*, *context*, and *provisioning*.

incremental zone transfer   Process by which a *primary DNS server*, in response to an IXFR request from a *secondary DNS server*, transfers only changes (new, deleted, or modified zone information) from its zone

file to the secondary server. See also *zone transfer* and *full zone transfer.*

influence   To produce an effect on by imperceptible or intangible means.

infrastructure master   A domain controller assigned the responsibility of managing cross-domain references between users and groups. At any given time there can be only one infrastructure master in the domain.

inheritance   In Windows 2000, refers to the capability of an object to receive its parent object's attributes, such as security and access permissions.

Intelligent Input/Output (I$_2$O)   A specification that aims to provide an I/O device driver architecture that is independent of both the device being controlled and the host OS.

IntelliMirror   A set of powerful features native to Windows 2000 for desktop change and configuration management; combines the advantages of centralized computing with the performance and flexibility of distributed computing.

Internet Engineering Task Force (IETF)   A large, international community of network designers, operators, vendors, and researchers concerned with the evolution of Internet architecture and the smooth operation of the Internet. It is open to any interested individual.

inter-site replication   Replication between domain controller bridgehead servers and sites.

intra-site replication   Replication between domain controllers in the same site.

IP security (IPsec)   IPsec is a means by which IP data transmissions may be encrypted to provide enhanced security.

IPX/SPX   Internetwork Packet Exchange/Sequenced Packet Exchange; a protocol utilized by Novell NetWare networks for LAN and WAN networking.

ISO 3166 country codes   International Standards Organization listing of two-character country codes, found at: `http://www.din.de/gremien/nas/nabd/iso3166ma/codlstp1.html`.

IT centric   Categorizes a company relative to the way its IT organization is viewed within the company. IT-centric companies typically center strategic business movement around IT.

iterative queries   Used primarily by servers during a recursive query process requested by a client. If the first *DNS server* cannot resolve the name, it uses an iterative process between itself and other DNS servers to resolve the name for the client.

K

KDC   See *Key Distribution Center*.

Kerberos   Industry standard and core Windows 2000 authentication protocol. Developed during MIT's project Athena, it is based on symmetric key cryptography and is widely supported throughout the distributed computing industry.

Key Distribution Center   Trusted intermediary between a client and a server. The KDC is responsible for authenticating users and granting shared secret keys.

Knowledge Consistency Checker (KCC)   A service that runs on all domain controllers. Its purpose is to create connection objects between domain controllers in the same site. Windows 2000 uses these connection objects to establish replication partners and redundancy.

L

LAN (local area network)   A network that is physically located in a single location. A single LAN does not overlap any *WAN* connections. Compare with *MAN* and **WAN**.

latency   Lag time between replication occurrences. This is especially prominent during scheduled *intersite replication* that occurs only once per day.

laws and regulations   Rules and codes of conduct designed to govern a process.

LDAP C API   A low-level API that allows for direct programmatic access to Active Directory.

Lightweight Directory Access Protocol (LDAP)   A scaled-down (lightweight) version of MIT's X.500 Directory Access Protocol. LDAP is the core protocol of Active Directory.

.local   Root namespace reserved by InterNIC for internal use. Similar to private IP address schemes.

long-term session key   Granted to a user after successful Kerberos authentication. It is derived by sending the user's password through a one-way hashing algorithm and is returned to the user encrypted in a *Ticket-Granting Ticket*.

LSDOU   Term used within this text (and others) meaning local policy, site, domain, or organizational unit.

M

MAN (Metropolitan Area Network)   An extension of a LAN utilizing high-speed fiber-optic cable capable of stretching several kilometers without signal degradation. Compare with *LAN* and *WAN*.

mandatory attribute   A schema attribute that must be given a value before an object containing it can be instantiated in the directory.

merger   In business, the act of two or more companies joining to become one.

Messaging Application Programming Interface (MAPI)   A set of interrelated functions that serve as a programmatic entry point to compliant messaging systems such as Microsoft Exchange.

Microsoft Directory Synchronization Services (MSDSS)   Synchronization technology that can be used between Active Directory and just about any NetWare configuration.

Microsoft Installer File (MSI)   New "package" file format that replaces setup.exe. MSI files are rich with granular control over application installation options, just-in-time installations, and resiliency.

Microsoft Readiness Framework (MRF)   Helps you identify and develop the competencies and skills you need to introduce new or changing technologies into the environments and business practices of your clients.

Miller-Heiman   Among the global leaders in sales development, with many published books such as *Conceptual Selling, Strategic Selling*, and *The New Strategic Selling*.

mixed mode   The mode of Active Directory operation that permits replication with down-level Windows NT backup domain controllers. This is the default mode for Active Directory and does not offer several of the new key benefits that *native mode* does.

Msinfo32   See *System Information Utility*.

N

name resolution   In *DNS*, the process of matching a fully qualified domain name with an IP address.

namespace   A bounded region within which a friendly name of an object can be resolved to the internal system name for that object.

native mode   The mode of Active Directory operation in which multi-master replication, nested groups, and other key new Windows 2000 features are enabled. Replication with down-level Windows NT 4.0 domain controllers is not enabled. Contrast with *mixed mode*.

NBTSTAT   Utility that may be used to view the NetBIOS connection information on a workstation or server.

nesting   In Active Directory, nesting refers to the design practice of including multiple levels of containers within containers so that each "child" container has exactly one "parent" container, which itself could be a child of another parent.

Network File System (NFS)   Standard file sharing protocol across many UNIX platforms.

Network Information Service (NIS)   Client/server protocol for distributing system configuration data such as user- and host names between computers on a network.

Network Load Balancing Services (NLBS)   Enables you to put up to 32 servers in a "cluster" and balance the load of incoming TCP/IP traffic between them.

Network Monitor   Windows NT/2000 utility that can be used to monitor the packet-level traffic on the physical network cable. Requires that Network Monitor Agents be installed.

network segment   Area of the internal network separated by IP subnets, which usually results in increased efficiency both within and between network segments.

network topology   General term referencing the high-level network infrastructure. References network type, internetwork links, network size, bandwidth, traffic patterns, and protocols.

No Override   Option that administrators can enable on a *Group Policy object* to force that GPO upon all child objects. No Override supersedes *Block Policy Inheritance.*

Novell Directory Services (NDS)   Novell's implementation of directory services for its NetWare network operating system.

NTLM   Windows NT LAN Manager authentication. Core authentication protocol supported by Windows NT. Used in Windows 2000 primarily to support interoperability with down-level Windows 9x and Windows NT systems.

O

object identifier (OID)   A globally unique number used to reference each schema object; represented as a dotted-decimal string, such as 1.2.840.1.1.1.1, in which 1.2.840 is assigned to the United States, and the remaining four values are reserved for corporations to use internally.

objective   Something worked toward; a plan.

OID   See *object identifier.*

operational model   A term used to describe how a company operates relative to *geographical scope* and other operational factors. Examples are regional, national, and international.

operations masters   Special servers designated to be the "single master" of some operation that does not implement well in a distributed environment (such as changing passwords, naming objects, and so on).

optional attribute   A schema attribute that does not require a value when an object containing it is instantiated in the directory.

OU security policy   In Windows 2000, an OU security policy refers to a *Group Policy object* defining security settings that is attached to a specific *OU.* These security settings may be used at the OU level to override domain security settings for that OU only.

outsourcing   Action of a company allowing an outside entity to occupy some position(s) or handle some task(s) that normally would belong to its own employees.

P

parent domain   A domain located in DNS namespace directly above the domain with the current focus.

partial replica   A partial version of a foreign *domain* partition sitting on a *global catalog server.* It contains all of the domain's objects, but only a select number of each object's attributes.

PDC emulator   A domain controller assigned the additional responsibility of acting as a PDC to service down-level client logon or replication with down-level BDCs. In native mode, PDC emulator domain controllers receive preferential replication of password changes performed by other domain controllers; so if a client from a third domain attempts to log on and cannot, that logon request can be forwarded to the PDC emulator for another try. At any given time, there can be only one PDC emulator master in the domain.

Performance Monitor   Windows NT-based utility that contains system resource objects and object counters that capture statistics on server resource utilization.

policy propagation   Term used to describe how Windows 2000 security policies process updates.

Pre-boot eXecution Environment (PXE)
Architecture for bootstrapping a computer.

Primary DNS server The authoritative DNS server for a zone; contains the master read/write copy of the zone database.

priority-one applications Mission-critical application list collaboratively compiled during an application inventory.

priority-three applications Applications that may or may not be used on a daily basis in an organization, and are collaboratively deemed to be tertiary to mission-critical and daily-use applications.

priority-two applications Applications utilized on a daily basis that have a stake in the efficiency of an organization's operation, but are collaboratively deemed not to be mission critical.

problem-objective table Used to map stated business problems to project objectives.

project objective An action item created with the intent of solving one business problem. No individual project objective should be directed at more than one business problem.

protocol binding Process by which a protocol such as *TCP/IP* or *IPX/SPX* attaches to a network adapter.

provisioning A function within the *identity administration* module of the *digital nervous system* that defines how actions are taken based on context.

Proxy and Forwarding Boolean flags set within a *session ticket* to allow servers to obtain session tickets for other servers on behalf of the client.

pruning and grafting A technique used to restructure objects contained within a domain. Pruning is loosely associated with "cutting," and grafting is loosely associated with "pasting."

PTR resource record DNS resource record that maps the IP address of host to its host name.

public key infrastructure (PKI) Refers to the set of OS and application services that makes it easy and convenient to use public key cryptography. Gives you the ability to manage, publish, and use keys.

Published Application A feature of *Software Installation and Maintenance* that allows administrators to make applications available to users via the Control Panel or through document invocation.

PXE See *Pre-boot eXecution Environment.*

Q

QIP server Offers standards-based, many-to-one DHCP fail-over, IP address "check-before-assign" capabilities, the ability to assign IP addresses to older BOOTP clients, and the ability to update DDNS servers with client information.

QoS (Quality of Service) Technology that enables administrators to allocate segments of bandwidth with priority for specific applications to specific users.

R

RAID Redundant Array of Inexpensive Disks; basic levels of RAID configuration include RAID 0: Disk Striping, RAID 1: Mirroring, and RAID 5: Stripe Set with Parity.

Rapid Economic Justification (REJ) A five-step approach that provides IT professionals an efficient method to analyze the economic performance of IT investments, plan for resources, and gain capital appropriation for IT projects. It is essentially a framework for performing *ROI* assessments.

realm Kerberos equivalent of a Windows 2000 domain.

recursive queries Used primarily by clients when requesting *name resolution* from a *DNS server*. Client expects either an IP address (a resolved query) or a failure notice from the servers. The server, in turn, must do extra work by forwarding the request on behalf of the client to the proper *DNS domain* for resolution.

Remote Installation Services (RIS) Services that run under Windows 2000 Server that simplify the task of installing an OS on computers throughout the organization; these provide a mechanism for computers to connect to a network server during the initial boot process, while the server controls a local installation of Windows 2000 Professional.

remote OS installation Process by which client computers with PXE-capable ROM may download and install operating software from a remote installation server.

rendezvous The process of bringing people together in a collaborative environment so that they may connect to resources and other people.

replication Process by which attribute-level data from one *domain controller* is passed to another domain controller in the same *domain*.

resilient application An *assigned application* deployed with *Windows Installer* and therefore able to detect and repair damaged application-related system files, possibly eliminating user downtime and the need for help desk support.

resolver A software component that ships as part of the TCP/IP stack on both Windows 2000 clients and servers whose purpose it to create and resolve name resolution queries.

resource distribution Disbursement of administrative employees across the *geographical scope* of the company.

Return on Investment Analysis of the current or potential impact a new technology has on business objectives and on *Total Cost of Ownership*.

RID master A domain controller assigned the responsibility of providing pools of *relative IDs* (RIDs) to domain controllers within its domain to assist with object naming. Domain controllers then couple a domain *security ID* (SID) with a RID to form a unique security identifier for an object. At any given time there can be only one RID master in the domain.

RIPrep Image Format Function of *Remote OS Installation* that enables administrators to clone entire Windows 2000 Professional installations, including all applications, services, and settings. This image file is then made available to RIS clients wanting to install it.

risk The possibility of suffering harm or loss.

ROI See *Return on Investment*.

Root DNS namespace The top-level DNS namespace for a given scope.

router A device that forwards packets between networks. Packets are forwarded based on routing tables, which can be manually created or automatically generated based on routing protocols.

Routing Information Protocol (RIP) A companion protocol to *IPX* in a Novell network for the exchange of routing information. Also, a distance-vector protocol used to update routing tables of *routers*.

RPC-based replication RPC over IP replication is used for all *intra-site replication* and can be used for *inter-site replication*.

S

Scatter/Gather I/O Enables increased I/O throughput for application data stored in noncontiguous memory.

schema A database that represents the types of object classes, object attributes, and attribute syntax that can be utilized by Active Directory.

Schema Admins   Only members of this group have the ability to modify the schema, an action that affects every object and attribute throughout the entire forest. You must tightly control membership to this group!

Schema Master   Domain controller given the responsibility of updating the schema. At any given time, there can be only one Schema Master in the entire Active Directory forest.

scope   In terms of Active Directory, refers to the boundaries of the namespace.

SDOU   Term used within this text (and others) meaning site, domain, or organizational unit.

secondary DNS server   Backup DNS servers that receive all their zone information via zone transfers with *primary DNS servers.*

Secure Server (require security)   IPsec security policy in which data transfers must be secured; otherwise, they will not work.

security descriptor   Defines the access permissions for an object. Each object has a security descriptor that stores the following: owner SID, group SID, DACL, SACL.

security group   Group used by Windows 2000 to assign permissions to allow users to gain access to resources.

security principal   Any entity that can force an action, such as a human element or a service.

Security Service Provider Interface (SSPI)   In Windows 2000, used to provide generic abstraction to support multiple authentication mechanisms based on shared secret or public key protocols.

Server (request security)   IPsec security policy in which data transfers will request IPsec encryption, but not require it. If necessary, it will communicate without security.

service   Responsible for making the information in a directory useful to requesting users or applications.

Service Advertising Protocol (SAP)   Novell NetWare protocol that allows file, print, and application servers to advertise their services.

service and product life cycle   The circular process of preparing, deploying, maintaining, and removing software or other products in a computing environment.

service level agreement (SLA)   An agreement between an IT organization and its business customers that describes the characteristics, parameters, and types of service and support the IT organization will provide.

service resource record (SRV)   DNS resource record that maps to the name of the server for a specific service, protocol, or domain.

Services for NetWare (SFN)   Software that provides for the synchronization of NetWare (NDS or Bindery) with Active Directory.

Services for UNIX (SFU)   Software that provides for the integration and/or coexistence of Active Directory and various UNIX platforms.

session key   Used in the Kerberos authentication process; granted by the KDC to a client requesting access to a server resource; used by both client and server to present a secure conversation.

session ticket   Kerberos ticket used by the client when requesting access to a network resource. Contains a shared secret session key that is known to be authentic and also known by only the KDC and the two computers that need to communicate.

shortcut trust   Shortcut trusts are manually created between two adjacent Windows 2000 domains; they are either one-way or coupled with another shortcut trust to form a two-way trust. They are one- or two-way transitive trusts. The shortcut trust is used to provide a shorter trust path from one domain to another in the same forest but different trees.

Single Sign-On Capability of Windows 2000 and some other operating systems to support the requesting of security credentials only once per logon session. Subsequent authentication requests are handled transparently.

site One or more well-connected IP *subnets* that, as a whole, act as a physical replication boundary.

site link The link between one or more sites that contains replication parameters such as the schedule, cost, frequency, and protocol to use.

site link bridge Used to connect sites and model the routing behavior of a network.

SMTP-based replication SMTP-based replication is available only for the configuration and schema containers during *inter-site replication*.

SNMP Simple Network Management Protocol; a TCP/IP-based protocol developed to manage nodes on an IP network.

Software Installation and Maintenance Feature of *IntelliMirror* designed to facilitate policy-based deployment and management of software centrally through the use of Group Policy, without having to visit each individual desktop.

SRV Record See *service resource record*.

SSL/TLS Secure Sockets Layer/Transport Layer Security; used by Windows 2000 in conjunction with X.509 certificates to provide mutual authentication, message integrity, and confidentiality.

Start of Authority The first record in a DNS zone, which identifies a primary DNS name server for the zone as the best source for information within that zone and as the entity for processing updates within that zone.

Static Inheritance A form of security attribute inheritance implemented by Windows 2000, also known as *Create Time Inheritance*. An object will inherit its parents attributes at the time of creation, but may or may not inherit parent attributes in the future based on specific settings.

strategic solution An elaborate and systematic scheme, program, or method worked out beforehand for the accomplishment of an objective.

strategy influences Factors that influence the strategic direction of company, such as priorities, *laws and regulations*, and *TCO*.

structural class Used to create the structure of Active Directory; derived from another structural class or *abstract class*.

subclass Schema class derived from another class. All schema classes are subclasses of top.

superclass Schema class from which other classes may be derived.

switch Network device that enables point-to-point communication between two or more computers or network devices. Uses virtual circuits to reduce collision zones to virtually nil.

symmetric multiprocessing (SMP) Two or more processors connected by a high-bandwidth bus and managed by one OS.

system access control list (SACL) Contains a list of events that can be audited for an object.

System Information Utility Collects your computer's system configuration information and provides a menu for displaying the associated system topics.

System Monitor Windows 2000–based utility that contains system resource objects and object counters that capture statistics on server resource utilization. This product is the upgraded version of the Performance Monitor from Windows NT.

System Monitor object counters Entities that report system utilization statistics back to the System Monitor utility.

System Monitor objects System resource, network, protocol–related entities that contain one or more counters that report system utilization statistics.

T

tactical solution An expedient for achieving a goal.

TCO See *Total Cost of Operations/Ownership.*

telecommuting The increasingly popular practice of working at home and connecting to the corporate office via phone line and modem or other technologies.

Ticket-Granting Ticket Special type of Kerberos session ticket kept in the client cache after a successful logon. When a client requests a network resource, the TGT is sent to the KDC, which responds with a *session ticket* for that client to use when accessing that resource.

ticket referral A process by which a *Key Distribution Center* refers requests for services or resources to the KDC managing the appropriate resource.

Token Ring A computer arbitration scheme in which conflicts in the transmission of messages are avoided by the granting of "tokens," which give permission to send. A station keeps a token while transmitting a message as long as it has a message to transmit, and then passes the token on to the next station.

Total Cost of Operations/Ownership A comprehensive model that helps managers understand the direct, budgeted costs and the indirect, unbudgeted costs associated with a particular asset throughout its life cycle.

transitive trust Implicit two-way trust relationship created automatically between same-domain domain controllers within the same site. This functionality enables users to authenticate anywhere within a forest and have access to their assigned resources.

Transmission Control Protocol/Internet Protocol (TCP/IP) A suite of protocols for transfering data of networks; used as the Internet standard protocol.

trust Relationship established between domains that enables users from one domain to be recognized by a domain controller in another domain.

U

unified directory A directory in which all object identities are maintained in a single instance and all services utilize those single instances throughout the directory.

Update Sequence Number A numeric trigger attached to each directory object and incremented whenever an attribute for that object is changed.

User Computer Settings Management Feature of *IntelliMirror* that enables administrators to centrally define computing environments for groupings of users and computers.

User Data Management Feature of *IntelliMirror* that ensures that a user's data is easily accessible, readily available, and always protected.

user principal name (UPN) A "friendly" name given to an object, which is easier to remember than the distinguished name.

user principal name suffix The part of the user *principal name* to the right of the at character (@). By default, the UPN suffix for a user account is the DNS domain name that references the Active Directory domain in which the user account resides.

V

value acceleration   Refers to using a technology to realize benefits now rather than later. *See value creation.*

value creation   Defines how a company expects to gain capital based on an expenditure. Usually expressed in one of four ways: *value restructuring, value acceleration, value linking,* or *flexibility.*

value linking   Refers to the snowball effect that added benefits in technology in one area can have on another area. See *value creation.*

value restructuring   Refers to using a technology solution to restructure the way a company does business, resulting in fundamental improvement. See *value creation.*

vision   Theoretical statement, usually backed by research and evidence, about how a company will operate sometime in the future.

W

WAN (Wide Area Network)   A network consisting of more than one LAN connected by leased line, ISDN, or some other WAN connection. Compare with *LAN* and *MAN.*

What if? analysis   A tactic used in business analysis involving asking "What if...?" questions with the goal of instigating thought and communications relative to what people want to accomplish.

WHOIS   An Internet directory service that enables, among other things, lookup of DNS domain names as a preparatory step toward registration.

Windows 2000 Readiness Analyzer   Utility that compares the devices and applications on your system against a list of known issues with their operation under Windows 2000.

Windows Installer   New installation and maintenance technology designed to work with *Software Installation and Maintenance* to help overcome the problems inherent in deploying and managing software throughout an organization. Delivers a higher level of sophistication than previous installation technology by providing for custom installation, resilient (self-healing) applications, and clean software removal.

Windows Internet Naming Service (WINS)   A Microsoft-created technology for mapping NetBIOS names to IP addresses.

Windows management instrumentation (WMI)   Represents a uniform model in which management data from any source can be managed in a standard way.

Windows management services   Provides a well-managed Windows environment, designed around management disciplines and roles, that will operate efficiently within the context of both a homogeneous Windows environment and a heterogeneous enterprise.

WINS   See *Windows Internet Naming Service.*

workload characterization   The categorization of servers by workload, such as domain controllers, Web servers, application servers, database servers, and so on.

X-Y

X.500   The OSI directory standard, defining a namespace, information model, functional model, and an authentication framework. Additionally, it defines the *Directory Access Protocol (DAP).*

X.509 certificate   Certificate issued by a *Certificate Authority* and used for Internet authentication.

Z

ZAP file   A text file that can be analyzed and executed by *Software Installation and Maintenance*. This type of file enables administrators to deploy non-Windows Installer applications, with some limitations.

zone transfer   Process by which a DNS server shares its database zone file with other DNS servers participating in the zone. See also *incremental zone transfer* and *full zone transfer*.

Overview of the Certification Process

You must pass rigorous certification exams to become a Microsoft Certified Professional. These closed-book exams provide a valid and reliable measure of your technical proficiency and expertise. Developed in consultation with computer industry professionals who have experience with Microsoft products in the workplace, the exams are conducted by two independent organizations. Sylvan Prometric offers the exams at more than 2,000 authorized Prometric Testing Centers around the world. Virtual University Enterprises (VUE) testing centers offer exams at more than 1,400 locations as well.

To schedule an exam, call Sylvan Prometric Testing Centers at 800-755-EXAM (3926) (or register online at **http://www.2test.com/register**) or VUE at 888-837-8734 (or register online at **http://www.vue.com/ms/msexam.html**). At the time of this writing, Microsoft offered eight types of certification, each based on a specific area of expertise. Please check the Microsoft Certified Professional Web site for the most up-to-date information (**www.microsoft.com/mcp/**).

TYPES OF CERTIFICATION

◆ **Microsoft Certified Professional (MCP).** Persons with this credential are qualified to support at least one Microsoft product. Candidates can take elective exams to develop areas of specialization. MCP is the base level of expertise.

◆ **Microsoft Certified Professional+Internet (MCP+Internet).** Persons with this credential are qualified to plan security, install and configure server products, manage server resources, extend service to run CGI scripts or ISAPI scripts, monitor and analyze performance, and trouble-shoot problems. Expertise is similar to that of an MCP but with a focus on the Internet.

◆ **Microsoft Certified Professional+Site Building (MCP+Site Building).** Persons with this credential are qualified to plan, build, maintain, and manage Web sites using Microsoft technologies and products. This credential is appropriate for people who manage sophisticated, interactive Web sites that include database connectivity, multimedia, and searchable content.

◆ **Microsoft Certified Database Administrator (MCDBA).** Qualified individuals can derive physical database designs, develop logical data models, create physical databases, create data services by using Transact-SQL, manage and maintain databases, configure and manage security, monitor and optimize databases, and install and configure Microsoft SQL Server.

◆ **Microsoft Certified Systems Engineer (MCSE).** These individuals are qualified to analyze the business requirements for a system architecture; design solutions; deploy, install, and configure architecture components; and troubleshoot system problems.

◆ **Microsoft Certified Systems Engineer+Internet (MCSE+Internet).** Persons with this credential are qualified in the core MCSE areas and also are qualified to enhance, deploy, and manage sophisticated intranet and Internet solutions that include a browser, proxy server, host servers, database, and messaging and commerce components. An MCSE+Internet-certified professional is able to manage and analyze Web sites.

◆ **Microsoft Certified Solution Developer (MCSD).** These individuals are qualified to design and develop custom business solutions by using Microsoft development tools, technologies, and platforms. The new track includes certification exams that test the user's ability to build Web-based, distributed, and commerce applications by using Microsoft products such as Microsoft SQL Server, Microsoft Visual Studio, and Microsoft Component Services.

◆ **Microsoft Certified Trainer (MCT).** Persons with this credential are instructionally and technically qualified by Microsoft to deliver Microsoft Education Courses at Microsoft-authorized sites. An MCT must be employed by a Microsoft Solution Provider Authorized Technical Education Center or a Microsoft Authorized Academic Training site.

NOTE: For up-to-date information about each type of certification, visit the Microsoft Training and Certification Web site at `http://www.microsoft.com/mcp`. You can also contact Microsoft through the following sources:

- Microsoft Certified Professional Program: 800-636-7544

- `mcp@msource.com`

- Microsoft Online Institute (MOLI): 800-449-9333

CERTIFICATION REQUIREMENTS

The following sections describe the requirements for the various types of Microsoft certifications.

NOTE: An asterisk following an exam in any of the following lists means that it is slated for retirement.

How to Become a Microsoft Certified Professional

To become certified as an MCP, you need only pass any Microsoft exam (with the exceptions of Networking Essentials, #70-058* and Microsoft Windows 2000 Accelerated Exam for MCPs Certified on Microsoft Windows NT 4.0, #70-240).

How to Become a Microsoft Certified Professional+Internet

To become an MCP specializing in Internet technology, you must pass the following exams:

◆ Internetworking with Microsoft TCP/IP on Microsoft Windows NT 4.0, #70-059*

◆ Implementing and Supporting Microsoft Windows NT Server 4.0, #70-067*

◆ Implementing and Supporting Microsoft Internet Information Server 3.0 and Microsoft Index Server 1.1, #70-077*

 OR Implementing and Supporting Microsoft Internet Information Server 4.0, #70-087*

How to Become a Microsoft Certified Professional+Site Building

To be certified as an MCP+Site Building, you need to pass two of the following exams:

◆ Designing and Implementing Web Sites with Microsoft FrontPage 98, #70-055

◆ Designing and Implementing Commerce Solutions with Microsoft Site Server 3.0, Commerce Edition, #70-057

◆ Designing and Implementing Web Solutions with Microsoft Visual InterDev 6.0, #70-152

How to Become a Microsoft Certified Database Administrator

There are two MCDBA tracks, one tied to Windows 2000, the other based on Windows NT 4.0.

Windows 2000 Track

To become an MCDBA in the Windows 2000 track, you must pass three core exams and one elective exam.

Core Exams

The core exams required to become an MCDBA in the Windows 2000 track are as follows:

◆ Installing, Configuring, and Administering Microsoft Windows 2000 Server, #70-215

 OR Microsoft Windows 2000 Accelerated Exam for MCPs Certified on Microsoft Windows NT 4.0, #70-240 (only for those who have passed exams #70-067*, #70-068*, and #70-073*)

◆ Administering Microsoft SQL Server 7.0, #70-028

◆ Designing and Implementing Databases with Microsoft SQL Server 7.0, #70-029

Elective Exams

You must also pass one elective exam from the following list:

◆ Implementing and Administering a Microsoft Windows 2000 Network Infrastructure, #70-216 (only for those who have *not* already passed #70-067*, #70-068*, and #70-073*)

OR Microsoft Windows 2000 Accelerated Exam for MCPs Certified on Microsoft Windows NT 4.0, #70-240 (only for those who have passed exams #70-067*, #70-068*, and #70-073*)

◆ Designing and Implementing Distributed Applications with Microsoft Visual C++ 6.0, #70-015

◆ Designing and Implementing Data Warehouses with Microsoft SQL Server 7.0 and Microsoft Decision Support Services 1.0, #70-019

◆ Implementing and Supporting Microsoft Internet Information Server 4.0, #70-087*

◆ Designing and Implementing Distributed Applications with Microsoft Visual FoxPro 6.0, #70-155

◆ Designing and Implementing Distributed Applications with Microsoft Visual Basic 6.0, #70-175

Windows NT 4.0 Track

To become an MCDBA in the Windows NT 4.0 track, you must pass four core exams and one elective exam.

Core Exams

The core exams required to become an MCDBA in the Windows NT 4.0 track are as follows:

◆ Administering Microsoft SQL Server 7.0, #70-028

◆ Designing and Implementing Databases with Microsoft SQL Server 7.0, #70-029

◆ Implementing and Supporting Microsoft Windows NT Server 4.0, #70-067*

◆ Implementing and Supporting Microsoft Windows NT Server 4.0 in the Enterprise, #70-068*

Elective Exams

You must also pass one elective exam from the following list:

◆ Designing and Implementing Distributed Applications with Microsoft Visual C++ 6.0, #70-015

◆ Designing and Implementing Data Warehouses with Microsoft SQL Server 7.0 and Microsoft Decision Support Services 1.0, #70-019

◆ Internetworking with Microsoft TCP/IP on Microsoft Windows NT 4.0, #70-059*

◆ Implementing and Supporting Microsoft Internet Information Server 4.0, #70-087*

◆ Designing and Implementing Distributed Applications with Microsoft Visual FoxPro 6.0, #70-155

◆ Designing and Implementing Distributed Applications with Microsoft Visual Basic 6.0, #70-175

How to Become a Microsoft Certified Systems Engineer

You must pass operating system exams and two elective exams to become an MCSE. The MCSE certification path is divided into two tracks: Windows 2000 and Windows NT 4.0.

The following lists show the core requirements for the Windows 2000 and Windows NT 4.0 tracks and the electives.

Windows 2000 Track

The Windows 2000 track requires you to pass five core exams (or an accelerated exam and another core exam). You must also pass two elective exams.

Core Exams

The Windows 2000 track core requirements for MCSE certification include the following for those who have *not* passed #70-067, #70-068, and #70-073:

◆ Installing, Configuring, and Administering Microsoft Windows 2000 Professional, #70-210

◆ Installing, Configuring, and Administering Microsoft Windows 2000 Server, #70-215

◆ Implementing and Administering a Microsoft Windows 2000 Network Infrastructure, #70-216

◆ Implementing and Administering a Microsoft Windows 2000 Directory Services Infrastructure, #70-217

The Windows 2000 Track core requirements for MCSE certification include the following for those who have passed #70-067*, #70-068*, and #70-073*:

◆ Microsoft Windows 2000 Accelerated Exam for MCPs Certified on Microsoft Windows NT 4.0, #70-240

All candidates must pass one of these three additional core exams:

◆ Designing a Microsoft Windows 2000 Directory Services Infrastructure, #70-219

   OR Designing Security for a Microsoft Windows 2000 Network, #70-220

   OR Designing a Microsoft Windows 2000 Infrastructure, #70-221

Elective Exams

Any MCSE elective exams that are current (not slated for retirement) when the Windows 2000 core exams are released can be used to fulfill the requirement of two elective exams. In addition, core exams #70-219,

#70-220, and #70-221 can be used as elective exams, as long as they are not already being used to fulfill the "additional core exams" requirement outlined previously. Exam #70-222 (Upgrading from Microsoft Windows NT 4.0 to Microsoft Windows 2000) can also be used to fulfill this requirement. Finally, selected third-party certifications that focus on interoperability may count for this requirement. Watch the Microsoft MCP Web site (`www.microsoft.com/mcp`) for more information on these third-party certifications.

Windows NT 4.0 Track

The Windows NT 4.0 track is also organized around core and elective exams.

Core Exams

The four Windows NT 4.0 track core requirements for MCSE certification are as follows:

◆ Implementing and Supporting Microsoft Windows NT Server 4.0, #70-067*

◆ Implementing and Supporting Microsoft Windows NT Server 4.0 in the Enterprise, #70-068*

◆ Microsoft Windows 3.1, #70-030*

   OR Microsoft Windows for Workgroups 3.11, #70-048*

   OR Implementing and Supporting Microsoft Windows 95, #70-064*

   OR Implementing and Supporting Microsoft Windows NT Workstation 4.0, #70-073*

   OR Implementing and Supporting Microsoft Windows 98, #70-098

◆ Networking Essentials, #70-058*

Elective Exams

For the Windows NT 4.0 track, you must pass two of the following elective exams for MCSE certification:

◆ Implementing and Supporting Microsoft SNA Server 3.0, #70-013

   OR Implementing and Supporting Microsoft SNA Server 4.0, #70-085

◆ Implementing and Supporting Microsoft Systems Management Server 1.2, #70-018

   OR Implementing and Supporting Microsoft Systems Management Server 2.0, #70-086

◆ Designing and Implementing Data Warehouse with Microsoft SQL Server 7.0, #70-019

◆ Microsoft SQL Server 4.2 Database Implementation, #70-021*

   OR Implementing a Database Design on Microsoft SQL Server 6.5, #70-027

   OR Implementing a Database Design on Microsoft SQL Server 7.0, #70-029

◆ Microsoft SQL Server 4.2 Database Administration for Microsoft Windows NT, #70-022*

   OR System Administration for Microsoft SQL Server 6.5 (or 6.0), #70-026

   OR System Administration for Microsoft SQL Server 7.0, #70-028

◆ Microsoft Mail for PC Networks 3.2-Enterprise, #70-037*

◆ Internetworking with Microsoft TCP/IP on Microsoft Windows NT (3.5–3.51), #70-053*

   OR Internetworking with Microsoft TCP/IP on Microsoft Windows NT 4.0, #70-059*

◆ Implementing and Supporting Web Sites Using Microsoft Site Server 3.0, #70-056

◆ Implementing and Supporting Microsoft Exchange Server 4.0, #70-075*

   OR Implementing and Supporting Microsoft Exchange Server 5.0, #70-076

   OR Implementing and Supporting Microsoft Exchange Server 5.5, #70-081

◆ Implementing and Supporting Microsoft Internet Information Server 3.0 and Microsoft Index Server 1.1, #70-077*

   OR Implementing and Supporting Microsoft Internet Information Server 4.0, #70-087*

◆ Implementing and Supporting Microsoft Proxy Server 1.0, #70-078

   OR Implementing and Supporting Microsoft Proxy Server 2.0, #70-088

◆ Implementing and Supporting Microsoft Internet Explorer 4.0 by Using the Internet Explorer Resource Kit, #70-079

   OR Implementing and Supporting Microsoft Internet Explorer 5.0 by Using the Internet Explorer Resource Kit, #70-080

◆ Designing a Microsoft Windows 2000 Directory Services Infrastructure, #70-219

◆ Designing Security for a Microsoft Windows 2000 Network, #70-220

◆ Designing a Microsoft Windows 2000 Infrastructure, #70-221

◆ Upgrading from Microsoft Windows NT 4.0 to Microsoft Windows 2000, #70-222

How to Become a Microsoft Certified Systems Engineer+Internet

You must pass seven operating system exams and two elective exams to become an MCSE specializing in Internet technology.

Core Exams

The following seven core exams are required for MCSE+Internet certification:

- ◆ Networking Essentials, #70-058*

- ◆ Internetworking with Microsoft TCP/IP on Microsoft Windows NT 4.0, #70-059*

- ◆ Implementing and Supporting Microsoft Windows 95, #70-064*

  OR Implementing and Supporting Microsoft Windows NT Workstation 4.0, #70-073*

  OR Implementing and Supporting Microsoft Windows 98, #70-098

- ◆ Implementing and Supporting Microsoft Windows NT Server 4.0, #70-067*

- ◆ Implementing and Supporting Microsoft Windows NT Server 4.0 in the Enterprise, #70-068*

- ◆ Implementing and Supporting Microsoft Internet Information Server 3.0 and Microsoft Index Server 1.1, #70-077*

  OR Implementing and Supporting Microsoft Internet Information Server 4.0, #70-087*

- ◆ Implementing and Supporting Microsoft Internet Explorer 4.0 by Using the Internet Explorer Resource Kit, #70-079

  OR Implementing and Supporting Microsoft Internet Explorer 5.0 by Using the Internet Explorer Resource Kit, #70-080

Elective Exams

You must also pass two of the following elective exams for MCSE+Internet certification:

- ◆ System Administration for Microsoft SQL Server 6.5, #70-026

  OR Administering Microsoft SQL Server 7.0, #70-028

- ◆ Implementing a Database Design on Microsoft SQL Server 6.5, #70-027

  OR Designing and Implementing Databases with Microsoft SQL Server 7.0, #70-029

- ◆ Implementing and Supporting Web Sites Using Microsoft Site Server 3.0, # 70-056

- ◆ Implementing and Supporting Microsoft Exchange Server 5.0, #70-076

  OR Implementing and Supporting Microsoft Exchange Server 5.5, #70-081

- ◆ Implementing and Supporting Microsoft Proxy Server 1.0, #70-078

  OR Implementing and Supporting Microsoft Proxy Server 2.0, #70-088

- ◆ Implementing and Supporting Microsoft SNA Server 4.0, #70-085

How to Become a Microsoft Certified Solution Developer

The MCSD certification has undergone substantial revision. Listed here are the requirements for the new track as well as the old.

New Track

For the new track, you must pass three core exams and one elective exam.

Core Exams

The core exams are as follows. You must pass one exam in each of the following groups:

Desktop Applications Development (one required)

◆ Designing and Implementing Desktop Applications with Microsoft Visual C++ 6.0, #70-016

  OR Designing and Implementing Desktop Applications with Microsoft Visual FoxPro 6.0, #70-156

  OR Designing and Implementing Desktop Applications with Microsoft Visual Basic 6.0, #70-176

Distributed Applications Development (one required)

◆ Designing and Implementing Distributed Applications with Microsoft Visual C++ 6.0, #70-015

  OR Designing and Implementing Distributed Applications with Microsoft Visual FoxPro 6.0, #70-155

  OR Designing and Implementing Distributed Applications with Microsoft Visual Basic 6.0, #70-175

Solution Architecture (required)

◆ Analyzing Requirements and Defining Solution Architectures, #70-100

Elective Exam

You must pass one of the following elective exams:

◆ Designing and Implementing Distributed Applications with Microsoft Visual C++ 6.0, #70-015

◆ Designing and Implementing Desktop Applications with Microsoft Visual C++ 6.0, #70-016

◆ Designing and Implementing Data Warehouses with Microsoft SQL Server 7.0, #70-019

◆ Developing Applications with C++ Using the Microsoft Foundation Class Library, #70-024

◆ Implementing OLE in Microsoft Foundation Class Applications, #70-025

◆ Implementing a Database Design on Microsoft SQL Server 6.5, #70-027

◆ Implementing a Database Design on Microsoft SQL Server 7.0, #70-029

◆ Designing and Implementing Web Sites with Microsoft FrontPage 98, #70-055

◆ Designing and Implementing Commerce Solutions with Microsoft Site Server 3.0, Commerce Edition, #70-057

◆ Programming with Microsoft Visual Basic 4.0, #70-065*

◆ Application Development with Microsoft Access for Windows 95 and the Microsoft Access Developer's Toolkit, #70-069

◆ Designing and Implementing Solutions with Microsoft Office 2000 and Microsoft Visual Basic for Applications, #70-091

◆ Designing and Implementing Database Applications with Microsoft Access 2000, #70-097

◆ Designing and Implementing Collaborative Solutions with Microsoft Outlook 2000 and Microsoft Exchange Server 5.5, #70-105

◆ Designing and Implementing Web Solutions with Microsoft Visual InterDev 6.0, #70-152

◆ Designing and Implementing Distributed Applications with Microsoft Visual FoxPro 6.0, #70-155

◆ Designing and Implementing Desktop Applications with Microsoft Visual FoxPro 6.0, #70-156

◆ Developing Applications with Microsoft Visual Basic 5.0, #70-165

◆ Designing and Implementing Distributed Applications with Microsoft Visual Basic 6.0, #70-175

◆ Designing and Implementing Desktop Applications with Microsoft Visual Basic 6.0, #70-176

Old Track

For the old track, you must pass two core technology exams and two elective exams for MCSD certification. The following lists show the required technology exams and elective exams needed for MCSD certification.

Core Exams

You must pass the following two core technology exams to qualify for MCSD certification:

◆ Microsoft Windows Architecture I, #70-160*

◆ Microsoft Windows Architecture II, #70-161*

Elective Exams

You must also pass two of the following elective exams to become an MSCD:

◆ Designing and Implementing Distributed Applications with Microsoft Visual C++ 6.0, #70-015

◆ Designing and Implementing Desktop Applications with Microsoft Visual C++ 6.0, #70-016

◆ Designing and Implementing Data Warehouses with Microsoft SQL Server 7.0, #70-019

◆ Microsoft SQL Server 4.2 Database Implementation, #70-021*

   OR Implementing a Database Design on Microsoft SQL Server 6.5, #70-027

   OR Implementing a Database Design on Microsoft SQL Server 7.0, #70-029

◆ Developing Applications with C++ Using the Microsoft Foundation Class Library, #70-024

◆ Implementing OLE in Microsoft Foundation Class Applications, #70-025

◆ Programming with Microsoft Visual Basic 4.0, #70-065

   OR Developing Applications with Microsoft Visual Basic 5.0, #70-165

   OR Designing and Implementing Distributed Applications with Microsoft Visual Basic 6.0, #70-175

◆ Designing and Implementing Desktop Applications with Microsoft Visual Basic 6.0, #70-176

◆ Microsoft Access 2.0 for Windows-Application Development, #70-051*

OR Microsoft Access for Windows 95 and the Microsoft Access Development Toolkit, #70-069

OR Designing and Implementing Database Applications with Microsoft Access 2000, #70-097

◆ Developing Applications with Microsoft Excel 5.0 Using Visual Basic for Applications, #70-052*

◆ Programming in Microsoft Visual FoxPro 3.0 for Windows, #70-054*

OR Designing and Implementing Distributed Applications with Microsoft Visual FoxPro 6.0, #70-155

OR Designing and Implementing Desktop Applications with Microsoft Visual FoxPro 6.0, #70-156

◆ Designing and Implementing Web Sites with Microsoft FrontPage 98, #70-055

◆ Designing and Implementing Commerce Solutions with Microsoft Site Server 3.0, Commerce Edition, #70-057

◆ Designing and Implementing Solutions with Microsoft Office (code-named Office 9) and Microsoft Visual Basic for Applications, #70-091

◆ Designing and Implementing Collaborative Solutions with Microsoft Outlook 2000 and Microsoft Exchange Server 5.5, #70-105

◆ Designing and Implementing Web Solutions with Microsoft Visual InterDev 6.0, #70-152

Becoming a Microsoft Certified Trainer

To fully understand the requirements and process for becoming an MCT, you need to obtain the Microsoft Certified Trainer Guide document from the following WWW site:

`http://www.microsoft.com/mcp/certstep/mct.htm`

At this site, you can read the document as a Web page or display and download it as a Word file. The MCT Guide explains the process for becoming an MCT. The general steps for the MCT certification are as follows:

1. Complete and mail a Microsoft Certified Trainer application to Microsoft. You must include proof of your skills for presenting instructional material. The options for doing so are described in the MCT Guide.

2. Obtain and study the Microsoft Trainer Kit for the Microsoft Official Curricula (MOC) courses for which you want to be certified. Microsoft Trainer Kits can be ordered by calling 800-688-0496 in North America. Those of you in other regions should review the MCT Guide for information on how to order a Trainer Kit.

3. Take and pass any required prerequisite MCP exam(s) to measure your current technical knowledge.

4. Prepare to teach a MOC course. Begin by attending the MOC course for which you want to be certified. This is required so that you understand how the course is structured, how labs are completed, and how the course flows.

5. Pass any additional exam requirement(s) to measure any additional product knowledge that pertains to the course.

6. Submit your course preparation checklist to Microsoft so that your additional accreditation may be processed and reflect on your transcript.

> **WARNING** You should consider the preceding steps a general overview of the MCT certification process. The precise steps that you need to take are described in detail on the Web site mentioned earlier. Do not misinterpret the preceding steps as the exact process you must undergo.

If you are interested in becoming an MCT, you can obtain more information by visiting the Microsoft Certified Training WWW site at `http://www.microsoft.com/train_cert/mct/` or by calling 800-688-0496.

What's on the CD-ROM

This appendix is a brief rundown of what you'll find on the CD-ROM that comes with this book. For a more detailed description of the newly developed *ExamGear, Training Guide Edition* exam simulation software, see Appendix D, "Using the ExamGear, Training Guide Edition Software." All items on the CD-ROM are easily accessible from the simple interface. In addition to *ExamGear, Training Guide Edition*, the CD-ROM includes the electronic version of the book in Portable Document Format (PDF), several utility and application programs, and a complete listing of the test objectives and where they are covered in the book.

EXAMGEAR, TRAINING GUIDE EDITION

ExamGear is an exam environment developed exclusively for New Riders Publishing. It is, we believe, the best exam software available. In addition to providing a means of evaluating your knowledge of the *Training Guide* material, *ExamGear, Training Guide Edition* features several innovations that help you to improve your mastery of the subject matter.

For example, the practice tests allow you to check your score by exam area or category to determine which topics you need to study more. In another mode, *ExamGear, Training Guide Edition* allows you to obtain immediate feedback on your responses in the form of explanations for the correct and incorrect answers.

Although *ExamGear, Training Guide Edition* exhibits most of the full functionality of the retail version of *ExamGear*, including the exam format and question types, this special version is written to the Training Guide content. It is designed to aid you in assessing how well you understand the Training Guide material and enable you to experience most of the question formats you will see on the actual exam. It is not as complete a simulation of the exam as the full *ExamGear* retail product. It also does not include some of the features of the full retail product, such as access to the mentored discussion groups. However, it serves as an excellent method for assessing your knowledge of the Training Guide content and gives you the experience of taking an electronic exam.

Again, for a more complete description of *ExamGear, Training Guide Edition* features, see Appendix D, "Using the ExamGear, Training Guide Edition Software."

EXCLUSIVE ELECTRONIC VERSION OF TEXT

The CD-ROM also contains the electronic version of this book in Portable Document Format (PDF). The electronic version comes complete with all figures as they appear in the book. You will find that the search capabilities of the reader come in handy for study and review purposes.

COPYRIGHT INFORMATION AND DISCLAIMER

Using the ExamGear, Training Guide Edition Software

This training guide includes a special version of *ExamGear*—a revolutionary new test engine that is designed to give you the best in certification exam preparation. *ExamGear* offers sample and practice exams for many of today's most in-demand technical certifications. This special Training Guide edition is included with this book as a tool to utilize in assessing your knowledge of the Training Guide material while also providing you with the experience of taking an electronic exam.

In the rest of this appendix, we describe in detail what *ExamGear, Training Guide Edition* is, how it works, and what it can do to help you prepare for the exam. Note that although the Training Guide edition includes nearly all the test simulation functions of the complete, retail version, the questions focus on the Training Guide content rather than on simulating the actual Microsoft exam. Also, this version does not offer the same degree of online support that the full product does.

EXAM SIMULATION

One of the main functions of *ExamGear, Training Guide Edition* is exam simulation. To prepare you to take the actual vendor certification exam, the Training Guide edition of this test engine is designed to offer the most effective exam simulation available.

Question Quality

The questions provided in the *ExamGear, Training Guide Edition* simulations are written to high standards of technical accuracy. The questions tap the content of the Training Guide chapters and help you review and assess your knowledge before you take the actual exam.

Interface Design

The *ExamGear, Training Guide Edition* exam simulation interface provides you with the experience of taking an electronic exam. This enables you to effectively prepare for taking the actual exam by making the test experience a familiar one. Using this test simulation can help eliminate the sense of surprise or anxiety that you might experience in the testing center, because you will already be acquainted with computerized testing.

STUDY TOOLS

ExamGear provides you with several learning tools to help prepare you for the actual certification exam.

Effective Learning Environment

The *ExamGear, Training Guide Edition* interface provides a learning environment that not only tests you through the computer, but also teaches the material you need to know to pass the certification exam. Each question comes with a detailed explanation of the correct answer and provides reasons why the other options were incorrect. This information helps to reinforce the knowledge you have already and also provides practical information you can use on the job.

Automatic Progress Tracking

ExamGear, Training Guide Edition automatically tracks your progress as you work through the test questions. From the Item Review tab (discussed in detail later in this appendix), you can see at a glance how well you are scoring by objective, by unit, or on a question-by-question basis (see Figure D.1). You can also configure *ExamGear* to drill you on the skills you need to work on most.

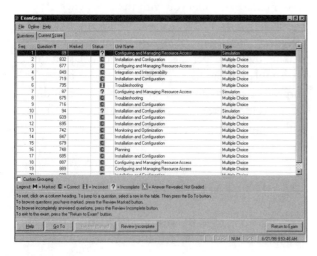

FIGURE D.1
Item review.

How ExamGear, Training Guide Edition Works

ExamGear comprises two main elements: the interface and the database. The *interface* is the part of the program that you use to study and to run practice tests. The *database* stores all the question-and-answer data.

Interface

The *ExamGear, Training Guide Edition* interface is designed to be easy to use and provides the most effective study method available. The interface enables you to select from the following modes:

◆ **Study Mode.** In this mode, you can select the number of questions you want to see and the time you want to allow for the test. You can select questions from all the chapters or from specific chapters. This enables you to reinforce your knowledge in a specific area or strengthen your knowledge in areas pertaining to a specific objective. During the exam, you can display the correct answer to each question along with an explanation of why it is correct.

◆ **Practice Exam.** In this mode, you take an exam that is designed to simulate the actual certification exam. Questions are selected from all test-objective groups. The number of questions selected and the time allowed are set to match those parameters of the actual certification exam.

◆ **Adaptive Exam.** In this mode, you take an exam simulation using the adaptive testing technique. Questions are taken from all test-objective groups. The questions are presented in a way that ensures your mastery of all the test objectives. After you have a passing score or if you reach a point where it is statistically impossible for you to pass, the exam is ended. This method provides a rapid assessment of your readiness for the actual exam.

Database

The *ExamGear, Training Guide Edition* database stores a group of test questions along with answers and explanations. At least three databases are included for each Training Guide edition product. One includes the questions from the ends of the chapters. Another includes the questions from the Practice Exam. The third is a database of new questions that have not appeared in the book. Additional exam databases may also be available for purchase online and are simple to download. Look ahead to the section "Obtaining Updates" in this appendix to find out how to download and activate additional databases.

INSTALLING AND REGISTERING EXAMGEAR, TRAINING GUIDE EDITION

This section provides instructions for *ExamGear, Training Guide Edition* installation and describes the process and benefits of registering your Training Guide edition product.

Requirements

ExamGear requires a computer with the following:

◆ Microsoft Windows 95, Windows 98, Windows NT 4.0, or Windows 2000.

   A Pentium or later processor is recommended.

◆ Microsoft's Internet Explorer 4.01 or later version.

   Internet Explorer 4.01 (or a later version) must be installed. (Even if you use a different browser, you still need to have Internet Explorer 4.01 or later installed.)

◆ A minimum of 16MB of RAM.

   As with any Windows application, the more memory, the better your performance.

◆ A connection to the Internet.

   An Internet connection is not required for the software to work, but it is required for online registration, product updates, downloading bonus question sets, and for unlocking other exams. These processes are described in more detail later.

Installing ExamGear, Training Guide Edition

Install *ExamGear, Training Guide Edition* by running the setup program that you found on the *ExamGear, Training Guide Edition* CD. Follow these instructions to install the Training Guide edition on your computer:

1. Insert the CD in your CD-ROM drive. The Autorun feature of Windows should launch the software. If you have Autorun disabled, click Start, and choose Run. Go to the root directory of the CD and choose START.EXE. Click Open and OK.

2. Click the button in the circle, and you see the welcome screen. From here you can install *ExamGear*. Click the ExamGear button to begin installation.

3. The Installation Wizard appears onscreen and prompts you with instructions to complete the installation. Select a directory on which to install *ExamGear, Training Guide Edition* (the Installation Wizard defaults to C:\Program Files\ExamGear).

4. The Installation Wizard copies the *ExamGear, Training Guide Edition* files to your hard drive, adds ExamGear, Training Guide Edition to your Program menu, adds values to your Registry, and installs test engine's DLLs to the appropriate system folders. To ensure that the process was successful, the Setup program finishes by running *ExamGear, Training Guide Edition.*

5. The Installation Wizard logs the installation process and stores this information in a file named INSTALL.LOG. This log file is used by the uninstall process in the event that you choose to remove *ExamGear, Training Guide Edition* from your computer. Because the *ExamGear* installation adds Registry keys and DLL files to your computer, it is important to uninstall the program appropriately (see the section "Removing *ExamGear, Training Guide Edition* from Your Computer").

Registering ExamGear, Training Guide Edition

The Product Registration Wizard appears when *ExamGear, Training Guide Edition* is started for the first time, and *ExamGear* checks at startup to see whether you are registered. If you are not registered, the main menu is hidden, and a Product Registration Wizard appears. Remember that your computer must have an Internet connection to complete the Product Registration Wizard.

The first page of the Product Registration Wizard details the benefits of registration; however, you can always elect not to register. The Show This Message at Startup Until I Register option enables you to decide whether the registration screen should appear every time *ExamGear, Training Guide Edition* is started. If you click the Cancel button, you return to the main menu. You can register at any time by selecting Online, Registration from the main menu.

The registration process is composed of a simple form for entering your personal information, including your name and address. You are asked for your level of experience with the product you are testing on and whether you purchased *ExamGear, Training Guide Edition* from a retail store or over the Internet. The information will be used by our software designers and marketing department to provide us with feedback about the usability and usefulness of this product. It takes only a few seconds to fill out and transmit the registration data. A confirmation dialog box appears when registration is complete.

After you have registered and transmitted this information to New Riders, the registration option is removed from the pull-down menus.

Registration Benefits

Remember that registration allows you access to download updates from our FTP site using *ExamGear, Training Guide Edition* (see the later section "Obtaining Updates").

Removing ExamGear, Training Guide Edition from Your Computer

In the event that you elect to remove the *ExamGear, Training Guide Edition* product from your computer, an uninstall process has been included to ensure that it is removed from your system safely and completely. Follow these instructions to remove *ExamGear* from your computer:

1. Click Start, Settings, Control Panel.

2. Double-click the Add/Remove Programs icon.

3. You are presented with a list of software that is installed on your computer. Select ExamGear, Training Guide Edition from the list and click the Add/Remove button. The *ExamGear, Training Guide Edition* software is then removed from your computer.

It is important that the INSTALL.LOG file be present in the directory where you have installed *ExamGear, Training Guide Edition* should you ever choose to uninstall the product. Do not delete this file. The INSTALL.LOG file is used by the uninstall process to safely remove the files and Registry settings that were added to your computer by the installation process.

USING EXAMGEAR, TRAINING GUIDE EDITION

ExamGear is designed to be user friendly and very intuitive, eliminating the need for you to learn some confusing piece of software just to practice answering questions. Because the software has a smooth learning curve, your time is maximized because you start practicing almost immediately.

General Description of How the Software Works

ExamGear has three modes of operation: Study Mode, Practice Exam, and Adaptive Exam (see Figure D.2).

All three sections have the same easy-to-use interface. Using Study Mode, you can hone your knowledge as well as your test-taking abilities through the use of the Show Answers option. While you are taking the test, you can expose the answers along with a brief description of why the given answers are right or wrong. This gives you the ability to better understand the material presented.

The Practice Exam section has many of the same options as Study Mode, but you cannot reveal the answers. This way, you have a more traditional testing environment with which to practice.

The Adaptive Exam questions continuously monitor your expertise in each tested topic area. If you reach a point at which you either pass or fail, the software ends the examination. As in the Practice Exam, you cannot reveal the answers.

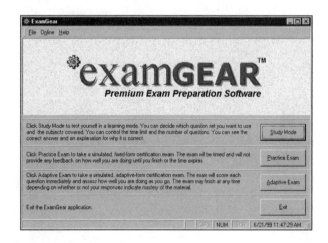

FIGURE D.2
The opening screen offers three testing modes.

Menu Options

The *ExamGear, Training Guide Edition* interface has an easy-to-use menu that provides the following options:

Menu	Command	Description
File	Print	Prints the current screen.
	Print Setup	Allows you to select the printer.
	Exit ExamGear	Exits the program.
Online	Registration	Starts the Registration Wizard and allows you to register online. This menu option is removed after you have successfully registered the product.
	Check for Product Updates	Downloads product catalog for Web-based updates.
	Web Browser	Opens the Web browser. It appears like this on the main menu, but more options appear after the browser is opened.
Help	Contents	Opens *ExamGear, Training Guide Edition*'s help file.
	About	Displays information about *ExamGear, Training Guide Edition*, including serial number, registered owner, and so on.

File

The File menu allows you to exit the program and configure print options.

Online

In the Online menu, you can register *ExamGear, Training Guide Edition*, check for product updates (update the *ExamGear* executable as well as check for free, updated question sets), and surf Web pages. The Online menu is always available, except when you are taking a test.

Registration

Registration is free and allows you access updates. Registration is the first task that *ExamGear, Training Guide Edition* asks you to perform. You will not have access to the free product updates if you do not register.

Check for Product Updates

This option takes you to *ExamGear, Training Guide Edition*'s Web site, where you can update the software. Registration is required for this option to be available. You must also be connected to the Internet to use this option. The *ExamGear* Web site lists the options that have been made available since your version of *ExamGear* was installed on your computer.

Web Browser

This option provides a convenient way to start your Web browser and connect to the New Riders Web site while you are working in *ExamGear, Training Guide Edition*. Click the Exit button to leave the Web browser and return to the *ExamGear* interface.

Help

As it suggests, this menu option gives you access to *ExamGear's* help system. It also provides important information like your serial number, software version, and so on.

Starting a Study Mode Session

Study Mode enables you to control the test in ways that actual certification exams do not allow:

◆ You can set your own time limits.

◆ You can concentrate on selected skill areas (units).

◆ You can reveal answers or have each response graded immediately with feedback.

◆ You can restrict the questions you see again to those missed or those answered correctly a given number of times.

◆ You can control the order in which questions are presented—random order or in order by skill area (unit).

To begin testing in Study Mode, click the Study Mode button from the main Interface screen. You are presented with the Study Mode configuration page (see Figure D.3).

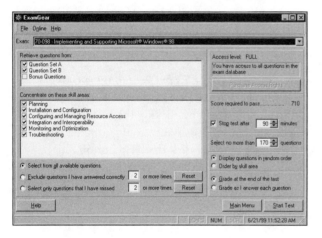

FIGURE D.3
The Study Mode configuration page.

At the top of the Study Mode configuration screen, you see the Exam drop-down list. This list shows the activated exam that you have purchased with your *ExamGear, Training Guide Edition* product, as well as any other exams you may have downloaded or any Preview exams that were shipped with your version of *ExamGear*. Select the exam with which you want to practice from the drop-down list.

Below the Exam drop-down list, you see the questions that are available for the selected exam. Each exam has at least one question set. You can select the individual

question set or any combination of the question sets if there is more than one available for the selected exam.

Below the Question Set list is a list of skill areas or chapters on which you can concentrate. These skill areas or chapters reflect the units of exam objectives defined by Microsoft for the exam. Within each skill area you will find several exam objectives. You can select a single skill area or chapter to focus on, or you can select any combination of the available skill areas/chapters to customize the exam to your individual needs.

In addition to specifying which question sets and skill areas you want to test yourself on, you can also define which questions are included in the test based on your previous progress working with the test. *ExamGear, Training Guide Edition* automatically tracks your progress with the available questions. When configuring the Study Mode options, you can opt to view all the questions available within the question sets and skill areas you have selected, or you can limit the questions presented. Choose from the following options:

◆ **Select from All Available Questions.** This option causes *ExamGear, Training Guide Edition* to present all available questions from the selected question sets and skill areas.

◆ **Exclude Questions I Have Answered Correctly** *X* **or More Times.** *ExamGear* offers you the option to exclude questions that you have previously answered correctly. You can specify how many times you want to answer a question correctly before *ExamGear* considers you to have mastered it (the default is two times).

◆ **Select Only Questions That I Have Missed** *X* **or More Times.** This option configures *ExamGear, Training Guide Edition* to drill you only on questions that you have missed repeatedly. You may specify how many times you must miss a question before *ExamGear* determines that you have not mastered it (the default is two times).

At any time, you can reset *ExamGear, Training Guide Edition's* tracking information by clicking the Reset button for the feature you want to clear.

At the top-right side of the Study Mode configuration sheet, you can see your access level to the question sets for the selected exam. Access levels are either Full or Preview. For a detailed explanation of each of these access levels, see the section "Obtaining Updates" in this appendix.

Under your access level, you see the score required to pass the selected exam. Below the required score, you can select whether the test will be timed and how much time will be allowed to complete the exam. Select the Stop Test After 90 Minutes check box to set a time limit for the exam. Enter the number of minutes you want to allow for the test (the default is 90 minutes). Deselecting this check box allows you to take an exam with no time limit.

You can also configure the number of questions included in the exam. The default number of questions changes with the specific exam you have selected. Enter the number of questions you want to include in the exam in the Select No More than *X* Questions option.

You can configure the order in which *ExamGear, Training Guide Edition* presents the exam questions. Select from the following options:

♦ **Display Questions in Random Order.** This option is the default option. When selected, it causes *ExamGear, Training Guide Edition* to present the questions in random order throughout the exam.

♦ **Order by Skill Area.** This option causes *ExamGear* to group the questions presented in the exam by skill area. All questions for each selected skill area are presented in succession. The test progresses from one selected skill area to the next, until all the questions from each selected skill area have been presented.

ExamGear offers two options for scoring your exams. Select one of the following options:

♦ **Grade at the End of the Test.** This option configures *ExamGear, Training Guide Edition* to score your test after you have been presented with all the selected exam questions. You can reveal correct answers to a question, but if you do, that question is not scored.

♦ **Grade as I Answer Each Question.** This option configures *ExamGear* to grade each question as you answer it, providing you with instant feedback as you take the test. All questions are scored unless you click the Show Answer button before completing the question.

You can return to the *ExamGear, Training Guide Edition* main startup screen from the Study Mode configuration screen by clicking the Main Menu button. If you need assistance configuring the Study Mode exam options, click the Help button for configuration instructions.

When you have finished configuring all the exam options, click the Start Test button to begin the exam.

Starting Practice Exams and Adaptive Exams

This section describes the Practice and Adaptive Exams, defines the differences between these exam options and the Study Mode option, and provides instructions for starting them.

Differences Between the Practice and Adaptive Exams and Study Modes

Question screens in the Practice and Adaptive Exams are identical to those found in Study Mode, except that the Show Answer, Grade Answer, and Item Review buttons are not available while you are in the process of taking a practice or adaptive exam. The Practice Exam provides you with a report screen at the end of the exam. The Adaptive Exam gives you a brief message indicating whether you've passed or failed the exam.

When taking a practice exam, the Item Review screen is not available until you have answered all the questions. This is consistent with the behavior of most vendors' current certification exams. In Study Mode, Item Review is available at any time.

When the exam timer expires, or if you click the End Exam button, the Examination Score Report screen comes up.

Starting an Exam

From the *ExamGear, Training Guide Edition* main menu screen, select the type of exam you want to run. Click the Practice Exam or Adaptive Exam button to begin the corresponding exam type.

What Is an Adaptive Exam?

To make the certification testing process more efficient and valid and therefore make the certification itself more valuable, some vendors in the industry are using a testing technique called *adaptive testing*. In an adaptive exam, the exam "adapts" to your abilities by varying the difficulty level of the questions presented to you.

The first question in an adaptive exam is typically an easy one. If you answer it correctly, you are presented with a slightly more difficult question. If you answer that question correctly, the next question you see is even more difficult. If you answer the question incorrectly, however, the exam "adapts" to your skill level by presenting you with another question of equal or lesser difficulty on the same subject. If you answer that question correctly, the test begins to increase the difficulty level again. You must correctly answer several questions at a predetermined difficulty level to pass the exam. After you have done this successfully, the exam is ended and scored. If you do not reach the required level of difficulty within a predetermined time (typically 30 minutes) the exam is ended and scored.

Why Do Vendors Use Adaptive Exams?

Many vendors who offer technical certifications have adopted the adaptive testing technique. They have found that it is an effective way to measure a candidate's mastery of the test material in as little time as necessary. This reduces the scheduling demands on the test taker and allows the testing center to offer more tests per test station than they could with longer, more traditional exams. In addition, test security is greater, and this increases the validity of the exam process.

Studying for Adaptive Exams

Studying for adaptive exams is no different from studying for traditional exams. You should make sure that you have thoroughly covered all the material for each of the test objectives specified by the certification exam vendor. As with any other exam, when you take an adaptive exam, either you know the material or you don't. If you are well prepared, you will be able to pass the exam. *ExamGear, Training Guide Edition* allows you to familiarize yourself with the adaptive exam testing technique. This will help eliminate any anxiety you might experience from this testing technique and allow you to focus on learning the actual exam material.

ExamGear's Adaptive Exam

The method used to score the Adaptive Exam requires a large pool of questions. For this reason, you cannot use this exam in Preview mode. The Adaptive Exam is presented in much the same way as the Practice Exam. When you click the Start Test button, you begin answering questions. The Adaptive Exam does not allow item review, and it does not allow you to mark questions to skip and answer later. You must answer each question when it is presented.

Assumptions

This section describes the assumptions made when designing the behavior of the *ExamGear, Training Guide Edition* adaptive exam.

◆ You fail the test if you fail any chapter or unit, earn a failing overall score, or reach a threshold at which it is statistically impossible for you to pass the exam.

◆ You can fail or pass a test without cycling through all the questions.

◆ The overall score for the adaptive exam is Pass or Fail. However, to evaluate user responses dynamically, percentage scores are recorded for units and the overall score.

Algorithm Assumptions

This section describes the assumptions used in designing the *ExamGear, Training Guide Edition* Adaptive Exam scoring algorithm.

Unit Scores

You fail a unit (and the exam) if any unit score falls below 66%.

Overall Scores

To pass the exam, you must pass all units and achieve an overall score of 86% or higher.

You fail if the overall score percentage is less than or equal to 85% or if any unit score is less than 66%.

Inconclusive Scores

If your overall score is between 67 and 85%, it is considered to be *inconclusive*. Additional questions will be asked until you pass or fail or until it becomes statistically impossible to pass without asking more than the maximum number of questions allowed.

Question Types and How to Answer Them

Because certification exams from different vendors vary, you will face many types of questions on any given exam. *ExamGear, Training Guide Edition* presents you with different question types to allow you to become familiar with the various ways an actual exam may test your knowledge. The Solution Architectures exam, in particular, offers a unique exam format and utilizes question types other than multiple choice. This version of *ExamGear* includes cases—extensive problem descriptions running several pages in length, followed by a number of questions specific to that case. Microsoft refers to these case/question collections as *testlets*. This version of *ExamGear, Training Guide Edition* also includes regular questions that are not attached to a case study. We include these question types to make taking the actual exam easier because you will already be familiar with the steps required to answer each question type. This section describes each of the question types presented by *ExamGear* and provides instructions for answering each type.

Multiple Choice

Most of the questions you see on a certification exam are multiple choice (see Figure D.4). This question type asks you to select an answer from the list provided. Sometimes you must select only one answer, often indicated by answers preceded by option buttons (round selection buttons). At other times, multiple correct answers are possible, indicated by check boxes preceding the possible answer combinations.

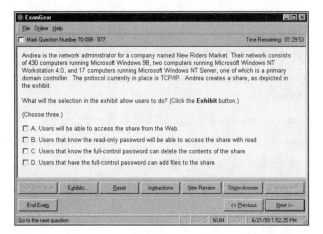

FIGURE D.4
A typical multiple-choice question.

You can use three methods to select an answer:

◆ Click the option button or check box next to the answer. If more than one correct answer to a question is possible, the answers will have check boxes next to them. If only one correct answer to a question is possible, each answer will have an option button next to it. *ExamGear, Training Guide Edition* prompts you with the number of answers you must select.

◆ Click the text of the answer.

◆ Press the alphabetic key that corresponds to the answer.

You can use any one of three methods to clear an option button:

◆ Click another option button.

◆ Click the text of another answer.

◆ Press the alphabetic key that corresponds to another answer.

You can use any one of three methods to clear a check box:

◆ Click the check box next to the selected answer.

◆ Click the text of the selected answer.

◆ Press the alphabetic key that corresponds to the selected answer.

To clear all answers, click the Reset button.

Remember that some of the questions have multiple answers that are correct. Do not let this throw you off. The *multiple correct* questions do not have one answer that is more correct than another. In the *single correct* format, only one answer is correct. *ExamGear, Training Guide Edition* prompts you with the number of answers you must select.

Drag and Drop

One form of drag-and-drop question is called a *Drop and Connect* question. These questions present you with a number of objects and connectors. The question prompts you to create relationships between the objects by using the connectors. The gray squares on the left side of the question window are the objects you can select. The connectors are listed on the right side of the question window in the Connectors box. An example is shown in Figure D.5.

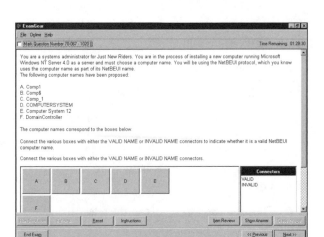

FIGURE D.5
A typical Drop and Connect question.

FIGURE D.6
The error message.

To select an object, click it with the mouse. When an object is selected, it changes color from a gray box to a white box. To drag an object, select it by clicking it with the left mouse button and holding the left mouse button down. You can move (or drag) the object to another area on the screen by moving the mouse while holding the left mouse button down.

To create a relationship between two objects, take the following actions:

1. Select an object and drag it to an available area on the screen.

2. Select another object and drag it to a location near where you dragged the first object.

3. Select the connector that you want to place between the two objects. The relationship should now appear complete. Note that to create a relationship, you must have two objects selected. If you try to select a connector without first selecting two objects, you are presented with an error message like that illustrated in Figure D.6.

Initially, the direction of the relationship established by the connector is from the first object selected to the second object selected. To change the direction of the connector, right-click the connector and choose Reverse Connection.

You can use either of two methods to remove the connector:

◆ Right-click the text of the connector that you want to remove, and then choose Delete.

◆ Select the text of the connector that you want to remove, and then press the Delete key.

To remove from the screen all the relationships you have created, click the Reset button.

Keep in mind that connectors can be used multiple times. If you move connected objects, it will not change the relationship between the objects; to remove the relationship between objects, you must remove the connector that joins them. When *ExamGear, Training Guide Edition* scores a drag-and-drop question, only objects with connectors to other objects are scored.

Another form of drag and drop question is called the *Select and Place* question. Instead of creating a diagram as you do with the Drop and Connect question, you are asked a question about a diagram. You then drag and drop labels onto the diagram in order to correctly answer the question.

Ordered-List Questions

In the *ordered-list* question type (see Figure D.7), you are presented with a number of items and are asked to perform two tasks:

1. Build an answer list from items on the list of choices.

2. Put the items in a particular order.

FIGURE D.7
A typical ordered-list question.

You can use any one of the following three methods to add an item to the answer list:

◆ Drag the item from the list of choices on the right side of the screen to the answer list on the left side of the screen.

◆ From the available items on the right side of the screen, double-click the item you want to add.

◆ From the available items on the right side of the screen, select the item you want to add; then click the Move button.

To remove an item from the answer list, you can use any one of the following four methods:

◆ Drag the item you want to remove from the answer list on the left side of the screen back to the list of choices on the right side of the screen.

◆ On the left side of the screen, double-click the item you want to remove from the answer list.

◆ On the left side of the screen, select the item you want to remove from the answer list, and then click the Remove button.

◆ On the left side of the screen, select the item you want to remove from the answer list, and then press the Delete key.

To remove all items from the answer list, click the Reset button.

If you need to change the order of the items in the answer list, you can do so using either of the following two methods:

◆ Drag each item to the appropriate location in the answer list.

◆ In the answer list, select the item that you want to move, and then click the up or down arrow button to move the item.

Keep in mind that items in the list can be selected twice. You may find that an ordered-list question will ask you to list in the correct order the steps required to perform a certain task. Certain steps may need to be performed more than once during the process. Don't think that after you have selected a list item, it is no longer available. If you need to select a list item more than once, you can simply select that item at each appropriate place as you construct your list.

Ordered-Tree Questions

The *ordered-tree* question type (see Figure D.8) presents you with a number of items and prompts you to create a tree structure from those items. The tree structure includes two or three levels of nodes.

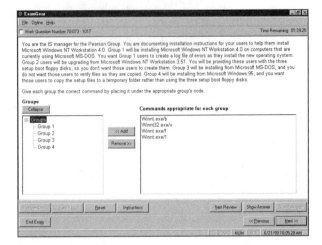

FIGURE D.8
A typical ordered-tree question.

An item in the list of choices can be added only to the appropriate node level. If you attempt to add one of the list choices to an inappropriate node level, you are presented with the error message shown in Figure D.9

FIGURE D.9
The Invalid Destination Node error message.

Like the ordered-list question, realize that any item in the list can be selected twice. If you need to select a list item more than once, you can simply select that item for the appropriate node as you construct your tree.

Also realize that not every tree question actually requires order to the lists under each node. Think of them as simply tree questions rather than ordered-tree questions. Such questions are just asking you to categorize hierarchically. Order is not an issue.

You can use either of the following two methods to add an item to the tree:

◆ Drag the item from the list of choices on the right side of the screen to the appropriate node of the tree on the left side of the screen.

◆ Select the appropriate node of the tree on the left side of the screen. Select the appropriate item from the list of choices on the right side of the screen. Click the Add button.

You can use either of the following two methods to remove an item from the tree:

◆ Drag an item from the tree to the list of choices.

◆ Select the item and click the Remove button.

To remove from the tree structure all the items you have added, click the Reset button.

Simulations

Simulation questions (see Figure D.10) require you to actually perform a task.

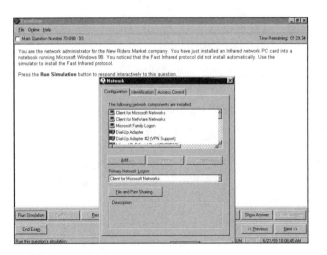

FIGURE D.10
A typical simulation question.

The main screen describes a situation and prompts you to provide a solution. When you are ready to proceed, you click the Run Simulation button in the lower-left corner. A screen or window appears on which you perform the solution. This window simulates the actual software that you would use to perform the required task in the real world. When a task requires several steps to complete, the simulator displays all the necessary screens to allow you to complete the task. When you have provided your answer by completing all the steps necessary to perform the required task, you can click the OK button to proceed to the next question.

You can return to any simulation to modify your answer. Your actions in the simulation are recorded, and the simulation appears exactly as you left it.

Simulation questions can be reset to their original state by clicking the Reset button.

Hot Spot Questions

Hot spot questions (see Figure D.11) ask you to correctly identify an item by clicking an area of the graphic or diagram displayed. To respond to the question, position the mouse cursor over a graphic. Then press the right mouse button to indicate your selection. To select another area on the graphic, you do not need to deselect the first one. Just click another region in the image.

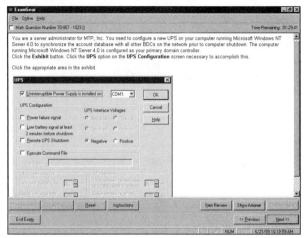

FIGURE D.11
A typical hot spot question.

Standard ExamGear, Training Guide Edition Options

Regardless of question type, a consistent set of clickable buttons enables you to navigate and interact with questions. The following list describes the function of each of the buttons you may see. Depending on the question type, some of the buttons will be grayed out and will be inaccessible. Buttons that are appropriate to the question type are active.

◆ **Run Simulation.** This button is enabled if the question supports a simulation. Clicking this button begins the simulation process.

◆ **Exhibits.** This button is enabled if exhibits are provided to support the question. An *exhibit* is an image, video, sound, or text file that provides supplemental information needed to answer the question. If a question has more than one exhibit, a dialog box appears, listing exhibits by name. If only one exhibit exists, the file is opened immediately when you click the Exhibits button.

◆ **Reset.** This button clears any selections you have made and returns the question window to the state in which it appeared when it was first displayed.

◆ **Instructions.** This button displays instructions for interacting with the current question type.

◆ **Item Review.** This button leaves the question window and opens the Item Review screen. For a detailed explanation of the Item Review screen, see the "Item Review" section later in this appendix.

◆ **Show Answer.** This option displays the correct answer with an explanation of why it is correct. If you choose this option, the current question will not be scored.

◆ **Grade Answer.** If Grade at the End of the Test is selected as a configuration option, this button is disabled. It is enabled when Grade as I Answer Each Question is selected as a configuration option. Clicking this button grades the current question immediately. An explanation of the correct answer is provided, just as if the Show Answer button were pressed. The question is graded, however.

◆ **End Exam.** This button ends the exam and displays the Examination Score Report screen.

◆ **<< Previous.** This button displays the previous question on the exam.

◆ **Next >>.** This button displays the next question on the exam.

◆ **<< Previous Marked.** This button is displayed if you have opted to review questions that you have marked using the Item Review screen. This button displays the previous marked question. Marking questions is discussed in more detail later in this appendix.

◆ **<< Previous Incomplete.** This button is displayed if you have opted to review questions that you have not answered using the Item Review screen. This button displays the previous unanswered question.

◆ **Next Marked >>.** This button is displayed if you have opted to review questions that you have marked using the Item Review screen. This button displays the next marked question. Marking questions is discussed in more detail later in this appendix.

◆ **Next Incomplete>>.** This button is displayed if you have opted to review questions, using the Item Review screen, that you have not answered. This button displays the next unanswered question.

Mark Question and Time Remaining

ExamGear provides you with two methods to aid in dealing with the time limit of the testing process. If you find that you need to skip a question or if you want to check the time remaining to complete the test, use one of the options discussed in the following sections.

Mark Question

Check this box to mark a question so that you can return to it later using the Item Review feature. The adaptive exam does not allow questions to be marked because it does not support item review.

Time Remaining

If the test is timed, the Time Remaining indicator is enabled. It counts down minutes remaining to complete the test. The adaptive exam does not offer this feature because it is not timed.

Item Review

The Item Review screen allows you to jump to any question. *ExamGear, Training Guide Edition* considers an *incomplete* question to be any unanswered question or any multiple-choice question for which the total number of required responses has not been selected. For example, if the question prompts for three answers and you selected only A and C, *ExamGear* considers the question to be incomplete.

The Item Review screen enables you to review the exam questions in different ways. You can enter one of two *browse sequences* (series of similar records): Browse Marked Questions or Browse Incomplete Questions. You can also create a custom grouping of the exam questions for review based on a number of criteria.

When using Item Review, if Show Answer was selected for a question while you were taking the exam, the question is grayed out in item review. The question can be answered again if you use the Reset button to reset the question status.

The Item Review screen contains two tabs. The Questions tab lists questions and question information in columns. The Current Score tab provides your exam score information, presented as a percentage for each unit and as a bar graph for your overall score.

The Item Review Questions Tab

The Questions tab on the Item Review screen (see Figure D.12) presents the exam questions and question information in a table. You can select any row you want by clicking in the grid. The Go To button is enabled whenever a row is selected. Clicking the Go To button displays the question on the selected row. You can also display a question by double-clicking that row.

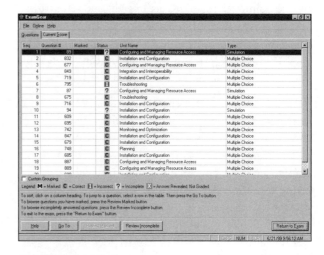

FIGURE D.12
The Questions tab on the Item Review screen.

Columns

The Questions tab contains the following six columns of information:

- ◆ **Seq.** Indicates the sequence number of the question as it was displayed in the exam.

- ◆ **Question Number.** Displays the question's identification number for easy reference.

- ◆ **Marked.** Indicates a question that you have marked using the Mark Question check box.

- ◆ **Status.** The status can be M for Marked, ? for Incomplete, C for Correct, I for Incorrect, or X for Answer Shown.

◆ **Unit Name.** The unit associated with each question.

◆ **Type.** The question type, which can be Multiple Choice, Drag and Drop, Simulation, Hot Spot, Ordered List, or Ordered Tree.

To resize a column, place the mouse pointer over the vertical line between column headings. When the mouse pointer changes to a set of right and left arrows, you can drag the column border to the left or right to make the column more or less wide. Simply click with the left mouse button and hold that button down while you move the column border in the desired direction.

The Item Review screen enables you to sort the questions on any of the column headings. Initially, the list of questions is sorted in descending order on the sequence number column. To sort on a different column heading, click that heading. You will see an arrow appear on the column heading indicating the direction of the sort (ascending or descending). To change the direction of the sort, click the column heading again.

The Item Review screen also allows you to create a *custom grouping*. This feature enables you to sort the questions based on any combination of criteria you prefer. For instance, you might want to review the question items sorted first by whether they were marked, then by the unit name, then by sequence number. The Custom Grouping feature allows you to do this. Start by checking the Custom Grouping check box (see Figure D.13). When you do so, the entire questions table shifts down a bit onscreen, and a message appear at the top of the table that reads `Drag a column header here to group by that column`.

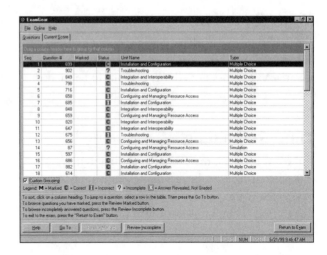

FIGURE D.13
The Custom Grouping check box allows you to create your own question sort order.

Simply click the column heading you want with the left mouse button, hold that button down, and move the mouse into the area directly above the questions table (the custom grouping area). Release the left mouse button to drop the column heading into the custom grouping area. To accomplish the custom grouping previously described, first check the Custom Grouping check box. Then drag the Marked column heading into the custom grouping area above the question table. Next, drag the Unit Name column heading into the custom grouping area. You will see the two column headings joined together by a line that indicates the order of the custom grouping. Finally, drag the Seq column heading into the custom grouping area. This heading will be joined to the Unit Name heading by another line indicating the direction of the custom grouping.

Notice that each column heading in the custom grouping area has an arrow indicating the direction in which items are sorted under that column heading. You can reverse the direction of the sort on an individual column-heading basis using these arrows. Click the column heading in the custom grouping area to change the direction of the sort for that column heading only. For example, using the custom grouping created previously, you can display the question list sorted first in descending order by whether the question was marked, in descending order by unit name, and then in ascending order by sequence number.

The custom grouping feature of the Item Review screen gives you enormous flexibility in how you choose to review the exam questions. To remove a custom grouping and return the Item Review display to its default setting (sorted in descending order by sequence number), simply uncheck the Custom Grouping check box.

The Current Score Tab

The Current Score tab of the Item Review screen (see Figure D.14) provides a real-time snapshot of your score. The top half of the screen is an expandable grid. When the grid is collapsed, scores are displayed for each unit. Units can be expanded to show percentage scores for objectives and subobjectives. Information about your exam progress is presented in the following columns:

◆ **Unit Name.** This column shows the unit name for each objective group.

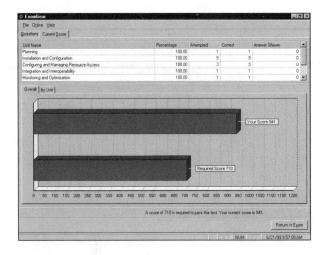

FIGURE D.14
The Current Score tab on the item review screen.

◆ **Percentage.** This column shows the percentage of questions for each objective group that you answered correctly.

◆ **Attempted.** This column lists the number of questions you answered either completely or partially for each objective group.

◆ **Correct.** This column lists the actual number of questions you answered correctly for each objective group.

◆ **Answer Shown.** This column lists the number of questions for each objective group that you chose to display the answer to using the Show Answer button.

The columns in the scoring table are resized and sorted in the same way as those in the questions table on the Item Review Questions tab. Refer to the earlier section "The Item Review Questions Tab" for more details.

A graphical overview of the score is presented below the grid. The graph depicts two red bars: The top bar represents your current exam score, and the bottom bar represents the required passing score. To the right of the bars in the graph is a legend that lists the required score and your score. Below the bar graph is a statement that describes the required passing score and your current score.

In addition, the information can be presented on an overall basis or by exam unit. The Overall tab shows the overall score. The By Unit tab shows the score by unit.

Clicking the End Exam button terminates the exam and passes control to the Examination Score Report screen.

The Return to Exam button returns to the exam at the question from which the Item Review button was clicked.

Review Marked Items

The Item Review screen allows you to enter a browse sequence for marked questions. When you click the Review Marked button, questions that you have previously marked using the Mark Question check box are presented for your review. While browsing the marked questions, you will see the following changes to the buttons available:

◆ The caption of the Next button becomes Next Marked.

◆ The caption of the Previous button becomes Previous Marked.

Review Incomplete

The Item Review screen allows you to enter a browse sequence for incomplete questions. When you click the Review Incomplete button, the questions you did not answer or did not completely answer are displayed for your review. While browsing the incomplete questions, you will see the following changes to the buttons:

◆ The caption of the Next button becomes Next Incomplete.

◆ The caption of the Previous button becomes Previous Incomplete.

Examination Score Report Screen

The Examination Score Report screen (see Figure D.15) appears when the Study Mode, Practice Exam, or Adaptive Exam ends—as the result of timer expiration, completion of all questions, or your decision to terminate early.

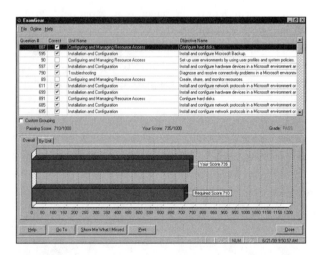

FIGURE D.15
The Examination Score Report screen.

This screen provides you with a graphical display of your test score, along with a tabular breakdown of scores by unit. The graphical display at the top of the screen compares your overall score with the score required to pass the exam. Buttons below the graphical display allow you to open the Show Me What I Missed browse sequence, print the screen, or return to the main menu.

Show Me What I Missed Browse Sequence

The Show Me What I Missed browse sequence is invoked by clicking the Show Me What I Missed button from the Examination Score Report or from the configuration screen of an adaptive exam.

Note that the window caption is modified to indicate that you are in the Show Me What I Missed browse sequence mode. Question IDs and position within the browse sequence appear at the top of the screen, in place of the Mark Question and Time Remaining indicators. Main window contents vary, depending on the question type. The following list describes the buttons available within the Show Me What I Missed browse sequence and the functions they perform:

- ◆ **Return to Score Report.** Returns control to the Examination Score Report screen. In the case of an adaptive exam, this button's caption is Exit, and control returns to the adaptive exam configuration screen.

- ◆ **Run Simulation.** Opens a simulation in Grade mode, causing the simulation to open displaying your response and the correct answer. If the current question does not offer a simulation, this button is disabled.

- ◆ **Exhibits.** Opens the Exhibits window. This button is enabled if one or more exhibits are available for the question.

- ◆ **Instructions.** Shows how to answer the current question type.

- ◆ **Print.** Prints the current screen.

- ◆ **Previous or Next.** Displays missed questions.

Checking the Web Site

To check the New Riders Home Page or the *ExamGear, Training Guide Edition* Home Page for updates or other product information, choose the desired Web site from the Web Sites option of the Online menu. You must be connected to the Internet to reach these Web sites. When you select a Web site, the Internet Explorer browser opens inside the *ExamGear, Training Guide Edition* window and displays the Web site.

OBTAINING UPDATES

The procedures for obtaining updates are outlined in this section.

The Catalog Web Site for Updates

Selecting the Check for Product Updates option from the Online menu shows you the full range of products you can either download for free or purchase. You can download additional items only if you have registered the software.

Product Updates Dialog Box

This dialog box appears when you select Check for Product Updates from the Online menu. *ExamGear, Training Guide Edition* checks for product updates from the New Riders Internet site and displays a list of products available for download. Some items, such as *ExamGear* program updates or bonus question sets for exam databases you have activated, are available for download free of charge.

Types of Updates

Several types of updates may be available for download, including various free updates and additional items available for purchase.

Free Program Updates

Free program updates include changes to the *ExamGear, Training Guide Edition* executables and runtime libraries (DLLs). When any of these items are downloaded, *ExamGear* automatically installs the upgrades. *ExamGear, Training Guide Edition* will be reopened after the installation is complete.

Free Database Updates

Free database updates include updates to the exam or exams that you have registered. Exam updates are contained in compressed, encrypted files and include exam databases, simulations, and exhibits. *ExamGear, Training Guide Edition* automatically decompresses these files to their proper location and updates the *ExamGear* software to record version changes and import new question sets.

CONTACTING NEW RIDERS PUBLISHING

At New Riders, we strive to meet and exceed the needs of our customers. We have developed *ExamGear, Training Guide Edition* to surpass the demands and expectations of network professionals seeking technical certifications, and we think it shows. What do you think?

If you need to contact New Riders regarding any aspect of the *ExamGear, Training Guide Edition* product line, feel free to do so. We look forward to hearing from you. Contact us at the following address or phone number:

New Riders Publishing
201 West 103rd Street
Indianapolis, IN 46290
800-545-5914

You can also reach us on the World Wide Web:

`http://www.newriders.com`

Technical Support

Technical support is available at the following phone number during the hours specified:

317-581-3833

Monday through Friday, 10:00 a.m.–3:00 p.m. Central Standard Time.

Customer Service

If you have a damaged product and need a replacement or refund, please call the following phone number:

800-858-7674

Product Updates

Product updates can be obtained by choosing *ExamGear, Training Guide Edition*'s Online pull-down menu and selecting Products Updates. You'll be taken to a private Web site with full details.

Product Suggestions and Comments

We value your input! Please email your suggestions and comments to the following address:

`certification@mcp.com`

LICENSE AGREEMENT

YOU SHOULD CAREFULLY READ THE
FOLLOWING TERMS AND CONDITIONS
BEFORE BREAKING THE SEAL ON THE
PACKAGE. AMONG OTHER THINGS, THIS
AGREEMENT LICENSES THE ENCLOSED
SOFTWARE TO YOU AND CONTAINS
WARRANTY AND LIABILITY DISCLAIMERS.
BY BREAKING THE SEAL ON THE PACKAGE,
YOU ARE ACCEPTING AND AGREEING TO
THE TERMS AND CONDITIONS OF THIS
AGREEMENT. IF YOU DO NOT AGREE TO
THE TERMS OF THIS AGREEMENT, DO NOT
BREAK THE SEAL. YOU SHOULD PROMPTLY
RETURN THE PACKAGE UNOPENED.

LICENSE

Subject to the provisions contained herein, New Riders
Publishing (NRP) hereby grants to you a nonexclusive,
nontransferable license to use the object-code version of
the computer software product (Software) contained in
the package on a single computer of the type identified
on the package.

SOFTWARE AND DOCUMENTATION

NRP shall furnish the Software to you on media in
machine-readable object-code form and may also
provide the standard documentation (Documentation)
containing instructions for operation and use of the
Software.

LICENSE TERM AND CHARGES

The term of this license commences upon delivery
of the Software to you and is perpetual unless earlier
terminated upon default or as otherwise set forth
herein.

TITLE

Title, ownership right, and intellectual property
rights in and to the Software and Documentation
shall remain in NRP and/or in suppliers to NRP of
programs contained in the Software. The Software is
provided for your own internal use under this license.
This license does not include the right to sublicense
and is personal to you and therefore may not be
assigned (by operation of law or otherwise) or transferred without the prior written consent of NRP. You
acknowledge that the Software in source code form
remains a confidential trade secret of NRP and/or its
suppliers and therefore you agree not to attempt to
decipher or decompile, modify, disassemble, reverse
engineer, or prepare derivative works of the Software
or develop source code for the Software or knowingly
allow others to do so. Further, you may not copy the
Documentation or other written materials accompanying the Software.

UPDATES

This license does not grant you any right, license, or interest in and to any improvements, modifications, enhancements, or updates to the Software and Documentation. Updates, if available, may be obtained by you at NRP's then-current standard pricing, terms, and conditions.

LIMITED WARRANTY AND DISCLAIMER

NRP warrants that the media containing the Software, if provided by NRP, is free from defects in material and workmanship under normal use for a period of sixty (60) days from the date you purchased a license to it.

THIS IS A LIMITED WARRANTY AND IT IS THE ONLY WARRANTY MADE BY NRP. THE SOFTWARE IS PROVIDED "AS IS" AND NRP SPECIFICALLY DISCLAIMS ALL WARRANTIES OF ANY KIND, EITHER EXPRESS OR IMPLIED, INCLUDING, BUT NOT LIMITED TO, THE IMPLIED WARRANTY OF MERCHANTABILITY AND FITNESS FOR A PARTICULAR PURPOSE. FURTHER, COMPANY DOES NOT WARRANT, GUARANTEE, OR MAKE ANY REPRESENTA-TIONS REGARDING THE USE, OR THE RESULTS OF THE USE, OF THE SOFTWARE IN TERMS OR CORRECTNESS, ACCURACY, RELIABILITY, CURRENTNESS, OR OTHERWISE AND DOES NOT WARRANT THAT THE OPERATION OF ANY SOFTWARE WILL BE UNINTERRUPTED OR ERROR FREE. NRP EXPRESSLY DISCLAIMS ANY WARRANTIES NOT STATED HEREIN. NO ORAL OR WRITTEN INFORMATION OR ADVICE GIVEN BY NRP, OR ANY NRP DEALER, AGENT, EMPLOYEE, OR OTHERS SHALL CREATE,

MODIFY, OR EXTEND A WARRANTY OR IN ANY WAY INCREASE THE SCOPE OF THE FOREGOING WARRANTY, AND NEITHER SUBLICENSEE OR PURCHASER MAY RELY ON ANY SUCH INFORMATION OR ADVICE. If the media is subjected to accident, abuse, or improper use, or if you violate the terms of this Agreement, then this warranty shall immediately be terminated. This warranty shall not apply if the Software is used on or in conjunction with hardware or programs other than the unmodified version of hardware and programs with which the Software was designed to be used as described in the Documentation.

LIMITATION OF LIABILITY

Your sole and exclusive remedies for any damage or loss in any way connected with the Software are set forth below.

UNDER NO CIRCUMSTANCES AND UNDER NO LEGAL THEORY, TORT, CONTRACT, OR OTHERWISE, SHALL NRP BE LIABLE TO YOU OR ANY OTHER PERSON FOR ANY INDIRECT, SPECIAL, INCIDENTAL, OR CONSEQUENTIAL DAMAGES OF ANY CHARACTER INCLUDING, WITHOUT LIMITATION, DAMAGES FOR LOSS OF GOODWILL, LOSS OF PROFIT, WORK STOPPAGE, COMPUTER FAILURE OR MALFUNCTION, OR ANY AND ALL OTHER COMMERCIAL DAMAGES OR LOSSES, OR FOR ANY OTHER DAMAGES EVEN IF NRP SHALL HAVE BEEN INFORMED OF THE POSSIBILITY OF SUCH DAMAGES, OR FOR ANY CLAIM BY ANOTHER PARTY. NRP'S THIRD-PARTY PROGRAM SUPPLIERS MAKE NO WARRANTY, AND HAVE NO LIABILITY WHATSOEVER, TO YOU. NRP's sole and exclusive obligation and liability and your exclusive remedy shall be: upon NRP's election, (i) the replacement of our defective media; or (ii) the repair or correction of your defective media if NRP is able, so that it will conform to the above warranty; or (iii) if NRP is unable to replace or repair, you may terminate this license by returning the Software. Only if you inform NRP of your problem during the applicable warranty period will NRP be obligated to honor this warranty. SOME STATES OR JURISDICTIONS DO NOT ALLOW THE EXCLUSION OF IMPLIED WARRANTIES OR LIMITATION OR EXCLUSION OF CONSE-QUENTIAL DAMAGES, SO THE ABOVE LIMITATIONS OR EXCLUSIONS MAY NOT APPLY TO YOU. THIS WARRANTY GIVES YOU SPECIFIC LEGAL RIGHTS AND YOU MAY ALSO HAVE OTHER RIGHTS WHICH VARY BY STATE OR JURISDICTION.

MISCELLANEOUS

If any provision of the Agreement is held to be ineffective, unenforceable, or illegal under certain circumstances for any reason, such decision shall not affect the validity or enforceability (i) of such provision under other circumstances or (ii) of the remaining provisions hereof under all circumstances, and such provision shall be reformed to and only to the extent necessary to make it effective, enforceable, and legal under such circumstances. All headings are solely for convenience and shall not be considered in interpreting this Agreement. This Agreement shall be governed by and construed under New York law as such law applies to agreements between New York residents entered into and to be performed entirely within New York, except as required by U.S. Government rules and regulations to be governed by Federal law.

YOU ACKNOWLEDGE THAT YOU HAVE READ THIS AGREEMENT, UNDERSTAND IT, AND AGREE TO BE BOUND BY ITS TERMS AND CONDITIONS. YOU FURTHER AGREE THAT IT IS THE COMPLETE AND EXCLUSIVE STATE-MENT OF THE AGREEMENT BETWEEN US THAT SUPERSEDES ANY PROPOSAL OR PRIOR AGREEMENT, ORAL OR WRITTEN, AND ANY OTHER COMMUNICATIONS BETWEEN US RELATING TO THE SUBJECT MATTER OF THIS AGREEMENT.

U.S. GOVERNMENT RESTRICTED RIGHTS

Use, duplication, or disclosure by the Government is subject to restrictions set forth in subparagraphs (a) through (d) of the Commercial Computer-Restricted Rights clause at FAR 52.227-19 when applicable, or in subparagraph (c) (1) (ii) of the Rights in Technical Data and Computer Software clause at DFARS 252.227-7013, and in similar clauses in the NASA FAR Supplement.

Index

C

D

O

P

Q-R

X-Z

Additional Tools for Certification Preparation

Taking the author-driven, no-nonsense approach that we pioneered with our *Landmark* books, New Riders proudly offers something unique for Windows 2000 administrators—an interesting and discriminating book on Windows 2000 Server, written by someone in the trenches who can anticipate your situation and provide answers you can trust.

ISBN: 1-56205-929-7

ISBN: 0-7357-0869-X

Architected to be the most navigable, useful, and value-packed reference for Windows 2000, this book uses a creative "telescoping" design that you can adapt to your style of learning. It's a concise, focused, and quick reference for Windows 2000, providing the kind of practical advice, tips, procedures, and additional resources that every administrator will need.

Understanding the Network is just one of several new titles from New Riders' acclaimed *Landmark Series*. This book addresses the audience in practical terminology, and describes the most essential information and tools required to build high-availability networks in a step-by-step implementation format. Each chapter could be read as a stand-alone, but the book builds progressively toward a summary of the essential concepts needed to put together a wide area network.

ISBN: 0-7357-0977-7

New Riders
Windows 2000 Resources

Advice and Experience for the Windows 2000 Networker

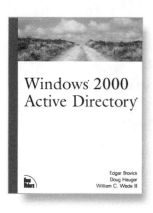

LANDMARK SERIES

We know how important it is to have access to detailed, solution-oriented information on core technologies. *Landmark* books contain the essential information you need to solve technical problems. Written by experts and subjected to rigorous peer and technical reviews, our *Landmark* books are hard-core resources for practitioners like you.

ESSENTIAL REFERENCE SERIES

The *Essential Reference* series from New Riders provides answers when you know what you want to do but need to know how to do it. Each title skips extraneous material and assumes a strong base of knowledge. These are indispensable books for the practitioner who wants to find specific features of a technology quickly and efficiently. Avoiding fluff and basic material, these books present solutions in an innovative, clean format—and at a great value.

CIRCLE SERIES

The *Circle Series* is a set of reference guides that meet the needs of the growing community of advanced, technical-level networkers who must architect, develop, and administer Windows NT/2000 systems. These books provide network designers and programmers with detailed, proven solutions to their problems.

The Road to MCSE Windows 2000

The new Microsoft Windows 2000 track is designed for information technology professionals working in a typically complex computing environment of medium to large organizations. A Windows 2000 MCSE candidate should have at least one year of experience implementing and administering a network operating system.

MCSEs in the Windows 2000 track are required to pass **five core exams and two elective exams** that provide a valid and reliable measure of technical proficiency and expertise.

See below for the exam information and the relevant New Riders title that covers that exam.

Core Exams

MCSE Candidates (Who Have Not Already Passed Windows NT 4.0 Exams) t Take All 4 of the Following Core Exams:

n 70-210: Installing, Configuring Administering Microsoft® dows® 2000 Professional

n 70-215: Installing, Configuring Administering Microsoft dows 2000 Server

n 70-216: Implementing Administering a Microsoft dows 2000 Network structure

n 70-217: Implementing Administering a Microsoft dows 2000 Directory ices Infrastructure

ISBN 0-7357-0965-3   ISBN 0-7357-0968-8

ISBN 0-7357-0966-1   ISBN 0-7357-0976-9

or

MCPs Who Have Passed 3 Windows NT 4.0 Exams (Exams 70-067, 70-068, and 70-073) Instead of the 4 Core Exams at Left, May Take:

Exam 70-240: Microsoft Windows 2000 Accelerated Exam for MCPs Certified on Microsoft Windows NT 4.0.

(This accelerated, intensive exam, which will be available until December 31, 2001, covers the core competencies of exams 70-210, 70-215, 70-216, and 70-217.)

ISBN 0-7357-0979-3

MCSE Training Guide: Core Exams (Bundle)

ISBN 0-7357-0976-9

PLUS - All Candidates - 1 of the Following Core Elective Exams Required:

am 70-219: Designing a Microsoft Windows 2000 Directory ices Infrastructure

am 70-220: Designing Security for a Microsoft Windows 2000 Network

am 70-221: Designing a Microsoft Windows 2000 vork Infrastructure

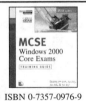

ISBN 0-7357-0983-1   ISBN 0-7357-0984-X   ISBN 0-7357-0982-3

US - All Candidates - 2 of the Following Elective Exams Required:

current MCSE electives (visit www.microsoft.com for a list of current electives)

cted third-party certifications that focus on interoperability will be accepted as an alternative to one ve exam. Please watch for more information on the third-party certifications that will be acceptable.)

am 70-219: Designing a Microsoft Windows 2000 Directory Services Infrastructure

am 70-220: Designing Security for a Microsoft Windows 2000 Network

am 70-221: Designing a Microsoft Windows 2000 Network Infrastructure

m 70-222: Upgrading from Microsoft Windows NT 4.0 to Microsoft Windows 2000

e exams that can also be used as elective exams may only be counted once toward a certification; that is, if a candidate receives t for an exam as a core in one track, that candidate will not receive credit for that same exam as an elective in that same track.

ISBN 0-7357-0983-1   ISBN 0-7357-0984-X   ISBN 0-7357-0982-3

New Riders

WWW.NEWRIDERS.COM

Books for Networking Professionals

Windows NT/2000 Titles

Windows 2000 TCP/IP
By Karanjit Siyan, Ph.D.
2nd Edition
700 pages, $34.99
ISBN: 0-7357-0992-0
Available August 2000

Windows 2000 TCP/IP cuts through the complexities and provides the most informative and complex reference book on Windows 2000-based TCP/IP topics. The book is a tutorial-reference hybrid, focusing on how Microsoft TCP/IP works, using hands-on tutorials and practical examples. Concepts essential to TCP/IP administration are explained thoroughly, and are then related to the practical use of Microsoft TCP/IP in a serious networking environment.

Windows 2000 DNS
By Roger Abell, Herman Knief, Andrew Daniels, and Jeffrey Graham
2nd Edition
450 pages, $39.99
ISBN: 0-7357-0973-4

The Domain Name System is a directory of registered computer names and IP addresses that can be instantly located. Without proper design and administration of DNS, computers wouldn't be able to locate each other on the network, and applications like email and Web browsing wouldn't be feasible. Administrators need this information to make their networks work. *Windows 2000 DNS* provides a technical overview of DNS and WINS, and how to design and administer them for optimal performance in a Windows 2000 environment.

Windows 2000 Registry
By Sandra Osborrne
2nd Edition
550 pages, $34.99
ISBN: 0-7357-0944-0
Available August 2000

Windows 2000 Registry is a powerful tool for accomplishing many important administration tasks, but little information is available on registry settings and how they can be edited to accomplish these tasks. This title offers unique insight into using registry settings to software or configure client systems in a Windows 2000 environment. The approach of the book is that of revealing the GUI through the registry, allowing system administrators to edit the registry settings to efficiently accomplish critical tasks such as configuration, installation, and management.

Windows 2000 Server Professional Reference
By Karanjit Siyan, Ph.D.
3rd Edition
1800 pages, $75.00
ISBN: 0-7357-0952-1

Windows 2000 Server Professional Reference is the benchmark of references available for Windows 2000. Although other titles take you through the setup and implementation phase of the product, no other book provides the user with detailed answers to day-to-day administration problems and tasks. Real-world implementations are key to help administrators discover the most viable solutions for their particular environments. Solid content shows administrators how to manage, troubleshoot, and fix problems that are specific to heterogeneous Windows networks, as well as Internet features and functionality.

Windows 2000 Professional
By Jerry Honeycutt
350 pages, $34.99 US
ISBN: 0-7357-0950-5

Windows 2000 Professional explores the power available to the Windows workstation user on the corporate network and Internet. The book is aimed directly at the power user who values the security, stability, and networking capabilities of NT alongside the ease and familiarity of the Windows 95/98 user interface. This book covers both user and administration topics, with a dose of networking content added for connectivity.

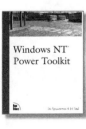

Windows NT Power Toolkit
By Stu Sjouwerman and Ed Tittel
1st Edition
800 pages, $49.99
ISBN: 0-7357-0922-X

This book covers the analysis, tuning, optimization, automation, enhancement, maintenance, and troubleshooting of Windows NT Server 4.0 and Windows NT Workstation 4.0. In most cases, the two operating systems overlap completely. Where the two systems diverge, each platform is covered separately. This advanced title comprises a task-oriented treatment of the Windows NT 4.0 environment. By concentrating on the use of operating system tools and utilities, resource kit elements, and selected third-

party tuning, analysis, optimization, and productivity tools, this book will show you how to carry out everyday and advanced tasks.

Windows 2000 User Management
By Lori Sanders
300 pages, $34.99
ISBN: 1-56205-886-X

With the dawn of Windows 2000, it has become even more difficult to draw a clear line between managing the user and managing the user's environment and desktop. This book, written by a noted trainer and consultant, provides comprehensive, practical advice to managing users and their desktop environments with Windows 2000.

Windows 2000 Deployment & Desktop Management
By Jeffrey A. Ferris, MCSE
1st Edition
400 pages, $34.99
ISBN: 0-7357-0975-0

More than a simple overview of new features and tools, *Windows 2000 Deployment & Desktop Management* is a thorough reference to deploying Windows 2000 Professional to corporate workstations. Incorporating real-world advice and detailed excercises, this book is a one-stop resource for any system administrator, integrator, engineer, or other IT professional.

Planning for Windows 2000

By Eric K. Cone, Jon Boggs, and Sergio Perez
1st Edition
400 pages, $29.99
ISBN: 0-7357-0048-6

Windows 2000 is poised to be one of the largest and most important software releases of the next decade, and you are charged with planning, testing, and deploying it in your enterprise. Are you ready? With this book, you will be. *Planning for Windows 2000* lets you know what the upgrade hurdles will be, informs you of how to clear them, guides you through effective Active Directory design, and presents you with detailed rollout procedures. Eric K. Cone, Jon Boggs, and Sergio Perez give you the benefit of their extensive experiences as Windows 2000 Rapid Deployment Program members by sharing problems and solutions they've encountered on the job.

Inside Windows 2000 Server

By William Boswell
2nd Edition
1533 pages, $49.99
ISBN: 1-56205-929-7

Finally, a totally new edition of New Riders' best-selling *Inside Windows NT Server 4.* Taking the author-driven, no-nonsense approach pioneered with the *Landmark* books, New Riders proudly offers something unique for Windows 2000 administrators—an interesting, discriminating book on Windows 2000 Server written by someone who can anticipate your situation and give you workarounds that won't leave a system unstable or sluggish.

BackOffice Titles

Implementing Exchange Server

By Doug Hauger, Marywynne Leon, and William C. Wade III
1st Edition
400 pages, $29.99
ISBN: 1-56205-931-9

If you're interested in connectivity and maintenance issues for Exchange Server, this book is for you. Exchange's power lies in its capability to be connected to multiple email subsystems to create a "universal email backbone." It's not unusual to have several different and complex systems all connected via email gateways, including Lotus Notes or cc:Mail, Microsoft Mail, legacy mainframe systems, and Internet mail. This book covers all of the problems and issues associated with getting an integrated system running smoothly, and it addresses troubleshooting and diagnosis of email problems with an eye toward prevention and best practices.

Exchange System Administration

By Janice Rice Howd
1st Edition
300 pages, $34.99
ISBN: 0-7357-0081-8

Your Exchange server is installed and connected—now what? Email administration is one of the most critical networking jobs, and Exchange can be particularly troublesome in large, heterogeneous environments. Janice Howd, a noted consultant and teacher with more than a decade of email administration experience, has put together this advanced, concise handbook for daily, periodic, and emergency administration. With in-depth coverage of topics like managing disk resources, replication, and disaster recovery, this is the one reference every Exchange administrator needs.

SQL Server System Administration

By Sean Baird,
Chris Miller, et al.
1st Edition
352 pages, $29.99
ISBN: 1-56205-955-6

How often does your SQL Server
go down during the day when everyone
wants to access the data? Do you spend
most of your time being a "report
monkey" for your coworkers and bosses?
SQL Server System Administration helps you
keep data consistently available to your
users. This book omits introductory
information. The authors don't spend
time explaining queries and how they
work. Instead, they focus on the information you can't get anywhere else, like
how to choose the correct replication
topology and achieve high availability of
information.

Internet Information Services Administration

By Kelli Adam
1st Edition,
200 pages, $29.99
ISBN: 0-7357-0022-2

Are the new Internet technologies in
Internet Information Services giving you
headaches? Does protecting security on
the Web take up all of your time? Then
this is the book for you. With hands-on
configuration training, advanced study of
the new protocols, the most recent version
of IIS, and detailed instructions on authenticating users with the new Certificate
Server and implementing and managing
the new e-commerce features, *Internet
Information Services Administration* gives
you the real-life solutions you need. This
definitive resource prepares you for
upgrading to Windows 2000 by giving
you detailed advice on working with
Microsoft Management Console, which
was first used by IIS.

SMS 2 Administration

By Michael Lubanski
and Darshan Doshi
1st Edition
350 pages, $39.99
ISBN: 0-7357-0082-6

Microsoft's new version of its Systems
Management Server (SMS) is starting
to turn heads. Although complex, it allows
administrators to lower their total cost of
ownership and more efficiently manage
clients, applications, and support operations. If your organization is using or
implementing SMS, you'll need some
expert advice. Michael Lubanski and
Darshan Doshi can help you get the most
bang for your buck with insight, expert
tips, and real-world examples. Michael and
Darshan are consultants specializing in
SMS and have worked with Microsoft
on one of the most complex SMS rollouts
in the world, involving 32 countries, 15
languages, and thousands of clients.

SQL Server Essential Reference

By Sharon Dooley
1st Edition
500 pages, $35.00 US
ISBN: 0-7357-0864-9

SQL Server Essential Reference is a comprehensive reference of advanced how-
tos and techniques for SQL Server 7
administrators. This book provides solid
grounding in fundamental SQL Server 7
administrative tasks to help you tame
your SQL Server environment. With
coverage ranging from installation,
monitoring, troubleshooting security,
and backup and recovery plans, this
book breaks down SQL Server into its
key conceptual areas and functions. This
easy-to-use reference is a must-have for
any SQL Server administrator.

UNIX/Linux Titles

Solaris Essential Reference
By John P. Mulligan
1st Edition
300 pages, $24.95
ISBN: 0-7357-0023-0

Looking for the fastest and easiest way to find the Solaris command you need? Need a few pointers on shell scripting? How about advanced administration tips and sound, practical expertise on security issues? Are you looking for trustworthy information about available third-party software packages that will enhance your operating system? Author John Mulligan—creator of the popular "Unofficial Guide to The Solaris™ Operating Environment" Web site (sun.icsnet.com)—delivers all that and more in one attractive, easy-to-use reference book. With clear and concise instructions on how to perform important administration and management tasks, and key information on powerful commands and advanced topics, *Solaris Essential Reference* is the book you need when you know what you want to do and only need to know how.

Linux System Administration
By M. Carling, Stephen Degler, and James Dennis
1st Edition
450 pages, $29.99
ISBN: 1-56205-934-3

As an administrator, you probably feel that most of your time and energy is spent in endless firefighting. If your network has become a fragile quilt of temporary patches and work-arounds, this book is for you. Have you had trouble sending or receiving email lately? Are you looking for a way to keep your network running smoothly with enhanced performance? Are your users always hankering for more storage, services, and speed? *Linux System Administration* advises you on the many intricacies of maintaining a secure, stable system. In this definitive work, the authors address all the issues related to system administration, from adding users and managing file permissions, to Internet services and Web hosting, to recovery planning and security. This book fulfills the need for expert advice that will ensure a trouble-free Linux environment.

GTK+/Gnome Application Development
By Havoc Pennington
1st Edition
492 pages, $39.99
ISBN: 0-7357-0078-8

This title is for the reader who is conversant with the C programming language and UNIX/Linux development. It provides detailed and solution-oriented information designed to meet the needs of programmers and application developers using the GTK+/Gnome libraries. Coverage complements existing GTK+/Gnome documentation, going into more depth on pivotal issues such as uncovering the GTK+ object system, working with the event loop, managing the Gdk substrate, writing custom widgets, and mastering GnomeCanvas.

Developing Linux Applications with GTK+ and GDK
By Eric Harlow
1st Edition
490 pages, $34.99
ISBN: 0-7357-0021-4

We all know that Linux is one of the most powerful and solid operating systems in existence. And as the success of Linux grows, there is an increasing interest in developing applications with graphical user interfaces that take advantage of the power of Linux. In this book, software developer Eric Harlow gives you an indispensable development handbook focusing on the GTK+ toolkit. More than an overview of the elements of application or GUI design, this is a hands-on book that delves into the technology. With in-depth material on the various GUI programming tools and loads of examples, this book's unique focus will give you the information you need to design and launch professional-quality applications.

Linux Essential Reference
By Ed Petron
1st Edition
350 pages, $24.95
ISBN: 0-7357-0852-5

This book is all about getting things done as quickly and efficiently as possible by providing a structured organization for the plethora of available Linux information. We can sum it up in one word—value. This book has it all: concise instructions

on how to perform key administration tasks, advanced information on configuration, shell scripting, hardware management, systems management, data tasks, automation, and tons of other useful information. This book truly provides groundbreaking information for the growing community of advanced Linux professionals.

Lotus Notes and Domino Titles

Domino System Administration
By Rob Kirkland, CLP, CLI
1st Edition
850 pages, $49.99
ISBN: 1-56205-948-3

Your boss has just announced that you will be upgrading to the newest version of Notes and Domino when it ships. How are you supposed to get this new system installed, configured, and rolled out to all of your end users? You understand how Lotus Notes works—you've been administering it for years. What you need is a concise, practical explanation of the new features and how to make some of the advanced stuff work smoothly by someone like you, who has worked with the product for years and understands what you need to know. *Domino System Administration* is the answer—the first book on Domino that attacks the technology at the professional level with practical, hands-on assistance to get Domino running in your organization.

Lotus Notes & Domino Essential Reference

By Tim Bankes, CLP
and Dave Hatter, CLP, MCP
1st Edition
650 pages, $45.00
ISBN: 0-7357-0007-9

You're in a bind because you've been asked to design and program a new database in Notes for an important client who will keep track of and itemize myriad inventory and shipping data. The client wants a user-friendly interface that won't sacrifice speed or functionality. You are experienced (and could develop this application in your sleep), but feel you need something to facilitate your creative and technical abilities—something to perfect your programming skills. The answer is waiting for you: *Lotus Notes & Domino Essential Reference*. It's compact and simply designed. It's loaded with information. All of the objects, classes, functions, and methods are listed. It shows you the object hierarchy and the relationship between each one. It's perfect for you. Problem solved.

Networking Titles

Network Intrusion Detection: An Analyst's Handbook

By Stephen Northcutt
1st Edition
267 pages, $39.99
ISBN: 0-7357-0868-1

Get answers and solutions from someone who has been in the trenches. The author, Stephen Northcutt, original developer of the Shadow intrusion detection system and former director of the United States Navy's Information System Security Office at the Naval Security Warfare Center, gives his expertise to intrusion detection specialists, security analysts, and consultants responsible for setting up and maintaining an effective defense against network security attacks.

Understanding Data Communications, Sixth Edition

By Gilbert Held
Sixth Edition
600 pages, $39.99
ISBN: 0-7357-0036-2

Updated from the highly successful fifth edition, this book explains how data communications systems and their various hardware and software components work. More than an entry-level book, it approaches the material in textbook format, addressing the complex issues involved in internetworking today. A great reference book for the experienced networking professional that is written by the noted networking authority, Gilbert Held.

Other Books By New Riders

Microsoft Technologies

ADMINISTRATION

Inside Windows 2000 Server
1-56205-929-7 • $49.99 US / $74.95 CAN
Windows 2000 Essential Reference
0-7357-0869-X • $35.00 US / $52.95 CAN
Windows 2000 Active Directory
0-7357-0870-3 • $29.99 US / $44.95 CAN
Windows 2000 Routing and Remote Access
Service
0-7357-0951-3 • $34.99 US / $52.95 CAN
Windows 2000 Deployment & Desktop
Management
0-7357-0975-0 • $34.99 US / $52.95 CAN
Windows 2000 DNS
0-7357-0973-4 • $39.99 US / $59.95 CAN
Windows 2000 User Management
1-56205-886-X • $34.99 US / $52.95 CAN
Windows 2000 Professional
0-7357-0950-5 • $34.99 US / $52.95 CAN
Planning for Windows 2000
0-7357-0048-6 • $29.99 US / $44.95 CAN
Windows 2000 Server Professional Reference
0-7357-0952-1 • $75.00 US / $111.95 CAN
Windows 2000 Security
0-7357-0991-2 • $39.99 US / $59.95 CAN
Available September 2000
Windows 2000 TCP/IP
0-7357-0992-0 • $34.99 US / $52.95 CAN
Available August 2000
Windows 2000 Registry
0-7357-0944-0 • $34.99 US / $52.95 CAN
Available August 2000
Windows 2000 Terminal Services and Citrix
MetaFrame
0-7357-1005-8 • $39.99 US / $59.95 CAN
Available October 2000
Windows NT/2000 Network Security
1-57870-253-4 • $45.00 US / $67.95 CAN
Available August 2000
Windows NT/2000 Thin Client Solutions
1-57870-239-9 • $45.00 US / $67.95 CAN
Windows 2000 Virtual Private Networking
1-57870-246-1 • $45.00 US / $67.95 CAN
Available September 2000
Windows 2000 Active Directory Design &
Migration
1-57870-242-9 • $45.00 US / $67.95 CAN
Available September 2000
Windows 2000 and Mainframe Integration
1-57870-200-3 • $40.00 US / $59.95 CAN
Windows 2000 Server: Planning and Migration
1-57870-023-X • $40.00 US / $59.95 CAN
Windows 2000 Quality of Service
1-57870-115-5 • $45.00 US / $67.95 CAN
Windows NT Power Toolkit
0-7357-0922-X • $49.99 US / $74.95 CAN
Windows NT Terminal Server and Citrix
MetaFrame
1-56205-944-0 • $29.99 US / $44.95 CAN

Windows NT Performance: Monitoring,
Benchmarking, and Tuning
1-56205-942-4 • $29.99 US / $44.95 CAN
Windows NT Registry: A Settings Reference
1-56205-941-6 • $29.99 US / $44.95 CAN
Windows NT Domain Architecture
1-57870-112-0 • $38.00 US / $56.95 CAN

SYSTEMS PROGRAMMING

Windows NT/2000 Native API Reference
1-57870-199-6 • $50.00 US / $74.95 CAN
Windows NT Device Driver Development
1-57870-058-2 • $50.00 US / $74.95 CAN
DCE/RPC over SMB: Samba and Windows NT
Domain Internals
1-57870-150-3 • $45.00 US / $67.95 CAN

APPLICATION PROGRAMMING

Delphi COM Programming
1-57870-221-6 • $45.00 US / $67.95 CAN
Windows NT Applications: Measuring and
Optimizing Performance
1-57870-176-7 • $40.00 US / $59.95 CAN
Applying COM+
ISBN 0-7357-0978-5 • $49.99 US / $74.95 CAN
Available August 2000

WEB PROGRAMMING

Exchange & Outlook: Constructing Collaborative
Solutions
ISBN 1-57870-252-6 • $40.00 US / $59.95 CAN

SCRIPTING

Windows Script Host
1-57870-139-2 • $35.00 US / $52.95 CAN
Windows NT Shell Scripting
1-57870-047-7 • $32.00 US / $45.95 CAN
Windows NT Win32 Perl Programming:
The Standard Extensions
1-57870-067-1 • $40.00 US / $59.95 CAN
Windows NT/2000 ADSI Scripting for System
Administration
1-57870-219-4 • $45.00 US / $67.95 CAN
Windows NT Automated Deployment and
Customization
1-57870-045-0 • $32.00 US / $45.95 CAN

BACK OFFICE

SMS 2 Administration
0-7357-0082-6 • $39.99 US / $59.95 CAN
Internet Information Services Administration
0-7357-0022-2 • $29.99 US / $44.95 CAN
SQL Server System Administration
1-56205-955-6 • $29.99 US / $44.95 CAN
SQL Server Essential Reference
0-7357-0864-9 • $35.00 US / $52.95 CAN

Open Source

MySQL
0-7357-0921-1 • $49.99 US / $74.95 CAN
Web Application Development with PHP
0-7357-0997-1 • $45.00 US / $67.95 CAN

Available June 2000
PHP Functions Essential Reference
0-7357-0970-X • $35.00 US / $52.95 CAN
Available August 2000
Python Essential Reference
0-7357-0901-7 • $34.95 US / $52.95 CAN
Autoconf, Automake, and Libtool
1-57870-190-2 • $35.00 US / $52.95 CAN
Available August 2000

Linux/Unix

ADMINISTRATION

Linux System Administration
1-56205-934-3 • $29.99 US / $44.95 CAN
Linux Firewalls
0-7357-0900-9 • $39.99 US / $59.95 CAN
Linux Essential Reference
0-7357-0852-5 • $24.95 US / $37.95 CAN
UnixWare 7 System Administration
1-57870-080-9 • $40.00 US / $59.99 CAN

DEVELOPMENT

Developing Linux Applications with GTK+ and
GDK
0-7357-0021-4 • $34.99 US / $52.95 CAN
GTK+/Gnome Application Development
0-7357-0078-8 • $39.99 US / $59.95 CAN
KDE Application Development
1-57870-201-1 • $39.99 US / $59.95 CAN

GIMP

Grokking the GIMP
0-7357-0924-6 • $39.99 US / $59.95 CAN
GIMP Essential Reference
0-7357-0911-4 • $24.95 US / $37.95 CAN

SOLARIS

Solaris Advanced System Administrator's Guide,
Second Edition
1-57870-039-6 • $39.99 US / $59.95 CAN
Solaris System Administrator's Guide, Second
Edition
1-57870-040-X • $34.99 US / $52.95 CAN
Solaris Essential Reference
0-7357-0023-0 • $24.95 US / $37.95 CAN

Networking

STANDARDS & PROTOCOLS

Cisco Router Configuration & Troubleshooting,
Second Edition
0-7357-0999-8 • $34.99 US / $52.95 CAN
Understanding Directory Services
0-7357-0910-6 • $39.99 US / $59.95 CAN

Understanding the Network: A Practical Guide to
Internetworking
0-7357-0977-7 • $39.99 US / $59.95 CAN

Understanding Data Communications, Sixth
Edition
0-7357-0036-2 • $39.99 US / $59.95 CAN
LDAP: Programming Directory Enabled
Applications
1-57870-000-0 • $44.99 US / $67.95 CAN
Gigabit Ethernet Networking
1-57870-062-0 • $50.00 US / $74.95 CAN
Supporting Service Level Agreements
on IP Networks
1-57870-146-5 • $50.00 US / $74.95 CAN
Directory Enabled Networks
1-57870-140-6 • $50.00 US / $74.95 CAN
Differentiated Services for the Internet
1-57870-132-5 • $50.00 US / $74.95 CAN
Quality of Service on IP Networks
1-57870-189-9 • $50.00 US / $74.95 CAN
Designing Addressing Architectures for
Routing and Switching
1-57870-059-0 • $45.00 US / $69.95 CAN
Understanding & Deploying LDAP Directory
Services
1-57870-070-1 • $50.00 US / $74.95 CAN
Switched, Fast and Gigabit Ethernet, Third
Edition
1-57870-073-6 • $50.00 US / $74.95 CAN
Wireless LANs: Implementing Interoperable
Networks
1-57870-081-7 • $40.00 US / $59.95 CAN
Wide Area High Speed Networks
1-57870-114-7 • $50.00 US / $74.95 CAN
The DHCP Handbook
1-57870-137-6 • $55.00 US / $81.95 CAN
Designing Routing and Switching Architectures for
Enterprise Networks
1-57870-060-4 • $55.00 US / $81.95 CAN
Local Area High Speed Networks
1-57870-113-9 • $50.00 US / $74.95 CAN
Available June 2000
Network Performance Baselining
1-57870-240-2 • $50.00 US / $74.95 CAN
Economics of Electronic Commerce
1-57870-014-0 • $49.99 US / $74.95 CAN

SECURITY

Intrusion Detection
1-57870-185-6 • $50.00 US / $74.95 CAN
Understanding Public-Key Infrastructure
1-57870-166-X • $50.00 US / $74.95 CAN
Network Intrusion Detection: An Analyst's
Handbook
0-7357-0868-1 • $39.99 US / $59.95 CAN
Linux Firewalls
0-7357-0900-9 • $39.99 US / $59.95 CAN

LOTUS NOTES/DOMINO

Domino System Administration
1-56205-948-3 • $49.99 US / $74.95 CAN
Lotus Notes & Domino Essential Reference
0-7357-0007-9 • $45.00 US / $67.95 CAN

Software Architecture & Engineering

Designing for the User with OVID
1-57870-101-5 • $40.00 US / $59.95 CAN
Designing Flexible Object-Oriented Systems with
UML
1-57870-098-1 • $40.00 US / $59.95 CAN
Constructing Superior Software
1-57870-147-3 • $40.00 US / $59.95 CAN
A UML Pattern Language
1-57870-118-X • $45.00 US / $67.95 CAN

Professional Certification

TRAINING GUIDES

MCSE Training Guide: Networking Essentials,
2nd Ed.
156205919X • $49.99 US / $74.95 CAN
MCSE Training Guide: Windows NT Server 4,
2nd Ed.
1562059165 • $49.99 US / $74.95 CAN
MCSE Training Guide: Windows NT
Workstation 4, 2nd Ed.
1562059181 • $49.99 US / $74.95 CAN
MCSE Training Guide: Windows NT Server 4
Enterprise, 2nd Ed.
1562059173 • $49.99 US / $74.95 CAN
MCSE Training Guide: Core Exams Bundle, 2nd
Ed.
1562059262 • $149.99 US / $223.95 CAN
MCSE Training Guide: TCP/IP, 2nd Ed.
1562059203 • $49.99 US / $74.95 CAN
MCSE Training Guide: IIS 4, 2nd Ed.
0735708657 • $49.99 US / $74.95 CAN
MCSE Training Guide: SQL Server 7
Administration
0735700036 • $49.99 US / $74.95 CAN
MCSE Training Guide: SQL Server 7
Database Design
0735700044 • $49.99 US / $74.95 CAN
CLP Training Guide: Lotus Notes 4
0789715058 • $59.99 US / $84.95 CAN
MCSD Training Guide: Visual Basic 6 Exams
0735700028 • $69.99 US / $104.95 CAN
MCSD Training Guide: Solution Architectures
0735700265 • $49.99 US / $74.95 CAN
MCSD Training Guide: 4-in-1 Bundle
0735709122 • $149.99 US / $223.95 CAN
CCNA Training Guide
0735700516 • $49.99 US / $74.95 CAN
A+ Certification Training Guide, 2nd Ed.
0735709076 • $49.99 US / $74.95 CAN
Network+ Certification Guide
073570077X • $49.99 US / $74.95 CAN
Solaris 2.6 Administrator Certification Training
Guide, Part I
157870085X • $40.00 US / $59.95 CAN
Solaris 2.6 Administrator Certification Training
Guide, Part II
1578700868 • $40.00 US / $59.95 CAN

MCSE Training Guide: Windows 2000
Professional
0735709653 • $49.99 US / $74.95 CAN •
MCSE Training Guide: Windows 2000 Server
0735709688 • $49.99 US / $74.95 CAN •
MCSE Training Guide: Windows 2000 Network
Infrastructure
0735709661 • $49.99 US / $74.95 CAN
MCSE Training Guide: Windows 2000 Network
Security Design
073570984X • $49.99 US / $74.95 CAN
MCSE Training Guide: Windows 2000 Network
Infrastructure Design
0735709823 • $49.99 US / $74.95 CAN
MCSE Training Guide: Windows 2000 Directory
Svcs. Infrastructure
0735709769 • $49.99 US / $74.95 CAN
MCSE Training Guide: Windows 2000 Directory
Services Design
0735709831 • $49.99 US / $74.95 CAN
MCSE Training Guide: Windows 2000
Accelerated Exam
0735709793 • $59.99 US / $89.95 CAN
MCSE Training Guide: Windows 2000 Core
Exams Bundle
0735709882 • $149.99 US / $223.95 CAN

How to Contact Us

IF YOU NEED THE LATEST UPDATES ON A TITLE THAT YOU'VE PURCHASED:

1) Visit our Web site at www.newriders.com.

2) Enter the book ISBN number, which is located on the back cover in the bottom right-hand corner, in the site search box on the left navigation bar.

3) Select your book title from the list of search results. On the book page, you'll find available updates and downloads for your title.

IF YOU ARE HAVING TECHNICAL PROBLEMS WITH THE BOOK OR THE CD THAT IS INCLUDED:

1) Check the book's information page on our Web site according to the instructions listed above, or

2) Email us at nrfeedback@newriders.com, or

3) Fax us at 317-581-4663 ATTN: Tech Support.

IF YOU HAVE COMMENTS ABOUT ANY OF OUR CERTIFICATION PRODUCTS THAT ARE NON-SUPPORT RELATED:

1) Email us at nrfeedback@newriders.com, or

2) Write to us at New Riders, 201 W. 103rd St., Indianapolis, IN 46290-1097, or

3) Fax us at 317-581-4663.

IF YOU ARE OUTSIDE THE UNITED STATES AND NEED TO FIND A DISTRIBUTOR IN YOUR AREA:

Please contact our international department at international@mcp.com.

IF YOU ARE INTERESTED IN BEING AN AUTHOR OR TECHNICAL REVIEWER:

Email us at opportunities@newriders.com. Include your name, email address, phone number, and area of technical expertise.

IF YOU WISH TO PREVIEW ANY OF OUR CERTIFICATION BOOKS FOR CLASSROOM USE:

Email us at nrmedia@newriders.com. Your message should include your name, title, training company or school, department, address, phone number, office days/hours, text in use, and enrollment. Send these details along with your request for desk/examination copies and/or additional information.

IF YOU ARE A MEMBER OF THE PRESS AND WOULD LIKE TO REVIEW ONE OF OUR BOOKS:

Email us at nrmedia@newriders.com. Your message should include your name, title, publication or website you work for, mailing address, and email address.

To better serve you, we would like your opinion on the content and quality of this book. Please complete this card and mail it to us or fax it to 317-581-4663.

Name _____

Address _____

City _____ State _____ Zip _____

Phone_____ Email Address _____

Occupation _____

Which certification exams have you already passed? _____
_____
_____
_____

Which certification exams do you plan to take? _____
_____
_____
_____

What influenced your purchase of this book?
❑ Recommendation   ❑ Cover Design
❑ Table of Contents   ❑ Index
❑ Magazine Review   ❑ Advertisement
❑ Reputation of New Riders ❑ Author Name

How would you rate the contents of this book?
❑ Excellent   ❑ Very Good
❑ Good   ❑ Fair
❑ Below Average   ❑ Poor

What other types of certification products will you buy/have you bought to help you prepare for the exam?
❑ Quick reference books   ❑ Testing software
❑ Study guides   ❑ Other

What do you like most about this book? Check all that apply.
❑ Content   ❑ Writing Style
❑ Accuracy   ❑ Examples
❑ Listings   ❑ Design
❑ Index   ❑ Page Count
❑ Price   ❑ Illustrations

What do you like least about this book? Check all that apply.
❑ Content   ❑ Writing Style
❑ Accuracy   ❑ Examples
❑ Listings   ❑ Design
❑ Index   ❑ Page Count
❑ Price   ❑ Illustrations

What would be a useful follow-up book to this one for you?_____
Where did you purchase this book? _____
Can you name a similar book that you like better than this one, or one that is as good? Why?_____
_____
_____

How many New Riders books do you own? _____
What are your favorite certification or general computer book titles? _____
_____

What other titles would you like to see us develop? _____

Any comments for us? _____
_____
_____

Fold here and tape to mail

New Riders Publishing
201 W. 103rd St.
Indianapolis, IN 46290